Essential Papers on
Posttraumatic Stress Disorder

ESSENTIAL PAPERS IN PSYCHOANALYSIS
General Editor: Leo Goldberger

Essential Papers on Posttraumatic Stress Disorder

Edited by
Mardi J. Horowitz, M.D.

NEW YORK UNIVERSITY PRESS

New York and London

NEW YORK UNIVERSITY PRESS
New York and London

Library of Congress Cataloging-in-Publication Data
Essential papers on posttraumatic stress disorder / edited by Mardi J.
Horowitz.
p.   cm. — (Essential papers in psychoanalysis)
Includes bibliographical references and index.
ISBN 0-8147-3558-4 (alk. paper). — ISBN 0-8147-3559-2 (pbk. :
alk. paper)
1. Post-traumatic stress disorder—Miscellanea.   I. Horowitz,
Mardi Jon, 1934-   .   II. Series.
RC552.P67E77   1999
616.85'21—dc21   98-34012
                         CIP

New York University Press books are printed on acid-free paper,
and their binding materials are chosen for strength and durability.

Manufactured in the United States of America

10   9   8   7   6   5   4   3   2   1

Contents

Introduction

Mardi J. Horowitz, M.D.

This introduction, like the book, is divided into three parts: diagnosis, explanation, and treatment. It will provide the reader with an overview of agreements and controversies concerning posttraumatic stress disorder. The individual papers provide detailed elaborations about these issues.

The contemporary era finds a high degree of agreement on diagnosis. There is also an encouraging level of agreement on explanation. Even in the area of treatment, where one may expect controversy, there is growing agreement on integrating biological, psychological, and social approaches. This introduction will model such a biopsychosocial approach.

DIAGNOSIS

Clarification of trauma-relevant diagnoses has progressed rapidly in the last two decades. Currently, the fourth version of the American Psychiatric Association's Diagnostic and Statistical Manual (DSM-IV), contains several stress response syndromes. Of these, the diagnosis of Posttraumatic Stress Disorder (PTSD) is central, and is summarized in table 1. There are other relevant diagnoses. These include Acute Stress Disorder, Brief Psychotic Disorder, with marked stressors, Adjustment Disorder, trauma-induced Dissociative Disorder such as Depersonalization Disorder, and a potential new diagnosis of Complicated Grief Disorder (Prigerson et al., 1996; Horowitz, et al., 1997). In addition, traumatic responses can flare up other symptom clusters into heightened psychopathology, leading to disorders of depression, anxiety, and pathological change in personality.

The diagnosis of PTSD emerged officially in 1980, after a controversy that involved difficult forensic issues as well as scientific observations. A polarization of causation was argued: Did the traumatic event in and of itself cause a psychiatric problem? Were pre-existing features of the victim's personality and vulnerability heavily involved? If trauma were the main cause of symptoms, the institutions or people responsible for causing or not preventing the traumatic events could be held legally responsible for damage to victims. If

Table 1. Official Diagnostic Criteria for Posttraumatic Stress Disorder (DSM-IV)

1. The person has been exposed to a traumatic event in which both of the following were present:
   a. the person experienced, witnessed, or was confronted with an event or events that involved actual or threatened death or serious injury, or a threat to the physical integrity of self or others
   b. the person's response involved intense fear, helplessness, or horror. Note: In children, this may be expressed instead by disorganized or agitated behavior
2. The traumatic event is persistently re-experienced in one (or more) of the following ways:
   a. recurrent and intrusive distressing recollections of the event, including images, thoughts, or perceptions. Note: In young children, repetitive play may occur in which themes or aspects of the trauma are expressed
   b. recurrent distressing dreams of the event. Note: In children, there may be frightening dreams without recognizable content
   c. acting or feeling as if the traumatic event were recurring (includes a sense of reliving the experience, illusions, hallucinations, and dissociative flashback episodes, including those that occur on awakening when intoxicated). Note: In young children, trauma-specific re-enactment may occur
   d. intense psychological distress at exposure to internal and external cues that symbolize or resemble an aspect of the traumatic event
   e. physiological reactivity on exposure to internal or external cues that symbolize or resemble an aspect of the traumatic event
3. Persistent avoidance of stimuli associated with the trauma and numbing of general responsiveness (not present before the trauma), as indicated by three (or more) of the following:
   a. efforts to avoid thoughts, feelings, or conversations associated with the trauma
   b. efforts to avoid activities, places, or people that arouse recollections of the trauma
   c. inability to recall an important aspect of the trauma
   d. markedly diminished interest or participation in significant activities
   e. feeling of detachment or estrangement from others
   f. restricted range of affect (e.g., unable to have loving feelings)
   g. sense of a foreshortened future (e.g., does not expect to have a career, marriage, children, or a normal life span)
4. Persistent symptoms of increased arousal (not present before the trauma), as indicated by two (or more) of the following.
   a. difficulty falling asleep or staying asleep
   b. irritability or outbursts of anger
   c. difficulty concentrating
   d. hypervigilance
   e. exaggerated startle response
   f. duration of the disturbance (symptoms in Criteria B, C, and D) is more than one month
   g. the disturbance causes clinically significant distress or impairment in social, occupational, or other important areas of functioning
Specify if:
      Acute: If duration of symptoms is less than three months
      Chronic: If duration of symptoms is three months or more
      With Delayed Onset: If onset of symptoms is at least six months after the stressor

prior personality or other predispositions were the cause, and the traumatic event was only a precipitant, then individual or institutional responsibility would be less. We know now this is a "both-and" rather than an "either-or" polarity.

The exposure of combatants to episodes of horror and terror led to high frequencies of psychological war casualties. Earlier conditions were labeled "shell shock," "combat neuroses," or "combat exhaustion." The equivalent term for civilian syndromes was "traumatic neurosis." The many clinical observations of the effects of trauma were then amplified by systematic epidemiological field studies and experiments (e.g., Horowitz, 1969, 1975; Horowitz and Becker, 1971; Horowitz, Alvarez, and Wilner, 1979). Repetition of unbidden mental experiences, recapitulation of trauma-related perceptions, emotions, and ideational associations were clarified as phenomena that increased in intensity and frequency as a person was closer to the center of a traumatic event. This confirmed the modern diagnosis of PTSD.

EXPLANATION

Freud (1914, 1920) pointed to repression of traumatic memories as a pathological defense that preserved emotional equilibrium but prevented mastery of the shocking experience. But shock mastery is not the entire picture. Some posttraumatic symptoms are due to both a lack of shock mastery and a failure to reschematize inner cognitive maps of self and the world to accord with a new reality (Horowitz, 1997b). Freud's early theory of abreaction and catharsis, emotional recall and expression of hitherto repressed traumas, as the necessary and sufficient mode for working through, is outmoded. His theory of repression of trauma itself has required considerable revision. However, Freud did accurately point to many posttraumatic effects upon memory.

In PTSD, a cardinal set of symptoms involves intrusive, unbidden repetitions of memory. Such memories can be experienced as re-enactments with pangs of strong negative emotions, and images that have an intensity bordering on perception. Some people react to such intrusions with secondary anxiety due to their sense of loss of control.

Real prior events can be recalled as if they were only daydreams, and fantasied events can be recalled as if they really occurred. The latter have been called false memories. Even during an event, the experience of traumatic perceptions can seem unreal, and the person can feel as if in a dream. Later, in memory, the reality of the event and the self as participant within it can be added. It is difficult to know, on the basis of recollection alone, what exact

Table 2. Memory

Unresolved	Resolved
1. Excessively imagistic and quasi-real	1. Less vivid recollection
2. Non-volitional repetitions	2. Voluntary recollection
3. Emotionally evocative (alarms and emotional pangs)	3. Less sharp emotional activation.
4. Difficult to dispel	4. Can shift attention away from memory
5. Unclear if real or unreal	5. Clearer sense of what is memory and what is fantasy
6. Hard to relate to identity	6. An aspect of identity

realities once occurred. Nonetheless, there are some qualities that, taken as a whole, can differentiate resolved and unresolved memories of prior traumatic experiences. These are shown in table 2.

Conscious and Unconscious Mental Processes

The process of forming the signs and symptoms of a posttraumatic syndrome is largely non-conscious: it takes place in the deep functions of the mind/brain, and it occurs in a social relationship and biological context. Memories of the trauma, erupting intrusively, are the most significant deflections from ordinary conscious experience. But a variety of avoidance and numbing behaviors also occur. There are times when memories are forgotten and later retrieved, or emotions are blunted that can be felt later. Explanation can begin by understanding different phases that can occur after the external aspects of the traumatic event are largely concluded.

These phases, a prototype of stress response, are modeled in figure 1 and figure 2. Figure 2 adds a spectrum from stress response states to greater psychopathological intensification of posttraumatic tendencies. While these are useful conceptual models, the reader should note that both intrusions and avoidances can, and often do, oscillate during the same time period. The range of response from resilient, to normally stressed, to psychopathologically stressed levels of response is given in more detail in table 3.

States of Mind

Posttraumatic omissions (denial, numbing, avoidance) are often due to the operation of unconscious control processes. These defensive operations func-

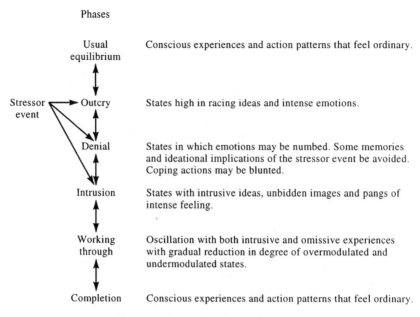

Figure 1. Phases of Response to Trauma

tion to restore emotional equilibrium, prevent emotional flooding, and reduce conceptual disorganization. Posttraumatic intrusions break through such defensive efforts. Sometimes a phase with more intrusions follows a phase of numbing. Paradoxically, these intrusions often begin just when the person begins to feel safe.

A phase of intrusion can contain horror, floods of unbidden images, and pangs of intense feeling. Such dreaded states of *intrusive horror* contrast sharply with what people want, often a desired state of calm equilibrium. The desired state of calm cannot be achieved and the dreaded state threatens to emerge repeatedly. People react with heightened defensive control, attempting to stabilize themselves. Phases of denial often contain such compromise states.

One common but problematic compromise state contains symptoms of both tension and avoidance. It is commonly experienced as a state of *anxious hypervigilance*. The person will both approach and avoid contemplating memories of the trauma or activities that remind him or her of the traumatic episode. They have a sense of shimmering toward and away from recollection.

Another less problematic compromise state can be called a quasi-adaptive

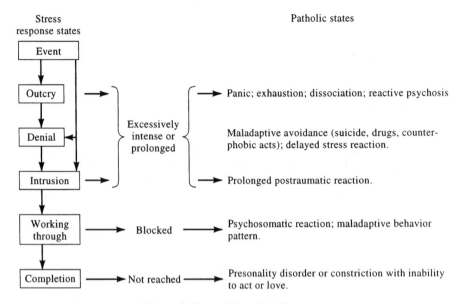

Figure 2. States Induced by Traumas

state because it reduces negative emotions to tolerable levels by use of more insistent but rigid defensive avoidances. Such overmodulated states of *denial and emotional numbing* are the result of disavowal and inhibition of memories and reactions to them.

The person might seem recovered, but neither a fully adaptive resolution nor the restoration of a desired state of *calm equilibrium* has been achieved. The distortions of thought required to blunt emotion make these denial and numbing states only quasi-adaptive.

Such common configurations of posttraumatic states of mind are illustrated in figure 3. These states of mind, and many individual variations, can have social, biological, and psychological causes.

Social Causes

Man-made disasters are especially cruel. The victim sustains the fright, injury, and loss caused by the disaster and the horror that perceived malevolence or lack of protection induces. PTSD and dreaded states of mind are more common with poor leadership, torture, sadism, and lack of human caring. Warfare stands out as a huge cause of PTSD in both military and civilian

Table 3. Types of Response to Stressor Events

Time	Resilient response	Normal stress response	Pathological stress response
Before event	Equilibrium	Equilibrium	Equilibrium (or pre-event turbulence)
During event	Emotional perturbation	Outcry	Prolonged or too intense outcry
After event	Equilibrium	Denial phase	Excessive and prolonged denial, repression, dissociation
		Intrusion phase	Excessive and prolonged intrusion and flooding
		Combined denial and intrusion, a working through phase with reduced denial and intrusion	Combined denial and intrusion without reduction over time
		Equilibrium	Reschematization into a pathological equilibrium (e.g., character distortion)

populations. However, even in peace some people are suddenly stripped of personal identity or worth by others; where the person expected fidelity, constancy, and support, he or she is assaulted and abused. Within families, for example, traumatic reactions increase with inconstancy, lack of control, self-centeredness, and exploitation of the weak by the strong.

Social causation includes cultural attitudes about how people ought or should respond to stress. In some cultures, responding to stress with physical illness is a "good response" and mental illness a "bad" or stigmatized response. In others, the reverse may be true. Stigmatization will worsen any condition because it undermines crucial supports of self-esteem, personal identity, and coping efforts. Failures in leaders, in social coherence, and social support may make the difference between a resilient or normal stress response and the more pathological levels of signs and symptoms shown in table 3. For example, American servicemen returning from the war in Vietnam were often treated not as heroes but as if they were responsible for the war. Many felt depreciated, neglected, and stigmatized (Horowitz and Solomon, 1975; Figley, 1978).

Another aspect of social traumas includes those who help after a disaster.

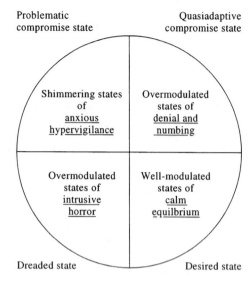

Figure 3. Desired, Dreaded, and Defensive-Compromise States of Mind
After Traumas

Seeing terrible sights, as in dismembered bodies, can combine with stress
and lead to posttraumatic symptoms in rescue workers who are not socially
perceived as victims (Marmar et al., 1995; Weiss et al., 1995).

Biological Causes

There are clear signs of mind/body interactions after stressor events. Selye
(1976) pioneered studies of heightened corticosteroid alterations. Changes in
these and other neurotransmitters and hormones after stressor events are under
current study (Charney et al., 1993). It appears that catecholamine chemistry
changes in times of stress. This involves neural networks that connect the
limbic, frontal cortical, basal gangliar, and hypothalamic structures. Disturbances in these networks and regions can disturb arousal control and alter the
regulation of emotional responses (as in fright and rage attacks). The amygdala may alter its danger-recognition set points, the hippocampus its memory-
encoding properties, and the medial prefrontal cortex its abilities to establish
or reduce associational connections. Such disturbances may partially explain
turbulent shifts in states.

   A prominent catecholamine in the physiologic reaction to stress may be
dopamine, which is concentrated in the norepinephrine-rich areas of the brain
such as the locus ceruleus and frontal cortex, which are connected to the

emotional-arousal-regulating functions of the amygdala. These chemicals may be involved in heightening biological propensities for low-threshold arousals leading to vulnerability to sudden alarm reactions to trigger stimuli. A series of stressor life events can chronically alter the synaptic transmission of brain-alerting systems, thereby altering the capacity to avoid startle reactions and disturbing disruptions of volitional attention. This sensitization can cause repeated alarms leading to fatigue and the further dysregulation of cognitive-emotional functioning (Southwick et al., 1993). Serotonin subtypes and their receptors regulate complex brain activities, and are involved in the production of stress hormones: trauma-induced alterations in this chemistry can also lead to anxiety-type arousals of the autonomic nervous system.

Some persons with PTSD may have been predisposed to this condition as a result of a variety of prior vulnerabilities. Some biological systems may have been hypersensitive before the stressor event. A vicious cycle can ensue, each stressor rendering the person more susceptible to the next (McFarlane, Weber, and Clark, 1993; Hamner, Diamond, and Hitri, 1994).

Psychological Causes

There is an encouraging level of agreement across different psychological schools of theory (dynamic, cognitive, and behavioral-learning theory) on how to explain some posttraumatic processes. These theories concur in use of associational concepts. A person can forge strong new connections between bits of memory when experiencing a traumatic event. These include conditioned associations that link perceptual stimuli, such as a loud noise from an explosion, with ideas of high danger and emotions of fright. Later stimuli with similar characteristics, but without the importance of real danger, are likely to trigger the same fright. Such generalizations to non-threatening stimuli may be reduced over time by calming experiences. This reduction in stimulus generalization is called shock mastery.

Traumatic events also establish vivid, emotional, and active memories. These are coded as high priority for review because they are so threatening to personal well-being. Some reviews are so intense that they feel like a reliving of the traumatic experience. Such active memories tend toward repeated representation in spite of inhibitory controls. This repetition may continue indefinitely, or may cease when the memory is adequately processed for personal meanings.

Shock mastery, then, has at least two features: (1) a gradual reduction in the strong associational linkages between stimuli that co-occurred with traumatic horror, terror, and the threat of annihilation, and (2) attenuation in the tendency to repetition of the memories.

Shock mastery is complicated by efforts to protect emotional equilibrium. Defensive control processes can inhibit conscious recollections and preconsciously processed associational connections. The purpose of such defensive control processes is to reduce emotion to tolerable limits, to prevent entry into dreaded, negative, and out of control states of mind such as intrusive horror. Breakthroughs of inhibitory efforts are experienced as unbidden ideas, images, and pangs of emotional response. Highly defensive inhibitions are experienced as states of denial and emotional numbing, and maladaptive avoidance behaviors may be signs observed by other people.

Another set of processes involves modification of cognitive maps. The maps are schemas that articulate self with the world. They contain beliefs and expectations that do not match the new traumatic information. Enduring preexisting attitudes are in sharp discord with the experiences produced by traumatic events (Horowitz, 1997b). This leads to signs and symptoms such as alarm emotions and the intrusive repetition of traumatic perceptions. Such symptoms can be reduced through processes of reschematization that bring cognitive maps into accord with new realities. These are not contradictory explanatory principles; issues of shock mastery and cognitive reschematization intersect.

The mismatch of the new stress-associated information with the active expectations of the person excites emotional reactions. States of alarm may occur. Alarm emotions such as fear motivate new efforts at coping with the information. But the amount of information requiring changes in schemas is vast. Complete integration of new meanings into existing schemas is impossible in a short time. The emotional implications to identity, attachment, and safety are too overwhelming. Long-lasting information processing is set in motion and may be essential to optimum adaptation.

If latent, weak, damaged, defective, or bad self-or other-person-concepts are activated by association with the traumatic event, negative emotions and even hopelessness, giving up, or self-disgust may occur. Fear and despair are less likely if resilient, competent, strong, or good self-concepts and/or other-person-concepts serve as dominant person-schematic organizers of the current state of mind. This cognitive-psychodynamic view, reported in more detail elsewhere (Horowitz, 1991, 1997a, 1998), is an integration of some psychoanalytic (Furst, 1967) and some cognitive-behavioral theoretical concepts (Bandura, 1982; Beck and Emery, 1985; Foa and Kozak, 1988).

Activation of relatively competent self-schemas from an individual's repertoire is likely to lead to response tactics that emphasize effective action, mobility, and assertiveness. Activation of less competent self-schemas is more likely to lead to a selection of maladaptive coping styles such as paralytic hiding, apathetic energy conservation, and an unnecessary placing of self as dependent and subordinate to others. Working through can lead not only to shock mastery but also to a strengthened sense of identity as a person who can endure, cope with, and master extreme events. A failure to reach such completion can impoverish one's sense of self-competence. Depression, rage, shame, and fear may become chronic emotional vulnerabilities.

Traumatic events impact on identity and may lead to a variety of self concept disturbances such as identity diffusion (a chaotic sense of self-fragmentation) or depersonalization. To bolster a sense of identity during stress, an individual often turns for reflectance of self to others. Attachment and bonding impulses are heightened. In such instances, victims may even bond with their aggressors if they are isolated from better sources of support. This can lead to dissociative experiences, in which the aggressor is bad, and in which the aggressor is good. Such segregations of person schematization make it harder to work over and work through memories and fantasies of traumatic events.

TREATMENT

Social Interventions

Right after a disaster, it is helpful to tell others what happened. This promotes understanding and reduces irrational fantasies about why events occurred; people need emotional support at such times. Even so, everyone has his or her own coping style and not everyone wants to review events in the same way. Some people seek out every bit of information, others need time for "dosing," to take in one tolerable bit of meaning at a time, and still others need to take some time off for recovery.

Children, especially, may seem to get off the topic of the disaster quickly. But that does not mean they do not care, have forgotten, or will not return to the meanings later. It means that they should not be criticized if they play when adults cry with grief; criticism will only confuse them about their own good/badness. In addition, children may believe that TV news repetitions (of the same disaster clips) mean that the event is going on and on in real time, repeating itself over and over. They may need frequent assurances from adults that this is not the case.

Feeling in control rather than helpless, and feeling group solidarity rather than selfishness makes a big difference in coping with disaster and processing memories. It is helpful to give people useful activities by assigning clear even if small tasks, and involving them in decisions; so does keeping track of time, and having timelines for future strategies of restoration.

Traumatic events decline in intensity but the internal stress endures; memories return and capture one's attention and affect one's sleep and alertness. Taking sedatives, tranquilizers, alcohol, or too many caffeinated beverages can make accidents more likely to happen. The person needs to be more careful, and allow more time for rest and sleep. But fear of flashbacks and other intrusive experiences may make victims reluctant to relax: leaving lights on, having a companion watch over them during sleep, sleeping with a pet, or similar changes can be helpful.

After the external traumatic events subside, the mind continues to process the meanings of the events internally to the self, focusing especially on how the events relate to enduring expectancies of how the world will be. Topics related to the events and to their impact on the person's inner fabric of beliefs will return to consciousness, while awake or in dreams, perhaps in surprising ways and at surprising intervals even months after the traumatic experiences. This is not a sign of "losing control over the mind," but rather that the mind is at work even beyond conscious expectations. Often a sense of increasing safety can release these topics for more attention and understanding. Patience and willingness by others to go over memories repeatedly is indicated.

Every event activates many themes that need processing later on, when the person feels safe. Some of these themes may seem very unsafe to consider. The person dreads entering an emotionally negative state of mind that feels like it will be out of control, and so avoids reminders and thoughts about threatening themes. When attempting to bring up a threatening topic with others, he or she may do so with lower emotional control or describe the event in a halting, obscure, or tense way. It is especially important to avoid telling the person to "forget about it," "brace up," or that "everything will be fine." This is where giving time with patience and tact can be extremely helpful even though the helper may feel that he or she cannot make up the loss or give clear counsel on exactly what to do.

Sometimes a traumatic event leads to a collapsing-dominoes effect. There is a disaster in which a loved one dies. Then the bereaved person becomes irritable with fatigue and frustration as well as sad with grief; this offends other disaster survivors or friends who might otherwise provide emotional support. They leave the victim because they do not perceive any gratitude.

The victim becomes more distressed, and this manifests itself in poor performance at work. The next dominoes fall, as the victim is reprimanded, threatened, or fired. Early social, culturally sensitive interventions can sometimes stop this cascade of catastrophes.

Biological Treatment

While relationship support is the first line of intervention, antianxiety medications are sometimes used to prevent extremes of fatigue, emotional flooding, agitation, and racing thoughts. These agents can often be used in a single dose, or as night by night sedation. Very transient use of benzodiazepines has sometimes been effective as a way of reducing explosive entry into extremely undermodulated states.

A variety of antidepressant medications have been used not just for depressive disorders exacerbated or precipitated by stressor events, but also for specific symptoms of PTSD or panic attacks following traumatic events. Selective serotonin reuptake inhibitors, tricyclics, and monoamine oxidase inhibitors have been tried with some reported success. Medications that reduce autonomic nervous system arousal, such as the beta adrenergic blockers have also been tried.

New research has also shown that some recurrent schizophrenic episodes may be precipitated by life events. At such times prescriptions of antipsychotic medications (or increase in dosage of such agents) may be indicated.

Psychotherapy

The major areas of focus across all psychotherapies include the trauma itself and its association with other meanings, such as beliefs, attitudes, expectations, and intentions. The major area of focus also includes discussion of how to restore functional capacity in the future. Some therapies focus in addition on the effect of traumas on affectional ties with others.

Shock mastery and reschematization processes are facilitated in psychotherapy. These processes are encouraged (1) by focusing on links between traumatic memories and personal meanings, and (2) by focusing on links between trauma responses and activated maladaptive personality traits. These foci are summarized in table 4. Most approaches to psychotherapy include several or even all of the domains listed. This overview may help readers to see the similarities of approach across different schools of technique, such as those of dynamic, cognitive, and behavioral clinicians.

Table 4. Levels of Focus in Treatment

Goal	Content areas
Link trauma memory to personal meanings and plans	Stressors, stress responses, and urgent coping choices
	Dreaded states and triggers of symptoms
	Differentiation of realistic from irrational beliefs
	Avoidance of adaptive challenges
	Long-range coping choices
Link trauma responses to activated and maladaptive personality issues	Repetitive maladaptive interpersonal patterns
	Problems with self-esteem and identity
	Alternative views of self and others
	Life plans and goals

Diagnosis alone does not lead to optimum treatment plans. Formulation is required to put together the biopsychosocial factors that cause specific signs and symptoms. I use a configurational analysis method for such case formulation (Horowitz, 1997a). It addresses 1) symptomatic phenomena, 2) states of mind, 3) topics of concern and defensive control of emotion, and 4) self-other beliefs (person schemas). This leads to 5) an integrated treatment plan.

Phenomena that increase after traumas include deflections from ordinary conscious expression. Reassurance that intrusions and omissions are not abnormal, and that they will usually abate in time, is often helpful. Otherwise the patient may be vulnerable to losing an already fragile sense of self-regulatory capacity.

The *states* that increase after trauma range from under-to overmodulated. Therefore, treatment plans should be progressively revised. Undermodulated states may be countered with empathy, support, and ideational linkages that provide clear and rational conceptual structuring. Overmodulated states may be countered by work on resistance to fuller expression. Therapy can be phase oriented, using different techniques as states shift. Treatment can moderate extreme states and facilitate a working-through state.

The *defensive control processes* that can lead to overmodulated states may depend on pre-existing cultural and personal coping practices and beliefs. In some cases, these social and personality-based habits of avoidance and reality-distortion should be addressed, especially if they unduly limit the expression of intense negative feelings, or the communication of personal needs for more social support.

Person schemas include beliefs about self and others, and the place of self in the social world. Trauma can induce ideas that are contradictory to these prior beliefs and expectations. Psychotherapy facilitates the integration of these mismatched ideas. When personality is involved—when traumas have activated latent conflicts about values, identity, and relationships—then treatment must sometimes confront deep-seated conflict. The result can be a growth in character. This may call for longer treatment aimed at using the trauma for growth and development, so that future stressors are less likely to be traumatic for the individual (Horowitz, 1998).

People everywhere are victims or terrorized eyewitnesses to human and natural disasters. A third of them may be vulnerable to develop PTSD. Many clinicians, through their research efforts, are engaged in improving diagnoses, explanations, and treatments of such conditions. New theories will undoubtedly illuminate how to prevent these disorders. Our current agreement on the validity of trauma-induced disorders empowers such research. Our need to know more about causation and treatment makes future clinical research in this area essential and challenging.

REFERENCES

Bandura A: The self and mechanisms of agency. In Suls J (ed): Psychological Perspectives of the Self, Vol 1. Hillsdale, NJ, Erlbaum, 1982

Beck A T, and Emery G: Anxiety Disorders and Phobias: A Cognitive Perspective. New York, Basic Books, 1985

Charney D S, Deutch A, Krystal J, Southwick S M, and Nagy L: Psychobiological mechanisms of post-traumatic stress disorder. Arch Gen Psychiatry 50:294, 1993

Figley C R (ed): Stress Disorders among Vietnam Veterans: Theory, Research and Treatment. New York, Brunner/Mazel, 1978

Foa E B, and Kozak M J: Emotional processing of fear: Exposure to corrective information. Psych Bull 99: 20–35, 1988

Freud S: Beyond the Pleasure Principle, Standard Edition (Strachey, editor) 18: 7–66, 1920. London, Hogarth Press, 1955

Freud S: Remembering, Repeating and Working Through, Standard Edition (Strachey, editor) 14: 69–102, 1914. London, Hogarth Press, 1955

Furst S S: Psychic trauma: A survey. In S S Furst (ed): Psychic Trauma, pp 3–50. New York, Basic Books, 1967

Hamner M B, Diamond B I, and Hitri A: Plasma norepinephrine and MHPG responses to exercise stress in PTSD. In Murbing M M (ed) : Catecholamine Function in Posttraumatic Stress Disorder: Emerging Concepts, pp 221–232. Washington, DC, American Psychiatric Press, 1994

Horowitz M J: Psychic trauma: Return of images after a stress film. Arch Gen Psychiatry 25:552–559, 1969

Horowitz M J: Intrusive and repetitive thoughts after experimental stress. Arch Gen Psychiatry *32: 1457–1463, 1975*

Horowitz M J: Person schemas. In Horowitz M (ed): Person Schemas and Maladaptive Interpersonal Behaviors, *pp 13–31. Chicago, U Chicago Press, 1991*

Horowitz M J: Formulation for Planning Psychotherapy. *Washington, DC, American Psychiatric Press, 1997a*

Horowitz M J: Stress Response Syndromes, *third edition, Northvale, NJ, Aronson, 1997b*

Horowitz M J: Cognitive Psychodynamics: From Conflict to Character, *New York, Wiley, 1998*

Horowitz M J, Alvarez W, and Wilner N: Impact of Event Scale: A measure of subjective stress. Psychosomatic Med *41:209–218, 1979*

Horowitz M J, and Becker S S: Cognitive response to stressful stimuli. Arch Gen Psychiatry *25:419–428, 1971*

Horowitz M J, Siegel B, Holen A, Bonanno G, Milbrath C, and Stinson C: Diagnostic criteria for complicated grief disorders. Am J Psychiatry *154:904–911, 1997*

Horowitz M J, and Solomon G F: A prediction of stress response syndromes in Vietnam veterans: Observations and suggestions for treatment. J Soc Issues *31:67–80, 1975*

Marmar C R, Weiss D S, Metzler T, Ronfeldt H, and Foreman C: Stress responses of emergency services personnel to the Loma Prieta earthquake interstate 880 freeway collapse and control traumatic incidents. J Traumatic Stress *9:63–85, 1995*

McFarlane A C, Weber D, and Clark R: Abnormal stimulus processing in posttraumatic stress disorder. Biological Psychiatry *34:311–320, 1993*

Prigerson H G, Frank E, Bierhals A J, Kasl S V, Reynolds III C F, Anderson B, Zubenko G S, Houck P R, George C J, and Kupfer D J: Complicated grief and bereavement-related depression as distinct disorders. Am J Psychiatry *152:22–30, 1996*

Selye H: Stress in Health and Disease. *Boston, Butterworths, 1976*

Southwick S M, Krystal J H, Morgan C A, Johnson D, Nagy L M, Nicolaou A, Heninger G R, and Charney D S: Abnormal noradrenergic function in posttraumatic stress disorder. Arch Gen Psychiatry *50:266–280, 1993*

Weiss D S, Marmar C R, Metzler T, and Ronfeldt H: Predicting symptomatic distress in emergency services personnel, JCCP *63:361–368, 1995*

Additional Books of Relevance

Appley M H, Trumbull R: Dynamics of Stress. *New York, Plenum, 1986*

Everly G S: A Clinical Guide to the Treatment of the Human Stress Response. *New York, Plenum, 1989*

Everstine D F, and Everstine L: The Trauma Response. *New York, Norton, 1993*

Gray J A: The Psychology of Fear and Stress. *Cambridge, Cambridge University Press, 1987*

Herman J L: Trauma and Recovery. *New York, Basic Books, 1992*

Kleber R J, and Bron D: Coping with Trauma. *Amsterdam, Swets and Zeitlinger, 1992*

Kulka R A, et al.: Trauma and the Vietnam War Generation. *New York, Brunner/Mazel, 1990*

Lazarus R S, and Folkman F: Stress, Appraisal, and Coping. *New York, Springer, 1984*

Meek C L (ed): Posttraumatic Stress Disorder: Assessment, Differential Diagnosis, and Forensic Evaluation. *Sarasota, FL, Professional Resource Exchange, 1990*

Peterson K C, Prout M F, and Schwarz R A: Posttraumatic Stress Disorder. *New York, Plenum, 1991*

Raphael B: When Disaster Strikes. *New York, Basic Books, 1986*

Scott M J, and Stradling S G: Counseling for Posttraumatic Stress Disorder. *London, Sage, 1992*

Solomon Z: Combat Stress Reaction. *New York, Plenum, 1993*

Sonnenberg S M, Blank A S, and Talbott J A: The Trauma of War. *Washington, DC, American Psychiatric Press, 1985*

Ulman R B, and Brothers D: The Shattered Self. *Hillsdale, NJ, Analytic Press, 1988*

Wilson J P, and Lindy J D: Countertransference and the Treatment of PTSD. *New York, Guilford, 1994*

Wilson J T, Harel Z, and Kahana B: Human Adaptation to Extreme Stress. *New York, Plenum, 1988*

PART I

Introduction

This section begins with a delineation of PTSD and then delves into the complex diagnostic issues. The paper by Freud in this section illustrates early disputes about posttraumatic symptoms. In this paper, Freud reasserted his then controversial view that neurotic symptoms stemmed from psychological conflict. He asserted that wishes to flee the terrors of war were repressed because shame would result if such aims were consciously known. By unconscious symptom formation the soldier tried to avoid the shame and guilt of not fulfilling obligations to comrades, society, and ideals.

During World War I, some German military physicians treated psychological casualties from what was then called "shell-shock" with quite painful electric currents. Their aim was to cause the disabled soldier more distress if he retreated from the front than if he returned to combat. Some soldiers were physically injured or even killed by this treatment, while others escaped from all horrors by suicide. Protests from family members forced the government to inquire about the propriety of this medical treatment. Freud was asked to give his expert opinion. He decried the use of such techniques, and formulated a psychodynamic route of symptom formation.

The German government's lawyers used Freud's psychodynamic formulations after World War II. After the release of concentration camp survivors, these victims of Nazi inhumanity sought reparation for physical and psychological damage. The government did not want to pay for their posttraumatic impairments. After all, the psychoanalytic theories of that time stated that all neuroses stemmed from reactions to childhood events. The adult war victims with a diagnosis of posttraumatic neuroses must have been abused as children, before incarceration and other horrors.

Clinical research, as in the paper by Eitinger, resolved this legal argument in favor of the victims. Eitinger found that two-thirds of all Norwegian concentration camp victims seeking reparation had experienced severe psychic reactions during captivity and 99% still displayed symptoms after the war. The main signs were poor memory and inability to concentrate (present in 87%); nervousness, irritability, and restlessness (86%); increased fatigue

(84%); and sleep disturbance (66%). Symptom frequency and intensity correlated with the severity of events during imprisonment. His conclusion was that adult traumatization had caused the disorders.

Some scientists hope to support the validity of the diagnosis of PTSD by finding biological substrates for consciously experienced symptoms. Such investigators seek measures of physiological responses to stimuli that remind victims of traumatic memories. For example, in the paper by Pitman and his colleagues, data from seven patients with PTSD and seven patients with anxiety disorders, all exposed to stimuli reminiscent of combat experiences, are compared. Five of the PTSD subjects and none of the anxiety subjects were identified by a statistical analysis using a discriminate function for identifying which subjects had heightened physiological responses.

Positive adaptation can occur as a consequence of working through responses to dire events. Nadelson and colleagues observed some women who became more serious, more careful, more self-reliant, and stronger in self-conceptualization after mastery of their traumatic rape experiences. Negative effects of the rape were, of course, pronounced. The authors found that only a third of forty-one rape victims recovered within the first few months. Others had symptoms persisting one to two and a half years after the rape. These symptoms included suspiciousness of others (76%), restriction in going out (61%), sexual difficulties (51%), and fear of being alone (49%).

The Terr paper deals with childhood trauma. Terr describes four characteristics of symptomatology in traumatized children: insistent and strongly visualized memories, trauma-related repetitive behaviors, trauma-specific contextual fears, and changed attitudes about self and others. A sense of omens, misperceptions, and mistimings was prominent after single, highly traumatic experiences. After repeated exposure the children were prone to massive denials, experiences of numbing, anesthesias of self, and personality pattern disturbances. Terr characterizes self-hypnosis, depersonalization, and dissociative states as possible personality traits developed after repeated trauma. Her emphasis on the consequences of chronic rage, including anger turned against the self, echoes findings by Lindemann in adult studies of grief.

Herman emphasized the adult consequences of trauma during childhood. She noted an increased adult tendency to hypervigilance, horror, and feeling dissociated. Symptoms of victimization in adulthood also included insomnia, exaggerated startle reactions, extreme agitation, headaches, gastrointestinal disturbances, as well as back and other pains. Herman also observed characterological changes such as a malignant sense of the self as contaminated, guilty, and evil. From prolonged victimization, such beliefs about self, even held unconsciously, might lead to repetitive self-mutilation. Adults abused as children were found to be at a high risk for rape, sexual harassment, battering, and becoming an aggressor.

As a group, the papers in this section show the validity of the PTSD diagnosis. The signs and symptoms of PTSD and related stress response syndromes cover the gamut from acute signs of loss of control over cognition, emotion, and bodily reaction to chronic problems that seem like stress-induced traits.

1. Signs and Symptoms of Posttraumatic Stress Disorder

Mardi J. Horowitz, Nancy Wilner, Nancy Kaltreider, and William Alvarez

AFTER SERIOUS life events some persons develop stress response syndromes characterized by phases of intrusive ideas and feelings and phases of ideational denial and emotional numbing. Review of clinical, field, and experimental studies has confirmed the characteristic configuration of this syndrome, which is described in detail elsewhere.[1] Because of the concordant findings from a variety of investigations, the Task Force on Nomenclature and Statistics of the American Psychiatric Association has included a new classification, the posttraumatic stress disorder, in the latest diagnostic system, DSM III.[2] We report the frequency and intensity of the characteristic signs and symptoms of this disorder. Awareness of these signs and symptoms is important; early recognition of the syndrome can lead to appropriate brief treatment and the probable prevention of chronic disorders.

BACKGROUND

Phenomenological description of stress response syndromes has been difficult because psychological reactions always combine response keyed to a recent serious life event with previous inner models of the self and the world. Prior attitudes, conflicts, developmental arrests, personality styles, cultural premises, and networks of social support are invariably combined with recent meanings and implications. Because of the mixture of past with present themes, classification of problems resulting from serious life events has oscillated between such diagnoses as "traumatic neurosis" and "neurosis precipitated by trauma." The existence of less formal and more specific diagnoses such as pathological grief,[3] combat neuroses,[4] rape-trauma syndrome,[5] and post-Vietnam syndrome[6] have both clarified and complicated the issue.

Reprinted by permission from *Archives of General Psychiatry,* 37, 85–92. Copyright © 1980 by the American Medical Association.

In the first official American Psychiatric Diagnostic System (DSM-I), stress response syndromes were included under the heading of "gross stress reactions." In the subsequent revision (DSM-II), still in effect at this writing, the diagnostic dilemma was reflected by deletion of this reaction. Instead, in formal classification, the diagnostic terms were those of the neuroses, such as "anxiety neurosis," or "transient situational disturbance." In the new revision (DSM-III), diagnoses of stress response syndromes are now possible because of a newly defined classification—the posttraumatic stress disorder. The diagnostic criteria as they appear in the draft of DSM-III are shown in table 1.1.

While consensual validation and clinical observation have resulted in substantial agreement in defining posttraumatic stress disorder, there is a need for data about the prevalence, within the syndrome, of various significant signs and symptoms. A considerable literature on traumatic reactions has been reviewed by Grinker and Spiegel,[4] Lazarus,[7] Janis,[8] Parad et al.,[9] Parkes,[10] Clayton,[11] and Horowitz.[1] Data reported by the studies that were reviewed are limited in applicability to examination of the signs and symptoms specific to stress response syndromes. Much of it was derived from field

*Table 1.1. Diagnostic Criteria for Posttraumatic Stress Disorder**

A. A recognizable stressor that would be expected to evoke significant symptoms of distress in almost all individuals
B. Re-experiencing the traumatic event either by
  (1) Recurrent and intrusive recollections of the event; or
  (2) Recurrent dreams of the event; or
  (3) Suddenly acting or feeling as if the traumatic event were occurring because of an association with an environmental or ideational stimulus
C. Numbing of responsiveness to, or involvement with, the external world, beginning some time after the traumatic event(s) as shown by either
  (1) Markedly diminished interest in one or more significant activities; or
  (2) Feelings of detachment or estrangement from others; or
  (3) Marked constriction of affective responses
D. At least two of the following (not present prior to the traumatic event)
  (1) Hyperalertness or exaggerated startle response;
  (2) Initial, middle, or terminal sleep disturbance;
  (3) Guilt about surviving when others have not, or about behavior required to achieve survival;
  (4) Memory impairment or trouble concentrating;
  (5) Avoidance of activities that arouse recollection of the traumatic event;
  (6) Intensification of symptoms by exposure to events that symbolize or resemble the traumatic event

---

*From Task Force on Nomenclature and Statistics, 1978, pp. N4–N5.

studies of persons investigated because they shared in the experience of a particular event, not because a particular syndrome developed. Data were collected through the use of instruments and interviews that focused on emotional manifestations and behavioral states, and omitted many qualities of the altered experiences of consciousness described in the DSM-III criteria. We provide data on a clinical population of persons with posttraumatic stress disorder, so defined by themselves and by clinicians through instruments and interviews designed with the intention of exploring the quality of these experiences.

METHODS

Design

A special unit developed for the treatment of stress response syndromes has been in operation at the University of California Medical Center for more than five years. It is staffed by faculty and advanced trainees in psychiatry, psychology, and social work. After initial screening and securing of informed consent, persons who sought help were evaluated and, when appropriate, treatment interviews were scheduled. After each evaluation interview, a set of rating scales was completed by the patient, and another set was completed by the clinician. These rating scales were specifically designed to formalize inquiry into the signs and symptoms of stress response syndromes.

Subjects

Persons evaluated at the clinic were usually referred by local community mental health centers, crisis clinics, other counselors, or, most often, by the university outpatient psychiatry service. Occasionally, persons aware of the clinic were self-referred. After a psychiatric social worker determined that the case seemed appropriate for the clinic, an evaluation interview was scheduled.

The most essential criteria for acceptance included responses at the neurotic level to the experience within the past year of a serious life event such as bodily damage resulting from accident, assault, illness, or surgery, or object loss, such as the death of a loved one. Criteria for rejection, with referral elsewhere, included having had psychotherapy since the event occurred, chronic misuse of drugs or alcohol, syndromes at the psychotic level, involvement with litigation concerning the event, and any reservations about giving written consent for participation in the research procedures. Persons with cancer or other serious continuing illnesses were also excluded, as were those involved in turbulent separations such as divorce, when there was a real possibility of reunion. Those with severe characterological disturbances, chronically chaotic lives, or complex and mixed syndromes were considered inappropriate for treatment at this clinic, with its focus on brief therapy, and were also referred elsewhere.

However, the acceptance criteria were flexible, and minor discrepancies could be set aside if the person met the essential guidelines: a neurotic level of symptomatic distress linked to a serious event, motivation for treatment, and a syndrome that might be helped by brief, focal therapy. Accordingly, 66 patients with stress response syndromes were evaluated and 44 were subsequently referred for brief, time-limited therapy within the clinic.[12] Among the 22 who were not referred to our clinic were persons who decided to seek private treatment, those who were unwilling to agree to the research requirements, and those who decided against treatment at the time of evaluation but agreed to follow-up interviews at a later date. Comparison of the 44 patients who received treatment with the 22 persons who were evaluated but not treated at this clinic showed that the 44 treated persons reported substantially higher levels of symptoms on the rating scales, but did not report symptoms different from those described by the group of 22. Therefore, to give the most comprehensive picture of the initial syndrome, the data analyses that follow include the entire evaluated sample of 66 persons. It was composed of 16 men and 50 women between 20 and 75 years of age, with a mean age of 34. Note that there is a bias in our consecutive sample toward more women than men.

Inciting Events

The life event that preceded the development of a stress response syndrome varied among patients. About half (34) experienced the death of someone close to them; the remainder (32) had sustained personal injuries including violence, accidents, and illnesses. Time from the occurrence of the event to the evaluation interview averaged 25 weeks, with a range of 1 to 136 weeks. The evaluation interview was then scheduled to occur within a few days of the incoming call initiated by the patient or referral source.

MAJOR RATING SCALES

Three scales provide the primary data on the configuration of the stress response syndrome: two self-report instruments and one clinical rating.

Impact of Event Scale: A Self-Report Instrument

The items on this instrument were abstracted from samples of earlier interviews with nonpatient subjects exposed to serious events in experimental studies of stress reactions,[13] and patients seen in the beginning phases of the stress clinic. The focus of the scale is on the form and quality of conscious experiences during a recent period with the event specific to the individual written on the form as the referent for response to the list of experiences. Responses cover the past seven days, not the entire period since the event occurred. This was found to be the best time unit for clinically valid reports of current subjective distress and states of mind related to a particular life event.[14]

As previously reported,[14] the Impact of Event Scale was developed through sequential refinement of items and studies of reliability and validity of the instrument. The result was a 15-item scale with four points for rating the intensity of each item. Subscales of coherent items were found to be both logically and empirically consistent, and yielded intrusion and avoidance scores. The internal consistency of these subscales, using Cronbach's Alpha, was 0.78 and 0.82, respectively. Test-retest reliability for the total stress score (intrusion and avoidance combined) was 0.87.

Symptom Checklist: A Self-Report Instrument

The 90-item symptom checklist[15] was used as a general indicator of a broad range of symptom dimensions and also as a reliable instrument that would allow articulation of data reported by this specialized sample with groups of patients and nonpatients in other clinical studies.[16] It consists of the following subscales: anxiety, depression, somatization, hostility, interpersonal sensitivity, phobic anxiety, paranoid ideation, obsessive-compulsive, and psychoticism.

Stress Response Rating Scale: An Instrument for Clinicians

This instrument was completed by clinicians after interviews with subjects. It has been refined several times on the basis of continuing experience with stress response syndromes. Like the Impact of Event Scale, it consists of intrusion and denial subsets.[17] The reliability of these subscales, using Cronbach's Alpha, was 0.89 and 0.86, respectively. However, the denial subset of this scale is unlike the avoidance subsets of the Impact of Event Scale in that it reflects processes observed by clinicians that may be beyond the conscious awareness of the subjects.

Other Rating Scales

Other scales provided supplementary information. For clinicians, these included a general symptom rating instrument (Brief Psychiatric Rating Scale)and a scale for classifying and scoring personality and information processing styles (Personality Typology). For subjects there was a Life Events Questionnaire and a global rating of experience and adjustment to stress (Experience of Stress Scale). Data on these instruments were examined and indicated results similar to the data to be presented in more detail. Since they did not contribute salient information for this presentation, these scales will be only briefly described.

Brief Psychiatric Rating Scale: An Instrument for Clinicians

Developed by Overall and Gorham,[18] this instrument consists of 16 categories of observable signs and symptoms, each rated on a 7-point scale, from "not present" to "extremely severe." Only 8 of the 16 categories were used, eliminating that half of the scale applicable to psychotic conditions, since patients with problems at the level were excluded from our sample.

Personality Typology: An Instrument for Clinicians

This instrument, currently being refined and tested, was used by clinicians to rate patients for goodness of fit to several typologies of neurotic styles. It included hysterical and obsessional patterns as well as other typologies, and rated expressive, interactional, and information-processing styles by operational definitions.[19] Preliminary findings will be discussed in the "Results" section.

Life Events Questionnaire: A Self-Report Instrument

This is the short form of a comprehensive questionnaire asking for reports of experienced life events of a relatively serious nature. In previous studies, weightings were developed for each event, according to the recency or remoteness in time from occurrence of the event, indicating the degree of stress that might be imposed.[20] As with other life event questionnaires,[21-23] the total score is a measure of presumptive cumulative stress from life changes. Scores on this instrument were compared to see if persons with greater cumulative changes might find a specific life event more stressful than those who had experienced less change.

Experience of Stress Scale: A Self-Report Instrument

On three separate "thermometer" scales, subjects are asked to rate their level of upset when the event occurred, their current level of upset, and the amount of adjustment they have made thus far. Each of these estimates is based on a scale of 1 to 100, with 100 being the most upset they can imagine for themselves.

RESULTS

Specific Forms of Experience

Data on the Impact of Event Scale, as mentioned, covered the person's recognition of states of stress during the previous seven days; these data,

Table 1.2. Impact of Event Scale: Experiences Reported by 66 Subjects

Intrusion items	%*	Group mean†	SD
I had waves of strong feelings about it.	88	3.8	1.9
Things I saw or heard suddenly reminded me of it.	85	3.7	1.9
I thought about it when I didn't mean to.	76	3.3	2.2
Images related to it popped into my mind.	76	3.2	2.2
Any reminder brought back emotions related to it.	76	3.0	2.1
I have difficulty falling asleep because of images or thoughts related to the event.	64	2.6	2.4
I had bad dreams related to the event.	44	1.7	2.2
Avoidance items			
I knew that a lot of unresolved feelings were still there, but I kept them under wraps.	71	3.0	2.2
I avoided letting myself get emotional when I thought about it or was reminded of it.	70	2.8	2.1
I wished to banish it from my store of memories.	65	2.8	2.3
I made an effort to avoid talking about it.	61	2.2	2.0
I felt unrealistic about it, as if it hadn't happened or as if it wasn't real.	58	2.2	2.3
I stayed away from things or situations that might remind me of it.	53	2.2	2.3
My emotions related to it were kind of numb.	59	2.1	2.1
I didn't let myself have thoughts related to it.	50	1.8	2.2

*Percent positive endorsement.
† On a scale of intensity where 5 is severe; 3, moderate; 1, mild; 0, not at all (within the past seven days).

ordered according to means, are summarized in table 1.2. Note that all items on the scale were reported rather frequently. The experiences reported most often were waves of strong feeling about the event, sudden triggers to recollection of the event, and unintended or intrusive thoughts, images, and emotions.

The judgments by clinicians for these same patients were also estimated for the previous seven days and are reported in order of means in table 1.3. Pangs of emotion about the event, preoccupation with it, and intrusive ideas

Table 1.3. Stress Response Rating Scale: Signs and Symptoms Reported by Clinicians for 66 Subjects

Intrusion items	%*	Group mean†	SD
Pangs of emotion	95	3.1	1.3
Rumination or preoccupation	90	2.9	1.4
Fear of losing bodily control or hyperactivity in any bodily system	82	2.6	1.5
Intrusive ideas (in word form)	77	2.3	1.5
Difficulty in dispelling ideas	74	2.1	1.6
Hypervigilance	69	1.6	1.4
Bad dreams	54	1.6	1.7
Intrusive thoughts or images when trying to sleep	51	1.6	1.8
Re-enactments	57	1.5	1.5
Intrusive images	51	1.4	1.6
Startle reactions	34	0.6	1.0
Illusions	26	0.6	1.1
Hallucinations, pseudohallucinations	8	0.2	0.8
Denial Items			
Numbness	69	1.8	1.5
Avoidance of associational connections	69	1.7	1.4
Reduced level of feeling responses to outer stimuli	67	1.7	1.5
Rigidly role-adherent or stereotyped	62	1.5	1.5
Loss of reality appropriacy of thought by switching attitudes	64	1.4	1.2
Unrealistic narrowing of attention, vagueness, or disavowal of stimuli	52	1.2	1.3
Inattention, daze	48	1.2	1.5
Inflexibility or constriction of thought	46	1.0	1.2
Loss of train of thoughts	44	0.9	1.2
Loss of reality appropriacy of thought by sliding meanings	41	0.8	1.2
Memory failure	34	0.8	1.2
Loss of reality appropriacy of thought by use of disavowal	25	0.6	1.2
Warding off trains of reality-oriented thought by use of fantasy	15	0.3	0.8

*Percent positive endorsement.
†On a scale of intensity where 5 is major; 3, moderate; 1, minor, 0, not present (within the past seven days).

related to it are again among the most commonly reported experiences. The denial items on the clinicians' form include signs that are difficult for patients to report; these are inferences drawn by the clinician from observation of defensive operations such as avoiding associational connections (69%), switching of attitudes (64%), and sliding meanings (41%). These processes and signs were described in previous clinical studies as control operations especially prominent in stress response syndromes.[1,17]

General Symptom Responses

The highest response levels on the 90-item Symptom Checklist were noted on the subscales of depression, anxiety, obsessive-compulsive, anger-hostility, and somatization. The most frequent symptoms, endorsed by more than 92% of the group, were feeling blue, worrying, feeling tense, feeling nervous, feeling lonely, and having trouble concentrating, as shown in tables 1.4 and

Table 1.4. Two Subscales of the Symptom Checklist:
Symptom Frequencies Reported by 64 Subjects*

	%
Depression	
Feeling blue	97
Worrying too much about things	97
Feeling lonely	92
Feeling low in energy or slowed down	91
Blaming yourself for things	89
Crying easily	84
Feeling everything is an effort	81
Feeling no interest in things	78
Feeling hopeless about the future	75
Feelings of worthlessness	72
Loss of sexual interest or pleasure	66
Feeling of being trapped or caught	62
Thoughts of ending your life	45
Anxiety	
Feeling tense or keyed-up	95
Nervousness or shakiness inside	94
Feeling fearful	75
Feeling so restless you couldn't sit still	72
Feeling pushed to get things done	70
Heart pounding or racing	67
Trembling	66
Suddenly scared for no reason	56
Spells of terror or panic	48
Feeling that familiar things are strange or unreal	36

* In the early phase of this study, two subjects did not fill out the Symptom Checklist.

Table 1.5. *Three Subscales of the Symptom Checklist:*
Symptom Frequencies Reported by 64 Subjects

	%
Obsessive-Compulsive	
Trouble concentrating	92
Unwanted thoughts, words, or ideas that won't leave your mind	90
Difficulty making decisions	88
Feeling blocked in getting things done	77
Trouble remembering things	75
Worried about sloppiness or carelessness	64
Your mind going blank	64
Having to check and double-check what you do	59
Having to do things very slowly to insure correctness	58
Having to repeat the same actions such as touching, counting, washing	35
Anger-Hostility	
Feeling easily annoyed or irritated	82
Temper outbursts that you could not control	42
Getting into frequent arguments	42
Having urges to break or smash things	41
Shouting or throwing things	31
Having urges to beat, injure, or harm someone	20
Somatization	
Headaches	79
Feeling weak in parts of your body	77
Nausea or upset stomach	70
Soreness of your muscles	66
Hot or cold spells	59
Pains in lower back	58
Faintness or dizziness	56
Numbness or tingling in parts of your body	55
Heavy feelings in your arms or legs	55
A lump in your throat	53
Pains in heart or chest	52
Trouble getting your breath	43

1.5. The clinically important experiences of suicidal thoughts and spells of terror or panic were present in 45% and 48%, respectively. As a kind of cross-reliability of items on the stress-specific instruments, the general Symptom Checklist again showed that intrusion was a frequent symptom: 90% reported unwanted thoughts, words, or ideas that were difficult to dispel.

Correlations

Intercorrelations of the subscales on the self-report instruments indicated that they measured different responses. Within the self-report scale for the more stress-specific experiences (Impact of Event), the intrusion and avoidance subscales correlated significantly (r = .47, P< .001). Correlations between the Impact of Event subscales and the subscales of the Symptom Checklist showed that the intrusion subscale of the Impact of Event Scale correlated significantly with only one subscale of the Symptom Checklist. This was a positive correlation between intrusive experiences on the Impact of Event Scale and experiences of anxiety on the Symptom Checklist (r = .36, P < .01), shown in table 1.6. The avoidance subscale (Impact of Event) correlated positively and significantly with every subscale of the Symptom Checklist and most cogently with the anxiety subscale (r = .42, P < .001). These data support the accepted premise that traumatic events tend to precipitate anxiety reactions, as is outlined in the diagnostic decision tables of DSM-III.

Time between the Life Event and the Evaluation

Studies of serious life events and symptomatic responses, such as those reviewed by Clayton,[11] indicated a gradual decline over time in the intensity of experience of signs and symptoms. Our own previous studies of estimates of distress from a variety of life events confirmed this impression.[20,24] But such studies involve field populations, not persons seeking help because of distress. In a patient population one would not necessarily expect a decrease in symptoms from time since the event to first evaluation. That, indeed, was our finding. The only correlation in the direction of reduced experiences with time was between time and the intrusion subset of the Impact of Event Scale (r = −.15, not significant).

Cumulative Stress

A presumptive cumulative stress score[20] for each person was derived from the Life Events Questionnaire and correlated with self-report of symptomatic experiences on the Impact of Event Scale and the Symptom Checklist. The aim was to see if persons with greater presumptive cumulative stress from various life events would experience more distress related to a specific, recent, serious event than persons with fewer life changes. If cumulative stress was a relevant issue, one would expect significant positive correlations between scores on the Life Events Questionnaire and scores on the Impact of Event Scale and other symptom measures. To some extent, this was the case. Correlation between the presumptive stress score from the Life Events Questionnaire and the total stress score (Intrusion plus Avoidance) from the Impact of Event Scale was positive although small and not significant (r = .17).

Table 1.6. *Self-Report Scales: Correlations of Subscales of Impact of Event Scale with Symptom Checklist**

Impact of event scale	Symptom Checklist									
	Depression	Anxiety	Obsessive-compulsive	Anger-hostility	Someti-zation	Interpersonal sensitivity	Phobic anxiety	Paranoid ideation	Psychot-icism	Total
Intrusion	0.18	0.36‡	0.14	0.16	0.19	0.12	0.07	0.17	0.07	0.23†
Avoidance	0.26†	0.42§	0.33‡	0.24†	0.22†	0.27†	0.22†	0.21†	0.26†	0.36‡

*N = 65.
†P < .05.
‡P < .01.
§P < .001.

Significant, positive, but low effect size correlations were noted between presumptive stress scores derived from life event reports and the Symptom Checklist subscales for anxiety ($r = .29$, P $<$ .01), anger ($r = .21$, P $<$ .05) and somatization ($r = .21$, P $<$ .05). Marginal correlation was noted in the depression subscale ($r = .20$, P $<$ .06). Correlations with the other five subscales of the Symptom Checklist were positive but not significant.

Comparison with Other Clinical and Normative Populations

As suggested by Waskow and Parloff,[16] the Symptom Checklist can be used to articulate clinical studies. When our data on severity of symptoms are compared with normal and clinical data from other centers, they substantiate the population we studied as similar to other psychiatric outpatient populations. For example, the scores from our group are similar in severity to those of 100 Johns Hopkins psychiatric outpatients and different from their sample of 48 normal, obese women[13] (table 1.7).

Age Effects

To examine the effect of age on the configuration of a stress response syndrome, a frequency histogram was constructed, and a cutoff point, both logical and empirical, was found at the 30-year period. The scores of the 38 persons under 30 were compared with those of 28 persons aged 30 or over. On inspection, no important trends were noted for these or any other more

Table 1.7. Comparison of Symptom Checklist Subscale Scores

	Stress clinic (n = 64)		Hopkins psychiatry outpatients (n = 100)			Hopkins obese normal women (n = 48)		
	Mean	SD	Mean	SD	t	Mean	SD	t
Depression	1.93	0.74	1.84	1.05	—	1.12	0.88	5.2†
Obsessive-compulsive	1.69	0.96	1.51	1.01	—	0.96	0.65	4.4†
Anxiety	1.61	0.88	1.51	1.00	—	0.83	0.67	5.0†
Interpersonal sensitivity	1.31	1.01	1.40	0.96	—	0.96	0.80	2.0
Paranoid ideation	1.21	0.98	1.34	1.08	—	0.73	0.57	3.0*
Somatization	1.12	0.67	1.05	0.97	—	0.72	0.58	3.3*
Phobic anxiety	0.99	0.97	0.88	0.97	—	0.48	0.58	3.2*
Psychoticism	0.99	0.75	0.99	0.84	—	0.43	0.44	4.5†
Hostility	0.88	0.89	1.29	1.05	3.0*	0.68	0.49	1.4

*$P <$ .01.
†$P <$ .001.

discrete age groups. Statistical comparison, using two-tailed t tests, showed only five of 78 possible contrasts beyond the P <.05 level. Since four significant differences could be expected by chance alone, we concluded that there were no noteworthy differences between the older and the younger subgroups.

Sex Effects

Similar comparisons of 78 contrasts between 50 women and 16 men showed only six significant differences. We interpret these findings as showing no major sex differences. However, because of our small sample of men, caution should be used in such interpretation of these data. Two of the six differences were on the self-ratings of the Impact of Event Scale: (1) "I knew that a lot of unresolved feelings were still there, but I kept them under wraps"; the mean score for women was 3.5 $\pm$ 2.1; the mean score for men was 1.4 $\pm$ 1.9 (t =3.5, P < .001); and (2) "I avoided letting myself get emotional when I thought about it or was reminded of it." On this item, the mean score for women was 3.2 $\pm$ 2.0; the mean score for men was 1.4 $\pm$ 1.9 (t = 3.2, P < .05). Women also scored higher on the total avoidance subscales, with mean scores of 20.6 $\pm$ 11.3 as compared with men, who had mean scores of 14.1 $\pm$ 12.0 (t = 2.0, P <.05).

The Stress Response Rating Scale, scored by clinicians, also showed significant differences on two items with women again scoring higher. They were: (1) "Warding off trains of reality oriented thoughts by use of fantasy," with the mean score for women at 0.4 $\pm$ 0.9, and the mean score for men at 0.1 $\pm$ 0.3 (t = 2.0, P <.05); and (2) "Inflexibility or constriction of thought," with the mean score for women at 1.1 $\pm$ 1.2, and the mean score for men at 0.4 $\pm$ 0.8 (t = 2.2, P <.05).

Men scored higher on the sixth area of significant differences between the sexes, the "Resistiveness" subscale of the Brief Psychiatric Rating Scale, where they had mean scores of 8.9 $\pm$ 2.8, as compared with the women, who had mean scores of 7.2 $\pm$ 2.7 (t = 2.1, P < .05).

Quality of the Serious Life Event

The generality of response can also be examined by comparing groups according to the type of serious life event that traumatized them. In the present sample, 28 women who sustained the loss of another were compared with 19 women who had sustained personal injuries. Of the 78 item contrasts, only three were significant at a level of P <.05, a number to be expected by chance alone. The women with injuries to the self had more somatic concerns, fewer intrusive images, and reported less avoidance of reminders of the event: all of these responses were expectable because of the obvious qualities of the discrete events.

Neurotic Character Styles

In previous publications,[1,19,25,26] predisposing variables were discussed in terms of expressive, interactional, and information-processing styles. Clinical judgment of these styles was included for the present sample. The reliability of the method has not yet been tested, and only some persons fit into a particular type. It will be necessary to accumulate a larger consecutive sample and to evolve a reliable method before any conclusions can be drawn on the interaction of information-processing styles and the experiential qualities of stress response states. Only the most tentative results can be reported herein, but they are worthy of mention in order to underscore the importance of the eventual inclusion of such variables.

Among the 66 patients in the sample, 14 had a good to excellent fit to the obsessional type and 13 had a good to excellent fit to the hysterical type. As would be expected from clinical theory, the hysterical group (12 women and one man) reported more symptoms than the obsessional group (11 women and three men). On the intrusion subset of the Impact of Event Scale, the hysterical group produced a mean score of 23 ± 8.0, as compared with a mean score of 17 ± 11.0 for the obsessional group. On the avoidance subset, the mean score for the hysterical group was 20 ± 10.0, as compared with 15 ± 13.0 for the obsessional group. Three of the 15 items of the Impact of Event Scale significantly differentiated the groups with levels of at least P .05, with the hysterical group always higher. On responses to the Symptom Checklist and other variables, the groups were similar.

Two of the items on the Impact of Event Scale were in the intrusion subset. They were: (1) "Things I saw or heard suddenly reminded me of it," with a mean score for the hysterical group of 4.4 ± 1.0, as compared with the obsessional group, who had mean scores of 2.9 ± 2.1 ($t = 2.5$, P < .05); and (2) "Images related to it popped into my mind," with a mean score for the hysterical group of 4.2 ± 1.5, as compared with the obsessional group who had mean scores of 2.0 ± 2.2 ($t = 2.9$, P < .05. The third item was from the avoidance subset: "I avoided letting myself get emotional when I thought about it or was reminded of it." The mean score for the hysterical group was 3.4 ± 1.4, and the mean score for obsessionals was 1.9 ± 2.2 (t = 2.0, P < .05). These data can be accounted for, perhaps, on the increased readiness of the hysterical personality to admit to emotional qualities of experience.

On the Stress Response Rating Scale, the hysterical group scored higher on "inattention, daze," with mean scores of 1.8 ± 1.3, than the obsessional group, who had mean scores of 0.7 ± 1.1 (t = 2.4, P < .03). The obsessional group scored higher on "inflexibility or constriction of thought," with mean scores of 1.6 ± 1.3, as compared with the hysterical group, who had mean scores of 0.5 ± 1.0 (t = 2.4, P < .05).

On the Brief Psychiatric Rating Scale, the hysterical group scored higher on the item "conceptual disorganization," with mean scores of 2.6 ± 1.1, than the obsessional group, who had mean scores of 1.6 ± 0.8 (t = 2.6, P < .05). The hysterical group also scored higher on the total intrusiveness subscale, with mean scores of 12.5 ± 1.7, while obsessionals had mean scores of 10.7 ± 2.5 (t = 2.2, P < .05). However, the obsessional group scored higher on the subscale score for somatic concerns, with mean scores of 4.9 ± 2.1, as compared with the hysterical group, who had mean scores of 3.2 ± 2.1 (t = 2.0, P < .05). On the Symptom Checklist, the groups were similar.

Review of the data indicated that these personality types, as differentiated by a measure still being refined, do not seem to have exerted strong effects on the quality or intensity of responses. It must also be noted that these subgroups were drawn from a sample of persons already self-selected because of problem states and a desire for help.

COMMENT

The most frequent signs and symptoms of stress response syndromes, present in three-quarters of the population studied, are intrusive ideas and feelings that tend to repeat aspects of the experience of the inciting event and reactions to it. We believe that important other experiences—episodes of numbing and ideational avoidance—are the result of control efforts aimed at prevention of such intrusive episodes.

The states of stress that are largely the result of the experience of serious life events are extremes of normal everyday experiences. That is, the person experiences and manifests more state lability than is usual for him, and enters more intensely and frequently into states characterized by intrusive, repetitive thought and/or by denial and numbing. Intrusive and avoidant states are not unique as reactions to serious life events, they are simply more frequent and intense after such events occur.

In the population we studied, the serious life events were the loss of a relationship with another, the loss of self-esteem, or the loss of a physical aspect of the self. A process was set in motion by these losses that allowed previous inner models, now recognized as discrepant with new realities, to be revised so that they were in accord with the current event. Dormant or active conflicts and developmental crises were inextricably woven into this process of examination, assimilation, and accommodation to new meanings. Results were achieved slowly, with interruptions in the progress that was made.

How might this situation lead to the various intrusive and avoidant episodes that characterize these syndromes? Because the integration and revision process is slow, and because the event is serious and important (and often sudden, intense, and unanticipated), perception of the event and representation of immediate associations to it are recorded in a form of active memory which, we hypothesize, has an intrinsic property of repeated representation. The process of integration, of a synthesis between new and enduring information, is set in motion by each representation. When inner models accord with the news, however it has been reinterpreted, a point of completion is reached. The active repetitive property is terminated as the event becomes a part of both long-term memory and expectancy schemata. Until such relative completion, episodic representation related to the serious event occurs, whether the person is awake or dreaming.

Each representation leads to reactive ideation that reflects the discrepancy between the recent event and inner models of how it was, or was fantasized to be, in the past. This leads to pangs of emotions of various quality, depending on the nature of the event and the discrepancies it evokes. The kinds of thoughts and feeling that result may be intense and painful, instigating control operations. These controls may accomplish coping strategies, such as gradual self-dosing of elements of the extensive implications of any loss, or defensive operations, as in maladaptive failures to recognize painful realities and the requisite patterns of action.

When the repetition of coded perceptions and reactive thoughts occurs despite controls, the episodes will be experienced as intrusive. When controls dominate and triggers to repetition are avoided, the result will be episodes of unusual constriction of ideational range, with dampening of emotional responsivity. It is of interest that the person may himself experience awareness of these constricted and numbed states. As the processing of information concerning the serious life event results in appropriate revision of inner models, the states of experience of intrusive and avoidant episodes of thought and feeling will be reduced, and symptoms related to these states will abate.

This study was supported by Clinical Research Grant MH30899–02 from the National Institute of Mental Health. Anne Wallace, MA, and Janice Krupnick, CSW, made important contributions to clinical assessment. Anthony Leong, MS, assisted in data analysis, and Phyllis Cameron and Marsha Jackson helped in preparation of the article. William Hargreave, PhD, Clifford Attkisson, PhD, and Robert Wallerstein, MD, provided consultations on the evaluation approach.

REFERENCES

1. *Horowitz M J:* Stress Response Syndromes. *New York, Jason Aronson Inc, 1976.*
2. *American Psychiatric Association* Diagnostic and Statistical Manual of Mental Disorders, *ed 3. Washington, DC, American Psychiatric Association, 1978.*
3. *Lindemann E: Symptomatology and management of acute grief.* Am J Psychiatry *101:141–148, 1944.*
4. *Grinker K, Spiegel S:* Men Under Stress. *Philadelphia, Blakiston, 1945.*
5. *Burgess A W, Holstrum L: The rape trauma syndrome.* Am J Psychiatry *131:981–986, 1974.*
6. *Figley CF (ed):* Stress Disorders Among Vietnam Veterans. *New York, Brunner/Mazel Inc, 1978.*
7. *Lazarus R:* Psychological Stress and the Coping Process. *New York, McGraw-Hill Book Co Inc, 1966.*
8. *Janis I:* Stress and Frustration. *New York, Harcourt, Brace, Jovanovich, 1969.*
9. *Parad H, Resnik H, Parad L:* Emergency Mental Health Services and Disaster Management. *New York, Prentice Hall, 1976.*
10. *Parkes C M:* Bereavement. *New York, International Universities Press, 1972.*
11. *Clayton P: Widowhood and grief. Read before the American Psychiatric Association, Atlanta, May 5, 1978.*
12. *Horowitz M J, Kaltreider N: Brief therapy of stress response syndromes, in Karasu T, Bellak L (eds):* Specialized Techniques in Individual Psychotherapy. *New York, Brunner/Mazel, 1979.*
13. *Horowitz M J, Wilner N: Stress films, emotions and cognitive response.* Arch Gen Psychiatry *30:1339–1344, 1976.*
14. *Horowitz M J, Wilner N, Alvarez W: Impact of event scale: A measure of subjective stress.* Psychosom Med *41: 209–218, 1979.*
15. *Derogatis L R, Lipman R S, Covi L: The SCL-90: An outpatient psychiatric rating scale.* Psychopharm Bull *9:13–28, 1973.*
16. *Waskow I, Parloff M (eds):* Psychotherapy Change Measures. *Roekville, Md, National Institute of Mental Health, 1975.*
17. *Horowitz M J: Psychological response to serious life events, in Hamilton V, Warburton D (eds):* Human Stress and Cognition: An Information Processing Approach. *New York, John Wiley & Sons, 1979.*

18. *Overall J, Gorham D: The Brief Psychiatric Rating Scale.* Psychol Re *10:799, 1962.*
19. *Horowitz M J: Stress response syndromes: Character style and brief psychotherapy.* Arch Gen Psychiatry *31:768–781, 1974.*
20. *Horowitz M J, Schaefer C, Hiroto D, et al.: Life event questionnaires for measuring presumptive stress.* Psychosom Med *39:413–431, 1977.*
21. *Holmes T, Rahe R H: The social readjustment rating scale.* J Psychosom Res *11: 213–218, 1967.*
22. *Dohrenwend B, Dohrenwend B (eds):* Stressful Life Events: Their Nature and Effects. *New York, John Wiley & Sons, 1974.*
23. *Gunderson E, Rahe R H:* Life Stress and Illness. *Springfield, Ill, Charles C Thomas Publisher, 1974.*
24. *Horowitz MJ, Schaefer C, Cooney P: Life event scaling for recency of experience, in Gunderson E, Rahe R H (eds):* Life Stress and Illness. *Springfield, Ill, Charles C Thomas Publisher, 1974.*
25. *Shapiro D:* Neurotic Styles. *New York, Basic Books, 1965.*
26. *Horowitz MJ: Sliding meanings: A defense against threat in narcissistic personalities.* Int J Psychoanal Psychother *4:167–180, 1975.*

2. Conflict between Current Knowledge about Posttraumatic Stress Disorder and Its Original Conceptual Basis

Rachel Yehuda and Alexander C. McFarlane

THE EMPIRICAL findings that have emerged since the original definition of posttraumatic stress disorder (PTSD) in 1980 have contradicted the original theoretical proposition that the response to trauma as described by the diagnosis of PTSD is essentially a normative one (1–5). This has led to an unusual tension between those with a strong allegiance to the social achievements that have been met by the existence of the disorder and the clinical researchers. In particular, as clinical researchers continue to make observations such as the relative rareness of the disorder following exposure to trauma (6–16), the existence of risk factors other than the trauma as predictors of PTSD (6–9, 12, 15–25), the atypical rather than normative nature of the biological stress response in PTSD (26, 27), and the prevalence of pre-and posttraumatic comorbidity (6, 7, 14, 15, 28, 29), there arises a conflict between those who wish to normalize the status of victims and those who wish to define and characterize PTSD as a psychiatric illness (30). The future of the traumatic stress field depends upon an acknowledgment of the competing agendas and paradigms that have emerged in the last 15 years since the inception of the diagnosis, a clarification of theoretical inconsistencies that have arisen, and a reformulation of the next generation of conceptual issues. Because PTSD is a prototypic illness in that it allows a characterization of the effects of environmental factors in psychiatric illness, clarification and resolution of divergent philosophical conceptions are imperative to a broader understanding of the role of stress in mental illness.

This chapter will review some of the conceptual origins of PTSD. We will address primarily the forces that provided the major impetus for establishing a diagnosis that defined a normative process of coping and adaptation in

Reprinted by permission from *American Journal of Psychiatry*, 152 (12), 1705–1713. Copyright © 1995 by the American Psychiatric Association.

response to exposure to trauma. After a review of the relevant research findings that have emerged in the last decade regarding the prevalence, longitudinal course, and neurobiology of PTSD, it will be suggested that although current data have supported PTSD as a distinct diagnostic entity, some of the specific features of the disorder are different from those originally developed. The implications of these differences will be explored.

FACTORS THAT GAVE RISE TO THE DEVELOPMENT OF PTSD

Conceptual Origins

The diagnosis of PTSD was established to fill a gap in the prevailing mental health field by acknowledging that extremely traumatic events could produce chronic clinical disorder in normal individuals (1–5). Although the idea that stress could contribute to psychiatric symptoms had been accounted for in previous diagnostic systems, those models primarily viewed enduring symptoms as being caused by premorbid vulnerability (1–5, 27, 31). In DSM-I and DSM-II, for example, the categories of gross stress reaction and transient situational disturbance, respectively, were used to describe acute symptomatic distress following adversity, whereas more prolonged disorders were conceptualized as being anxiety or depressive neuroses. Regardless of whether these conditions were considered as resulting from developmental fixation or genetic predisposition, the role of environmental stress was at best considered a nonspecific trigger that might serve to release, exacerbate, or prolong a predictable diathesis to psychiatric symptoms. Thus, the primary philosophical shift involved in including PTSD in DSM-III was to create a diagnostic category that resolved a previous quandary of how to classify a chronic condition in normal people who developed long-term symptoms following an extremely traumatic event (1, 2). This formulation postulated a general concept of a "posttraumatic stress disorder" and implied that PTSD involved a natural process of adaptation to extraordinarily adverse situations and that the pattern of symptoms did not depend on a constitutional vulnerability.

Historical Context

The idea that stress triggers psychiatric illness in normal individuals had even earlier origins than the formal nosologic classification systems. For example, before the development of his libidinal theory of neurosis, Freud's initial theory was that hysteria had traumatic origins (32). Freud subsequently rejected this idea in favor of more developmental models (33) but, nonetheless, continued to assert that the phenomenology of responses to actual trauma (traumatic neurosis) could be differentiated from those that were the product of developmental fixation (34). Similarly, Janet's observation of dissociative responses following exposure to trauma (35), Kardiner's description of the physioneurosis in traumatic war neuroses (36), studies of concentration camp survivors that emerged in the aftermath of World War II (37–42), and studies of the psychological consequences following burn injury (43, 44) were also perspectives that validated the idea that exposure to trauma may have mental health consequences.

The issue that was raised by the proponents of PTSD was not whether extreme stress or trauma could cause psychological damage—it would have been difficult to argue that trauma could not be a major factor in precipitating psychological symptoms. Rather, the question was how should people who succumb to the effects of trauma be viewed, and treated, by the mental health field. Thus, the formulation of PTSD as a normative or adaptive response to trauma in DSM-III addressed a social and political issue as well as a mental health one. Although DSM-III focused on differentiating stressful from traumatic events and articulating the nature of the actual syndrome of PTSD, the very existence of this disorder raised the issue of how to best conceptualize the phenomenon of individuals who decompensate following exposure to trauma (1–5). For example, were trauma survivors to be viewed as psychologically damaged by the experiences that befell them or was it more appropriate to validate the experience of trauma from a humanistic and existential perspective by viewing their responses as an adaptation to frightening environmental events? These formulations had substantial implications for the treatment of trauma survivors (A. C. McFarlane and R. Yehuda, unpublished paper).

The question of how to view the trauma survivor was fueled by other social and moral agendas. For example, the human rights issues that emerged in the investigation of the effects of torture and political repression, civil rights issues, and the rise of feminism all resulted in an increasing urgency to address the plight of the traumatized individual (5). These social and political developments gave rise to a humanitarian concern that was championed by some proponents in the mental health field (45).

NORMATIVE STRESS RESPONSE: IMPLICATIONS FOR THE ESTABLISHMENT OF PTSD

The earlier discussion highlights the historical, social, and political impetus for establishing a diagnosis that normalized an individual's symptoms following adversity. However, it was equally important to support the rationale for PTSD with scientific evidence about the direct effects of trauma. In the absence of empirical data about the effects of trauma, support for the original conceptualizations of PTSD was derived largely from other areas of theory and research.

A major intellectual cornerstone for early conceptions of PTSD was the field of biological studies of stress, which essentially justified a normal continuum of responses to adversity (46–48). Indeed, during the formative years of empirical biological studies of PTSD, most theoreticians hypothesized that neurobiological alterations in this disorder would be similar to those observed in studies exploring the neurobiology of stress (49–51). In particular, Selye's findings that any adversity could provoke a biological stress response (47) provided a scientific validity of the conception of PTSD that was derived from scientific observations and not from the need to advocate on behalf of victims. Furthermore, the Selye formulation suited the political and social agenda because it shifted the emphasis away from the victim's vulnerability as the etiologic factor and focused on the responsibility of the perpetrator. The concept of a prior biological stress response was an appropriate counterargument to critics who attacked the diagnosis of PTSD as having a political and philosophical origin, and it provided a post hoc scientific hypothesis that a biological response to trauma reflects a natural physiologic process.

A second body of literature that was compatible with Selye's ideas about stress was the life events literature (52–57). This literature provided indirect support for the notion of PTSD as a normative stress response by demonstrating a temporal relationship between adverse life events and the development of psychiatric and physical symptoms. Similarly, the crisis intervention and bereavement fields provided clinical support for the observation that transient traumatic events could produce symptoms that were amenable to intervention (2, 58–61). These fields were important to the mental health conceptions of PTSD because they provided a therapeutic model of how to address the "event" in treatment (62–67). Ultimately, the focus on the traumatic event brought to bear the need to carefully define the universality and commonalities inherent in confrontation with death and helplessness and underscored the need to examine typical reactions of trauma survivors. The crisis intervention literature formed the conceptual basis for viewing chronic PTSD as a prolongation of the normal response to stress, as well as for the use of preventive debriefing treatments that are currently used following exposure to trauma (67).

Although these areas of theory and research likely influenced original conceptions of PTSD, the relevance of these notions to current knowledge of PTSD requires reevaluation. For example, as discussed later in this paper, empirical data on the biology of PTSD suggest a formulation that differs from the one that might have been predicted by the Selye model (26). Furthermore, studies of the prevalence, course, and comorbidity of PTSD have raised issues regarding the role of the stressor as the true etiologic factor in the development of this disorder. In the next section, findings from empirical studies of PTSD will be reviewed to illustrate that contrary to what might have been predicted at the time that the diagnosis of PTSD was established, many recent findings are inconsistent with the notion that traumatic events are the primary cause of symptoms and challenge the idea of PTSD as a typical stress response. Paradoxically, other data, such as the emerging evidence of a distinct and biological basis of PTSD, provide strong support for the validity of this diagnosis as well as insights into its nature.

EMPIRICAL OBSERVATIONS AND THEIR RELATIONSHIP TO PTSD SOCIAL AND CLINICAL THEORY

The conceptual underpinnings of PTSD have been addressed through a wide variety of research methodologies. First, prevalence studies have examined whether PTSD is the expected response following exposure to trauma. Second, the role of vulnerability factors as predictors of PTSD has raised questions regarding whether PTSD is a distinct disorder that arises from exposure to trauma or, rather, some other factor or combination of factors. Third, studies on the longitudinal course of the disorder have provided information about the process that separates the chronic and disabling form of the disorder from the normal process of adaptation and restitution. Studies of comorbidity have challenged the idea that PTSD can be clearly differentiated from other psychiatric disorders. Finally, the biological studies of PTSD have allowed an independent test of the distinctness of the disorder and its similarity to neurobiological alterations observed following stress and trauma.

Epidemiological Studies of the Prevalence of PTSD

Epidemiological studies of "high-risk" individuals (e.g., defined as those surviving a traumatic event, such as combat veterans or rape victims) have generally suggested that the occurrence of PTSD following a traumatic event is the exception rather than the rule (6–16, 68, 69). In DSM-IV, estimates of the prevalence of PTSD among those exposed to a criterion A stressor range from 3% to 58%.

One of the classic epidemiological studies found a 15% prevalence of current PTSD and a 30% prevalence of lifetime PTSD among Vietnam veterans (15). The prevalence of PTSD in Desert Storm veterans was found to be substantially lower. Only 9% of Desert Storm soldiers could be diagnosed with PTSD 6 months following their return from the Persian Gulf (16). Studies of civilians have also shown that PTSD is relatively rare compared to the prevalence of trauma. A study of a random sample of 1,007 young adults from a large health maintenance organization in Detroit found that of the 39% of individuals exposed to trauma, only 23.6% had developed PTSD at some time in their life (12).

Studies of the prevalence of PTSD in civilian populations exposed to specific traumatic events yield similar statistics. The study of the Mount Saint Helens volcanic eruption demonstrated that only 3.6% of those exposed to this natural disaster had PTSD and that most of the symptoms had resolved in the 2 years following the traumatic event (8). Similarly, in a representative sample of 469 volunteer firefighters exposed to severe bushfires, a PTSD prevalence rate of 16% was observed immediately following exposure, and less than half of those cases had gone into remission at 42 months (29).

In evaluating these results it is important to consider the nature and severity of the traumatic event, since a number of investigators have documented a relationship between severity of the trauma and the development of chronic PTSD (70, 71). Indeed, it is likely that some types of events are more traumatic than others and produce different rates of PTSD. In contrast to the low prevalence rates reported for natural disasters, for example, the lifetime prevalence rates of PTSD among crime victims has been estimated to vary from 19% to 75% (72). Also of note is the relatively high prevalence rate of persistent and chronic PTSD (47%–50%) among prisoners of war and concentration camp survivors (73–75). However, even among those who are exposed to very severe and prolonged trauma, there is usually a substantial number of individuals who do not develop PTSD or other psychiatric illnesses (76). Moreover, in documented epidemiological studies it is difficult to find even transitory symptoms in more than 50% of the population, and in the majority the symptoms will have usually resolved within 2–3 years (77). Thus, the available epidemiological data show that PTSD, and certainly chronic PTSD, is more unusual than usual following exposure to a variety of traumatic events.

Vulnerability Factors

The observation that trauma is not a sufficient determinant of PTSD raises the possibility that there may be risk factors that account for a given individual's vulnerability to developing this disorder. A variety of possible candidates have been investigated including genetic risk factors (17, 78), family history (12, 24), the individual's personality (16, 79), past history of trauma (21, 22), past history of behavioral or psychological problems (6), nature of parental relationships (23), and other life events at the time of the trauma (17), as well as posttraumatic factors such as social support (80) and exposure to subsequent reactivating stressors (73, 81). There has been an increasing exploration of these issues in recent years that has suggested that some vulnerability factors exert their effects at relatively low thresholds (25), whereas others come into play at a relatively high level (82) of exposure.

To date, it is unclear whether the risk factors for PTSD suggest a specific predisposition to PTSD or reflect a general predisposition to mental illness that is triggered by adversity. Nonetheless, the issue that is raised by the demonstrated role of vulnerability factors is that decompensation following trauma is neither a random process nor an outcome entirely predictable by the nature of the traumatic event. This observation appears to call into question the most fundamental assumption of PTSD as potentially occurring in any individual as a result of exposure to a traumatic event.

Longitudinal Course

The role of longitudinal studies is to describe the time course of symptom development and to determine whether there are a range of symptom patterns among victims who have undergone similar traumas (83). These studies provide information about the normative process of response to stress, the factors that might modify this process, and patterns of dysregulation. In particular, prospective longitudinal studies of non-treatment-seeking individuals have allowed a more systematic examination of Horowitz's influential formulation that following a traumatic event, there is a process of oscillation between the states of intrusion and avoidance that is part of the normal process of integrating an experience of extraordinary magnitude (2). Horowitz's model, which has been considered to be one of the major ideological bases for PTSD (84), implied that the symptoms of PTSD are a continuation of the normal acute traumatic phenomena or, rather, the failure of restitution of this process. Thus, an implicit prediction of the model was that the severity and chronicity of symptoms would be proportional to the magnitude of the trauma. Although many studies have supported the view that the intensity of the trauma has a bearing on severity and chronicity of PTSD symptoms (2, 10, 70, 85), other studies have highlighted the complexity of this relationship and its lack of predictive power (7, 17, 21, 76, 83, 85). Furthermore, recent prospective epidemiological studies have given rise to the suggestion that the acute stress response may be quite different in individuals who develop PTSD and in those who do not.

For example, in a study of the survivors of a terrorist attack on a bus, Shalev (86) failed to demonstrate that the early intensity of the intrusive affects and cognitions related to longer-term outcome. A second study, of train drivers involved in fatal accidents, similarly demonstrated that the pattern of hyperarousal did not emerge simultaneously with the intrusions and that the avoidance phenomena developed after an initial delay (87). A third study demonstrated that the symptom profile that emerges within 2 weeks following a traumatic event may be quite different from that observed at a 3-month follow-up (88). These observations imply that the intrusive phenomena in the immediate aftermath of a trauma may be different from those that occur 3 to 4 months later, or those that occur more chronically (29). Thus, the passage of time may be required before a demarcation emerges between the normal response and disorder.

The nature of acute traumatic reactions may be modified by a range of factors other than the severity of trauma, such as the history of prior trauma. Resnick and colleagues demonstrated that women with a prior rape history were three times more likely to develop PTSD than were women raped for the first time (25, 89). In that study, a prior rape history was associated with significantly lower cortisol levels in the hours after the trauma of rape. In contrast, the higher cortisol levels in women without an assault history were positively correlated with the severity of rape (89). These results suggest that acute responses to stress are not homogeneous and depend on variables other than those associated with the focal trauma. Furthermore, distinct biological responses to acute trauma that are a function of prior experience may affect the long-term course of PTSD.

The importance of these recent prospective studies is that they call into question the idea that PTSD is a continuation of the normal stress response. The very fact of heterogeneity of acute stress responses is incompatible with Horowitz's model of symptom formation in PTSD because it implies that certain acute responses to trauma may be adaptive, whereas others may be maladaptive and result in disorder. Studies of the spectrum of acute stress responses and their long-term consequences will be critical for future conceptualizations of PTSD. For now, however, emerging data appear to challenge earlier ideas of the homogeneity and universality of the early response to trauma and raise the possibility that the emergence of chronic symptoms may be predicted by discrete biological and psychological features of the acute response to trauma.

Comorbidity

The presence of psychiatric comorbidity is another issue that poses a dilemma for the initial conceptualization of PTSD as a normative stress response. The prevalence of comorbid psychiatric conditions has been investigated in a number of traumatized groups with PTSD, and these studies have found that anywhere from 50% to 90% of individuals with chronic PTSD also meet diagnostic criteria for another psychiatric disorder, including substance abuse (14, 15). Recent studies of community samples have also demonstrated high rates of comorbidity in both disaster victims and subjects selected in the North Carolina cohort of the Epidemiologic Catchment Area study (28, 68). In general, psychiatric comorbidity appears to develop over time in traumatized individuals with PTSD. In the study by North et al. of the victims of a mass shooting, for example, rates of comorbidity 1 month after the trauma were much lower than those in other populations studied (90). Thus, there may be a cascade in the months following the onset of PTSD that suggests the unfolding of a secondary psychopathological process. Regardless, the findings suggest that it is the exception rather than the rule for individuals to meet diagnostic criteria for PTSD in the absence of meeting criteria for another psychiatric disorder (91).

An important consideration in unpacking the question of psychiatric comorbidity is that these conditions may be a result of the overlap of symptoms between diagnoses as they are formulated in current nosologic conceptions and may not necessarily represent distinct disorders (91). Even so, the existence of these symptoms raises the possibility that they might be considered secondary to these comorbid disorders rather than being secondary to PTSD.

A particular irony of the findings about comorbidity is that most patients would satisfy the diagnostic criteria for either depressive neurosis or anxiety neurosis, which would have been the diagnoses previously used to describe these patients. The formulation of DSM-I argued that these were sufficient to explain the long-term effects of traumatic stress, and there is some substance to this as a parsimonious argument.

The presence of psychiatric comorbidity is a complex issue that overlaps with some of the conundrums raised by the complex longitudinal course of PTSD and existence of vulnerability factors. The relative rareness of "pure PTSD" (i.e., a frequently used term that denotes a syndrome uncomplicated by the presence of symptoms of other psychiatric disorders), compared to the presence of more complex forms, suggests that traumatic stress may precipitate a whole host of symptoms and conditions. As such, the emergence of PTSD following exposure to a trauma may represent the manifestation of an underlying diathesis rather than a normative adaptation to environmental challenge.

Emerging Neurobiology of PTSD

Although a comprehensive review of the neurobiology of PTSD is beyond the scope of this paper, there are essential implications of neurobiological studies to the philosophical conceptions of PTSD. The most important conclusion to date from these studies has been that there is a distinct set of biological alterations that serves to characterize the state of prolonged or persistent symptoms in response to a traumatic event (92, 93). However, the nature of these disturbances suggests that the biological correlates of long-term psychological responses to trauma are far more complex than what was originally anticipated.

Initially, biological studies of PTSD were almost exclusively driven by the hypothesis that the alterations in symptomatic individuals would be analogous to those observed in animal and human studies of stress (48, 49, 94, 95). A series of biological findings have now emerged that show changes in stress-responsive systems that are quite different from what would be predicted on the basis of the stress literature (26, 27, 94, 96–104). Furthermore, the alterations in individuals with PTSD have been found to be distinct from those of similarly exposed individuals without PTSD (98, 99, 105–108). Moreover, the abnormalities observed in PTSD have been found to be different from those in other psychiatric disorders that have been associated with stress, such as mood and other anxiety disorders (98–104, 109–111). Together, these points suggest that the biology of PTSD is not simply a reflection of the normative biology of stress, as has been consistently hypothesized.

A salient demonstration of the previously discussed conclusions consists of the findings of hypothalamic-pituitary-adrenal (HPA) axis alterations in PTSD (26, 27). These studies have suggested that rather than showing the classic profile of increased adrenocortical activity and resultant dysregulation of this system described in studies of stress and major depression, PTSD sufferers show evidence of a highly sensitized HPA axis characterized by decreased basal cortisol levels (98, 100–103) and increased negative feedback regulation (99, 104). Studies of psychophysiologic (105–108), electrophysiologic (109–112), and neurochemical (109, 110, 113–118) alterations in PTSD have revealed similar abnormalities of the sympathetic nervous system and other neuromodulatory systems. Many of these studies have demonstrated that PTSD patients have exaggerated and more finely tuned biological responses both to stimuli that are reminders of the traumatic event (105–108, 116) and to perturbations, such as neuroendocrine challenge (113, 114) and other laboratory stressors like loud tones and exercise (108, 118). In the aggregate, the biological data suggest that individuals with PTSD may show a sensitization of several biological systems. The sensitization observed in PTSD can be contrasted to the attenuated or dysregulated biological and behavioral responses characteristically associated with habituation and adaptation to chronic stress (47) and major depression (119). Observations of biological sensitization have prompted theorists to more recently consider the application of animal models of kindling (120) and time-dependent change (121) as relevant to the neurobiology of PTSD (95, 122).

A concluding statement that can be made concerning the neurobiology of PTSD, on the basis of the findings to date, is that there are biological changes following exposure to a trauma that are particularly associated with the symptoms of PTSD and that do not appear to be present as a result of exposure to trauma per se. Although, as described previously in this paper, earlier formulations might have seen a resemblance between the biology of stress and PTSD as a rationale for the diagnosis, the distinctness of the biology of PTSD and the biology of stress provides an even stronger validation of PTSD as a discrete disorder. It is likely, however, that the significance of the neurobiological data could not be fully appreciated without the increasing knowledge derived from descriptive studies. That is, in the context of the prevalence and other data that challenge the normative nature of PTSD, biological findings that depart from classic stress paradigms appear quite reasonable. In tandem, then, the descriptive and biological data have moved

the field toward a more sophisticated notion of PTSD and a greater understanding of the heterogeneous nature of the response to traumatic events.

CONCLUSIONS

The contribution of PTSD to psychiatry is that it provides an observational
framework for studying the effects of stress and trauma. From a social and
political perspective, PTSD as a concept has done much to assist in the
recognition of the rights and needs of victims who have been stigmatized,
misunderstood, or ignored by the mental health field. The existence of this
diagnosis has allowed the emergence of the much needed data about the
effects of trauma that did not previously exist and could not have been
systematically collected without this diagnosis. The original conceptual basis
of PTSD provided the constructs for the development of hypotheses about
the effects of trauma that the field of psychiatry has had to address. To date,
empirical knowledge derived from investigation of the effects of trauma has
substantiated the importance of these humanistic concerns to a large degree
and has allowed a further clarification of the concept of PTSD that extends
its original conceptual roots.

It is now clear that PTSD does provide a model for a process of adjustment
and destabilization to trauma that has biological, psychological, and phenomenological dimensions. The biological investigations have demonstrated that
the substrates of the disorder may not, in fact, be similar to the "normative
stress response" described by Selye but, rather, may be a progressive sensitization of biological systems that leave the individual hyperresponsive to a
variety of stimuli. PTSD has provided a model for the further development
of a series of sophisticated ideas about the phenotypic expression of vulnerability, perhaps through use of models such as kindling (120), sensitization
(120, 121), and parallel distributed processing (123). The finding that PTSD
is not an inevitable consequence of trauma requires theorists to be more
precise in their formulation of the effects of trauma and to search for other
vulnerability factors that give rise to and perpetuate the course of PTSD.

The current challenge in the field of traumatic stress studies is to address
the emerging empirical basis of PTSD as central to the validity of the disorder
while placing in proper historical perspective that the diagnosis came to be
by acceptance of the political and social rights of traumatized groups. Now
that PTSD's place in psychiatric nosology is safely established, it is the
scientific process that must provide the organizing philosophy for the field.

REFERENCES

1. Andreasen N C: Posttraumatic stress disorder, in Comprehensive Textbook of Psychiatry, 3rd ed, vol 2. Edited by Kaplan H I. Freedman A M, Sadock B J. Baltimore, Williams & Wilkins, 1980, pp. 1517–1525
2. Horowitz M J: Stress Response Syndromes, 2nd ed. New York, Jason Aronson, 1986
3. Figley C R: Helping Traumatized Families. San Francisco, Jossey-Bass, 1989
4. Green B L, Wilson J P, Lindy J D: Conceptualizing posttraumatic stress disorder: a psychosocial framework, in Trauma and Its Wake: The Study and Treatment of Post-Traumatic Stress Disorder. Edited by Figley C R. New York. Brunner/Mazel, 1985, pp. 53–69
5. Herman J L: Trauma and Recovery. New York, Basic Books, 1992
6. Helzer J E, Robins L N. McEvoy L: Posttraumatic stress disorder in the general population. N Engl J Med 1987; 317: 1630–1634
7. Davidson J R T, Hughes D, Blazer D, George L K: Posttraumatic stress disorder in the community: an epidemiological study. Psychol Med 1991; 21:1–9
8. Shore J H, Vollmer W M, Tatum E L: Community patterns of posttraumatic stress disorders. J Nerv Ment Dis 1989; 177:681–685
9. Card J J: Epidemiology of PTSD in a national cohort of Vietnam veterans. J Clin Psychol 1987; 43:6–17
10. Pynoos R S, Frederick C, Nader K, Arroyo W, Steinberg A, Eth S, Nunez F, Fairbanks L: Life threat and posttraumatic stress in school-age children. Arch Gen Psychiatry 1987; 12:1057–1063
11. Health status of Vietnam veterans, I: psychological characteristics. The Centers for Disease Control Vietnam Experience Study. JAMA 1988; 259:2701–2707
12. Breslau N, David G C, Andreski P, Peterson E: Traumatic events and posttraumatic stress disorder in an urban population of young adults. Arch Gen Psychiatry 1991; 48:216–222
13. Goldberg J, True W R, Eisen S A, Henderson W G: A twin study of the effects of the Vietnam war on posttraumatic stress disorder. JAMA 1990; 263:1227–1232
14. Freedy J R, Shaw D L, Jarrell M P: Towards an understanding of the psychological impact of natural disaster: an application of the conservation resources stress model. J Traumatic Stress 1992; 5:441–454
15. Kulka R A, Schlenger W E, Fairbank J A, Hough R L, Jordan B K, Marmar C R, Weiss D S: Trauma and the Vietnam War Generation: Report of Findings from the National Vietnam Veterans Readjustment Study. New York, Brunner/Mazel, 1990
16. Southwick S M, Morgan A, Nagy L M, Bremner D, Nicholaou A L, Johnson D R, Rosenheck R, Charney D S: Trauma-related symptoms in veterans of Operation Desert Storm: a preliminary report. Am J Psychiatry 1993; 150:1524–1538
17. McFarlane A C: The aetiology of post-traumatic morbidity: predisposing, precipitating and perpetuating factors. Br J Psychiatry 1989; 154:221–228
18. Shore J H, Tatum E L, Vollmer W M: Evaluation of mental health effects of

disaster: Mt St Helens eruption. Am J Public Health 1986; 76(March Suppl):76–83

19. Shore J H, Tatum E L, Vollmer W M: Psychiatric reactions to disaster: the Mount St Helens experience. Am J Psychiatry 1986; 143:590–595

20. Pitman R K, Orr S P, Lownhagen M H, Macklin M L, Altman A: Pre-Vietnam contents of PTSD veterans' service medical and personnel records. Compr Psychiatry 1991; 32:1–7

21. Bremner J D, Southwick S M, Johnson D R, Yehuda R, Charney D S: Childhood physical abuse and combat-related posttraumatic stress disorder in Vietnam veterans. Am J Psychiatry 1993; 150:235–239

22. Zaidi L Y, Foy D W: Childhood abuse and combat-related PTSD. J Traumatic Stress 1994; 7:33–42

23. Emery V O, Emery P E, Shama D K, Quiana N A, Jassani A K: Predisposing variables in PTSD patients. J Traumatic Stress 1991; 4:325–343

24. Davidson J, Swartz M, Storck M, Krishnan R R, Hammett E: A diagnostic and family study of posttraumatic stress disorder. Am J Psychiatry 1985; 142:90–93

25. Resnick H S, Kilpatrick D G, Best C L, Kramer T L: Vulnerability-stress factors in development of posttraumatic stress disorder. J Nerv Ment Dis 1992; 180:424–430

26. Yehuda R, Giller E L, Levengood R A, Southwick S M, Siever L J: Hypothalamic-pituitary-adrenal functioning in PTSD: expanding the concept of the stress response spectrum, in Neurobiological and Clinical Consequences of Stress: From Normal Adaptation to PTSD. Edited by Friedman M J, Charney D S, Deutch A W. New York, Raven Press, 1996

27. Yehuda R, Resnick H, Kahana B, Giller E L: Longlasting hormonal alterations in extreme stress in humans: normative or maladaptive? Psychosom Med 1993; 55:287–297

28. Green B L, Lindy J D, Grace M C, Leonard A C: Chronic posttraumatic stress disorder and diagnostic comorbidity in a disaster sample. J Nerv Ment Dis 1992; 180:760–766

29. McFarlane A C: Multiple diagnoses in posttraumatic stress disorder in the victims of a natural disaster. J Nerv Ment Dis 1992; 180:498–504

30. McFarlane A C: The Ash Wednesday bushfires in South Australia; implications for planning future post-disaster services. Med J Australia 1984; 141:286–291

31. Green B L, Lindy J D, Grace M C: Posttraumatic stress disorder: toward DSM-IV. J Nerv Ment Dis 1985; 173:406–411

32. Breuer J, Freud S: Studies on Hysteria: Physical Mechanisms of Hysteria. Translated by Strachey J. New York, Penguin, 1973

33. Brown J A: Freud and the Post-Freudians. New York, Penguin, 1961

34. Freud S: Introductory Lectures on Psychoanalysis: Fixation to Traumas—The Unconscious. Translated by Strachey J. New York, Penguin, 1973

35. van der Kolk V A, van der Hart O: Pierre Janet and the breakdown of adaptation in psychological trauma. Am J Psychiatry 1989; 146:1530–1540

36. Kardiner A: The Traumatic Neurosis of War. New York, Paul Hoeber, 1941

37. Dor-Shav N K: On the long-range effects of concentration camp internment on Nazi victims: twenty-five years later. J Consult Clin Psychol 1978; 46:1–11

38. Niederland W G: Clinical observations on the "survivor syndrome." Int J Psychoanal 1968; 49:313–315

39. Antonovsky A, Maoz B, Dowty N, Wijsenbeek B: Twenty-five years later: a limited study of the sequelae of the concentration camp experience. Soc Psychiatry 1971; 6:186–193

40. Chodoff P: Late effects of the concentration camp syndrome. Arch Gen Psychiatry 1963; 8:323–333

41. Eitinger L: Pathology of the concentration camp syndrome. Arch Gen Psychiatry 1961; 5:371–380

42. Krystal H: Massive Psychic Trauma. New York, International Universities Press, 1968

43. Andreasen N J, Norris A S: Long-term adjustment and adaptation mechanisms in severely burned adults. J Nerv Ment Dis 1972; 154:352–362

44. Andreasen N J, Noyes R Jr, Hartford C E, Brodland G, Proctor S: Management of emotional reactions in seriously burned adults. N Engl J Med 1972; 286:65–69

45. Lifton R J: Home from the War: Vietnam Veterans—Neither Victims nor Executioners. New York, Simon and Schuster, 1973

46. Cannon W B: The emergency function of the adrenal medulla in pain and the major emotions. Am J Physiol 1914; 3:356–372

47. Selye H: The Stress of Life. New York, McGraw-Hill, 1956

48. Mason J W: A historical view of the stress field. J Human Stress 1975; 6–12

49. Krystal J H, Kosten T R, Perry B D, Southwick S M, Mason J W, Giller E L: Neurobiological aspects of PTSD: review of clinical and preclinical studies. Behavior Therapy 1989; 20:177–198

50. van der Kolk B, Greenberg M, Boyd H, Krystal J: Inescapable shock, neurotransmitters, and addition to trauma: toward a psychobiology of posttraumatic stress disorder. Biol Psychiatry 1985; 20:314–325

51. Kolb L C: A neuropsychological hypothesis explaining the posttraumatic stress disorders. Am J Psychiatry 1987; 144:989–995

52. Rabkin J G, Struening E L: Life events, stress and illness. Science 1976; 194:1013–1020

53. McFarlane A C: The effects of stressful life events and disasters: research and theoretical issues. Aust NZ J Psychiatry 1985; 19:409–421

54. Bidzinska E J: Stress factors in effective diseases. Br J Psychiatry 1984; 144:161–166

55. Swann A C, Secunda S K, Stokes P E, Croughan J, Davis J M, Koslow S H, Maas J W: Stress, depression, and mania: relationship between perceived role of stressful events and clinical and biochemical characteristics. Acta Psychiatr Scand 1990; 81:389–397

56. Post R M, Rubinow D R, Ballenger J C: Conditioning and sensitisation in the longitudinal course of affective illness. Br J Psychiatry 1986; 149:191–201

57. Ghaziuddin M, Ghaziuddin N, Stein G S: Life events and the recurrence of depression. Can J Psychiatry 1990; 35:239–242

58. Raphael B: The Anatomy of Bereavement. New York, Basic Books, 1983

59. Cranshow R: Reactions to a disaster. Arch Gen Psychiatry 1963; 9:157–162

60. Kinston W, Rosser K: Disaster: effects on mental and physical state. J Psychosom Res 1974; 19:437–456

61. Lifton R J, Olson E: The human meaning of total disaster: the Buffalo Creek experience. Psychiatry 1976; 39:1–18

62. Mitchell J: When disaster strikes . . . : the critical incident stress debriefing process. J Emergency Med Services 1983; 8:36–39

63. Blaufarb H, Levine J: Crisis intervention in an earthquake. Soc Work 1972; 17: 16–19

64. Lindemann E: Symptomatology and management of acute grief. Am J Psychiatry 1944; 101:141–148

65. Raphael B: When Disaster Strikes: A Handbook for the Caring Professions. London, Hutchinson, 1986

66. Raphael B: Preventative intervention with the recently bereaved. Arch Gen Psychiatry 1977; 34:1450–1454

67. Austin L: Responding to Disaster: A Guide for Mental Health Professionals. Washington, DC, American Psychiatric Press, 1992

68. de Girolamo G, McFarlane A C: Epidemiology of posttraumatic stress disorders: a comprehensive review of the literature, in Ethnocultural Aspects of Post-Traumatic Stress Disorder: Issues, Research, and Directions. Edited by Marsella A J, Friedman M, Gerrity E, Scurfield R. Washington, DC, American Psychological Association, 1996

69. Davidson J R T, Fairbank J A: The epidemiology of posttraumatic stress disorder, in Posttraumatic Stress Disorder: DSM-IV and Beyond. Edited by Davidson J R T, Foa E B. Washington, DC, American Psychiatric Press, 1993, pp 147–172

70. Foy D W, Sipprelle R C, Rueger D B, Carroll E M: Etiology of posttraumatic stress disorder in Vietnam veterans. J Consult Clin Psychol 1984; 40:1323–1328

71. March J S: What constitutes a stressor: the "criterion A" issue, in Posttraumatic Stress Disorder: DSM-IV and Beyond. Edited by Davidson J R T, Foa E B. Washington, DC, American Psychiatric Press, 1993, pp 130–145

72. Kilpatrick D G, Resnick H S: Posttraumatic stress disorder associated with exposure to criminal victimization in clinical and community populations. Ibid, pp 147–172

73. Yehuda R, Kahana B, Schmeidler J, Southwick S M, Wilson S, Giller E L: Impact of cumulative lifetime trauma and recent stress on current posttraumatic stress disorder symptoms in Holocaust survivors. Am J Psychiatry 1995; 152:1815–1818

74. Kluznick J C, Speed N, Van Valkenburg C, Magraw R: Forty-year follow-up of United States prisoners of war. Am J Psychiatry 1986; 143:1443–1446

75. Goldstein G, van Kammen W, Shelly C, Miller D J, van Kammen D P: Survivors of imprisonment in the Pacific theater during World War II. Am J Psychiatry 1987; 144:1210–1213

Current Knowledge about Posttraumatic Stress Disorder 57

76. McFarlane A C: *Vulnerability to posttraumatic stress disorder, in Posttraumatic Stress Disorder: Etiology, Phenomenology, and Treatment. Edited by Wolf M E, Mosnaim A D. Washington, DC, American Psychiatric Press, 1990*

77. Green B: *Traumatic stress and disaster: mental health factors influencing adaptation, in Annual Review of Psychiatry. Washington, DC, American Psychiatric Press, 1996*

78. True W R, Rise J, Eisen S, Heath A C, Goldberg J, Lyons M, Nowak J: *A twin study of genetic and environmental contributions to liability for posttraumatic stress symptoms. Arch Gen Psychiatry 1993; 50:257–264*

79. Schnurr P P, Friedman M J, Rosenberg S D: *Premilitary MMPI scores as predictors of combat-related PTSD symptoms. Am J Psychiatry 1993; 150:479–483*

80. Solomon S, Smith E: *Social support and perceived controls as moderators of responses to dioxin and flood exposure, in Individual and Community Responses to Trauma and Disaster: The Structure of Human Chaos. Edited by Ursano R J, McCaughey B G, Fullerton C S. New York, Cambridge University Press, 1994*

81. Solomon Z, Prager E: *Elderly Israeli Holocaust survivors during the Persian Gulf War: a study of psychological distress. Am J Psychiatry 1992; 149:1707–1710*

82. McCraine E W, Hyer L A, Boudewyns P A, Woods M G: *Negative parenting behaviour, combat exposure, and PTSD symptom severity: test of a person-event interaction model. J Nerv Ment Dis 1992; 180:432–438*

83. Blank A S: *The longitudinal course of posttraumatic stress disorder, in Posttraumatic Stress Disorder: DSM-IV and Beyond. Edited by Davidson J R T, Foa E B. Washington, DC, American Psychiatric Press, 1993, pp 3–22*

84. Brett E A, Ostroff R: *Imagery and posttraumatic stress disorder: an overview. Am J Psychiatry 1985; 142:417–424*

85. Yehuda R, Southwick S M, Giller E L Jr: *Exposure to atrocities and severity of chronic posttraumatic stress disorder in Vietnam combat veterans. Am J Psychiatry 1992; 149:333–336*

86. Shalev A Y: *Posttraumatic stress disorder among injured survivors of a terrorist attack: predictive value of early intrusion and avoidance symptoms. J Nerv Ment Dis 1992; 180:505–509*

87. Karlehage S, Malt U, Hoff H: *The effect of major railway accidents on the psychological health of train drivers—II: a longitudinal study of the one-year outcome after the accident. J Psychosom Res 1993; 37:807–817*

88. Rothbaum B O, Foa E B, Riggs D S, Murdock T, Walsh W: *A prospective examination of posttraumatic stress disorder in rape victims. J Traumatic Stress 1992; 5:455–475*

89. Resnick H S, Yehuda R, Pitman R K, Foy D W: *Effect of previous trauma on acute plasma cortisol level following rape. Am J Psychiatry 1995; 152:1675–1677*

90. North C S, Smith E M, Spitznagel E L: *Posttraumatic stress disorder in survivors of a mass shooting. Am J Psychiatry 1994; 151:82–88*

91. Friedman M J, Yehuda R: *PTSD and comorbidity: psychological approaches to differential diagnosis, in Neurobiological and Clinical Consequences of Stress:*

    *From Normal Adaptation to PTSD. Edited by Friedman M J, Charney D S,
    Deutch A Y. New York, Raven Press, 1996*

 92. *Giller M J: Biological Assessment and Treatment of Post-Traumatic Stress Dis-
     order. Washington, DC, American Psychiatric Press, 1991*
 93. *Murburg M M (ed): Catecholamine Function in Posttraumatic Stress Disorder:
     Emerging Concepts. Washington, DC, American Psychiatric Press, 1994*
 94. *Yehuda R, Giller E L, Southwick S M, Lowy M T, Mason J W: Hypothalamic-
     pituitary-adrenal dysfunction in PTSD. Biol Psychiatry 1991; 30:1031–1048*
 95. *Charney D S, Deutch A, Krystal J, Southwick S M, Nagy L: Psychobiological
     mechanisms of post-traumatic stress disorder. Arch Gen Psychiatry 1993; 50:
     294–305*
 96. *Mason J, Southwick S, Yehuda R. Wang S, Riney S, Johnson D, Lubin H, Blake
     D, Zhou G, Charney D S: Elevation of serum free triiodothyronine, total triio-
     dothyronine, thyroxine-binding globulin, and total thyroxine levels in combat-
     related posttraumatic stress disorder. Arch Gen Psychiatry 1994; 51:629–641*
 97. *Mason J W, Giller E L Jr, Kosten T R, Yehuda R: Psychoendocrine approaches
     to the diagnosis and pathogenesis of posttraumatic stress disorder, in Biological
     Assessment and Treatment of Posttraumatic Stress Disorder. Edited by Giller
     E L Jr. Washington, DC, American Psychiatric Press, 1991, pp 65–86*
 98. *Yehuda R, Kahana B, Binder-Brynes K, Southwick S M, Mason J W, Giller E L:
     Low urinary cortisol excretion in Holocaust survivors with posttraumatic stress
     disorder. Am J Psychiatry 1995; 152:982–986*
 99. *Yehuda R, Boisoneau D, Lowy M T, Giller E L Jr: Dose-response changes in
     plasma cortisol and lymphocyte glucocorticoid receptors following dexametha-
     sone administration in combat veterans with and without posttraumatic stress
     disorder. Arch Gen Psychiatry 1995; 52:583–593*
100. *Yehuda R, Boisoneau D, Mason J W. Giller E L: Relationship between lympho-
     cyte glucocorticoid receptor number and urinary-free cortisol excretion in mood,
     anxiety, and psychotic disorder. Biol Psychiatry 1993; 34:18–25*
101. *Mason J W, Giller E L, Kosten T R, Ostroff R B, Podd L: Urinary free-cortisol
     levels in post-traumatic stress disorder patients. J Nerv Ment Dis 1986; 174:
     145–159*
102. *Yehuda R, Southwick S M, Nussbaum G. Wahby V, Mason J W, Giller E L: Low
     urinary cortisol excretion in patients with PTSD. J Nerv Ment Dis 1990; 178:
     366–369*
103. *Yehuda R, Teicher M H, Levengood R. Trestman R, Siever L J: Circadian rhythm
     of cortisol regulation in PTSD. Biol Psychiatry, 1996*
104. *Yehuda R, Southwick S M, Krystal J H, Bremner D, Charney D S, Mason J W:
     Enhanced suppression of cortisol following dexamethasone administration in
     posttraumatic stress disorder. Am J Psychiatry 1993; 150:83–86*
105. *Pitman R K, Orr S P, Forgue D F, DeJong J B, Clairborn J M: Psychophysio-
     logic assessment of posttraumatic stress disorder imagery in Vietnam combat
     veterans. Arch Gen Psychiatry 1987; 44:970–975*
106. *Shalev A, Rogel-Fuchs Y: Psychophysiology of the PTSD: from sulfur fumes to
     behavioral genetics. Psychosom Med 1993; 55:413–423*
107. *Shalev A Y, Orr S P, Pitman R K: Psychophysiologic assessment of traumatic*

imagery in Israeli civilian patients with posttraumatic stress disorder. Am J Psychiatry 1993; 150:620–624

108. Shalev A Y, Orr S P, Peri P, Schreiber S, Pitman R K: Physiologic responses to loud tones in Israeli post-traumatic stress disorder patients. Arch Gen Psychiatry 1992; 40:870–975

109. Southwick S M, Yehuda R, Charney D S: Neurobiological alterations in posttraumatic stress disorder: a review of the clinical literature, in Acute and Longterm Responses to Trauma and Disaster. Edited by Fullerton C S, Ursano R J. Washington, DC, American Psychiatric Press, 1996

110. Kosten T R, Mason J W, Giller E L, Ostroff R, Harkness L: Sustained urinary norepinephrine and epinephrine elevations in post-traumatic stress disorder. Psychoneuroendocrinology 1987; 12:13–20

111. McFarlane A C, Weber D, Clark R: Abnormal stimulus processing in posttraumatic stress disorder. Biol Psychiatry 1993; 34:311–320

112. Paige S R, Reid G M, Allen M G, Newton J E: Psychophysiological correlates of posttraumatic stress disorder in Vietnam veterans. Biol Psychiatry 1990; 27: 419–430

113. Southwick S M, Krystal J H, Morgan C A, Johnson D, Nagy L M, Nicolaou A, Heninger G R, Charney D S: Abnormal noradrenergic function in posttraumatic stress disorder. Arch Gen Psychiatry 1993; 50:266–274

114. Rainey J M Jr, Aleem A, Ortiz A, Yeragani V, Pohl R, Berchou R: A laboratory procedure for the induction of flashbacks. Am J Psychiatry 1987; 144:1317–1319

115. Perry B D, Southwick S M, Yehuda R, Giller E L: Adrenergic receptor regulation in post-traumatic stress disorder, in Biological Assessment and Treatment of Post-traumatic Stress Disorder. Edited by Giller E L. Washington, DC, American Psychiatric Press, 1990, pp 87–114

116. McFall M, Murburg M, Ko G: Autonomic response to stress in Vietnam combat veterans with post-traumatic stress disorder. Biol Psychiatry 1990; 27:1165–1175

117. Yehuda R, Southwick S M, Ma X, Giller E L, Mason J W: Urinary catecholamine excretion and severity of symptoms in PTSD. J Nerv Ment Dis 1992; 180:321–325

118. Hamner M B, Diamond B I, Hitri A: Plasma norepinephrine and MHPG responses to exercise stress in PTSD, in Catecholamine Function in Posttraumatic Stress Disorder: Emerging Concepts. Edited by Murburg M M. Washington, DC, American Psychiatric Press, 1994, pp 221–232

119. Siever L J, Davis K L: Overview: toward a dysregulation hypothesis of depression. Am J Psychiatry 1985; 142:1017–1031

120. Post R M: Transduction of psychosocial stress into the neurobiology of recurrent effective disorder. Am J Psychiatry 1992; 149:999–1010

121. Antelman S M, Yehuda R: Time-dependent change following acute stress: relevance to the chronic and delayed aspects of posttraumatic stress disorder, in Catecholamine Function in Posttraumatic Stress Disorder: Emerging Concepts. Edited by Murburg M M. Washington, DC, American Psychiatric Press, 1994, pp 87–98

122. Yehuda R, Antelman S M: Criteria for rationally evaluating animal models of posttraumatic stress disorder. Biol Psychiatry 1993; 33:479–486
123. McFarlane A C, Yehuda R, Clark R: Biological models of symptoms formation in PTSD: the role of neural networks. Biol Psychiatry, 1996

3. Childhood Traumas

An Outline and Overview

Lenore C. Terr

MENTAL CONDITIONS brought on by horrible external events in childhood present a wide range of findings. If one looks only at the clinical manifestations of trauma in a given day in the life of the traumatized child, one could diagnose conduct disorder, borderline personality, major affective disorder, attention deficit hyperactivity, phobic disorder, dissociative disorder, obsessive-compulsive disorder, panic disorder, adjustment disorder, and even such conditions, as yet unofficial in the nomenclature, as precursors of multiple personality or acute dissociative disorder, and not be wrong. If one projects this multiplicity of technically correct diagnoses onto a traumatized child's adulthood, one finds even more diagnostic leeway.

We must organize our thinking about childhood trauma, however, or we run the risk of never seeing the condition at all. Like the young photographer in Cortázar's short story and Antonioni's film, "Blow Up," we may enlarge the diagnostic fine points of trauma into such prominence that we altogether lose the central point—that external forces created the internal changes in the first place. We must not let ourselves forget childhood trauma just because the problem is so vast.

Studies of adults in mental hospitals (1), adults suffering from multiple personalities (2), adults who are borderline (3), and adolescents who go on to commit murder (4) show that these adults and adolescents very often were abused or shocked in their own childhoods. Studies of adult rape victims demonstrate that they often were raped or incestuously abused as children and that they are quite prone to being raped again—and again—in their adult lives (5). Those who harm children have often been harmed themselves as children (6). And some of those who indulge in self-mutilation or who make repeated suicide attempts give vivid past histories of long-standing childhood horrors (7).

Reprinted by permission from *American Journal of Psychiatry*, 148 (1), 10–20. Copyright © 1991 by the American Psychiatric Association.

One could say that childhood trauma is so ubiquitous to the psychiatric disorders of adolescence and adulthood that we should forget it, that it cancels itself out. We know, however, that not every child is directly shocked or personally subjected to terror from the outside. Most children come from relatively kind, non-abusive families. Most youngsters are never enrolled in a pedophilic day-care center or happen upon a satanic cult. The chances of experiencing a frightening flood, hurricane, or earthquake are not that great. The chances of witnessing a murder or of being kidnapped are not overwhelmingly high. Numbers of children should be able to get through their childhoods without any direct exposure to a traumatic event or series of terrible events. And they apparently do so (8, 9).

Even if we were to broaden the diagnosis of childhood trauma, as I will propose in this paper, to allow in any child mentally harmed enough by a single external event or a long-standing series of such events to qualify for a trauma-related diagnosis, we could not possibly cover everything that we see in adults as a result of these early traumas—the borderline patients, the patients with multiple personality disorder, and the chronic victims or victimizers, for instance. We will still need our adult diagnostic schemes and our adult treatment plans. But perhaps, if we looked in a more organized fashion at childhood psychic trauma and at what it does, we would recognize it as the important etiologic determinant that it actually is. We could begin to see how childhood trauma works. And we could study it better.

Like childhood rheumatic fever, which causes a number of conditions in adulthood ranging from mitral stenosis to subacute bacterial endocarditis to massive heart failure, childhood psychic trauma leads to a number of mental changes that eventually account for some adult character problems, certain kinds of psychotic thinking, considerable violence, much dissociation, extremes of passivity, self-mutilative episodes, and a variety of anxiety disturbances. Even though heart failure and subacute bacterial endocarditis in adulthood look very different from one another and demand specific treatments, their original cause—the childhood rheumatic fever—gives an organizing pattern to the physician's entire approach. Every good internist knows how to obtain and assess a history of rheumatic fever, even though it was the pediatrician who originally diagnosed and treated the sick child.

In this paper, I will define childhood trauma and point to four features that characterize almost all of the conditions resulting from extreme fright in childhood. These four features are seen in children suffering the results of events that were single, sudden, and unexpected, the classical Freudian traumas (10, 11), and in children responding to long-standing and anticipated blows, those resulting in the various child abuse syndromes (12, 13) or survivor syndromes (14–16). These four features appear to last for years in the course of the condition. They are often seen in adults who were traumatized as children, even though the adults now carry other diagnoses. Only one or two of these four features may be evident in an individual traumatized as a child; but from the history it is often evident that the other features played an important part in the person's life.

I will divide all of the trauma-stress conditions of childhood into two rough categories and call them type I and type II childhood traumas. I will propose that children suffering from type I traumas, the results of one sudden blow, differ in certain ways from children suffering from type II traumas, the results of long-standing or repeated ordeals. I will conclude with a note on the crossover conditions, childhood traumas that appear to settle between the two major types that I propose.

This paper is largely theoretical, although each point will be illustrated with a clinical example. It is based, in part, upon three studies: the Chowchilla kidnapping study (8, 17, 18), a retrospective study of 20 pre-schoolers suffering from a wide range of traumas that were documented by third parties (19), and a study of normal latency-aged children's and adolescents' responses to the Challenger space shuttle explosion (9). The paper is primarily based, however, upon my clinical notes taken from more than 150 individual children who came for evaluation or treatment after a variety of externally generated horrors. The paper is an attempt to organize and to provide a scheme of thinking about childhood psychic trauma. It is not meant in any way as a last-minute addition to the *DSM-IV* process or as a proposal for a new and revisionary *DSM-V*. Instead, it is an outline and overview of a group of phenomena that may go their various ways into the adult diagnostic groups but that should still hold together in our thinking because of their association with the earliest traumas.

I will define childhood trauma as the mental result of one sudden, external blow or a series of blows, rendering the young person temporarily helpless and breaking past ordinary coping and defensive operations. As the reader will note, I have broadened the concept of trauma to include not only those conditions marked by intense surprise but also those marked by prolonged and sickening anticipation. All childhood traumas, according to my definition, originate from the outside. None is generated solely within the child's own mind. Childhood trauma may be accompanied by as yet unknown biological changes that are stimulated by the external events. The trauma begins with events outside the child. Once the events take place, a number of internal changes occur in the child. These changes last. As in the case of rheumatic fever, the changes stay active for years—often to the detriment of the young victim.

FOUR CHARACTERISTICS COMMON TO MOST CASES OF CHILDHOOD TRAUMA

There are several well-known characteristics that distinguish the traumas of childhood. Thought suppression, sleep problems, exaggerated startle responses, developmental regressions, fears of the mundane, deliberate avoidances, panic, irritability, and hypervigilance are prominent among these.

I consider four characteristics, however, particularly important in traumatized children no matter when in the course of the illness one observes the child and no matter what age the child is at the time. They are: 1) strongly visualized or otherwise repeatedly perceived memories, 2) repetitive behaviors, 3) trauma-specific fears, and 4) changed attitudes about people, aspects of life, and the future.

One note on traumatic dreams, the classic Freudian sign of trauma that I have not included in my list of four: the repetitive dream is a hallmark of trauma, but it is not always seen in childhood trauma, especially in children under age 5. Dreaming appears to be something that develops into what we recognize as dreaming by about age 3 or 4 (20). Before that, infants physically demonstrate that they are dreaming by making mouthing movements or little sounds in their sleep. Toddlers may scream from sleep without awakening, but this kind of dreaming is often too primitive and inexpressive to establish that traumatic dreams are actually taking place (21). In a study of 20 children with documented traumas that occurred before the age of 5, only four of them verbalized the contents of their dreams (19). The repeated dream apparently is very difficult to find in most traumas before the age of 5. Furthermore, these dreams often take deeply disguised forms as time progresses after the traumatic event. In those children old enough to dream and to remember their dreams, traumatic dreaming may occur at intervals several years apart or in such deeply disguised forms that the process becomes extremely difficult to distinguish from other forms of dreaming.

Visualized or Otherwise Repeatedly Perceived Memories

The ability to re-see or, occasionally but less frequently, to re-feel a terrible event or a series of events is an important common characteristic of almost all externally generated disorders of childhood (22). Re-seeing is so important that it sometimes occurs even when the original experience was not at all visual (22). Tactile, positional, or smell memories may also follow from long-standing terrors or single shocks. But the tendency to revisualize appears to be the strongest of all of these re-perceptions in childhood trauma. Visualizations are most strongly stimulated by reminders of the traumatic event, but they occasionally come up entirely unbidden.

The vivid and unwelcome nature of returning traumatic visualizations marks them as special to these externally generated conditions. Children tend to see their traumas and old ordeals at leisure—during times when they are bored with classes, at night before falling asleep, and when they are at rest listening to the radio or watching television. As opposed to those traumatized as adults, traumatized children rarely find themselves abruptly interrupted by sudden, dysphoric visualizations.

Even those who were infants or toddlers at the time of their ordeals and thus were unable to lay down, store, or retrieve full verbal memories of their traumas tend to play out, to draw, or to re-see highly visualized elements from their old experiences (19). In cases in which the facts of a sexual abuse are not known, for instance, children may indicate their internalized visions of the abuse by sketching what they see in their mind or acting it out almost like a movie picture. Such children may use their visual and positional senses, senses that may outlast the verbal memory itself, to draw pictures of themselves "at the most scary moments of [their] life." Of course, other posttraumatic features should be present, too, if the child actually was a trauma victim.

Three and a half years after experiencing a series of traumatic events, a 5-year-old child was discovered (through pornographic photographs confiscated by U.S. Customs agents) to have been sexually misused in a day-care home between the ages of 15 and 18 months. The girl's parents did not dare speak to her about what they had learned from the investigators. They, in retrospect, realized that she had been sketching hundreds of nude adults beginning from the time when she had first begun to draw.

While playing in my office, this child told me that a baby she had just drawn was "all naked" and "a bad girl." Unknowingly, she had just depicted herself. Despite the fact that the little girl's only verbal memory of the events was "I think there was grave danger at a lady—MaryBeth's—house," her volumes of drawings represented strongly visualized elements that she had retained and had needed to recreate from these very early, nonverbal experiences.

A 40-year-old mental health professional began working at a facility for male juvenile delinquents. On his long rides home he began seeing himself as a toddler—attacked in a shack by a group of older children. The man drove to the town where he had lived until he was 4 years old, and he found the shack that he had "pictured." The shack stood catercornered to his old house.

Repetitive Behaviors

Play and behavioral reenactments are frequent manifestations of both the single blow and the long-standing terrors of childhood. Psychophysiologic repetitions are less frequently observed in ordinary practice, but they gain particular importance in certain cultures (23). Posttraumatic play, defined by the players as "fun," is a grim, long-lasting, and particularly contagious form of childhood repetitive behavior (24). Although reenactments lack the element of "fun," they also repeat aspects of the terrible events. Reenactments can occur as single behaviors, repeated behaviors, or bodily responses. Repetitive behaviors may even be seen in children who were exposed to traumatic events before the age of 12 months (19). In other words, children who have no verbal memory whatsoever of their traumas may be seen to feel physical sensations or play or act in a manner that evokes what they originally experienced at the time of the event. The 5-year-old girl described in the previous case vignette, for instance, experienced "funny feelings" in her "tummy" every time she saw a finger pointed at her. The pornographic pictures confiscated by the customs authorities showed an erect penis jabbing the very spot on the 15–18-month-old child's belly that she had indicated when, at age 5, she spoke of the "funny feelings."

The childhood survivors of single shocks and of long-standing terrors are usually entirely unaware that their behaviors and physical responses repeat something of the original set of thoughts or emergency responses. Thus, the presence or absence of behavioral reenactments may at times be better determined from interviews with third parties.

Behavioral reenactments may recur so frequently as to become distinct personality traits. These may eventually gather into the personality disorders of adulthood, or they may recur so physiologically as to represent what seems to be a physical disease. Long after most repeated nightmares have disappeared into deeply disguised form, reenactments continue to characterize the behaviors of traumatically stressed children. Recent psychiatric investigation into the lives and works of important artists—Edgar Allen Poe, Edith Wharton, René Magritte, Alfred Hitchcock, and Ingmar Bergman (25), Stephen King (26), and Virginia Woolf (27)—show that these artists reenacted childhood traumas behaviorally throughout their lifetimes and also played out their traumas in artistic works spanning their entire careers. If one could live a thousand years, one might completely work through a childhood trauma by playing out the terrifying scenario until it no longer terrified. The lifetime allotted to the ordinary person, however, does not appear to be enough.

A 6-year-old girl walked into a circus tent and was suddenly attacked by a runaway lion. The animal tore open her scalp and bit into her face. The girl had to undergo several surgical procedures to repair what happened within a few seconds' time. She was left with an uneven hairline and a large bald spot. After the extraordinary experience, the little girl preferred "Beauty Parlor" to all other games of pretend. She combed her younger sister's hair repeatedly, often bringing the younger child to tears over the roughness of the combing. The little girl's dolls developed bald spots and uneven hairlines without anyone ever observing exactly how these anomalies came into being. The child, previously outgoing and friendly, stuck close to home and rarely ventured out into her neighborhood. At age 6, her main hopes for the future were to grow up and become a runway model or a "beauty parlor lady."

Trauma-Specific Fears

Some of the specific fears related to the shocks and long-standing extreme external stresses of childhood can be avoided by moving out of town or by changing houses or neighborhoods. Fears can be conditioned away by repeatedly facing the feared object. Most extremely stressed or psychically traumatized children continue to harbor one or two trauma-related fears, however, well into adulthood. Fears of specific things that are related to experiences precipitated by traumatic events are fairly easy to spot, once one knows what the trauma might have been. This type of literal, specific fear is pathognomonic of the childhood traumas. Whereas neurotically or developmentally phobic children may fear *all* dogs, the dog-bitten youngster will fear the German shepherds, the Dobermans, or whatever species actually created the traumatic state. Whereas neurotically anxious children fear growing up or getting married, traumatized youngsters fear (and re-create) oral sex, anal intercourse, or whatever particular sexual abuse they originally experienced.

Traumatized children tend also to fear mundane items—the dark, strangers, looming objects, being alone, being outside, food, animals, and vehicles, for instance. In fact, fears of the dark and of being alone are strongly connected with sudden shocks in the early years (9). But these mundane fears may also be connected with a number of other emotional disorders and developmental stages of childhood. The panic and extreme avoidances observed following terrifying events, in connection with this mundane group of fears, *do* make them important to childhood trauma. But the specific, literal kinds of fear noted in the preceding paragraph almost "label" the traumatic condition. When one sees this literal kind of fear lasting throughout the years despite the natural tendencies toward spontaneous desensitization, childhood trauma is the most likely cause.

A girl was sexually misused by her father from age 5 to age 15, at which time she ran away from home, never to return. As a married adult of 38, she feared sex with her husband unless she initiated the act herself. She responded to the female-on-top or side-to-side positions, positions that had not originally been taken by her father. Any sexual positioning that was evocative of the incestuous set of sexual postures stimulated fear, pain, and revulsion.

Changed Attitudes about People, Life, and the Future

The sense of a severely limited future, along with changed attitudes about people and life, appears to be important in the trauma and extreme stress disorders originating in childhood. The limitation of future perspective is particularly striking in traumatized children because ordinary youngsters exhibit almost limitless ideas about the future. Truisms, such as "I live one day at a time" or "I can't guess what will happen in my lifetime," come from the rethinkings that occur in the years after traumatic events. Ideas such as "You can't trust the police" or "You can't count on anything or anyone to protect you" also follow from single and long-standing, repeated traumas. Sexually traumatized girls may shrink away from men or accost them with overfriendly advances. Part of this behavior is reenactment, but part reflects attitudinal changes. Limitations in scope and future perspective in childhood trauma victims seem to reflect the ongoing belief that more traumas are bound to follow. Traumatized children recognize profound vulnerability in all human beings, especially themselves. This shattering of what Lifton and Olson call "the shield of invincibility" (28) and what Erikson terms "basic trust" and "autonomy" (29) appears to characterize almost all event-engendered disorders of childhood. The feeling of futurelessness of the traumatized child is quite different from that of the depressed youngster. For the traumatized, the future is a landscape filled with crags, pits, and monsters. For the depressed, the future is a bleak, featureless landscape stretched out to infinity.

A 17-year-old boy, searching for a freeway shoulder on which to stop his disabled car, was hit from the rear by a speeder. The boy's automobile exploded. He flew out completely unscathed but watched helplessly as his best friend burned to death in the passenger seat.

For months after the event the boy could not work and spent most of his days moping. He was plagued with bad dreams and fears of further disaster. He began psychotherapy; and when I said to him at the end of an early session, "See you next week," he asked, "How do you know it will be next week? Who knows? I may die on my way out of your office. I may be killed out there on the sidewalk. I don't count on seeing you next week. I live day to day—day to day."

A 15-year-old girl came for psychiatric treatment because, since she was attacked at age 8, she had failed to volunteer or speak up in class. Since her acceptance in an academic high school, she could achieve no more than Bs because she was too quiet.

The girl had experienced significant changes in her attitudes about life and people while she was lying in a hospital room for 3 months, following repairs to her vagina, anus, and peritoneum. A man had grabbed her from a Chinatown sidewalk on her way home from school. He had taken her into an abandoned garage and attacked her vagina with a pair of chopsticks. The girl had decided after her ordeal that she was "chosen" by the deranged man because she had "showed too much." Never again, she had vowed to herself, would she ever "show." People could not be trusted, she believed. Life must be endured, not savored.

FEATURES CHARACTERISTIC OF THE SINGLE-BLOW TRAUMAS, TYPE I DISORDERS

The type I traumatic conditions of childhood follow from unanticipated single events. These are classical childhood traumas by Anna Freud's definition (30). These are also the most typical posttraumatic stress disorders that one finds in childhood, usually meeting the criteria of repetition, avoidance, and hyperalertness that represent the major divisions in our diagnostic manual, *DSM-III-R*. Those children who suffer the results of single blows appear to exhibit certain symptoms and signs that differentiate their conditions from those resulting from the more complicated events. The findings special to single, shocking, intense terrors are 1) full, detailed, etched-in memories, 2) "omens" (retrospective reworkings, cognitive reappraisals, reasons, and turning points), and 3) misperceptions and mistimings. Type I traumas do not appear to breed the massive denials, psychic numbings, self-anesthesias, or personality problems that characterize the type II disorders of childhood.

Full, Detailed Memories

With the exception of youngsters below the approximate age of 28 to 36 months, almost every previously untraumatized child who is fully conscious at the time that he or she experiences or witnesses one terrible event demonstrates the ability to retrieve detailed and full memories afterward (19). Verbal recollections of single shocks in an otherwise trauma-free childhood are delivered in an amazingly clear and detailed fashion. Children sometimes sound like robots as they strive to tell every detail as efficiently as possible. As a matter of fact, children are sometimes able to remember more from a single event than are the adults who observed the same event (24). A few details from a traumatic event of childhood may be factually wrong because the child initially misperceived or mistimed the sequence of what happened. But children with type I disorders seem to remember the event and to give impressively clear, detailed accounts of their experiences.

This remarkable retrieval of full, precise, verbal memories of almost all single-blow traumas makes one conclude that these memories stay alive in a very special way, no matter how much conscious suppression the traumatized child is attempting. Memories of prolonged or variably repeated childhood abuses, on the other hand, appear to be retained in spots, rather than as clear, complete wholes (19). Amnesias, as a matter of fact, are often reported in children who seem to be heading for the multiple personality disorders of adulthood (31). Children who have been repeatedly physically or sexually abused may waver in their accusations of abusers and waver in the completeness and the detail of their memories. But children who have been traumatized a single time do not often forget. As Malle says at the conclusion of his autobiographical film, *Au Revoir Les Enfants* (1987), a tale of a single, terrible event from his boyhood in occupied France, "Over forty years have passed, but I will remember every second of that January morning until the day I die."

The first time that he visited the psychiatrist, a 5-year-old boy minutely described his stepfather's murder of his baby brother. The incident had occurred 2 weeks earlier. The boy knew just where under the television table in a motel room he had been hiding. He reported exactly where he had been sitting and lying before taking cover. He described the types of blows that fell upon his younger sibling and meticulously repeated the attacker's phrases and threats. He said that he had been trying to forget all of this but could not. The boy's teacher had been reprimanding him for repeatedly hiding under the desks and tables at school, but neither teacher nor student recognized the significance of this "bad behavior."

Omens

During and after single-blow shocks, children tend frequently to ask themselves "Why?" and "Why me?" In this way they attempt to gain retrospective mastery over the randomness, the lack of control, and the "less-than-humaneness" of the trauma that they endured. When children traumatized by a single event belatedly develop a reason why everything happened, a purpose to the entire affair, or a way that the disaster could have been averted, considerable mental energy goes into these reworkings of the past. I have termed these belated reshiftings, reasons, and warnings "omens" (17), while Pynoos et al. call them "cognitive reappraisals" (11). I believe that we are describing the same phenomenon. This kind of rethinking and reworking occurs much more often after one sudden external shock than it does after a prolonged series of terrible experiences. Children who have found omens or reasons to explain why they suffer often feel intensely guilty. Although victims of type II childhood trauma also experience profound guilt, the sense of guilt does not often consciously align itself to the "Why me?" question. The repetitions and long-standing nature of the type II stressors make the inquiry "How could I have avoided it?" far less pressing than the question "How will I avoid it the next time?"

The omen or cognitive reappraisal is a belated way in which the singly traumatized child tries to deal retroactively with what had been entirely unexpected—a sudden, surprising psychological blow. Because repeated horrors encourage a sense of anticipation and expectation, different means of coping come to be employed. These means of coping eventually create the defining characteristics of the type II disorders, characteristics that are unmatched in the type I disorders.

An 8-year-old boy's mother bought him a fancy skateboard, admonishing him to ride only on the sidewalk. The first Saturday morning the boy rode his skateboard on the sidewalk, he was run over by a car backing out of a neighbor's driveway. The boy commented a year later, "I can't help thinking many, many times about what Mom said about riding skateboards on sidewalks."

A 16-year-old girl received a slice of pizza from her best friend as a birthday present. Biting into the pizza, she was poisoned by a corrosive toxin. The girl suffered from internal injuries for more than 6 weeks. Even though the real source of the poison was found by health officials at the pizza parlor, the injured girl thought again and again about the nature of her relationship with the friend who had purchased the pizza. In minutest detail she tried to figure out at what point her friend had decided to kill her.

Misperceptions

Misidentifications, visual hallucinations, and peculiar time distortions often occur to children who have experienced single, intense, unexpected shocks

(22, 32). In contrast to this, the long-standing, extreme external stresses that affect children are often engineered by perpetrators known to them—caretakers, teachers, or family members, for instance. Because of a child's familiarity with such perpetrators, the chances of early misperceptions become slim. Two important exceptions to this general rule are when a type II victim thinks that he or she "sees" a once-familiar abuser years after losing track of the person and when a known, long-standing perpetrator was never perceived correctly by the child because of a disguise that he or she was wearing (as in satanism and cults).

Many of the type I childhood traumas include visual misperceptions and hallucinations. These perceptual distortions may seem to indicate organic mental conditions or psychoses, but a few bizarre sightings do not "make" a brain disorder or a schizophrenic episode. Visual hallucinations and illusions are observed in children shortly after traumatic events and, at times, long after sudden, unanticipated shocks. Massive releases of neurotransmitters in the brain at the time of the terror may account for these problems with perception. But the types of substances and mechanisms are, as yet, unknown.

A 7-year-old girl rode in a station wagon alongside her sister and two cousins on a family outing to the mountains. A loose boulder from an adjacent hillside smashed into the roof of the girl's car, killing one cousin and the girl's older sister, while sparing the girl and her other young cousin. For the ensuing year, the surviving girl "saw" her sister at her bedside almost every night. The dead sister visited the living child dressed in pink, green, and orange outfits. She appeared fully fleshed, as she was in life. The vision said nothing. The young survivor felt upset by a sense of menace emanating from her sister's "ghost," yet, at the same time, she felt oddly comforted by the sight.

FEATURES CHARACTERISTIC OF VARIABLE MULTIPLE, OR LONG-STANDING TRAUMAS, TYPE II DISORDERS

Type II disorders follow from long-standing or repeated exposure to extreme external events. The first such event, of course, creates surprise. But the subsequent unfolding of horrors creates a sense of anticipation. Massive attempts to protect the psyche and to preserve the self are put into gear. The defenses and coping operations used in the type II disorders of childhood—massive denial, repression, dissociation, self-anesthesia, self-hypnosis, identification with the aggressor, and aggression turned against the self—often lead to profound character changes in the youngster. Even though a repeatedly abused youngster may not settle into a recognizable form of adult character disorder until the late teens or early twenties, extreme personality problems may emerge even before the age of 5.

The emotions stirred up by type II traumas are 1) an absence of feeling, 2) a sense of rage, or 3) unremitting sadness. These emotions exist side by side with the fear that is ubiquitous to the childhood traumas. Type II disorders, under the scrutiny of able mental health professionals, may come to be diagnosed in childhood as conduct disorders, attention deficit disorders, depression, or dissociative disorders. Recognition of the expanded group of traumas that I am suggesting here may help to define a common etiology and range of findings for many of these childhood conditions. Of course, if a child originally was traumatized, one would expect to find vestiges of the repeated visualizations, repeated behaviors and physiologic sensations, specific fears, and revised ideas about people, life, and the future that appear to characterize the childhood traumas.

Denial and Psychic Numbing

Denial and psychic numbing have long been considered classic findings of the posttraumatic stress disorders. Diagnostic problems often arise, however, because massive denial and emotional shutdown are so often evanescent or absent in children who have gone through single shocks (17). Although conscious suppression of thoughts will take place in any kind of trauma, and although brief, limited denial and numbing may last from moments to hours after a shocking event, massive denial and psychic numbing are primarily associated with the long-standing horrors of childhood, what I would call the type II traumas. Children who experience this type of stress may employ such extreme numbing and denial that they look extremely withdrawn or inhuman. When very young, they may assume the guise of Spitz's "hospitalism" babies (33) or of "hail fellow well met" superficiality (34), both of which are signs of failure of attachment and of personality organization.

Children who experience type II traumas do not complain of going "numb." The sense of going dead is one that depends upon years of subjectively knowing what it was to feel alive. On the other hand, children who have been repeatedly brutalized or terrorized do exhibit massive denial to the eyes of the trained observer. Such children avoid talking about themselves. They often go for years without saying a thing about their ordeals. They valiantly try to look normal at school, in the neighborhood, and on the playground. They may tell their stories once or twice and entirely deny them later. (This is quite different from some children who have experienced type I traumas, who may tell their stories even at kindergarten Show and Tell.)

Children who experience type II traumas often forget. They may forget whole segments of childhood—from birth to age 9, for instance. Where one sees the difference between these "forgetful" children and ordinary youngsters is in the multiply traumatized child's relative indifference to pain, lack of empathy, failure to define or to acknowledge feelings, and absolute avoidance of psychological intimacy. Repeatedly brutalized, benumbed children employ massive denial—and when their denial-related behaviors cluster together, the resultant childhood personality disorder (one that cuts across adult narcissistic, antisocial, borderline, and avoidant categories) is massive.

Profound psychic numbing in children occurs as an accommodation to the most extreme, long-standing, or repeated traumatic situations. Childhood physical and sexual abuse represent two of these extremes. What still makes the underlying idea of "trauma" the correct etiology and pathogenesis here is the fact that the specific fears, the repeated play, the behavioral and physiologic reenactments, the tendencies toward visualizations, and the revised ideas about life, people, and the future seem to persist in so many of these children for years after the last abuse stops.

Suzanna was 6 years old when her teenaged brother began sexually molesting her. (It turned out that he, in turn, had been sexually molested by a junior high school teacher before he began abusing Suzanna.) Suzanna once tried to tell her mother, "Nobody's supposed to touch you in your—" (she pointed at her genitals). But after that she said nothing further to her parents, teachers, or friends until the school nurse discovered what was happening 2½ years after it began.

On psychiatric examination when she was age 9, Suzanna spent much of the first hour pushing her index finger back and forth through a small hole she had made with the rest of her fingers. She repeatedly rubbed the loose couch pillows over one another. She said of her experiences with her brother, "He put his penis where I pooped. It hurt. I told him it hurt, but he said nuttin' back. I didn't like that at all. It didn't really frighten me. Not really. I just made up my mind to think about other things."

When Suzanna was asked how she was able to do this mind trick, "to think about other things," she replied, "I say 'I don't know' over and over to myself. When I say my prayers I keep saying the last word of the prayer. Sometimes I do it a hundred times. I say 'I don't know' a lot of times in my mind each day. . . . Sometimes now I find myself not feeling things. I don't feel sad or mad when I should be. I'm not afraid when I should be. I act silly and crazy a lot. The people at my school think I'm funny because of it."

Self-Hypnosis and Dissociation

Spontaneous self-hypnosis, depersonalization, and dissociation are important outcomes of repeated, long-standing terrors (the type II traumas). Children who have been the victims of extended periods of terror come to learn that the stressful events will be repeated. Some of these children, the ones, perhaps, who have an innate ease of hypnotizability, spontaneously fall upon the technique of self-hypnosis. This mechanism enables a child mentally to escape. Suzanna, the child described in the previous paragraph, used the repetition of a single word, the last word of her prayers, to accomplish this escape from pain and worry. She also lulled herself into minitrances by saying "I don't know" in her mind. The children at school recognized her affect to be unusual. But nobody but the child herself could recognize the self-hypnosis.

Traumatized children who use a great deal of self-hypnosis may, in fact, go on to develop adult multiple personality disorders (35). This is probably a rare condition. Spontaneous dissociation, however, accounts for a number of more commonly observed findings in abused children—bodily anesthesias, feelings of invisibility, and amnesias for certain periods of childhood life.

Multiple personality disorder, a syndrome in search of its own place in our diagnostic manuals, belongs here, at least in terms of etiology—the repeated, extreme, long-standing traumas of childhood. In children, periods of time that cannot be accounted for, problem behaviors, visual and auditory hallucinations, and headaches appear to indicate that the child is suffering from multiple personality precursors (36). Most self-hypnotizing children who are type II trauma victims fall short of the multiple personality or precursor diagnoses, however. They develop, instead, anesthesias to bodily pain, sexual anesthesias, and extreme emotional distancings. Children who come to expect the repetition of terrors remove themselves in any way that they can. These emotional removals are not possible for the ordinary type I trauma victim.

Frederick was 7 years old when he was sent to live with his aunt because his mother found out, through a tape recording set up to catch her husband at infidelity, that Frederick's stepfather had been throwing him against walls while she worked the evening shift. Frederick did not tell anyone his year-long story, despite two visits to the emergency room and one neighbor-instigated protective service investigation.

While in his aunt's custody, Frederick glanced down at the playground pavement one day and saw blood. After several seconds of searching for a wounded companion, Frederick realized that it was *he* who was bleeding. The boy realized he could feel no pain.

In a psychotherapy session I asked Frederick how he could make this sort of thing happen. "It jus' happens now," he said. "I used to pretend I was at a picnic with my head on Mommy's lap. The first time my stepdaddy hit me, it hurt a lot. But then I found out that I could make myself go on Mommy's lap [in imagination], and Winston couldn't hurt me that way. I kept goin' on Mommy's lap—I didn't have to cry or scream or anything. I could *be* someplace else and not get hurt. I don't know how many times Winston punched me out. I wasn't always payin' attention. Like I told you, first I'd be at a picnic on Mom's lap. Later I didn't have to think of no picnic—

jus' her lap. Now if somethin' makes me bleed, I don't think of no lap at all. I jus' don't feel no pain."

Jamie was repeatedly abused by his alcoholic father. He had also repeatedly observed his father beat his mother. At age 8, he witnessed his mother shoot his father to death. When he was 9, the child was psychologically evaluated. At that time he told me, "I started some planets. I made my planets up as a game. But it's real now. It's no game anymore." Jamie described a safe planet he had invented long ago, his own planet. He also had invented a number of very unsafe planets where people "got killed." He said that he had come to achieve invisibility by repeatedly visiting his own safe planet and avoiding the unsafe ones. "Starting when I was 6," he said, "I began to feel invisible. When my Mom pointed a gun at my Dad . . . I was thinking like 'I didn't see it,' like 'This didn't happen.' I blinked to see if I was dreaming. . . . I remember at first pretending I wasn't there—that I didn't see it—that I was on my own planet. I had gone there a lot before. When Mom and Dad would fight, I would try not to hear, not to see. I'd try to go to sleep. Normally I couldn't. I'd try to get out of the room where they were. I'd try to visit my planet. But now my mind, yes, it just goes blank. Mostly it happens at home. A few minutes at a time."

Jamie repeatedly dreamed by night about his father's death. And he visualized the killing by day. But from the moment that his dad was shot, Jamie wondered if he himself could turn invisible. "I know I can," he said. "I do it here on earth. I do it all the time on my planet. You're just going to have to believe me. My friends believe it. . . . When my father was being shot I felt invisible. But if I turned invisible in front of everybody, they'd take away my powers."

Rage

Rage, including anger turned against the self, is a striking finding in those posttraumatic disorders that are brought on by repeated or long-standing abuses, the type II disorders. One observes rage and its negative, extreme passivity, in those type II disorders originating in places where trust originally resided. Dorothy Otnow Lewis and her group reported that among adolescent delinquents who go on to commit murder, chronic physical abuse is a key finding within a cluster of several other key findings (36). The rage of the repeatedly abused child cannot safely be underestimated.

Reenactments of anger may come so frequently in the type II trauma disorders that habitual patterns of aggressiveness are established. The rage may become so fearsome to the child as to create extremes of passivity. Wild fluctuations of both active anger and extreme passivity may so dominate the clinical picture that the young person is eventually given a diagnosis of borderline personality. Defenses against rage such as passive into active and identification with the aggressor also put their own peculiar stamps on the type II child. Type II children have been known to attack their own bodies.

Self-mutilations or physically damaging suicide attempts occur. The festering anger of the repeatedly abused child is probably as damaging a part of the condition as is the chronic numbing. Both of these, in fact, the numbing and rage, probably figure later in the antisocial, borderline, narcissistic, and multiple personality diagnoses that are so often part of the picture of the type II traumatized child grown up.

A 5-year-old boy whose new stepmother had been tying him with ropes and leaving him locked up in closets behaved well at kindergarten. At home, however, he took scissors to his stepmother's best lingerie. He sprinkled India ink twice into the family wash. He consistently managed not to eat the food his stepmother prepared for him. The boy's stepmother said he was asking for the punishments she gave him. And so the abuses escalated.

A 45-year-old woman had been a teenager in summer camp when the atomic bomb destroyed her home in Hiroshima. (Her immediate family was spared; all were out of town on Aug. 6, 1945.) As an adult, the woman could not get along well with her American-born husband, alternately accusing him of laziness, ineptitude at work, and infidelity. From the time her daughter turned 13, the woman began believing the girl to be promiscuous, a liar, a drug addict, and a thief. The woman could not get along with her co-workers at the international law office where she worked. She was able, she said, to relate only to customers from Japan. They reminded her "of the people [she] used to know at home when [she] was a girl." I invited the woman to come to my office to talk about her experiences with the bomb. She made two appointments for this purpose but failed to appear for either. Obviously, too much time had elapsed to prove any cause-and-effect hypothesis here. It is interesting, however, that the woman's anger and suspiciousness rested only with American and American-influenced people. Native Japanese persons, the victims, not the perpetrators of the atomic bomb, were entirely spared her wrath.

CROSSOVER TYPE I–TYPE II TRAUMATIC CONDITIONS OF CHILDHOOD

When a single psychological shock takes a child's parent's life, leaves a child homeless, handicapped, or disfigured, or causes a child to undergo prolonged hospitalization and pain, the ongoing stresses tend to push the changes in the child toward those characteristic of the type II childhood traumas. In these cases one often finds features of both the type I and the type II conditions. Those children with permanent handicaps, longstanding pain, or loss of significant objects are often forced into making significant character changes or using numbing tricks to minimize their pain. They may still retain, however, the characteristics typical of responses to single events—clear memory, perceptual distortions, and omens.

Perpetual Mourning and Depression

Psychic shock interferes with childhood bereavement and vice versa (37). The combined psychological effects of shock and grief continue to drag on throughout childhood. As time goes by, and the childhood mourning does not proceed through its ordinary stages (38), the young trauma victim is reinjured—from the inside this time—through prolonged exposure to sadness and loss. The psychological condition of mixed mourning and trauma in youth may take the guise of major affective disorder and may have to be treated as such, at least at first. There is a high rate of depression in refugee children from brutal regimes (15, 16). An explanation for this finding may be the unresolved trauma that potentiates and extends the unresolved grief, the grief that furthers the trauma, or both.

A 4-year-old boy watched his older sister's evisceration in a freak accident in a children's swimming pool. Before the disaster she had asked him to play, but he had refused. The little girl then sat down on an exposed drain pipe. The boy spent a couple of years after the accident using wooden blocks to build his own perfect pool. He blamed himself for not agreeing to play with his sister, an act, he felt, that caused his sister's injury. The boy retained a clear memory of all of the events. He showed symptoms typical of type I trauma.

Following his sister's death in transplantation surgery 2 years after the accident, the boy began to retreat from his friends, avoid participating in class, and stay silent much of the time. His teachers complained about his extreme passivity and said he was losing ground in subjects in which he had already proved himself. He lost some weight and stopped sleeping through the night. He lost his playfulness and began losing his friends. His 2 years of mourning had introduced type II characteristics into a previously pure type I disorder.

Childhood Disfigurement, Disability, and Pain

Children who are physically injured in psychically traumatic accidents tend perpetually to mourn old selves, personas that were previously intact and perfect. Even when perpetual grief is not the problem, posttraumatic physical handicaps frequently demand considerable personality reorganization in order that the child can live with a new, limited self. In children, character rearrangements may become massive. To deal with the pain and procedures accompanying traumatic accidents, children may employ self-hypnosis. They may experience self-revulsion, unremitting guilt and shame, impotent rage at their peers who shun and tease them, and sadness. Suicide attempts are not infrequent in this group. Robert Stoller suggested in a recent paper that some extremes of adult sadomasochistic behavior may originate in painful illnesses, injuries, and procedures during childhood. Rather than self-hypnotizing, these children may divert themselves from the pain by self-stimulating—and thus perpetually associate their pain with sexuality (39). Childhood syndromes of injury and shock do not consistently qualify, under *DSM-III-R* criteria, as posttraumatic stress disorders (40). But these mixed syndromes of depression, numbing, rage, and fright often carry many of the four characteristics that I associate with childhood traumas. Adjustment to a sudden surprise, coupled with a prolonged ordeal, often lies at the origin of the problem.

A kindergartner climbed onto a large department store display table, causing it to fall over onto her face as her grandmother paid the clerk for a purchase. The child's facial bones were smashed, and although they were beautifully reconstructed, she looked quite different than she had before the accident. Old friends did not recognize her, and other kindergartners told the child that she must be pretending to be Belinda— she could not actually *be* Belinda.

The little girl, previously outgoing, mischievous, and vivacious, took on a quiet, remote, and perfectly well-behaved mode of behavior. Two years after the accident she said, "I was a devil before, but I was punished for it. Now I'm good." Despite the fact that she experienced bad dreams, liked to play alone under chairs, and tended to mutilate her dolls' faces, Belinda's character change dominated all other posttraumatic findings.

SUMMARY

There appears to be a group of problems brought on in childhood by the experience of extreme fright generated by outside events. Some of these childhood problems are created by one external shock, and others are created by a multiplicity of blows. Untreated, all but the mildest of the childhood traumas last for years. The child's responses, in fact, may create a number of different kinds of problems in adult life. There are four characteristics, however, that seem to affect almost everyone subjected to extreme terrors in childhood. These findings seem to last and can be retrieved in histories. They include repeated visualizations or other returning perceptions, repeated behaviors and bodily responses, trauma-specific fears, and revised ideas about people, life, and the future. These four findings appear to remain clustered together in childhood trauma victims even when other diagnoses seem more appropriate. Like rheumatic fever, childhood trauma creates changes that may eventually lead to a number of different diagnoses. But also like rheumatic fever, childhood trauma must always be kept in mind as a possible underlying mechanism when these various conditions appear.

If one takes all of the disorders of childhood brought on by extreme external events and puts them into the general category of trauma, they can be roughly subdivided into two groupings: type I, which is brought on by one sudden shock, and type II, which is precipitated by a series of external blows. Crossover conditions are quite common and develop when one blow creates a long-standing series of childhood adversities.

REFERENCES

1. Carmen E(H), Rieker P P, Mills T: Victims of violence and psychiatric illness. Am J Psychiatry 1984; 141:378–383
2. Bliss E: Multiple Personality, Allied Disorders, and Hypnosis. New York, Oxford University Press, 1986
3. Walsh R: The family of the borderline patient, in The Borderline Patient. Edited by Grinker F, Werble B. New York, Jason Aronson, 1977
4. Lewis D O, Lovely R, Yaeger C, et al.: Toward a theory of the genesis of violence. J Am Acad Child Psychiatry 1989; 28:431–436
5. Russell D: The Secret Trauma. New York, Basic Books, 1986
6. Silver L B, Dublin C C, Lourie R S: Does violence breed violence? contributions from a study of the child abuse syndrome. Am J Psychiatry 1969; 126:404–407
7. Herman J, Van Der Kolk B: Traumatic antecedents of borderline personality, in Psychological Trauma. Edited by Van Der Kolk B. Washington, DC, American Psychiatric Press, 1987
8. Terr L: Life attitudes, dreams, and psychic trauma in a group of "normal" children. J Am Acad Child Psychiatry 1983; 22:221–230
9. Terr L: Children's responses to the Challenger disaster, in New Research Program and Abstracts, American Psychiatric Association 143rd Annual Meeting. Washington, DC, APA, 1990
10. Freud S: Beyond the pleasure principle (1920), in Complete Psychological Works, standard ed, vol 18. London, Hogarth Press, 1955
11. Pynoos R, Frederick C, Nader K, et al.: Life threat and posttraumatic stress in school age children. Arch Gen Psychiatry 1987; 44:1057–1063
12. Green A: Dimensions of psychological trauma in abused children. J Am Acad Child Psychiatry 1983; 22:231–237
13. McLeer S, Deblinger E, Atkins M, et al.: Post-traumatic stress disorder in sexually abused children. J Am Acad Child Adolesc Psychiatry 1988; 27:650–659
14. Kinzie J D, Sack W. Angell R, et al.: The psychiatric effects of massive trauma on Cambodian children. J Am Acad Child Adolesc Psychiatry 1986; 25:370–383
15. Kinzie J D, Sack W, Angell R, et al.: A three-year follow-up of Cambodian young people traumatized as children. J Am Acad Child Adolesc Psychiatry 1989; 28: 501–504
16. Kestenberg J: Child survivors of the Holocaust—40 years later. J Am Acad Child Psychiatry 1985; 24:408–412
17. Terr L: Children of Chowchilla. Psychoanal Study Child 1979; 34:547–623

18. Terr L C: Chowchilla revisited: the effects of psychic trauma four years after a school-bus kidnapping. Am J Psychiatry 1983; 140:1543–1550

19. Terr L: What happens to the memories of early childhood trauma? J Am Acad Child Adolesc Psychiatry 1988; 27:96–104

20. Mack J: Nightmares and the Human Conflict. Boston, Little, Brown, 1970

21. Terr L: Children's nightmares, in Sleep and Its Disorders in Children. Edited by Guilleminault C. New York, Raven Press, 1987

22. Terr L: Remembered images in psychic trauma. Psychoanal Study Child 1985; 40:493–533

23. Kinzie J D: Severe posttraumatic stress syndrome among Cambodian refugees, in Disaster Stress Studies. Edited by Shore J. Washington, DC, American Psychiatric Press, 1986

24. Terr L: "Forbidden games." J Am Acad Child Psychiatry 1981; 20:740–759

25. Terr L: Childhood trauma and the creative product. Psychoanal Study Child 1987; 42:545–572

26. Terr L: Terror writing by the formerly terrified. Psychoanal Study Child 1989; 44:369–390

27. Terr L: Who's afraid in Virginia Woolf? Psychoanal Study Child 1990; 45:531–544

28. Lifton R, Olson E: The human meaning of total disaster. Psychiatry 1976; 39:1–18

29. Erikson E: Childhood and Society. New York, Norton, 1950

30. Freud A: Comments on trauma, in The Writings of Anna Freud, vol V, 1956–1965: Research at the Hampstead Child Therapy Clinic and Other Papers. New York, International Universities Press, 1969

31. Kluft R: Childhood multiple personality disorder, in Childhood Antecedents of Multiple Personality. Edited by Kluft R. Washington, DC, American Psychiatric Press, 1985

32. Terr L: Too Scared to Cry. New York, Harper & Row, 1990

33. Spitz R: Hospitalism. Psychoanal Study Child 1945; 1:64–72

34. Terr L C: A family study of child abuse. Am J Psychiatry 1970; 127: 665–671

35. Spiegel D: Multiple personality as a posttraumatic stress disorder. Psychiatr Clin North Am 1984; 7:101–110

36. Lewis D O, Moy E, Jackson L D, et al.: Biopsychosocial characteristics of children who later murder: a prospective study. Am J Psychiatry 1985; 142: 1161–1167

37. Eth S, Pynoos R: Interaction of trauma and grief in childhood, in Post-traumatic Stress Disorder in Children. Edited by Eth S, Pynoos P. Washington, DC, American Psychiatric Press, 1985

38. Osterweis M, Solomon F, Green M (eds): Bereavement. Washington, DC, National Academy Press, 1984

39. Stoller R: Consensual sadomasochistic perversions, in the Psychoanalytic Core. Edited by Blum H, Weinshel E M, Rodman F R. New York, International Universities Press, 1989

40. Stoddard F J, Norman D K, Murphy J M: A diagnostic outcome study of children and adolescents with severe burns. J Trauma 1989; 29:471–477

4. Complex PTSD

A Syndrome in Survivors of Prolonged and Repeated Trauma

Judith Lewis Herman

THE CURRENT diagnostic formulation of PTSD derives primarily from observations of survivors of relatively circumscribed traumatic events: combat, disaster, and rape. It has been suggested that this formulation fails to capture the protean sequelae of prolonged, repeated trauma. In contrast to the circumscribed traumatic event, prolonged, repeated trauma can occur only where the victim is in a state of captivity, unable to flee, and under the control of the perpetrator. Examples of such conditions include prisons, concentration camps, and slave labor camps. Such conditions also exist in some religious cults, in brothels and other institutions of organized sexual exploitation, and in some families.

Captivity, which brings the victim into prolonged contact with the perpetrator, creates a special type of relationship, one of coercive control. This is equally true whether the victim is rendered captive primarily by physical force (as in the case of prisoners and hostages), or by a combination of physical, economic, social, and psychological means (as in the case of religious cult members, battered women, and abused children). The psychological impact of subordination to coercive control may have many common features, whether that subordination occurs within the public sphere of politics or within the supposedly private (but equally political) sphere of sexual and domestic relations.

This paper reviews the evidence for the existence of a complex form of posttraumatic disorder in survivors of prolonged, repeated trauma. A preliminary formulation of this complex posttraumatic syndrome is currently under consideration for inclusion in DSM-IV under the name of DESNOS (Disorders of Extreme Stress). In the course of a larger work in progress, I have

Reprinted by permission from *Journal of Traumatic Stress*, 3 (1) 377–391. Copyright © 1992 by Plenum Publishing.

recently scanned literature of the past 50 years on survivors of prolonged domestic, sexual, or political victimization (Herman, 1992). This literature includes first-person accounts of survivors themselves, descriptive clinical literature, and, where available, more rigorously designed clinical studies. In the literature review, particular attention was directed toward observations that did not fit readily into the existing criteria for PTSD. Though the sources include works by authors of many nationalities, only works originally written in English or available in English translation were reviewed.

The concept of a spectrum of posttraumatic disorders has been suggested independently by many major contributors to the field. Kolb, in a letter to the editor of the *American Journal of Psychiatry* (1989), writes of the "heterogeneity" of PTSD. He observes that "PTSD is to psychiatry as syphilis was to medicine. At one time or another PTSD may appear to mimic every personality disorder," and notes further that "It is those threatened over long periods of time who suffer the long-standing severe personality disorganization." Niederland, on the basis of his work with survivors of the Nazi Holocaust, observes that "the concept of traumatic neurosis does not appear sufficient to cover the multitude and severity of clinical manifestations" of the survivor syndrome (in Krystal, 1968, p. 314). Tanay, working with the same population, notes that "the psychopathology may be hidden in characterological changes that are manifest only in disturbed object relationships and attitudes towards work, the world, man and God" (Krystal, 1968, p. 221). Similarly, Kroll and his colleagues (1989), on the basis of their work with Southeast Asian refugees, suggest the need for an "expanded concept of PTSD that takes into account the observations [of the effects of] severe, prolonged, and/or massive psychological and physical traumata." Horowitz (1986) suggests the concept of a "post-traumatic character disorder," and Brown and Fromm (1986) speak of "complicated PTSD."

Clinicians working with survivors of childhood abuse also invoke the need for an expanded diagnostic concept. Gelinas (1983) describes the "disguised presentation" of the survivor of childhood sexual abuse as a patient with chronic depression complicated by dissociative symptoms, substance abuse, impulsively, self-mutilation, and suicidality. She formulates the underlying psychopathology as a complicated traumatic neurosis. Goodwin (1988) conceptualizes the sequelae of prolonged childhood abuse as a severe posttraumatic syndrome which includes fugue and other dissociative states, ego fragmentation, affective and anxiety disorders, reenactment and revictimization, somatization and suicidality.

Clinical observations identify three broad areas of disturbance which transcend simple PTSD. The first is symptomatic: the symptom picture in survivors of prolonged trauma often appears to be more complex, diffuse, and tenacious than in simple PTSD. The second is characterological: survivors of prolonged abuse develop characteristic personality changes, including deformations of relatedness and identity. The third area involves the survivor's vulnerability to repeated harm, both self-inflicted and at the hands of others.

SYMPTOMATIC SEQUELAE OF PROLONGED VICTIMIZATION

Multiplicity of Symptoms

The pathological environment of prolonged abuse fosters the development of a prodigious array of psychiatric symptoms. A history of abuse, particularly in childhood, appears to be one of the major factors predisposing a person to become a psychiatric patient. While only a minority of survivors of chronic childhood abuse become psychiatric patients, a large proportion (40–70%) of adult psychiatric patients are survivors of abuse (Briere and Runtz, 1987; Briere and Zaidi, 1989, Carmen *et al.*, 1984; Jacobson and Richardson, 1987).

Survivors who become patients present with a great number and variety of complaints. Their general levels of distress are higher than those of patients who do not have abuse histories. Detailed inventories of their symptoms reveal significant pathology in multiple domains: somatic, cognitive, affective, behavioral, and relational. Bryer and his colleagues (1987), studying psychiatric inpatients, report that women with histories of physical or sexual abuse have significantly higher scores than other patients on standardized measures of somatization, depression, general and phobic anxiety, interpersonal sensitivity, paranoia, and "psychoticism" (dissociative symptoms were not measured specifically). Briere (1988), studying outpatients at a crisis intervention service, reports that survivors of childhood abuse display significantly more insomnia, sexual dysfunction, dissociation, anger, suicidality, self-mutilation, drug addiction, and alcoholism than other patients. Perhaps the most impressive finding of studies employing a "symptom check-list" approach is the sheer length of the list of symptoms found to be significantly related to a history of childhood abuse (Browne and Finkelhor, 1986). From this wide array of symptoms, I have selected three categories that do not readily fall within the classic diagnostic criteria for PTSD: these are the somatic, dissociative, and affective sequelae of prolonged trauma.

Somatization

Repetitive trauma appears to amplify and generalize the physiologic symptoms of PTSD. Chronically traumatized people are hypervigilant, anxious, and agitated, without any recognizable baseline state of calm or comfort (Hilberman, 1980). Over time, they begin to complain, not only of insomnia, startle reactions and agitation, but also of numerous other somatic symptoms. Tension headaches, gastrointestinal disturbances, and abdominal, back, or pelvic pain are extremely common. Survivors also frequently complain of tremors, choking sensations, or nausea. In clinical studies of survivors of the Nazi Holocaust, psychosomatic reactions were found to be practically universal (Hoppe, 1968; Krystal and Niederland, 1968: De Loos, 1990). Similar observations are now reported in refugees from the concentration camps of Southeast Asia (Kroll et al., 1989; Kinzie et al., 1990). Some survivors may conceptualize the damage of their prolonged captivity primarily in somatic terms. Nonspecific somatic symptoms appear to be extremely durable and may in fact increase over time (van der Ploerd, 1989).

The clinical literature also suggests an association between somatization disorders and childhood trauma. Briquet's initial descriptions of the disorder which now bears his name are filled with anecdotal references to domestic violence and child abuse. In a study of 87 children under twelve with hysteria, Briquet noted that one-third had been "habitually mistreated or held constantly in fear or had been directed harshly by their parents." In another 10%, he attributed the children's symptoms to traumatic experiences other than parental abuse (Mai and Merskey, 1980). A recent controlled study of 60 women with somatization disorder (Morrison, 1989) found that 55% had been sexually molested in childhood, usually by relatives. The study focused only on early sexual experiences; patients were not asked about physical abuse or about the more general climate of violence in their families. Systematic investigation of the childhood histories of patients with somatization disorder has yet to be undertaken.

Dissociation

People in captivity become adept practitioners of the arts of altered consciousness. Through the practice of dissociation, voluntary thought suppression, minimization, and sometimes outright denial, they learn to alter an unbearable reality. Prisoners frequently instruct one another in the induction of trance states. These methods are consciously applied to withstand hunger, cold, and pain (Partnoy, 1986; Sharansky, 1988). During prolonged confinement and isolation, some prisoners are able to develop trance capabilities ordinarily seen only in extremely hypnotizable people, including the ability to form positive and negative hallucinations, and to dissociate parts of the personality. [See first-person accounts by Elaine Mohamed in Russell (1989) and by Mauricio Rosencof in Weschler (1989).] Disturbances in time sense, memory, and concentration are almost universally reported (Allodi *et al.*, 1985; Tennant *et al.*, 1986; Kinzie *et al.*, 1984). Alterations in time sense begin with the obliteration of the future but eventually progress to the obliteration of the past (Levi, 1958). The rupture in continuity between present and past frequently persists even after the prisoner is released. The prisoner may give the appearance of returning to ordinary time, while psychologically remaining bound in the timelessness of the prison (Jaffe, 1968).

In survivors of prolonged childhood abuse, these dissociative capacities are developed to the extreme. Shengold (1989) describes the "mind-fragmenting operations" elaborated by abused children in order to preserve "the delusion of good parents." He notes the "establishment of isolated divisions of the mind in which contradictory images of the self and of the parents are never permitted to coalesce." The virtuosic feats of dissociation seen, for example, in multiple personality disorder, are almost always associated with a childhood history of massive and prolonged abuse (Putnam *et al.*, 1986; Putnam, 1989; Ross *et al.*, 1990). A similar association between severity of childhood abuse and extent of dissociative symptomatology has been documented in subjects with borderline personality disorder (Herman *et al.*, 1989), and in a nonclinical, college-student population (Sanders *et al.*, 1989).

Affective Changes

There are people with very strong and secure belief systems, who can endure the ordeals of prolonged abuse and emerge with their faith intact. But these are the extraordinary few. The majority experience the bitterness of being forsaken by man and God (Wiesel, 1960). These staggering psychological losses most commonly result in a tenacious state of depression. Protracted depression is reported as the most common finding in virtually all clinical studies of chronically traumatized people (Goldstein *et al.*, 1987; Herman, 1981; Hilberman, 1980; Kinzie *et al.*, 1984; Krystal, 1968; Walker, 1979). Every aspect of the experience of prolonged trauma combines to aggravate depressive symptoms. The chronic hyperarousal and intrusive symptoms of

PTSD fuse with the vegetative symptoms of depression, producing what Niederland calls the "survivor triad" of insomnia, nightmares, and psychosomatic complaints (in Krystal, 1968, p. 313). The dissociative symptoms of PTSD merge with the concentration difficulties of depression. The paralysis of initiative of chronic trauma combines with the apathy and helplessness of depression. The disruptions in attachments of chronic trauma reinforce the isolation and withdrawal of depression. The debased self-image of chronic trauma fuels the guilty ruminations of depression. And the loss of faith suffered in chronic trauma merges with the hopelessness of depression.

The humiliated rage of the imprisoned person also adds to the depressive burden (Hilberman, 1980). During captivity, the prisoner cannot express anger at the perpetrator; to do so would jeopardize survival. Even after release, the survivor may continue to fear retribution for any expression of anger against the captor. Moreover, the survivor carries a burden of unexpressed anger against all those who remained indifferent and failed to help. Efforts to control this rage may further exacerbate the survivor's social withdrawal and paralysis of initiative. Occasional outbursts of rage against others may further alienate the survivor and prevent the restoration of relationships. And internalization of rage may result in a malignant self-hatred and chronic suicidality. Epidemiologic studies of returned POWs consistently document increased mortality as the result of homicide, suicide, and suspicious accidents (Segal et al., 1976). Studies of battered women similarly report a tenacious suicidality. In one clinical series of 100 battered women, 42% had attempted suicide (Gayford, 1975). While major depression is frequently diagnosed in survivors of prolonged abuse, the connection with the trauma is frequently lost. Patients are incompletely treated when the traumatic origins of the intractable depression are not recognized (Kinzie et al., 1990).

CHARACTEROLOGICAL SEQUELAE OF PROLONGED VICTIMIZATION

Pathological Changes in Relationship

In situations of captivity, the perpetrator becomes the most powerful person in the life of the victim, and the psychology of the victim is shaped over time by the actions and beliefs of the perpetrator. The methods which enable one human being to control another are remarkably consistent. These methods were first systematically detailed in reports of so-called "brainwashing" in American prisoners of war (Biderman, 1957; Farber et al., 1957). Subsequently. Amnesty International (1973) published a systematic review of methods of coercion, drawing upon the testimony of political prisoners from widely differing cultures. The accounts of coercive methods given by battered women (Dobash and Dobash, 1979; NiCarthy, 1982, Walker, 1979), abused children (Rhodes, 1990), and coerced prostitutes (Lovelace and McGrady, 1980) bear an uncanny resemblance to those hostages, political prisoners, and survivors of concentration camps. While perpetrators of organized political or sexual exploitation may instruct each other in coercive methods, perpetrators of domestic abuse appear to reinvent them.

The methods of establishing control over another person are based upon the systematic, repetitive infliction of psychological trauma. These methods are designed to instill terror and helplessness, to destroy the victim's sense of self in relation to others, and to foster a pathologic attachment to the perpetrator. Although violence is a universal method of instilling terror, the threat of death or serious harm, either to the victim or to others close to her, is much more frequent than the actual resort to violence. Fear is also increased by unpredictable outbursts of violence, and by inconsistent enforcement of numerous trivial demands and petty rules.

In addition to inducing terror, the perpetrator seeks to destroy the victim's sense of autonomy. This is achieved by control of the victim's body and bodily functions. Deprivation of food, sleep, shelter, exercise, personal hygiene, or privacy are common practices. Once the perpetrator has established this degree of control, he becomes a potential source of solace as well as humiliation. The capricious granting of small indulgences may undermine the psychological resistance of the victim far more effectively than unremitting deprivation and fear.

As long as the victim maintains strong relationships with others, the perpetrator's power is limited; invariably, therefore, he seeks to isolate his victim. The perpetrator will not only attempt to prohibit communication and material support, but will also try to destroy the victim's emotional ties to others. The final step in the "breaking" of the victim is not completed until she has been forced to betray her most basic attachments, by witnessing or participating in crimes against others.

As the victim is isolated, she becomes increasingly dependent upon the perpetrator, not only for survival and basic bodily needs, but also for information and even for emotional sustenance. Prolonged confinement in fear of death and in isolation reliably produces a bond of identification between captor and victim. This is the "traumatic bonding" that occurs in hostages, who come to view their captors as their saviors and to fear and hate their rescuers. Symonds (1982) describes this process as an enforced regression to "psychological infantilism" which "compels victims to cling to the very person who is endangering their life." The same traumatic bonding may occur between a battered woman and her abuser (Dutton and Painter, 1981; Graham *et al.*, 1988), or between an abused child and abusive parent (Herman, 1981; van der Kolk, 1987). Similar experiences are also reported by people who have been inducted into totalitarian religious cults (Halperin, 1983; Lifton, 1987).

With increased dependency upon the perpetrator comes a constriction in initiative and planning. Prisoners who have not been entirely "broken" do not give up the capacity for active engagement with their environment. On the contrary, they often approach the small daily tasks of survival with extraordinary ingenuity and determination. But the field of initiative is increasingly narrowed within confines dictated by the perpetrator. The prisoner no longer thinks of how to escape, but rather of how to stay alive, or how to make captivity more bearable. This narrowing in the range of initiative becomes habitual with prolonged captivity, and must be unlearned after the prisoner is liberated. [See, for example, the testimony of Hearst (Hearst and Moscow 1982) and Rosencof in Weschler, 1989.]

Because of this constriction in the capacities for active engagement with the world, chronically traumatized people are often described as passive or helpless. Some theorists have in fact applied the concept of "learned helplessness" to the situation of battered women and other chronically traumatized people (Walker, 1979; van der Kolk, 1987). Prolonged captivity undermines or destroys the ordinary sense of a relatively safe sphere of initiative, in which there is some tolerance for trial and error. To the chronically traumatized person, any independent action is insubordination, which carries the risk of dire punishment.

The sense that the perpetrator is still present, even after liberation, signifies a major alteration in the survivor's relational world. The enforced relationship, which of necessity monopolizes the victim's attention during captivity, becomes part of her inner life and continues to engross her attention after release. In political prisoners, this continued relationship may take the form of a brooding preoccupation with the criminal careers of specific perpetrators or with more abstract concerns about the unchecked forces of evil in the world. Released prisoners continue to track their captors, and to fear them (Krystal, 1968). In sexual, domestic, and religious cult prisoners, this continued relationship may take a more ambivalent form: the survivor may continue to fear her former captor, and to expect that he will eventually hunt her down; she may also feel empty, confused, and worthless without him (Walker, 1979).

Even after escape, it is not possible simply to reconstitute relationships of the sort that existed prior to captivity. All relationships are now viewed through the lens of extremity. Just as there is no range of moderate engagement or risk for initiative, there is no range of moderate engagement or risk for relationship. The survivor approaches all relationships as though questions of life and death are at stake, oscillating between intense attachment and terrified withdrawal.

In survivors of childhood abuse, these disturbances in relationship are further amplified. Oscillations in attachment, with formation of intense, unstable relationships, are frequently observed. These disturbances are described most fully in patients with borderline personality disorder, the majority of whom have extensive histories of childhood abuse. A recent empirical study, confirming a vast literature of clinical observations, outlines in detail the specific pattern of relational difficulties. Such patients find it very hard to tolerate being alone, but are also exceedingly wary of others. Terrified of abandonment on the one hand, and domination on the other, they oscillate between extremes of abject submissiveness and furious rebellion (Melges and Swartz, 1989). They tend to form "special" dependent relations with idealized caretakers in which ordinary boundaries are not observed (Zanarini *et al.*, 1990). Very similar patterns are described in patients with MPD, including the tendency to develop intense, highly "special" relationships ridden with boundary violations, conflict, and potential for exploitation (Kluft, 1990).

Pathologic Changes in Identity

Subjection to a relationship of coercive control produces profound alterations in the victim's identity. All the structures of the self—the image of the body, the internalized images of others, and the values and ideals that lend a sense of coherence and purpose—are invaded and systematically broken down. In some totalitarian systems (political, religious, or sexual/domestic), this process reaches the extent of taking away the victim's name (Hearst and Moscow, 1982; Lovelace and McGrady, 1980). While the victim of a single acute trauma may say she is "not herself" since the event, the victim of chronic trauma may lose the sense that she has a self. Survivors may describe themselves as reduced to a nonhuman life form (Lovelace and McGrady, 1980;

Timerman, 1981). Niederland (1968), in his clinical observations of concentration camp survivors, noted that alterations of personal identity were a constant feature of the survivor syndrome. While the majority of his patients complained, "I am now a different person," the most severely harmed stated simply, "I am not a person."

Survivors of childhood abuse develop even more complex deformations of identity. A malignant sense of the self as contaminated, guilty, and evil is widely observed. Fragmentation in the sense of self is also common, reaching its most dramatic extreme in multiple personality disorder. Ferenczi (1932) describes the "atomization" of the abused child's personality. Rieker and Carmen (1986) describe the central pathology in victimized children as a "disordered and fragmented identity deriving from accommodations to the judgments of others." Disturbances in identity formation are also characteristic of patients with borderline and multiple personality disorders, the majority of whom have childhood histories of severe trauma. In MPD, the fragmentation of the self into dissociated alters is, of course, the central feature of the disorder (Bliss, 1986; Putnam, 1989). Patients with BPD, though they lack the dissociative capacity to form fragmented alters, have similar difficulties in the formation of an integrated identity. An unstable sense of self is recognized as one of the major diagnostic criteria for BPD, and the "splitting" of inner representations of self and others is considered by some theorists to be the central underlying pathology of the disorder (Kernberg, 1967).

REPETITION OF HARM FOLLOWING PROLONGED VICTIMIZATION

Repetitive phenomena have been widely noted to be sequelae of severe trauma. The topic has been recently reviewed in depth by van der Kolk (1989). In simple PTSD, these repetitive phenomena may take the form of intrusive memories, somato-sensory reliving experiences, or behavioral reenactments of the trauma (Brett and Ostroff, 1985; Terr, 1983). After prolonged and repeated trauma, by contrast, survivors may be at risk for repeated harm, either self-inflicted, or at the hands of others. These repetitive phenomena do not bear a direct relation to the original trauma; they are not simple reenactments or reliving experiences. Rather, they take a disguised symptomatic or characterological form.

About 7–10% of psychiatric patients are thought to injure themselves deliberately (Favazza and Conterio, 1988). Self-mutilation is a repetitive behavior which appears to be quite distinct from attempted suicide. This compulsive form of self-injury appears to be strongly associated with a history of prolonged repeated trauma. Self-mutilation, which is rarely seen after a single acute trauma, is a common sequel of protracted childhood abuse (Briere, 1988; van der Kolk *et al.*, 1991). Self-injury and other paroxysmal forms of attack on the body have been shown to develop most commonly in those victims whose abuse began early in childhood.

The phenomenon of repeated victimization also appears to be specifically associated with histories of prolonged childhood abuse. Widescale epidemiologic studies provide strong evidence that survivors of childhood abuse are at increased risk for repeated harm in adult life. For example, the risk of rape, sexual harassment, and battering, though very high for all women, is approximately doubled for survivors of childhood sexual abuse (Russell, 1986). One clinical observer goes so far as to label this phenomenon the "sitting duck syndrome" (Kluft, 1990).

In the most extreme cases, survivors of childhood abuse may find themselves involved in abuse of others, either in the role of passive bystander or, more rarely, as a perpetrator. Burgess and her collaborators (1984), for example, report that children who had been exploited in a sex ring for more than one year were likely to adopt the belief system of the perpetrator and to become exploitative toward others. A history of prolonged childhood abuse does appear to be a risk factor for becoming an abuser, especially in men (Herman, 1988; Hotaling and Sugarman, 1986). In women, a history of witnessing domestic violence (Hotaling and Sugarman, 1986), or sexual victimization (Goodwin *et al.*, 1982) in childhood appears to increase the risk of subsequent marriage to an abusive mate. It should be noted, however, that contrary to the popular notion of a "generational cycle of abuse," the great majority of survivors do not abuse others (Kaufman and Zigler, 1987). For the sake of their children, survivors frequently mobilize caring and protective capacities that they have never been able to extend to themselves (Coons, 1985).

CONCLUSIONS

The review of the literature offers unsystematized but extensive empirical support for the concept of a complex posttraumatic syndrome in survivors of prolonged, repeated victimization. This previously undefined syndrome may coexist with simple PTSD, but extends beyond it. The syndrome is characterized by a pleomorphic symptom picture, enduring personality changes, and high risk for repeated harm, either self-inflicted or at the hands of others.

Failure to recognize this syndrome as a predictable consequence of prolonged, repeated trauma contributes to the misunderstanding of survivors, a misunderstanding shared by the general society and the mental health professions alike. Social judgment of chronically traumatized people has tended to be harsh (Biderman and Zimmer, 1961; Wardell *et al.*, 1983). The propensity to fault the character of victims can be seen even in the case of politically organized mass murder. Thus, for example, the aftermath of the Nazi Holocaust witnessed a protracted intellectual debate regarding the "passivity" of the Jews, and even their "complicity" in their fate (Dawidowicz, 1975). Observers who have never experienced prolonged terror, and who have no understanding of coercive methods of control, often presume that they would show greater psychological resistance than the victim in similar circumstances. The survivor's difficulties are all too easily attributed to underlying character problems, even when the trauma is known. When the trauma is kept secret, as is frequently the case in sexual and domestic violence, the survivor's symptoms and behavior may appear quite baffling, not only to lay people but also to mental health professionals.

The clinical picture of a person who has been reduced to elemental concerns of survival is still frequently mistaken for a portrait of the survivor's underlying character. Concepts of personality developed in ordinary circumstances are frequently applied to survivors, without an understanding of the deformations of personality which occur under conditions of coercive control. Thus, patients who suffer from the complex sequelae of chronic trauma commonly risk being misdiagnosed as having personality disorders. They may be described as "dependent," "masochistic," or "self-defeating." Earlier concepts of masochism or repetition compulsion might be more usefully supplanted by the concept of a complex traumatic syndrome.

Misapplication of the concept of personality disorder may be the most stigmatizing diagnostic mistake, but it is by no means the only one. In general, the diagnostic concepts of the existing psychiatric canon, including simple PTSD, are not designed for survivors of prolonged, repeated trauma, and do not fit them well. The evidence reviewed in this paper offers strong support for expanding the concept of PTSD to include a spectrum of disorders (Brett, 1992), ranging from the brief, self-limited stress reaction to a single acute trauma, through simple PTSD, to the complex disorder of extreme stress (DESNOS) that follows upon prolonged exposure to repeated trauma.

REFERENCES

Allodi, F., et al., (1985). Physical and psychiatric effects of torture: Two medical studies. In Stover, E., and Nightingale, E. (eds.), The Breaking of Bodies and Minds: Torture. Psychiatric Abuse, and the Health Professions, Freeman, New York, pp. 58–78.

Amnesty International (1973). Report on Torture, Farrar, Straus and Giroux, New York.

Biderman, A. D. (1957). Communist attempts to elicit false confessions from Air Force prisoners of war. Bull. New York Acad. Med. 33: 616–625.

Biderman, A. D., and Zimmer, H. (1961). The Manipulation of Human Behavior, Wiley, New York (Introduction), pp. 1–18.

Bliss, E. L. (1986). Multiple Personality, Allied Disorders, and Hypnosis, Oxford University Press, New York.

Brett, E. A. (1992). Classification of PTSD in DSM-IV as an anxiety disorder, dissociative disorder, or stress disorder. In Davidson, J., and Foa, E. (eds.), PTSD in Review: Recent Research and Future Directions. American Psychiatric Press, Washington, D.C.

Brett, E. A., and Ostroff, R. (1985). Imagery in post-traumatic stress disorder: An overview. Am. J. Psychiatry 142: 417–424.

Briere, J. (1988). Long-term clinical correlates of childhood sexual victimization. Annal. New York Acad. Sci. 528: 327–334.

Briere, J., and Runtz, M. (1987). Post-sexual abuse trauma: Data and implications for clinical practice. J. Interpers. Viol. 2: 367–379.

Briere, J., and Zaidi, L. (1989). Sexual abuse histories and sequelae in female psychiatric emergency room patients. Am. J. Psychiatry 146: 1602–1606.

Brown, D. P., and Fromm, E. (1986). Hypnotherapy and Hypnoanalysis. Laurence Erlbaum, Hillsdale, N.J.

Browne, A., and Finkelhor, D., (1986). Impact of child sexual abuse: A review of the literature. Psychological Bull. 99: 55–77.

Bryer, J. B., Nelson, B. A., Miller, J. B., and Krol, P. A. (1987). Childhood sexual and physical abuse as factors in adult psychiatric illness. Am. J. Psychiatry 144: 1426–1430.

Burgess, A. W., Hartman. C. R., McCausland, M. P., et al. (1984). Response patterns in children and adolescents exploited through sex rings and pornography. Am. J. Psychiatry 141: 656–662.

Carmen, E. H., Rieker, P. P., and Mills, T. (1984). Victims of violence and psychiatric illness. Am. J. Psychiatry 141: 378–383.

Coons, P. M. (1985). Children of parents with multiple personality disorder. In Kluft, R. P. (ed.), Childhood Antecedents of Multiple Personality Disorder, American Psychiatric Press, Washington, D.C., pp. 151–166.

Dawidowicz, L. (1975). The War against the Jews, Weidenfeld and Nicolson, London.

De Loos, W. (1990). Psychosomatic manifestations of chronic PTSD. In Wolf, M. E., and Mosnaim. A. D. (eds.), Posttraumatic Stress Disorder: Etiology, Phenomenology, and Treatment. American Psychiatric Press, Washington, DC, pp. 94–105.

Dobash, R. E., and Dobash, R. (1979). Violence against Wives: A Case against the Patriarchy, *Free Press, New York.*

Dutton, D., and Painter, S. L. (1981). Traumatic bonding: The development of emotional attachments in battered women and other relationships of intermittent abuse. Victimology *6: 139–155.*

Farber, I. E., Harlow, H. F., and West, L. J. (1957). Brainwashing, conditioning, and DDD (debility, dependency, and dread). Sociometry, *23: 120–147.*

Favazza, A. R., and Conterio, K. (1988). The plight of chronic self-mutilators. Community Mental Health Journal *24: 22–30.*

Ferenczi, S. (1932/1955). Confusion of tongues between adults and the child: The language of tenderness and of passion. In Final Contributions to the Problems and Methods of Psychoanalysis. *Basic Books, New York.*

Gayford, J. J. (1975). Wife-battering: A preliminary survey of 100 cases. Brit. Med. J. *1: 194–197.*

Gelinas, D. (1983). The persistent negative effects of incest. Psychiatry *46: 312–332.*

Goldstein, G., van Kammen, V., Shelley, C., et al., (1987). Survivors of imprisonment in the Pacific theater during World War II. Am. J. Psychiatry *144: 1210–1213.*

Goodwin, J. (1988). Evaluation and treatment of incest victims and their families: A problem oriented approach. In Howells, J. G. (ed.), Modern Perspectives in Psycho-Social Pathology; *Brunner/Mazel, New York.*

Goodwin, J., McMarty, T., and DiVasto, P. (1982). Physical and sexual abuse of the children of adult incest victims. In Goodwin, J. (ed.), Sexual Abuse: Incest Victims and Their Families. *John Wright, Boston, pp. 139–154.*

Graham, D. L., Rawlings, E., and Rimini, N. (1988). Survivors of terror: Battered women, hostages, and the Stockholm syndrome. In Yllo, K., and Bograd, M. (eds.), Feminist Perspectives on Wife Abuse, *Sage, Beverly Hills, pp. 217–233.*

Halperin, D. A. (1983). Group processes in cult affiliation and recruitment. In Psychodynamic Perspectives on Religion, Sect, and Cult, *John Wright, Boston.*

Hearst, P. C., and Moscow, A. (1982). Every Secret Thing, *Doubleday, New York.*

Herman, J. L. (1981). Father-Daughter Incest, *Harvard University Press, Cambridge, Mass.*

Herman, J. L. (1988). Considering sex offenders: A model of addiction. Signs J. Women Culture Soc. *13: 695–724.*

Herman, J. L. (1992). Trauma and Recovery; *Basic Books, New York.*

Herman, J. L., Perry, J. C., and van der Kolk, B. A. (1989). Childhood trauma in borderline personality disorder. Am. J. Psychiatry *146: 490–495.*

Hilberman, E. (1980). The "wife-beater's wife" reconsidered. Am. J. Psychiatry *137: 1336–1347.*

Hoppe, K. D. (1968). Resomatization of affects in survivors of persecution. Int. J. Psychoanal. *49: 324–326.*

Horowitz, M. (1986). Stress Response Syndromes, *Jason Aronson, Northvale, N.J., quote on p. 49.*

Hotaling, G., and Sugarman, D. (1986). An analysis of risk markers in husband to wife violence: The current state of knowledge. Viol. Vict. *1: 101–124.*

Jacobson, A., and Richardson, B. (1987). Assault experiences of 100 psychiatric inpatients: *Evidence of the need for routine inquiry.* Am. J. Psychiatry *144: 908–913.*

Jaffe, R. *(1968). Dissociative phenomena in former concentration camp inmates.* Int. J. Psychoanal. *49: 310–312.*

Kaufman, J., and Zigler, E. *(1987). Do abused children become abusive parents?* Am. J. Orthopsych *57: 186–192.*

Kernberg, O. *(1967). Borderline personality organization.* J. Am. Psychoanal. Assoc. *15: 641–685.*

Kinzie, J. D., Boehnlein, J. K., Leung, P. K., et al., *(1990). The prevalence of posttraumatic stress disorder and its clinical significance among Southeast Asian refugees.* Am. J. Psychiatry *147: 913–917.*

Kinzie, J. D., Fredrickson, R. H., Ben, R., et al. *(1984). PTSD among survivors of Cambodian concentration camps.* Am. J. Psychiatry *141: 645–650.*

Kluft, R. P. *(1990). Incest and subsequent revictimization: The case of therapist-patient sexual exploitation, with a description of the sitting duck syndrome. In* Incest-Related Syndromes of Adult Psychopathology. *American Psychiatric Press, Washington, D.C., pp. 263–289.*

Kolb, L. C. *(1989). Letter to the editor.* Am. J. Psychiatry *146: 811–812.*

Kroll, J., Habenicht, M., Mackenzie, T., et al. *(1989). Depression and posttraumatic stress disorder in Southeast Asian refugees.* Am. J. Psychiatry *146: 1592–1597, quote on p. 1596.*

Krystal, H. *(ed.) (1968).* Massive Psychic Trauma, *International Universities Press, New York.*

Krystal, H., and Niederland, W. *(1968). Clinical observations on the survivor syndrome. In Krystal, H. (ed.),* Massive Psychic Trauma, *International Universities Press, New York, pp. 327–348.*

Levi, P. *(1958/1961).* Survival in Auschwitz: The Nazi Assault on Humanity, *Trans. Woolf, S., Collier, New York.*

Lifton, R. J. *(1987). Cults: Religious totalism and civil liberties. In* The Future of Immorality and Other Essays for a Nuclear Age, *Basic Books, New York.*

Lovelace, L., and McGrady, M. *(1980).* Ordeal, *Citadel, Secaucus, N.J.*

Mai, F. M., and Merskey, H. *(1980). Briquet's treatise on hysteria: Synopsis and commentary.* Arch. Gen. Psychiatry *37: 1401–1405, quote on p. 1402.*

Melges, F. T., and Swartz, M. S. *(1989). Oscillations of attachment in borderline personality disorder.* Am. J. Psychiatry *146: 1115–1120.*

Morrison, J. *(1989). Childhood sexual histories of women with somatization disorder.* Am. J. Psychiatry *146: 239–241.*

NiCarthy, G. *(1982).* Getting Free: A Handbook for Women in Abusive Relationships, *Seal Press, Seattle.*

Niederland, W. G. *(1968). Clinical observations on the 'survivor syndrome.'* Int. J. Psychoanal. *49: 313–315.*

Partnoy, A. *(1986).* The Little School: Tales of Disappearance and Survival in Argentina, *Cleis Press, San Francisco.*

Putnam, F. W. *(1989).* Diagnosis and Treatment of Multiple Personality Disorder, *Guilford, New York.*

Putnam, F. W., Guroff, J. J., Silberman, E. K., et al. (1986). The clinical phenomenology of multiple personality disorder: Review of 100 recent cases. J. Clin. Psychiatry 47: 285–293.

Rhodes, R. (1990). A Hole in the World, Simon and Schuster, New York.

Rieker, P. P., and Carmen, E. (1986). The victim-to-patient process: The disconfirmation and transformation of abuse. Am. J. Orthopsychiat. 56: 360–370.

Ross, C. A., Miller, S. D., Reagor, P., et al. (1990). Structured interview data on 102 cases of multiple personality disorder from four centers. Am. J. Psychiatry 147: 596–601.

Russell, D. (1986). The Secret Trauma, Basic Books, New York.

Russell, D. (1989). Lives of Courage: Women for a New South Africa, Basic Books, New York.

Sanders, B., McRoberts, G., and Tollefson, C. (1989). Childhood stress and dissociation in a college population. Dissociation 2: 17–23.

Segal, J., Hunter, E. J., and Segal. Z. (1976) Universal consequences of captivity: Stress reactions among divergent populations of prisoners of war and their families. Int. J. Social Sci. 28: 593–609.

Sharansky, N. (1988). Fear No Evil (Trans. Hoffman, S.), Random House, New York.

Shengold, L. (1989). Soul Murder: The Effects of Childhood Abuse and Deprivation, Yale University Press. New Haven, quote on p. 26.

Strentz, T. (1982). The Stockholm syndrome: Law enforcement policy and hostage behavior. In Ochberg, F. M., and Soskis, D. A. (eds.), Victims of Terrorism, Westview, Boulder, Colo., pp. 149–163.

Symonds, M. (1982). Victim responses to terror: Understanding and treatment. In Ochberg, F. M., and Soskis. D. A. (eds.), Victims of Terrorism, Westview, Boulder, Colo., pp. 95–103, quote on p. 99.

Tennant, C. C., Gouston, K. J., and Dent, O. F. (1986). The psychological effects of being a prisoner of war: Forty years after release. Am. J. Psychiatry 143: 618–622.

Terr, L. C. (1983). Chowchilla revisited: The effects of psychic trauma four years after a school-bus kidnapping. Am. J. Psychiatry 140: 1543–1550.

Timerman, J. (1981). Prisoner Without a Name, Cell Without a Number (Trans. Talbot, T.), Vintage, New York.

van der Kolk, B. A. (1987). Psychological Trauma, American Psychiatric Press, Washington, D.C.

van der Kolk, B. A. (1989). Compulsion to repeat the trauma: Reenactment, revictimization, and masochism. Psychiatr Clin. North Am. 12: 389–411.

van der Kolk, B. A., Perry, J. C., and Herman, J. L. (1991). Childhood origins of self-destructive behavior. Am J. Psychiatry 148: 1665–1671.

van der Ploerd, H. M. (1989). Being held hostage in the Netherlands: A study of long-term aftereffects. J. Traum Stress 2: 153–170.

Walker, L., (1979). The Battered Woman, Harper and Row, New York.

Wardell, L., Gillespie D., and Leffler, A. (1983). Science and violence against wives. In Finkelhor, D., Gelles, R., Hotaling, G., et al. (eds.), The Dark Side of Families: Current Family Violence Research. Sage, Beverly Hills, pp. 69–84.

Weschler, L. (1989). The great exception: I: Liberty, New Yorker, April 3.
Wiesel, E. (1960). Night (Trans. Rodway, S.), Hill and Wang, New York.
Zanarini, M., Gunderson, J., Frankenburg, F., et al. (1990). Discriminating borderline personality disorder from other Axis II disorders. Am. J. Psychiatry 147: 161–167.

5. Introduction to *Psycho-Analysis* and the *War Neuroses*

Sigmund Freud

THIS SMALL BOOK on the war neuroses—the opening volume of our *Internationale Psychoanalytische Bibliothek*—deals with a subject which until recently enjoyed the advantage of being in the greatest degree topical. When it came up for discussion at the Fifth Psycho-Analytical Congress, which was held in Budapest in September, 1918, official representatives from the highest quarters of the Central European Powers were present as observers at the papers and other proceedings. The hopeful result of this first contact was that the establishment of psycho-analytic Centres was promised, at which analytically trained physicians would have leisure and opportunity for studying the nature of these puzzling disorders and the therapeutic effect exercised on them by psycho-analysis. Before these proposals could be put into effect, the war came to an end, the state organizations collapsed and interest in the war neuroses gave place to other concerns. It is, however, a significant fact that, when war conditions ceased to operate, the greater number of the neurotic disturbances brought about by the war simultaneously vanished. The opportunity for a thorough investigation of these affections was thus unluckily lost—though, we must add, the early recurrence of such an opportunity is not a thing to be desired.

But this episode, though it is now closed, was not without an important influence on the spread of psycho-analysis. Medical men who had hitherto held back from any approach to psycho-analytic theories were brought into closer contact with them when, in the course of their duties as army doctors, they were obliged to deal with war neuroses. The reader will be able to gather from Ferenczi's paper with what hesitations and under what disguises these closer contacts were made. Some of the factors which psycho-analysis had

"Four Prefaces: Psychoanalysis and War Neuroses" from *The Collected Papers*, vol. 5 by Sigmund Freud. Edited by James Strachey. Published by Basic Books, Inc., by arrangement with The Hogarth Press, Ltd., and the Institute of Psycho-Analysis, London. Reprinted by permission of Basic Books, a division of HarperCollins Publishers, Inc.

recognized and described long before as being at work in peace-time neuroses—the psycho-genic origin of the symptoms, the importance of *unconscious* instinctual impulses, the part played in dealing with mental conflicts by the primary gain from being ill ('the flight into illness')—were observed to be present equally in the war neuroses and were accepted almost universally. Simmel's studies show, too, what successes could be achieved by treating war neurotics by the method of catharsis, which, as we know, was the first step towards the psycho-analytic technique.

There is, however, no need to consider that these approaches to psycho-analysis imply any reconciliation or any appeasement of opposition. Suppose someone has hitherto rejected the whole of a complex of interdependent propositions, but now suddenly finds himself in a position to convince himself of the truth of one portion of the whole. It might be thought that he will begin to hesitate about his opposition in general and permit himself some degree of deferent expectation that the other portion, about which he has had no personal experience and can consequently form no judgement of his own, may also turn out to be true. This other portion of psycho-analytic theory, with which the study of the war neuroses did not come into contact, is to the effect that the motive forces which are expressed in the formation of symptoms are sexual and that neuroses arise from a conflict between the ego and the sexual instincts which it repudiates. ('Sexuality' in this context is to be understood in the extended sense in which it is used in psycho-analysis and is not to be confused with the narrower concept of 'genitality'.) Now it is quite true, as Ernest Jones remarks in his contribution to this volume, that this portion of the theory has not yet been proved to apply to the war neuroses. The work that might prove it has not yet been taken in hand. It may be that the war neuroses are altogether unsuitable material for the purpose. But the opponents of psycho-analysis, whose dislike of sexuality is evidently stronger than their logic, have been in a hurry to proclaim that the investigation of the war neuroses has finally disproved this portion of psycho-analytic theory. They have been guilty here of a slight confusion. If the investigation of the war neuroses (and a very superficial one at that) has *not shown* that the sexual theory of the neuroses is *correct*, that is something very different from its *showing* that that theory is *incorrect*. With the help of an impartial attitude and a little good will, it should not be hard to find the way to a further clarification of the subject.

The war neuroses, in so far as they are distinguished from the ordinary neuroses of peace-time by special characteristics, are to be regarded as traumatic neuroses whose occurrence has been made possible or has been promoted by a conflict in the ego. Abraham's paper affords good evidence for this conflict, which has also been recognized by the English and American writers quoted by Jones. The conflict is between the soldier's old peaceful ego and his new warlike one, and it becomes acute as soon as the peace-ego realizes what danger it runs of losing its life owing to the rashness of its newly formed, parasitic double. It would be equally true to say that the old ego is protecting itself from a mortal danger by taking flight into a traumatic neurosis or to say that it is defending itself against the new ego which it sees is threatening its life. Thus the pre-condition of the war neuroses, the soil that nourishes them, would seem to be a national [conscript] army; there would be no possibility of their arising in an army of professional soldiers or mercenaries.

Apart from this, the war neuroses are only traumatic neuroses, which, as we know, occur in peace-time too after frightening experiences or severe accidents, without any reference to a conflict in the ego.

The theory of the sexual aetiology of the neuroses, or, as we prefer to say, the libido theory of the neuroses, was originally put forward only in relation to the transference neuroses of peace-time and is easy to demonstrate in their case by the use of the technique of analysis. But its application to the other disorders which we later grouped together as the narcissistic neuroses already met with difficulties. An ordinary dementia praecox, a paranoia or a melancholia are essentially quite unsuitable material for demonstrating the validity of the libido theory or for serving as a first introduction to an understanding of it; and it is for that reason that psychiatrists, who neglect the transference neuroses, are unable to come to terms with it. But the traumatic neuroses of peace-time have always been regarded as the most refractory material of all in this respect; so that the emergence of the war neuroses could not introduce any new factor into the situation that already existed.

It only became possible to extend the libido theory to the narcissistic neuroses after the concept of a 'narcissistic libido' had been put forward and applied—a concept, that is, of an amount of sexual energy attached to the ego itself and finding satisfaction in the ego just as satisfaction is usually found only in objects. This entirely legitimate development of the concept of sexuality promises to accomplish as much for the severer neuroses and for the psychoses as can be expected of a theory which is feeling its way forwards on an empirical basis. The traumatic neuroses of peace will also fit into the scheme as soon as a successful outcome has been reached of our investigations into the relations which undoubtedly exist between fright, anxiety and narcissistic libido.

The traumatic neuroses and war neuroses may proclaim too loudly the effects of mortal danger and may be silent or speak only in muffled tones of the effects of frustration in love. But, on the other hand, the ordinary transference neuroses of peace-time set no aetiological store by the factor of mortal danger which, in the former class of neuroses, plays so mighty a part. It is even held that the peace-time neuroses are promoted by indulgence, good living and inactivity—which would afford an interesting contrast to the living-conditions under which the war neuroses develop. If they were to follow the example of their opponents, psycho-analysts, finding that their patients had fallen ill owing to frustration in love (owing to the claims of the libido being unsatisfied) would have to maintain that there can be no such things as danger-neuroses or that the disorders that appear after frightening experiences are not neuroses. They have, of course, no notion of maintaining any such thing. On the contrary, a convenient possibility occurs to them of bringing the two apparently divergent sets of facts together under a single hypothesis. In traumatic and war neuroses the human ego is defending itself from a danger which threatens it from without or which is embodied in a shape assumed by the ego itself. In the transference neuroses of peace the enemy from which the ego is defending itself is actually the libido, whose demands seem to it to be menacing. In both cases the ego is afraid of being damaged—in the latter case by the libido and in the former by external violence. It might, indeed, be said that in the case of the war neuroses, in contrast to the pure traumatic neuroses and in approximation to the transference neuroses, what is feared is nevertheless an internal enemy. The theoretical difficulties standing in the way of a unifying hypothesis of this kind do not seem insuperable: after all, we have a perfect right to describe repression, which lies at the basis of every neurosis, as a reaction to a trauma—as an elementary traumatic neurosis.

APPENDIX

Memorandum on the Electrical Treatment of War Neurotics;[1]

(1955 [1920])

There were plenty of patients even in peace-time who, after traumas (that is, after frightening and dangerous experiences such as railway accidents, etc.) exhibited severe disturbances in their mental life and in their nervous activity, without physicians having reached an agreed judgement on these states. Some supposed that with such patients it was a question of severe injuries to the nervous system, similar to the haemorrhages and inflammations occurring in non-traumatic illnesses. And when anatomical examination failed to establish such processes, they nevertheless maintained their belief that finer changes in the tissues were the cause of the symptoms observed. They therefore classed these traumatic cases among the organic diseases. Other physicians maintained from the first that these states could only be regarded as functional disturbances, and that the nervous system remained anatomically intact. But medical opinion had long found difficulty in explaining how such severe disturbances of function could occur without any gross injury to the organ.

The war that has recently ended produced and brought under observation an immense number of these traumatic cases. In the result, the controversy was decided in favour of the functional view. The great majority of physicians no longer believe that the so-called 'war neurotics' are ill as a result of tangible organic injuries to the nervous system, and the more clear-sighted among them have already decided, instead of using the indefinite description of a 'functional change', to introduce the unambiguous term 'mental change'.

Although the war neuroses manifested themselves for the most part as motor disturbances—tremors and paralyses—and although it was plausible to suppose that such a gross impact as that produced by the concussion due to the explosion of a shell near by or to being buried by a fall of earth would lead to gross mechanical effects, observations were nevertheless made which left no doubt as to the psychical nature of the causation of these so-called war neuroses. How could this be disputed when the same symptoms appeared behind the Front as well, far from the horrors of war, or immediately after a return from leave? The physicians were therefore led to regard war neurotics in a similar light to the nervous subjects of peace-time.

What is known as the psycho-analytic school of psychiatry, which was brought into being by me, had taught for the last twenty-five years that the neuroses of peace could be traced back to disturbances of emotional life. This explanation was now applied quite generally to war neurotics. We had further asserted that neurotic patients suffered from mental conflicts and that the wishes and inclinations which were expressed in the symptoms were unknown to the patients themselves—were, that is to say, unconscious. It was therefore easy to infer that the immediate cause of all war neuroses was an unconscious inclination in the soldier to withdraw from the demands, dangerous or outrageous to his feelings, made upon him by active service. Fear of losing his own life, opposition to the command to kill other people, rebellion against the ruthless suppression of his own personality by his superiors—

these were the most important affective sources on which the inclination to escape from war was nourished.

A soldier in whom these affective motives were very powerful and clearly conscious would, if he was a healthy man, have been obliged to desert or pretend to be ill. Only the smallest proportion of war neurotics, however, were malingerers; the emotional impulses which rebelled in them against active service and drove them into illness were operative in them without becoming conscious to them. They remained unconscious because other motives, such as ambition, self-esteem, patriotism, the habit of obedience and the example of others, were to start with more powerful until, on some appropriate occasion, they were overwhelmed by the other, unconsciously-operating motives.

This insight into the causation of the war neuroses led to a method of treatment which seemed to be well-grounded and also proved highly effective in the first instance. It seemed expedient to treat the neurotic as a malingerer and to disregard the psychological distinction between conscious and unconscious intentions, although he was known not to be a malingerer. Since his illness served the purpose of withdrawing him from an intolerable situation, the roots of the illness would clearly be undermined if it was made even more intolerable to him than active service. Just as he had fled from the war into illness, means were now adopted which compelled him to flee back from illness into health, that is to say, into fitness for active service. For this purpose painful electrical treatment was employed, and with success. Physicians are glossing over the facts in retrospect when they assert that the strength of this electrical current was the same as had always been employed in functional disorders. This would only have been effective in the mildest cases; nor did it fit in with the underlying argument that a war neurotic's illness had to be made painful so that the balance of his motives would be tipped in favour of recovery.

This painful form of treatment introduced in the German army for therapeutic purposes could no doubt also be employed in a more moderate fashion. If it was used in the Vienna Clinics, I am personally convinced that it was never intensified to a cruel pitch by the initiative of Professor Wagner-Jauregg.[2] I cannot vouch for other physicians whom I did not know. The psychological education of medical men is in general decidedly deficient and more than one of them may have forgotten that the patient whom he was seeking to treat as a malingerer was, after all, not one.

This therapeutic procedure, however, bore a stigma from the very first. It did not aim at the patient's recovery, or not in the first instance; it aimed, above all, at restoring his fitness for service. Here Medicine was serving purposes foreign to its essence. The physician himself was under military command and had his own personal dangers to fear—loss of seniority or a charge of neglecting his duty—if he allowed himself to be led by considerations other than those prescribed for him. The insoluble conflict between the claims of humanity, which normally carry decisive weight for a physician, and the demands of a national war was bound to confuse his activity.

Moreover, the successes of treatment by a strong electric current, which were brilliant to begin with, turned out afterwards not to be lasting. A patient who, having been restored to health by it, was sent back to the Front, could repeat the business afresh and have a relapse, by means of which he at least gained time and escaped the danger which was at the moment the immediate one. If he was once more under fire his fear of the electric current receded, just as during the treatment his fear of active service had faded. In the course of the war years, too, a rapidly increasing fatigue in the popular spirit made itself felt more and more, and a growing dislike of fighting, so that the treatment I have described began to fail in its effects. In these circumstances some of the army doctors gave way to the inclination, characteristic of Germans, to carry through their intentions regardless of all else—which should never have happened. The strength of the current, as well as the severity of the rest of the treatment, were increased to an unbearable point in order to deprive war neurotics of the advantage they gained from their illness. The fact has never been contradicted that in German hospitals there were deaths at that time during treatment and suicides as a result of it. I am quite unable to say, however, whether the Vienna Clinics, too, passed through this phase of therapy.

I am in a position to bring forward conclusive evidence of the final breakdown of the electrical treatment of the war neuroses. In 1918 Dr. Ernst Simmel, head of a hospital for war neuroses at Posen, published a pamphlet in which he reported the extraordinarily favourable results achieved in severe cases of war neurosis by the psychotherapeutic method introduced by me. As a result of this publication, the next Psycho-Analytical Congress, held in Budapest in September 1918,[3] was attended by official delegates of the German, Austrian and Hungarian Army Command, who promised that Centres should be set up for the purely psychological treatment of war neuroses. This promise was made although the delegates can have been left in no doubt that with this considerate, laborious and tedious kind of treatment it was impossible to count on the quickest restoration of these patients to fitness for service. Preparations for the establishment of Centres of this kind were actually under way, when the revolution broke out and put an end to the war and to the influence of the administrative offices which had hitherto been all-powerful. But with the end of the war the war neurotics, too, disappeared— a final but impressive proof of the psychical causation of their illnesses.

Vienna, 23.2.20.

NOTES

1. [At the end of the first World War, after the break-up of the Austro-Hungarian Empire, many reports became current in Vienna that men suffering from war neuroses had been brutally treated by the army doctors. An enquiry into the matter was therefore instituted by the Austrian War Ministry, in the course of which Freud was called upon to give an expert opinion. He accordingly submitted a memorandum to the commission responsible for the enquiry, and subsequently appeared before them for oral examination. His memorandum was traced in the Archives of the War Ministry by Professor Josef Gicklhorn, of the University of Vienna, who has most generously put a photostat at our disposal. We are further indebted to Dr. K. R. Eissler, of New York (Secretary of the Sigmund Freud Archives), for having first drawn our attention to the document. The original MS occupies five and a half of the large foolscap sheets used habitually by Freud. The document is headed, in his handwriting: 'Gutachten über die elektrische Behandlung der Kriegsneurotiker von Prof. Dr. Sigm. Freud', and is dated by him: 'Wien, 23.2.20'. An official stamp at the top of the first page records that the memorandum was received by the 'Kommission zur Erhebung militärischer Pflichtverletzungen' (Commission for Enquiry into Violations of Military Duty) on February 25, 1920. Each page also bears the official stamp of the State Archives.— The English translation, which appears here for the first time, is by James Strachey; the original German has not yet (1955) been published.]

2. [Julius von Wagner-Jauregg was Professor of Psychiatry at the University of Vienna from 1893 to 1928.]

3. [In the original MS. this date is quite clearly written '1818'.]

6. Organic and Psychosomatic Aftereffects of Concentration Camp Imprisonment

Leo Eitinger

THE AIM of this presentation is to describe briefly some of the changes that were found in a group of Norwegian concentration camp prisoners. This very select group was investigated thoroughly by a medical commission headed by Axel Strøm, M.D., professor of Social Medicine at the University of Oslo. The results of this teamwork were published by the different authors and edited by Strøm in a monograph [4]. The following is a review of the main psychiatric findings and remarks concerning a followup of the patients investigated earlier.

There were 214 men and 13 women. At the time of arrest most were between 20 and 30 years of age. At the time of the examination half of the patients were 50 or more years old.

EXAMINATION

All were admitted to the Neurological Department of the Rikshospital in Oslo. The following examinations were carried out routinely: clinical neurological examination, electroencephalography, examination of the spinal fluid, pneumoencephalography, psychiatric examination, psychological examination, sociomedical examination, including collection of information from family, workmates, and so forth, and a careful study of all documents relating to the case.

The patients were examined further at the outpatients' department of internal medicine, ear, nose, and throat, and eye diseases. The following laboratory tests were carried out: sedimentation rate, serological testing for syphilis, determination of hemoglobin, red and white blood cells, potassium, calcium,

Reprinted by permission of Lippincott-Raven Publishers from "Organic and Psychosomatic Aftereffects of Concentration Camp Imprisonment." In H. Krystal and W. G. Niederland, eds., *Psychic Traumatization*, 205–215. 1971. Boston: Little Brown.

phosphorus, and cholesterol in the blood, sugar tolerance test, electrocardiogram, basal metabolism, and determination of 17-keto-steroids in the urine.

Each case was evaluated by a commission consisting of neurologists, psychiatrists, and specialists in social medicine. At least five members of the commission took part in each evaluation. Evaluation embraced diagnosis, prognosis, consideration of etiology and pathogenesis, and whether any disability was caused by imprisonment (war-conditioned disability). Whenever it was felt that therapeutic or rehabilitation measures might achieve results, attempts were made to apply them.

HISTORY

The majority of the patients were of working or lower middle-class origin. Educational standards were relatively low; 60 percent had only the 7-year primary school, and 43 percent had received no special training for their work. Otherwise the group was in no way different from the general population. *Health prior to arrest* was good in 187 cases (82 percent), reasonable in 33 (15 percent), and poor in 7 cases (3 percent). One hundred sixty-eight (74 percent) were harmonious, mentally stable individuals, 19 were somewhat sensitive persons, 15 less harmonious or unstable individuals, and 21 had other deviating personality traits. Two hundred eight (92 percent) were socially well adjusted before the war and in regular employment. Eighteen had some adjustment difficulties, and 11 had abused alcohol, 3 of them to a considerable degree.

One hundred twenty-four (55 percent) had been systematically tortured, 80 very brutally indeed. The period of imprisonment was generally of long duration. Sixty-seven percent had been in captivity for 2 years or more, 32 percent for more than 3 years. One-third were *Nacht und Nebel* prisoners, i.e., prisoners in extermination camps.

Imprisonment was marked by severe undernourishment and a high incidence of disease. Sixty percent had lost more than 30 percent of their body weight; more than a third had lost more than 40 percent. More than half had suffered from serious diarrhea, edema, and head injuries with loss of consciousness. Between 40 and 50 percent had had cellulitis and other skin infections as well as back injuries. Other diseases and injuries were also common, as were mental disturbances.

The majority of ex-prisoners said that their health had improved in the first years after release. Then a deterioration had set in, and this had in most cases been progressive. Altogether, 224 complained that they were in poorer health after imprisonment than before.

Premature aging and frequent illness were general. Besides the neurological and mental diseases, most common were diseases of the digestive organs, cardiovascular diseases, and diseases of the respiratory system. Altogether, 184 (81 percent) of the ex-prisoners were so affected.

Among the digestive diseases, diarrhea and peptic ulcers were the most common. There was a clear correlation between a current persistent tendency to diarrhea and diarrhea (including dysentery) during imprisonment. A similar correlation existed between the occurrence of peptic ulcers and emotional disturbances in the post-war years. Among diseases of the respiratory organs, chronic bronchitis was predominant, often combined with asthma, emphysema, bronchiectasis, and chronic sinusitis. A lowered resistance to respiratory infections was common.

PSYCHIATRIC ASPECTS

Of the 227 ex-prisoners, 226 were examined by psychiatrists. The special objectives of this examination were the premorbid personality, psychic reactions to arrest and captivity, and the actual symptomatology at the time of examination and its possible connection with wartime stresses.

As a whole the examined persons represented a positive selection in regard to premorbid health. The majority must be described as harmonious, socially well-adjusted individuals. Only 10 had exhibited signs of mental disease before arrest.

During captivity two-thirds had experienced psychic reactions in the form of anxiety, tension, despair, serious depressive reactions, and psychic anesthesia. The psychic disorders appeared with greater frequency among those who were under the age of 25 at the time of arrest, and among individuals who had suffered from mental disturbances before the war. The degree of hardship during captivity was also of essential importance.

Psychic deviations were verified in 223 (99 percent) of those examined. The main symptoms were: poor memory and inability to concentrate (87.2 percent); nervousness, irritability, restlessness (85.5 percent); increased fatigue (83.7 percent); sleep disturbances (65.5 percent); loss of initiative (60.4 percent); anxiety phenomena (57.7 percent); emotional lability (56.8 percent); dysphoric moodiness (55.9 percent); vertigo (53.7 percent); and nightmares (52.0 percent). Such symptoms as feelings of insufficiency, headaches, vegetative lability, depressive disturbances, tendency to social withdrawal, and abuse of alcohol tolerance occurred in less than 50 percent of the investigated persons.

Being of the opinion that no single *isolated* symptom can be of any diagnostic importance, we tried to find both a quantitative and qualitative expression for the constellation of symptoms which is known under the name *concentration camp syndrome*. Our starting point was the following group of symptoms: failing memory and difficulty in concentration, nervousness, irritability, restlessness, fatigue, sleep disturbances, headaches, emotional instability, dysphoric moodiness, vertigo, loss of initiative, vegetative lability, and feelings of insufficiency.

With regard to the etiology of the concentration camp syndrome, this proved to be *completely independent* of age either at the time of arrest or at the time the examination was carried out. The existence of "hereditary tainting," i.e., financial conditions or harmony during the patient's childhood, schooling, or training received prior to arrest, could also be excluded, as well as the state of health before arrest. Mental illnesses and deviating traits of character were not of significance. The same applied to special factors in the patients' lives prior to arrest, e.g., abuse of alcohol and social adjustment. In fact we find that nothing from the precaptivity period was of significance in the development of the concentration camp syndrome.

There was, however, a closer correlation with the *severity of torture*, the incidence of *head injuries*, and loss of weight, and with the *severity of imprisonment*.

The findings permit us to conclude that it is *primarily the more somatic aspects which were of significance in the development of the concentration camp syndrome* and that it is especially the cumulative stress as expressed in "degree of severity of captivity" which is the decisive factor for the development of the concentration camp syndrome.

It has been stated that the concentration camp syndrome, as it may be seen in the ex-prisoners today, may be unrelated to the patients' wartime experiences but can arise from stress situations occurring later. We found no evidence in our investigation which could confirm this supposition inasmuch as none of the factors revealed in the patients' lives and conditions after release (such as social environment, interpersonal relationship after their return, marital conditions, and so forth) have shown any statistically valid relation to the presence or absence of the concentration camp syndrome.

The general conclusion must be that it is only the traumatization of concentration camp treatment which is causative in the etiology of the concentration camp syndrome. Although this will never be proved with absolute certainty, it appears very probable when one takes all the available data into consideration.

There was a high degree of correlation between the neurological status and the results of the psychiatric examinations. This was true for the total psychiatric examination, and also when the concentration camp syndrome and the psychiatric status were considered separately.

Particularly striking was the correlation between the neurological status and the findings from the psychiatric examinations, if one correlated the neurological status with a positive psychiatric status combined with at least seven concentration camp symptoms. This combination was found in 85 of the 115 ex-prisoners with a positive neurological status, as against 43 of the 101 with a negative neurological status ($p < 0.01$).

It is remarkable that the combination of concentration camp syndrome and positive psychiatric status was observed only in patients with positive neurological status or with positive laboratory tests (excluding seven cases not fully examined). *This particular combination, therefore, appears to be a very strong indication of organic cerebral damage.*

Certain symptoms which contribute to the concentration camp syndrome showed a clearly positive correlation to the neurological status; these include increased fatigability, vertigo, and feelings of insufficiency. The other symptoms—dysphoria, emotional lability, disturbance of sleep, nervousness, irritability and restlessness, vegetative disturbances, headache, loss of initiative, impairment of memory and concentration ability—bore no statistically significant correlation to the neurological status, although the last two showed borderline values ($0.10 > p > 0.05$). All these symptoms are clinical phenomena which often accompany organic brain disease, and the more of them that are present, the greater the likelihood of organic cerebral damage.

Headache showed a definite correlation with head injury suffered during imprisonment. Of the 129 cases with a history of severe head injuries, 88 were troubled by headaches (68 percent), as compared to 48 of 98 (49 percent) without such injuries ($p < 0.01$).

Anxiety symptoms were of special interest in this material. We know that anxiety is a very common symptom among psychiatric patients, occurring both periodically in attacks, or free-floating. There were 98 (43 percent) cases in our group, a relatively modest incidence. We have, however, been very strict in our assessment and have annotated only those cases in which we ourselves noted clear signs of anxiety during examinations. Anxiety was very clearly associated with nightmares and sleep disturbances.

Anxiety phenomena showed no correlation with the ex-prisoners' lives prior to arrest. It did not seem to be of importance whether his personality had deviated from normal or whether he had been socially maladjusted. The postwar circumstances, such as social conditions, interpersonal relationships, or abuse of alcohol, do not appear to be significant either. On the other hand we did find a clear connection with the appearance of *psychic disturbances during imprisonment,* especially anxiety. There were also more cases of anxiety among those who had suffered the severest types of imprisonment, but this difference was not statistically significant.

Since the development of anxiety seems to depend on whether the patient showed signs of psychic disturbances and anxiety during imprisonment, the objection might be raised here that the question put to certain patients by their examiner may have concentrated too much on this problem. But if the method used is that whereby one doctor first notes the patient's experiences and his reactions during captivity without touching on the actual symptoms, then this objection is not valid. It is, of course, possible that ex-prisoners who were troubled with anxiety find it easier to recall corresponding emotions from the time of their captivity and were more preoccupied with them than those who no longer suffered from anxiety. But this is something that always has to be reckoned with when a patient's *subjective* reactions are being examined. On the other hand it is also likely that patients who developed intense mental unbalance and anxiety resulting from their sufferings were not able to work through them satisfactorily after the war, nor to abreact them on their own. They had received no psychiatric treatment either, and their symptoms had become chronic. When we remember that it was the youngest, the least stable, and the most emaciated who developed these symptoms, then this anxiety reaction becomes even more understandable. We wish to emphasize again that the nightmares described by our patients were always related to actual circumstances in the past and that their contents were thus very real.

From the neurological examination it appeared that of the 98 patients with anxiety, 82 (84 percent) had definite encephalopathy. Of the 128 without this symptom, 102 (80 percent) had encephalopathy. Accordingly, we found no correlation between anxiety and encephalopathy. Anxiety seems to be a consequence of the psychic stress suffered during imprisonment, but the causes of encephalopathy must be looked for among the other types of stress they suffered in the camps.

Impotence was observed in 76 male ex-prisoners with the following age distribution (Table 6.1):

Table 6.1. Impotence in Male Ex-Prisoners

Age group	Impotent	Total	Percentage of impotence
35	9	27	33.3
40	12	43	27.9
45	16	36	44.4
50	20	44	45.4
55	11	27	40.7
60	6	26	}
65	2	10	21.6
70 and over	0	1	}
Total	76	214	35.5

According to Kinsey, 1 percent of men are impotent at the age of 40; this percentage increases to 3 percent in the fifties and to 10 percent in the sixties, and 24 percent in the seventies [3]. In the eighties 77 percent are impotent. We see that in the age group under sixty we find a remarkably high incidence of impotence. Since anxiety was a characteristic feature in a number of ex-prisoners, it was natural to look at impotence in relation to this. According to Ellis (1961) impotence of a psychogenic origin based on anxiety shows itself either in the form of ejaculatio praecox or an erective impotence with retained morning erection [1]. None of our patients suffered from ejaculatio praecox, and few had morning erections. Neither did they suffer from severe endocrine disturbances which could explain their impotence. Depressive reactions in the form of melancholia can form impotence, especially where loss of libido is concerned. The affective reactions in these patients, however, did not show depression. Impotence in their cases seems to stem from a condition of the central nervous system, a general exhaustion. Ford (1951) and his co-workers describe the sexual inactivity of animals after the removal of the cortex [2].

Impotence showed in our cases a clear correlation to the neurological status and to the degree of encephalopathy. Of 142 prisoners with an encephalopathy point count of 2.5 or more, impotence was present in 57 cases (40 percent), compared to 19 (22 percent) of the 85 with a point count of 2.0 or less ($0.02 > p > 0.01$). Accordingly, impotence seems to be connected with the organic cerebral changes.

One hundred ninety-three of the former prisoners were examined with a battery of psychological tests. A study of 50 other patients with verified brain damage had been made earlier, and the findings from this study were used as control material. The same quantitative scoring system was used for both groups. The Wechsler Adult Intelligence Scale, the Goldstein Scheerer Cube Test, the Trail Making Test, and the Halstead-Wepman Test were the methods elected for evaluating intellectual and other impairment, and the final analysis with a summary diagnostic judgment was termed K-score.

Psychometric changes were found in a high percentage of cases from the ex-prisoners' group and in all cases of the brain-damaged control group. One hundred eighty ex-prisoners showed impairment of intellectual functioning and ability which ranged from slight to severe. Impaired functioning was found which primarily affected mental speed, visuomotor learning, retention, "social anticipation," ability to plan and organize when presented with special problems, visual perception, and the ability to maintain sustained effort.

The analysis of behavior in this study recorded very clearly those trends of impairment which are supposed to be caused by organic brain damage. In addition to this fact a high degree of correlation was found between the psychological classifications and the diagnosis of encephalopathy (p < 0.01) and the neurological status (p < 0.01). It would seem, therefore, that the intellectual impairment revealed by poor psychological test performance can be best explained in terms of behavioral parameters which depend upon the full functioning of an undamaged brain.

Intellectual impairment shown by psychological examination was related to the severity of the brain damage: the more serious the intellectual defects, the higher the incidence of positive neurological signs and symptoms, including abnormal pneumo-encephalographic findings.

One hundred fifty-six of the 227 patients had been reexamined during the observation period from 1957, roughly according to the same methods as outlined earlier. In no case was there reason to change the diagnoses, and in practically all the cases a slight reduction of the working capacity could be demonstrated. We are not certain that this can be considered a sign of a progressive tendency of the chronic brain syndrome. It seems, however, that the compensating power of the individuals is reduced, thus giving a picture of clinical deterioration.

CONCLUSIONS

In conclusion it may be stated that a chronic brain syndrome was found in the majority of 227 Norwegian concentration camp survivors examined in this study. This could be attributed to the stress suffered during imprisonment. Head injuries, torture, severe malnutrition, and hard captivity conditions in general seemed to be the most important etiological factors. In most cases several factors probably worked together. Both these and other factors during captivity seem to have provoked psychic disturbances during imprisonment, especially anxiety. These again caused personality changes (*erlebnissbedingte Personlichkeitwandel*—Venzlaff) of a very deeply penetrating and generalized nature with few tendencies to recovery [5].

REFERENCES

1. Ellis, A. Coitus. In A. Ellis and A. Horsbanel (Eds.), The Encyclopedia of Sexual Behavior. *New York: Hawthorn, 1961.*
2. Ford, C. S., and Bloch, F. A. Patterns of Sexual Behavior. *New York: Harper and Brothers, 1951.*
3. Kinsey, A. C., et al. Sexual Behavior in the Human Male. *Philadelphia: Saunders, 1948.*
4. Strøm, A., Eitinger, L., Grønvik, O., Lønnum, A., Engens, A., Oswik, K., and Rogan, A. Undersøklse av Norske tidlingere konsentrasjonsleisfanger. Tidsskr. Norske Laeforening, *No. 13/14, 803–816, 1961.*
5. Venzlaff, U. Erlebnishintfergrund und Dynamik seelischer Verfolgungsschaeden. In H. Paul and H. Herberg (Eds.), Psychische Spaetschaeden nach politischer Verfolgung. *Basel; New York: Karger, 1963, Pp. 157–173.*

7. Pierre Janet and Modern Views of Dissociation

Frank W. Putnam

P IERRE JANET'S numerous important contributions to our understanding of dissociative phenomena and the psychological effects of trauma grew out of a life-long interest in hypnosis and mystical states of consciousness tempered by his passion for precise observation and classification. Janet's successive accomplishments in philosophy, psychology and psychiatry represented in his own words, ". . . a question of conciliating scientific tastes and religious sentiments, which was not an easy task" (Janet, 1930, p. 123). As a young philosophy student he was drawn to the work of Charcot, who was resurrecting the study of hypnosis (Ellenberger, 1970). His doctoral thesis, *L'Automatisme Psychologique* (1889), published over a century ago was a brilliant study of hypnosis and clinical dissociation that immediately thrust Janet into the circle of luminaries of the day.

In recognition of his expertise, Janet was permitted extensive freedom during his medical training to examine patients on Charcot's wards at the Salpêtriére (Ellenberger, 1970). There he applied the standards of observation and documentation gleaned from his earlier psychological studies. In marked contrast to the flamboyant Charcot who was celebrated for his dramatic public demonstrations of hysterical symptoms, Janet insisted on interviewing his patients alone. He documented everything that they said or did in extensive case histories scrutinizing the patient's entire life and course of therapy (Ellenberger, 1970). Eventually he accumulated more than 5000 cases which served as a data base for his observations and theories.

Janet explored dissociative symptoms extensively and first articulated most of the basic clinical principles. He made the connection between dissociative psychopathology and traumatic experiences and pioneered hypnotic and abreactive treatment techniques to recover and rework what he termed the

---

Reprinted by permission from *Journal of Traumatic Stress*, 2 (2), 199–223. Copyright © 1989 by Plenum Publishing.

". . . traumatic memory of an unassimilated event" (Janet, 1930, p. 370). In particular, Janet recognized the role of altered states of consciousness with their attendant state-dependent memory and cognition in producing dissociative pathology. He identified the long-term somatic repercussions of dissociated memories and affects observing, "One should go through the entire field of mental diseases and a part of physical diseases to show the mental and bodily disturbances resulting from the banishment of a thought from personal consciousness." (Janet, quoted in Ellenberger, 1970, p. 361).

In the century following the publication of *L'Automatisme Psychologique* Janet's reputation was eclipsed by Freud and only now is he receiving the belated recognition owed him as the first and foremost investigator of dissociation. In addition to his seminal contributions to our understanding of dissociation and trauma, Janet made many other important contributions to modern psychiatry including the first articulation of a transference theory of psychotherapy (Haule, 1986) and the first systematic descriptions of obsessive-compulsive disorder and bulimia (Pitman, 1987; Pope *et al.*, 1985).

PRINCIPLES OF DISSOCIATION

The Dissociative Continuum

Janet differs from his contemporaries and modern authorities, however, on one fundamental principle of dissociation. Janet viewed dissociation as a discontinuous phenomenon that was experienced only by people with certain psychiatric disorders, primarily hysteria, and was absent in normal individuals (Janet, 1989; Perry and Laurence, 1984; van der Hart and Horst, 1989; White and Shevach, 1942). This difference reflects, in part, Janet's limited and precise use of the term dissociation (déagrégation = dissociation) which for him referred only to those cases in which there was a pathological separation between ideas and behaviors and consciousness. The cardinal feature of this pathological separation was amnesia. The result was that

Things happen as if an idea, a partial system of thoughts, emancipated itself, became independent and developed itself on its own account. The result is, on the one hand, that it develops far too much, and, on the other hand, that consciousness appears no longer to control it. (Janet, 1926, p. 42)

His peers and later investigators, however, generally disregarded his criterion of pathological insulation, amnesia, and viewed dissociation as a process that exists on a continuum from such normal everyday experiences as daydream-

ing to psychiatric disorders such as psychogenic amnesia and multiple personality disorder (Bernstein and Putnam, 1986). There is indirect evidence,
however, that Janet acknowledged this continuum and as he later observed
while discussing the nature of suggestion, "Pathological phenomena are only
exaggerations of normal phenomena . . ." (Janet, 1925/1976, p. 274).

Evidence supporting the concept of a dissociative continuum comes from
studies of hypnotizability by Hilgard (1986), Spiegel (1963), and others and
from studies of depersonalization and dissociation using questionnaires and
rating scales (Bernstein and Putnam, 1986). Figure 7.1 demonstrates the
smoothed distribution of dissociative experiences reported on the Dissociative
Experiences Scales (DES), by a variety of psychiatric patients and normal
subjects.

The DES is a reliable and valid questionnaire for quantifying dissociative
phenomena (Bernstein and Putnam, 1986; Ross et al., 1989). Both normal
and patient groups demonstrate the classic left (leptokurtic) skewing found in
virtually all distribution studies of dissociative phenomena. Similar data have
been published for the distribution of hypnotizability as measured by standardized instruments, though the latter tends towards bimodality in some
samples (Hilgard, 1986). These data demonstrate that dissociation, or correlates of dissociation such as hypnotizability, exists along a continum from
minor to major degrees though the distribution is not a normal (Gaussian)
probability curve. Most normal individuals report relatively few significant
dissociative experiences and these generally involve "spacing out" in monotonous situations or becoming "entranced" by movies, television, or books.

Pathological Dissociation

As a consequence of this continuum most clinical definitions focus on the
question of what separates pathological dissociation from normal dissociative
experiences. Many of Janet's contemporaries, including Morton Prince and
William James, conceptualized dissociation as a normative process that becomes pathological only in certain circumstances (Putnam, 1989). Similar
formulations have been proposed by modern investigators, most cogently by
Ernest Hilgard (1986) with his "neodissociative" model of or human behavior. Indeed, as Hilgard (1973) observes, "daily life is full of many small
dissociations if we look for them" (p. 406).

Nemiah (1981) has identified two principles that can be used to differentiate pathological from nonpathological dissociation. The first is that the individual undergoing a pathological dissociative reaction experiences a signifi-

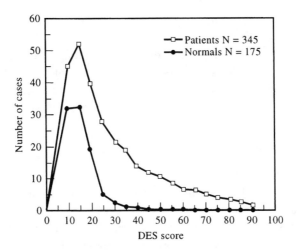

Figure 7.1. Distribution of the scores.

cant alteration in his sense of identity. This may take several forms. For example, in psychogenic amnesia the individual often becomes amnesic for personal and/or self-referential information, typically including identity. These are the "John" or "Jane Doe" cases brought to the emergency room by the police.

In psychogenic fugue states, individuals often, but not always, assume a secondary identity and are amnesic for part or all of the history of their primary identity. In multiple personality disorder (MPD) the individual's sense of self is composed of a series of separate and distinct identities that exchange control over the individual's behavior. In depersonalization syndrome, individuals experience disturbances in the reality of self so that they report feeling as if they were "dead," "a robot," or "unreal." In dissociative symptoms, such as flashbacks, the individual may experience an alteration in sense of self along dimensions such as age and body image.

The second principle is that the individual manifests disturbance of memory, typically amnesia (partial or complete), for events in the dissociated state. This is similar to Janet's original requirement of amnesia for dissociated behavior. Significant degrees of amnesias can be demonstrated in the vast majority of MPD cases and other dissociative disorders (Markowtisch, 1988; Putnam *et al.,* 1986). The presence of amnesia is a DSM-III-R diagnostic criterion for psychogenic amnesia and psychogenic fugue and presently there is considerable support for inclusion of amnesia as a DSM-IV criterion for the diagnosis of multiple personality disorder.

Other disturbances of memory may occur, however, such as the dreamlike recall described in depersonalization syndrome so that while the information is available to voluntary recall it is distorted or lacking a first person experiential quality. Individuals often report that depersonalized experiences are remembered as if "it happened to someone else" or as if "I was watching myself from a safe place."

Linkage to Trauma

A review of the clinical literature on dissociation rapidly convinces one of the existence of a third principle. Dissociative symptoms and disorders are closely linked to traumatic experiences (Henderson and Moore, 1944; Putnam, 1985; Sargent and Slater, 1941; Spiegel, 1986; van der Kolk, 1987). In fact, most authorities conceptualize dissociative reactions occurring in the context of acute trauma as an adaptive process that protects the individual and allows him to continue to function, though often in an automaton-like manner (Ludwig, 1983; Spiegel, 1986; van der Kolk and Kadish, 1987). Janet was among the first to conceptualize dissociation as a defense against trauma and to systematically work with the traumatic memories and affects behind the dissociative symptoms (van der Hart and Horst, 1989).

Psychogenic amnesia and psychogenic fugue states are frequently associated with acute situational traumas such as the death of a buddy in combat, the break-up of an important relationship or a serious financial reverse (Abeles and Schilder, 1935; Kanzer, 1939; Kennedy and Neville, 1957; Kiersch, 1962; Putnam, 1985). Multiple personality disorder is significantly correlated with severe, repetitive child abuse typically occurring before puberty (Bliss, 1980; Coons et al., 1988; Putnam et al., 1986).

Depersonalization syndrome often appears in individuals suffering torture or abusive confinement as adolescents or adults (Dor-Shav, 1978; Jacobson, 1977; Putnam, 1985). Transient depersonalization reactions may occur in individuals experiencing life-threatening trauma (Fullerton et al., 1981; Noyes and Kletti, 1977; Putnam, 1985). Unlike the other dissociative disorders, however, depersonalization syndrome is not inevitably associated with traumatic antecedents and appears to develop "spontaneously" in some individuals. Symptoms of depersonalization are common across a wide range of psychiatric and neurological disorders (Putnam, 1985). Transient experiences of depersonalization are normative in adolescence and diminish with age (Bernstein and Putnam, 1986).

Dissociative reactions and disorders occurring acutely in the context of immediate trauma are typically short-lived and often resolve spontaneously (Putnam, 1985). There may, however, be subsequent dissociative symptoms such as flashbacks and abreactions that periodically reoccur causing significant distress years after the trauma (van der Kolk and Kadish, 1987). In some individuals, particularly those suffering from sustained repetitive trauma, a chronic dissociative disorder such as depersonalization syndrome or multiple personality disorder develops. In such cases, the initially adaptive role of dissociation in blunting the impact of the traumatic experience becomes a maladaptive chronic process that seriously interferes with the functioning of the individual (Spiegel, 1986).

Dissociation as an Adaptive Response to Acute Trauma

Janet recognized the adaptive nature of dissociation in the context of acute trauma and the long-term pathological consequences for the individual if the dissociated memories and affects (idées fixes) were not reworked and assimilated into the individual's awareness. Other investigators have subsequently explored the adaptive functions of dissociation in the context of acute trauma (Bliss, 1984; Braun and Sachs, 1985; Frankel, 1976; Spiegel, 1984). Ludwig (1983) states:

This mechanism [dissociation] has great individual and species survival value. Under certain conditions, it serves to facilitate seven major functions: (1) the automatization of certain behaviors, (2) efficiency and economy of effort, (3) the resolution of irreconcilable conflicts, (4) escape from the constraints of reality, (5) the isolation of catastrophic experiences, (6) the cathartic discharge of certain feelings, and (7) the enhancement of herd sense (e.g. the submersion of the individual ego for the group identity, greater suggestibility, etc.). (p. 93)

An additional adaptive function associated with dissociated states of consciousness is analgesia. This capacity has been well demonstrated in hypnosis laboratories and in operating theaters (Hilgard and Hilgard, 1975). When faced with pain, many victims of repetitive trauma report being able to activate analgesia in response to environmental cues or by using trance-inducing strategies, e.g., staring at a point in space or repeating a rhyme. Like the other adaptive functions of dissociation, chronic analgesia may become maladaptive contributing to feelings of depersonalization or provoking self-mutilation or other self-destructive behavior.

THE DISSOCIATIVE DISORDERS

The DSM-III-R recognizes four distinct dissociative disorders and a fifth catch-all category, Dissociative Disorder NOS (APA, 1987). Dissociative symptoms such as depersonalization, flashbacks and abreaction may make a major contribution to the psychopathology of a number of other disorders including: posttraumatic stress disorder (PTSD) (Blank, 1985; Kolb, 1985, 1987; Spiegel, 1986); eating disorders (Pettinati et al., 1985; Torem, 1986; Vanderlinden and Vandereycken, 1988); phobic disorders (Frankel and Orne, 1976); conversion disorder (Putnam, 1989) and obsessive-compulsive disorder (Ross and Anderson, 1988; Torch, 1981).

Dissociative symptoms, particularly feelings of depersonalization, are widespread across a range of psychiatric disorders (Cattell, 1972; Putnam, 1985). A survey of 311 psychiatric patients who did not meet DSM-III-R diagnostic criteria for a dissociative disorder found that 41% still reported significant dissociative symptoms (Putnam—unpublished data).

There are little data on the incidence or prevalence of any of the dissociative disorders and guesstimates of the prevalence of MPD, for example, range from one in a million up to 10% of psychiatric inpatients (Bliss and Jeppsen, 1985; Coons et al., 1988). There are mixed data regarding a possible higher incidence of dissociative disorders in females. There is no evidence of a gender association with psychogenic amnesia or psychogenic fugue (Putnam, 1985). Some case series would suggest an increased incidence of depersonalization symptoms in females but others report an equal incidence (Putnam, 1985; Shimizu and Sakamoto, 1986). Several case series have reported a significantly higher incidence of MPD in females (Coons et al., 1988; Putnam, 1985) but others have argued that male MPD cases are simply being missed because they present in atypical ways; are in the criminal justice system or alcohol and drug rehabilitation programs rather than mainstream mental health settings; and/or that females are at higher risk for abuse (Putnam, 1989). The question of a possible gender association remains open for MPD but does not seem to exist for the other dissociative disorders.

There are some intriguing data suggesting that the age of the individual at the time of the trauma may influence the form of the dissociative symptoms (Putnam, 1985). Multiple personality disorder appears to be the result of severe repetitive trauma prior to puberty typically occurring between ages 4 and 10 years (Coons et al., 1988; Putnam et al., 1986). Recent child and adolescent case reports (Fagan and McMahon, 1984; Kluft, 1985, 1986; Riley and Mead, 1988; Vincent and Pickering, 1988; Weiss *et al.,* 1985) support the position that the onset of MPD occurs in childhood but that it is rarely diagnosed before the third decade (Bliss, 1980; Coons *et al.,* 1988; Putnam *et al.,* 1986).

Psychogenic amnesia and psychogenic fugue are thought to be exceptionally rare during early to middle adolescence and typically occur between ages 20 to 40 years. It is possible however, that like MPD, child and adolescent cases are simply being missed because of a low index of suspicion or that the dissociative symptoms are explained away by other diagnoses (Kluft, 1985). Depersonalization syndrome typically has its onset during late adolescence to early adulthood and almost always first occurs before age 40 years (Putnam, 1985; Shimizu and Sakamoto, 1986). Thus the scanty data available suggest that in general, like posttraumatic stress disorder (Kolb, 1987), the dissociative disorders are more likely to occur in younger individuals.

While the core features of the dissociative disorders are disturbances in sense of self and memory, patients rarely present with initial complaints referable to those symptoms. Instead, most MPD patients, for example, present with symptoms suggestive of depression and anxiety coupled with somatic complaints, particularly headaches and gastrointestinal problems (Bliss, 1980; Coons *et al.,* 1988; Putnam *et al.,* 1986). Typically they are refractory to the standard treatments for these symptoms and usually acquire a range of psychiatric and medical diagnoses, spending an average of seven years in the mental health system prior to diagnoses of MPD (Coons *et al.,* 1988; Putnam *et al.,* 1986). Common misdiagnosis include: depression, schizophrenia, bipolar affective disorder, and borderline personality disorder.

Patients with depersonalization syndrome often present with sensory complaints such as visual disturbances, typically microscopic or the sense of looking at the world through a fog or smoky veil or with complaints of feeling as if they were in a dream or of feeling enclosed in a glass bubble and cut off from the world. Psychogenic amnesia and psychogenic fugue patients rarely present voluntarily but may be brought in by the police as "John Does." During a fugue state there is little that would suggest to someone who did not know the patient well that anything was amiss. As Janet observed:

In fact, they are mad people in full delirium; nevertheless, they take railway tickets, they dine and sleep in hotels, they speak to a great number of people. We are, it is true, sometimes told that they were thought a little odd, that they looked preoccupied and dreamy, but after all, they are not recognized as mad people ... (quoted in Rapaport, 1942, p. 201)

Dissociation is believed to play an important role in the pathology of a number of other psychiatric disorders, most notably posttraumatic stress disorder (Kolb, 1987; Spiegel *et al.*, 1988; van der Kolk *et al.*, 1984). Studies of spontaneous dissociation as measured by the DES (Bernstein and Putnam, 1986; Loewenstein and Putnam, 1989) and of hypnotizability (Spiegel *et al.*, 1988; Stutman and Bliss, 1985) indicate that combat veterans suffering PTSD have significantly higher levels of spontaneous dissociation or correlates of dissociation than comparison groups of other psychiatric patients. Flashbacks, abreactions and intrusive imagery are common clinical manifestations of the dissociative process in PTSD victims (Kolb, 1987; Spiegel, 1986).

NORMATIVE DISSOCIATION

This chapter honoring the centennial of Janet's original contribution to our understanding of dissociation is focused on pathological dissociation as a response to trauma. No survey of modern views of dissociation would be complete, however, without briefly touching on research into dissociation as a normative process. Dissociative phenomena have been the centerpiece of models of the mind for over 150 years (Carlson, 1986; Crabtree, 1986) and continue to play a central role over 150 years thinking about mental processes, particularly those involving "unconscious" mental mechanisms (e.g., see Bowers and Meichenbaum, 1984).

In addition to the many minor dissociations of everyday life, laboratory research on normative dissociation has focused on several experimental paradigms, most notably (1) posthypnotic amnesia, (2) interference phenomena affecting the ability of subjects to perform two tasks simultaneously, (3) hypnotically induced perceptual alterations and trance logic, and (4) hidden observer phenomena. The last is the demonstration that in about half of highly hypnotizable subjects in whom hypnotic analgesia has been induced, the experimenter can communicate with a "hidden part" of the person that perceives the pain although the subject denies an awareness of the pain. (Hilgard, 1986). Kihlstrom (1984) has cogently reviewed the range of experimental data on normative dissociative phenomena and integrated these findings with current cognitive theory of mental processes.

MODELS AND MECHANISMS OF DISSOCIATION

The major models of dissociation and dissociated behavior in current vogue today are largely derived from the work and speculations of Janet and his contemporaries. This reflects the clarity of observation and quality of clinical work of that era and the constancy of dissociative phenomena over time and across cultures. Most of the models overlap at several points and are not mutually exclusive.

Dissociation as an Autohypnotic Disorder

Janet recognized the connection between dissociation and hypnosis, which he defined as a form of dissociation. "Hypnosis may be defined as the momentary transformation of the mental state of an individual, artificially induced by a second person, and sufficing to bring about dissociations of personal memory" (Janet quoted in Haule, 1986, p. 86). The link between hypnosis and clinical dissociation continues to be a major focus of modern investigation. Bliss (1983, 1984) maintains that "self-hypnosis" is the operative mechanism in the dissociative disorders. Others (Carlson and Putnam, 1989; Spiegel *et al.,* 1988) suggest that hypnotizability and pathological dissociation share overlapping phenomena but are not necessarily identical processes. Claims that multiple personality disorder can be induced in suggestible individuals by hypnosis, however, have been demonstrated to be false (Braun, 1984; Greaves, 1980; Kluft, 1982).

Central to the autohypnotic model is the observation that individuals with dissociative symptoms uniformly score in the highly hypnotizable range on standard scales (Bliss, 1983, 1984; Spiegel *et al.,* 1988). J. R. Hilgard (1972) has suggested that there may be two separate developmental pathways leading to such high hypnotizability in adulthood. The first is the preservation into adulthood of childhood imaginative capacities and capacity for intense absorption. She found a high correlation between hypnotizability and a composite measure of adult involvement in reading, drama, creativity and childhood imagination. The second pathway is through the experience of strict discipline, severe punishment, and abuse in childhood. A high correlation between childhood trauma and adult levels of hypnotizability has been found by a number of investigators (Cooper and London, 1976; Hilgard, 1972; Nash *et al.,* 1984; Nowlis, 1969).

Recent data correlating spontaneous dissociative experiences with hypnotizability support J. R. Hilgard's hypothesis of two developmental pathways to high hypnotizability (Carlson and Putnam, 1989). It appears as if individuals with high levels of spontaneous dissociation in everyday life are also highly hypnotizable, but highly hypnotizable individuals need not have high levels of spontaneous dissociation. Prospective studies and longitudinal studies of alterations in hypnotizability by trauma are necessary to confirm this hypothesis.

States of Consciousness Model

The states of consciousness model of dissociative disorders is an expansion of the autohypnotic or trance state model discussed above. It differs in that it emphasizes the properties of states of consciousness, irrespective of type of state, as the mechanistic principles involved in the dissociative disorders. From the early 1800s to the present, clinicians have conceptualized dissociative reactions as altered states of consciousness. Janet viewed dissociative disorders as the existence within an individual of two or more states of consciousness isolated from each other by a cleft of amnesia and operating with apparent independence (Haule, 1986). Janet's colleague, Ribot (1891), first proposed that the principles of state-dependent learning and memory were operative in MPD, a hypothesis subsequently confirmed by a number of investigators (Ludwig *et al.,* 1972; Nissen *et al.,* 1988; Silberman *et al.,* 1985). Janet, himself, was acutely aware of the role of state-dependent learning and memory in a range of mental disturbances associated with strong emotions.

Popular observation noticed long ago that the individual, when overcome by emotion, is 'not himself,' that he is 'beside himself.' And I have shown on numerous occasions that the characteristics which have been acquired by education and moral development may suffer a complete change under the influence of emotion. . . . Oblivescence of the event which occasioned the emotion and inability to remember facts which immediately preceded, have frequently been found to accompany intensely emotional experiences in the form of continuous and retrograde amnesia. But it must not be thought that these phenomena are merely pathological caprices. They are an exaggerated form of a general disturbance of memory which is characteristic of all emotions. (Janet, 1905, p. 107).

Recent studies suggest that different states of consciousness (e.g., affective, dissociative, anxiety and catatonic states) share a set of basic principles and properties (Putnam, 1988). Transitions or "switches" between states are associated with rapid, nonlinear changes in (1) affect, (2) attention and cognition, (3) retrieval of memories and access to learned skills, (4) autonomic physiology, and (5) sense of self. Dramatic examples of such switches include: transitions between depressed and manic states in bipolar illness; panic attacks; abreactions in PTSD; onset/offset of conversion reactions, switches into and out of catatonic states; and switches between alter personalities in

MPD. Work by Wolff (1987) and others on normal infants indicates that states are the basic building block of human behavior. Interestingly, infants demonstrate many of the same psychophysiological markers of switching observed in pathological state switches in adults (Putnam, 1988).

Dissociative disorders can thus be conceptualized as the creation of highly discrete states of consciousness in the context of severe trauma. These dissociative states are imbued with a strong predominate affect (e.g., fear, anger, depression, etc.), a cognitive style, a state-dependently bound set of memories and behaviors and a state-dependent sense of self. The amnesias that separate dissociative states from normal consciousness are an extreme form of state-dependent memory retrieval. The alterations in identity represent profound state-dependent shifts in sense of self. In response to a single acute traumatic experience, one dissociative state may be created. In the face of repetitive or sustained trauma, a range of dissociative states may arise.

The abrupt onset and offset of these states (e.g., in psychogenic amnesia and fugue, flashbacks and abreactions) or the transitions among a series of dissociative states (e.g., multiple personality disorder) are examples of a universal switch mechanism. Activation of these dissociative states by environmental or internal triggers (e.g., cognitive trains of thought) are responsible for symptoms such as flashbacks, abreactions or recapitualtive behaviors in traumatized individuals.

Neurobiological Theories of Dissociation

Not surprisingly, dissociative phenomena have spawned a range of neurobiological theories and models. At the beginning of the nineteenth century, the great American psychiatrist, Benjamin Rush, suggested that MPD was the result of a disconnection between the two hemispheres of the brain (Carlson, 1986). This explanation was repeatedly reinvoked over the next century and reached an absurd level when a French psychiatrist proposed that there must actually be five "hemispheres" because his patient have five alter personalities. Analyses of split brain studies (Sidtis, 1986) and physiological studies of differential autonomic nervous system activity across alter personalities of MPD patients (Putnam et al., 1990) do not support a hemispheric disconnection or laterality model of MPD or dissociation.

Charcot first proposed that MPD was actually a form of epilepsy (Charcot and Marie, 1892). Modern cases of MPD associated with epilepsy or temporal lobe abnormalities continue to be reported (Benson et al., 1986; Mesulam, 1981; Putnam, 1986). Recent investigations of dissociative symptoms in patients with documented epilepsy (Devinsky *et al.*, 1989; Loewenstein and Putnam, 1989; Ross *et al.*, 1989) and video/EGG-monitored MPD patients (Devinsky *et al.*, 1989) cast considerable doubt on the hypothesis that dissociation is either an ictal or interictal manifestation of epilepsy. Symptoms of depersonalization were, however, significantly more likely to be associated with a dominant hemisphere seizure foci (Devinsky *et al.*, 1989).

While still preliminary, psychophysiological studies of MPD indicate that the alter personalities states of MPD patients exhibit differential physiological responses to the same stimuli (Coons, 1988; Putnam, 1986). This work is augmented by the burgeoning research into the psychophysiology of the trauma response. Animal models of learned helplessness and conditioned fear indicate that trauma produces neurobiological alterations at many levels (e.g., cellular, endocrine, autonomic and central nervous system) as well as producing behaviors (e.g., freezing and stress-induced analgesia) that appear analogous to clinical phenomena observed in trauma victims. (Kolb, 1987; van der Kolk, 1987). These preliminary studies have enormous potential for integrating our understanding of the biological basis of psychological and somatic sequelae of trauma.

Social Role Playing Models of Dissociative Behavior

Janet first raised the possibility of role-playing in MPD, noting that his patient Léonie had a personality who was a role played to please the hypnotist (Ellenberger, 1970). Subsequently others have suggested that MPD in particular, may simply be a fabricated role adopted by the patient to deceive or please the therapist (Orne *et al.*, 1984; Spanos *et al.*, 1986). Similar critiques have been leveled at laboratory demonstrations of dissociation such as the hidden observer.

Clinically it is usually apparent that the cost to the patient far outweighs any secondary gain derived from such symptoms. Experimentally extensive replication employing variations in the demand characteristics of the laboratory situation have established that the hidden observer phenomenon is not simply a response to subject expectations or experimenter cues (Kihlstrom, 1984). With regard to socially-cued simulations of MPD, even a cursory reading of the experiments of Spanos *et al.* (1986) is sufficient to establish that the experimental entities produced in these contrived demonstrations using psychology undergraduates have no relevance to the clinical phenomena observed in dissociative patients.

THE TREATMENT OF DISSOCIATIVE DISORDERS

The treatment of dissociative disorders is an empirical process grounded in clinical reality (Putnam, 1986). Pragmatic observations of what works and what does not, however, generally support the autohypnotic and/or state models of pathological dissociation. In general, medications are only useful as adjunctive treatments for associated depression, anxiety and some posttraumatic symptoms but do not affect the primary dissociative symptoms (Barkin *et al.*, 1986; Friedman, 1987; Loewenstein *et al.*, 1988; Putnam, 1989). As Janet (1925/1976) eloquently articulated, an eclectic treatment approach using psychotherapy focused on recovery and reworking of memories of traumatic events seems to be the most effective intervention (Braun, 1986; Putnam, 1989; Torch, 1987). In many instances, these memories must first be accessed through the induction of an altered state of consciousness, e.g., by amytal interview or hypnosis.

The use of therapeutic abreaction for recovery of traumatic material was pioneered by Janet, though the existence of such reactions had long been recognized by the early hypnotists. At times he would deliberately trigger abreactions by placing the patient in hypnotic trance and reenacting the traumatic scene. In one case, Vof, the patient was amnesic for an attack by a rabid dog and other traumatic events covering a six-week period. At first Janet attempted to recover these memories through automatic writing and his technique of automatic talking which predated Freud's free association techniques. When this failed, Janet had her relive the traumatic experiences under hypnosis. The memories flooded back now accompanied by headaches and suicidal impulses (Ellenberger, 1970). In the case of Justine, he joined her recurrent abreactive crises, becoming an actor in the drama and gaining a therapeutic entree to the material. Later, in each case, he worked in psychotherapy with hypnosis to transform and integrate the traumatic material.

Unfortunately most of Janet's contributions were dismissed or forgotten as free association techniques developed by Freud as an alternative to hypnosis were adopted by the spreading psychoanalytic movement. Only now, as we once again acknowledge the reality and psychological impact of trauma, are we able to appreciate the legacy of Janet's careful work.

CONCLUSIONS

Pierre Janet's careful analysis of dissociated behavior laid the foundation for modern understanding of the dissociative disorders and the role of dissociation in a range of other psychiatric disorders. Modern views of dissociation stress the concept of a continuum process and differ from Janet's view more as a matter of definition than conceptualization. Janet recognized the role of traumatically generated discrete states of consciousness with their attendant state-dependent memories, sense of self and psychophysiology in dissociation. He pioneered the basic treatment techniques aimed at the recovery and reworking of underlying traumata, leaving us an important legacy. Further studies of dissociation seek to clarify the basic psychobiological mechanisms, identify subgroups of dissociative patients, and teach us more about psychiatric disorders characterized by rapid shifts in state of consciousness.

REFERENCES

Abeles, M., and Schilder, P. (1935). Psychogenic loss of personal identity. Arch. Neurol. Psychiat. 34: 587–604.

American Psychiatric Association (1987). Diagnostic and Statistical Manual of Mental Disorders, Third Edition Revised, American Psychiatric Association, Washington, D.C.

Barkin, R., Braun, B. G., and Kluft, R. P. (1986). The dilemma of drug therapy for multiple personality disorder. In Braun, B. G. (ed.), Treatment of Multiple Personality Disorder, American Psychiatric Press, Washington, D.C., pp. 107–132.

Benson, D. F., Miller, B. L., and Signer, S. F. (1986). Dual personality associated with epilepsy. Arch. Neurol. 43: 417–474.

Bernstein, E. M., and Putnam, F. W. (1986). Development, reliability, and validity of a dissociation scale. J. Nerv. Ment. Dis. 174: 727–735.

Blank, A. S. (1985). The unconscious flashback to the war in Vietnam veterans: Clinical mystery, legal defense and community problem. In Sonneberg, S. M., Blank, A. S., and Talbott, J. A. (eds.), The Trauma of War: Stress and Recovery in Vietnam Veterans, American Psychiatric Press, Washington, D.C., pp. 293–309.

Bliss, E. L. (1980). Multiple personalities: A report of 14 cases with implications for schizophrenia and hysteria. Arch. Gen. Psychiat. 37: 1388–1397.

Bliss, E. L. (1983). Multiple personalities, related disorders and hypnosis. Am. J. Clin. Hypnos. 26: 114–123.

Bliss, E. L. (1984). Spontaneous self-hypnosis in multiple personality disorder. Psychiat. Clin. N. Am. 7: 135–148.

Bliss, E. L., and Jeppsen, E. A. (1985). Prevalence of multiple personality among inpatients and outpatients. Am. J. Psychiat. 142: 250–251.

Bowers, K. S., and Meichenbaum, D. (eds.) (1984). The Unconscious Reconsidered, Wiley, New York.

Braun, B. G. (1984). Hypnosis creates multiple personality: Myth or reality Int. J. Clin. Exp. Hypn. 32: 191–197.

Braun, B. G. (1986). Treatment of Multiple Personality Disorder, American Psychiatric Press, Washington, D.C.

Braun, B. G., and Sachs, R. G. (1985). The development of multiple personality disorder: Predisposing, precipitating, and perpetuating factors. In Kluft, R. P. (ed.), The Childhood Antecedents of Multiple Personality, American Psychiatric Press, Washington, D.C.

Carlson, E. B., and Putnam, F. W. (1989). Integrating research in dissociation and hypnotic susceptibility. Are there two pathways to hypnotizability? Dissociation, 2(1), 32–38.

Carlson, E. T. (1986). The history of dissociation until 1880. In Quen, J. M. (ed.), Split Minds Split Brains, New York University Press, New York.

Cattell, J. P. (1972). Depersonalization phenomena. In Arieti, S. (ed.), American Handbook of Psychiatry, Basic Books, New York.

Charcot, J. M., and Marie, P. (1892). On hystereoepilepsy. In Tuke, H. (ed.), A Dictionary of Psychological Medicine, Churchill, London.

Coons, P. M. (1988). Psychophysiologic aspects of multiple personality disorder: A review. Dissociation 1: 47–53.

Coons, P. M., Bowman, E. S., and Milstein, V. (1988). Multiple personality disorder: A clinical investigation of 50 cases. J. Nerv. Ment. Dis. 176: 519–527.

Cooper, L. M., and London, P. (1976). Children's hypnotic susceptibility, personality and EEG patterns. Internatl J. Clin. Hypn. 24: 140–166.

Crabtree, A. (1986). Explanations of dissociation in the first half of the twentieth century. In Quen, J. M. (ed.), Split Minds Split Brains, New York University Press, New York.

Devinsky, O., Putnam, F. W., Grafman, J., Bromfield, E., and Theodore, W. H. (1989). Dissociative states and epilepsy. Neurol, 39, 835–840.

Dor-Shav, K. N. (1978). On the long-range effects of concentration camp internment on Nazi victims: 35 years later. Journal of Consulting and Clinical Psychology. 46:1–11.

Ellenberger, H. F. (1970). The Discovery of the Unconscious: The History and Evolution of Dynamic Psychiatry, Basic Books, New York.

Fagan, J., & McMahon, P. P. (1984). Incipient multiple personality in children. Four cases. J Nerv Ment Dis. 172(1): 26–36.

Frankel, F. H. (1976). Hypnosis: Trance as a Coping Mechanism, Plenum, New York.

Frankel, F. H., Orne, M. T. (1976). Hypnotizability and phobic behavior. Archives of General Psychiatry. 37: 1036–1040.

Friedman, M. J. (1987). Toward rational pharmacotherapy for posttraumatic stress disorder. Am J Psychiatry. 145: 281–285.

Fullerton, D. T., Harvy, R. F., Klein, M. H., Howell, T. (1981). Psychiatric disorders in patients with spinal cord injuries. Archives of General Psychiatry. 38:1369–1371.

Greaves, G. B. (1980). Multiple personality. 165 years after Mary Reynolds. J Nerv Ment Dis. 168(10):577–96.

Haule, J. (1986). Pierre Janet and dissociation: The first transference theory and its origins in hypnosis. American Journal of Clinical Hypnosis. 29: 86–94.

Henderson, J. L., Moore, M. (1944). The psychoneuroses of war. New England Journal of Medicine. 230: 273–279.

Hilgard, E. R. (1973). A neodissociative interpretation of pain reduction in hypnosis. Psychological Review. 80: 396–411.

Hilgard, E. R. (1986). Divided consciousness: Multiple controls in human thought and action (Revised Edition), Wiley, New York.

Hilgard, E. R. and Hilgard, J. R. (1975). Hypnosis in Relief of Pain, William Kaufmann, Inc. Los Altos, Calif.

Hilgard, J. R. (1972) Evidence for a developmental-interactive theory of hypnotic susceptibility. In Fromm, E., Shor, R. E. (eds.) Hypnosis: Research Developments and Perspectives, Chicago, Aldine Atherton.

Jacobson, E. (1977). Depersonalization. Journal of the American Psychoanalytic Association. 7: 581–609.

Janet, P. (1889). L'automatisme psychologique, Pans Balliere, Paris.

Janet, P. (1905). Mental pathology. The Psychological Review. 12: 98–117.

Janet, P. (1925/1976). Psychological healing: A historical and clinical study [Translation of Les Medications Psychologiques, 1925 edition, MacMillian, New York] Arno Press, New York.

Janet, P (1926). The major symptoms of hysteria (2nd Edition), MacMillian, New York.

Janet, P. (1930). Psychological autobiography. In Murchison, C. (ed.), A History of Psychology in Autobiography, vols. 1, Clark University Press, Worcester.

Kanzer, M. (1939). Amnesia: A statistical study. Am J Psychiatry. 96: 711–716.

Kennedy A., and Neville J. (1957). Sudden loss of memory. British Medical Journal. vii: 428–433.

Kiersch, T. A. (1962). Amnesia: A clinical study of ninety-eight cases. Am J Psychiatry. 119: 57–60.

Kihlstrom, J. F. (1984). Conscious, subconscious, unconscious: A cognitive perspective. In Bowers, K. S., Meichenbaum, D. (eds). The Unconscious Reconsidered, Wiley & Sons, New York.

Kluft, R. P. (1982). Varieties of hypnotic intervention in the treatment of multiple personality. Am. J. Clin. Hypn. 26: 73–83.

Kluft, R. P. (1985). Childhood multiple personality disorder: Predictors, clinical findings and treatment results. In Kluft, R. P. (ed.), Childhood Antecedents of Multiple Personality, American Psychiatric Press, Washington, D.C.

Kluft, R. P. (1986). Treating children who have multiple personality disorder. In Braun, B. G. (ed.), Treatment of Multiple Personality Disorder, Washington, D.C., American Psychiatric Press, pp. 79–106.

Kolb, L. C. (1985). The place of narcosynthesis in the treatment of chronic and delayed stress reactions of war. In Sonneberg, S. M., Blank, A. S., and Talbott, J. A. (eds.), The Trauma of War: Stress and Recovery in Vietnam Veterans, American Psychiatric Press, Washington, D.C., pp. 211–226.

Kolb, L. C. (1987). A neuropsychological hypothesis explaining posttraumatic stress disorders. Am. J. Psychiatry. 144: 989–995.

Loewenstein, R. J., Hornstein, N., and Farber, B. (1988). Open trial of Clonazepam in the treatment of posttraumatic stress symptoms in multiple personality disorder. Dissociation, 3: 3–12.

Loewenstein, R. J., and Putnam, F. W. (1989). A comparison study of dissociative *symptoms in patients with complex partial seizures, multiple personality disorder, and posttraumatic stress disorder.* Dissociation. *1(4): 17–23.*

Ludwig, A. M. (1983). *The psychobiological functions of dissociation.* Am. J. Clin. Hypn. *26: 93–99.*

Ludwig, A. M., Brandsma, J. M., Wilbur, C. B., Bendfeldt., F., and Jameson, H. (1972). *The objective study of a multiple personality.* Arch. Gen. Psychiat. *26: 298–310.*

Markowtisch, H. J. (1988). *Transient psychogenic amnesia.* Ital. J. Neurol. Sci. *(Suppl) 9: 49–51.*

Mesulam, M. M. (1981). *Dissociative states with abnormal temporal lobe EEG: Multiple personality and the illusion of possession.* Arch. Neurol. *38: 176–181.*

Nash, M. R., Lynn, S. J., and Givens, D. L. (1984). *Adult hypnotic susceptibility, childhood punishment, and child abuse: A brief communication.* Int. J. Clin. Exp. Hypn. *32: 6–11.*

Nemiah, J. C. (1981). *Dissociative disorders. In Freedman, A. M., and Kaplan, H. I. (eds.),* Comprehensive Textbook of Psychiatry, *(third edition), Williams and Wilkins, Baltimore, pp. 1544–1561.*

Nissen, M. J., Ross, J. L., Willingham, D. B., MacKenzie, T. B., and Schacter, D. L. (1988). *Memory and awareness in a patient with multiple personality disorder.* Brain Cogn. *8: 117–134.*

Nowlis, D. P. (1969). *The child-rearing antecedents of hypnotic susceptibility and of naturally occurring hypnotic-like experiences.* Int. J. Clin. Exp. Hypn. *25: 125–146.*

Noyes, R., and Kletti, R. (1977). *Depersonalization in response to life-threatening danger.* Psychiatry. *18: 375–384.*

Orne, M. T., Dinges, D. F., and Orne, E. C. (1984). *On the differential diagnosis of multiple personality in the forensic context.* Int. J. Clin. Exp. Hypn. *32: 118–169.*

Perry, C., and Laurence, J. R. (1984). *Mental processing outside of awareness: The contributions of Freud and Janet. In Bowers, K. S., and Meichenbaum, D. (eds.),* The Unconscious Reconsidered, *Wiley, New York.*

Pettinati, H. M., Horne, R. L., and Staats, J. M. (1985). *Hypnotizability in patients with anorexia nervosa and bulimia.* Arch. Gen. Psychiat. *42: 1014–1016.*

Pitman, R. K. (1987). *Pierre Janet on obsessive-compulsive disorder (1903).* Arch. Gen. Psychiatry. *44: 226–232.*

Pope, H. G., Hudson, J. I., and Mialet, J. P. (1985). *Bulimia in the late nineteenth century: The observations of Pierre Janet.* Psychol. Med. 15: 739–743.

Putnam, F. W. (1985). Dissociation as a response to extreme trauma. The Childhood Antecedents of Multiple Personality, *American Psychiatric Press, Washington, D.C. pp. 65–98.*

Putnam, F. W. (1986). *The treatment of multiple personality disorder: State of the art. In Braun, B. G. (ed.),* Treatment of Multiple Personality Disorder, *American Psychiatric Press, Washington, D.C., pp. 175–198.*

Putnam, F. W. (1988). *The switch process in multiple personality disorder and other state-change disorders.* Dissociation 1: 24–32.

Putnam, F. W. (1989). Diagnosis and Treatment of Multiple Personality Disorder, *Guilford, New York.*

Putnam, F. W. (1992). *Conversion symptoms. In Joseph, A. B., Young, R. R. (eds).*

Movement Disorders in Neurology and Neuropsychiatry. *Blackwell Scientific Publications, Boston.*

Putnam, F. W., Guroff, J. G., Siberman, E. K., Barban, L., and Post, R. M. *(1986). The clinical phenomenology of multiple personality disorder: Review of 100 recent cases.* J. Clin. Psychiat. *47: 285–293.*

Putnam, F. W., Zahn, T. P., and Post, R. M. *(1990). Differential autonomic nervous system activity in multiple personality disorder.* Psychiat Res. *31: 251–260.*

Rapaport, D. *(1942).* Emotions and Memory *(Menninger Clinic Monograph Series No. 2), Williams and Wilkins, Baltimore.*

Ribot, T. *(1891).* The Diseases of the Personality, *Open Court Publishing, Chicago.*

Riley, R. L., and Mead, J. *(1988). The development of symptoms of multiple personality disorder in a child of three.* Dissociation *1: 41–46.*

Ross, C. A., and Anderson, G. *(1988). Phenomenological overlap of multiple personality disorder and obsessive-compulsive disorder.* J. Nerv. Dis. *176: 295–299.*

Ross, C. A., Heber, S., Anderson, G., Norton, G. R., Anderson, B., del Campo, M., and Pillay, N. *(1989). Differentiating multiple personality disorder and complex partial seizures.* Gen. Hosp. Psychiat. *11: 54–58.*

Ross, C. A., Norton, G. R., and Anderson, G. *(1988). The Dissociative Experiences Scale: A replication study.* Dissociation *1: 21–22.*

Sargent, W., and Slater, E. *(1941). Amnesic syndromes in war.* Proc. Roy. Soc. Med. *34: 757–764.*

Shimizu, M., and Sakamoto, S. *(1986). Depersonalization in adolescence.* Japanese J. Psychiat. Neurol. *40: 603–608.*

Sidtis, J. J. *(1986). Can neurological disconnection account for psychiatric dissociation? In Quen, J. M. (ed.),* Spilt Minds Split Brains, *New York University Press, New York.*

Silberman, E. K., Putnam, F. W., Weingartener, H., Braun, B. G., and Post, R. M. *(1985). Dissociative states in multiple personality disorder: A quantitative study.* Psychiat. Res. *15: 253–260.*

Spanos, N. P., Weekes, J. R., Menary, E., and Bertrand, L. D. *(1986). Hypnotic interview and age regression procedures in the elicitation of multiple personality symptoms: A simulation study.* Psychiatry *49: 298–311.*

Spiegel, D. *(1984). Multiple personality as a post-traumatic stress disorder.* Psychiat. Clin. N. Am. *7: 101–110.*

Spiegel, D. *(1986). Dissociating damage.* Am. J. Clin. Hypn. *29: 123–131.*

Spiegel, D., Hunt, T., and Dondershine, H. E. *(1988). Dissociation and hypnotizability in post-traumatic stress disorder:* Am. J. Psychiat. *145: 301–305.*

Spiegel, H. *(1963). The dissociation-association continuum.* J. Nerv. Ment. Dis. *136: 374–378.*

Stutman, R., and Bliss, E. L. *(1985). The post-traumatic stress disorder (the Vietnam syndrome), hypnotizability and imagery.* American Journal of Psychiatry. *142: 741–743.*

Torch, E. M. *(1981). Depersonalization syndrome: An overview.* Psychiatr. Quart. *53: 249–258.*

Torch, E. M. *(1987). The psychotherapeutic treatment of depersonalization disorder.* Hillside J. Clin. Psychiatry *9: 133–151.*

Torem, M. S. (1986). Dissociative states presenting as an eating disorder. Am. J. Clin. Hypn. *29: 137–142.*

van der Hart, O., and Horst, R. (1989). The dissociation theory of Pierre Janet. J. Traum. Stress *2: 399–414.*

van der Kolk, B. (1987). Psychological Trauma, *American Psychiatric Press, Washington, D.C.*

van der Kolk, B., Blitz, R., Burr, W., Sherry, S., and Hartmann, E. (1984). Nightmares and trauma: A comparison of nightmares after combat with lifelong nightmares in veterans, Am. J. Psychiat. *141: 187–190.*

van der Kolk, B., and Kadish, W. (1987). Amnesia, dissociation, and the return of the repressed. In van der Kolk, B. (ed.). Psychological Trauma, *American Psychiatric Press, Washington, D.C.*

Vanderlinden, J., and Vandereycken, W. (1988). The use of hypnotherapy in the treatment of eating disorders. Int. J. Eating Dis. *7: 381–387.*

Vincent, M., and Pickering, M. R. (1988). Multiple personality disorder in childhood. Can. J. Psychiatry *33: 524–529.*

Weiss, M., Sutton, P. J., and Utecht, A. J. (1985). Multiple personality in a 10-year-old girl. J. Am. Acad. Child Psychiat. *24: 495–501.*

White, R. W., and Shevach, B. J. (1942). Hypnosis and the concept of dissociation. J. Abnorm. Soc. Psychol. *37: 309–328.*

Wolff, P. H. (1987). The Development of Behavioral States and the Expression of Emotions in Early Infancy, *University of Chicago Press, Chicago.*

8. Symptomatology and Management of Acute Grief

Erich Lindemann

AT FIRST GLANCE, acute grief would not seem to be a medical or psychiatric disorder in the strict sense of the word but rather a normal reaction to a distressing situation. However, the understanding of reactions to traumatic experiences, whether or not they represent clear-cut neuroses, has become of ever-increasing importance to the psychiatrist. Bereavement or the sudden cessation of social interaction seems to be of special interest because it is often cited among the alleged psychogenic factors in psychosomatic disorders. The enormous increase in grief reactions due to war casualties, furthermore, demands an evaluation of their probable effect on the mental and physical health of our population.

The points to be made in this paper are as follows:

1. Acute grief is a definite syndrome with psychological and somatic symptomatology.
2. This syndrome may appear immediately after a crisis; it may be delayed; it may be exaggerated or apparently absent.
3. In place of the typical syndrome there may appear distorted pictures, each of which represents one special aspect of the grief syndrome.
4. By appropriate techniques these distorted pictures can be successfully transformed into a normal grief reaction with resolution.

Our observations comprise 101 patients. Included are 1) psychoneurotic patients who lost a relative during the course of treatment, 2) relatives of patients who died in the hospital, 3) bereaved disaster victims (Cocoanut Grove Fire) and their close relatives, 4) relatives of members of the armed forces.

The investigation consisted of a series of psychiatric interviews. Both the

Reprinted from *American Journal of Psychiatry*, 101, 141–148. Copyright © 1944 by the American Psychiatric Association.

timing and the content of the discussions were recorded. These records were subsequently analysed in terms of the symptoms reported and of the changes in mental status observed progressively through a series of interviews. The psychiatrist avoided all suggestions and interpretations until the picture of symptomatology and spontaneous reaction tendencies of the patients had become clear from the records. The somatic complaints offered important leads for objective study. Careful laboratory work on spirograms, g.-i. functions, and metabolic studies are in progress and will be reported separately. At present we wish to present only our psychological observations.

SYMPTOMATOLOGY OF NORMAL GRIEF

The picture shown by persons in acute grief is remarkably uniform. Common to all is the following syndrome: sensations of somatic distress occurring in waves lasting from twenty minutes to an hour at a time, a feeling of tightness in the throat, choking with shortness of breath, need for sighing, and an empty feeling in the abdomen, lack of muscular power, and an intense subjective distress described as tension or mental pain. The patient soon learns that these waves of discomfort can be precipitated by visits, by mentioning the deceased, and by receiving sympathy. There is a tendency to avoid the syndrome at any cost, to refuse visits lest they should precipitate the reaction, and to keep deliberately from thought all references to the deceased.

The striking features are 1) the marked tendency to sighing respiration; this respiratory disturbance was most conspicuous when the patient was made to discuss his grief. 2) The complaint about lack of strength and exhaustion is universal and is described as follows: "It is almost impossible to climb up a stairway." "Everything I lift seems so heavy." "The slightest effort makes me feel exhausted." "I can't walk to the corner without feeling exhausted." 3) Digestive symptoms are described as follows: "The food tastes like sand." "I have no appetite at all." "I stuff the food down because I have to eat." "My saliva won't flow." "My abdomen feels hollow." "Everything seems slowed up in my stomach."

The sensorium is generally somewhat altered. There is commonly a slight sense of unreality, a feeling of increased emotional distance from other people (sometimes they appear shadowy or small), and there is intense preoccupation with the image of the deceased. A patient who lost his daughter in the Cocoanut Grove disaster visualized his girl in the telephone booth calling for him and was much troubled by the loudness with which his name was called by her and was so vividly preoccupied with the scene that he became oblivious of his surroundings. A young navy pilot lost a close friend; he remained a vivid part of his imagery, not in terms of a religious survival but in terms of an imaginary companion. He ate with him and talked over problems with him, for instance, discussing with him his plan of joining the Air Corps. Up to the time of the study, six months later, he denied the fact that the boy was no longer with him. Some patients are much concerned about this aspect of their grief reaction because they feel it indicates approaching insanity.

Another strong preoccupation is with feelings of guilt. The bereaved searches the time before the death for evidence of failure to do right by the lost one. He accuses himself of negligence and exaggerates minor omissions. After the fire disaster the central topic of discussion for a young married woman was the fact that her husband died after he left her following a quarrel, and of a young man whose wife died that he fainted too soon to save her.

In addition, there is often disconcerting loss of warmth in relationship to other people, a tendency to respond with irritability and anger, a wish not to be bothered by others at a time when friends and relatives make a special effort to keep up friendly relationships.

These feelings of hostility, surprising and quite inexplicable to the patients, disturbed them and again were often taken as signs of approaching insanity. Great efforts are made to handle them, and the result is often a formalized, stiff manner of social interaction.

The activity throughout the day of the severely bereaved person shows remarkable changes. There is no retardation of action and speech; quite to the contrary, there is a push of speech, especially when talking about the deceased. There is restlessness, inability to sit still, moving about in an aimless fashion, continually searching for something to do. There is, however, at the same time, a painful lack of capacity to initiate and maintain organized patterns of activity. What is done is done with lack of zest, as though one were going through the motions. The bereaved clings to the daily routine of prescribed activities; but these activities do not proceed in the automatic, self-sustaining fashion which characterizes normal work but have to be carried on with effort, as though each fragment of the activity became a special task. The bereaved is surprised to find how large a part of his customary activity was done in some meaningful relationship to the deceased and has now lost its significance. Especially the habits of social interaction—meeting friends, making conversation, sharing enterprises with others—seem to have been lost. This loss leads to a strong dependency on anyone who will stimulate the bereaved to activity and serve as the initiating agent.

These five points—1) somatic distress, 2) preoccupation with the image of the deceased, 3) guilt, 4) hostile reactions, and 5) loss of patterns of conduct—seem to be pathognomonic for grief. There may be added a sixth characteristic, shown by patients who border on pathological reactions, which is not so conspicuous as the others but nevertheless often striking enough to color the whole picture. This is the appearance of traits of the deceased in the behavior of the bereaved, especially symptoms shown during the last illness, or behavior which may have been shown at the time of the tragedy. A bereaved person is observed or finds himself walking in the manner of his deceased father. He looks in the mirror and believes that his face appears just like that of the deceased. He may show a change of interests in the direction of the former activities of the deceased and may start enterprises entirely different from his former pursuits. A wife who lost her husband, an insurance agent, found herself writing to many insurance companies offering her services with somewhat exaggerated schemes. It seemed a regular observation in these patients that the painful preoccupation with the image of the deceased described above was transformed into preoccupation with symptoms or personality traits of the lost person, but now displaced to their own bodies and activities by identification.

COURSE OR NORMAL GRIEF REACTIONS

The duration of a grief reaction seems to depend upon the success with which a person does the *grief work*, namely, emancipation from the bondage to the deceased, readjustment to the environment in which the deceased is missing, and the formation of new relationships. One of the big obstacles to this work seems to be the fact that many patients try to avoid the intense distress connected with the grief experience and to avoid the expression of emotion necessary for it. The men victims after the Cocoanut Grove fire appeared in the early psychiatric interviews to be in a state of tension with tightened facial musculature, unable to relax for fear they might "break down." It required considerable persuasion to yield to the grief process before they were willing to accept the discomfort of bereavement. One assumed a hostile attitude toward the psychiatrist, refusing to allow any references to the deceased and rather rudely asking him to leave. This attitude remained throughout his stay on the ward, and the prognosis for his condition is not good in the light of other observations. Hostility of this sort was encountered on only occasional visits with the other patients. They became willing to accept the grief process and to embark on a program of dealing in memory with the deceased person. As soon as this became possible there seemed to be a rapid relief of tension and the subsequent interviews were rather animated conversations in which the deceased was idealized and in which misgivings about the future adjustment were worked through.

Examples of the psychiatrist's rôle in assisting patients in their readjustment after bereavement are contained in the following case histories. The first shows a very successful readjustment.

A woman, aged 40, lost her husband in the fire. She had a history of good adjustment previously. One child, ten years old. When she heard about her husband's death she was extremely depressed, cried bitterly, did not want to live, and for three days showed a state of utter dejection.

When seen by the psychiatrist, she was glad to have assistance and described her painful preoccupation with memories of her husband and her fear that she might lose her mind. She had a vivid visual image of his presence, picturing him as going to work in the morning and herself as wondering whether he would return in the evening, whether she could stand his not returning, then, describing to herself how he does return, plays with the dog, receives his child, and gradually tried to accept the fact that he is not there any more. It was only after ten days that she succeeded in accepting his loss and then only after having described in detail the remarkable qualities of her husband, the tragedy of his having to stop his activities at the pinnacle of his success, and his deep devotion to her.

In the subsequent interviews she explained with some distress that she had become very much attached to the examiner and that she waited for the hour of his coming. This reaction she considered disloyal to her husband but at the same time she could accept the fact that it was a hopeful sign of her ability to fill the gap he had left in her life. She then showed a marked drive for activity, making plans for supporting herself and her little girl, mapping out the preliminary steps for resuming her old profession as secretary, and making efforts to secure help from the occupational therapy department in reviewing her knowledge of French.

Her convalescence, both emotional and somatic, progressed smoothly, and she made a good adjustment immediately on her return home.

A man of 52, successful in business, lost his wife, with whom he had lived in happy marriage. The information given him about his wife's death confirmed his suspicions of several days. He responded with a severe grief reaction, with which he was unable to cope. He did not want to see visitors, was ashamed of breaking down, and asked to be permitted to stay in the hospital on the psychiatric service, when his physical condition would have permitted his discharge, because he wanted further assistance. Any mention of his wife produced a severe wave of depressive reaction, but with psychiatric assistance he gradually become willing to go through this painful process, and after three days on the psychiatric service he seemed well enough to go home.

He showed a high rate of verbal activity, was restless, needed to be occupied continually, and felt that the experience had whipped him into a state of restless overactivity.

As soon as he returned home he took an active part in his business, assuming a post in which he had a great many telephone calls. He also took over the rôle of amateur psychiatrist to another bereaved person, spending time with him and comforting him for his loss. In his eagerness to start anew, he developed a plan to sell all his former holdings, including his house, his furniture, and giving away anything which could remind him of his wife. Only after considerable discussion was he able to see that this would mean avoiding immediate grief at the price of an act of poor judgment. Again he had to be encouraged to deal with his grief reactions in a more direct manner. He has made a good adjustment.

With eight to ten interviews in which the psychiatrist shares the grief work, and with a period of from four to six weeks, it was ordinarily possible to settle an uncomplicated and undistorted grief reaction. This was the case in all but one of the 13 Cocoanut Grove fire victims.

MORBID GRIEF REACTIONS

Morbid grief reactions represent distortions of normal grief. The conditions mentioned here were transformed into "normal reactions" and then found their resolution.

a. Delay of Reaction— The most striking and most frequent reaction of this sort is *delay* or *postponement*. If the bereavement occurs at a time when the patient is confronted with important tasks and when there is necessity for maintaining the morale of others, he may show little or no reaction for weeks or even much longer. A brief delay is described in the following example.

A girl of 17 lost both parents and her boy friend in the fire and was herself burned severely, with marked involvement of the lungs. Throughout her stay in the hospital her attitude was that of cheerful acceptance without any sign of adequate distress. When she was discharged at the end of the three weeks she appeared cheerful, talked rapidly, with a considerable flow of ideas, seemed eager to return home and assume the rôle of parent for her two younger siblings. Except for slight feelings of "lonesomeness" she complained of no distress.

This period of griefless acceptance continued for the next two months, even when the household was dispersed and her younger siblings were placed in other homes. Not until the end of the tenth week did she begin to show a true state of grief with marked feelings of depression, intestinal emptiness, tightness in her throat, frequent crying, and vivid preoccupation with her deceased parents.

That this delay may involve years became obvious first by the fact that patients in acute bereavement about a recent death may soon upon exploration be found preoccupied with grief about a person who died many years ago. In this manner a woman of 38, whose mother had died recently and who had responded to the mother's death with a surprisingly severe reaction, was found to be but mildly concerned with her mother's death but deeply engrossed with unhappy and perplexing fantasies concerning the death of her brother, who had died twenty years ago under dramatic circumstances from metastasizing carcinoma after amputation of his arm had been postponed too long. The discovery that a former unresolved grief reaction may be precipitated in the course of the discussion of another recent event was soon demonstrated in psychiatric interviews by patients who showed all the traits of a true grief reaction when the topic of a former loss arose.

The precipitating factor for the delayed reaction may be a deliberate recall of circumstances surrounding the death or may be a spontaneous occurrence in the patient's life. A peculiar form of this is the circumstance that a patient develops the grief reaction at the time when he himself is as old as the person who died. For instance, a railroad worker, aged 42, appeared in the psychiatric clinic with a picture which was undoubtedly a grief reaction for which he had no explanation. It turned out that when he was 22, his mother, then 42, had committed suicide.

b. Distorted Reactions— The delayed reactions may occur after an interval which was not marked by any abnormal behavior or distress, but in which there developed an *alteration* in the patient's *conduct* perhaps not conspicuous or serious enough to lead him to a psychiatrist. These alterations may be considered as the surface manifestations of an unresolved grief reaction, which may respond to fairly simple and quick psychiatric management if recognized. They may be classified as follows: 1) *overactivity without a sense of loss*, rather with a sense of well-being and zest, the activities being of an expansive and adventurous nature and bearing semblance to the activities formerly carried out by the deceased, as described above; 2) *the acquisition of symptoms belonging to the last illness of the deceased.* This type of patient appears in medical clinics and is often labeled hypochondriasis or hysteria. To what extent actual alterations of physiological functions occur under these circumstances will have to be a field of further careful inquiry. I owe to Dr. Chester Jones a report about a patient whose electrocardiogram showed a definite change during a period of three weeks, which started two weeks after the time her father died of heart disease.

While this sort of symptom formation "by identification" may still be considered as conversion symptoms such as we know from hysteria, there is another type of disorder doubtlessly presenting 3) a recognized *medical disease*, namely, a group of psychosomatic conditions, predominately ulcerative colitis, rheumatoid arthritis, and asthma. Extensive studies in ulcerative colitis have produced evidence that 33 out of 41 patients with ulcerative colitis developed their disease in close time relationship to the loss of an important person. Indeed, it was this observation which first gave the impetus for the present detailed study of grief. Two of the patients developed bloody diarrhea at funerals. In the others it developed within a few weeks after the loss. The course of the ulcerative colitis was strikingly benefited when this grief reaction was resolved by psychiatric technique.

At the level of social adjustment there often occurs a conspicuous 4) *alteration in relationship to friends and relatives* The patient feels irritable, does not want to be bothered, avoids former social activities, and is afraid he might antagonize his friends by his lack of interest and his critical attitudes. Progressive social isolation follows, and the patient needs considerable encouragement in re-establishing his social relationships.

While overflowing hostility appears to be spread out over all relationships, it may also occur as 5) *furious hostility against specific persons*; the doctor or the surgeon are accused bitterly for neglect of duty and the patient may assume that foul play has led to the death. It is characteristic that while patients talk a good deal about their suspicions and their bitter feelings, they are not likely to take any action against the accused, as a truly paranoid person might do.

6) Many bereaved persons struggled with much effort against these feelings of hostility, which to them seem absurd, representing a vicious change in their characters and to be hidden as much as possible. Some patients succeed in hiding their hostility but become wooden and formal, with affectivity and conduct *resembling schizophrenic pictures*. A typical report is this, "I go through all the motions of living. I look after my children. I do my errands. I go to social functions, but it is like being in a play; it doesn't really concern me. I can't have any warm feelings. If I were to have any feelings at all I would be angry with everybody." This patient's reaction to therapy was characterized by growing hostility against the therapist, and it required considerable skill to make her continue interviews in spite of the disconcerting hostility which she had been fighting so much. The absence of emotional display in this patient's face and actions was quite striking. Her face had a mask-like appearance, her movements were formal, stilted, robot-like, without the fine play of emotional expression.

7) Closely related to this picture is a *lasting loss of patterns of social interaction*. The patient cannot initiate any activity, is full of eagerness to be active—restless, can't sleep—but throughout the day he will not start any activity unless "primed" by somebody else. He will be grateful at sharing

activities with others but will not be able to make up his mind to do anything alone. The picture is one of lack of decision and initiative. Organized activities along social lines occur only if a friend takes the patient along and shares the activity with him. Nothing seems to promise reward; only the ordinary activities of the day are carried on, and these in a routine manner, falling apart into small steps, each of which has to be carried out with much effort and without zest.

8) There is, in addition, a picture in which a patient is active but in which most of his activities attain a coloring which is *detrimental to his own social and economic existence*. Such patients with uncalled for generosity, give away their belongings, are easily lured into foolish economic dealings, lose their friends and professional standing by a series of "stupid acts," and find themselves finally without family, friends, social status or money. This protracted self-punitive behavior seems to take place without any awareness of excessive feelings of guilt. It is a particularly distressing grief picture because it is likely to hurt other members of the family and drag down friends and business associates.

9) This leads finally to the picture in which the grief reaction takes the form of a straight *agitated depression* with tension, agitation, insomnia, feelings of worthlessness, bitter self-accusation, and obvious need for punishment. Such patients may be dangerously suicidal.

A young man aged 32 had received only minor burns and left the hospital apparently well on the road to recovery just before the psychiatric survey of the disaster victims took place. On the fifth day he had learned that his wife had died. He seemed somewhat relieved of his worry about her fate; impressed the surgeon as being unusually well-controlled during the following short period of his stay in the hospital.

On January 1st he was returned to the hospital by his family. Shortly after his return home he had become restless, did not want to stay at home, had taken a trip to relatives trying to find rest, had not succeeded, and had returned home in a state of marked agitation, appearing preoccupied, frightened, and unable to concentrate on any organized activity. The mental status presented a somewhat unusual picture. He was restless, could not sit still or participate in any activity on the ward. He would try to read, drop it after a few minutes, or try to play pingpong, give it up after a short time. He would try to start conversations, break them off abruptly, and then fall into repeated murmured utterances: "Nobody can help me. When is it going to happen? I am doomed, am I not?" With great effort it was possible to establish enough rapport to carry on interviews. He complained about his feeling of extreme tension, inability to breathe, generalized weakness and exhaustion, and his frantic fear that something terrible was going to happen. "I'm destined to live in insanity or I must die. I know that it is God's will. I have this awful feeling of guilt." With intense morbid guilt feelings, he reviewed incessantly the events of the fire. His wife had stayed behind.

When he tried to pull her out, he had fainted and was shoved out by the crowd. She was burned while he was saved. "I should have saved her or I should have died too." He complained about being filled with an incredible violence and did not know what to do about it. The rapport established with him lasted for only brief periods of time. He then would fall back into his state of intense agitation and muttering. He slept poorly even with large sedation. In the course of four days he became somewhat more composed, had longer periods of contact with the psychiatrist, and seemed to feel that he was being understood and might be able to cope with his morbid feelings of guilt and violent impulses. On the sixth day of his hospital stay, however, after skillfully distracting the attention of his special nurse, he jumped through a closed window to a violent death.

If the patient is not conspicuously suicidal, it may nevertheless be true that he has a strong desire for painful experiences, and such patients are likely to desire shock treatment of some sort, which they picture as a cruel experience, such as electrocution might be.

A 28-year-old woman, whose 20 months-old son was accidentally smothered developed a state of severe agitated depression with self-accusation, inability to enjoy anything, hopelessness about the future, overflow of hostility against the husband and his parents, also with excessive hostility against the psychiatrist. She insisted upon electric-shock treatment and was finally referred to another physician who treated her. She responded to the shock treatments very well and felt relieved of her sense of guilt.

It is remarkable that agitated depressions of this sort represent only a small fraction of the pictures of grief in our series.

PROGNOSTIC EVALUATION

Our observations indicate that to a certain extent the type and severity of the grief reaction can be predicted. Patients with obsessive personality make-up and with a history of former depressions are likely to develop an agitated depression. Severe reactions seem to occur in mothers who have lost young children. The intensity of interaction with the deceased before his death seems to be significant. It is important to realize that such interaction does not have to be of the affectionate type; on the contrary, the death of a person who invited much hostility, especially hostility which could not well be expressed because of his status and claim to loyalty, may be followed by a severe grief reaction in which hostile impulses are the most conspicuous feature. Not infrequently the person who passed away represented a key person in a social system, his death being followed by disintegration of this social system and by a profound alteration of the living and social conditions for the bereaved.

In such cases readjustment presents a severe task quite apart from the reaction to the loss incurred. All these factors seem to be more important than a tendency to react with neurotic symptoms in previous life. In this way the most conspicuous forms of morbid identification were found in persons who had no former history of a tendency to psychoneurotic reactions.

MANAGEMENT

Proper psychiatric management of grief reactions may prevent prolonged and serious alterations in the patient's social adjustment, as well as potential medical disease. The essential task facing the psychiatrist is that of sharing the patient's grief work, namely, his efforts at extricating himself from the bondage to the deceased and at finding new patterns of rewarding interaction. It is of the greatest importance to notice that not only over-reaction but under-reaction of the bereaved must be given attention, because delayed responses may occur at unpredictable moments and the dangerous distortions of the grief reaction, not conspicuous at first, be quite destructive later and these may be prevented.

Religious agencies have led in dealing with the bereaved. They have provided comfort by giving the backing of dogma to the patient's wish for continued interaction with the deceased, have developed rituals which maintain the patient's interaction with others, and have counteracted the morbid guilt feelings of the patient by Divine Grace and by promising an opportunity for "making up" to the deceased at the time of a later reunion. While these measures have helped countless mourners, comfort alone does not provide adequate assistance in the patient's grief work. He has to accept the pain of the bereavement. He has to review his relationships with the deceased, and has to become acquainted with the alterations in his own modes of emotional reaction. His fear of insanity, his fear of accepting the surprising changes in his feelings, especially the overflow of hostility, have to be worked through. He will have to express his sorrow and sense of loss. He will have to find an acceptable formulation of his future relationship to the deceased. He will have to verbalize his feelings of guilt, and he will have to find persons around him whom he can use as "primers" for the acquisition of new patterns of conduct. All this can be done in eight to ten interviews.

Special techniques are needed if hostility is the most marked feature of the grief reaction. The hostility may be directed against the psychiatrist, and the patient will have such guilt over his hostility that he will avoid further interviews. The help of a social worker or a minister, or if these are not available, a member of the family, to urge the patient to continue coming to see the psychiatrist may be indispensable. If the tension and the depressive features are too great, a combination of benzedrine sulphate, 5–10 mgm. b.i.d., and sodium amytal, 3 gr. before retiring, may be useful in first reducing emotional distress to a tolerable degree. Severe agitated depressive reactions may defy all efforts of psychotherapy and may respond well to shock treatment.

Since it is obvious that not all bereaved persons, especially those suffering because of war casualties, can have the benefit of expert psychiatric help, much of this knowledge will have to be passed on to auxiliary workers. Social workers and ministers will have to be on the look-out for the more ominous pictures, referring these to the psychiatrist while assisting the more normal reactions themselves.

ANTICIPATORY GRIEF REACTIONS

While our studies were at first limited to reactions to actual death, it must be understood that grief reactions are just one form of separation reactions. Separation by death is characterized by its irreversibility and finality. Separation may, of course, occur for other reasons. We were at first surprised to find genuine grief reactions in patients who had not experienced a bereavement but who had experienced separation, for instance with the departure of a member of the family into the armed forces. Separation in this case is not due to death but is under the threat of death. A common picture hitherto not appreciated is a syndrome which we have designated *anticipatory grief.* The patient is so concerned with her adjustment after the potential death of father or son that she goes through all the phases of grief—depression, heightened preoccupation with the departed, a review of all the forms of death which might befall him, and anticipation of the modes of readjustment which might be necessitated by it. While this reaction may well form a safeguard against the impact of a sudden death notice, it can turn out to be of a disadvantage at the occasion of reunion. Several instances of this sort came to our attention when a soldier just returned from the battlefront complained that his wife did not love him any more and demanded immediate divorce. In such situations apparently the grief work had been done so effectively that the patient has emancipated herself and the readjustment must now be directed towards new interaction. It is important to know this because many family disasters of this sort may be avoided through prophylactic measures.

BIBLIOGRAPHY

Many of the observations are, of course, not entirely new. Delayed reactions were described by Helene Deutsch (1). Shock treatment in agitated depressions due to bereavement has recently been advocated by Myerson (2). Morbid identification has been stressed at many points in the psychoanalytic literature and recently by H. A. Murray (3). The relation of mourning and depressive psychoses has been discussed by Freud (4), Melanie Klein (5), and Abraham (6). Bereavement reactions in wartime were discussed by Wilson (7). The reactions after the Cocoanut Grove fire were described in some detail in a chapter of the monograph on this civilian disaster (8). The effect of wartime separations was reported by Rosenbaum (9). The incidence of grief reactions among the psychogenic factors in asthma and rheumatoid arthritis has been mentioned by Cobb *et al.* (10, 11).

1. *Deutsch, Helene. Absence of grief. Psychoanalyt Quart., 6:12, 1937.*
2. *Myerson, Abraham. The use of shock therapy in prolonged grief reactions. New England J. Med., 230:9, Mar. 2, 1944.*
3. *Murray, H. A. Visual manifestations of personality. Jr. Abn. & Social Psychol., 32:161–184, 1937.*
4. *Freud, Sigmund. Mourning and melancholia. Collected Papers IV, 152– 170; 288–317.*
5. *Klein, Melanie. Mourning and its relation to manic-depressive states. Internat. J. Psychoan., 21:125–153, 1940.*
6. *Abraham, C. Notes on the psycho-analytical investigation and treatment of the libido, viewed in the light of mental disorder. Selected Papers of Carl Abraham. New York: Int. Univ. Press, 1940.*
7. *Wilson, A. T. M. Reactive emotional disorders. Practitioner, 146: 254–258.*
8. *Cobb, S., & Lindemann, E. Neuropsychiatric observations after the Cocoanut Grove fire. Ann. Surg., June 1943.*
9. *Rosenbaum, Milton. Emotional aspects of wartime separations. Family, 24:337– 341, 1944.*
10. *Cobb, S., Bauer, W., and Whitney, I. Environmental factors in rheumatoid arthritis. J.A.M.A., 113:668–670, 1939.*
11. *McDermott, N., and Cobb, S. Psychogenic factors in asthma. Psychosom. Med., 1:204–341, 1939.*

9. Psychiatric Reactions to Disaster

The Mount St. Helens Experience

James H. Shore, Ellie L. Tatum, and
William M. Vollmer

THE VOLCANIC ERUPTION of Mount St. Helens on May 18, 1980, focused on national attention on the magnitude of the geological phenomena and created a human disaster of significant proportion. The pyroplastic eruption, flooding, and explosion of volcanic ash into the atmosphere have been studied extensively to assess their environmental impact on human health. Although more than 50 people lost their lives in the major eruption, the potential for subsequent eruption and flooding gave a dual aspect to this disaster and posed an ongoing long-term threat to human health. The public health reports focused on immediate disaster planning, autopsy findings, emergency services, and potential pulmonary effects (1–5). In this paper we present the initial psychiatric findings of a community-based study of the Mount St. Helens experience. This study represents the first application of a new criterion-based diagnostic method in the study of human reactions to the stress resulting from a major disaster. The results address long-standing controversies in this field.

There have been several comprehensive reviews of the psychological consequences of natural disasters (6–8). We also reviewed this literature with selected studies from the Mount St. Helens disaster (9). These articles summarize the findings of major disaster studies and highlight the methodological limitations of previous studies. Leivesley (10) identified three major difficulties in disaster research: a wide variation in sampling, observation, and nomenclature; significant variation in types of disasters occurring in many cultures; and different interpretations applied to the same data.

In addition, there have been at least three major interpretive approaches to disaster research. First, the psychiatric approach has attempted to define the

Reprinted from *American Journal of Psychiatry*, 143, 590–595. Copyright © 1986 by the American Psychiatric Association.

extent to which disaster victims have suffered from significant mental illness. Another viewpoint, held primarily by sociologists, has focused on behavioral response to disaster as a group process and social adaptation to disaster stress, assuming minimal negative mental health consequences to individuals. A third approach has emphasized the disruption of interpersonal and social linkages and the use of support systems in response and recovery. Quarantelli, from the disease research center at Ohio State University, has been an articulate spokesman for the sociological view. He has argued that "the individual trauma approach [psychiatric] still assumes that disaster victims respond primarily to the disaster agent or its immediate effect and [investigators] have not fully seen that the surrounding social context is by far the most important factor" (11).

We agree that the surrounding social context and interpersonal networks are important variables. However, the sociological view discounts the importance of individual psychiatric impairment and morbidity. Our findings of psychiatric reactions to the Mount St. Helens disaster provide new data in this controversy and emphasize the significance of stress-induced psychiatric disorder among disaster victims.

METHOD

The Sample

The study included two rural Northwest logging communities. Castle Rock, Wash., and the adjoining Toutle River Valley were affected severely by the Mount St. Helens eruption and flood. This area served as our exposed community. Estacada, Ore., and the surrounding Eagle Creek neighborhood were chosen as a comparable control community. The sampling procedure included several steps. First, residence lists for both communities were compiled from a variety of sources. For the exposed community we also had access to a property damage survey following the May 1980 eruption. To maximize the number of disaster victims in the study, we stratified the sample from our exposed community to include all households with property damage. A systematic random sample was taken of the remaining households. For the control community the subjects consisted of a systematic random sample of all households. A single respondent was selected from each household using a sampling scheme designed to provide to provide an age and sex distribution which would approximate that of the total population (12). All respondents were required to be between the ages of 18 and 79 years, Caucasian, and continuously residing in the study area since May 18, 1980. Only single-family or noninstitutional small group residences were included.

Initial contact with potential households was guided by a protocol that required multiple attempts at contact both by telephone and in the field. Overall, 81.4% (N=2,152) of all households selected for screening were contacted. The contact rates for the Oregon and Washington samples were comparable with the exception of the property-damage group, where contact was more efficient (96.1%, N=128). The greater efficiency of contact among households with property damage reflects both a real difference in the composition of this group and the different manner in which the sampling list for this group was derived. Among eligible individuals who were contacted, compliance rates were virtually identical (76%–78%, N = 1,257) among the three sampling groups. Comparison with available census data indicates that our samples underrepresented the younger, single, and lower socioeconomic status individuals to a similar degree for both of the communities.

Interviews were conducted between July 1 and October 31, 1983–38 to 42 months after the disaster. After our initial interviews were completed, we identified all individuals who reported either significant residential damage (a total dollar loss of at least $5,000) or the death of a family member or other relative due to the Mount St. Helens eruption. To further increase the disaster group, we then attempted to interview a member of the opposite sex in all such households having at least two eligible adults. This resulted in an additional 60 subjects, giving a total sample size of 1,025. We divided the subjects into three groups—high exposure, low exposure, and control—on the basis of information obtained from their questionnaires. Specifically, the 138 subjects who suffered at least $5,000 in property loss or the death of a family member or close relative were defined as the high-exposure. The remaining 410 subjects in the exposed community were classified as the low-exposure group, and the 477 Oregon subjects constituted the control group. Thus, the classification of subjects from the disaster community into high-or low-exposure groups was based on major criteria. We were able to externally validate these criteria for approximately 80% of the subjects through examination of tax assessor records or interview with the subject's spouse.

The mean ± SD ages for the control, low-exposure, and high-exposure groups were 45 ± 15, 45 ± 16, and 47 ± 13 years, respectively. Other characteristics of the sample are presented in table 9.1. Overall, the control and low-exposure groups were comparable with respect to sociodemographic makeup. One exception was employment status: more Oregon than Washington subjects were unemployed. In contrast with these two groups, the high-

Table 9.1. Characteristics of a Control Group and Subjects Exposed to the Mount St. Helens Disaster

	Control subjects (n = 477)		Subjects exposed to disaster			
			Low exposure (n = 410)		High exposure (n = 138)	
Characteristic	N	%	N	%	N	%
Sex						
Male	238	50	213	52	61	44
Female	239	50	197	48	77	56
Marital status						
Married	358	75	328	80	124	90
Widowed, separated, or divorced	81	17	49	12	11	8
Never married	38	8	33	8	3	2
Household socioeconomic status[a]						
High	105	22	66	16	32	23
Medium	200	42	168	41	51	37
Low	172	36	176	43	55	40
Unemployment rate						
Men	43	9	25	6	8	6
Women	33	7	25	6	7	5
Evacuated on May 18, 1980	5	1[b]	144	35	97	70
Any residence damage	0	0	53	13	81	59
Residence severely damaged or destroyed	0	0	0	0	55	40[c]

[a] By Hollingshead scale: high = 1 and 2, medium = 3, low = 4 and 5.
[b] Five control subjects indicated that they "left the area they were in at the time of the disaster [May 18, 1980] for reasons of safety."
[c] Loss of over 33% of dollar value of house.

exposure group was older, more affluent, and more likely to be married. The larger proportion of women in the high-exposure group does not reflect a real difference in the makeup of the high-exposure population but rather resulted from an altered sampling protocol during the initial weeks of screening.

Additional information in table 9.1 further describes the nature of the impact of the disaster in the high-and low-exposure groups. A much larger proportion of the high-exposure subjects reported some damage to their primary residence; the median dollar loss to either residence or other property was $40,000–$60,000. The impact in the low-exposure group was much less severe; only a small proportion reported damage to their primary residence, and there was little dollar loss reported. This information further supports the notion of the low-exposure group as an intermediate-exposure group and not merely as a second, unaffected control sample.

Procedure

The field interview research instrument was developed to address multiple variables in the study of psychiatric disorder and disaster stress. The variables studied with individual components of the research questionnaire included past and present mental health status, physical health history, sociodemographic and occupational status, support networks, the perception of the threat of and the impact of the disaster, sense of psychological well-being, present state symptoms at the time of the field interview, and use of recovery assistance services. The subjects' mental health status was measured with the Diagnostic Interview Schedule (13) and four subscales of the Symptom Checklist-90 SCL-90) (14).

The Diagnostic Interview Schedule was developed by selected universities through support from the National Institute of Mental Health. It is a structured interview patterned after *DSM-III* and is designed for administration by trained paraprofessionals. This new method allows broad application of criterion-based diagnostic assessment for the study of psychiatric epidemiology. Findings from the Diagnostic Interview Schedule have recently been reported from three community-wide studies as part of the national epidemiology catchment area project (15). In the development of our research methodology for the Mount St. Helens disaster, we incorporated the Diagnostic Interview Schedule as the first application of this new technique to a disaster community.

The onset and prevalence rates of disaster-related psychiatric disorders reported for our two Washington groups represent simple averages from among the low-and high-exposure subjects. More sophisticated estimation procedures using stratification weights led to essentially the same results. Statistical methods for comparing onset rates included both logistic regression and a chi-square test for trend in proportions. All analyses were stratified by sex. Information from the Diagnostic Interview Schedule data was generated with a computer program supplied by Washington University in St. Louis. Eighteen field interviewers underwent an intensive 2-week training session and successfully demonstrated their mastery of the interview protocol, especially the Diagnostic Interview Schedule. The interrater reliability for case rating with the schedule was demonstrated with a kappa of .93.

RESULTS

Using age-at-onset data obtained through the Diagnostic Interview Schedule, we calculated the postdisaster onset rates for primary psychiatric disorders in the exposed and control communities. We identified three psychiatric disorders that showed marked exposure-related onset patterns following the volcanic eruption. These three were single-episode depression, generalized anxiety disorder, and Mount St. Helens-related posttraumatic stress disorder. They will be referred to as the Mount St. Helens disorders. Figure 9.1 shows cumulative lifetime prevalence rates for the Mount St. Helens disorders for men and women in the 10 years preceding the research interview. The prevalence at any given point—for example, 4 years before the interview—represents the proportion of subjects who, 4 years earlier, would have reported a

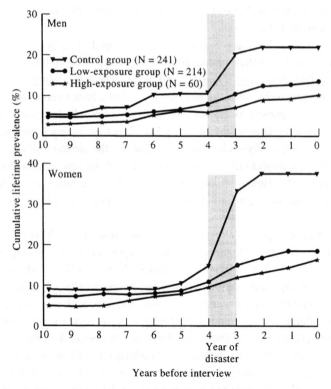

Figure 9.1. Lifetime Prevalence of Single-Episode Depression, Generalized Anxiety Disorder, and Posttraumatic Stress Disorder in Men and Women before and after the Mount St. Helens Disaster

history of one of the Mount St. Helens disorders. Thus, by definition, these are nondecreasing curves. Since the major eruption had occurred, on average, 3 years and 4 months before the interview, we would expect that most of the disaster-related effects if they existed) would appear at the 3-year point. The prevalence rates demonstrate that this is precisely what happened. Both men and women displayed a statistically significant "dose-response" onset pattern in the period between 3 and 4 years before the interview (table 9.2). For men these onset rates ranged from 0.9% in the control sample to 11.1% in the high-exposure group. Among women the differences were even more pronounced, with rates ranging from 1.9% to 20.9%. In subsequent years the rate of onset in the high-exposure group dropped sharply. Two years following the eruption, no new cases were observed in this high-exposure group.

When we further stratified our analysis by age, employment status, physical health history, and a number of other variables, we consistently found this dose-response pattern among all subgroups. In addition, we tested to see if the disaster response was different for individuals experiencing bereavement versus other forms of loss. In our definition of high exposure we included respondents who suffered a major property loss and those who lost a family member or other relative. There were 15 subjects in the latter category, half of whom also reported major property damage. An additional 65 subjects reported the death of a friend due to the Mount St. Helens eruption. Among this latter group, 12 were classified as high-exposure, 50 as low-exposure,

Table 9.2. Rates of Single-Episode Depression, Generalized Anxiety Disorder, and Posttraumatic Stress Disorder in Men and Women after the Mount St. Helens Disaster

Group	N^a	Subjects with Disorders after the Disaster[b]			
		First year		Total	
		N	%	N	%
Men					
Control	227	2	0.9	9	4.0
Low-exposure	198	5	2.5	12	6.1
High-exposure	54	6	11.1	7	13.0
Women					
Control	212	4	1.9	14	6.6
Low-exposure	177	10	5.6	17	9.6
High-exposure	67	14	20.9	18	26.9

[a] Population at risk for onset of disorders after the disaster. Subjects with earlier onset of psychiatric disorders were excluded.
[b] All trends were significant p<.025, chi-square test for trend in binomial proportions.

and 3 as control subjects. Additional information about deaths was available from the coping section of our interview schedule. Subjects were asked to describe the most stressful event during the past few years. From this question we identified 138 subjects who reported the death of a relative or friend unrelated to the Mount St. Helens eruption.

The Diagnostic Interview Schedule distinguishes between depressive feelings associated only with bereavement and significant affective illness. Only the latter were included in our definition of the Mount St. Helens disorders. Nonetheless, our dose-response pattern could have been due in part to exacerbation of preexisting depressive symptoms and increased generalized anxiety in the bereavement group. We therefore excluded from our analysis the 80 subjects who reported a death related to the Mount St. Helens eruption. We still saw a highly significant dose-related onset pattern for the Mount St. Helens disorders in the first year after the eruption. Among men, the onset of disorders was 2.3% (N = 172) in the low-exposure group, 8.9% (N = 45) in the high-exposure group, and 0.9% (N= 227) in the control group; among women, the corresponding figures were 4.4% (N= 158), 21.2% (N = 52), and 1.9% (N = 211). Both of the trends were significant (for the men, χ^2 = 10.7, df = 1, p<.005, and for the women, χ^2 = 31.9, df = 1, p<005, test for trend in binomial proportions).

Table 9.3 compares the relative influence of deaths, other deaths, and no known deaths. The total postdisaster onset rates are presented, since some of the "other deaths" may have occurred after the first year following the disaster. Although the number of deaths reported among subjects who experienced major property loss was small, there was clearly a trend for the

Table 9.3. Rates of Single-Episode Depression, Generalized Anxiety Disorder, and Posttraumatic Stress Disorder in Subjects Reporting a Disaster-Related Death, Other Death, or No Death after the Mount St. Helens Disaster

Type of death	Control (n = 438)		Low-Exposure (n = 384)		High-exposure (n = 112)		Significance[a]
	N	Percent with postdisaster disorder	N	Percent with postdisaster disorder	N	Percent with postdisaster disorder	
Disaster-related	0	0	54	14.8	15	40.0	p<.05
Other	71	7.0	50	4.0[b]	9	11.1	n.s.
None known	367	4.9	280	6.8[c]	88	20.4[c]	p<.005

[a] One-sided significance levels based on test for trend in binomial proportions.
[b] Trend toward significant difference from the group with a disaster-related death (p<.10).
[c] Significantly different from the group with a disaster-related death (p<.05).

disaster-related deaths to be associated with increased morbidity. There was no evidence of higher morbidity among the "other death" group than among the group with no known deaths.

The preceding analysis looks only at the pattern of new cases (i.e., onsets) after the eruption. A related question is to what extent the stress of the disaster exacerbated the recurrence of symptoms among individuals who met the *DSM-III* criteria for psychiatric disorders before the eruption. Only symptoms associated with diagnosable disorders were considered in our calculation of recurrence rates. Because of the relatively small number of prior cases, the low-and high-exposure groups have been combined. Among women with prior depression or generalized anxiety, the recurrence of symptoms of one or more of the Mount St. Helens disorders after the eruption was significantly greater among those exposed to the disaster than among the control subjects (36 of 49 women or 73%, versus 18 of 34 women or 53%; $\chi^2 = 2.86$, df $= 1$, p<.05, one-sided value based on corrected chi-square). Among the men, the differences in the recurrence rates were not statistically significant (14 of 24, or 58% of men exposed to the disaster, versus 11 of 21, or 52% of the male control subjects; $\chi^2 = 0.01$, df$=1$, n.s.).

In addition to the Diagnostic Interview Schedule, we also included four subscales from the SCL-90 (depression, hostility, anxiety, and somatization) (14). Mean scores for each individual scale were calculated. Despite the highly significant dose-response onset of Mount St. Helens disorders observed during the first year after the disaster, we found no significant differences in the four subscales for present state symptoms 3½ years following the eruption.

DISCUSSION AND CONCLUSIONS

To our knowledge, this is the first study of behavioral response to disaster that has used the Diagnostic Interview Schedule with a research method that included an unaffected control community. The findings indicate that there was a significant difference in subsequent psychiatric morbidity among three groups exposed to varying levels of disaster stress. These differences are reflected in the differential onset of three specific psychiatric disorders, the so-called Mount St. Helens disorders. The observed onset pattern is consistent with a dose-response relationship to disaster stress and is associated with major property loss or death of a family member or close relative due to the disaster. In the first year after the eruption, high exposure subjects of both sexes evidenced onset rates 11 to 12 times higher than those observed in the control community. Subsequent onset patterns suggest that the disaster stress, particularly among the high-exposure subjects, may have saturated the at-risk population, since no new onsets occurred in this group after the initial 18 months following the eruption. The increased onset of three stress-related psychiatric disorders and the dose-response pattern for these new cases indicate that disaster stress significantly increased psychiatric morbidity for this population. Further analysis has shown that this increased morbidity cannot be explained by mediating variables such as education, income, or employment history.

Three potential sources of bias for this study include sample selection, classification in assigning individuals to exposure groups, and accuracy of respondent reporting during the interview. Concerning the first bias, comparisons with available census data indicate that younger, single, and lower socioeconomic status individuals were underrepresented in our samples. This is also a common finding among other studies with community samples (16). Nonetheless, our data suggest that the magnitude of this bias is stable across exposure groups and that between group-comparisons are valid. In order to minimize classification bias we developed objective criteria that represented a substantial level of impact. Between tax assessor records and double-sample confirmation, we were able to verify the loss in a large proportion of our high-exposure subjects. Reporting bias was undoubtedly also present to some degree. Several factors suggest, however, that it was not a major problem. First, we were careful in the interview procedure not to allow control community subjects to know that they were serving as such. Second, we found significant differences between exposure groups only for the Mount St. Helens disorders, all of which we had hypothesized a priori as being most likely to be influenced by disaster stress. Third, lifetime prevalence rates for the remaining disorders measured by the Diagnostic Interview Schedule were similar to those recently reported in the national epidemiology catchment area studies (15). Finally, present state symptoms as measured by four subscales of the SCL-90 (14) showed no significant differences between the exposure groups. Were reporting bias a real problem in this study, we would have expected it to manifest itself across a broad range of disorders and to be most pronounced on present state symptom questions, since these are much easier to influence artificially than the interview schedule's criterion-based diagnoses.

The Diagnostic Interview Schedule offered the advantage of providing a retrospective review of symptoms, impairment, and treatment history. By anchoring disorder onset and duration patterns to the stress event, we were able to gain a longitudinal perspective both pre-and posteruption. The method allowed for identification of predisaster baseline rates, onset rates, and recurrence patterns for both experimental and control communities. By entering the field 3–4 years after the Mount St. Helens eruption, we could identify all postdisaster onset rates and demonstrate their duration. While there is a debate about the validity of Diagnostic Interview Schedule diagnosis by paraprofessional field interviewers when compared with *DSM-III* diagnoses by experienced clinicians, in this study the control community provided a comparison that identified true differences in the rates of the interview schedule diagnoses.

It is not surprising that no significant differences were found among the exposure groups on the SCL-90 subscales. Our analysis of symptom duration has shown that most symptoms of depression and anxiety had abated by the third year after the eruption, although symptoms of posttraumatic stress disorder tended to persist longer. Bromet et al. (17) did find significant differences for symptoms of depression and anxiety between mothers of preschoolers at Three Mile Island and a control community. These were measured by the SCL-90 both 9 and 12 months after that disaster. Eleven months after the major eruption of Mount St. Helens, Murphy (18) interviewed those who had lost family members and those who suffered major damage to their primary residence as a result of the volcano. She found that these groups had elevated scores on the SCL-90 somatization and depression subscales when compared to control subjects. However, we found no differences in present state symptoms 3½ years after the eruption.

This disaster research represents a psychiatric perspective in defining the extent to which disaster victims suffer in their response to significant stress. A particular pattern of stress response symptoms begins to emerge from the Mount St. Helens disorders. The findings demonstrate that stress response disorders due to a natural disaster, as measured by strict diagnostic criteria, can be highly significant and can occur in a dose-response pattern according to different levels of stress.

REFERENCES

1. Baxter P J, Ing R, Faulk H, et al.: Mount St Helens eruptions, May 18 to June 12, 1980: an overview of the acute health impact. JAMA 246:2585–2589. 1981
2. Baxter P J, Ing R, Faulk H, et al.: Mount St Helens eruptions: the acute respiratory effects of volcanic ash in a North American community. Arch Environ Health 38:138–143, 1983

3. *Buist A S: Are volcanoes hazardous to your health? West J Med 237: 294–301, 1982*

4. *Nania J, Bruya T E: In the wake of Mount St. Helens. Ann Emerg Med 11:184–191, 1982*

5. *Buist A S, Bernstein R S (eds): Health Effects of Volcanoes: An Approach to Evaluating the Health Effects of an Environmental Hazard. Am J Public Health 76 (March suppl), 1986*

6. *Kinston W, Rosser R: Disaster: effects on mental and physical state. J. Psychosom Res 18: 437–456, 1974*

7. *Logue J N, Melick M E, Hansen H: Research issues and directions in the epidemiology of health effects of disasters. Epidemiol Rev 3:140–162, 1981*

8. *Berren M R, Beigel A, Ghertner S: A typology for the classification of disasters. Community Ment Health J 16:103–111, 1980*

9. *Shore J H, Tatum E L, Vollmer W M: Evaluation of mental health effects of disaster, Mount St. Helens eruption. Am J Public Health 76 (March suppl): 76–83, 1986*

10. *Leivesley S: Psychological response to disaster, in Epidemiology of Natural Disasters, vol 5: Contributions to Epidemiology and Biostatistics. Edited by Seman J, Leivesley S, Hogg C. Basel, Karger Publications, 1984*

11. *Quarantelli E L: The Consequences of Disasters for Mental Health, Conflicting Views: Preliminary Paper 62. Columbus, Ohio State University, 1979, p 21*

12. *Bryant B E: Respondent selection in a time of changing household composition, in Readings in Survey Research. Edited by Ferber R. Chicago, American Marketing Association, 1978*

13. *Robins L N, Helzer J E, Crough J, et al. National Institute of Mental Health Diagnostic Interview Schedule. Arch Gen Psychiatry 38:318–389, 1981*

14. *Derogatis L R, Lipman R S, Covi L.: SCL-90: an outpatient psychiatric rating scale—preliminary report. Psychopharmacol Bull 9: 13–28, 1973*

15. *Robins L N, Helzer J E, Weissman M M, et al.: Lifetime prevalence of specific psychiatric disorders in three sites. Arch Gen Psychiatry 41: 949–958, 1984*

16. *Weber D, Burt R C: Who's Home When: Working Paper 37, Washington, DC, US Bureau of the Census, 1972*

17. *Bromet E J, Parkinson D K, Schulberg H C, et al.: Mental health of residents near the Three Mile island reactor: a comparative study of selected groups. J Preventive Psychiatry 1:255–276, 1982*

18. *Murphy S: Stress levels and health status of victims of a natural disaster. Res Nurs Health 7:205–215, 1984*

10. A Follow-Up Study of Rape Victims

Carol C. Nadelson, Malkah T. Notman, Hannah
Zackson, and Janet Gornick

In THE LAST DECADE, rape has attracted widespread attention from the media, social scientists, and the mental health professions. However, there is little empirical literature on the effects of rape beyond the end of the first year following the rape (1).

Most researchers agree that during the first days and months a wide array of responses, affecting nearly every aspect of the victim's life, is prevalent. Victims experience behavioral symptoms, including altered sleeping habits, nightmares, and changes in eating patterns, and somatic symptoms such as headaches, nausea, exhaustion, and overall discomfort and tension. The range of emotional and cognitive responses in vast. Victims report fears, general anxiety, difficulties in concentrating, intrusive thoughts about the event, lethargy, irritability, anger, guilt, and self-blame. In these early weeks and months, functioning at work, school, or in the home is disrupted and social relationships are affected. Victims move their residences, travel, or sharply curtail their activities as they struggle to adapt (2–5).

Most previous work on rape based on 1-year follow-up studies suggests that the rape victim recovers from the acute trauma by the end of this time (2, 3, 6). Two recent studies cast some doubt on this conclusion. McCahill and associates (7) followed up 213 victims and found that at the end of 1 year at least one-third of the victims still reported rape-related "adjustment problems." These included fear and decreased social activities, disruptions in eating habits and sleeping patterns, and worsened sexual relations with their partners. In 1978 Burgess and Holmstrom (1) published a 4–6 year follow-up study. They reinterviewed 81 of the original group of women they had reported on and found that the majority of these women (74%) felt that they had "recovered" by the time they were interviewed, 4 to 6 years after the

Reprinted from *American Journal of Psychiatry,* 139 (10), 1226–1270. Copyright © 1982 by the American Psychiatric Association.

rape. However, half of the women felt that it "took years." Only one-third of the total sample reported feeling "recovered" within a period of months.

The major theoretical framework that has been applied to rape response has been crisis theory (2, 8, 9). It describes a period of disequilibrium lasting up to approximately 6 weeks, after which the crisis is resolved and the individual returns to a precrisis level of functioning, although some victims exhibit a postresolution level of functioning that may be different from that of the precrisis state (10, 11).

Although crisis theory provides a useful framework for understanding the dynamics of the short-term effects of rape, its applicability to the analysis and modeling of long-term effects can be questioned. An alternative conceptualization, posttraumatic stress disorder (which originated in the studies of post-traumatic neuroses after World War II) encompasses the recognition that the effects of exposure to a severely stressful event may persist for many years (12–17). Tyhurst (18), Titchener and Kapp (19), and others have applied this model to other traumatic situations. Notman and Nadelson (4) placed rape in this group of stressful events and focused on both the crisis response to rape and the potential long-term consequences.

The study described here was undertaken to explore effects of rape persisting 1–2½ years after the occurrence.

METHOD

We selected for the follow-up study all women (N; eq 130) reporting rape who had come to the Beth Israel Hospital Rape Crisis Intervention Program during a 12-month period in the late 1970s. Rape was determined by self-report. The program is based jointly in the hospital's social service and emergency departments (20) and serves an urban area with a large student population.

Contact was initiated by calling the telephone numbers listed on the records. If the woman could not be found in this manner, a more intensive search was made. When she was reached, the purpose of the study was explained and the woman was asked to participate in a study designed to learn about the aftermath of rape. She was advised of her right to decline participation or to terminate the interview at any time. Table 10.1 summarizes the results of contacts with the study population.

We were able to interview 41 women. The interview focused specifically on 1) the recalled effect of the emergency room experience, counseling, and police and trial experiences; 2) the interventions of supportive professional

Table 10.1. Reasons for Nonparticipation in Follow-Up Study
among 130 Rape Victims

Reason	Number of women
Not included in study	42
Under age 18 at time of rape	19
Incomplete records or missing data	13
Recorded history of previous psychiatric hospitalizations and/or severe psychotic episodes	6
Mental retardation	2
Spanish-speaking	1
Deaf	1
Included in study but not located	46
No longer living at recorded address, no forwarding address or telephone number	20
Telephone number on records changed to unpublished	8
Telephone disconnected or no current listing in directory	8
No answer on repeated calls or no response to message	6
Moved to Europe	3
Family refused to leave message	1
Included in study and located	42
Refused interview	1
Interviewed	41

and nonprofessional individuals; and 3) the woman's reactions to the rape, including life changes associated with it and any long-term effects. Specific symptoms, physical and emotional, that had developed since the rape were also elicited.

A response was coded as "yes" if the victim reported that the symptom she developed after the rape was still present at the time of interview, "improved" if the symptom appeared after the rape but subsequently subsided and was no longer present, and "no" if the symptom was not present after the rape or was of the same intensity as before the rape. We also asked open-ended questions about life changes: if multiple responses were given, all responses were counted. All questions were asked of each individual in the same manner and in the same order.

RESULTS

The interviewed group was comparable to the group not interviewed with regard to age and marital status. The ages of the interviewed victims ranged from 18 to 60 years, with 86% being between 18 and 29 years; 73% were single and 20% were married or divorced. The time between the rape and the interview ranged from 15 to 30 months. The median interval was 22 months.

We will present the data in three sections summarizing the victims' responses to "On looking back on the rape experience, what feelings stand out for you most?" and "Have there been any changes in your life which you related to the rape?" and their comments on a list of several common postrape symptoms. Because particular postrape experiences, such as sexual difficulties, were elicited in more than one of these contexts, what sounds like repetition actually indicates that a particular experience was elicited first as an associative response and later confirmed by a response to direct questioning. Likewise, some women did not report symptoms when open-ended questions were asked but they did respond affirmatively when they were presented with a symptom list.

Response to Initial Open-Ended Questions

The responses to the question, "On looking back on the rape experience, what feelings stand out for you?" are summarized in table 10.1. Almost half of the women mentioned intense terror, horror, fear, and/or fright about the possibility of being killed by the rapist. About three-quarters of those interviewed spontaneously discussed fears acquired after the rape, including, in order of decreasing frequency, walking alone, going out alone, men, sleeping, being left alone, noise, another rape, and darkness.

Other postrape reactions, which persisted for weeks to months, included nausea, feelings of degradation and devastation, loss of self-esteem, frustration, indignation, nervousness, pervasive anxiety or anxiety attacks, depression, sleep disturbances, lack of concentration, recurring and intrusive thoughts, and a sense of unreality and depersonalization. One woman reported still feeling guilty about not having prevented the rape.

In recalling the experience, several emphasized that they experienced post-rape sexual difficulties. They commented, "I'm all screwed up about men now" and "I just don't like sex anymore." Many women stated that they experienced changes in affect such as increased anger, hate, bitterness, or aloofness.

More than one-quarter of the women interviewed spontaneously stated that the rape had a lasting impact on their lives. Illustrative comments include "I'll never get rid of it," "I think of it every day," "I can never forget it," "I don't think I'll ever get over it," "It will never leave me," "It was the most significant experience of my life," "It crippled me," "It ruined my life," "I must suffer." One woman noted that she could no longer watch violence on television or films. Other reactions involved the rapist: some women felt desire for revenge and retaliation, and others expressed pity for the rapist as a "sick man."

Life Changes Related to Rape

When the women were asked directly about changes in their lives that they related to the rape, three-quarters noted changes which they directly attributed to the experience, as shown in table 10.2. Some could be viewed as positive, such as seeing themselves as stronger or more careful, self-reliant, independent, serious, thoughtful, or selective in choosing friends. One woman noted that the rape had led her to seek psychotherapy, and another reported that it fostered closer relationship with her mother.

More negative outcomes, including some form fear, anxiety, and/or depressive symptomatology were reported by almost half of the women. Others mentioned that they were more fearful of being alone and restricted about going out.

However, the victims also indicated that they worried; experienced intrusive thoughts, sleep disturbances, increased emotional susceptibility, and feelings of vulnerability; and feared retaliation. With this question, over one-third

Table 10.2. Feelings and Life Changes Associated with Rape among 41 Women

Response	N	%
Feelings		
Terror of rape	17	41
Postrape fear	31	76
Other postrape reactions	16	32
Postrape sexual difficulties	9	22
Character changes	18	44
Lasting impact of rape	11	27
Other	7	17
Don't know	1	2
None	1	2
No answer	1	2
Life changes		
Personality maturation	18	44
Fear, anxiety, depressive symptoms	17	41
Changed sexual attitudes and relationships	15	37
Specific actions (e.g., moving, increasing security)	14	34
No changes	11	27

of those interviewed commented on changes in sexual attitudes and/or relationships, including new suspiciousness of men. The respondents also told of changed behavior in husbands and boyfriends, including two who reported rape-related separations.

In addition, 14 women (34%) described measures they had taken since the rape, including moving residence or increasing security precautions. Two women stated they lost jobs because the rape had made it difficult for them to continue to function as they previously had done.

Specific Symptoms

The responses to specific questions about symptoms are summarized in table 10.3. The most common symptom reported as still present at the time of interview was a pervasive suspiciousness of others. Almost all of the women were troubled by continued feelings of fear and distrust of others. More than half reported that they felt restricted and would venture out only with friends. A few noted that they feared walking alone even in daylight.

Strikingly, more than half of the sample, when specifically asked about sexual problems, reported current difficulties, including 11 women (25%) who described avoidance of any sexual relationship since the rape. They also made comments about their answers, including, "I don't want to get in-volved." "I stay away from men now." "The thought of sex makes me sick," "I've lost my desire," "I haven't been able to get close to anyone." Three women dreaded oral sex because it recalled the rape, and I woman was still plagued with flashbacks of the rape. Two women reported that they were unable to experience orgasm since the rape: "I've got to fake a lot now," "I just get cold inside."

Table 10.3. Specific Symptoms among 41 Rape Victims 1–2½ Years after Rape

	Still present		Improved		Not experienced		No answer	
Type of symptom	N	%	N	%	N	%	N	%
Suspicious of others	31	76	4	10	4	10	2	5
Restricted going out	25	61	9	22	5	12	2	5
Sexual difficulties	21	51	7	17	10	24	3	7
Fear of being alone	20	49	12	29	7	17	2	5
Depression	17	41	13	31	9	22	2	5
Fatigue	16	39	7	17	16	39	2	5
Sleep disturbances	10	24	23	56	6	15	2	5
Lack of concentration	10	24	15	37	14	34	2	5

Of the 41% who stated that they experienced depressive feelings related to the rape, some experienced continuous sadness and others noted intermittent episodes of severe depression.

Sleep disturbances present early in the postrape period showed the greatest improvement. More than half the respondents acknowledged previous problems that had subsided by the time of interview. The most common difficulties were nightmares and/or waking at night with an inability to fall back asleep.

DISCUSSION

Rape victims are difficult to locate because many disconnect telephones, change to unlisted numbers, or change residences (21). Coupled with the transient life styles common in late adolescent and young adult populations, this makes it difficult to follow them and perhaps also accounts for the scarcity of studies. Considering these factors, our 47% (42/88) location rate was high for this population. Moreover, the participation rate of those who were located approached 100% (41/42). We were impressed with the victims' cooperation, willingness to be interviewed, and this desire to help other victims. This may alleviate some concerns that additional psychological trauma could result if a victim is recontacted and reminded of the rape.

This follow-up study of rape occurred 15–30 months after the experience. Although the overall characteristics of victims who do not seek professional aid are unknown and the study did not control for differences between those who enter the health care system and those who do not, the data indicate some ongoing responses of rape victims that are present at an average of 22 months postrape. We also do not know with certainty the life changes that occur during a similar time period in an ordinary population which has undergone no trauma. However, because those with overt mental illness or even mental health contacts were not included in the sample we can presume to have a "normal" population. The fact that this group did report a large number of symptoms attributed to the rape is important. Although we must acknowledge the potential in using retrospective recall, the intensity of the memories and extent of the symptoms seem to indicate that the subjects' recall of the impact of the experience has validity even if the specific memories might not be exact. These symptoms are consistent with the diagnosis of posttraumatic stress disorder (*DSM-III*).

This group of women also reported positive adaptational outcomes, including becoming more serious, more careful, more self-reliant, and, to some extent, stronger. This reinforces the view that for many people stressful life events can be growth promoting and foster maturation. Even if symptoms persist for some time, the individual can master the trauma and resume control of his/her life, and this positive adaptation is facilitated when external supports provide validation (4). Our finding that a highly stressful experience such as rape can also be growth promoting is in agreement with recent evidence from the abortion literature which indicates that the experience of abortion can also lead to a positive developmental outcome, depending on previous life experience and adaptive capacity (22, 23).

A striking finding was the large number of women who reported sexual difficulties after the rape. The fact that many victims did not spontaneously volunteer this information but that it was easily elicited by direct questioning is not surprising because sexual functioning is clearly not an everyday topic of conversation for many people, and for those who have been sexually traumatized it has special meanings and negative implications (4).

The data from this study and clinical impressions (unpublished data of C. Nadelson) that a high proportion of women who seek treatment of sexual dysfunction have histories of early sexual trauma suggest that a follow-up evaluation must include comprehensive sexual and psychological histories (1). Counselors must be aware of the connection between sexual trauma and sexual dysfunction and recognize that long-term symptoms may occur. Rape victims do not necessarily revert to their previous state of functioning readily. The positive and negative effects are not yet entirely clear. Maturational effects such as feelings of great self-reliance, inner strength, thoughtfulness, and seriousness may serve to counteract invasive fears. Short-term, issue-oriented therapy is crucial for the rape victim, although many victims who are struggling to master the immediate experience report active rape-related symptoms in a number of areas well beyond the first year after the rape and may need help at later times.

REFERENCES

1. Burgess A W, Holmstrom L L: Recovery from rape and prior life stress. Res Nurs Health 1: 165–174, 1978
2. Burgess A W, Holmstrom L L: Rape: Victims of Crisis. Bowie, Md. Robert J Brady Co. 1974
3. Sutherland S, Scherl D S: Patterns of response among victims of rape. Am J Orthopsychiatry 40:503–511, 1970
4. Notman M T, Nadelson C C: The rape victim: psychodynamic considerations. Am J Psychiatry 133:408–413, 1976.

5. *Kilpatrick D M, Veronen L J. Resnick P A: The aftermath of rape: recent empirical findings. Am J Orthopsychiatry 49: 658–669, 1979*
6. *Katz S, Mazur M: Understanding the Rape Victim: A Synthesis of Research Findings. New York, John Wiley & Sons. 1979*
7. *McCahill T W, Meyer L C. Fischman A M: The Aftermath of Rape. Lexington, Mass, Lexington Books, 1979*
8. *McCombie S L: Characteristics of rape victims seen in crisis intervention. Smith College Studies in Social Work 46: 137–158, 1976*
9. *Hoff L A, Williams T: Counseling the rape victim and her family Crisis Intervention 6(4):2–13, 1975*
10. *Lindemann E: Symptomatology and management of acute grief, in Stress and Coping. Edited by Monat A, Lazarus R. New York, Columbia University Press. 1944*
11. *Caplan G: Principles of Preventive Psychiatry. New York. Basic Books. 1964*
12. *Glover E: Notes on the psychological effects of war conditions on the civilian population. I: the Munich crisis. Int J Psychoanal 22: 132–146, 1941*
13. *Glover E: Notes on the psychological effects of war conditions on the civilian population. III: the blitz. Int J Psychoanal 23: 17–37, 1942*
14. *Grinker R, Spiegel J: Men Under Stress. Philadelphia. Blakiston, 1945*
15. *Kardiner A, Spiegel J, War Stress and Neurotic Illness. New York. Hocher. 1941*
16. *Rado S: Pathodynamics and treatment of traumatic war neurosis (traumatophobia). Psychosom Med 4: 362–369, 1942*
17. *Schmideberg M: Some observations on individual reactions to air raids. Int J Psychoanal 23: 146–176, 1942*
18. *Tyhurst J S: Individual reactions to community disaster: the natural history of psychiatric phenomena. Am J Psychiatry 107:764–769, 1951*
19. *Titchener J L, Kapp F T: Family and character change at Buffalo Creek, Am J Psychiatry 133: 295–299, 1976*
20. *McCombie S L, Bassuk E. Savitz R. et al.: Development of a medical center rape crisis intervention program. Am J Psychiatry 133: 418–421, 1976*
21. *Holmes K A, Williams J E: Problems and pitfalls of rape victim research: an analysis of selected methodological, ethical, and pragmatic concerns. Victimology: An International Journal 4(1): 17–28, 1979*
22. *Payne E. Kravitz A. Notman M. et al.: Outcome following therapeutic abortion. Arch Gen Psychiatry 33: 725–733, 1976*
23. *Gilligan C, Belensky M F: Crisis and transition: a naturalistic study of abortion decisions, in Clinical Development Psychology. Edited by Selman R. Yando R. San Francisco. Jossey-Bass, 1980*

11. Psychophysiologic Responses to Combat Imagery of Vietnam Veterans with Posttraumatic Stress Disorder versus Other Anxiety Disorders

Roger K. Pitman, Scott P. Orr, Dennis F. Forgue,
Bruce Altman, Jacob B. de Jong, and
Lawrence R. Herz

A MAJOR SOURCE of support for the validity of the diagnosis posttraumatic stress disorder (PTSD: American Psychiatric Association, 1987) has been the finding that war veterans with this condition are more physiologically responsive to combat-related stimuli than are other individuals. The various groups of comparison subjects used in this research have included non-veterans (Blanchard et al., 1982), mentally healthy combat veterans (Blanchard et al., 1986; Malloy et al., 1983; Pallmeyer et al., 1986; Pitman et al., 1987) and non-PTSD psychiatric patients (Malloy et al., 1983; Pallmeyer et al., 1986). Non-PTSD psychiatric comparison subjects are important, because it is only by including them that PTSD's validity as a separate mental disorder can be tested. However, the utility of one of the two psychophysiologic studies that included psychiatric control subjects (Malloy et al., 1983) was compromised by the fact that these subjects were not combat veterans; it may not be surprising that persons with no prior exposure to combat should be unresponsive to combat-related stimuli. Although another study (Pallmeyer et al., 1986) did include 5 psychiatric combat control subjects, no measure of severity of combat exposure was provided, and only 1 of the 5 had a diagnosis in the same category as PTSD, namely, generalized anxiety. The other diagnoses were alcoholism (for 3 subjects) and bipolar affective disorder (for 1 subject). Although these 5 non-PTSD psychiatric subjects appeared less physiologically responsive than the PTSD subjects to the standard auditory, com-

Reprinted from *Journal of Abnormal Psychology*, 99 (1), 49–54. Copyright © 1990 by the American Psychological Association.

bat-related stimulus used in that study, this finding was statistically significant at only one of several stimulus intensity levels used.

We previously reported that physiologic responses to imagery of past combat events successfully discriminated PTSD Vietnam veterans from mentally healthy combat Vietnam veterans (Pitman et al., 1987). The goal of the present study was to extend this research by using a comparison group of combat Vietnam veterans with anxiety disorders, as these disorders are from the same category of the revised third edition of the *Diagnostic and Statistical Manual of Mental Disorders (DSM-III-R*, American Psychiatric Association, 1987) as PTSD. Suitable subjects who were Vietnam combat veterans with non-PTSD anxiety disorders were not in abundance. Possible reasons for this include unfitness of persons with anxiety disorders for military duty in the first place, a greater risk of their developing PTSD when in combat, less contact of such persons with the Veterans Administration (VA) afterwards, and their disinclination to undergo the required medication-free period prior to the study. Nevertheless, over several years, we were able to recruit and study 7 such subjects as well as an equal number of previously unstudied PTSD subjects.

METHOD[1]

Subjects

The sample consisted of White male veterans with combat experience in Vietnam as defined by Fairbank, Keane, and Malloy (1983). Subjects were recruited both from the population of active and former VA outpatients and Vet Center clients and from advertisements in the media. One of us (RKP or LRH) performed an initial screening interview, described the study, and obtained informed consent. Patients on psychotropic medication or medication with potentially confounding autonomic effects were asked to abstain from its use for 2 weeks prior to the laboratory session. Patients for whom medication abstinence was contraindicated and patients with potentially interfering medical conditions were excluded. RKP or LRH also rated each subject's degree of combat exposure on the 14-point Revised Combat Scale (RCS; Egendorf et al., 1981).

Following screening, the subject was given a diagnostic interview by either a psychiatrist (LRH or JBdJ) or a clinical psychologist (BA), who used the Structured Clinical Interview for *DSM-III-R* (SCID), version NP-V (Spitzer & Williams, 1985), which is designed for research with Vietnam veterans.

All interviewers were trained by the SCID's authors in its use prior to the study. The interviewer noted which elements of the diagnostic criteria for PTSD were satisfied, if any, and whether the subject met criteria for any other mental disorders. Subjects with a diagnosis of an organic mental, schizophrenic, paranoid, bipolar manic, or other psychotic disorder, or with active substance dependence, were excluded. Subjects with a current diagnosis of PTSD, with or without another nonexcluding mental disorder, were classified into the PTSD group ($n = 7$). Of the 7 PTSD subjects, 2 met criteria for one or more accompanying mental disorders: 1 had panic disorder: the other had panic disorder, obsessive compulsive disorder, and major depression. Subjects with a diagnosis of an anxiety disorder but not current or past PTSD were classified into the anxious group ($n = 7$). The anxiety disorders represented in this group included two panic disorders, two generalized anxiety disorders, one obsessive compulsive disorder, one social phobia, and one simple phobia. None of the 7 anxious subjects had another accompanying mental disorder. Three of the PTSD and 3 of the anxious subjects were in outpatient treatment at the time of the study; none were inpatients.

Psychometrics

Each subject completed the following psychometric tests and questionnaires: (a) Questionnaire upon Mental Imagery (Sheehan, 1967), which provides an estimate of a subject's imagery ability (a lower score indicates better imagery ability); (b) Mississippi Scale for Combat-Related PTSD (Keane, Caddell, & Taylor, 1988), on which a cutoff score of 107 has been found to best discriminate PTSD from non-PTSD subjects; (c) PTSD subscale of the Minnesota Multiphasic Personality Inventory (MMPI), on which a cutoff score of 30 has been reported to be the best discriminator (Keane, Malloy, & Fairbank, 1984); and (d) State-Trait Anxiety Inventory (Spielberger et al., 1970). The demographic and psychometric profiles of the PTSD and anxious groups are presented in table 11.1. These results indicate that the groups were closely matched for age, educational level, and imagery ability. The PTSD subjects reported significantly greater combat exposure; their mean fell into the heavy combat range of the RCS. The mean of the anxious subjects fell into the medium combat range, though 3 had heavy combat exposure. There was a significant group difference on the Mississippi scale, and this supported the PTSD diagnostic distinction between the groups. However, on the MMPI PTSD scale, the group difference was not significant (see Orr et al., 1990). Their Mississippi scale and MMPI PTSD scores indicate that the PTSD

Table 11.1. Demographic, Psychometric, and Baseline Physiologic Data

Variable	PTSD (n = 7) M	SD	Anxious (n = 7) M	SD	t(12)	p
Age	40.1	3.5	38.9	3.6	<1	ns
Education	14.3	2.1	12.9	2.3	1.2	ns
Revised Combat Scale (0–14)*	12.3	2.4	8.0	4.2	2.3	0.4
Questionnaire upon Mental Imagery (35–245)	82.1	22.0	79.1	35.3	<1	ns
Mississippi PTSD Scale (35–175)	110.6	20.0	79.1	11.3	3.6	<.01
MMPI PTSD Scale (0–49)	22.0	11.2	16.0	6.9	1.2	ns
Trait Anxiety (20–80)	49.9	12.0	47.1	5.7	<1	ns
State Anxiety (20–80)	57.0	14.0	44.4	10.1	1.9	ns
Baseline physiologic levels						
Heart rate (beats per min)	70.8	12.0	73.6	7.9	<1	ns
Skin conductance (µmhos)	2.8	4.1	2.6	2.8	<1	ns
Frontalis EMG (µV)	1.8	0.5	2.7	0.9	2.3	.04
Individual combat events						
Severity (0–12)	11.1	0.4	10.5	1.0	1.6	ns
Symptomatic impact (IOES)						
Intrusion (0–21)	11.6	1.9	4.0	3.6	4.9	<.01
Avoidance (0–24)	13.9	3.0	2.2	1.8	8.9	<.01
Individual precombat traumatic event						
Severity (0–12)	9.4	2.6	6.0	1.7	2.9	.02
Symptomatic impact (IOES)						
Intrusion (0–21)	1.7	4.5	3.7	4.7	<1	ns
Avoidance (0–24)	2.6	6.8	2.7	4.5	<1	ns

NOTE. PTSD = posttraumatic stress disorder; MMPI = Minnesota Multiphasic Personality Inventory; EMG = electromyogram; IOES = Impact of Event Scale.
ªFigures in parentheses after instruments indicate range of possible scores.

subjects did not have severe PTSD. The groups were closely matched on trait anxiety, which supported their shared diagnostic status as anxiety disorders. The (nonsignificantly) higher state anxiety of the PTSD group may reflect their anticipation of participating in a PTSD research study.

Scripts

Following the diagnostic interview and psychometric tests, the subject was scheduled for an appointment with a psychiatric social worker experienced in working with Vietnam veterans (DF), who was blind to group membership. DF composed five individualized scripts portraying actual experiences from the subject's past after the method of Lang's group (Lang et al., 1983; Levin et al., 1982), including the two most stressful combat experiences that the subject could recall, a precombat traumatic experience, a positive experience, and a neutral experience. The subject was first asked to describe each experience in writing on a script preparation form (available from the authors on request) and then to select, from a "menu" of subjective visceral and muscular reactions appearing at the bottom of the form, those that he remembered as having accompanied the experience. DF reviewed the subject's written responses, asked him to clarify or expand on the details when necessary, and then composed a script approximately 30 s in duration that portrayed each experience in the second person, present tense, incorporating five different visceral and muscular reactions or as many as the subject selected, whichever was less. An example of a previous subject's individualized combat script has been presented elsewhere (Pitman et al., 1987).

After the subject finished an individual script preparation form, he was asked to complete the Impact of Event Scale (IOES: Horowitz et al., 1979; Zilberg et al., 1982) as it pertained to the experience that he had just described. The IOES measures, on 0–3, Likert-type scales, the frequency during the past week of various PTSD-related symptoms connected with the experience. Two scores were calculated from this instrument for each individualized script: an intrusion score (here referred to as IOES-I) and an avoidance score (IOES-A). The use of the IOES in this study differed from the use of the Mississippi and MMPI PTSD scales in that the latter provided an estimate of the overall severity of combat-related PTSD symptomatology, whereas the IOES provided an estimate of the PTSD-symptomatic impact of a discrete combat event.

In addition to the individualized scripts, we used six standard scripts portraying various hypothetical experiences; these were the same for all subjects. The standard scripts (available from the authors on request) included two neutral experiences (sitting in a lawn chair, looking out a living room window), a combat experience (an incoming mortar and rocket attack), a positive experience (at the beach), an action experience (riding a bicycle), and a fear experience (speaking in public). The standard scripts also incorporated visceral and muscular responses that might be expected in the respective situations. The standard scripts, with the exception of the combat script, were the same as those previously used by Lang et al. (1983). Each script was recorded in a neutral voice by one of us (SPO) to be played back in the laboratory.

Transcripts of the individualized combat and precombat traumatic scripts obtained for each subject were prepared for review in scrambled order by four experts who were Vet Center staff members experienced in counseling Vietnam veterans, blind as to subjects' diagnoses. These raters were asked to judge each script on a 0–12, Likert-type scale for the amount of trauma that event would have produced for the average Vietnam veteran (not how much trauma the event appeared to produce for the specific individual involved). Interrater reliability for this measure has previously been reported to be .61 (intraclass R: Pitman et al., 1987). The four ratings were averaged for each script, providing a measure of the apparent severity of the event.

Apparatus

The laboratory session took place in an 11 ft $\times$ 9 ft (3.4 m $\times$ 2.7 m) humidity- and temperature-controlled, sound-attenuated subject room, connected by wires to an adjoining portion of the laboratory in which the experimental apparatus was located. The subject was seated in a comfortable armchair. A monitor in the subject room was used to display the emotion self-report scales, and subjects' self-reports were entered into the computer through a joystick. A Coulbourn Modular Instrument System was used in the recording of physiologic analog signals, which were monitored by Hitachi V-212 oscilloscopes. Dependent physiologic measures included heart rate, skin conductance, and electromyogram (EMG) of the left lateral frontalis facial muscle. The EMG was obtained through Beckman silver/silver chloride mini-electrodes that were placed according to published specifications (Fridlund & Cacioppo, 1986), connected to a Coulbourn Hi-Gain Bioamplifier (S75–01), and integrated by means of a 0.5-s time constant through a Coulbourn Contour-Following Integrator (S76–01). Skin conductance level was obtained through Beckman silver/silver chloride electrodes that were placed on the subject's left palm and connected to a Coulbourn Skin Conductance Module (S71–11), which used a constant (0.5 V) voltage and was used in the direct-coupled mode (Fowles et al., 1981). Heart rate was obtained through standard limb electrocardiogram leads connected to a Coulbourn Hi-Gain Bioamplifier (S75–01) that input to a Coulbourn Tachometer (S77–26). Analog outputs of the physiologic modules were digitized by a Coulbourn Analog-to-Digital Converter (S25–12) prior to sampling. An IBM-XT computer was used to control the tape recorder and the self-report graphics monitor and to sample and store the digitized physiologic signals. The computer was interfaced with the instrument system through a Coulbourn Lablink Computer Interface.

Procedure

After orientation to the subject room, electrodes were attached and subjects listened to a 3-min relaxation instruction tape. The subject was informed that a series of scripts would be presented after this tape. Each script presentation consisted of four sequential 30-s periods: baseline, reading, imagery, and recovery. The subject was instructed to listen carefully during the playing of the scripts and to attempt to imagine as vividly as possible each experience as it was presented (read period) and, after the script terminated, to continue to imagine the experience from beginning to end (imagery period) until he heard a tone. He was further instructed to stop imagining the script at the tone and to relax (recovery period) until a second tone was heard. At this time, he made his self-reports on 12-point, Likert-type scales (see table 11.2). The computer was programmed to start the baseline period for the next script after a rest period of 1 min or after heart rate had returned to within 5% of its value during the previous baseline period, whichever was longer. For all scripts, all subjects' heart rates returned to this criterion within 3 min; usually heart rate returned to criterion within 1 min.

There were 11 script presentations. Following the first (standard neutral) script, there were two blocks of five scripts each. Each block contained one of the individualized combat scripts, one of the remaining neutral scripts, one

Table 11.2. Self-Report Ratings of the Individualized Combat Scripts

Rating	PTSD		Anxious			
	M	*SD*	*M*	*SD*	*t*(12)	*p*
Vividness	11.4	1.5	8.7	2.6	2.4	.02
Emotion dimensions						
Arousal	11.2	1.2	7.9	2.3	3.3	<.01
Valence (pleasantness)	0.4	0.9	2.7	2.1	2.6	.01
Dominance (control)	0.8	1.2	4.6	2.4	3.8	<.01
Discrete emotions						
Happiness	0	0.0	0.4	1.1	1.0[a]	*ns*
Sadness	9.4	3.5	3.6	3.8	2.9	<.01
Fear	10.2	2.8	5.3	3.2	3.1	<.01
Surprise	10.6	1.4	4.7	2.9	4.7	<.01
Anger	11.3	1.3	3.4	4.3	4.7[a]	<.01
Disgust	8.7	3.0	3.1	4.3	2.8	.01

NOTE. All ratings on 0–12 scale. PTSD = posttraumatic stress disorder.
[a] t test for unequal variances.

of the positive scripts, either the individualized precombat traumatic script or the standard fear script, and either the action or the standard combat script. No two of the combat, precombat traumatic, or fear scripts were presented sequentially. Within these constraints, the order of script presentation was randomized. For each script, the physiologic variables were sampled two times per s.

At the conclusion of the experiment, each subject was debriefed and treatment options were discussed with him if he wished.

Data Reduction and Analysis

For each script, a change score was calculated for each physiologic dependent variable by subtracting the preceding baseline period mean from the imagery period mean. The responses to the two individualized combat scripts were averaged prior to analysis. The hypothesis regarding these responses was clearly of a directional nature; that is, there was no reason to predict that the anxious subjects would be more responsive to the combat scripts than the PTSD subjects. This allowed for the use of one-tailed t tests in the analysis of these results.

RESULTS

Baseline Physiologic Levels

The mean levels for each physiologic variable for the PTSD and anxious subjects during the baseline period preceding the first script, and results of univariate analyses, appear in table 11.1. The only significant group difference was for EMG, the PTSD subjects being lower at baseline than the anxious subjects.

Physiologic Responses to Scripts

The only scripts on which the physiologic responses of the PTSD and anxious subjects differed significantly were the individualized combat scripts. There was a nonsignificant trend for the PTSD subjects to be more responsive to the individualized precombat traumatic script, but at lower magnitudes than their responses to the individualized combat scripts. Neither group was very responsive to either the standard combat or the standard fear script. Therefore, the remaining report will be limited to the averaged responses to the individ-ualized combat scripts.

The judged severity of subjects' individual combat events did not differ significantly between the two groups (see table 11.1). However, these ex-periences produced much greater symptomatology in the PTSD than in the anxious subjects, as revealed by the difference in IOES scores. Figure 11.1 presents the physiologic responses (change scores) to imagery of these experiences. As shown, t tests revealed significant group differences for skin conductance and EMG, whereas for heart rate there was only a trend.[2]

In our previous study in which we used this methodology, a discriminant function was empirically derived from the heart rate, skin conductance, and EMG responses to the individualized combat scripts of 18 PTSD and 15 mentally healthy Vietnam combat veterans. Application of this function to the present physiologic responses resulted in the correct identification of 5 of the 7 PTSD subjects (sensitivity = 71%) and all of the 7 anxious subjects (specificity = 100%). The chance occurrence of this distribution is $p = .01$ (Fisher's exact test). The two physiologically nonresponsive PTSD subjects (false negatives) had the lowest and third lowest Mississippi scale scores and were the only PTSD subjects who did not meet the *DSM-III-R* criterion of physiologic reactivity to events resembling the traumatic event.

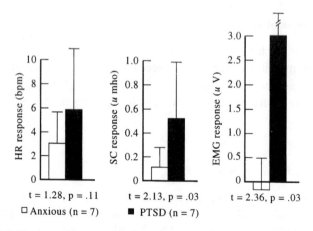

Figure 11.1. Mean physiologic responses (change scores) to the individualized combat scripts. (*SD* of the electromyogram response for the posttraumatic stress disorder [PTSD] group [broken line] = 3.7 μv. For all *t* tests. *df* = 12.)

Emotion Self-Reports

Table 11.2 presents the self-report ratings of the individualized combat scripts. The PTSD and anxious groups differed significantly in the predicted direction: that is, the PTSD subjects reported more disturbed subjective reactions than the anxious subjects on all self-report variables except happiness.

DISCUSSION

The physiologic responses to the individualized combat scripts of the PTSD and anxious subjects studied here are remarkable for their close correspondence in pattern and magnitude to those obtained for the PTSD and mentally healthy combat control subjects we previously studied, using the same methodology (Pitman et al., 1987). A discriminant function derived from the previous study's physiologic data classified the present subjects with slightly greater accuracy. These results replicate our previous finding of increased physiologic responsivity to imagery of past traumatic combat events in individuals diagnosed as having PTSD. As found before, the method has greater specificity than sensitivity; a proportion of PTSD patients (about one third) do not appear to be physiologically responsive to imagery of their past combat experiences. The results further indicate that, unlike PTSD patients, combat Vietnam veterans with non-PTSD anxiety disorders are not very physiologically responsive to imagery of their past combat experiences. This supports the specificity of the psychophysiologic imagery method for PTSD, in that the method is able to successfully differentiate PTSD subjects not only from mentally healthy Vietnam combat veterans but also from their closest diagnostic neighbors.

Previously reported psychophysiologic investigations of PTSD (Blanchard et al., 1986; Blanchard et al., 1982; Malloy et al., 1983; Pallmeyer et al., 1986; Pitman et al., 1987), in addition to finding elevated responsiveness to combat-related stimuli, also revealed elevated baseline heart rates in PTSD subjects. This has led to speculation that tonic arousal may be as useful as phasic arousal in characterizing PTSD. Results from the present study contradict this notion, in that the PTSD subjects did not have higher baseline physiologic levels than anxious subjects but did have larger physiologic responses to imagery of their past combat events.

By successfully separating PTSD patients from patients with other anxiety disorders, the present results indicate that there is more to combat-related

PTSD than just being "nervous in the service." Instead, the findings demonstrate a specific physiologic responsivity to imagery of past events that are presumed to be etiologic in the disorder. Because linkage of symptoms to specific past experience is critical to the definition of PTSD, our results further support the validity of PTSD as a diagnostic entity.

NOTES

1. Because the methodologies overlapped, portions of this section appeared in Pitman et al., 1987.
2. During the preparation of the individualized combat scripts, 3 anxious subjects, but only 1 PTSD subject, selected fewer than five pertinent, subjective, visceral and muscular reactions from the menu. In order to ascertain whether the consequent inclusion of a lesser number of these reactions in their individualized combat scripts may have biased the anxious group toward lower mean physiologic responses, the responses of the 4 anxious subjects for whom the full five subjective reactions were included in each combat script were calculated separately and found to be as follows: heart rate $M = 4.0$, $SD = 2.4$; skin conductance $M = 0$. $SD = 0.5$; EMG $M = 0$, $SD = 0.5$. Thus, even the anxious subjects whose scripts contained the prescribed maximum number of subjective visceral and muscular reactions showed nil skin conductance and EMG responding.

We were unable to match the groups for overall combat exposure as measured by the RCS (Egendorf et al., 1981), as we did in our previous study (Pitman et al., 1987). In an attempt to control for this potentially confounding factor, from the pool of the 7 PTSD subjects reported in this study combined with the 18 PTSD subjects reported in the previous study (Pitman et al., 1987), the 7 with the lowest RCS scores (designated PTSD') were compared with the 7 anxious subjects. The mean RCS scores of these two groups were both in the moderate range and did not significantly differ: PTSD' $M = 9.0$, $SD = 1.4$; anxious $M = 8.0$, $SD = 4.2$, $t(12) < 1$. Their responses to the individualized combat scripts were as follows: for heart rate. PTSD' $M = 2.3$, $SD = 5.0$, anxious $M = 3.1$, $SD = 2.2$, $t(12) < 1$; for skin conductance, PTSD' $M = 0.47$, $SD = 0.48$, anxious $M = 0.11$, $SD = 0.15$, $t(12) = 1.9$, $p = .04$; for EMG, PTSD' $M = 1.50$ $SD = 2.20$, anxious $M = -0.36$, $SD = 0.77$, $t(12) = 2.1$, $p = .03$. Thus, a subgroup of PTSD subjects matched for overall combat exposure to the anxious control subjects showed significantly higher skin conductance and EMG responses to the individualized combat scripts. (We acknowledge a limitation of this retrospective analysis, namely, that the low measured combat exposure of the PTSD' subjects may to some extent reflect error variance in the RCS, and the actual combat exposure could be somewhat higher.)

REFERENCES

American Psychiatric Association. (1987). Diagnostic and statistical manual of mental disorders *(3rd ed., revised). Washington, DC: Author.*

Blanchard, E. B., Kolb, L. C., Gerardi, R. J., Ryan, P., & Pallmeyer, T. P. (1986). *Cardiac response to relevant stimuli as an adjunctive tool for diagnosing post-traumatic stress disorder in Vietnam veterans.* Behavior Therapy; 17, 592–606.

Blanchard, E. B., Kolb, L. C., Pallmeyer, T. P., & Gerardi, R. J. (1982). *A psychophysiological study of post traumatic stress disorder in Vietnam veterans.* Psychiatric Quarterly, 54, 220–229.

Egendorf, A., Kadushin, C., Laufer, R. S., Rothbart, G., & Sloan, L. (1981). *Legacies of Vietnam: Comparative adjustment of veterans and their peers. Washington: U.S. Government Printing Office.*

Fairbank, J. A., Keane, T. M., & Malloy, P. F. (1983). *Some preliminary data on the psychological characteristics of Vietnam veterans with posttraumatic stress disorders.* Journal of Consulting and Clinical Psychology, 51, 912–919.

Fowles, D. C., Christie, M. J., Edelberg, R., Grings. W. W., Lykken, D. T., & Venables, P. H. (1981). *Publication recommendations for electrodermal measurements.* Psychophysiology, 18, 232–239.

Fridlund, A. J., & Cacioppo, J. T. (1986). *Guidelines for human electromyographic research.* Psychophysiology, 23, 567–589.

Horowitz, M., Wilner, N., & Alvarez, W. (1979). *Impact of Event Scale: A measure of subjective stress.* Psychosomatic Medicine, 41, 209–218.

Keane, T. M., Caddell, J. M., & Taylor, K. L. (1988). *Mississippi Scale for Combat-Related Posttraumatic Stress Disorder: Three studies in reliability and validity.* Journal of Consulting and Clinical Psychology, 56, 85–90.

Keane, T. M., Malloy, P. F., & Fairbank, J. A. (1984). *Empirical development of an MMPI subscale for the assessment of combat-related posttraumatic stress disorder.* Journal of Consulting and Clinical Psychology, 52, 888–891.

Lang, P. J., Levin, D. N., Miller, G. A., & Kozak, M. J. (1983). *Fear behavior, fear imagery, and the psychophysiology of emotion: The problem of affective response integration.* Journal of Abnormal Psychology; 92, 276–306.

Levin, D. N., Cook. E. W., & Lang, P. J. (1982). *Fear imagery and fear behavior: Psychophysiological analysis of clients receiving treatment for anxiety disorders.* Psychophysiology, 19, 571–572.

Malloy, P. F., Fairbank, J. A., & Keane, T. M. (1983). *Validation of a multimethod assessment of posttraumatic stress disorders in Vietnam veterans.* Journal of Consulting and Clinical Psychology, 51, 488–494.

Orr, S. P., Claiborn, J. M., Altman, B., de Jong, J. B., Forgue, D. F., Herz, L. R., & Pitman, R. K. (1990). *Psychometric profile of PTSD, anxious, and healthy Vietnam veterans: Correlations with psychophysiologic responses.* Journal of Consulting and Clinical Psychology.

Pallmeyer, T. P., Blanchard, E. B., & Kolb, L. C. (1986). *The psychophysiology of combat-induced post-traumatic stress disorder in Vietnam veterans.* Behavior Research and Therapy, 24, 645–652.

Pitman, R. K., Orr, S. P., Forgue, D. F., de Jong, J. B., & Claiborn, J. M. (1987). *Psychophysiologic assessment of posttraumatic stress disorder imagery in Vietnam combat veterans.* Archives of General Psychiatry, 44, 970–975.

Sheehan, P. Q. (1967). *A shortened form of Bett's Questionnaire upon Mental Imagery.* Journal of Clinical Psychology, 223, 380–389.

Spielberger, C. D., Gorsuch, R. L., & Lushene, R. E. (1970). Manual for the State-Trait Anxiety Inventory (self-evaluation questionnaire). *Palo Alto, CA: Consulting Psychologists Press.*

Spitzer, R. L., & Williams, J. B. W. (1985). Structured Clinical Interview for DSM-III-R. *Non-patient version-Vietnam. New York: New York State Psychiatric Institute, Biometrics Research Department.*

Zilberg, N. J., Weiss, D. S., & Horowitz, M. J. (1982). Impact of Event Scale: A cross-validation study and some empirical evidence supporting a conceptual model of stress response syndromes. Journal of Consulting and Clinical Psychology, 50, 407–414.

PART II

Introduction

As you know, this book is divided into diagnostic, etiological, and therapeutic considerations. Since it is a selection of papers previously published, it is no surprise that not just one, but two or three domains may be covered in each article within a section. This section contains material on diagnoses and treatments as well as on causation. The papers provide a spread of hypotheses. Limitations of space made it mandatory for me to leave out many superb contributions. I simply selected a set to provide the beginning reader of literature on PTSD with a possible range of explanations for symptom formation. These papers have lists of references that will help such readers find excellent works I could not include.

In my general introduction I provided a rough sketch of social, biological, and psychological levels of explanation. I think the following papers will be clear in their use of these levels. There is, however, one issue I would like to comment on in order to prepare the less experienced reader. This issue concerns repression and dissociation.

Repression was a term used by Freud to refer to unconscious mental processes that blocked ideas, memories, fantasies, feelings, and impulses from gaining conscious expression. We now know that a great variety of cognitive and emotional inhibitory control processes operate to form such defensive maneuvers. These include a range from conscious to unconscious avoidances of recollection, imagination, and contemplation of mental contents that might otherwise lead to flooding of consciousness with unwanted emotions.

The early use of terms such as repression and dissociation tended to lead to circular reasoning. The defense mechanism of repressing memories was seen as a process that led to outcomes called the repression of memory. Then people who had a disposition to repression were called repressors. Similarly, the process of dissociating otherwise amenable aggregates of self-knowledge led to outcomes called dissociative experiences, and might occur in people with "dissociative personality traits." In contemporary terms, we now try to limit terms like "repression" and "dissociation" to observable phenomena.

We then try to explain personality dispositions and unconscious mental processes that form such experiences in other terms.

Both repressive and dissociative phenomena can occur because of conflicts about what it is proper or desirable to think, and feel, and do, as well as deficiencies in cognitive, emotional, and coping capacities. A person might defensively inhibit recollection of a horrifying memory or he might be unable to represent the ideas clearly and consciously with reflective self-awareness. Both could lead to states of apparent forgetting of a subsequently recalled memory. Another person might unconsciously segregate seemingly incompatible views of personal identity, and relationship transactions with others, to avoid shame or guilt. Or he might be unable to combine the identity experience of this state of mind with the identity experience of an alternate state, perhaps because of a deficiency in the supraordinate, self-organizing schemas that are required to make that kind of linkage in reflective self-awareness. Both conflict and deficiency could explain a lack of continuity or coherence in a sense of identity over diverse states of mind of that person.

Controversies occur because some theoreticians emphasize conflicts between expressive impulses and defensive operations and others emphasize stress-induced deficits. I suggest to the reader that it may be best to take a "both-and" rather than an "either-or" stance on such causation of repressive and dissociative phenomena; there is a great deal that is unknown, and some theory is more hypothetical than proven.

Another controversy is, in my opinion, a false controversy. That is the struggle to create a mind-brain dichotomy between psychological and biological levels of causation. Again, a "both-and" stance is suggested to the reader. Any psychological process rests upon biological substrates. We do not yet know for sure what they are. We do agree that they exist mainly in the brain and that they operate as complex neural networks, neurotransmitter-hormonal systems, and genetic governors of physiology and anatomy. We can focus on psychological and social meanings and their changes after stressor events without denying biology, using a stance of biological "substrate neutrality." We can use PTSD to investigate neurophysiological shifts and neuroanatomical dispositions or changes, and can use medications to determine their effects on symptoms, mental states, and social functioning. Focusing at times on these chemistries and physiologies does not reduce our concern for the totalities and complexities that are involved in mental emotions, social relationships, and assemblies of personal meaning.

While this section reveals controversies about the cause of PTSD, we do know and agree on a lot. PTSD is caused by stressor events which then evoke shifts in social, biological, and psychological processes. We understand some of the processes, we realize there are interactions, and we are relatively well along in defining outcomes. We even know a bit about what disposes some people to have more intense, extended, or complicated responses to stressor events. This combination of the known and the unknown, and the need for more hypotheses to add to existing theory, might encourage more research in this interesting field.

12. Functional Disorders

Michael R. Trimble

In PREVIOUS WRITINGS, the terms 'hysteria' and 'functional' were mentioned on several occasions and their meanings not made very clear. This was because the users of the words were often imprecise. Thus, for example, Erichsen (1882) wrote:

'We will now proceed to the consideration of a condition of the nervous system that occasionally occurs as a result of spinal concussion, which appears in its clinical history, in its symptoms and probably in its pathology, closely allied to anaemia of the cord, and which for want of a better name we are apt to call "hysteria". . . . '

And two pages later: 'The symptoms indicative of this emotional or hysterical condition are. . . . ' While he was unclear in his usage of the word hysteria, he nevertheless suggested that the origins of the emotional symptoms were of the same pathology as other symptoms of 'spinal concussion'. Putnam (1881), as mentioned, was far more precise on the matter, and referred to the works of Charcot and his colleagues in Paris. However, Charcot's ideas were not representative of all thinkers on the subject. It is germane to consider therefore, in brief, the origins and ideas surrounding the concepts of hysteria, and their relationship to the problems of 'railway spine', and also to discuss the closely related terms 'functional' and 'psychogenic'.

The term hysteria, as outlined by Veith (1965), had its origins in Egyptian and Greek medicine, being derived from the word 'hystera', meaning uterus. The symptoms of hysteria were thought initially to be related to this organ and its wandering, which having dried up, was supposed to search the body for moisture, and the patient's complaints thus depended on where it came to rest. Several ingenious methods were designed by physicians to entice the errant organ back to its proper anatomical location, including vaginal fumigations. This mode of thinking assumed a unity between physical and psychological symptoms, which continued well into the Middle Ages. The latter

Reprinted by permission of John Wiley & Sons, Ltd., from Michael Trimble *Post-Traumatic Neurosis: From Railway Spine to the Whiplash*, by 33–35. 1981.

however was an era pervaded by devils and demons who were held responsible for patients' maladies, and many people were persecuted as witches who would now be diagnosed as suffering from hysteria or neurosis.

An advance in understanding about hysteria came in the sixteenth century from Edward Jorden (1569–1632). This little-known English physician wrote a book with the grand title:

A BRIEFE DISCOURSE OF A DISEASE CALLED THE SUFFOCATION OF THE MOTHER. WRITTEN UPON OCCASION WHICH HATH BEENE OF LATE TAKEN THEREBY, TO SUSPECT POSSESSION OF AN EVIL SPIRIT, OR SOME SUCH LIKE SUPERNATURAL POWER. WHEREIN IS DECLARED THAT DIVERS STRANGE ACTIONS AND PASSIONS OF THE BODY OF MAN WHICH IN THE COMMON OPINION, ARE IMPUTED TO THE DEVIL, HAVE THEIR TRUE NATURALL CAUSES, AND DO ACCOMPANIE THIS DISEASE.

Not only did this book contain notes on the signs and symptoms of psychiatric disorders but, as the title suggests, also claimed that such disorders were natural, rather than supernatural, and presumably were within the realm of the study of medicine. Jorden, while still persisting in uterine aetiologies, suggested that:

'it is an affect of the mother or wombe wherein the principall parts of the bodie by consent do suffer diversly according to the diversitie of the causes and diseases wherewith the matrix is offended. . . . The principall parts of the body are the seates of the three faculties, which do governe the whole body. The braine of the animall, the hart of the vitall, the liver of the naturall. . . . These parts are affected in this disease, and do suffer in *their functions* as they are diminished, depraved, or abolished, according to the nature and plenty of the humor, and the temperament and situation of the mother.'

He, for the first time thus implied that the brain was involved in the origins of hysteria, and that the brain's *functions* were altered in the disease.

The idea that the brain was affected in hysteria was taken up and elaborated by both Willis and Sydenham. Thomas Willis (1621–73), often called the founder of modern neurology, was one of the great seventeenth century English physicians. He clearly implicated the brain as the seat of hysteria, and explained the situation in the following way (Willis, 1664): ' . . . the passions commonly called hysterical, arise most often, from the animal spirits, possessing the beginning of the nerves within the head, and infected with some taint.' He took his ideas further by providing post-mortem evidence to demonstrate that the uterus of patients who had died but suffered hysteria were normal. The animal spirits concept, supported by Willis, was still essentially monistic, and did not invoke, as did his contemporary Sydenham

(1624–83) the Cartesian dualism which was later to become the order of the day. Thus Descartes (1596–1650), the seventeenth century philosopher, brought to completion or nearly so, the dualism of mind and matter which was perhaps originally formulated by Plato, and which was cultivated for religious reasons by the Christian theologians. In this scheme, mind and matter were two separate independent worlds. Since mind did not move the body, animal spirits ceased to be the cornerstone of the link between mind and body. As Descartes himself recorded (Descartes, 1649):

'. . . I regard the human body as a machine so built and put together of bone, nerve, muscle, vein, blood and skin, that still, although it had no mind, it would not fail to move in all the same ways as at present, since it does not move by the direction of its will, nor consequently by means of the mind, but only by the arrangement of its organs.'

With regard to the mind he commented:

'I knew then that I was a substance, whose whole essence or nature is, but to think and who to be, hath need of no place, nor depends on any materiall thing. So that this me, to wit, my soul by which I am what I am, is wholly distinct from the body, and more easie to be known than it; . . . '

These ideas permitted the expression of new theories in medical thinking, in that they allowed doctors to postulate natural causes for disease without treading on religious ideology. The influence of Descartes is clear in the writings of Sydenham who observed many cases of hysteria and thought it was prevalent: 'Of all chronic disease hysteria . . . is the commonest . . . few of the maladies of miserable mortality are not imitated by it . . . ' (Sydenham, 1740). Hysteria, however, had its origins in the mind: 'The remote or external causes of hysteria are over-ordinate actions of the body, and still oftener over-ordinate commotions of the mind.'

The term 'neurologie' was originally used by Willis (1667) in his book *Pathologiae Cerebri et Nervosi Generis Specimen*, and subsequently became widely used. Robert Whytt (1714–66), the first Scottish 'neurologist', was the first person to define precisely the meaning of the term 'nervous'. For him 'nervous' clearly implied conditions arising from a disordered nervous system, and hysteria was included under the category 'nervous'. He wrote (Whytt, 1768):

'Those disorders may, peculiarly, deserve the name nervous, which, on account of an unusual delicacy, or unnatural state of the nerves, are produced by causes, which in people of a sound constitution, would either have no such effects, or at least in a much less degree.'

It was, however, William Cullen (1710–90), another Scottish physician from Edinburgh, who made the most significant contribution of this era. He was especially interested in the classification of diseases, and his views had a lasting influence on medical thought. He recognized in his taxonomy four principal categories, namely fevers, cachexias, local disorders, and neuroses. The 'neuroses' were further subdivided to include comata, adynamae, spasmi, and vesaniae. The first three subcategories included such disorders as paralysis and tetanus, and the vesaniae were the disorders of the 'intellectual functions'. He thus used the term 'neuroses' for nervous disorders in general, those which 'depend on a more general affection of the nervous system'. For him these diseases all arose in disturbed brain activity and

'These affections of the mind must be considered as depending upon a certain state of our corporeal part. . . . We cannot doubt that the operations of our intellect always depend upon certain motions taking place in the brain. . . . It is very probable that the state of the intellectual *functions* depends chiefly upon the state and condition of what is termed nervous power. . . . ' (Cullen, 1772)

This distinction of the neuroses being dependent on disordered nerve 'motions' was very influential. As time progressed, and knowledge of neurology advanced, many of the conditions described by Cullen became discrete neurological entities, and underlying structural brain pathology identified or at least suggested. However, the neuroses and in particular the disorders he classified under vesaniae, were still associated with disturbed nerve power.

Although other writers around the same time were expressing similar views to those of Cullen, the first use of the word 'functional' in reference to nervous diseases was by another Edinburgh physician in the nineteenth century, Andrew Coombe (1797–1847). It is perhaps no accident that his ideas follow from Whytt and Cullen, since both these men had been at Edinburgh before him.

'Function' as a term had been in use in the English language about 300 years before this, although its use as meaning 'a special kind of activity' had more recent origins (Dallenbach, 1915). There are, from the point of view of this discussion, two main lines of reference. One pertains to a physiological use, that is the activity of an organ, the other to its psychological use, as activity of the intellectual or emotional faculties. In these senses the word does not appear in the writings of, for example Hobbes (1588–1679), Locke (1632–1704), Berkeley (1685–1753), or Hume (1711–1776), in spite of the fact that all wrote extensively on psychology, and Locke had a medical training. Hartley (1705–1757), in his *Observations on Man* (1748) used the word 20 times, mainly in the physiological sense, writing for example about the structure and functions of several organs. Many authors around this time used the word in both senses. Brown (1778–1820), in his *Sketch of a System of the Philosophy of the Human Mind* (1820), however, made specific reference to mental phenomena:

'The innumerable changes, corporeal and mental, we reduce, by generalising, to a few classes; and we speak, in reference to the mind, of its faculties or *functions* of perception, memory, reason. . . . '

Cullen, as noted above, also made reference to 'intellectual functions'.

It was, however, according to Dallenbach, through phrenology that the use of the psychological, as opposed to the physiological sense, of the term became more widespread. Gall (1758–1828) and Spurzheim (1776–1832), lectured widely on such doctrines throughout Europe. While in earlier work, Gall wrote only of 'functions of the brain', later the extended use of the term for psychological reference is clear, and 'function' became synonymous with the older terms such as power or faculty.

Coombe was a supporter of the 'new science of phrenology', which led him to consider the brain and its functions. He said (1831):

' . . . In prosecuting our researches into what are erroneously called mental diseases, we must . . . study the nature of the organic disorder which disturbs *mental functions*.'

However, he then reverted to the physiological use of the term:

'In accordance with the view we have elsewhere taken the exciting causes may be divided into the two great classes of local and *functional*.'

He continued:

'The *functional causes*, then, which have a reference to the brain as the seat of feeling and thought, are not only the most frequent and most important, but in the strictest sense *functional*. . . . The term *functional* has a reference to disorder in the action of the organs of mind. . . . '

The psychological meaning of the term functional continued in use alongside the physiological, both often being used in the same text. Some neurologists, however, following the lead of Coombe, split neurological illness into 'organic' and 'functional' categories, using the latter in its physiological sense.

The ideas of Reynolds and Gowers provide examples of such thinking. Reynolds (1828–96), writing on the symptoms of disease said that they 'resolve themselves into modifications of structure such as hypertrophy, variolous pustules, etc., and of *function*, as for example paralysis, convulsions, flux and the like'. He took up the challenge of some contemporary authors that functional disease did not exist, by pointing out that there was an obvious relation between functional and structural disease. Thus 'the immediate conditions of all such symptoms as result from modified functions being the intimate organic (vegetal) processes of the tissues . . . the mechanical changes . . . do not cause the symptoms directly, but by the intervention of secondary induced alterations in the minute organic processes' (Reynolds, 1855). The two were thus mutually interdependent and related.

Gowers (1893) in his well-known textbook *A Manual of Diseases of the Nervous System* divided neurological disorders into organic and functional disease. The latter included 'those diseases that consist only in a disturbance of *function* . . . and many diseases which have this in common with true *functional* disease, that they are transient and not permanent, and that they are not known to depend on organic changes'. He went on to say:

'Molecular changes in nutrition, considered as such, must be colossal to be detected. Such alterations, not sufficient to be seen, but still considerable, probably constitute the morbid process in many diseases that are commonly classed as *"functional"*.'

In his text, under the heading 'functional' are included such disorders as chorea, paralysis agitans, tetanus, epilepsy, and migraine. They keep company with hysteria, of which Gowers said:

'The primary derangement is in the higher cerebral centres, but the functions of the lower centres in the brain, of the spinal cord, and of the sympathetic system, may be secondarily disordered.'

Hughlings Jackson (1835–1911) (Taylor 1958) also considered the use of the term functional. He said:

'it is sometimes used as a name for minute changes, or for those the existence of which we are obliged to discover post-mortem. For instance, it is said that epilepsy and chorea are functional diseases, it being meant that the changes on which the symptoms depend are so slight that they do not involve alteration of structure, but only of function. . . . I have . . . used the term "functional" to describe the morbid alterations of the *normal function* of nerve tissue.'

He went on to consider two fundamental kinds of alteration of function by disease, namely loss of function and over-function. 'In the latter, more nerve force is stored up than in health, and more is therefore expended; the nerve tissue is highly unstable.' He was anxious to point out that functional abnormalities are physiological states, rather than pathological conditions, and that while certain diseases (e.g. tumours) are said to 'cause' convulsions, what really was happening was that the tumour led to neuronal instability.

Of particular relevance to the issue of posttraumatic neurosis are the ideas of the German physician Oppenheim (1858–1919), who originally used the term 'traumatic neuroses'. Oppenheim was a pupil of Westphal, who favoured the view that functional symptoms were due to small myelitic or encephalitic lesions. Oppenheim's *Textbook of Nervous Diseases for Physicians and Students* (1911) was widely known towards the end of the last century. He abandoned the views of Westphal, and attributed the symptoms of concussion to functional disturbances which he assumed 'are produced by molecular changes in the central nervous system' (Oppenheim, 1911). He felt that the term 'railway brain' was more appropriate than 'railway spine', in that the brain rather than the spine was the seat of many of the conditions. Incidentally, he made the very interesting observation not only that any injury can induce posttraumatic neurosis, but that it may also develop after surgical operations—for some reason especially after operations on the ear.

Erichsen, in his book, had not totally ignored the concept of functional illness and discussed briefly hysteria and its role in the production of symptoms. However, he felt that 'hysteria' was a word that 'serves as a cloak to ignorance, and which simply means a group of symptoms all subjective and each one separately common to many morbid states'. He was quite emphatic about its incidence:

'During a hospital practice of thirty years I can scarcely recall to mind a single case in which the emotional or hysterical state . . . has been met with after, or as a consequence of, any of the ordinary accidents of civil life.'

He did suggest nevertheless that it was seen after railway accidents, this he felt being due to the marked difference between such accidents and 'ordinary accidents'.

'The crash and confusion, the uncertainty attendant on the railway collision, the shrieks of the sufferers, possibly the sight of the victims of the catastrophe, produce a mental impression of a far deeper and more vivid character than is occasioned by the more ordinary accidents of civil life.'

Erichsen, however, was confident that making the distinction between hysteria and 'concussion of the spine' was simple. 'It certainly has always appeared extraordinary to me' he wrote 'that so great an error of diagnosis could so easily be made'.

Others, including Page, were not so sure or dogmatic. Paget (1902), invented the name 'neuromimesis' for these disorders, 'because the symptoms thereof are so prone to mimic those which are due to undoubted pathological change'. Page, acknowledging Paget, devoted a whole chapter to 'Functional or Neuromimetic Disorders'. Differing from the views of Erichsen he felt that it was very common to mistake hysteria for structural disease, and that hysteria was a common sequel to railway accidents. Moreover, there was no evidence that functional disorders ever progressed to become cases of organic disease. In one passage Page was again critical of Erichsen. He had just described a case history of a healthy 30 year-old male who developed back pains following a collision, and then had an abnormal gait. The patient received a large compensation award, and three and a half years later was apparently in perfect health.

'That there never was any lesion of the spinal cord the issue of the case has abundantly proved, and we cannot help thinking that such a diagnosis would never have been raised were the influences of the mind upon the body more fully recognised, and were it not unfortunately regarded as almost a matter of course that the injuries received in, and the symptoms seen after, railway collision must be due to "concussion of the spine" and be followed by the chronic meningitis and the myelitis, and the "inflammatory irritation of the membranes" of which we hear so much but which no man has ever seen.'

Page then, unlike Erichsen, clearly felt that nervous shock and hysteria were responsible for many of the symptoms of patients seen following railway accidents. It was a simple step, as already seen, for the classification of the sequelae of accidents to be made logical, by Hodges, into organic and functional. However the term 'functional' was soon to alter radically in meaning. First the works of Charcot must be discussed.

Jean-Martin Charcot, the son of a Paris carriage builder, became Médecin de l'Hospice de la Salpêtrière in 1862, at the age of 37. Of the hospital he wrote:

'This great asylum holds a population of 5,000 persons, among whom are to be counted a large number who have been admitted for life as incurables. . . . We are . . . in possession of a sort of museum of living pathology of which the resources are great.'

He was soon to become one of the most famous neurologists of all time, and by the year of his death in 1893 the framework of modern neurology had been laid down. The neuroses were studied at the Salpêtrière between 1862 and 1892, and Charcot was particularly interested in the subject of the post-traumatic neuroses. His work in this field was considered to be great. Pierre Marie said after his death:

'But what dominates the work of Charcot on hysteria, that which will never perish and will continue to serve as a guide to future medical generations, was his demonstration of the existence of hysteria in the male, and his indomitable studies on traumatic hysteria. . . . ' (Guillain, 1959)

It is often thought that Charcot was deceived by his patients and that his results were influenced by this, particularly with regard to the work on hysteria. His biographer, Guillain, refutes this. Thus of malingering Charcot himself said (1889):

'It is found in every phase of hysteria and one is surprised at times to admire the ruse, the sagacity and the unyielding tenacity that especially the women, who are under the influence of a severe neurosis, display in order to deceive . . . especially when the victim of the deceit happens to be a physician . . . '

Charcot began to investigate hysteria using the same methods he had used for studying organic neurological disease. Although he elaborated a more psychological theory of hysteria than others of his time, it was still clearly neurophysiological, and concerned with abnormal function of the brain in various hysterical states. He recognized and described the stigmata which are found in patients with hysteria, such as the anaesthesias and the reduction in visual fields, and attempted to explain them. For example the hemi-anaesthesia 'such as is presented in hysteria—may, in certain cases, be produced by a circumscribed lesion of the cerebral hemispheres' (Charcot, 1877). He acknowledged Briquet's advance in the field of establishing 'beyond dispute that hysteria is governed in the same way as other morbid conditions, by rules and laws which attentive and sufficiently numerous observations always permit us to establish. . . . Thus we are brought to recognize that the principles which govern pathology as a whole are applicable to neuroses . . . '.

He recognized that hysteria affected men as well as women, and suggested it was often found in males after railway accidents. Railway spine and railway brain he felt were in fact manifestations of hysteria.

'These serious and obstinate nervous states which present themselves after collisions of this kind, and which render their victims incapable of working . . . are very often hysteria.' (Charcot, 1889).

He opposed the ideas of Oppenheim and the German school of establishing a separate category of 'traumatic neurosis' for these conditions, and suggested that a common mechanism was responsible for the production of the symptoms in all types of the disorder, whether traumatic or otherwise. He supported his ideas with the experimental induction of symptoms in patients by hypnosis. For example, he would suggest to a patient that when out of the hypnotic state they would become paralyzed after a slap on the back. In that the symptoms he suggested were induced in this way, and were exactly the same as a posttraumatic monoplegia, it seemed as if he had demonstrated the mechanism for the production of symptoms.

Charcot used the term 'functional' in the physiological sense that several others outlined above suggested. Thus in discussing the aetiology of a hysterical upper limb paralysis he said:

'There is without doubt a lesion of the nervous centres, but where is it situated, and what is its nature? It is, I opine, in the grey matter of the cerebral hemisphere on the side opposite the paralysis, and more precisely in the motor zone of the arm. . . . But certainly it is not of the nature of a circumscribed organic lesion of a destructive nature . . . We have here unquestionably one of those lesions which escape our present means of anatomical investigation, and which, for want of a better term, we designate dynamic or *functional* lesions.' (Charcot, 1889)

Perhaps even more significant than Charcot's work on posttraumatic hysteria was his bringing together of two other key figures in the history of neurology and psychiatry. Sigmund Freud (1856–1939) applied for, and received, from the University of Vienna, a six-month travelling grant, and chose to visit Paris and study under Charcot. There he was introduced to Pierre Janet (1859–1947), and was able to discuss with him the related problems of hypnosis and the unconscious. Later in his life Freud wrote: 'Pierre Janet, Bleuler and others were able to formulate a theory of the neuroses which was scientifically acceptable because of Charcot's concepts.' Both Janet and Freud broadened the notion of hysteria, and with it ideas on the aetiology of the neuroses and in particular the posttraumatic neuroses. Janet paid great attention to unconscious factors in the formation of hysterical symptoms, and actually used the word 'unconscious' in his writings. He was, however, unable to take the step made by Freud, and still held on to the notion that the brain in hysteria was in some way abnormal and weak. He rejected both a neurological theory, and ideas which suggested symptoms were faked, considering hysteria as a 'psychogenic' disease. There was a basic feature, namely narrowing of the field of consciousness.

'The hysterical personality cannot perceive all the phenomena: it definitely sacrifices some of them. It is a kind of autotomia and the abandoned phenomena develop independently without the subject being aware of them.' (Janet, 1893)

Discussion of the term psychogenic should at this stage be briefly introduced. According to Lewis (1972) it first appeared in the early nineteenth century, and was considered to refer to the 'origin of the mind, or to evolutionary development which had been due to the activity of mind in animals and human beings'. Sommer (1894) introduced it into psychiatry in a discussion on the nature of hysteria, a disorder which he felt was 'evoked by ideas, and influenced by ideas'. It soon established itself to mean 'caused by psychological factors', although various authors, including Janet, discussed the relative contribution of premorbid personality in association with other factors that led to the appearance of symptoms. His theories were not, however, 'psychogenic' in the same sense as those developed by Freud.

In the German literature towards the end of the last century the term psychogenesis was used imprecisely, but the concept flourished with the developing ideas of Freud. While it is not intended to discuss his writings in any detail, his ideas are crucial for the profound influence they have had, not only on the history of ideas generally, but particularly on the development of psychiatry and the split that occurred, in some countries at least, with neurology. Before his time the speciality psychiatry, as an independent speciality from neurology, was not universally recognized. Freud himself numbered neuropathology amongst early specialist interest, and worked with Brucke and Meynert prior to his visit to Paris. After this, however, he devoted the rest of his professional life to psychiatry. He said:

'I abandoned the treatment of organic nervous disease, but that was of little importance. For on the one hand the prospects in the treatment of such disorders were in any case never promising, while on the other hand, in the private practice of a physician working in a large town, the quantity of such patients was nothing compared to the crowds of neurotics, whose number seemed further multiplied by the manner in which they hurried, with their troubles unsolved, from one physician to another.' (Freud, 1946)

He returned to Vienna and was keen to spread the news of Charcot's work and discoveries to his colleagues. In 1886 he presented a paper to the Viennese medical society which has direct bearing on the subject of posttraumatic neurosis. Freud began by telling the members present of his visit to Paris, and of Charcot's concepts of hysteria. He explained the differences between 'grande hystérie' (when special types of convulsions were present), and 'petite hystérie'. He pointed out that hysteria was not due to disease of the genital organs, that it was not malingering, and that it commonly occurred in males. This last point was contentious in that it was still generally considered that hysteria was confined to women. Although, as Veith (1965) points out,

Galen ascribed to men a condition resembling hysteria, and this was repeated by several physicians throughout history including Sydenham (1740) (who referred to the male version of hysteria as hypochondriasis, in that the hypochondrium in males behaved similarly to the uterus in females), in Austria, at the time Freud was reporting, hysteria was still considered by many to be a condition of women, and in any case was thought unrelated to posttraumatic illness. Charcot referred to male hysteria both in the 'classical' sense, and also as seen in the posttraumatic cases. Freud presented these ideas and supported his argument by discussing a case of Charcot's whom he had seen in Paris. The patient was a young man who had an industrial accident, and then developed paralysis of an arm. The patient had a range of 'stigmata', and Freud argued that such cases, and also cases of railway spine, should be considered examples of hysteria.

The ensuing discussion on Freud's paper was heated. Ellenberger (1970) suggests that the Viennese physicians were not, however, in conflict over Freud's presentation of a case of male hysteria; several of them attested the condition by commenting on cases of their own, but the main dissent was about his equating posttraumatic neuroses with hysteria.

In 1893 Charcot died in Paris, and with him his ideas and prestige. According to Ellenberger (1970), the good of Charcot, like all great men, was interred with his bones. At the Salpêtrière his legend turned to that of 'the despot scientist whose belief in his own superiority blinded him . . . ', and the controversy about traumatic neurosis and male hysteria continued for a few years only.

Nevertheless research into the neuroses continued in Vienna. Freud, through his friendship with Josef Breuer, developed further his ideas about neurosis, psychogenesis, and hysteria. Initially working on cathartic hypnosis they found many patients who did not respond to treatment, and altered their methods to develop what was referred to as the 'talking treatment.' Freud became very impressed with the idea of unconscious psychological motivation and went on to develop a complete psychological theory of hysteria. In *Studies in Hysteria*, published jointly with Breuer in 1895, the idea was expressed that the symptoms of hysteria were due to repressed memories of traumatic events, which were emotionally arousing in that they were not permitted expression, and thus symptoms developed in their place. They likened hysteria to posttraumatic neurosis, commenting:

'Our experiences have shown us, however, that the most various symptoms, which are ostensibly spontaneous and, as one might say, idiopathic products of hysteria, are just as strictly related to the precipitating trauma as the phenomena to which we have just alluded and which exhibit the connection quite clearly.'

However, the trauma for them was a psychological, as opposed to a physical event, which was often not immediately apparent, and frequently was defined as an episode in childhood. Sometimes such events were clear, but often the cause was obscured by 'symbolic relations between the precipitating cause and the pathological phenomenon'. Precipitating causes, defined as 'psychical traumas', were 'ideogenic'.

Initially the necessity for some idiosyncrasy in the form of 'abnormal excitations of the nervous system' was invoked to explain the interaction between the person and the trauma such that: ' . . . in such people the excitation of the central organ can flow into the sensory nervous apparatuses which are normally accessible only to peripheral stimuli. . . . ' Later, as Freud developed his structuralized model of the mind, other factors were introduced, and a mechanism was suggested as follows:

'Accordingly the real traumatic moment is that in which the conflict thrusts itself upon the ego and the latter decides to banish it. Such banishment does not annihilate the opposing presentation but merely crowds it into the unconscious. This process, occurring for the first time, forms a nucleus and point of crystallization for the formation of a new psychic group separated from the ego, around which, in the course of time, everything collects in accord with the opposing presentation.' (Freud, 1920).

Freud himself did not write much on the specific topic of the posttraumatic neuroses following physical accidents, and it was left to his followers to develop ideas on the subject. With Breuer (1895) he commented:

'During the days following a railway accident, for instance, the subject will live through his frightful experiences again both in sleeping and waking, and always with the renewed affect of fright, till at last, after this period of "psychical working-out", or of "incubation", conversion into somatic phenomenon takes place.'

Further ideas are suggested by this short extract from *Psychopathology of Everyday Life* (1914):

'Similarly, to fall, to make a misstep, or to slip need not always be interpreted as an entirely accidental miscarriage of a motor action. The linguistic double meaning of these expressions points to diverse hidden fantasies, which may present themselves through the giving up of bodily equilibrium. I recall a number of lighter nervous ailments in women and girls which made their appearance after falling without injury, and which were conceived as traumatic hysteria as a result of the shock of the fall. At that time I already entertained the impression that these conditions had a different connection, that the fall was already a preparation of the neurosis, and an expression of the same unconscious fantasies of sexual content which may be taken as the moving forces behind the symptoms. Was not this very thing meant in the proverb which says "When a maiden falls, she falls on her back?".'

Otto Fenichel (1898–1946) wrote about the posttraumatic neurosis. In this condition he felt that there was blocking of ego functions associated with regressive phenomena of a variety of kinds. For him trauma that 'upset the entire economy of the mental energy also of necessity upset the equilibrium between the repressed impulses and the repressing forces' (Fenichel, 1946). In addition, the accidents were perceived as a threat of either loss of love or castration anxiety, feelings which until the accident the patient had successfully overcome.

Ideas in psychoanalysis altered with time, and the original theories of Freud were modified. One development, which occurred particularly in the United States of America, was that which increasingly emphasised ego function, as opposed to 'repressed impulses' and what may be called the more 'id'-orientated theories of Freud. Examples come from the works of Kamman and Kardiner. Kamman (1951) thus stated that posttraumatic neurosis 'is not an organic lesion but a failure in the victim's total possibilities for adaptation'. The neurosis was 'psychogenic' by which he meant the result of conflicting forces or drives within the personality structure of the individual. The posttraumatic neurosis was seen as a 'reaction', and was in no way related therefore to the type of injury causing it. In compensation neurosis, which he categorized separately from posttraumatic neurosis, although the patient consciously believes he is ill, careful examination reveals a 'volitional factor' with a foreconscious or unconscious desire for gain. The disorder, he felt, was precipitated by environmental factors, one of which was the prospect of compensation, acting in association with personality defects.

Kardiner (1941) undertook research on patients with posttraumatic neurosis that developed during war-time when many cases of neurosis and hysteria which developed on the battlefield were seen by doctors, and their presentation added much fuel to the psychological ideas of aetiology. Kardiner, like some other authors around at this time, concentrated on the ego and its disturbances. Examples of this type of thinking include such statements as:

'There is uniformity in the symptoms of the acute state; this uniformity yields to considerable diversification during the transitional phase; and when chronic, the symptoms tend to fall again into three or four main groups. The one conclusion warranted by this is that in the transitional phase the individual makes many efforts to master the anxiety and in doing so employs every resource found useful to him in his past experience.'

'The traumatic event creates excitations beyond the possibility of mastering and inflicts a severe blow to the total ego organisation. The activities involved in successful adaptation to the external environment become blocked in their usual outlets. . . . The adaptation to the external world is the result of a complicated series of integrations, which owe their existence in part to the narcissistic gratification of success. As a result of the trauma, that portion of the ego which normally helps the individual carry out automatically certain organised . . . *functions* . . . on the basis of innumerable successes in the past, is either destroyed or inhibited.'

Such ideas need not be elaborated further here, but it is important to recognize not only the shift to a psychological use of the term function, but also the advance in thought about psychogenesis which came about by the observations of patients with posttraumatic neurosis in the war situation which represented a fundamentally different approach to psychiatric patients than the earlier Freudian ideas had called for. Symptoms were not now thought of in terms of 'conflict' between two internal systems of the mind (ego and id), but were seen more in terms of a failure of the adaptation of the individual to a new (and changed) environment. 'Adaptation' said Kardiner 'is a series of manoeuvres in response to changes in the external environment, or to changes within the organisation, which counsel some activity in the outer world in order to continue existence, to remain intact or free from harm, and to maintain controlled contact with it.' In this scheme the posttraumatic neuroses were seen as 'the record of the lasting consequences of an abrupt change in the external environment to which the resources of the individual are unequal'. The ego thus fails in its adaptation to the situation and symptoms result.

By this time both the words 'functional' and 'psychogenic' had lost their original meanings. 'Psychogenic', instead of having, as for Freud, some concept of an internal mental mechanism, had become equated mainly with external events, stress, and pressure. As with the early history of 'functional', several authors came to use the term in a nondiscriminating way, for example Faergeman (1963) who suggested that 'psychogenic' could mean either 'growing out of innate constitutional factors' or a 'psychopathic condition covered by environmental factors with which the organism cannot cope'. Jorgensen (1956) despaired of the situation stating that ' . . . there exists no universally valid definition of the concept 'psychogenesis'. . . . Purely external psychic causes do not exist'. Lewis (1972) quoted several contemporary definitions to demonstrate the current 'shoddy state of the term'. For example: 'Psychogenic disorders of the personality are those that seem to arise largely because of disturbed interpersonal relations, social maladjustments and the like' (Cobb); or 'The psychogenic disorders of man are in fact sociogenic' (Wolf); to the meaningless statement 'Psychogenic, term usually employed of disorders which originate in mental conditions' (Drever). Lewis's own belief was that someone had done a disservice to psychiatry by giving it the term 'psychogenic' and felt it to be ' . . . at the mercy of inconsistent theoretical positions touching on the fundamental problems of causality, dualism, and normality. It would do well at this stage to give it a decent burial, along with some of the fruitless controversies whose fire it has stoked'.

'Functional' has been the subject of several manuscripts, likewise ending in disrepute. Gore (1922), a lecturer in neurology at Victoria University of Manchester, wrote a book entitled *Functional Nervous Disorders: Their Classification and Treatment.* After acknowledging the difficulties of defining 'functional diseases' he went on to state:

'Functional nervous disorders are the expressions of abnormally controlled emotional reactions, determined and adjusted by environmental factors and not by any gross or demonstrable pathological lesion.'

Ramsay (1939), in a personal series of injury cases found that 41% developed 'functional (as opposed to organic) disease' in response to the injury. He outlined four main types of disorder: post-concussion syndrome, hysteria, neurasthenia, and anxiety state. The first of these he actually felt 'may be more of an anxiety state', and the seemingly large number of such disorders in his series was a reflection of the fact that in general practice the incidence of 'functional disease' was itself high. The aetiology was explained thus:

' . . . in such cases the soil is ready for the seed; in other words, that some mental conflict or maladjustment to life was already present and that the injury acted as an exciting cause of the psychoneurotic symptoms which developed subsequently. They are usually more prone to suggestion. . . . '

It seems that he was using 'functional' as synonymous with a psychiatric diagnosis.

Nearer to the present, Blake Pritchard, physician to Maida Vale Hospital, while equating functional with hysterical and thus detracting from its broader meaning, discussed the word 'functional', and highlighted why difficulty had arisen with it. He emphasized that both 'functional' and 'hysterical' implied a positive diagnosis. These problems did not present, as is still commonly assumed, as a bizarre mélange of symptoms without uniformity, but had recognizable characteristics, repeated from patient to patient in a similar form. 'If the essential possible characteristics of a functional or hysterical disturbance are absent, judgement should be suspended, further observations made, and further help sought.' He suggested the use of the term functional 'does no more than describe a particular kind of behaviour disturbance, and is applicable when we do not know whether the cause is in the mind or the brain or in both'. He pointed out that the concept of functional disease as due to altered activity of neurones without physical change did not survive the rapid development of neurophysiology that occurred in this century.

'The reason why "functional" did not survive as a precise and useful term was that the notion of function was uncritically equated with that of activity . . . and ceased, on this basis to have any valid significance . . . the activities of nervous structures can be observed and demonstrated: their functions, although they may be inferred and may be asserted, can be neither observed or demonstrated' (Blake Pritchard, 1955)

Contemporary use of the word has floundered completely. Not only does it refer to psychiatric illness generally, but also to 'those conditions in which symptoms and signs result not from any primary physical disease but from conscious or sub-conscious mental processes . . . ' (Brain and Walton, 1969). Confusion is such that clinically patients are often diagnosed as 'functional', as if this were an end to the diagnostic process, and it is assumed that by using this term everyone understands, except the patient, what the cause of his symptoms are. The point is well made by this anecdote from Kessel (1979):

'A professor of medicine was consulted by a middle-aged lady with stomachache. On her second visit he looked one by one at her X-rays and then turned to her, beaming, and said: "I'm glad to be able to tell you that they don't show anything wrong." Seeing her crestfallen face he asked her if that was not what she wanted to hear. "Well *my* doctor told me", she explained indignantly, "that I've got a *large functional element.*" '

However, there still exists a line of thought handed down from beyond Charcot, essentially non-Cartesian. That is of a physiological psychology, based on an understanding of disturbed nerve function in 'functional disorders'. Kinnier Wilson (1930), for example, was critical of the clinico-anatomical method, and what he called the 'neurological school of medical thought'. He said:

'Accordingly clinical symptoms are to be considered as representing either excitation or cessation of function, or a series in which the latter follows the former. Without exception all are *functional* in the sense of being related to function. To attempt to distinguish "functional" from "organic" symptoms is therefore meaningless.'

He followed this with a personal anecdote from his teacher Bastian, who, when told there was a patient on the ward who suffered from functional fits, replied, 'Did you ever see a fit that was not functional?' and said, 'I then secured an insight into semeiology which I trust I have never since failed to maintain'.

Foster Kennedy served as a further stepping stone, and the recent discovery of the neurotransmitters as the final common path. He said:

'In the millions of nerves in the grey matter of the brain and cord, with their enormous aggregation of processes, there exists the complicated mechanism in which are represented our highest mental functions and the mainspring of physical action. In what manner mental processes and emotional states are evolved from or through nervous structure is as yet hidden from us. Our ignorance becomes more plain in those nervous disorders known as "functional", the symptoms of which are subjective. There is evidence, however, and overwhelming evidence, that structural nerve changes underlie subjective clinical manifestations. There must be organic change causing or paralleling our psychic phenomena. But what these may be, the finer strains of gold and silver and the most careful chemical analysis have as yet failed to disclose.' (Kennedy, 1930)

The theme of neurotransmission, and some other current neurobiological concepts of functional disorders will be discussed later. However, the point is made that even though a mainstream of thought developed in the light of writings of Janet and Freud that psychiatric illness and posttraumatic neurosis implied psychological psychiatric disturbance, throughout there has been an undercurrent arguing for a physiologically based psychiatry with all that it implied.

REFERENCES

Blake Pritchard, E. A. (1955) The functional symptoms of organic disease of the brain. Lancet i, 363.

Brain, W. R. and Walton, J. N. (1969) Diseases of the Nervous System. 7th Edition Oxford University Press, Oxford.

Brown, T. (1820) Sketch of a system of the philosophy of the human mind. Edinburgh.

Charcot, J. M. (1877) Lectures on the Diseases of the Nervous System. New Sydenham Society, London.

Charcot, J. M. (1889) Clinical Lectures on Diseases of the Nervous System. Vol. II. New Sydenham Society, London.

Coombe, A. (1831) Observations on Mental Derangement: Being an application of the principles of phrenology to the elucidation of the causes, symptoms, nature and treatment of insanity. Anderson, Edinburgh.

Cullen, W. (1772) Nosology: or a systematic arrangement of diseases by classes, order, genera, and species; with the distinguishing characters of each, and outlines of the systems of Sauvages, Linnaeus, Vogel, Sagar and MacBride. *Creech, Edinburgh.*

Dallenbach, K. M. *(1915) The history and derivation of the word 'function' as a systematic term in psychology.* Journal of Psychology 26, 473.

Descartes, R. *(1649)* Philosophical Works, *Trans. and ed. Haldane, E. S. and Ross, G. R. T. Cambridge University Press, Cambridge (1931).*

Ellenberger, H. F. *(1970)* The Discovery of the Unconscious. *Basic Books, New York.*

Erichsen, J. E. *(1882)* On Concussion of the Spine: Nervous shock and other obscure injuries of the nervous system in their clinical and medico-legal aspects. *Longmans, Green and Co., London.*

Faergeman, P. M. *(1963)* Psychogenic Psychoses. *Butterworths, London.*

Fenichel, O. *(1946)* The Psychoanalytic Theory of Neurosis. *Kegan Paul, Trench, London.*

Freud, S. *(1914)* Psychopathology of Everyday Life. *Trans. Brill, A. A. T. Fisher Unwin, London.*

Freud, S. *(1920)* Selected Papers on Hysteria. *Nervous and Mental Diseases Monograph Series No 4.*

Freud, S. *(1946)* An Autobiographical Study. *Trans. Strachey. J. Hogarth Press, London.*

Freud, S. and Breuer, J. *(1895)* Studies on Hysteria. *Trans. Strachey, J. Hogarth Press (1955), London.*

Gore, D. E. *(1922)* Functional Nervous Disorders: Their classification and treatment. *John Wright and Sons, Bristol.*

Gowers, W. R. *(1893)* A Manual of Diseases of the Nervous System. *Reprinted 1970. Hatner Publishing Co., Darien, Conn.*

Guillain, G. *(1959)* J. M. Charcot. His Life—His Work. *Trans. Bailey, P. Pitman, London.*

Hartley, D. *(1748)* Observations on man, his fame, his duty and his expectations. *London, J. Johnson.*

Janet, P. *(1893)* Contribution à l'étude des accidents mentaux chez les hysteriques. *Rueff et Cie., Paris.*

Jorgensen, E. G. *(1956) On the concepts psychogenesis and psychosomatics.* Acta Psychiatrica Scandinavica Suppl. **108,** 135.

Kamman, G. R. *(1951) Traumatic neurosis, compensation neurosis or attitude pathosis?* Archives of Neurology and Psychiatry **65,** 593.

Kardiner, A. *(1941)* The Traumatic Neurosis of War. *Psychosomatic Medicine Monograph II–III. Paul B. Hoeber, New York.*

Kennedy, F. *(1930) Neuroses following accident.* Bulletin of the New York Academy of Medicine **6,** 1.

Kessel, N. *(1979) Reassurance.* Lancet **i,** 1128.

Lewis, A. *(1972) 'Psychogenic': a word and its mutations.* Psychological Medicine **2,** 209.

Oppenheim, H. *(1911)* Textbook of Nervous Diseases for Physicians and Students. *Trans. Bruce, A. T. N. Foulis, London.*

Paget, J. *(1902)* Selected Essays and Addresses. *Longmans, Green and Co., London.*

Putnam, J. J. (1881) Recent investigations into patients of so-called concussion of the spine. Boston Medical and Surgical Journal *109*, *217*.

Ramsay, J. (1939) Nervous disorder after injury. British Medical Journal *2*, *385*.

Reynolds, J. R. (1855) The Diagnosis of Diseases of the Brain, Spinal Cord, Nerves and their Appendages. *J. Churchill, London.*

Sommer, R. (1894) Diagnostik der Geisteskrankheiten *Urban und Schwarzenberg, Wien.*

Sydenham, T. (1740) The Whole Works. *11th Edition. Pechey, J. Ware & Wellington, London.*

Taylor, J. (1958) Selected Writings of John Hughlings Jackson. *Ed. Taylor, J. Staples Press, London.*

Thorne, F. C. (1949) The attitudinal pathosis. Journal of Clinical Psychology *5, 1.*

Veith, I. (1965) Hysteria. The History of a Disease. *University of Chicago Press, Chicago.*

Whytt, R. (1768) Observations on the Nature, Causes and Cure of those Disorders which have been called Nervous, Hypochondriac or Hysteric, to which are prefixed some Remarks on the Sympathy of the Nerves. *Beckett and Du Hondt, Edinburgh.*

Willis, T. (1664) Cerebri Anatome. *J. Flesher, London.*

Willis, T. (1667) Pathologiae cerebri et nervosi generis specimin. *Oxon.*

Wilson, S. A. K. (1930) Nervous semeiology with special reference to epilepsy. British Medical Journal *2, 1.*

13. The Human Meaning of Total Disaster
The Buffalo Creek Experience

Robert Jay Lifton and Eric Olson

IN LATE 1972 we were asked by lawyers from the Washington, D.C., firm of Arnold and Porter to consult on the psychological effects of the Buffalo Creek, West Virginia, flood disaster. At that time a case claiming damages for "psychic impairment" was being prepared on behalf of more than 600 people who had survived the February 1972 flood. The flood resulted from massive corporate negligence in the form of dumping coal waste in a mountain stream in a manner that created an artificial dam, resulting in increasingly dangerous water pressure behind it. After several days of rain the dam gave way, and a massive, moving wall of "black water" (containing the coal waste), more than 30 feet high, roared through the narrow creek hollow, devastating the mining hamlets along the 17-mile valley. In less than an hour the water reached the foot of the hollow at Man, West Virginia, and in that time 125 people were killed and nearly 5000 made homeless.

The ensuing days and weeks after the flood constituted what Kai Erikson called a second trauma, the deepening awareness that the fabric of community life had been irreparably destroyed.[1] The claim of "psychic impairment" in the lawsuit against the Pittston Company, whose Buffalo Mining Company subsidiary had built the dam, was based on the effects on the survivors' psychological well-being of the flood experience itself as well as the destruction of the community. The lawsuit was settled out of court in August 1974 for 13.5 million dollars, approximately half of which was based on "psychic impairment."

In connection with our consultation in the case we made, together and individually, five trips to Buffalo Creek between April 1973 and August 1974 and have conducted a total of 43 interviews involving 22 Buffalo Creek survivors. In addition we have talked with several ministers and volunteer workers in the area, and read through the extensive documentation of the

---

disaster compiled by a variety of observers and professional consultants working with the survivors.

The psychological impact of the disaster has been so extensive that no one in Buffalo Creek has been unaffected. The overwhelming evidence is that everyone exposed to the Buffalo Creek disaster has experienced some or all of the following manifestations of the general constellation of the survivor (Lifton, 1968, pp. 479–541).

DEATH IMPRINT AND DEATH ANXIETY

The first category of these survivor patterns is that of the *death imprint* and related *death anxiety*. The death imprint consists of memories and images of the disaster, invariably associated with death, dying, and massive destruction. These memories were still extremely vivid during interviews conducted 30 months after the flood, so that one can speak of them as *indelible images*. The memories of destruction were all-encompassing, so that a sense very close to the feeling that "it was the end of time" was present in many survivors. As one man whom we interviewed in May 1974 put it: "Everything came to an end—just stopped. Everything was wiped out."

Over the period of our visits we could observe the extent to which the anxiety and fear associated with these images took on chronic form—fear so strong in many as to constitute permanent inner terror. The fear tends to be associated with flood and disaster, with nature and the elements, and especially with rain and water. As one man put it in May 1974:

When it rained hard last week it was like the past came out again. I took the family down to the cellar and [at times like this] I just know the whole flood is going to come back. . . . it's like you might step out of the trailer and get caught in something. Everytime it rains I get the feeling that it's a natural thing for the floods to come.

In other words, what is ordinarily "unnatural" destruction has become, psychologically speaking, "natural"—what one expects to happen. The same man, like many others, is unable to sleep when it rains, because "I don't want to be caught in bed with the flood." He goes on to recognize that the fear is irrational: "Knowing that the water couldn't get to me now doesn't help." He feels compelled to "keep checking the river" and to "keep pacing the house." For water has become the enemy—"I used to love to swim but I can't go back to water no more"—and "The weather more or less controls my thoughts."

And many others expressed similar feelings about the weather 27 months after the flood. One woman particularly troubled with insomnia stated: "When it starts raining I get afraid. I didn't use to be that way but now I am. I'm afraid of thunder and lightning." Another woman (interviewed at the same time): "I have a real scary feeling when it rains—even though there's no danger up there." And still another, greatly troubled by insomnia and general anxiety: "If it rains I get a very uneasy feeling. The clouding up now makes me feel uncomfortable."

A related symptom, also widespread, is a fear of crowds. Gatherings of large numbers of people become associated with the disaster. One man (in May 1974) told us that he avoids crowds because he imagines another disaster and "if there are 12 people in the crowd only some people would escape and some would be lost. If I was there by myself I could get away." He was expressing a characteristic feeling that his survival was a matter of luck, perhaps a fluke, and that in the grotesque competition for survival created by such a disaster he would be better off on his own. Involved here also is the shattering in the survivor of the illusion of invulnerability we carry with us in both ordinary and dangerous situations, and a related sense of having been rendered precariously vulnerable to the next threat. Another man said that he stays away from crowds because "I get nervous when I get with a crowd— all that feeling comes back," and added that "If you get around a crowd it seems like somebody will bring up the subject and I just don't like to hear it. I can't keep from crying like a baby."

Terrifying dreams, still recurring regularly 27 months after the disaster, are especially vivid expressions of death anxiety. Two such typical recurrent dreams we encountered were:

I dream I'm in a car on a pier surrounded by muddy water—or else in a pool of muddy water. I feel like I've got to hold on to the side of the pool. If I do I'm all right. I know that I can't get out. I have to stay in it.

I've never been to no funerals except the ones right after the flood . . . In the dream there is a big crowd at the funeral—the whole family is watching. I'm being buried. I'm scared to death. I'm trying to tell them I'm alive but they don't pay no attention. They act like I'm completely dead but I'm trying to holler to them that I'm alive. They cover me up and lower me down, but I can see the dirt on me. I'm panicked and scared. I become violent trying to push my way through the dirt . . . I think I'll suffocate if I don't fight my way out. I feel like I'm trying to shout that I'm alive.

In both cases the dreamer is threatened by a disaster-related form of death, and must struggle desperately to remain alive. The first dream suggests being locked in a continuous struggle without being able to leave the lethal environment (the muddy pool). The second dream reflects the state of being "as-if dead"—both dead and alive—characteristic of the most severe kinds of survivor experience. Both dreams reflect the survivor's perpetually fearful anticipation. As one man put it, "Sometimes me and my wife don't go to bed at all. . . . It's hard to live under a dread all the time."

That dread, moreover, tends to become a collective family experience in ways that further stimulate fear in each individual—as a father of four children told us in May 1974:

We all want to leave. . . . Me and my oldest son stayed in the house right after the flood. The boys [now ages 18 and 16] say, "I can't go to sleep in this bedroom." My youngest daughter [age 11] won't go upstairs by herself, even in the daytime. She seems afraid. The whole family seems afraid. They get most shook up when a storm comes up. Their nerves are already on edge. It don't take much to get everyone shook up. After a bad storm it's a couple days before they sleep. During the tornado warnings they were all shook up and I wanted to go to the school [on higher ground and the place where survivors congregated after the flood]

The tornado warnings (of April 1974) he mentions were especially traumatic to Buffalo Creek survivors, intensifying dread and reactivating the entire disaster experience. This phenomenon of reactivation contributes greatly to the survivor's sense of permanent vulnerability. As a Baptist minister explained in May 1974:

I told you [in a previous interview] people had quieted down a bit. But when they announced all those hurricanes people came to the church and stayed all night. . . . Just let something blow up and they flare up again.

This diffuse, death-related anxiety comes to pervade the Buffalo Creek environment to the point of contagion. As in other overwhelming disasters (such as Hiroshima), outsiders coming in, such as mental health professionals and clergymen, describe experiencing some of the fear and dread described by people exposed to the disaster.

We may sum up this first category by saying that Buffalo Creek survivors remain haunted not just by death but by grotesque and unacceptable forms of death; feel ever vulnerable to these forms of death; and perceive their overall environment—including nature itself—as threatening and lethal rather than life-sustaining.

DEATH GUILT

The second category is that of *death guilt*—the survivor's sense of painful self-condemnation over having lived while others died. Survivors we spoke to 30 months after the disaster were still plagued by the feeling, however irrational, that they could or should have done something to save close relatives who perished. One of the plaintiffs, who made a series of desperate efforts to save his wife before she went under, has since experienced a mixture of preoccupation with memories of her and his failure to save her, and anger at the coal company because "they killed my wife." Psychologically the two emotions merge, and like other survivors of extreme situations, he inwardly experiences a certain amount of personal responsibility for having "killed her." Also involved is the survivor's characteristic feeling that his life was purchased at the cost of another's—that the other person's death permitted him to live, that had he died the other might have lived instead. These feelings, very widespread in Buffalo Creek, are inseparable from the death-related fears already described and are among the most painful emotions known to humankind.

Death guilt is reflected in the preoccupation of survivors with dead relatives—for example, one plaintiff's constant thoughts about his many dead cousins, and another's brooding over his dead mother, sister, and three brothers. The latter, Mr. T., in addition to his persistent feeling that he should have done something to save them, told us in May 1974 that he would still "sit and study and wonder" because "so much happened at one time," asking himself again and again: "Why didn't the family get out after they were warned?" He would conclude that "You can't ever get that answer . . . as if there's something left out, and maybe it's better that I can't figure it out." Contributing greatly to that sense is his continuous struggle to fend off a sense of guilt and responsibility for those unacceptable deaths.

Death guilt is perhaps most vivid in recurrent dreams. Some of these dreams include the reappearance of dead relatives, either in everyday situations or in uneasy reunions in which it is not clear whether they are or are not actually alive. Much more disturbing, and still frequent after 27 months, were dreams in which death guilt was more direct. The wife of Mr. T. had been unusually close to his dead mother:

I dreamed we knew the dam was going to break. In the dream Mrs. T. had a white dress on. She asked me to follow her out in the yard. She just kept going back into a hole that looked like a mine. I don't know why she wanted me to come with her— she held out her hand, but I was afraid.

The dream suggests the dreamer's sense that she should have shared the disturbing fate—the death—of her mother-in-law.

Still more characteristic were recurrent dreams of actual disaster events or scenes resembling them in depicting grotesque death, as described by a survivor in May 1974:

I dreamt about the baby I found with half its face torn off, and the truck full of bodies. Sometimes in those dreams you're running, or trying to get hold of someone to help them out of the mud. Just last week I had that dream. I woke up pulling on my wife. After that you just can't go back to sleep. That was about 3:00 A.M. last Friday night. There's nothing you can do at that time of night until 7:00 or so in the morning when you see people out. . . .

In such dreams the survivor experiences an image of ultimate horror—a single image that comes to exemplify his entire disaster experience in the combination of fear, pity, and guilt that it evokes in him. Such images are especially likely to include children or women whose grotesque death one witnessed or failed to prevent—since in most cultures, ours included, those two groups (especially children) are viewed as particularly helpless and vulnerable, as beings whose lives the physically stronger members of society are particularly responsible for maintaining.

One survivor contrasted his capacity to absorb his World War II combat experience with his total inability to deal with residual guilt from the flood disaster, as expressed in an image of ultimate horror involving a mother pleading with him, while herself drowning, to save her baby:

When I was on the battlefield in World War II I was expecting the worst, and it didn't bother me at all like this. When my buddies got killed I knew I was no part of their getting killed. But when the flood came I didn't have time to help that lady and her baby who cried for help.

He went on to explain that "feelings about not helping people during the war went away after I came home," but those related to the flood had stayed with him for 27 months, both in his waking life and his dreams:

In my dreams I never get caught in the water. What hurts is the people calling for me to come and help them but I can't do it. The ending of the dreams is always the same—hitting my back on the railroad cars where I hid from the water.

People who have gone through this kind of experience are never quite able to forgive themselves for having survived. Another side of them, however, experiences relief and gratitude that it was *they* who had the good fortune to survive in contrast to the fate of those who died—a universal and all-too-human survivor reaction that in turn intensifies their guilt. Since the emotion is so painful, the sense of guilt may be suppressed and covered over by other emotions or patterns, such as rage or apathy.

But whether or not suppressed, that guilt continues to create in Buffalo Creek survivors a sense of a burden that will not lift. They feel themselves still bound to the dead, living a half-life devoid of pleasure and with limited vitality.

PSYCHIC NUMBING

The third category is that of *psychic numbing*—a diminished capacity for feeling of all kinds—in the form of various manifestations of apathy, withdrawal, depression, and overall constriction in living. Psychic numbing is perhaps the most universal response to the disaster, and the essence of what has been called the "disaster syndrome." Partly it is an extension of the "stunned" state experienced at the time of the flood. That state was a defense against feeling the full impact of the overwhelming death immersion. The numbing persists at Buffalo Creek because people still need to defend themselves against the kinds of death anxiety and death guilt discussed above. Numbing, then, is an aspect of persistent grief; of the "half-life" defined by loss, guilt, and close at times to an almost literal identification with the dead. As one of the plaintiffs put it: "I feel dead now. I have no energy. I sit down and I feel numb." Survivors withdrew from groups, from activities of various kinds, from one another. They describe being disinterested in seeing friends or in many cases in doing anything. Even in intimate relationships their capacity for both emotional and physical feeling—including sexual feeling—tends to be greatly diminished. Their withdrawal may be accompanied by a wide variety of psychosomatic symptoms, such as general fatigue, loss of appetite, gastrointestinal difficulties, and aches and pains and dysfunction that can involve just about any organ system. The pattern has been described in other disasters as a breakdown in the ordinary psychosomatic balance or equilibrium, resulting in what used to be called neurasthenia. At Buffalo Creek one can observe a vicious circle of withdrawal and abandonment—as one survivor made clear in an interview in May 1974: "I want to be left alone. Now you don't care so much about other people; it's like everything is destroyed. It's like you're left alone." That is, his sense of having been abandoned and his tendency to withdraw reinforce one another.

Very common aspects of numbing at Buffalo Creek have been such things as memory lapses, general sluggishness and unresponsiveness, and confusion about details of one's immediate surroundings and about the passage of time in general. Those lapses, as one survivor makes clear, tend to be specifically associated with the disaster: "I can remember things from 1932 to 1972 better than I can the past two years. This past two years I can't remember what I do—weeks and months just go by." Numbing or avoidance of feeling can also be expressed in overactivity. Thus one woman said of her very troubled husband: "He works all the time. He gets himself overtired. He says, 'If I just sit down I'd die.' "

Numbing is closely related to the psychological defense of denial, and people said again and again in a variety of ways: "It's hard to believe that all this happened" or "I still can't accept that it happened." Numbing and denial are sustained because of the survivor's inability to confront or work through the disaster experience. He is thus left psychologically imprisoned in death- and guilt-related conflicts that can neither be dealt with nor eliminated. Feeling stays muted; psychological pain remains silent; and life experience in general is drastically reduced.

In recent years, authorities on disaster have come to recognize that psychic numbing occurs not only in survivors but in observers and evaluators of disaster. Medical and psychological professionals have been known to experience strong tendencies to ward off anxieties of their own around death and guilt aroused by their contact with survivors, which has in turn led them to deny the existence of these emotions and ignore or underestimate the psychological cost of disaster.

COUNTERFEIT NURTURING AND UNFOCUSED RAGE

A fourth category is that of *impaired human relationships*, and consists especially of *conflict over need or nurturing as well as strong suspicion of the counterfeit*. So much of their lives having been so suddenly and totally destroyed, survivors feel themselves in great need of love and support but at the same time unable to accept as genuine whatever affection or nurturing may be offered to them. While some have been able to help one another, there have also been instances of breakdown of the closest human bonds. One such case is that of two of the plaintiffs, a young married couple. Both remember their relationship prior to the flood as "calm and peaceful and loving." Now, according to the wife, her husband is "touchy about everything. Things with me and him are at a kind of halt, a stand-still. . . . Something is always bothering him—it's constant—it never seems to stop." They very rarely have sexual relations or even sleep in the same room. The husband's perception is that life in general, since he lost many relatives in the flood, has consisted of "one aggravation after another." He says that his wife "has no desire for me. She's hateful and doesn't want to turn toward me."

Yet each realized that the other was suffering. The wife said of the husband that "He's still grieving—he cries out in his sleep. He still sees pictures of his relatives. He still says he'd like to kill Jim V. [the former manager of the Pittston mining operation at Buffalo Creek] because Jim said the dam wouldn't break." And then she added:

I still grieve too. It hurts me awful bad that you can't walk down the road and see them [she too was very close to her husband's relatives]. Sometimes I think I see one of them. It hurts when you suddenly realize that they're dead.

And she could conclude: "A big part of my touchiness does seem to be related to my grieving." Both, in other words, were so enmeshed in unrelieved grief reactions—unresolved death anxiety and death guilt—that neither could reach out to or even trust the other. They would go through brief periods of slight improvement in their relationship only to find the post-disaster pattern of mutual estrangement and distrust reasserting itself and still predominating 27 months after the flood.

Survivors have special need for family closeness, but also a particularly strong tendency to grate on one another in a way that intensifies each other's resentment and fear. As one man put it, "My kids seem to be doing all right but when I go to pieces now they go to pieces too."

Over the period since the disaster, the problem of anger and unfocused or unexpressed rage has increased. One woman, talking about the problem, said: "It's like that all over—everybody is angry and touchy." Often the touchiness is expressed toward fellow survivors in the various forms of envy, jealousy, and resentment that have been frequently observed following disasters, and are characteristic of people who feel themselves weakened and victimized. At public meetings or in casual conversations, even seemingly positive suggestions for better help and support are sometimes received with suspicion— either because they are reminders of weakness or because of a tendency among survivors, bound as they are to the dead, to view any sign of energy and vitality on the part of fellow survivors—any strong affirmation of life— as somehow inappropriate or immoral.

But the hostility tends to be very diffuse, and many survivors told us of the frequent experience since the flood of violent impulses toward anyone who irritated them, and of enormous intensification of whatever difficulty they had experienced in the past in controlling their tempers. One of the plaintiffs put the matter characteristically:

It used to be I could control my temper. Now my temper just goes. I just can't control it. When some little thing happens that seems unfair I get touchy.

And he added a bit later in the interview: "Since I lost my wife I can't get what I want. Nothing satisfies me." Anger, that is, continues to cover over grief and loss. And another male survivor: "I'm 46 years old. I've never been in jail. But if I could have got to some of those officials I probably would have hurt somebody. . . . I still get angry at times. I get all blurry and it flares up real quick. Before the flood if anything came up it seems like I could sit down and think and work things out." The quotation suggests the difficulty survivors have in finding adequate targets for their anger. Many select the former manager but seem to sense even as they do so that he as an individual is not an adequate target. Nor is it easy to personify an alternative target—as another man makes clear: "I can't say I feel angry at the people who built the dam, because I've never seen one of them. . . . And I've never seen Jim V., the general manager, since the flood." A good deal of anger is directed toward the mine company but it too ends in frustration:

There's a lot of people that's angry. They just don't care because what they worked on for years was completely destroyed. Then Pittston offers you just a little for all that. It makes you angrier than hell. To think they could treat old people that way, it makes you want to go out and fight somebody.

This inability to find a satisfying outlet or target tends to lead people either to suppress their anger or express instead their continuous grief—as another survivor explained in May 1974:

I feel angry at the coal company, but I don't feel like taking it out on someone. When the kids come in late I get upset, but the kids don't cause any trouble. If my wife gets upset she sits and cries. She doesn't get angry.

Some come to recognize, as one woman did, that anger too can be a painful burden:

I don't like to feel so angry. I don't like to lose control. I don't even like to talk about the road [a new road being built that angers many people]. The anger, a lot of it, is still there.

Later in the interview the same woman added: "Anger, if not vented in the right way, will only hurt yourself. . . . The Church of God has helped me to control my anger. I feel I can cope more. If I let myself get pressured then I get upset." Generally speaking, the fundamentalist religion that most of the survivors have some connection with tends to teach that anger is bad and is not a proper response.

Thirty months after the disaster, survivors are left with diffuse anger they themselves disapprove of, rage they cannot express, and an overall sense that everything (and everyone) is suspect and that life itself has been rendered counterfeit.

INNER FORM: THE STRUGGLE FOR SIGNIFICANCE

The fifth category has to do with the significance or meaning surrounding a disaster, the capacity of survivors *to give their death encounter significant inner form or formulation*. At issue here is the survivor's capacity to find sufficient explanation for his experience so as to be able to resolve the inner conflicts described under the other four categories. Only by coming to some such meaning and significance is he able to find meaning and significance in the rest of his life. In many disasters, survivors are able to find some comfort, or at least resignation, in the deep conviction that what happened was a matter of God's will or of some larger power that no mortal could influence. No such comfort or resignation can be found among the people of Buffalo Creek. Some of them have attempted to understand the experience within a religious context, and in a church service attended by one of us (E.O.), the minister (not a survivor himself) declared almost boastfully that he had predicted the flood as a punishment for sin in the valley. Survivors we interviewed did not express any such concept but could well be unconsciously affected by a related sense that their own evil or sinfulness had something to do with their miserable fate. That feeling would be consistent with one interpretation of their religion and with inner feelings about disaster and illness prevalent not only in Christian societies but in many non-Western cultures as well. Mostly, however, the Buffalo Creek survivors are left without any acceptable or consoling explanation for the disaster. Instead they expressed a bitter awareness that the disaster was man-made and a conviction that God had nothing to do with it. Those feelings have become increasingly intense and unshakeable. Some, for instance, make an angry point about terminology, in bitter response to public statements that God's will was involved—as the following quotations from three different people suggest:

I call this a disaster, not a flood. This wasn't a natural flood.

A few individuals in charge of the coal company are responsible for this. God didn't put the dam up there.

They call it a flood. I call it a dam that Pittston built up there that broke loose. . . . Governor Moore said it was an act of God but God wasn't up on that slate dump with a bulldozer.

Similar feelings were expressed to us by a Freewill Baptist minister: "I believe the dam was made by man, not by God, and it collapsed because it was not made right." The same man, able to observe large numbers of survivors closely, concluded that because of the disaster, "People are much more suspicious of God's justice." That last statement is of considerable importance because it suggests the extent to which people can no longer trust even a deity to put the moral world back in order. Precisely such a sense of the disruption of the moral universe occurs characteristically in the most severe forms of disaster, and is evident in every single survivor I interviewed in Buffalo Creek. That sense of moral inversion—of wrong-doing going unpunished and responsibility unacknowledged while innocent victims undergo pain and suffering—further prevents psychological resolution and leaves people embittered and confused. They remain locked in their death anxiety, survivor guilt, numbing, and impaired human relationships, bound to the disaster itself and to its destructive psychological influences.

TOTALITY OF DISASTER: SPECIAL CHARACTERISTICS OF BUFFALO CREEK

These five categories of course overlap, and together constitute Buffalo Creek's particular version of the "survivor syndrome." No one exposed to the disaster in Buffalo Creek, whatever his or her diagnosis, could escape from significant psychological suffering associated with the patterns and conflicts described above. Indeed, the great majority of people we interviewed showed evidence of most or all of these major patterns and conflicts. This impressive impact of the Buffalo Creek disaster is related to certain characteristics specific to this situation:

(1) The suddenness of the Buffalo Creek flood (as opposed to more gradual flooding or other kinds of disaster in which there is significant warning). Survivors were still, 27 months later, preoccupied with the abruptness of the transition from normal existence to the grotesque scenes of the disaster. They relate that suddenness to their inability, even now, to understand or accept what happened. Commenting on both suddenness and intensity, Dwight Harshbarger (1973) of West Virgin University has pointed out that "Unlike other flood disasters, this flood more resembled the destruction of a tornado or earthquake than a flood." He reports estimates of workers in the disaster area that during the first 24 hours after the flood "88% of the 4000 persons displaced by the water exhibited shock and incoherent thinking." Psychiatric

authorities have now recognized that the nature of a disaster—"and particularly its suddenness, which gives the ego no time to prepare its defenses"—is a "significant determinant of the post-traumatic states" (Leopold and Dillon, 1963, p. 919). Those findings confirmed an earlier conclusion by Alexandra Adler, who compared survivors of the Coconut Grove fire in Boston in 1942 with a group of patients who had undergone head injuries, that "Terrifying events . . . have a higher incidence of neurosis *traceable to the circumstances of the accident* than the everyday head injuries" (1945, p. 240). There is no doubt that the Buffalo Creek disaster qualified as such a "terrifying event." The general principle, in Buffalo Creek and elsewhere, is that the suddenness and terror of a disaster intensify both its immediate and long-range human influences.

(2) The relationship of the disaster to callousness and irresponsibility of other human beings. Beyond the confusion and bitterness we already noted around the recognition that the disaster was caused by other men, the survivors have, over time, expressed their sense of profound humiliation at the low value that the neglect seemed to place upon their own lives. For they knew that not only was the dam man-made but also it was widely understood (for some time prior to the flood) to be dangerous. Their inevitable conclusion was that they, the residents of Buffalo Creeks, were looked upon by the company as less than human. One man told us that when it was suggested to the company before the disaster that they put a pipe through the dam to relieve the water pressure, the company's spokesman said that it would not be a good idea to do so because if they let the water [full of coal waste] out it would "kill the fish in the creek." The miner then looked up with a bitter smile and said, "Hell, I ain't got nothing against taking care of the environment but there wasn't all that many fish in the creek . . . and besides I reckon one human life was worth the whole batch of them."

He was trying to say that the company either was making a hypocritical excuse for not doing what it should have done, or, if sincere, considered the lives of the fish more valuable than those of the human beings in the valley. In either case the survivor's sense of worth and dignity was radically undermined. A related kind of callousness is described by another survivor:

I think the company is responsible. They'd been warned. They disregarded the danger as the coal companies always have in Appalachia. They should be tried under criminal law. If you and I did something like that we'd be in jail. A friend of mine found a baby dead in the mud on his back porch. His house had been torn down. Island Creek Coal Company that I work for is not one bit better. They would do the same thing if it weren't for the government. They started work back right after the flood. It was hard on the employees. They had coal trains going down the hollow while they were still picking up bodies. That don't look a bit good. Of course it's their business, and they had a right to do it. But it was a hardship on the men.

This kind of perception confirms the feeling of the people of Buffalo Creek that the company cares only about coal and the dollars it brings and views the miners and their families, living or dead, as expendable. We would stress the relationship of this awareness of human callousness to survivors' specific psychological suffering. This was true in Hiroshima (Lifton, 1968), and an important study by the sociologist E. G. Luchterhand comparing the effects of an "ordinary" tornado, the Irish famine, and the Nazi holocaust came to the conclusion that "as the source of stress shifts from indiscriminate violence by nature to the discriminate oppression by man, the damage to human personality becomes less remediable" (1971, p. 47). The psychological principle involved, tragic in its effects at Buffalo Creek, is that people who feel their humanity violated and unrecognized by others internalize that diminished sense of themselves in ways that impair their capacity for recovery or even hope.

(3) The continuing relationship of survivors to the disaster. We would stress the psychological significance of the fact that the people of Buffalo Creek for the most part still work in the mines of the company whose policies and actions led to the flood, and thereby remain dependent for their livelihood upon the agents of their destruction. That situation has created a combination of bitter resentment and unrelieved dependency—a sense of counterfeit nurturance—which survivors have experienced as demeaning and psychologically painful. Those emotions were intensified by certain actions of the company in getting people to sign agreements for small financial settlements soon after the flood, which many Buffalo Creek people, and outside observers as well, perceived as taking advantage of survivors' numbed, confused, and suggestible post-disaster state. Some thought the company took special advantage of those who were most helpless, such as the elderly. In any case, survivors tended to view their present situation as part of a very old story— as one man in particular made clear:

At one time the coal companies ruled this part of West Virginia. Then when that ended they took to piling up stuff all over. . . . Before the union they done men awful bad. Then the miners and the workingman started to get a decent living out of it. It's like the coal company is bound and determined to take advantage of people one way or the other.

What is of considerable psychological importance (even apart from questions about the accuracy of that perception of the company) is the force of this combination of abuse, resentment, and dependency, a combination that is both specific to the post-disaster period and has roots in the historical past.

The survivors are also affected by the fact that the physical environment has never really been restored or repaired. There are physical reminders of the disaster everywhere. As one man said in May 1974, "Everything in the area brings all this [painful memories of the disaster] back to me." More than that, the extensive strip mining now taking place is perceived by survivors as further destruction of the land on which they live. "They're tearing up everything" is the way that one of the survivors described the situation, while fearing that "I could be next," meaning that he might actually be forced to move in order to make way for the strip mining because "the company's going to do what they want to do or else." So great is the discomfort caused by the dust produced by the process that another of the plaintiffs, in describing her simple desires for herself and her family, said: "All I want is found rooms and a bath and no dust."

People perceived the disaster to have altered the area permanently in ways that impoverished their lives, as another survivor explained:

The things that I could do, there is nothing to do them with. I'm in debt now — trailers are everywhere, where I leased some land for horses, 90 acres or so up above where Green Valley Trailer Camp was. And it's all on account of the flood. I don't hold it against the people in the trailers — they had to have somewhere to live. But you can't raise a garden on that land now. I raised about all the vegetables you could raise. I put all the vegetables in the freezer for the winter. I gave vegetables away to friends. . . . I don't have enough room to grow a garden now.

Others found, even when a plot of earth was available, that these various physical insults to the land had rendered it difficult or impossible to grow things that grew readily before. Overall, there was a sense that the land itself had ceased to be a source of life. Nature could no longer be relied upon to symbolize the experience of renewal, so crucial for victims of all forms of disaster. (Even in Hiroshima, the appearance of cherry blossoms during the spring following the disaster symbolized to many the possibilities for such renewal and rebirth.) As rural people with unusually strong attachments to the outdoors and to nature in general, Buffalo Creek survivors are uncomfortably sensitive to alterations of the landscape, as one of the plaintiffs makes clear:

If you were somewhere else and you had some pretty grass and pretty flowers to look at, at least you could feel a little happy. But up there [where he lives] you open the door and there's nothing but a rock pile.

It is felt not only that one's natural surroundings no longer sustain life but that they have been permanently impaired by the disaster. One of the plaintiffs spoke of "snakes coming back now, many more snakes than before the flood, black snakes and rattlers." Many other survivors had similar impressions, and a number have observed that unusual matings between different species of poisonous snakes have been taking place. Whatever the actual impact of the flood on the ecology of snakes in the area, the combination of their real dangerousness and their traditional (Biblical) symbolization of evil contributes to survivors' sense that the disaster turned nature against them so that the very land that nurtured them in the past is no more than a "disaster area" now. "Before, when I lived there it seemed like home to me, and warm. And now I don't even feel like I was born and raised there. It's still a disaster area to me," is the way that one of the plaintiffs put it.

(4) The isolation of the area and community. The Buffalo Creek community has long been rather isolated geographically, and inbred, strongly attached to its immediate land and surroundings, and placing enormous significance on home, family, and kin. Hence, after the disaster, it had only very limited connections with outside support, and few possibilities for involvement of a life-enhancing nature that could help the survivors move beyond the disaster itself. This isolation looms very large in the widespread conflict among survivors over whether to remain in Buffalo Creek or to leave. Many express a strong desire to get away from the area and from its ever-present reminders of the disaster. But even those with the strongest desire to leave are likely to experience strong doubts about doing so. A typical statement was:

We all want to leave. My wife don't have the heart to do nothing. I think I would like to get out of the valley . . . so the kids can go to school [in another place]. It's hard to pull up and move out when things are so hard.

Few have any other place to go and most are fearful about possible alternatives. As one very troubled survivor put it, "I hate to give up what I've got here without knowing that what I was getting would be better." Or, as in the case of another, they convey partial recognition that their conflicts have been so internalized that moving cannot help: "Some people I know have left the valley, but they're not satisfied." The combination of lack of outside connections and severe economic limitations is likely to result, even for those who express the strongest desire to get away, in little more than a utopian dream without foundation in their lives:

It seems like some day we'll find a little hollow with hills on both sides and we'd build a little house and we'd be all right.

But there are powerful emotions that hold disaster survivors to the place where they have suffered. These include the complex of psychological ties to people and place that we call "roots," but also the impulse to remain close to the dead. Thus, the survivor quoted above who spoke of wanting to leave but finding it difficult "when things are so hard," added later in the interview, with considerable anxiety: "If I move out of the valley I'm not running from nothing. I hope I'm moving *toward* something." He seemed to fear that he *was* running from something, broadly speaking from the horror of the experience, always epitomized for survivors by their images of the dead. To leave the dead can be still another source of guilt and fear.

The nature of the isolation of the people of Buffalo Creek, then, is such that they are trapped in the place of their suffering midst evidence and reminders of the disaster, held by ties to the living, the dead, and the land in ways that provide no solace.

(5) Totality of communal destruction. The Buffalo Creek disaster was unique in its combination of suddenness, destructive power within a limited circumscribed area, and resulting breakdown of community structure. Harshbarger has stated the matter well in comparing Buffalo Creek with other disasters and explaining his use of the term *"total loss* disaster":

I . . . feel that the Buffalo Creek disaster was, while smaller in the value of property lost, a more intense disaster than the later floods of hurricane Agnes, or other large disasters. It takes a considerable amount of searching to find this combination of *total loss*, i.e., of lives, properties, and the basic structure and social fabric of communities themselves. The San Francisco earthquake and the Chicago fire are reminiscent of larger, but comparable, *total loss* disaster. While there may be more recent examples, none come to mind (Rapid City [South Dakota, where a large flood took place], while comparable in some ways, retained its basic community structure; Buffalo Creek did not). [Harshbarger, 1972, p. 10]

Important factors in creating this totality of impact were the suddenness described earlier, the geography (narrowness of the hollow), and the demography (closely-bunched community) of the area. As Harshbarger also states, "Virtually no one who lives in the Valley was untouched by the disaster"

(1973, p. 8). And a survivor puts the matter still more simply: "This thing destroyed and hurt just about everybody in this hollow."

Also contributing to the destruction of the community were certain policies of federal and state relief agencies, notably the first-come-first-served basis for assigning people to the trailers in the mobile home parks rather than placement according to prior communal patterns; and the high population density of the new trailer parks, which resulted in a further sense of dislocation and an unrelieved feeling of temporariness. At the same time people live close enough to their former homes and landmarks to be reminded, frequently and painfully, of what they have lost. Survivors lack the human structures we all require to maintain orderly rhythms and consistent values in our lives. Since they still live more or less in their pre-disaster environment, it is as if a vast, destructive force decimated the elements of community, totally removing some and shaking up all the others so that they now exist in distorted and incoherent relationship to each other. On the basis of many psychiatric, psychological, and sociological studies (including those of Hinkle and Wolff, Cassel, Lindemann, Parkes, and Selye), there can be no doubt that this communal breakdown results in severe stress and contributes greatly to a wide variety of medical and psychiatric illnesses and disorders.

The totality of the Buffalo Creek disaster, then, encompasses this communal breakdown as well as the survivor conflicts described earlier. Both in fact merge in a final common pathway of individual suffering.

Throughout this discussion we have made an overall assumption, now well established by extensive observations, that every disaster shares certain common patterns with all other disasters; but that each disaster, in its overall combination of characteristics, becomes unique. Thus, one can find various combinations of the five characteristics listed above—suddenness, human callousness in causation, continuing relationship of survivors to the disaster, isolation of the community, and totality of destruction—in a number of other disasters. But the occurrence of *all* of them in a single disaster is highly unusual, and helps us understand the extensive human impact of the Buffalo Creek flood.

PATTERNS OF DESPAIR

The consistent psychological pattern in Buffalo Creek has been a sequence beyond protest or hope, coalescing into a lasting despair. Although philosophers have long emphasized the significance of despair, psychiatrists and psychoanalysts have also recently come to emphasize its clinical importance and the debilitating nature of its combination of chronic depression, uncon-nectedness, and hopelessness. Erikson, for instance, speaks of despair as the "lack or loss of . . . ego integration," and emphasizes its relationship to fear of death, and to "the feeling that . . . time is now short, too short for the attempt to start another life" (1963, p. 269). Despair has a close relationship to an impaired sense of connectedness and of continuity beyond the self, and to an inability to find meaning in relationship to one's past and imagined future (Lifton, 1973a). In Buffalo Creek we found despair to be especially widespread and to include a chronic form of depression and a sense that things would never change—one would never get over the disaster. As the minister-survivor quoted earlier put it, "People seem to be afraid that they are not going to recover, that they are going to be crazy forever." Survivors themselves come to be impressed by the length of time their symptoms have persisted, as one man made clear: "I feel like these fears should have left me after 27 months—there's hardly any illness that lingers on this long. The passing of time since the flood doesn't seem to help." He sees his life as prematurely over, precisely confirming the observation by Erikson quoted above:

I'm 52 years old now. My life is just about lived out now. I don't know what I could do now to begin a new life.

Another man expressed similar sentiments: "It's been two years since this happened. You'd think I'd be able to talk about it without crying." Still another man said: "I don't think I'll ever get back to where I was. I don't think that's possible." And one of the plaintiffs summed matters up for herself and others: "There ain't nobody who's going to get over that loss."

People contrast the relatively hopeful movement of life existing prior to the disaster with the hopeless stagnation after it—as expressed here by an incapacitated miner:

It's a split decision. There's the life you lived before and the life you live after. Before the disaster it seemed like you got up and you looked forward; there was something I was going ahead to—the garden, the horses, the job. The garden is gone; there are trailers where the horses were; there's no job left.

Also contributing to despair is the burden of anger and bitterness men-tioned earlier, which eventually takes the form of a sense of being over-whelmed by the negative and destructive aspects of all human beings. One survivor, in her associations to a dream about a trailer, talked about "the feeling of evil in the dream—it's like people are mean—I feel like I've been disillusioned with the government and everything else. . . . I never felt before that people had anything against me—but now I have to fight myself to keep from feeling that."

Another survivor expressed his despair still more generally: "You get the feeling, What the hell's the use of trying to do anything? It's like you really don't have any freedom—nobody don't pay any attention to you. . . . The little man is just stepped on and walked on." One is again reminded of the general principle mentioned earlier that the more a survivor of a disaster perceives the experience to reflect human callousness (rather than an act of nature or God), the more severe and long-lasting are the psychological effects.

This despair exists within a survivor bind—wanting very much to be able to dismiss the entire disaster from their minds and knowing that they are unable to do so. As one man put it, "You can keep these things down in your mind but not out." And he went on to say: "I feel the least I can talk about this the better off I am, and just let this be forgotten." Others at the same time (May 1974) expressed similar emotions. Nonetheless, all were extremely aware of the ways in which the disaster was still working on their minds— through nightmares, depression, fears, and the whole gamut of symptoms we have discussed. One could say that the overall solidity of this Appalachian subculture contributed to their sense that they simply had to carry on and not dwell on past horrors—just as their religion taught them that nurturing too much resentment was "un-Christian." The difficulty has been that the sup-pression of feeling has never been more than partially successful (because of the particularly malignant features of the Buffalo Creek disaster), and genuine healing has not taken place. The slightest symbolic reminder of the disaster propels the whole constellation of its images and emotions into the center of people's awareness. For as Leopold and Dillon have pointed out, "rather than time being a healer, psychological damage incurred in life-threatening trauma, if untreated, *tends* to grow worse with time" (italics ours; Leopold and Dillon, 1963; 1960, p. 385; 1961, p. 86; Leopold, 1962). That observation is consis-tent with a statement by J. S. Tyhurst that the posttraumatic period of a severe disaster lasts "for the remainder of the person's life, and includes the period of rehabilitation" (1950, p. 766).

Indeed, psychiatrists throughout the world have come to recognize post-traumatic neurosis as a condition that can take the most serious and incapac-itating forms. Kardiner states that "Traumatic neurosis is a disease very closely related to schizophrenia [generally considered the most malignant of all psychiatric syndromes], both from the point of view of central dynamics and from the ultimate withdrawal from the world which is set in motion. The deteriorations undergone in both conditions have a striking resemblance to each other" (1959, p. 256). Grauer, writing from Canada, states similarly that "in reactions due to extreme environmental stress we are dealing with a condition akin to psychosis or a borderline [psychotic] state" (1969, p. 621). Parkes and Bowlby in England, and many others making use of their work, have presented convincing evidence that various kinds of experiences of grief, separation, and loss are causative factors in a wide variety of mental and physical illnesses (Parkes, 1972; Bowlby, 1969, 1973). Lacey draws upon that work in his Aberfan research on children and concludes that, in view of the evidence that "many psychiatric problems of adult life appear to be connected with childhood bereavement . . . it seems very likely that many of the Aberfan children may experience psychiatric problems in later life" (1972, p. 259). Child psychiatrists examining children in Buffalo Creek have had similar impressions, and have noted that young children are particularly susceptible to the despair and other symptom manifestations of their parents.

We should hardly be surprised at the finding of Bennet that for survivors of the Bristol floods of 1968 (in England), "in all aspects studied the health of the flooded people was worse during the twelve months after the floods than the health of the not flooded; and for the older people there was an increased likelihood of dying within twelve months" (1970, p. 455).

There is, in fact, mounting evidence that the effects of disaster can extend over generations, and that adverse effects of significant proportion can occur in children of survivors, even when the children are born some years after a particular disaster. That has been true of children of concentration camp survivors, as Rakoff and his associates (among others) have demonstrated, because "there is not only a sick member, but the family itself is a collection of severely disturbed and traumatized individuals" (1966, p. 24). There was evidence of a similar phenomenon in Hiroshima, and while one cannot as yet speak of future generations at Buffalo Creek one can certainly observe many families to be "a collection of severely disturbed and traumatized individuals," who could well transmit various disaster-related conflicts to subsequent generations.

Still, many in Buffalo Creek continue to struggle to overcome their despair. One woman put it simply (in May 1974): "I just want to start living again." And a number of survivors expressed related aspirations toward restored vitality and renewal—whether through moving away from Buffalo Creek, adopting a child, being helped by family members, or in a few cases through medical, psychiatric, or psychological assistance. But many of the survivors, because of their limited educational and social background and equally limited financial resources, lack the capacity to take any significant steps toward renewal. Moreover, there are very limited community and professional facilities in the Buffalo Creek area. Ideally, survivors should have extensive community rebuilding in which they could have an active voice.

Survivors' overall psychological health could also be somewhat improved by any outcome in the situation which recognized their suffering, recognized also the responsibility of those whose actions or inaction caused the disaster, gave people who wished to leave the opportunity to do so, gave those who wished to rebuild on their land the opportunity to do so, and in a general sense conveyed to survivors the sense that at least a step had been taken to put the moral world back in order. Also of great psychological importance would be the capacity of people to embark upon a collective "survivor mission," consisting of actions or policies that might provide something of a sense of meaning and "survivor wisdom" from a situation that was otherwise totally destructive. Survivors of Hiroshima, for instance, have been able to benefit somewhat from the sense that conveying the horrors of their experience to the outside world could enable man to learn something about the effects of nuclear weapons and possibly avoid using them again. And at an individual level, parents whose children die of leukemia can derive solace from a "survivor mission" of energetically supporting scientific research that might prevent such tragedies in the future. Buffalo Creek survivors could, in a parallel way, derive some benefit from contributing to policies and programs that would insure greater safety and protection for mining areas and miners and prevent such disasters from occurring again.

The range of variations of the flood's effects upon survivors is difficult to estimate precisely. We can say that it brought about an extraordinary number of psychiatric disturbances, and that even those in the very small minority without formal psychiatric diagnoses, despite exposure to the disaster, tended to experience significant degrees of psychological suffering and conflict. The range of variation had to do with differing individual flood experiences and also with available postflood resources, both in terms of psychic resilience and material and social support. Without denying the existence of significant variation in psychological vulnerability, we have been far more impressed (as have other observers) by the degree to which the massive character of the trauma subsumed individual differences and produced strikingly consistent forms of impairment. We have also been impressed by the persistence of these expressions of psychological impairment, which in many cases increased rather than diminished over time.

BUFFALO CREEK AND THE WORLD

Our observations were all too consistent with a body of recent experience with "massive psychic trauma" of war, revolution, concentration camps, and severe disasters (Lifton, 1961, 1968, 1970, 1973b; Krystal, 1968; and Grosser et al., 1964)—psychiatrists have regularly observed that psychological impairment can result in virtually anyone, independently of estimates of predisposition. These observations have led a number of investigators to examine closely the nature and impact of massive trauma. Kardiner, for instance, beginning with observations on war, generalizes to explain that "The traumatic event breaks up . . . [the] balance between the ego and the environment by overwhelming the coping devices which the ego has at its disposal. The anxiety is overwhelming, and the ego shrinkage can be so complete that death can ensue. The entire adaptive equipment is thus disintegrated" (1959, p. 252). Those conclusions agree with many observations made in relationship to both world wars, the Korean War, and more recently the Vietnam War (Van Putten and Emory, 1973; and Lifton, 1973b). Hence the insistence of researchers working in these areas on such terms as "traumatic neurosis," "posttraumatic neurosis," or "the traumatic syndrome." Observations on those surviving Nazi concentration camps, and Lifton's work on survivors of Hiroshima (1968) have strongly confirmed the hypothesis that massive psychic trauma—that is, extreme stress, involving life-and-death situations, undergone by large numbers of people—always takes precedence over issues of predisposition. Hence Koranyi rightly observes that, under such conditions, "pre-existing pathology [predisposition] appeared to be obliterated in the final outcome and become buried under the unvaried likeness and monotony of the survivor syndrome" (1969, p. 172). Putting that observation in simpler words, if the stress is great enough it can produce strikingly similar psychological disturbances in virtually everyone exposed to it. For as another psychoanalytic observer put it, "One can say that the regenerative powers of the ego are not limitless, that the human spirit can be broken beyond repair . . ." (Rappaport, 1968, p. 730). And Hocking, an Australian, has reviewed a number of situations of extreme stress and concluded that "There was no correlation between the symptoms of the survivors and the pre-existing personality or any other factor in the patients' earlier life" (1970, p. 544), therefore suggesting that "when the duration and degree of stress are severe, pre-existing personality characteristics do little more than determine how long an individual can tolerate the situation before the onset of neurotic symptoms" (p. 542). Brüll makes a general statement very relevant to the Buffalo Creek situation: "The conception of trauma really conveys that time which has flowed on without meaning assumes a particular meaning in the sense of burden, pain, disappointment, injury, anxiety, fear, challenge" (1967–70, p. 97). And in a more immediate way, with specific reference toward disaster, Leopold and Dillon emphasize the importance of giving "cognizance . . . to the role of the accident itself in producing a discrete illness, which in all likelihood, would not have occurred had there been no accident" (1963, p. 920). All of these observations have been amply confirmed in Buffalo Creek.

The categories of survivor response within which we have here described the Buffalo Creek experience derive from a more general depth-psychological perspective or paradigm which emphasizes symbolization (rather than instinctual expression) as the essence of human mentation (Lifton, 1973a, 1976a, 1976b, 1968, 1973b; Lifton and Olson, 1974). Impairments to the process of symbolization result in various forms of numbing—decreased capacity to feel and to give form to experience. Beyond its centrality for the survivor syndrome, numbing is an overall manifestation of psychic impairment, and provides a broad context for examining specific forms of psychopathology.

The most fundamental symbolizations, those from which what we call motivation essentially derives, have to do with images and inner forms around life, being alive, and maintenance of life continuity. These symbolizations mediate between the immediate involvements of the self in day-to-day activity and the more ultimate expressions of the self's participation in ongoing collective life—its ties to continuing human community, to nature, and to intense forms of experience of self-renewal. This experiential dialectic between immediate-proximate involvements on the one hand, and ultimate-immortalizing continuity on the other, is radically interrupted by the experience (and in some degree the anticipation) of disaster. Overwhelming moment-to-moment conflict and debilitating loss of faith in human continuity combine and reinforce one another to produce the loss of vitality, the depression, and the despair of human beings no longer able to give inner form to their lives.

The Buffalo Creek disaster had a profound effect on all symbolization of life-continuity, and the persistence of resulting psychic numbing had to do with the collective inability to overcome imagery of disintegration, separation, and stasis, or to achieve any new sense of purpose that might reactivate imagery of integrity, connection, and movement. One sees with great clarity in Buffalo Creek the close relationship between communal viability and individual psychological process; and one becomes witness there to the anguish of people struggling to begin again, but without adequate grounding in symbolizations that might sustain hope. In all of these ways, Buffalo Creek epitomizes the tenuousness of so much of contemporary existence—our combination of survival of old and anticipation of new holocaust, and our struggles, equally inadequate, to confront that death-dominated precariousness as a source of new vitality and of transformation.

NOTE

1. See Kai T. Erikson, "Loss of Communality at Buffalo Creek," and James L. Titchener and Frederic T. Kapp, "Family and Character Change in Buffalo Creek," both presented at the Amer. Psychiatric Assn. meetings, Anaheim, Calif., in May 1975, at a symposium, "Disaster at Buffalo Creek: Studies of 160 Families," jointly sponsored with the Amer. Psychoanal. Assn. We worked closely with Erikson and Titchener throughout.

REFERENCES

Adler, A. "Two Different Types of Post-traumatic Neuroses," Amer. J. Psychiatry (1945) 102:237–240.

Bennet, G. "Bristol Floods 1968. Controlled Survey of Effects on Health of Local Community Disaster," British Med. J. (1970) 3:454–458.

Bowlby, J. Attachment and Loss, Vol. 1, Attachment, Vol. 2, Separation: Anxiety and Anger; Basic Books, 1969, 1973.

Brüll, F. "The Trauma: Theoretical, Considerations," Israel Annals Psychiatry (1967–70) 7–8:96–108.

Erikson, E. H. Childhood and Society (2d Ed.); Norton, 1963.

Grauer, H. "Psychodynamics of the Survivor Syndrome," Canad. Psychiatric Assn. J. (1969) 14:617–622.

Grosser, G. H., et al. The Threat of Impending Disaster; MIT Press, 1964.

Harshbarger, D. "Draft of Research and Intervention Project," 1972, quoted in G. H. Sage, "The Universal Effects of Mass Disaster upon People," manuscript.

Harshbarger, D. "An Ecological Perspective on Disastrous and Facilitative Disaster Intervention Based on the Buffalo Creek Disaster," presented at NIMH Continuing Education Seminar on Emergency Mental Health Services, Washington, D. C., June 22–24, 1973.

Hocking, F. "Psychiatric Aspects of Extreme Environmental Stress," Dis. Nerv. System (1970) 31:542–545.

Kardiner, A. "Traumatic Neuroses of War," in S. Arieti (Ed.), American Handbook of Psychiatry, Vol. 1; Basic Books, 1959.

Koranyi, E. K. "Psychodynamic Theories of the 'Survivor Syndrome,'" Canad. Psychiatric Assn. J. (1969) 14:165–174.

Krystal, I. (Ed.) Massive Psychic Trauma; *Int. Univ. Press, 1968.*

Lacey, G. N. "Observations on Aberfan," J. Psychosom. Res. *(1972) 16:257–260.*

Leopold, R. L. "Management of Post-Traumatic Neuroses," in J. H. Nodine and J. H. Moyer (Eds.), Psychosomatic Medicine: The First Hahnemann Symposium; *Lea & Febiger, 1962.*

Leopold, R. L., and Dillon, H. "Psychiatric Considerations in Whiplash Injuries of the Neck," Penn. Med. J. *(1960) 63:385–389.*

Leopold, R. L., and Dillon, H. "Children and the Post-Concussion Syndrome," J. Amer. Med. Assn. *(1961) 175:86–92.*

Leopold, R. L., and Dillon, H. "Psycho-anatomy of a Disaster: A Long Term Study of Post-traumatic Neuroses in Survivors of a Marine Explosion," Amer. J. Psychiatry *(1963) 119:913–921.*

Lifton, R. J. Thought Reform and the Psychology of Totalism; *Norton, 1961.*

Lifton, R. J. Death in Life; *Random House, 1968.*

Lifton, R. J. History and Human Survival; *Random House, 1970.*

Lifton, R. J. "The Sense of Immortality: On Death and the Continuity of Life." Amer. J. Psychoanal. *(1973) 33:3–15. (a)*

Lifton, R. J. Home from the War; *Simon & Schuster, 1973. (b)*

Lifton, R. J. The Life of the Self; *Simon & Schuster, 1976a.*

Lifton, R. J. "From Analysis to Form: Towards a New Psychological Paradigm," J. Amer. Acad. Psychoanal. *(1976b).*

Lifton, R. J., and Olson, E. Living and Dying; *Praeger, 1974.*

Luchterhand, E. G. "Sociological Approaches to Massive Stress in Natural and Man-Made Disasters," Int. Psychiatry Clinic *(1971) 8:29–53.*

Parkes, C. M. Bereavement: Studies of Grief in Adult Life; *Int. Univ. Press, 1972.*

Rakoff, V., et al. "Children and Families of Concentration Camp Survivors," Canada's Mental Health *(1966) 14:24–26.*

Rappaport, E. A. "Beyond Traumatic Neurosis," Int. J. Psycho-Anal. *(1968) 49:719–731.*

Tyhurst, J. S. "Individual Reactions to Community Disaster," Amer. J. Psychiatry *(1950) 107:764–769.*

Van Putten, T., and Emory, W. H. "Traumatic Neuroses in Vietnam Returnees," Arch. Gen. Psychiatry *(1973) 29:695–698.*

14. A Behavioral Formulation of Posttraumatic Stress Disorder in Vietnam Veterans

Terence M. Keane, Rose T. Zimering, and Juesta M. Caddell

Our participation in the Vietnam war was among the most tragic political and military involvements in American history. The ambiguity of purpose surrounding our presence in Vietnam has been highlighted by several excellent historical reviews (Karnow, 1983; Maclear, 1981). While the political and social strife that existed in America in the 60s and 70s as a function of our participation in Vietnam has ceased, the psychological problems of the men and women who fought that war appear to be increasing. A study conducted by the Center for Policy Research (Egendorf et al., 1981), conservatively estimated that 16–35% of the 2.8 million Americans who served in Vietnam were suffering from significant psychological problems as a result of their combat exposure. Unfortunately, this study did not include those potential subjects who were legally incarcerated, hospitalized for psychiatric or other reasons, or who were living in inaccessible or remote places, factors that would undoubtedly increase the rates of disorder reported. Although the exact incidence rate of problems experienced by Vietnam veterans awaits completion of the epidemiological study recently mandated by the United States Congress, the prevalence of psychological problems among Vietnam veterans represents a significant challenge to the health care delivery system of our nation.

Our purpose in this paper is to define the disorder that has been increasingly used to circumscribe the varied symptoms reported by combatants (i.e., posttraumatic stress disorder, PTSD), briefly present a conditioning model for the development of PTSD that we have found useful from both a clinical assessment and treatment standpoint, and to provide preliminary information on the empirical validity of the symptom criteria for the diagnosis of PTSD.

Reprinted by permission from *The Behavior Therapist*, 8, 9–12. Copyright © 1985 by the Association for Advancement of Behavior Therapy.

PTSD DEFINED

PTSD is a constellation of symptoms that describes the psychological response often observed in individuals following a discrete, life-threatening event. While such an event could occur in combat, it may also be the result of a rape, an assault, a natural disaster, a motor vehicle accident, etc. The primary symptoms of the disorder as presented in DSM-III are intrusive recollections of the event often accompanied by nightmares or flashbacks, an exaggerated startle response, disturbed sleep patterns, avoidance of close interpersonal relationships, guilt, constricted affect, and the impairment of memory and concentration. High levels of anxiety and depression are described as associated features of the disorder.

Although survivors of any traumatic event may report symptoms consistent with these diagnostic criteria, combatants are distinguishable from other survivors on the basis of the number of traumatic events to which they may have been exposed. That is, a combatant is likely to come into contact with several stressors or traumatic events during a tour of combat duty whereas others suffering from PTSD (rape victims, assault victims) are more likely to have been exposed to a single event. Data from several different research laboratories support the notion that with increased combat exposure there is a corresponding increase in psychological distress (e.g., Egendorf et al., 1981; Foy et al., 1984). Due to unprecedented capabilities in mobilization and mechanization, the typical Vietnam combat veteran saw extensive levels of combat during the 12–13 month tour. While initial reports of psychiatric casualties from Vietnam were low (cf., Bourne, 1969), more recent reports have indicated that the adverse psychological effects of combat in Vietnam are widespread and enduring (Egendorf et al., 1981; Keane et al., 1983). These men and women are now seeking mental health assistance from practitioners in both the public and private sectors. Operational models and testable theories are needed, therefore, to provide an understanding of the disorder that will benefit the individuals seeking assistance.

A LEARNING THEORY MODEL FOR PTSD

Conditioning and Instrumental Learning Factors. Our conceptualization proposes that the clinical symptoms of combat veterans can be best understood through a two-factor learning theory of psychopathology. Originally postulated by Mowrer (1947; 1960), two-factor theory states that psychopathology is a function of both (a) classical conditioning, wherein a fear response is learned through associative principles, and (b) instrumental learning whereby individuals will avoid those conditioned cues that evoke anxiety. In his pioneering studies, Pavlov found that presentation of electric shock to an organism led to reflexive withdrawal of the shocked extremity, as well as an array of behavioral responses indicative of fear. When a bell was repeatedly paired with the shock, the bell alone eventually came to elicit a similar fear response. The organism learned to respond both behaviorally and physiologically to a previously neutral stimulus (bell; conditioned stimulus; CS) when it was paired with an aversive event (shock; unconditioned stimulus; UCS).

The second factor in Mowrer's theory is that an organism will attempt to escape or avoid an aversive stimulus. Due to the pairing of the bell (CS) with the shock (UCS), the organism is motivated to escape from the CS. In experimental studies employing the shuttle-box, organisms repeatedly escaped from a single CS in order to avoid the UCS (cf., Mineka, 1979). Escaping the CS presumably results in a reduction of conditioned fear which reinforces this escape response. It is this escape and avoidance (of the UCS) pattern that parallels many forms of human psychopathology and that has been cited as a formulation for various anxiety mediated disorders. Unfortunately, this theory and model have been seriously criticized by clinicians since the typical laboratory avoidance models generally yield short-lived avoidance, whereas human psychopathology manifests remarkable persistence (e.g., Rachman, 1977). To address the inadequacies of the conditioning models, Solomon and his colleagues (Solomon, Kamin & Wynne, 1953; Solomon & Wynne, 1954) used an intense shock (traumatic) as the aversive UCS. Organisms exposed to this conditioning paradigm displayed avoidant behavior in the shuttlebox for many more trials than had been observed previously. However, subsequent research raised questions concerning factors other than shock intensity that might have actually accounted for the persistent responding in these studies (Brush, 1957).

Stampfl & Levis (1967) and their associates (Levis & Boyd, 1979; Levis & Hare, 1977) developed a conditioning model of psychopathology that when tested appeared to produce stable avoidant responding. Essentially, their adaptation of Mowrer's theory emphasized the importance of a serial presentation of several different CSs (e.g., tone, buzzer, light) prior to the presentation of the UCS. This simple procedural change resulted in avoidance behavior more closely paralleling the persistence of human psychopathology. It is, therefore, this model that we propose has immediate relevance to our understanding of and treatment for combat-related PTSD.

Two-Factor Theory and PTSD. It is likely that different organisms acquire fear through similar mechanisms. Just as the organism in Pavlov's studies learned to respond with fear to a previously neutral stimulus, humans exposed to a life-threatening experience can become conditioned to a wide assortment of stimuli present during the trauma. For example, sounds, smells, terrain, time of day, the people present, and even cognitions can become conditioned to the traumatic event. Thus, each stimulus can evoke anxiety responses similar to those experienced during the event. If a traumatized individual encounters one of these stimuli at a later time, it may result in a disruptive startle reaction or a conditioned emotional response (CER). However, it is clear that Vietnam veterans with PTSD display far more complex symptomatology than a simple startle reaction. Indeed, their stress disorder is not delimited to those cues associated with their traumatic events. Other cues not present during conditioning also elicit anxiety and contribute to their symptomatology. To explain the broad range of stimuli that can evoke anxiety in Vietnam veterans, we rely upon several widely accepted behavioral principles.

Higher-order conditioning in part can explain the wide array of anxiety-provoking stimuli. In a Pavlovian example, once the CS (bell) comes to evoke fear on its own, it can be paired with a new neutral stimulus (e.g., a light). With repeated pairings of the light and bell, the light becomes a higher order CS, capable of producing fear by itself. Similarly, cues that were conditioned by combat trauma can be paired with new stimuli that may in turn evoke anxiety.

A second and related principle, *stimulus generalization*, also helps to explain the gradual exacerbation of the PTSD condition over time. Stimulus generalization proposes that the more similar a novel stimulus is to a conditioned stimulus, the stronger the response will be to that new stimulus. For example, sudden loud noises (e.g., a car backfiring, firecracker exploding) are often similar enough to gunfire to evoke a defensive or aggressive response in combat veterans. With both higher-order conditioning and stimulus generalization, we can account for the wide range of stimuli capable of evoking the memory of the trauma and/or its physiological component in combatants with PTSD. The greater the number and variety of stimuli that can evoke the fear response, the more difficult it becomes for the traumatized combatant to successfully avoid these stimuli.

Perhaps the benchmark symptoms for a diagnosis of PTSD are (a) intrusive thoughts regarding the traumatic event, (b) vivid recollections of the traumatic event wherein the individual reports that he feels that the trauma is actually reoccurring (flashbacks), and (c) terrifying nightmares that contain specific details of the event (and can seriously disrupt sleep patterns). Most individuals with PTSD report that the memories of the trauma are so aversive that they strive to avoid thinking about them. While this strategy is reported to be initially successful (Horowitz, 1976), the growing number of stimuli that evoke memories of the traumatic event eventually makes these avoidance efforts more and more difficult. Accordingly, the traumatized individual is repeatedly exposed to aspects of the traumatic memory and its associated affective, behavioral, and physiological arousal. It is in this psychological condition that most individuals seek psychological intervention.

Incomplete Exposure to Memories. This element of the conceptualization yields an apparent paradox that may at first inspection compromise our understanding of the development of PTSD symptomatology. If the traumatized person is repeatedly exposed to elements of the traumatic memory, and does indeed experience the affect and physiological arousal associated with it, then why isn't a decrement in arousal observed? One of the principles basic to behavior therapy is that exposure to conditioned stimuli leads to anxiety reduction (extinction) (Mineka, 1979; Wilson and Davison, 1971). We explain this potential contradiction by emphasizing the need for exposure to all elements (CSs) of the memory. Exposure to all components of the memory would lead to extinction of the traumatic response and promote adaptive recovery from the life stressor. Unfortunately, for a number of reasons such complete exposure does not always occur.

In a previous article, we (Keane et al., 1986) proposed that following a traumatic event, a survivor attempts to review the event first to enhance memory consolidation and second to initiate coping and adaptive responding. However, when the anxiety, affect, and arousal surrounding elements of a memory reach extremely high levels, the person attempts to avoid thinking of the memory for any prolonged period. This avoidance is comparable in nature to the avoidance discussed in the preceding sections (Mowrer, 1960; Stampfl & Levis, 1967). As a result of the avoidance of exposure to all the cues of the memory, anxiety is maintained to these cues (Levis & Boyd, 1979). Solomon and Wynne (1954) referred to this phenomenon as the conservation of anxiety.

Other factors also limit exposure to the traumatic memories from combat. For example, the military environment does not reinforce the expression of appropriate emotion subsequent to combat events. Indeed, affective responding to combat-related trauma may for various reasons be discouraged, ignored, or even punished. For many Vietnam veterans, a similar response was reported when they returned to the United States. These individuals were openly discouraged from reviewing events by aversive encounters with persons who demonstrated little understanding of the traumatic nature of the combat experience. Many Vietnam veterans to this day have yet to discuss their Vietnam combat experiences with anyone. This virtual prohibition of discussing traumatic events both in Vietnam and upon return home may have limited the needed exposure to combat memories. Thus, the veteran's post-trauma environment (both in Vietnam and the USA) may have contributed to the maintenance of their fears and anxieties.

An additional factor may also have precluded exposure to traumatic memories. Individuals frequently are unable to report important components of the catastrophic event. Free recall of an event often reveals long periods of time for which the person is unable to account. Gradual imaginal exposure to the event (e.g., imaginal flooding), which presents many of the trauma-related cues, has accessed these previously unavailable memory components in many cases (Fairbank, Gross, & Keane, 1983; Keane & Kaloupek, 1982). To account for this clinical phenomenon, we have hypothesized that affective state dependent retention is operational (Bower, 1981; Keane et al. 1986, Weingartner, Miller, & Murphy, 1977). Basically state dependent retention refers to the storage of a memory in a physiological or cognitive state that is dramatically different from the state in which the memory is recalled. This change in state leads to impoverished recall of information unless specific cues are provided. In the instance of trauma, the memory for the event (and especially the most anxiety-producing elements of the event) is stored in a state of peak psychological and physiological arousal; when recall is attempted in a more relaxed state this change directly interferes with recollection of the specific cues surrounding the trauma. Although free recall of the traumatic memory may be poor, it is reasonable to speculate that the traumatic event may still have adverse psychological consequences without the individual attributing his disturbance to a specific event. Indeed, this is frequently observed in clinical work with Vietnam veterans with PTSD.

Additional Factors in Understanding PTSD. There are many other factors that influence the manifestation of symptoms in traumatized combat veterans. For example, behavioral expressions of anger, irritability, and aggression appear to be concomitants of the disorder. For combatants these behaviors are well learned as a function of their military training and are likely to be displayed in their civilian lives when other problem solving skills are unsuccessful in resolving conflicts. Moreover, expression of anger and aggression can be construed as emotions and behaviors that are incompatible with anxiety. Consequently, an individual using this approach to solving interpersonal problems may at once feel relieved of anxiety and also obtain an immediate short-term goal. The combination of negative reinforcement (i.e., anxiety relief) and positive reinforcement (goal attainment) increases the likelihood that displays of aggression will occur in the future under similar circumstances.

Vietnam veterans also appear to be lacking in the interpersonal competencies required for adaptive resolution of life's general crises. Perhaps due to the time in their lives in which they were exposed to trauma (mean age of the Vietnam veteran was 19.2; mode = 18), Vietnam veterans with PTSD appear less skillful in generating and evaluating alternative modes of action, problem solving, and negotiation abilities. Training in such skills when combined with anxiety-reduction techniques may be particularly beneficial to Vietnam veterans with PTSD in preventing future psychological distress. Vietnam veterans with PTSD also frequently report social alienation and diminished interest in both vocational and avocational activities. The social alienation experienced by survivors of trauma appears to be a function first of the survivors' unwillingness and/or inability to disclose information about the trauma to others in their environment, and second to the significant others' unwillingness and/or inability to address the topic of the trauma for fear of upsetting the survivor. While these problems exist for all survivors, the problem was particularly acute for the Vietnam veteran who fought an unpopular war for a country that often confused the combatant with the policymakers. This combination of factors has assuredly contributed to the poor levels of social support reported by Vietnam veterans (Keane et al., 1983).

While a number of factors might be responsible for the reports of diminished interest in activities by PTSD veterans (e.g., depression, guilt, poor social support) behavioral contrast also seems to play an important role. For combat veterans, the reinforcement value of current day activities pales in comparison with the action and the activities of Vietnam. The equipment used, the responsibility shouldered, and the life and death importance of their behavior was far more reinforcing than the often trite tasks and roles they were asked to assume upon return home. For some veterans this contrast effect led to various forms of thrill seeking and sensation seeking in efforts to compensate for the obvious change of excitement in lifestyles.

There are presumably many factors that interact to yield a traumatic stress disorder. Historical and familial factors, psychological stability, experience in coping with stressful events, social support systems, cognitive schemas, and perhaps biochemical factors, all possibly play a role in who does and who does not develop a chronic stress disorder following trauma. Research has just now begun to identify and tease apart these factors, but many more studies need to be conducted to gain further insight into understanding and treating this disorder.

OPERATIONALIZING AND VALIDATING PTSD DIAGNOSTIC CRITERIA

PTSD as a syndrome has the advantage of being introduced to mental health professionals with fairly well-specified descriptions of the disorder's symptoms. Yet the diagnosis is subject to many of the criticisms that have been leveled against the DSM-III itself. These criticisms have ranged from charges of unreliability, bias, and the mixed conceptual model found in the manual (Smith & Kraft, 1983), to the more political concerns over the boundaries of professional domain (Schacht & Nathan, 1977). However, underlying this range of criticisms is the common concern that empiricism must determine the overall utility and ultimate scientific success of DSM-III. Specifically, the new diagnosis of PTSD is defined by criteria that were clinically, rather than empirically, derived. To date, little research has been conducted on the validity of the symptoms included in the criteria.

Challenges to the validity of the PTSD criteria are particularly relevant for combat-related PTSD. Ambiguity in diagnostic criteria can result in a loss of government funding for treating and studying the disorder as well as the denial of service-connected disability compensation for the veterans themselves. The diagnostic category has also had important legal implications since Vietnam veteran offenders have claimed PTSD as their defense for an array of criminal acts.

A study from our laboratory (Zimering, Caddell & Keane, 1984) was designed to address the validity of the symptom criteria for PTSD. Several symptoms were assessed by evaluating veteran performance on cognitive and behavioral tasks, and questionnaires selected for their relationship to specific symptoms of the disorder. Responses of PTSD veterans on these tasks were compared to those of well-adjusted Vietnam combat veterans without PTSD. The following symptoms were assessed: (a) intrusive thoughts (an intrusive thought questionnaire), (b) concentration impairment (a sustained attention task), (c) decreased interpersonal contact (an affect recognition task), (d) anxiety (a motor steadiness task), (e) memory impairment (a short-term verbal memory task), and (f) increased symptomatology when exposed to cues associated with the trauma (presentation of neutral and combat sounds while measuring self-report of intrusive thoughts and psychophysiological arousal e.g., heart rate, skin resistance). We hypothesized that following the presentation of combat stimuli there would be impaired performance in the PTSD veterans and that their performance would be more impaired than the cohort group of well-adjusted combat veterans.

Results showed that performance on five of the six tasks was effective in distinguishing Vietnam veterans with PTSD from those who are currently well adjusted. PTSD veterans demonstrated increased physiological arousal, motoric agitation, and intrusive, combat-related cognitions when exposed to cues resembling the original traumatic event. These veterans also exhibited poor concentration when compared to their well-adjusted counterparts and they performed more poorly when asked to identify common affects (emotions) displayed on standardized tapes. Collectively these findings support the inclusion of all symptoms assessed with the sole exception of memory impairment. These results on the memory task indicate the need for greater specificity in defining the type of memory problems that may exist in Vietnam veterans. Yet, it is unclear if symptoms or tasks other than those included here would also separate these two groups, if other types of memory tasks would document the existence of this impairment, or if these tasks would discriminate other groups of Vietnam veterans. Future studies can provide this information, as well as add to the supporting evidence for the diagnostic criteria found in the present study.

In summary, there is a paucity of empirical investigations examining the etiology, symptomatology, assessment and treatment of PTSD. However, recent data based research suggests that a conditioning paradigm offers a viable framework within which to conceptualize the assessment and treatment of combat-related PTSD. Estimates of the prevalence of this disorder and its far-reaching social and political implications highlight the need for further intensive research in the area of PTSD.

REFERENCES

Bourne, P. G. (Ed.). (1969). The psychology and physiology of stress. New York: Academic.

Bower, G. H. (1981). Mood and memory, American Psychologist, 36, 129–148.

Brush, F. R. (1957). The effects of shock intensity on the acquisition and extinction of *an avoidance response in dogs.* Journal of Comparative and Physiological Psychology, 50, *547–552.*

Egendorf, A., Kadushin, C., Laufer, R. S., Rothbart, G., & Sloan, L. *(1981).* Legacies of veterans and their peers. *New York: Center for Policy Research.*

Fairbank, J. A., Gross, R. T., & Keane, T. M. *(1983). Behavioral assessment of intense anxiety during the treatment of posttraumatic stress disorders.* Behavior Modification, 7(4), *557–568.*

Foy, D. W., Sipprelle, R. C., Rueger, D. B., & Carroll, E. M. *(1984). Etiology of posttraumatic stress disorder in Vietnam veterans: Analysis of premilitary, military and combat exposure influence.* Journal of Consulting and Clinical Psychology, 52, *79–87.*

Horowitz *(1976).* Stress Response Syndromes. *New York: Aronson.*

Karnow, S. *(1983).* Vietnam a history. *New York: Viking.*

Keane, T. M., Caddell, J. M., Martin, B., Zimering, R. T., & Fairbank, J. A. *(1983). Substance abuse among Vietnam veterans with posttraumatic stress disorder.* Bulletin of the Society of Psychologists in Addictive Behaviors, 2(2), *117–122.*

Keane, T. M., Fairbank, J. A., Caddell, J. M., Zimering, R. T., & Beviler, M. E. *(1986). A behavioral approach to assessing and treating posttraumatic stress disorder in Vietnam veterans. Chapter in C. R. Figley (Ed.)* Trauma and its wake: The assessment and treatment of posttraumatic stress disorders.

Keane, T. M. & Kaloupek, D. G. (1982). Imaginal flooding in the treatment of a posttraumatic stress disorder. Journal of Consulting and Clinical Psychology, 50, *138–140.*

Levis, D. J. & Boyd, T. L. *(1979). Symptom maintenance: An infrahuman analysis and extension of the conservation of anxiety principle.* Journal of Abnormal Psychology, 88 (2), *107–120.*

Levis, D. J. & Hare, N. A. *(1977). Review of the theoretical rationale and empirical support for the extinction approach of implosive (flooding) therapy. In M. Hersen, R. M. Eisler, & P. M. Miller (Eds.),* Progress in behavior modification *(Vol. 4). New York: Academic.*

Maclear, M. *(1981).* Vietnam: The 10,000 Day War. *London: Thames/Methune.*

Mineka, S. *(1979). The role of fear in theories of avoidance learning, flooding and extinction.* Psychological Bulletin, 86, *985–1010.*

Mowrer, O. H. *(1947). On the dual nature of learning; A reinterpretation of "conditioning" and "problem solving."* Harvard Educational Review, 17, *102–148.*

Mowrer, O. H. *(1960).* Learning Theory and Behavior. *New York: Wiley.*

Rachman, S. *(1977). The conditioning theory of fear acquisition: A critical examination.* Behavior Research and Therapy, 15, *375–387.*

Schacht, T. & Nathan, P. E. *(1977). But is it good for psychologists? Appraisal and status of DSM-III.* American Psychologist, 32, *1017–1025.*

Smith, D. & Kraft, W. A. *(1983). DSM-III: Do psychologists really want an alternative?* American Psychologist, 38(7), *777–785.*

Solomon, R. L., Kamin, L. J., & Wynne, L. C. *(1953). Traumatic avoidance learning: The outcomes of several extinction procedures with dogs.* Journal of Abnormal & Social Psychology, 48, *291–302.*

Solomon, R. L. & Wynne, L. C. *(1954). Traumatic avoidance learning: The principles of anxiety conservation and partial irreversibility*. Psychological Review, 61, *353–385.*

Stampfl, T. G. & Levis, D. J., (1967). *Essentials of implosive therapy: A learning-theory-based psychodynamic behavioral therapy.* Journal of Abnormal Psychology, 72, *157–163.*

Weingartner, H., Miller, H., & Murphy, D. L. (1977). *Mood-state-dependent retrieval of verbal associations.* Journal of Abnormal Psychology, 86, *276–284.*

Wilson, G. T. & Davison, G. C. (1971) *Process of fear reduction in systematic desensitization: Animal studies.* Psychological Bulletin, 76, *1–14.*

Zimering, R. T., Caddell, J. M., & Keane, T. M. (1984) Posttraumatic stress disorder in Vietnam veterans: An empirical evaluation of the diagnostic criteria. *Unpublished manuscript.*

15. Dissociation and Hypnotizability in Posttraumatic Stress Disorder

David Spiegel, Thurman Hunt, and
Harvey E. Dondershine

D EFENSE MECHANISMS have received attention largely from the retrospective vantage point of psychoanalysis. They have been viewed as defenses against painful memories rather than painful experiences, and the reasons for the use of one particular defense mechanism rather than another have always been rather mysterious (1). More recently, attention has been directed toward the function of defense mechanisms as a protection against the overwhelming experience of trauma as it is inflicted. Individuals capable of profound dissociation and the analgesia associated with high hypnotizability might well mobilize such defenses during an episode of physical trauma. One example is the out-of-body experience often reported by women during rape or by patients suffering cardiac arrest. They describe the sensation of floating above their own bodies, feeling strangely detached from and even sorry for the person suffering beneath them.

Dissociation has been reported during many traumatic experiences (2). It may be that spontaneous reliving rather than simply remembering a traumatic event in posttraumatic stress disorder (PTSD) owes some of its hypnotic-like abreactive intensity to the fact that the patient was in a dissociated state during the trauma and is thus in a similar mental state while reliving it. Dissociation then becomes a defense against the painful affect associated with memories of the traumatic experience. Such abreactions can be elicited by a variety of stimuli, such as a tape recording of combat noises (3) and formal hypnotic age regression (4,5), which reactivate the dissociative response to the trauma.

The importance of imagery in posttraumatic symptoms has recently been observed (6). Theories about traumatic symptoms differ; some emphasize

Reprinted by permission from *American Journal of Psychiatry*, 145 (3), 301–305. Copyright ©
1988 by the American Psychiatric Association.

cognitive breakdown and withdrawal, with amnesia as a focal symptom (4,7), while others emphasize intrusive recollections and images (8). The *DSM-III* criteria include both types of symptoms: numbing of responsiveness on the one hand and intrusive recollections, sudden reliving of the traumatic events, and stimulus sensitivity on the other. Both observations may be fundamentally correct. What may occur in response to trauma is a polarization of experience in which trauma victims alternate between intense, vivid, and painful memories and images associated with the traumatic experience and a kind of pseudonormality in which the victims avoid such memories, using traumatic amnesia, other forms of dissociation, or repression, with a reduction in adaptive capacity and a constriction of the range of affective response. This polarization of consciousness can be seen in the hypnotic state, during which intense absorption in the hypnotic focal experience (9) can be achieved by means of the dissociation of experience at the periphery of consciousness (10,11). As in the hypnotic experience, traumatic imagery is either intense or absent. Thus, more frequent use of dissociative defenses, with their on-off quality, would be especially likely among victims of severe trauma.

A survey of the types of traumatic near-death experiences reveals a number of experiences that are dissociative in nature and resemble typical hypnotic phenomena: time distortion, visual hallucinations, and other sensory alterations (12–14). The presence of PTSD-related auditory hallucinations in non-schizophrenic patients has been shown to be related to the intensity of combat exposure and PTSD symptoms (15). These hallucinations generally took the form of voices of dying comrades, enemy soldiers, or civilians. These voices often suggested that the patient should commit suicide. The authors observed that such patients were especially sensitive to an imaginal flooding technique which recreated the state of physiological arousal experienced in combat (3). The relevance of hypnotic phenomena to the experience of trauma is also supported by reports of the usefulness of hypnosis to facilitate treatment of PTSD symptoms by enhancing such techniques as abreaction with modification of the details of the traumatic experience (4), grief work using hypnotic images (5), and hypnotic alteration of combat dreams (16).

The relationship between dissociation and trauma has had little empirical validation, in part because of the comparatively few studies of the association between the related construct of hypnotizability and trauma (2,17–19) and the absence, until recently, of measures of dissociation per se (20). The clinical use of hypnotizability testing can be helpful to differential diagnosis, since it can evoke and measure dissociation. Those who are hypnotizable often use the capacity spontaneously (8,21). Breuer (22), in fact, described dissociation as a "hypnoidal" state: "What we should be doing would be first to assign the phenomena of hysteria to hypnosis, and then to assert that hypnosis is the cause of those phenomena" (p. 248). Hypnotizability, which is the fundamental capacity to experience dissociation in a structured setting, should be high if extreme dissociative symptoms such as amnesia, fugue, hysterical psychosis, or multiple personality disorder occur (2,23,24). Thus, it can be helpful diagnostically to use a measure of hypnotizability (25,26), such as the Hypnotic Induction Profile (9) or the Stanford Hypnotic Clinical Scale (27), in the differential diagnosis of dissociative disorders.

In one study of hypnotizability in PTSD (28), 26 Vietnam combat veterans were divided into high and low symptom groups on the basis of posttraumatic symptoms, and those with high symptoms were found to be significantly more hypnotizable on the Stanford Hypnotic Susceptibility Scale. Form C (29). While no inference of cause and effect can be made, Hilgard (30) observed that self-report of punishment during childhood was one of three variables which were associated with later high hypnotizability in a population of normal college students ($r=0.30$, $N=187$). She speculated: "A possible tie between punishment and hypnotic involvement might come by way of dissociation. . . . Although we have no direct evidence, some of our case material . . . suggests that reading or other involvements may sometimes be an escape from the harsh realities of a punitive environment" (p. 221). When Frischholz (31) reanalyzed these data, he found that a multiple correlation combining imaginative involvement and punishment yielded a significantly higher correlation with hypnotizability ($r=0.40$) than did either variable alone. This suggests that the two variables (and presumably others) contribute independently to the development or preservation of hypnotizability.

The finding of higher hypnotizability among individuals with PTSD contrasts with the findings of generally lower hypnotizability and the absence of very high hypnotizability among patients with other severe psychiatric disorders, such as schizophrenia (32–34) and affective disorders (34,35). On the basis of these findings and the prominence of dissociative symptoms in PTSD, we predicted that patients with PTSD should have higher hypnotizability scores than other patient samples and a normal control sample.

METHOD

The 65 patients in the posttraumatic stress disorder sample represented half of a consecutive series of inpatients randomly assigned to one of two programs at the Menlo Park Division of the Palo Alto Veterans' Administration

Medical Center designed for the treatment of this disorder in veterans who had served in Vietnam. All met *DSM-III* criteria for PTSD, and their hypnotizability was assessed by one of us (H.E.D.) on the day of admission using the protocol for the Hypnotic Induction Profile (10). The other subject groups were derived from a sample of normal volunteers (N = 83) and in-and outpatients, primarily at the same medical center, who have been described previously (34). Informed consent for participation in the study was obtained from all subjects; only one patient refused. The comparison patients had diagnoses of schizophrenia (N = 23); generalized anxiety disorder (N = 18); major depression, bipolar disorder—depressed, and dysthymic disorder (N = 56); and miscellaneous disorders (N = 18). Hypnotizability scores were taken from the induction score of the Hypnotic Induction Profile. This scale is a 0–10 linear measure consisting of scores on five equally weighted items: dissociation, challenged hand levitation, an experience of reduced control in one hand, response to the cutoff signal, and instructed sensory alteration.

The data analytic technique was analysis of covariance with age as the covariate (time since latency has been shown to be inversely related to hypnotizability [10,36]), followed by post hoc t tests where permitted.

RESULTS

The mean ± SD hypnotizability score for the patients with PTSD was 8.04 ± 2.24. These patients had a mean induction score significantly higher than that of all the other patients and control subjects taken as a group (t=11.9, df=261, p<0.001). Their hypnotizability score was significantly higher than that of each of the other groups (see table 15.1). There was a significant main effect for age (F=7.17, df; eq1,256, p<0.008), but this did not account for the differences observed. A simple analysis of variance yielded significance values of the same magnitude, ruling out problems of colinearity in the analysis of covariance due to age differences.

DISCUSSION

Our findings are consistent with the hypothesis that many of the symptoms of posttraumatic stress disorder are dissociative in nature. This sample of Vietnam veterans with PTSD had higher hypnotizability scores than a normal control sample, and their scores were substantially higher than those of all the other psychiatric patient groups, including those with schizophrenia, dysthymia, major and bipolar depressive disorders, and generalized anxiety dis-

Table 15.1. Hypnotic Induction Profile Scores for Patients with PTSD, Control Subjects, and Patients with Other Psychiatric Diagnoses

| | | | | Hypnotic induction profile | | | | |
| | | Age (years) | | Score | | Comparison with mean score of PTSD patients[a] | | |
Group	N	Mean	SD	Mean	SD	t	df	p
Patients with PTSD	65	34.9	4.0	8.04	2.24			
Normal control subjects	83	28.1	8.8	7.23	2.24	2.48	146	0.01
Patients with schizophrenia	23	35.7	10.4	3.99	3.19	6.26	86	0.001
Patients with generalized anxiety disorder	18	38.8	12.2	4.06	3.30	5.39	81	0.001
Patients with affective disorders	56	43.1	13.1	5.76	3.19	3.83	19	0.001
Patients with miscellaneous disorders	18	37.4	14.2	5.96	2.85	2.80	81	0.01

[a] Analysis of covariance indicated a significant main effect for diagnosis (F = 12.3, df = 1, 5, p<0.001). Significance values are from post hoc t tests.

order. Thus, despite being quite symptomatic, patients with PTSD had hypnotizability scores more like those of the normal control sample than any of the other patient groups. Indeed, their scores were higher than normal and twice those of the small sample of patients with generalized anxiety disorder, which suggests the prominence of dissociative as opposed to anxiety-related symptoms in PTSD. Further, while age was found in this study, as in previous studies (10,36), to be correlated inversely with hypnotizability, the differences held when the effect of age was partialed out of the analysis.

The present study differs from previous work by Stutman and Bliss (28) in that we measured a large patient sample who had sought treatment, whereas the earlier investigators studied a community sample of veterans responding to a newspaper advertisement, finding that those high in the symptoms of posttraumatic stress disorder were more highly hypnotizable than those who were low in such symptoms. Clearly, the two studies are compatible, and, indeed, the Stutman and Bliss finding (28) provides evidence that it is not merely self-selection in seeking treatment that accounts for the high hypnotizability observed, but rather the prominence of PTSD symptoms.

Most of the symptoms associated with posttraumatic stress disorder in *DSM-III* have a flavor of dissociation: reexperiencing the event through intrusive recollections, nightmares, flashbacks, emotional numbing with feelings of detachment or isolation, stimulus sensitivity with the avoidance of environmental cues that are associated with recollections of the traumatic events, and difficulty concentrating. The phenomenon of dissociation implies an isolated set of interacting affects and memories that can be reactivated. They come as a unit, consistent with evidence in cognitive psychology for state-dependent memory (37). This body of work has shown that mental content can be more accurately retrieved when the mood state is congruent in the retrieval process to that in which the material was learned. Memories laid down in the company of strong affect might therefore be available only if the person were able to tolerate reexperiencing the associated intense affect. Such experiences are defensively avoided, and thus the memories and their association networks of affect are dissociated.

The study of dissociation began with observations of overlapping phenomena in hypnosis and multiple personality disorder patients (38). Hysterical patients prone to dissociative symptoms have been found to be highly hypnotizable (2,39) and are likely to use their dissociative capacities in the face of stress: "Hysterical patients . . . have an exaggerated, perhaps inborn, tendency toward mental dissociation that provides them with a ready-made mechanism of defense for dealing with emotionally painful events" (39, p. 947). Janet (40) emphasized dissociation as the primary defense, while Freud (41) acknowledged dissociation but emphasized repression. The major distinction between the two defense mechanisms can be understood in terms of the relationships among the material that is kept out of conscious awareness. In dissociation, specific memories and associated feelings seem to contain rules excluding other memories and feelings from conscious awareness, although these rules are not absolute, and the boundaries can be breached (31). For example, memories associated with depressive affect tend to prevent recall of happier memories (37). In repression, similar material may be kept out of awareness to exclude uncomfortable affects that accompany it, but there is no rule within one set of memories or associations which necessitates the exclusion of others. Many PTSD patients consider their memories to be incompatible with conducting an ordinary life and rewarding relationships. These two jarringly different images of the self must be kept apart. As Hilgard (11) has noted, dissociated mental states can be thought of as coexisting side by side, separated by amnesic barriers, while repression implies a more vertical or archaeological mental structure.

Freud (41) was troubled about the relationship between traumatic neuroses and his general theory that repression served as a means of keeping unacceptable wishes out of consciousness. Why would trauma be repressed when it was not wished for? His repression model fits the development of oedipal fears and wishes better than it does trauma. Much has recently been made of Freud's abandonment of the trauma theory as the general explanation for the neuroses. The possibility that different defenses are mobilized by trauma and by development problems is of greater interest. Dissociation may be elicited more by physical trauma, repression by longstanding developmental conflicts and warded-off wishes.

Trauma can be understood as the experience of being made into an object, a thing: the victim of someone else's rage, of nature's indifference, of one's own physical or psychological limitations. Along with the pain and fear that are associated with rape, combat trauma, or natural disaster comes an overwhelming and marginally bearable sense of helplessness, a realization that one's own will and wishes become irrelevant to the course of events; this leaves a view of the self that is damaged or contaminated by the humiliation, pain, and fear that the event imposed or a fragmented sense of self. The preexisting personality attempts to carry on as though nothing at all had happened. However, the need for the dissociation implies an association: that pain and humiliation were, in fact, inflicted. Thus, the person reconsolidates with a sense of fragmentation, and the real truth is the dissociated and warded-off self that was humiliated and damaged.

Thus, while dissociation serves the function of defending consciousness from the immediate experience of painful events—physical pain, fear, anxiety, and helplessness—it then becomes an entrenched part of the overall view of self. Once the self is divided in a powerful way, the experience of unity becomes problematic, since ordinary self-consciousness is no longer synonymous with the entirety of self and personal history. Rather, it becomes associated with the awareness of some warded-off tragedy, the moment of humiliation and fear, the act of cowardice, the sense of having been degraded. The person comes to feel that there is an inauthentic self which carries on the everyday functions of life but with the sense of numbing, the lack of genuine pleasure in otherwise pleasurable activities. The unconscious, warded-off memories exert censorship on conscious experience. The process of dissociation becomes part of the patient's identity, to be remobilized in the face of subsequent stress or even imagined situations reminiscent of this stress.

The experience of involuntariness may be a link among hypnosis, dissociation, and trauma. The importance of involuntariness in hypnosis was emphasized originally by Bernheim (42) and more recently by Weitzenhoffer (43). As discussed earlier, the kinds of events that mobilize dissociation as a defense also seem to be those in which the patient's volition is physically overridden. Thus, the natural involuntariness associated with the hypnotic state can be viewed as a repetition of an experience in which involuntariness is literally imposed by external circumstances.

The causal explanation for these findings remains obscure. Does the experience of trauma enhance hypnotizability, or are highly hypnotizable individuals more sensitive to the aftereffects of combat trauma? It is unlikely that individuals with low hypnotizability are impervious to the effects of combat. It may be that they assimilate the experience less symptomatically by maintaining their perspective on it as an external force imposed on them, thereby minimizing damage to their self-esteem. Or perhaps they develop other symptoms, such as alcohol and drug abuse, which may overshadow the intrusive recollections and other symptoms of PTSD. It would be interesting to see whether veterans with PTSD have drug and alcohol abuse rates that are lower than those of veterans with similar combat exposure but without PTSD. It is also possible that the experience of extreme physical violence is so psychologically devastating that equally extreme defenses are mobilized to deal with the experience. Such trauma may stimulate or reopen access to this form of dissociative experience, which normally begins to decline after latency (10,36). It is possible that combat and other forms of extreme trauma create a dissociative state which is reexperienced when the content and affect of the memories are retrieved. In any event, this and previous work lend credence to the importance of dissociation as an underlying factor in the symptoms of posttraumatic stress disorder and of hypnosis as a relevant modality in the treatment of these individuals.

REFERENCES

1. Freud A: The Ego and Mechanisms of Defense. New York, International Universities Press, 1946
2. Spiegel D, Fink R: Hysterical psychosis and hypnotizability. Am J Psychiatry 1979; 136:777–781
3. Kolb L C, Mutalipassi L R: The conditioned emotional response: a sub-class of the chronic and delayed post-traumatic stress disorder. Psychiatr Annals 1982; 12:979–987
4. Kardiner A, Spiegel H: War Stress and Neurotic Illness. New York, Paul Hoeber, 1947
5. Spiegel D: Vietnam grief work using hypnosis. Am J Hypn 1981; 24:33–40
6. Brett E A, Ostroff R: Imagery and posttraumatic stress disorder: an overview. Am J Psychiatry 1985; 142:417–424
7. Krystal H, Niederland W G: Psychic Traumatization. Boston, Little, Brown, 1971

8. *Horowitz M J: Stress Response Syndromes. New York, Jason Aronson, 1976*
9. *Tellegen A, Atkinson G: Openness to absorbing and self-altering experiences ("absorption"), a trait related to hypnotic susceptibility. J Abnorm Psychol 1974; 83:268–277*
10. *Spiegel D, Spiegel H: Trance and Treatment: Clinical Uses of Hypnosis. Washington, DC, American Psychiatric Press, 1987*
11. *Hilgard E R: Divided Consciousness: Multiple Controls in Human Thought and Action. New York, John Wiley & Sons, 1977*
12. *Grinker R, Spiegel J: Men under Stress. Philadelphia, Blakiston, 1945*
13. *Van Putten T, Emory WH: Traumatic neuroses in Vietnam returnees. Arch Gen Psychiatry 1973; 29:695–698*
14. *Greyson B: A typology of near-death experiences. Am J Psychiatry 1985; 142: 967–969*
15. *Mueser K T, Butler R W: Auditory hallucinations in combat-related chronic posttraumatic stress disorder. Am J Psychiatry 1987; 144:299–302*
16. *Eichelman B: Hypnotic change in combat dreams of two veterans with posttraumatic stress disorder. Am J Psychiatry 1985; 142:112–114*
17. *Spiegel H: The grade 5 syndrome: the highly hypnotizable person. Int J Clin Exp Hypn 1974; 22:303–319*
18. *Bliss E L: Multiple personalities: a report of 14 cases with implications for schizophrenia and hysteria. Arch Gen Psychiatry 1980; 37:1388–1397*
19. *Spiegel D: Multiple personality as a post-traumatic stress disorder. Psychiatr Clin North Am 1984; 7:101–110*
20. *Sanders S: The perceptual alteration scale: a scale measuring dissociation. Am J Clin Hypn 1986; 29:95–102*
21. *Shor R E, Orne M T, O'Connell D N: Psychological correlates of plateau hypnotizability in a special volunteer sample. J Pers Soc Psychol 1966; 3:80–95*
22. *Breuer, J, Freud S: Studies on hysteria (1893–1895), in Complete Psychological Works, standard ed, vol 2. London, Hogarth Press, 1955*
23. *Putnam F W: Dissociation as a response to extreme trauma, in Childhood Antecedents of Multiple Personality. Edited by Kluft R P. Washington, DC, American Psychiatric Press, 1985*
24. *Steingard S, Frankel F H: Dissociation and psychotic symptoms. Am J Psychiatry 1985; 142:953–955*
25. *Frankel F H, Apfel R H, Kelly S F, et al.: The use of hypnotizability scales in the clinic: a review after six years. Int J Clin Exp Hypn 1979; 27:63–73*
26. *Mott T: The clinical importance of hypnotizability. Am J Clin Hypn 1979; 21: 263–269*
27. *Hilgard E R, Hilgard J R: Hypnosis in the Relief of Pain. Los Altos, Calif, William Kaufman, 1975*
28. *Stutman R K, Bliss E L: Posttraumatic stress disorder, hypnotizability, and imagery. Am J Psychiatry 1985; 142:741–743*
29. *Weitzenhoffer A M, Hilgard E R: Stanford Hypnotic Susceptibility Scale, Form C. Palo Alto, Calif, Consulting Psychologists Press, 1962*
30. *Hilgard J R: Personality and Hypnosis: A Study of Imaginative Involvement, Chicago, University of Chicago Press, 1970*

31. *Frischholz E J: The relationship among dissociation, hypnosis, and child abuse in the development of multiple personality disorder, in Childhood Antecedents of Multiple Personality. Washington, DC, American Psychiatric Press, 1985*
32. *Lavoie G, Sabourin M: Hypnosis and schizophrenia: a review of experimental and clinical studies, in Handbook of Hypnosis and Psychosomatic Medicine. New York, Elsevier-North Holland, 1980*
33. *Pettinati H M: Measuring hypnotizability in psychotic patients. Int J Clin Exp Hypn 1982; 30:404–416*
34. *Spiegel D, Detrick D, Frischholz E: Hypnotizability and psychopathology. Am J Psychiatry 1982; 139:431–437*
35. *Spiegel D: Hypnotizability and psychoactive medication. Am J Clin Hypn 1980; 22:217–222*
36. *Morgan A H, Hilgard E R: Age differences in susceptibility to hypnosis, Int J Clin Exp Hypn 1973; 21:78–85*
37. *Bower G H: Mood and memory. Am Psychol 1981; 36:129–148*
38. *Ellenberger H F: Discovery of the Unconscious: The History and Evolution of Dynamic Psychiatry, New York, Basic Books, 1970*
39. *Nemiah J C: Dissociative disorders, in Comprehensive Textbook of Psychiatry, 4th ed, vol 1. Edited by Kaplan H I, Sadock B J. Baltimore, Williams & Wilkins, 1985*
40. *Janet P: Psychological Healing: A Historical and Clinical Study, vols 1, 2. Translated by Paul E. London, George Allen and Unwin, 1925*
41. *Freud S: New introductory lectures on psychoanalysis (1932–1936), in Complete Psychological Works, standard ed, vol 22. London, Hogarth Press, 1964*
42. *Bernheim H: Automatisme et Suggestion. Paris, Librarie Felix Alcan, 1917*
43. *Weitzenhoffer A M: Hypnotic susceptibility revisited. Am J Clin Hypn 1980; 22: 130–146.*

16. A Model of Mourning
Change in Schemas of Self and Other

Mardi J. Horowitz

U NCONSCIOUS PROCESSES lead to extremes of conscious experience during grief. Some time after a loved one dies, a preoccupation with the deceased may dominate the mourner's conscious experience. Visual or auditory images of the deceased may occur unexpectedly. The bereaved person may experience unwelcome and intrusive emotions: not just sadness, as expected, but also fear, rage, and guilt. An opposite extreme in conscious experience may also occur. The bereaved person may consciously attempt to recall a memory about the deceased, and fail. Or the mourner may try to cry, but cannot. Thus extremes of conscious representations in terms of intrusions and omissions may occur during mourning, and both extremes suggest unconscious conflict between impulsive and defensive aims. The following case excerpt illustrates both intrusive and omissive types of deflection from voluntary control of conscious representation:

Mary's elderly mother died when Mary was middle-aged. Mary felt sorrowful, cried at the funeral, took a week away from her work and usual social activities, and then went through her mother's belongings, quietly contemplating her memories. She then resumed her life as usual, until, weeks later, she found herself preoccupied with unbidden images of hostile exchanges with her mother. These malevolent and dominating images were based on memories and fantasies of the past. When Mary tried to deliberately recall her mother in the context of pleasant, loving memories, she could not conjure up any image at all of her mother's face.

Unconscious mental processes dictate much of the experience of mourning. The person in mourning seldom can accurately predict *when* he or she might enter a particular emotional mood, *what* memories of the deceased would then be recalled, *when or if* strong emotions would be triggered by some reminder of the loss, or *why* a new behavior emerged that exhibited traits of

Reprinted by permission from *Journal of American Psychoanalytic Association*, 38 (2), 297–324. Copyright © 1990 by International Universities Press, Inc.

the deceased. Few persons ever predict the quality of anniversary reactions accurately, yet most persons have them. The unconscious mind is tracking time and recording dates in ways not reported to consciousness, even after a psychoanalysis. The next two vignettes illustrate such phenomena.

A clinical psychologist attended a talk on the relation of unconscious factors to the phenomenology of grief experiences. At the coffee break, she said that just that morning she had finally put on the earrings left her by her mother upon her death two years before. Up until the day of the seminar, the psychologist had left them, untouched, in her jewelry box. She had attached no significance to the act that morning, but during the talk she realized she had decided—unconsciously—to symbolically complete her mourning by taking the earrings as her own. She thought she had also probably signed up for the conference for the same purpose.

A more detailed vignette indicates a series of unpredicted anniversary reactions following the death of a loved one:

The noted psychiatrist and psychoanalyst Engel (1975) wrote of his anniversary reactions after his twin brother died suddenly from a heart attack, like their father before him. His brother died at age 49; the father had died at age 58. When Engel heard of the death, at first he felt stunned disbelief, and then began crying, 20 minutes later. Within a few hours he was experiencing chest pains. On later examination it was discovered that Engel, too, showed evidence of coronary heart disease, although not an infarction. During the next months, Engel worried that he would have a heart attack. Eleven months after his twin brother died, he did have a coronary occlusion. Afterward, Engel felt relief: he no longer had to fear a heart attack would fell him at any moment.

As the years passed, he became less concerned by anniversaries, and so did not anticipate he would have any reaction on the fifth-year anniversary of his brother's death when Engel himself was 54 years old. When the date arrived, however, he had a dream on a theme of guilt at surviving a heart attack when his brother had died from one.

On the fifth-year anniversary of Engel's own heart attack, he had another dream wherein he remembered that a friend had died suddenly. In the dream, he felt sad and agitated and tried to tell a colleague about the death. He awakened in a depressed mood. This friend, in many associations, had the characteristics of Engel's twin brother. He then realized that he had been looking forward to the anniversary as a cause for celebration that he had survived for five years. Yet during the actual day, he blocked out any conscious memory of its significance. That significance was represented in the dream thoughts.

When Engel reached 58, the age his father had been when he died, Engel made a number of errors in conscious thought. He remembered his father as dying at age 59 instead of age 58, although for many years Engel had feared that he, too, would die at 58. In this way he passed his fifty-eighth year without conscious anxiety, since the threat of death was projected into the future. After the threat had passed and he had survived his fifty-ninth birthday, Engel recalled that his father had died at age 58.

Such anniversary phenomena indicate how unconscious defensive operations can serve to reduce levels of felt anxiety and guilt. The balance between impulsive aims at mastery by repetition in thought and unconscious defensive aims at avoidance of emotional pain varies over time, leading to phasic variation in what a person consciously experiences.

PHASES OF RESPONSE DURING MOURNING

Pollock (1978) described variations in affect as the mourning process progresses. The degree of conscious experience of affect provides an index of change. Parkes (1964, 1972) and Parkes and Weiss (1983) reviewed Freud's (1917), Lindemann's (1944), and subsequent models of the bereavement process, and differentiated specific phases of grief: (1) initial denial and avoidance of the loss, (2) subsequent alarm reactions, such as anxiety, with restlessness and physiological complaints, (3) searching to find the lost person, (4) anger and guilt, (5) feelings of internal loss, (6) adoption of traits or mannerisms of the deceased, and (7) acceptance and resolution, including appropriate changes in identity. To these seven phases Pollock (1972, 1978) added the importance of revived mourning on anniversaries and of phases of creativity during mourning. One can condense the phases of mourning into the phases already described for stress response syndromes in general: outcry, denial, intrusion, working through, and completion (Horowitz, 1986).

NORMAL AND PATHOLOGICAL GRIEF

Grief has normal forms and pathological variations. Pathological grief is often a highly intense and out-of-control experience of the kind of ideas and feelings normally found during mourning (Freud, 1917; Deutsch, 1937; Lindemann, 1944; Glick et al., 1974; Pollock, 1978; Bowlby, 1980; Raphael, 1983). Sometimes, however, it is a failure to mourn (Clayton, 1974; Horowitz et al., 1980; Osterweiss, et al., 1984; Windholtz et al, 1985). And at other times it is a set of signs and symptoms atypical of normal grief (Abraham, 1924). In one of his most important theoretical papers, "Mourning and Melancholia," Freud (1917) presented the decisive effects of the nature of the previous relationship with the deceased in predicting whether normal or pathological grief would occur. Preexisting ambivalence in this relationship predisposes the person to both more intense and turbulent affects and more extensive and regressive defenses.

Normal grief reactions, as already mentioned, may change in the quality of subjective experience during various phases of mourning. So, too, pathological grief reactions may have signs and symptoms with a phasic change pattern, as shown in table 16.1.

The phases of outcry, denial, intrusion, and working through shown in table 16.1 are generalizations. While the phases are often sequential as tabulated, no one person must necessarily follow the order presented, or even experience all of the phases. Personality style, current conflicts, and developmental level of the personality all affect the experience and length of the phases. Persons with compulsive personalities often remain longer in a low

Table 16.1. Common Experiences during Grief and Their Pathological Intensification

Phase	Normal response	Pathological intensifications
Dying	Emotional expression and immediate coping with the dying process	Avoidant; overwhelmed, dazed, confused; self-punitive; inappropriately hostile
Death and outcry	Outcry of emotions with news of the death and turning for help to others or isolating self with self-succoring	Panic; dissociative reactions; reactive psychoses
Warding off (denial)	Avoidance of reminders, social withdrawal, focusing elsewhere, emotional numbing, not thinking of implications to self or certain themes	Maladaptive avoidances of confronting the implications of the death. Drug or alcohol abuse, counterphobic frenzy, promiscuity, fugue states, phobic avoidance, feeling dead or unreal
Reexperience (intrusion)	Intrusive experiences including recollections of negative relationship experiences with the deceased, bad dreams, reduced concentration, compulsive enactments	Flooding with negative images and emotions, uncontrolled ideation, self-impairing compulsive reenactments, night terrors, recurrent nightmares, distraught from intrusion of anger, anxiety, despair, shame or guilt themes, physiological exhaustion from hyperarousal
Working through	Recollections of the deceased and contemplations of self with reduced intrusiveness of memories and fantasies, increased rational acceptance, reduced numbness and avoidance, more "dosing" of recollections and a sense of working it through	Sense that one cannot integrate the death with a sense of self and continued life. Persistent warded off themes may manifest as anxious, depressed, enraged, shame-filled or guilty moods, and psychophysiological syndromes
Completion	Reduction in emotional swings with a sense of self-coherence and readiness for new relationships. Able to experience positive states of mind	Failure to complete mourning may be associated with inability to work, create, to feel emotion or positive states of mind

emotion denial phase, while persons with histrionic personalities are often more prone to extended intrusive phases. Sometimes persons with narcissistic personalities show few direct manifestations of grief after a brief outcry phase. They may be too developmentally immature to have an adult type of relationship and so cannot exhibit an adult type of mourning at its loss.

Many aspects of the psychodynamics of the phases of grief have been worked out by the authors cited above. A great deal is now known in psychoanalytic theory about why preexisting ambivalence in the relationship complicates mourning. It can motivate excessive defensive avoidance of the grief process to avoid anxiety, shame, and guilt at feeling anger. Such ambivalence can lead to an interminable sense of bereavement as self-punishment. The ambivalence can be compulsively reenacted in transference reactions to other persons, leading to loss of social supports, and an ensuing, escalating sense of abandonment.

To such well-known aspects of classical theory, I aim to add further theories about how schemas of self and others change during a mourning process. After a very brief review of schema theory, I shall discuss each phase of experience during mourning in order to explain the prototypical set of experiences during that phase by such theory.

SCHEMA THEORY

A self-schema is an organized composite of multiple features that persists unconsciously to organize mental processes and perhaps produce derivatives for conscious representation. Self-schemas may be articulated to schemas of others in ways that organize a script of wishes, fears, and likely reactions. This larger-order schema is called a role relationship model in configurational analysis (Horowitz, 1987).

Researchers have postulated that *schemas* (the modern plural replacing *schemata*) are organizers of information processing whose forms both speed up appraisal and fill in for missing information (Bartlett, 1932; Piaget, 1937; Singer and Salovey, 1991). Higher-order schemas such as role relationship models maintain coherences between lower-order schemas such as those of bodies and body parts. Higher-order schemas operate as wholes, as more than the sum of parts.

Any individual has a repertoire of multiple schemas of self and others. Different ones might be regnant in different states of mind. Shifts in states of mind might occur as schemas varied in activity (Horowitz, 1988). Entry into states of high transference distortions from a state of more realistic recognition of the relationship with the analyst is a derivative of regression to role relationship models that are schemas of an earlier time (Slap and Saykin, 1983).

Freud (1912) based his theory of transference on the carry-over into new relationships of templates developed during key times of childhood development. He saw the development of the libido as having forms that included self-and object representations and figuration of self-and object activities. Jacobson (1964), Kernberg (1967), and Arlow (1969) were especially important in showing how these forms powerfully influenced the organization of drives and emotions. The British object relations school formed and utilized such theory, as has the recent self psychological school of psychoanalytic thought (Sutherland, 1980; Kohut, 1972; Slap and Saykin, 1983). Person schemas theory stems from this background and is articulated to classical dynamic and cognitive theories elsewhere (Horowitz, 1988).

THE PHASE OF OUTCRY

Outcry is a phase of immediate response to the first news of death or loss. It contains a rapid unconscious assessment of the implications to the self of the loss. The sudden confrontation with bad news leads to a sharp rise in the experience and expression of such raw emotions as fear, sadness, and anger, and to physiological changes in sympathetic, parasympathetic, histaminic, and immunological systems. The result may range from hyperarousal to shock. The phase of outcry is named for one of its features, the sudden expression of strong feelings. Because unconscious thought proceeds further and more swiftly than conscious thought, intrusive emotions can take subjective awareness by surprise. A cascade of emotional experiences occurs during this phase, as different implications of the death are touched upon. A deeper review of these topics will take place during subsequent phases of response, but the first emotional indicators of their importance are now present.

I found an insightful illustration of this power of emotion during the outcry phase in James Agee's *A Death in the Family* (1957). The following excerpt illustrates the outcry phase of a woman whose husband died in a car accident only a few days earlier. She dons her mourning veil for his funeral, thinking as she does so that she has grown up almost overnight, for she realizes her loss and knows that terrible pain lies ahead. As she leaves the bedroom shared with her husband, she is stunned by grief:

The realization came without shape or definability, save as it was focused in the pure physical acts of leaving the room, but came with such force, such monstrous piercing weight, in all her heart and soul and mind and body but above all in the womb, where it arrived and dwelt like a cold and prodigious, spreading stone, that groaned almost inaudibly, almost a mere silent breath, an *Ohhhhhh*, and doubled deeply over, hands to her belly, and her knee joints melted [pp. 305–306].

If a death is unexpected, emotional expression may be more intense than if the death was long anticipated. In anticipatory grief, a working model showing the deceased as dying develops. After confrontation with an unexpected death, a person may form a working model in which the deceased is viewed as seriously harmed and critically in need of help. This working model sharply arouses emotional systems. Because the deceased is modeled as harmed, the self is aroused to act to reduce threat. The alarm emotions prepare the body for action and motivate the conscious mind to interrupt other activities in order to plan this action. As a result, the person may undertake frantic but hopeless activity to repair the hazardous condition of the deceased. Some funeral rituals serve this obligation to "do something!" The working model can be a bit irrational in regard to the reality of permanent loss, since it depicts the other as harmed but not completely beyond help.

The nature of the working model will determine the contents of the crying out of alarming emotional ideas. The emotional expression of an outcry phase may come as actions and images, as well as words. There may be appeals for divine help ("Oh God!") or expressions of rage ("God damn it!") or remorse ("I'm so sorry!"). Rapid unconscious appraisals of the repercussions of the death may lead to defensive opposition to alarming ideas and emotions. Some form of denial can occur in the emotional exclamations that characterize this phase ("Oh no! It can't be! Say it isn't so!"). A rapid appraisal of the self during the outcry phase leads to conscious vows like "I'll survive this," or "I'll never enjoy life again—ever!" These inner assertions become an important part of the memory of receiving the bad news.

The term "working model" applies to a transient schema derived from both perception and enduring schemas (Bowlby, 1980; Bretherton and Waters, 1985). It is based heavily on immediate perceptions of external reality, although schemas organize (and potentially distort) that perception. An enduring schema of a role relationship model is less situationally dependent. It is activated by inner wishes. *Thus we may infer that the mind unconsciously compares the working role-relationship model and the enduring role-relationship model. If they do not match, intense emotions may arise, serving to motivate either plans for correcting the mismatch or defensive avoidances to reduce recognition of it.* This mismatch is the usual state of affairs in the outcry phase. The sharp expression of emotional alarms itself may serve an

evolutionary adaptive purpose. Sobbing may summon aid; shock and fear
may elicit protection; remorse, renewed support; and rage may alert others to
treat the subject with tact and caution.

THE PHASE OF DENIAL

There are a variety of defenses that reduce emotional flooding and help the
person cope with immediate needs. As a result of the initial defensive inhibitions of some emotional themes, the alarm reactions characteristic of the
outcry phase are reduced. One is often aware that denial is operating, and
one is conscious of feeling numb or insulated. The seventeenth-century poet
John Dryden, in "Threnodia Augustalis" (in Moffatt, 1982) spoke of this
when he wrote "Tears stand congealed and cannot flow/And the sad soul
retires into her inmost room." Emily Dickinson (1955) wrote, "After great
pain, a formal feeling comes. The Nerves sit ceremonious, like Tombs."

The avoidance of states of high emotion during a denial phase has been
explained as the consequence of active inhibitory efforts. If conscious, these
defensive maneuvers are called *suppression*; if unconscious, they are called
repression (Freud, 1915; Abraham, 1924; Deutsch, 1937; Lindemann, 1944).
Usually, unconscious defenses predominate and the person may not consciously know that themes are warded off. The purpose of the defenses is to
reduce emotional pain. This may be adaptive in allowing self-restorative
periods, or maladaptive in postponing indefinitely a desirable process of
working through. Defensive processes involve selection among themes, topics, and schemas that have sufficient motive force to gain conscious attention,
as in the following example from a psychoanalytic case.

Mr. F. was a professional man in his early forties. He sought psychoanalysis for the
resolution of neurotic difficulties involving rivalry with peers, with rages at them and
at superiors in his corporation. He had been in analysis for two years when there
came news of a sharp decline in the health of his mother. She was soon to die.

During the period before the news of her illness, Mr. F. had permitted himself to
regress into a gradually more intense transference neurosis characterized by oscillations between anxiously longing for the analyst's loving attention and experiencing
rivalrous, envious ambitions to triumph over him by proving himself the analyst's
sexual and mental superior. Derivative patterns of this relationship dilemma were
observed in Mr. F.'s current interactions with his father. His relationship as an adult
with him was conflicted, his adult relationship with his mother relatively less conflicted. Other important patterns occurred at work with his employer and in memories
of his father. Analytic work dealt also with the triangular oedipal relationship among
his mother, his father, and him, and his warded-off ambitions to win mother from
father, with guilt and anxiety over wishes to rid the family of his father.

When the news came that his mother, who lived in a distant city, had gone into the hospital for cancer surgery, Mr. F. talked of the possibility of her death, experienced worry, and expected sorrow. The operation revealed a malignant tumor that had spread to the point that his mother had to be regarded as terminally ill. When he received the news, Mr. F. left at once to visit her.

Upon his return, the analytic process continued much as before in terms of the intense level of transference manifestations. Mr. F. "held his breath" as he waited to hear of his mother's further decline. Meanwhile, the triangular relationship among Mr. F., his mother, and his father was further woven into the analysis of conflicts surrounding his persistent but warded-off love for the rivalry with his father. In other words, he treated the very bad news about his mother's illness much like other episodic stresses of everyday life: with negative feelings and some effect on the analytic process, but without cessation of the analytic process in its larger stream of transference regressions and resolving transference resistances. Anticipatory mourning was not conspicuous, although Mr. F. mentioned from time to time that he expected to hear of his mother's death.

Mr. F.'s mother stayed in touch but did not communicate great suffering. A few months later, she died. Mr. F. returned home at once for her funeral. He stayed for two weeks, having many interactions with his father. On Mr. F.'s return to the analysis, he expressed his feelings of sadness and his anger at aspects of his mother's medical care. His associations, however, revealed that this anger was a displacement of anger at his mother, and the defense was interpreted as such.

About three months of analysis followed, governed by somber moods and desultory movement in terms of transference work. The envious and rivalrous, yearning-and-seeking transference themes abated. Preoedipal transference issues about anger at abandonment did not emerge at this time, as they had on his return from the funeral. At times Mr. F. tried deliberately to think about the implications of his mother's death or about how he had experienced the analytic process before she died. These conscious efforts at restoring richness of emotion to the psychoanalytic situation were ineffective.

He was in a *phase of denial*, manifested in a broad limitation on degree of exploration of mourning themes that had surfaced briefly during an outcry phase and that would later emerge during an intrusive phase. During this denial phase there was a reduction of intensity of transference phenomena. The previous regression into a transference neurosis had been made possible by the growing experience of safety with the analyst. The threat of grief apparently reduced his sense of safety, and it seemed that he progressed out of the regressive transference position in order to handle this threat and gather his strength for the mourning experience he may have unconsciously anticipated.

Death of a loved one leads to too many implications to fully process in a short time. The mind unconsciously retains important memories for later processing. After a traumatic event the mind codes these memories not only in the computational unconscious, but also in a warded-off dynamic unconscious (Breuer and Freud, 1895; Freud, 1920; Horowitz, 1988). The latter is a form of *active memory* (Horowitz and Becker, 1971; Horowitz, 1986) because it has as a function the automatic re-representation of the information it contains. These memories become less active as they are assimilated into schemas. This repetition of active memory is a factor in the compulsion to repeat traumas until they are mastered, what Freud called the process of changing memories from "untamed" to "tamed" (Breuer and Freud, 1895; Freud, 1920).

During the denial phase of mourning, the active memory of some themes about the loss is avoided by an inhibition of topics for conscious representation that is unconsciously decided upon. The outcome is repression of topics, omission of recollection, avoidance of recognizing personal implications of the death, and often a conscious but vague sense of being frozen, insulated, derealized or depersonalized.

Unlike in certain other posttraumatic reactions, in bereavement total suppression or repression of the theme of loss is seldom observed. Some recognition of short-range consequences of the death to the self occurs, while many other long-range effects are not contemplated. The continued use of schemas that contain beliefs which model the deceased as alive is what is most prominent during this phase. We may see this as another, less discussed aspect of the repetition compulsion. The preserved role relationship model of the self with the deceased as alive contributes to such phenomena as the use of the present tense in describing the relationship with the deceased, as in, "*We* like to travel during vacations." In other words, there is some dissociation of role relationship models during the denial phase. The person preserves a role relationship model of the self as related to the living other, while separately developing a recognition of the self as alive and the deceased as dead when situational reminders force that recognition. The latter role relationship model is inhibited from organizing ideas and feelings in many states of mind during the denial phase.

THE PHASE OF INTRUSION

The denial phase may last for days, weeks, or even months. During this time, the mourner may have returned to many of the customary forms of his or her life. A sense of safety may be returning. It may be just then, surprisingly, that intrusive experiences increase in frequency and intensity. In the fourth century, the poet and courtier P'An Yueh (Rexroth, 1970) wrote "In Mourning for His Dead Wife." The poem indicates a year has passed since her death, and yet:

. . . Her perfume
Still haunts the bedroom. Her clothes
Still hang there in the closet.
She is always alive in
My dreams. I wake with a start.
She vanishes. And I
Am overwhelmed with sorrow . . .

A further fragment from the case of Mr. F. illustrates these phenomena.

Mr. F.'s mother had been dead for several months. Under no particular stress in terms of his external situation, and without much in the way of new analytic work, Mr. F. decided to look through his photographs of her. He viewed the pictures without particular emotional response, as he reported in the next day's analytic session. But that night he had a bad dream wherein he saw himself in the hospital, going through painful and frightening procedures like his mother had endured. This review of photographs, on the surface an apparently spontaneous decision, seemed to be due to an unconscious sense of readiness to enter a more active form of grief. The decision, action, and dream marked the onset of an *intrusive phase of reexperience.*

During this phase, Mr. F. had visual images about his mother even when he was trying to concentrate at his work. While driving, he would find himself ruminating emotionally about whether he had done enough for her before she died. He pined sadly for her return. At other times he felt irritable, with occasional pangs of anger at having no mother. He resented his wife at times because she could still speak to her mother on the telephone.

During the analysis his associational reveries led from relating these intrusive daily experiences of ideas and emotions to deeper themes of feeling abandoned by his mother. He was, angry at her for leaving him, then felt guilty for being angry. He effected a role reversal, putting himself in the role of the person abandoning the needful other, his mother. He castigated himself for being too devoted to his work to visit or even call his mother as much as he felt she would have liked; and he feared that she was yet alive, hovering between life and death, or just "somewhere," unavailable, but still angry at him.

During this period Mr. F. saw the analyst mainly as consistently "there for him," as listening closely and with sensitivity, and making periodic helpful clarifications. Several transference themes that had a clear relationship to ideas and feelings about his mother emerged during this period. These themes included fear that the analyst, like his mother, might leave him; anger at the analyst leaving him each weekend and on short professional trips, with guilt over being irrationally hostile; and expectations that the analyst would criticize him for having less interest than before in the analysis. These topics were like those that appeared in the analysis before the death, and had less "stickiness." Mr. F. experienced these transference themes and was able to quickly relate his transferred ideas and feelings to his relationship with his mother.

Conscious recognition of the significance of a loss to the self becomes prominent during the phase of intrusive reexperiencing of memories about the stressful event and the previous relationship to the person lost. There is less use of repression as an unconscious defensive operation. Conscious efforts at suppression, however, may continue to curb the sharp pangs of emotion associated with this phase. This conscious, suppressive, defensive avoidance paradoxically contributes to the intrusiveness of recollections at this time, because the conscious representations of ideas and feelings are a kind of breakthrough phenomenon.

During this phase one may become preoccupied with an aspect of identification with the deceased in which one views oneself as vulnerable to death. One may experience the physical symptoms of the disease that killed the other, or in fantasy reveries strike mental bargains with the gods to reduce fear and protect the self. One may feel guilty for worrying about dying when it is the other who is actually dead. This type of survivor guilt is just one of many motifs signaling development of new schemas of the self as alive and the deceased as dead.

Existing schemas still organize an expectation that the deceased will be alive and present in certain situations. Therefore, these situations feel particularly "empty." Cooking a meal, going out with friends, or going to the movies painfully emphasizes the absence of the habitual companion. Emotional reactions to such empty situations are heightened during this intrusive phase of bereavement, because the working schema of being alone still differs from the enduring schema of being together. This discrepancy between the role relationship models and the signal affects leads to renewed efforts to bring back the dead loved one, with an increase in pining and searching, use of magical offerings, and efforts to undo the incidents that led to the death.

Wishes for restoration of the deceased are long unsatisfied, obviously, and frustration mounts. In the face of death, the survivor mounts a last-ditch effort to fulfill his wish that the deceased be alive. Derivatives of desired role relationship models emerge in consciousness as the bereaved recalls the satisfaction of having the loved one present (Freud, 1900). These memories are dramatically different from the emptiness of the current situation, and this has sharp emotional consequences. For example, great joy during a dream of wish fulfillment is replaced by a great pang of sorrow upon awakening to the realization that the dream is not real. The same dream of being with the beloved deceased may be remembered with pleasure, not sorrow, in some later phase of mourning, when more grief work has been accomplished.

At the same time, ideation proceeds with lessened defensive inhibition. Unanswered questions during the outcry phase of initial realization, such as, "Who is to blame [for the death]?" and "Why did this [loss] happen to me?"

reemerge during the intrusive phase. These themes may be organized during this phase by usually dormant schemas, such as those wherein the self is viewed as bad and harmful to the other, or defective and abandoned by the other. Survivor guilt, guilt over anger with the deceased, shame over helplessness, and fear of future repetitive suffering may recur as intrusive preoccupations.

THE PHASE OF WORKING THROUGH

During the working-through phase, there are recurrences of avoidant and intrusive phenomena. These omissions and preoccupations oscillate, taking the edge off either extreme and helping to promote equilibrium. Periods of relaxation occur in which neither defensive numbness nor emotional flooding is prominent.

Intrusive memories of the deceased begin to change in form. Current concerns and relationships with living people blend with scenes involving the deceased. These blends occur prominently in dreams. Not infrequently in such dreams, the bereaved occupies the role of the deceased, and vice versa.

Between the initial unconscious view of the deceased as alive, yet lost to contact with the self, and the eventual, full, unconscious acceptance of the death, unconscious beliefs undergo many changes. These lead to varied conscious experiences during a working-through phase, as the following case example illustrates.

A young husband suffered the death of his wife in a scuba diving accident. Six months later, during his waking hours and in dreams, he had intrusive, intolerably sad and frightening images of her blue face when the body was recovered. These unbidden images gradually subsided in frequency during a brief psychodynamic psychotherapy.

Before his wife's death, he never experienced a sharp elevation in heart rate when he saw her or a woman who resembled her. After her death, during the earlier denial and intrusive phases of his grief experiences, he still did not have these sensations. The everyday situation of being with his wife, his earlier phase of grief after her death, and his later recognitions of his loss were very different contexts.

During the working-through period of the mourning process, however, he did develop this intrusive bodily sensation in a specific context. He worked as a trainer of personnel for a large corporation, and began a new class every two weeks. During this period, when he saw a woman in the class who resembled his wife, at first glance he would feel his pulse surge in his chest, wrists, and throat.

The everyday situation *before her death* was mainly one of calm belief in their continuing commitment to each other. The *intrusive phase of his grief* was characterized by visions of her as dead, primary-process beliefs in her continued life, and alarming pangs of sadness mixed with fear. The later phase of *working through* contained a growing recognition of loss, but still a pining for her return. With this phase near relative *completion*, the intrusion of physiologic arousal subsided.

During the phase in which he felt the sudden surges of pulse, he had no conscious ideas about the women who resembled his wife; his cardiac reaction felt instantaneous. Yet from our vantage point as observers, we may infer that there was some type of unconscious construction of meaning about the women that led to his excitation. He was hoping his wife had returned from death (primary process) while knowing that she was dead (secondary process). The primary process was rapid and unconscious, using ideas incorporated in a schema of finding and being reunited with his harmed, living wife. Fluctuation of that schema led to the emotional responses that would occur in such a reunion.

Changes in schemas occur most prominently in the working-through phase. Many repetitions of intrusive ideas and feelings will have occurred, and trains of thought will have been set in motion. These thoughts and the repetition of new situations and their working models will gradually build new, enduring role relationship models.

During the grief work, one reviews the relationship with the deceased in terms of all the varied self-concepts which have participated in working models of the attachment. This may include weak, dependent, childlike self-concepts in relation to the other as a parental figure, even when the real relationship was between peers. It may include strong, dominating, or rivalrous views of self and other. The good and bad, clean and dirty, selfish and caring, and loving and hating themes will all have their time on the stage of reminiscence and decision—I say "decision" because this review is not just a searching, inner magical, primary-process restoration of things now gone. As mentioned above, the process serves an evolutionary, survival-of-the-species function in that it prepares the person to make new commitments after a loss and to accept the self with a true view of the present situation. Before this adaptive end of mourning is reached, the schemas and memories of the relationship require review in order to decide what is now true, what is now fantasy, and to discriminate the present from the past.

Sometimes it is a relief when a frustrating, hated, significant other dies. Even so, *the more ambivalence and conflict found in the themes for review, the harder it will be to reach the conclusions that complete the mourning process* (Freud, 1920; Lindemann, 1944; Bowlby, 1980; Raphael, 1983). The reasons for this are these: the thinking process will be complex and contradictory, the negative emotional experience will be intense and threatening, and the avoidant defensive maneuvers will tend to disrupt thinking. Most especially, consciousness as a tool for decision-making will likely be obscured by repression, suppression, dissociation, denial, disavowal, isolation, and reaction formation.

Preexisting ambivalence will, all things being equal, intensify and lengthen, or delay and derail, a working-through process. These are two of the most common forms of pathological grief reactions. But all things are not equal, and a great deal depends on what may be termed either ego strength or the integrity and resilience of self-organization.

Preexisting neurotic character makes ambivalence and conflict more likely, and will also impair one's ability to use others for emotional support during the extended crises of mourning. Preexisting narcissistic and borderline character pathology will make more difficult the review and change of person schemas (Kernberg, 1967; Kohut, 1972; Horowitz, 1988). Reactive decompensation may result, as the absence of the bolstering functions of the deceased damages the bereaved's sense of self-organization. As a defense, mourning may be totally interrupted and the deceased replaced by imagined and distorted relationships with whomever or whatever is available for support.

Part of the task, at an unconscious level, is to decide in terms of schemas that the deceased is permanently, irrevocably dead. For example, with repetition of the current working model developed in the empty situations, a new, enduring role relationship model develops in which the self is related to the person in the past, but not in the present or future except through memories. Empty situations lose their threatening surprise; the person no longer dreads abandonment or losing contact; rather, the person is simply alone. Yearning remains but loses its component of alarm. The resulting state of mind may be *poignant sadness* rather than the more emotional *agitated sadness*.

The progressive changes in expected role relationship models during working through can be reversed by a process of regression. Anniversary dates may trigger this, as in the case of Engel, but then progression is easier, because developmental schemas for it have been forged by the working-through phase.

With the reduction in frequency of distraught states of mind during this phase, the person may attempt a new relationship of the sort that was lost. Another person is found to care for, relate to sexually, or serve as a companion. Commonly the new relationship is then colored by efforts to restore within it some aspects of the lost relationship. The discrepancy between the preexisting role relationship model with the deceased and the patterns occurring with the new person may lead to emotional responses like alarm. In effect, an illusion of restoration occurs until it is suddenly seen as an error. This illusion is a form of transference reaction.

The new companion may react to inappropriate transference-based expectations. This contributes to distress, confusion, and disruptions of poise. After spending time with the new person, and with the mourning process closer to completion, the bereaved is capable of separating the relationship with the new companion from the previous relationship with the deceased. A more committed and realistic attachment with the new person is now possible because a schema of the new person as different from the deceased has been established.

COMPLETION

Although listed as such in table 16.1, completion is not actually a phase so much as it is a milestone. It marks the relative end of mourning. It is "relative" because some mourning for a major loss persists throughout the lifetime, and may be reactivated by reminders such as anniversaries (Pollock, 1972, 1978). It is listed as a phase because it contains the sense of self-coherence and readiness for new relationships. In pathological grief this sense may never be achieved. There may be continuing impairment in work, creativity, or intimacy that can go on distorting the person's character for years. In contrast, in some states of completed mourning, the person feels an enhancement of competence, and a freeing from the work of grief as well as from its symptoms.

Some of that freedom is expressed by Mark Wolynn (1986) in his poem "Nothing but Snow." The title word "Nothing" is probably used to mean the absence of intrusive images and feelings. "Nothing" appears again at the end of the poem. The protagonist visits the graveyard where a loved one is buried. Various images are described, then the poem closes with the reference to "nothing," which may mean reaching completion of mourning:

> Tonight, I go into the graveyard,
> Where nothing is loose, not even God,
> And under a few stars I shout out,
> And wait, and shout again,
> My joy insurmountable, as nothing,
> Nothing at all, returns.

The surprise is the "joy insurmountable." One would expect sorrow that nothing returns. But there can be joy that the heavy burden of intrusive symptoms and the hard review of a relationship is over. Now the relationship lives on in the mind, a cherished memory that no longer brings haunting, external reminders of the loss.

SCHEMATIC CHANGE THROUGH PHASES OF GRIEF

The overall progression of schematic change discussed in the preceding text is outlined in figure 16.1.

The course of transference reactions in the psychoanalysis of an adult who suffered a traumatic bereavement during early adolescence reveals the readiness with which role relationship models can be tried out, one after the other, during the resumption of a mourning process interrupted for years by defensive inhibitions. Only when self-organization and relationship capacities develop may a warded-off mourning process be tolerable. This case followed shifting transference phenomena previously observed and reported by Wolfenstein (1966), Fleming and Altschul (1963), and Zients (1986).

The 27-year-old patient presented character problems involving phobic withdrawal from love and work, and avoidance of developing career-related skills. During the course of psychoanalysis, it gradually became apparent that he had never mourned his mother, who died when he was 13.

During the first two years of treatment he remained indifferent to the analyst's vacations or work-related trips. Weekends apart meant nothing. Then he threatened to leave analysis on a variety of pretexts, citing the analyst's inadequacy. With each challenge, he observed the analyst's reactions carefully. Because the analyst did not appear anxious and did not act firmly to urge him to stay in treatment, he decided—unconsciously, I believe—that the analyst could tolerate his own fear of losing the patient.

The patient identified with the analyst's ability to tolerate sadness and anxiety at impending separation and loss. For the first time, he began to feel the analyst's departure on vacations as painful. He mourned each weekend as a loss. Earlier childhood fears of abandonment surfaced in conscious memories. Missing the analyst, and being pleased at reunions, then awakened more positive memories of his mother. Only then, gradually, did he begin to grieve. He entered an intrusive phase, with sobbing, over vivid visual memories of his mother's funeral. He spent an extended period working through these reactions.

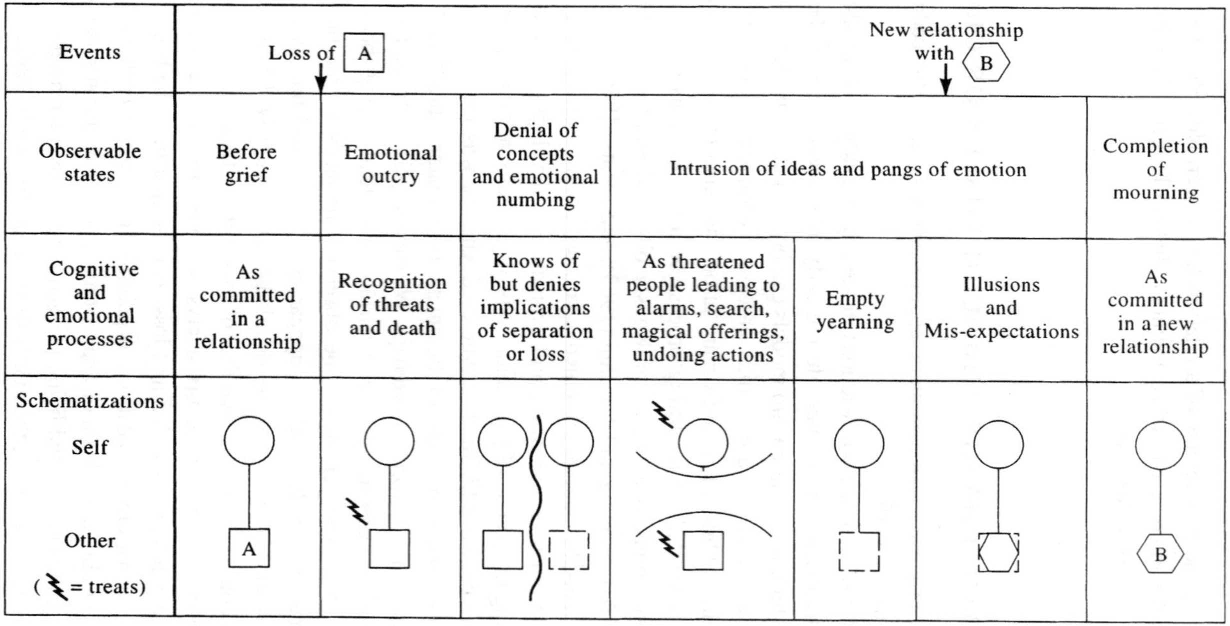

Events	Loss of A			New relationship with B			Completion of mourning
Observable states	Before grief	Emotional outcry	Denial of concepts and emotional numbing	Intrusion of ideas and pangs of emotion	Empty yearning	Illusions and Mis-expectations	As committed in a new relationship
Cognitive and emotional processes	As committed in a relationship	Recognition of threats and death	Knows of but denies implications of separation or loss	As threatened people leading to alarms, search, magical offerings, undoing actions			
Schematizations — Self, Other (~ = treats)							

Figure 16.1. Reprinted from *Introduction to Psychodynamics* (Horowitz, 1988).

CONCLUSION

The human species has evolved with a capacity for mourning that reaches its most complex expression in the adult. While replete with conscious experiences, the need to mourn and the organization of a sequence of mourning processes seem to be unconscious aspects of both impulses and defenses. During the outcry phase of mourning, alarming pangs of emotion may occur as the mind reacts to the serious mismatch between working models of the new situation and enduring schemas. The deceased may be modeled as harmed rather than dead. By the time of entry into a denial phase, the person has reconstituted the operation of unconscious defensive inhibitions. During this phase dissociations are prominent, with operative schemas of the deceased as both dead and alive.

With entry into an intrusive phase, both usual and warded-off role relationship models involving self and the deceased emerge, organizing not only conscious reviews, but unbidden ideas, hard-to-dispel images, and intrusive emotions.

In a working-through phase, the mourning person may more easily contemplate more themes. The new working models are repeated and so they begin to be established as enduring schemas. This work reduces alarm, emotion, and signal affects as it diminishes the discrepancy, or mismatch, between working models and enduring schemas. As the bereaved person slowly develops schemas that match the reality of permanent separation, the work of grief gradually enters the completion phase.

It takes a long time to reach such a point of relative completion; the work of schematic change is slow. While schemas enable people to perceive, plan, and act rapidly, the schemas themselves cannot be quickly altered. Like transference change and the developmental course of identification, the work of mourning cannot be rushed. Mourning is not heartbreak, it prevents the heart from being broken.

REFERENCES

Abraham, K. (1924). A short study of the development of the libido, viewed in the light of mental disorders. In Selected Papers. New York: Basic Books, 1953, pp. 418–501.

Agee, J. (1957). A Death in the Family. New York: McDowell, Obelin.

Arlow, J. A. (1969). Unconscious fantasy and disturbances of conscious experience. Psychoanalytic Q., 38:1–27.

Bartlett, R. C. (1932). Remembering: A Study in Experimental and Social Psychology. *Cambridge, Mass.: Cambridge Univ. Press.*

Bowlby, J. (1980). Attachment and Loss, Vol. III. Loss: Sadness and Depression. *New York: Basic Books.*

Bretherton, I. & Waters, E., Eds. (1985). Growing Points in Attachment Theory and Research: Monographs of the Society for Research in Child Development. *Chicago: Chicago Univ. Press.*

Breuer, J. & Freud, S. (1895). Studies on hysteria. S. E., 2.

Clayton, P. J. (1974). Mortality and morbidity in the first year of widowhood. Arch. Gen. Psychiat., *30:747–750.*

Deutsch, H. (1937). Absence of grief. Psychoanal. Q., *6:12–22.*

Dickinson, E. (1955). Poem #341. In The Poems of Emily Dickinson, *ed. T. H. Johnson. Cambridge, Mass.: Belknap/Harvard Univ. Press.*

Engel, G. L. (1975). The death of a twin: mourning and anniversary reactions. Int. J. Psychoanal., *56:23–40.*

Fleming, D. & Altschul., S. (1963). Activation of mourning and growth by psychoanalysis. Int. J. Psychoanal., *44:419–431.*

Freud, S. (1900). The interpretation of dreams. S. E., 4 & 5.

——— *(1912). The psychodynamics of transference.* S. E., 12.

——— *(1915). The unconscious.* S. E., 14.

——— *(1917). Mourning and melancholia.* S. E., 14.

——— *(1920). Beyond the pleasure principle.* S. E., 18.

Glick, I. O., Weiss, R. S. & Parkes, C. M. (1974). The First Year of Bereavement. *New York: Wiley.*

Horowitz, M. J. (1986). Stress Response Syndromes *(2nd ed.). Northvale, N. J.: Aronson.*

——— *(1987).* States of Mind *(2nd ed.). New York: Plenum.*

——— *(1988).* Introduction to Psychodynamics: A New Synthesis. *New York: Basic Books.*

——— *& Becker, S. S. (1971). The compulsion to repeat trauma: experimental study of intrusive thinking after stress.* J. Nerv. Ment. Dis., *153(1):32–40.*

——— *Wilner, N., Marmar, C. & Krupnick, J. (1980) Pathological grief and the activation of latent self images.* Amer. J. Psychiat., *137:1157–1162.*

Jacobson, E. (1964). The Self in the Object World. *New York: Int. Univ. Press.*

Kernberg, O. F. (1967). Borderline personality organization. J. Amer. Psychoanal. Assn., *15:41–68.*

Kohut, H. (1972). Thoughts on narcissism and narcissistic rage. Psychoanal. Study Child, *27:360–400.*

Lindemann, E. (1944). Symptomatology and management of acute grief. Amer. J. Psychiat., *101:141–148.*

Moffatt, M. J., Ed. (1982). In the Midst of Winter: Selections from the Literature of Mourning. *New York: Vintage Press.*

Osterweiss, M., Solomon, F. & Green, M. (1984). Bereavement: Reactions, Consequences, and Care. *Washington, D.C.: Natl. Acad. Sci. Press.*

Parkes, C. M. (1964). Recent bereavement as a cause of mental illness. Brit. J. Psychiat., *110:198–204.*

────── (1972). Bereavement. *New York: Int. Univ. Press.*

────── & Weiss, R. S. (1983). Recovery from Bereavement. *New York: Basic Books.*

Piaget, J. (1937). The Construction of Reality in the Child. *New York: Basic Books, 1954.*

Pollock, G. (1972). *The mourning-liberation process and creativity: the case of Kathe Kollwitz.* Annual Psychoanal., *10:333–354.*

────── (1978). *Process and affect: mourning and grief.* Int. J. Psychoanal., *59:255–276.*

Raphael, B. (1983). The Anatomy of Bereavement. *New York: Basic Books.*

Rexroth, K., Ed. (1970). Love and the Turning Year. *San Francisco: New Directions.*

Singer, J. & Salovey, P. (1991). *Organized knowledge structures and personality: person schemas, self-schemas, prototypes and scripts. In* Person Schemas and Maladaptive Interpersonal Behavior Patterns, *ed. M. J. Horowitz. Chicago: Chicago Univ. Press.*

Slap, J. W. & Saykin, A. J. (1983). *The schema: basic concept in a nonmetapsychological model of the mind.* Psychoanal. Contemp. Thought, *6:305–325.*

Sutherland, J. D. (1980). *The British object relation theorists: Balint, Winnicott, Fairbairn, Guntrip.* J. Amer. Psychoanal. Assn., *28:829–860.*

Windholz, M., Marmar, C. & Horowitz, M. (1985). *Review of research on conjugal bereavement.* Comprehen. Psychia., *26:433–447.*

Wolfenstein, M. (1966). *How is mourning possible?* Psychoanal. Study Child, *21:93–123.*

Wolynn, M. (1986). *Nothing but snow.* The New Yorker. *January, 1986.*

Zients, A. B. (1986). *Identification and its vicissitudes as viewed in adolescence: object loss and identification.* Int. J. Psychoanal., *67:77–85.*

17. Neurobiological Aspects of PTSD
Review of Clinical and Preclinical Studies

John H. Krystal, Thomas R. Kosten, Steven Southwick, John W. Mason, Bruce D. Perry, and Earl L. Giller

CLINICIANS DURING World War I suggested that posttraumatic disorders were caused by conditioned sympathetic activation, perhaps indicative of changes in brain function (Bury, 1918; Campbell, 1918). Consistent with this hypothesis, an early experimental study reported that veterans with "the irritable heart of soldiers" and "shell shock" exhibited greater increases in heart rate and respiratory rate than did healthy subjects when exposed in a laboratory to gunfire or sulfuric flame (Meakins & Wilson, 1918). Also, similar groups of patients responded to intravenous epinephrine administration with exaggerated arousal responses including severe anxiety, heart rate, and blood pressure increases (Fraser & Wilson, 1918; Peabody et al., 1918). In addition, Drury (1918) found that anxious war veterans with "irritable heart" were more sensitive to the effects of carbon dioxide inhalation which activates the sympathetic nervous system. During World War II, Crile (1940) bilaterally denervated the adrenal glands of war veterans with "neurocirculatory asthenia" in order to decrease sympathetic nervous activation. He reported clinical improvement in 107 of 152 cases in response to this extreme treatment approach.

Despite promising physiologic findings, biological theories were abandoned in favor of psychodynamic and behavioral approaches, perhaps due to the failure of biologists to demonstrate brain "lesions" in traumatized patients and the concomitant psychodynamic advances (Rado, 1942). Rado (1942) described the social costs which resulted from the withering of biological approaches to trauma:

Reprinted by permission from *Behavior Therapy*, 20, 177–198. Copyright © 1989 by the Association for the Advancement of Behavior Therapy.

"The cost of this progress was a misuse of (psychodynamic) terms by writers . . . who took such phrases as 'unconscious motivation' to refer to deliberate intent on the part of the patient, rather than to automatic biological reactions not subject to his control. This interpretation lent support to the frequently heard charge of malingering, leading to futile disciplinary measures and needless cruelty." (p. 362)

The abandonment of neurobehavioral studies of PTSD had additional costs. Physiological investigations begun during World War I were not pursued until psychophysiological PTSD studies began again in the 1960s. In addition, placebo-controlled clinical trials of pharmacologic treatments in PTSD have significantly lagged behind other diagnoses such as depression, panic disorder, and schizophrenia. In the 1980s however, clinical neuroscientific approaches to PTSD are reemerging in psychiatry (reviewed in van der Kolk et al., 1985; Kosten & Krystal, 1988). Paralleling these advances, the first double-blind placebo-controlled trials of pharmacotherapies for PTSD are currently being reported (Frank et al., 1988).

In evaluating neurobiologic advances relevant to PTSD, this review will proceed at two levels, clinical and preclinical. Clinical sections will consider recent psychophysiological, neuroendocrine, and psychopharmacologic findings in patients with PTSD. Preclinical sections will focus on the contributions of the central noradrenergic system to PTSD-like behavioral syndromes. The long-term course of PTSD symptoms will also be reviewed in the context of cellular models for short-and long-term changes in neuronal plasticity. Lastly, inescapable or uncontrollable stress will be reviewed as an integrative animal model for PTSD.

PSYCHOPHYSIOLOGICAL STUDIES OF PTSD

Psychophysiological studies conducted in populations formally diagnosed as PTSD validated the findings of the World War I studies. A number of studies (Blanchard et al., 1982; Pitman et al., 1987), but not all (Dobbs & Wilson, 1960), reported baseline autonomic activation in PTSD patients characterized by increased heart rate, systolic blood pressure or forehead EMG. Although Malloy and his associates (1983) did not observe this increased heart rate, they did note larger heart rate increases in PTSD patients than controls in response to neutral stimuli. PTSD patients also exhibited a more marked conditioned autonomic hyperactivity in the laboratory as evidenced by increased heart rate, respiratory rate, galvanic skin response, and EMG (Dobbs & Wilson, 1960; Blanchard et al., 1982; 1986; Pitman et al., 1987). Many of these studies also documented conditioned anxiety, agitation, and panic states in association with the physiologic measures. Also, Brende (1982) reported data on six patients suggesting that hypnotically induced war imagery produced predominately right-handed or left-handed electrodermal responses, thought to be indicative of lateralized cortical activation, in patients with prominent numbing or intrusive symptoms, respectively.

Peripheral Catecholamines: Evidence of Sympathetic and Central Noradrenergic Dysregulation in PTSD

Abnormally high levels of catecholamines and their metabolites have been found in the plasma and urine of people undergoing severe stress and in PTSD patients providing evidence of dysregulation of central and/or peripheral noradrenergic systems (Svensson, 1987). One study of severe stress exposure found that landing an airplane on an aircraft carrier produced increased plasma levels of the norepinephrine metabolite, 3-methoxy, 4-hydroxyphenethylene glycol (MHPG) (Rubin et al., 1970). In nine PTSD inpatients, levels of epinephrine and norepinephrine in urine samples collected over 24 hours were significantly higher than affective disorder patients or schizophrenics (Kosten et al., 1987). During hospitalization, the elevated catecholamine levels were sustained, actually increasing slightly, despite reduction of their symptoms. This contrasted with other diagnostic groups where catecholamine levels decreased during the hospital stay. Physical exertion and other potentially confounding variables did not account for the differences between PTSD and the other groups.

Lactate administration, which elicits panic attacks in panic patients, elicited PTSD-like flashbacks (7/7) and panic attacks (6/7) in 7 patients with PTSD, 6 of whom also met panic disorder criteria (Rainey et al., 1987). Since PTSD patients with panic disorder represent only a subgroup of all PTSD patients, further study in PTSD patients without panic disorder will be needed to evaluate the generalized applicability of these findings. However, central noradrenergic dysregulation has been implicated in lactate-induced panic and the findings of Rainey and his colleagues (1987) highlight possible common biological underpinnings for the observed clinical similarity of flashbacks and panic attacks in many PTSD patients (Mellman & Davis, 1985).

The assessment of peripheral adrenergic receptors on platelets and lymphocytes provides the first direct evidence of altered receptor function in PTSD. Perry and associates (1987a; 1987b) have demonstrated a 40% decrease in the numbers of platelet α_2 adrenergic receptors in 25 patients with PTSD. This reduction is associated with a relative loss of high-affinity α_2 receptor binding sites which, unlike low-affinity sites, are coupled to adenylate cyclase-linked second messenger systems (Delean et al., 1981; Perry et al., 1987a). In addition, this group has reported that following *in vitro* agonist exposure, α_2 receptors in intact platelets are down regulated four times faster in PTSD patients than controls (Perry et al., 1987b). The down regulation of platelet α_2 receptors may represent an adaptive response to excessive receptor stimulation produced by chronically elevated plasma catecholamines (consistent with Kosten et al., 1987). The authors speculate that the platelet studies may model α_2 receptor down regulation which may be occurring in the brain of PTSD patients in response to excessive central noradrenergic activation. Also, the relative loss of high-affinity platelet α_2 receptors suggests that noradrenergic receptor coupling to second messenger systems may also be reduced in PTSD patients. Consistent with the α_2 receptor findings, Lerer and his associates (1987b) also recently reported evidence of desensitization of adenylate cyclase-coupled adrenergic receptors on lymphocytes and platelets of individuals with PTSD.

Alterations in catecholamine function in PTSD also may be reflected in altered levels of the synthetic or digestive enzymes for these neurotransmitters. Davidson and his associates (1985a) found that veterans with PTSD exhibited lower platelet levels of the catecholamine metabolizing enzyme, monoamine oxidase (MAO). Low platelet MAO levels have been described in bipolar depression and alcoholism, but anxiety disorders have been associated with high MAO levels (Davidson et al., 1980; Gudeman et al., 1982). Thirteen of the 23 PTSD subjects in Davidson's study also carried the diagnosis of major depression, but their platelet MAO levels did not differ from the remaining 10 patients. However, the 10 patients with PTSD and alcoholism had lower MAO levels than subjects with PTSD but without alcoholism (3.8 vs. 6.6 nmol/hr mg.).

MAO activity is largely genetically determined and environmental factors may contribute only 12%–33% to inter-individual differences in platelet MAO activity (Nies et al., 1973; Reveley et al., 1983). These findings raise the possibility that low MAO activity levels may be associated with vulnerability to a spectrum of psychiatric disorders (Buchsbaum et al., 1976). The overlap of PTSD and alcoholism in this genetically influenced trait is interesting in light of the high incidence of alcoholism and substance abuse reported in the families of PTSD patients by this group (Davidson et al., 1985b). Another genetic link between stress response and alcohol consumption could be mediated by the last enzyme in the epinephrine synthetic pathways, phenylethanolamine N-methyltransferase (PNMT). Pharmacologic blockade of PNMT activity in rat brain diminishes the rewarding properties of alcohol (reviewed in Linnoila et al., 1987), while inherited differences in PNMT activity are associated with altered α_2 receptor levels which may alter stress response (Stolk et al., 1985). Future studies in other patient populations will be helpful in determining environmental and genetic contributions to the PTSD-alcoholism association.

THE HYPOTHALAMO-PITUITARY-ADRENAL (HPA) AXIS IN PTSD

Severe stress is associated with cortisol release through activation of the HPA axis (Selye, 1936; Mason, 1968). In the hypothalamus, several neurotransmitter systems cause the release of corticotropin-releasing factor (CRF) in response to stress. CRF induces pituitary secretion of adrenocorticotropic hormone (ACTH) which in turn causes the release of cortisol from the adrenal gland. Each end organ product in the HPA axis, i.e., ACTH or cortisol, inhibits the release of the preceding releasing factors, i.e., CRF or ACTH, making this system self-regulating (reviewed in Mason, 1968; McEwen, 1987).

Since PTSD is associated with chronic states of alarm, arousal, and depression, one might expect to find HPA activation in this disorder. Threat of combat, for example, has been reported to increase plasma glucocorticoid levels in officers and decrease levels in enlisted men in a small sample. (Bourne et al., 1968). Also, subgroups of depressed patients fail to suppress their cortisol in response to dexamethasone or show blunted ACTH responses to CRF (Carroll et al., 1981; Amsterdam et al., 1987). However, in a preliminary study, Mason and his associates (1986) found low 24-hour urinary cortisol levels in Vietnam veterans with PTSD. In a separate set of studies, PTSD patients exhibited blunted ACTH responses to CRF similar to depressed patients, but PTSD patients showed a decrease in cortisol, which did not reach statistical significance compared to controls. Basal cortisol levels were elevated in patients with major depression or patients with very high PTSD scores in this study (Smith et al., 1989). Also, 6 (21%) of 28 PTSD patients did not normally suppress their cortisol secretion in response to dexamethasone, but only 2 (7%) of their patients without co-existing major depression exhibited this abnormality (Kudler et al., 1987).

The precise nature of central noradrenergic, sympathetic, and HPA systems in PTSD patients remains unclear but studies in rodents suggest that their interaction may be significant. CRF infusion increases the activity of the noradrenergic locus coeruleus in the rat (Valentino et al., 1983). Also, gluco-corticoid receptors have been localized to several noradrenergic innervated brain regions including the locus coeruleus (Harfstrand et al., 1986). Adrena-lectomy appears to activate central noradrenergic systems as reflected in-creased baseline and stress-induced hypothalamic norepinephrine turnover (reviewed in McEwen, 1987). Glucocorticoids selectively affect norepineph-rine synthesis in a variety of brain regions and generally decrease α, receptor coupling to second messenger systems (reviewed in McEwen, 1987). In the periphery, adrenalectomy produces low plasma cortisol and elevated baseline and stress-induced levels of plasma norepinephrine, a pattern similar to that observed in PTSD patients (Brown & Fisher, 1986). Dexamethasone admin-istration reduces both the central and peripheral consequences of adrenalec-tomy (Brown & Fisher, 1986; McEwen, 1987).

Clinical Psychopharmacology and PTSD

A broad spectrum of agents have been introduced as possible pharmacologic treatments for PTSD during the past 20 years. With the exception of the antidepressants, the therapeutic efficacy of these medications has not been assessed with placebo-controlled studies. These medications have diverse mechanisms of action and preliminary experience suggests that some medi-cations either have limited efficacy or efficacy that is focused to subsets of PTSD symptoms. This section will briefly speculate on pathophysiologic mechanisms for PTSD based on known mechanisms of action of putative pharmacologic treatments for PTSD.

Several medications that decrease the magnitude of central noradrenergic activation or its postynaptic consequences have been reported to decrease arousal-related PTSD symptoms. Clonidine, which binds to inhibitory α, noradrenergic receptors, and alprazolam, which acts at inhibitor benzodiaze-pine receptors, decrease central noradrenergic activation or the behavioral consequences of noradrenergic activation (Charney et al., 1986) and have been reported to relieve hyperarousal symptoms in PTSD patients in open uncontrolled studies (Kolb et al., 1984; Dunner et al., 1985). Propranolol, which blocks beta-adrenergic receptors but not alpha-adrenergic receptors postsynaptic to central and peripheral noradrenergic neurons, has been re-ported to have a similar but perhaps lower efficacy for treating arousal symp-toms (Kolb et al., 1984).

Antidepressants also show a broad spectrum of efficacy in posttraumatic disorders (Birkhimer et al., 1985; Bleich et al., 1986). One series of 12 cases suggested that antidepressants were most effective in treating nightmares, depression, sleep disorders and startle reactions but were less able to relieve pathological avoidance of reminders of the trauma, shame, and the loss of warm feelings for others (Boehnlein et al., 1985). Some of these reports suggest that monoamine oxidase inhibitors (MAOI) may be more efficacious than tricyclic antidepressants, particularly in tricyclic-resistant patients (Hogben & Cornfield, 1981; Shen & Park, 1983; Milanes et al., 1984). One recent open study, however, found that MAOIs produced only modest gains in 25 Israeli combat veterans with PTSD (Lerer et al., 1987a). To date, the only controlled treatment study in PTSD supports the efficacy of both tricyclics and MAOIs (Frank et al., 1988; and unpublished data). There was a trend in this study for patients treated with MAOIs to show greater clinical improvement on anxiety ratings and on intrusion items from the Impact of Events scale.

Antidepressants have a variety of effects on central noradrenergic functioning including inhibition of central noradrenergic activity, down regulation of α, and beta-receptors, and increasing the amount of neurotransmitter released per neuronal activation (Charney et al., 1981). These changes effect both the magnitude of noradrenergic response to aversive environmental stimuli and the homeostatic regulation of monoamine systems. Such changes may be essential for enabling traumatized individuals, who exhibit biochemical evidence of loss of normal noradrenergic modulation, to return to normal levels of noradrenergic function. Antidepressants also have significant effects on serotonin and dopamine systems which are beyond the scope of this review.

Other putative treatments for PTSD, including lithium, carbamazepine, and neuroleptics implicate a diversity of neurotransmitter systems and treatment mechanisms for PTSD. Lithium and carbamazepine appear useful in controlling impulsive outbursts, decreasing intrusive symptoms, and improving sleep and mood disturbances observed in PTSD (Lipper et al., 1986; van der Kolk, 1987). The mechanism by which these medications produce therapeutic change in PTSD are unclear at this point. The capacity of carbemazepine for reversing certain types of neuronal sensitization will be discussed as a possible mechanism of action later in this review. Recent evidence suggests that neuroleptics may be less effective than antidepressants for alleviating many PTSD symptoms (Bleich et al., 1986). Neuroleptics block the effects of dopamine released from stress-activated meso-frontal dopamine systems (Deutch et al., 1985). They are generally most effective in decreasing psychotic symptoms and impulsive behavior observed in some individuals with

PTSD. They are not recommended for treating non-psychotic depression or anxiety in PTSD patients.

An additional reason for the diversity of pharmacologic treatments for PTSD is that patients with a number of psychiatric disorders acquire PTSD as a comorbid condition. PTSD comorbidity with panic (Rainey et al., 1987), depression (Kudler et al., 1987), and alcoholism (Davidson et al., 1985a) influence the neurobiologic findings of PTSD studies and clinical experience suggests that comorbid diagnoses influence treatment response. Treatments, such as the neuroleptics, might be ineffective in treating many PTSD symptoms but have therapeutic value through reducing psychosis arising from a comorbid condition, such as schizophrenia. However, even in "pure" PTSD, a number of neurotransmitter systems are likely to be involved and there may be variability in relative contributions of these systems between individuals. Even considering this diversity, though, many current treatments for PTSD are linked by their capacity to decrease the magnitude of noradrenergic tone, further implicating this system in PTSD pathophysiology.

PRECLINICAL STUDIES

The clinical studies highlighted in this review indicate the presence of long-lasting posttraumatic dysregulation of noradrenergic and HPA systems. The psychophysiological studies also provide evidence of learned alarm responses that become inappropriately displayed in "safe" environments. The learned responses and intrusive recollections in PTSD also indicate disturbances in memory regulation. In the following sections, we will present animal models for the dysregulation of alarm, the acquisition of avoidance, and the disturbance in memory function associated with PTSD. To begin with, we will build on the clinical studies implicating central noradrenergic dysregulation in PTSD. We will also review evidence that central noradrenergic disturbance could result in maladaptive states of alarm and cognitive disturbance. In contrast, the fear-enhanced startle model will provide cellular and pharmacologic insights into associative learning processes underlying a major PTSD symptom. However, the presence of baseline autonomic disturbances in PTSD suggests that the nervous dysregulation is not entirely associative. Non-associative and associative learning processes responsible for transient and long-term changes in alarm responses will be distinguished at both the behavioral and neuronal levels utilizing a review of avoidance learning in the snail, Aplysia. The response to inescapable, severe, or repeated stress, often called the "learned helplessness" model, will also be reviewed as an integrative model that highlights overlap and complementarity in the dysregulation and learning models for trauma.

Central Noradrenergic Systems and States of Alarm: A Dysregulation Model

Hypothetically, one might look for "trauma centers" that discriminate environmental danger, mediate the development of traumatic levels of arousal, and influence the appearance of alarm behaviors. Conditioned activation of these brain regions could underlie the alarm-like symptoms of PTSD. Because such brain nuclei presumably exist within well-characterized neurotransmitter systems, drugs that inhibit activation of these trauma centers would be predicted to have therapeutic value in PTSD.

The locus coeruleus (LC), the primary neuronal center for the ascending dorsal noradrenergic system in the brain, meets the criteria for a brain trauma center. The IC is located in the pons and innervates areas implicated in significance discrimination, fear, and memory formation in the limbic system and cerebral cortex (reviewed in Redmond, 1979; Sara, 1985). Threatening situations and stimuli associated with threat (conditioned stimuli) elicit LC activation that has been documented by electrical recordings from LC neurons in awake monkeys (Grant & Redmond, 1983), cats (Rasmussen & Jacobs, 1986), and rats (Weiss et al., 1987).

Central noradrenergic activation also elicits fear behaviors similar to the alarm-like symptoms of PTSD. In primates, direct LC stimulation, pharmacologic activation of the LC using yohimbine or piperoxane, and the noradrenergic hyperactivity associated with opiate withdrawal are associated with the display of fear or alarm behaviors (see Redmond, 1979; Redmond & Krystal, 1984). These alarm behaviors are similar to those observed when monkeys are confronted by predatory dogs (Leahy et al., 1980). After bilateral LC lesions, monkeys fail to display appropriate fear responses and may attack dominant monkeys and humans (reviewed in Redmond, 1979). LC lesion in rats also prevents stress-induced increases in brain MHPG, a biochemical index of norepinephrine release and turnover (Korf, 1976).

Consistent with predictions that inhibition of putative "trauma centers" would relieve PTSD symptoms, drugs which inhibit central noradrenergic systems decrease the acute biochemical response to stress, as well as the appearance of alarm-like PTSD symptoms. Clonidine, propranolol, antidepressants and benzodiazepines are examples of drugs with these properties (reviewed in Redmond, 1979; Kosten & Krystal, 1988). Antidepressants are more complicated in their action. However, their effects on noradrenergic systems may mediate aspects of their clinical efficacy in PTSD. Substances frequently abused by individuals with PTSD, including ethanol, benzodiaze-pines, barbiturates and opiates, also share the ability to inhibit noradrenergic activity and the anxiety-related symptoms of PTSD (reviewed in Redmond & Krystal, 1984; Kosten & Krystal, 1988).

The concept of trauma centers highlights the link between neurobiology, behavior, and pharmacotherapy. The LC, however, had many roles. Noradre-nergic systems have been implicated in "signal-to-noise" environmental dis-criminations which facilitate associative learning outside of traumatic settings (Woodward et al., 1979). Other groups also suggest that the LC regulates the attentional balance between interoceptive (internal) and exteroceptive (envi-ronmental) cues (Foote et al., 1980; Iverson, 1984). In this model, increasing levels of LC activity focus attention on external stimuli. These information-processing models also suggest that the LC primes the organism to detect danger and make appropriate defensive responses. Consistent with these roles, LC lesions or stress-induced noradrenergic depletion impair a wide spectrum of adaptive learning and defensive responses (Weiss et al., 1987; Minor et al., 1988; reviewed in Sara, 1985; McEwen, 1987).

Neurobiological Models for Learned Traumatic Responses in PTSD

Conditional Enhancement of the Startle Response and PTSD

Generalized dysregulation of brain alarm systems can account for only a component of PTSD symptoms. These patients also generally suffer from specific learned responses to specific environmental stimuli suggesting that associative learning plays an important role in the genesis of PTSD sympto-matology. Davis and his colleagues have demonstrated that a core PTSD symptom, fear-enhanced startle, may be reduced to an associative learning process arising from the convergence of simple sensory-motor pathways mediating basement startle and fear enhancement (reviewed in Davis, 1980, 1986). The central nucleus of the amygdala, a putative fear center, plays an important integrative role between the baseline and fear-enhanced startle pathways. In the fear-enhanced acoustic startle paradigm, a light previously paired with an electric shock produces an enhancement of the startle response elicited by a loud noise. Consistent with the clinical observations by Krystal

(1978) suggesting that extreme environmental stress produced alarm responses, as well as cognitive and behavioral "shutting down," behavioral freezing and increased startle are highly correlated in the fear-enhanced startle paradigm (Leaton & Borszcz, 1985).

Fear-enhanced startle is affected by manipulations of several neurotransmitter systems including the dopamine, norepinephrine, and endorphin systems (Davis, 1980). Clonidine, neuroleptics, alcohol, and opiates decrease the magnitude of the startle response. The ethanol abstinence syndrome and, to a lesser extent, the administration of the opiate antagonist, naloxone, enhance startle magnitude (Gibbins et al., 1971; Davis, 1980). While most drugs used therapeutically or illicitly by individuals with PTSD inhibit the startle enhancement, tricyclics fail to do so (Cassella & Davis, 1985). It is possible that the lack of tricyclic effects in this paradigm may underline reported clinical limitations of these drugs in treating PTSD (Hogben & Cornfield, 1981; Birkhimer et al., 1985).

Associative and Non-Associative Mechanism for Learned Traumatic Responses Lessons from Aplysia

Kandel (1983) contrasted associative and non-associative mechanisms for learned responses to aversive stimuli developed in the snail, Aplysia specific, cue-dependent enhancement of alarm and avoidance. In the Aplysia model, a neutral shrimp extract cue paired with shock enhances a gill withdrawal escape response. This associative learning depends on the transduction of temporally paired environment stimuli into paired neurochemical messages impacting on a common sensory-motor pathway. In the snail, serotonin application to the neurons in the gill withdrawal pathway simulates defensive arousal and produces "learned" alarm enhancement in the absence of an actual environmental cue (reviewed in Kandel, 1983).

Non-associative, cue independent, learned responses arise from repeated unpaired adversive stimulus presentation (Kandel, 1983). Unlike associative learning, which requires the convergence of at least two neuronal inputs, sensitization may be modeled monosynaptically. Walters (1987) has also demonstrated that non-associative learning may be behaviorally generalized, producing enhanced escape locomotion, release of ink, as well as gill withdrawal. However, consistent with the human psychophysiologic studies in PTSD, generalized responses are typically of a smaller magnitude in the Aplysia than cue-dependent associative processes (Walters & Byrne, 1985).

Thus at least two fundamental learning processes—associative and non-associative—must be considered in PTSD. Cue-dependent enhancement, such as panic attacks precipitated by helicopter noise, are evidence of associative conditioning. In contrast, neuronal kindling produced by repeated exposure to gunfire might produce non-associative learned responses. It is likely that associative and non-associative processes interact. Walters (1987) showed that both associative and non-associative learning take place concurrently in snails exposed to severe aversive stimulation, such as a simulated predator attack.

Molecular Substrates of Neural and Behavioral Plasticity: Models for Traumatic Alterations in Neural Activity and Memory

There are at least three significant paradoxes in the course of PTSD which highlight the importance of understanding the nature of long-lasting forms of memory and learned responses: (1) the actual trauma may be brief but may produce long-lasting, if not lifelong, disturbances; (2) in the initial posttraumatic period, recall of the trauma may be impaired although images and sensations associated with the trauma may be intrusively reexperienced in great detail decades after the trauma; (3) patients experiencing intrusive thoughts or exaggerated alarm responses may transiently improve in response to treatment analogous to phobic patients in whom desensitization sometimes appears to fade with time (Jacobs & Nadel, 1985). These paradoxes suggest that posttraumatic neuroendocrine responses, alarm responses and memories are the product of long-term forms of learning which contrast with the easily forgotten events of daily life associated with moderate or controllable levels of arousal. Presuming this situation to be the case, understanding the molecular mechanisms underlying long-lasting learned responses and memory formation could help to distinguish subtypes of PTSD (long-lasting versus transient), the spectrum of symptoms to be expected in acute versus chronic PTSD, and the degree of plasticity of particular PTSD symptoms or their capacity to respond to specific behavioral and pharmacologic interventions.

Although similar intracellular processes underlie generalized sensitization and operant learning, distinct intracellular mechanisms mediate the transient and long-term shock-induced changes. In Aplysia, short-term sensitization or habituation generally fades within one hour. Severe or repeated aversive stimulus exposure, however, produces enhanced reactivity which is still present one week later (reviewed in Goelet & Kandel, 1986). Transient avoidance learning in Aplysia operates through a spectrum of intracellular processes which up or down regulate the reactivity of a simple sensorimotor response system. These intracellular processes are organized in "second messenger" systems responsible for translating the chemical message carried by neuro-transmitters into changes in cellular response. The chemical messenger systems have not been completely delineated, but include many well-established cellular second messenger systems, such as an adenylate cyclase-cAMP-protein kinase system, a phosphoinositol-diacylglycerol-C kinase system, and a calcium-calmodulin-protein kinase system. The second messenger systems produce changes in membrane potential and cell metabolism by influencing the intercellular levels of potassium, calcium, and other ions through changes in protein phosphorylation (Castelluci et al., 1982; Goelet & Kandel, 1986).

Protein phosphorylation also appears to modulate neuronal reactivity in other systems by influencing the number of neurotransmitter receptors on the cell surface, the affinity of these receptors for neurotransmitters or drugs, and the coupling of neurotransmitter receptors to second messenger systems (Sibley et al., 1986; reviewed in Nestler & Greengard, 1984). Many of these phosphorylated regulatory proteins are quickly broken down, consistent with their role in transient forms of learning. Blockade of protein phosphorylation also prevents the biophysical changes associated with short-term learning (Castelluci et al., 1982). These studies suggest that organisms respond immediately to traumatic stressors with alterations in neuronal activity and neurotransmitter release which are translated into short-term cellular adaptations, learned responses, and short-term memory by a number of presynaptic and postsynaptic processes, such as transmembrane ion conductance and protein phosphorylation.

In addition to the mechanisms implicated in transient learned responses, long-term learned responses depend on the appearance of specific gene products which maintain the learned response or memory trace. The primary evidence for this view is that long-term, but not short-term, avoidance learning may be interrupted by the administration of drugs which inhibit transcription, the formation of RNA from DNA, and translation, the formation of proteins from RNA (reviewed in Davis & Squire, 1984: Goelet & Kandel, 1986). However, once the necessary gene products are produced, drugs which block transcription and translation are ineffective in reversing the response enhancement.

Recent findings introduce the possibility that microstructural changes play a role in long-lasting traumatic enhancement of alarm, avoidance and memory. Chen & Bailey (see Kandel, 1983; Goelet & Kandel, 1986) documented micro-structural neuronal changes in the sensory pathways which appear to mediate long-term enhancement of alarm responses in Aplysia: sensitized neurons approximately doubled the number of presynaptic varicosities and increased the number of active zones which could release neurotransmitters, the surface area of the active zones, and the amount of neurotransmitter vessicles released per site. Habituated neurons showed the opposite pattern of structural change.

The relevance of the Aplysia studies for human learning and traumatization derives from the similarity of invertebrate and mammalian cellular modes for producing stable alterations in neural and behavioral plasticity within the systems mediating alarm and memory. For example, a process similar to stable heterosynaptic facilitation takes place in the rat hippocampus, a region which plays a central role in the consolidation of long-term memory (Skelton et al., 1987). Paired activation of septal and entorhinal inputs produces long-term potentiation (LTP) of hippocampal neurons. This process seems to be necessary for long-term memory formation (Robinson & Racine, 1986; Larson & Lynch, 1986).

Similar to the Aplysia studies, the consolidation of long-term learned responses, perhaps through LTP, appears to require the production of specific gene products (reviewed in Davis & Squire, 1984). LTP also parallels long-term avoidance learning in Aplysia in involving phosphoprotein messenger systems and calcium-mediated processes in modifications of hippocampal neuronal structure (reviewed in Fifkova, 1985) and function (Lovinger et al., 1986). Intracellular levels of neuronal phosphoproteins, such as those in the cycle AMP second messenger system, vary in accordance with neuronal activity and may directly mediate alterations in gene expression (Comb et. al., 1987), perhaps influencing stress response (Lightman & Young, 1987).

Noradrenergic systems and the HPA, implicated by clinical studies of PTSD, appear to interact in LTP. Central noradrenergic depletion, associated with severe inescapable stresses, impairs LTP and produces learning deficits (reviewed in McEwen, 1987). Glucocorticoids antagonize the learning deficits associated with both noradrenergic depletion and drugs which interfere with gene expression at the level of protein synthesis (reviewed in McEwen et al., 1986; McEwen, 1987). It is conceivable that high glucocorticoid levels induced by stress protect adaptive learning acutely but that the low cortisol levels associated with chronic PTSD may contribute to adaptation impairments.

These recent animal findings suggest that PTSD could be associated with fundamental and long-lasting neuronal modifications including alterations in structure and gene expression. Situations which produce only transient forms of learning are unlikely to induce long-lasting neuronal adaptation and, thus are probably not eliciting the complete picture of traumatic response. This hypothesis suggests that many PTSD symptoms may have the indelible quality of long-term memory and that some treatments may, for example, cover long-lasting sensitization of alarm systems with transient habituation leading to the reemergence of symptoms when the short-term habituation fades. Thus it is quite likely that long-term or periodic treatments might be necessary to maintain clinical improvement in some PTSD patients.

PTSD as Inescapable Stress Responses: Toward Integrating Biological Approaches to PTSD

Stress Response and Mechanisms for Learning. Inescapable stress (IS) response, the "learned helplessness" model, has already been introduced as a powerful model for studying the interaction of biology and behavior in traumatic disorders (Krystal, 1978; van der Kolk et al., 1985). By longitudinally following animals exposed to severe or repeated inescapable aversive stimuli, the processes highlighted by animal models described earlier in this paper appear to be integrated in a single syndrome. IS exposure produces an initial alarm response. This is followed by conditioned alarm states and exaggerated reactivity to previously tolerated stressors. IS presentation is also followed by "helplessness" characterized by impaired avoidance learning, failure to employ previously successful escape strategies, and behavioral depression. In addition, IS produces opioid and non-opioid forms of analgesia, stomach ulceration, immunosuppression, lowered tumor resistance, and a delayed but not acute pattern of substance abuse (Visintainer et al., 1982; Shavit et al., 1982; Henke, 1985; reviewed in Kosten & Krystal, 1988).

IS, much like any human disaster, produces "traumatic" behavioral disturbances in only a portion of the exposed animals. The clinical relevance of this animal model is supported by the parallels between factors which influence IS vulnerability and variables influencing susceptibility to potential human psychological trauma. The central features of learned helplessness appear to be lack of control over stress presentation; and the severity, duration, and repetition of the aversive stimulus (Weiss et al., 1970; Anisman et al., 1978). Environmental or developmental factors, such as history of maternal deprivation, previous IS exposure, and the degree to which the stimulus requires an active coping response, increase vulnerability to IS effects. In contrast, presence of a "supportive" peer and previous escape experience have protective effects in animals. These factors influence learning, memory, cognitive appraisal, level of arousal, and response initiation processes (Anisman et al., 1978; Anisman & Sklar, 1981). Animals may also be bred for susceptibility to IS, suggesting that inherited biological factors also influence vulnerability to PTSD (Anisman et al., 1979a).

Central noradrenergic systems appear to be an important mediator of IS response. IS exposure produces massive noradrenergic activation, as indicated by increased norepinephrine turnover, increased levels of plasma catecholamines, depletion of central noradrenergic neurons, and increased amounts of noradrenergic metabolites in brain and plasma (Weiss et al., 1970; Korf, 1976; Anisman & Sklar, 1979; 1981). In addition, IS activation of locus coeruleus neurons correlates with the inhibition of adaptive responding during a post-IS swim stress situation (Weiss et al., 1987).

Central noradrenergic systems may be sensitized by IS exposure through both non associative and associative mechanisms. Animals repeatedly exposed to IS exhibit exaggerated noradrenergic responses to mild stress exposure consistent with the concept of generalized sensitization discussed earlier (Irwin et al., 1986; Tsuda et al., 1986; Walters, 1987). Noradrenergic depletion also sensitizes limbic and cortical neurons through kindling (McIntyre & Edson, 1981; 1982). Supporting the link between noradrenergic depletion and sensitization, drugs that deplete central catecholaminergic neurons decrease the number of shocks necessary to produce behavioral deficits after IS (Anisman & Sklar, 1979; Irwin et al., 1986). However, electrical stimulation of the locus coeruleus retards the development of kindling, suggesting that the facilitation described above is specific for neuronal depletion (Jimenez-Rivera et al., 1987). Although kindling is primarily studied as a model for seizure disorders, it may be relevant to a broad spectrum of behaviors (Post et al., 1986). Clinical studies also implicate kindling in PTSD. The reported efficacy of the anticonvulsant carbamazepine, in treating PTSD symptoms suggests that further studies of kindling mechanisms may be relevant to this disorder. (Lipper et al., 1986). IS presentation also increases noradrenergic reactivity through associative mechanisms. Animals exposed to sights, sounds, or odors similar to the IS setting exhibited behavioral alarm and noradrenergic activation (Cassens et al., 1980; Desiderato & Newman, 1971).

IS and Dysregulation Models

Some PTSD symptoms may arise purely from activation-induced disturbances in homeostatic neuronal systems and not as goal-directed learned responses. Alternatively, stress-induced dysregulation may produce learned behavioral syndromes which adaptively dampen arousal, in contrast to the learned fear states described earlier. This section will review evidence that IS produces massive multi-system brain activation resulting in depletion of noradrenergic neurons and alternations in receptor function which directly affect IS response, particularly the "negative" or behavioral inhibition symptoms of PTSD and IS response (van der Kolk et al., 1985).

The negative symptoms of PTSD, such as impaired concentration, loss of interest in people or activities, and psychomotor retardation, are similar in form to the "negative" behavioral changes observed after IS exposure. It produces a transient depletion of brain catecholamine systems which correlate with the behavioral deficits described above (Anisman et al., 1979a). Drugs which deplete brain catecholamines, such as tetrabenazine, DSP4, and alpha-methyl-para-tyrosine (AMPT) reproduce or exacerbate the cognitive and behavioral deficits produced by IS (Anisman et al., 1979b). In particular, chemical lesions of LC projections mimicked IS-induced learning deficits (Minor et al., 1988). In primates, IS produced depression of locomotor, explorator, and playful social behavior reminiscent of changes produced by the catecho amine synthesis inhibitor, alpha-methyl para-tyrosine (Redmond et al., 1971; 1973). Similarly, a subset of humans administered the amine neurotransmitter depleting drug, reserpine, exhibit behavioral inhibition, decreased motivation, and dysphoric mood (Goodwin & Bunney, 1971). Viewing the "helplessness", as a result of neuronal depletion may be a bit oversimplistic. Repeated stress exposure actually increases the level of norepinephrine by increasing its synthesis, a process facilitated by glucocorticoids under most conditions (reviewed in Stone, 1975; McEwen, 1987). This synthetic adaptation may have some protective value against repeated traumatization, "stress immunization" (Seligman & Maier, 1967). However, the overall utilization of this neurotransmitter continues to increase, consistent with the activation of this system by stress (Irwin et al., 1986). Meso-limbic and meso-frontal dopamine systems activated by inescapable stress exposure also influence response initiation. These systems may play a direct role in the initial behavioral deficits seen in learned helplessness (Reinhard et al., 1982; Deutch et al., 1985).

Clonidine, benzodiazepines, and antidepressants, noted earlier to be useful in treating PTSD symptoms, prevent the development of learned helplessness (Anisman et al., 1980; Petty & Sherman, 1980). Injection of desipramine or norepinephrine into LC innervated areas such as the hippocampus and frontal cortex, had a similar prophylactic effect (Petty & Sherman, 1980). Benzodiazepine injections into the LC, which inhibit its activation, also prevent the development of IS-induced behavioral deficits. Alternatively, benzodiazepine inverse agonists which elicit severe alarm responses in humans (Dorow et al., 1983), produces a behavioral syndrome similar to IS in animals which was reversed by the benzodiazepine antagonist Ro 15–1788 (Skolnick et al., 1984). These findings are consistent with the hypothesis that noradrenergic activation contributes etiologically to IS response and, perhaps, PTSD. It is not clear whether the activation, the subsequent neuronal depletion, or the disturbances in homeostatic neuronal function underlying sensitization are critical to the development of learned helplessness. However, the evidence suggests that pretreatment with a noradrenergic inhibiting substance may prevent some of the later sequelae of stress exposure.

Noradrenergic systems also play a role in the reversal of learned helplessness. Clonidine, atypical and tricyclic antidepressants, monoamine oxidase inhibitors, electroconvulsive shock, and acute benzodiazepine administration also ameliorate the IS-induced escape deficits (Petty & Sherman, 1979; Sherman et al., 1982; Anisman et al., 1980). However, substances abused by individuals with PTSD, including stimulants, barbiturates, ethanol, as well as chronic benzodiazepine administration, which may attenuate the severity of IS-induced arousal states, lack the ability to "treat" learned helplessness once it develops (Sherman et al., 1982). Neuroleptics, perhaps overused in the treatment of PTSD, exacerbate IS-induced behavioral deficits, an effect antagonized by clonidine (Anisman et al., 1981). Also, direct infusion of a monoamine oxidase inhibitor into the LC reversed the noradrenergic and behavioral deficits observed after IS (Goodman et al., 1983). In addition to the pharmacologic strategies, one study used a behavioral approach and reversed learned helplessness by forcing dogs across a barrier to teach active coping strategies (Seligman et al., 1968).

Traumatic disturbances in homeostatic brain function observed after IS exposure involve intracellular regulatory processes linked to transient forms of cellular plasticity in the snail, Aplysia. After massive noradrenergic activation and neuronal depletion, presynaptic α_2 adrenoceptors and intracellular calcium-mediated processes inhibit central noradrenergic activity, norepinephrine synthesis increases, and transmitter levels return to baseline (Andrade & Aghajanian, 1984; Stone, 1975). However, the presynaptic α_2 receptors adapt to the stress-induced bombardment with down regulation, potentially altering subsequent stress response. Postsynaptic α_2 and beta-receptors are similarly down regulated. The severe noradrenergic activation observed after IS, chronic α_2 antagonist administration, and opiate withdrawal also desensitize the adenylate cyclase-protein phosphorylation cascade (U'Prichard & Kvetnansky, 1980; Nathanson & Redmond, 1981; reviewed in Redmond & Krystal, 1984). In contrast, Stone and his colleagues (1985), studying brain slices from restrained animals, found that IS desensitized the α_2 but not the beta-receptor stimulated accumulation of cyclic AMP. However, there is evidence that following the initial traumatic receptor down regulation, animals may exhibit increases in receptor function. For example, in the rat, four weeks after LC stimulation, the number of α_2 receptors in the cortex, hypothalamus, and hippocampus are increased (Velley et al., 1985).

Conditions which massively, repeatedly, or continuously activate central noradrenergic systems such as IS, opiate withdrawal, or chonric α_2 antagonist administration produce superficially similar chronic syndromes (discussed in van der Kolk et al., 1985; Kosten & Krystal, 1988). These syndromes are characterized by a pattern of dampened oscillation of noradrenergic arousal characterized by periods of apparent hypoactivity or hyperactivity of this system. In animals, this oscillatory pattern appears to be mediated by pre-and post-synaptic regulatory systems (Nathanson & Redmond, 1981; Velley et al., 1985). This oscillatory pattern may have clinical correlates in acute and protracted opioid abstinence, as well as the stages which have been described in the course of PTSD symptoms (Redmond & Krystal, 1984; Horowitz, 1973).

IMPLICATIONS

As part of the resurgence of scientific investigations of traumatic stress response, clinical and basic neuroscience research is having increasing impact on PTSD theory and contributing new and improved treatments for this disorder. Although, to date, these investigations have lagged behind other psychiatric diagnoses, PTSD research has the advantage of studying a pathological process with identifiable etiologic agents, environmental stressors, that may be studied clinically and modeled in the laboratory. Building on current theoretical and clinical foundations, future investigations will continue to augment neuroscience contributions in this area.

REFERENCES

Amsterdam, J. D., Maislin, G., Winokur, A., Kling, M., & Gold, P. (1987). Pituitary and adrenocortical responses to the ovine corticotropin releasing hormone in depressed patients and healthy volunteers. Arch Gen Psychiatry, 44, 775–781.
Andrade, R., & Aghajanian, G. K. (1984). Locus coeruleus activity in vitro: Intrinsic

regulation by a calcium-dependent potassium conductance but not alpha 2 adrenoceptors. J Neurosci, 4, *161–170.*

Anisman, H., Beauchamp, C., & Zarchanko, R. M. *(1984). Effects of inescapable shock and not epinephrine depletion induced by DSP4 on escape performance.* Psychopharmacology, 83, *56–61.*

Anisman, H., deCatanzaro, D., & Remington, G. *(1978). Escape performance following exposure to inescapable shock: Deficits in motor response maintenance.* J Exp Psychol Animal Behavior Processes, 4, *197–218.*

Anisman, H., Grimmer, L., Irwin, J., Remington, G., & Sklar, L. S. *(1979a). Escape performance after inescapable shock in selectively bred lines of mice: Response maintenance and catecholamine activity.* J Comp Physiol Psychol, 93, *229–241.*

Anisman, H., Irwin, J., & Sklar, L. S. *(1979b). Deficits of escape performance following catecholamine depletion: Implications for uncontrollable stress.* Psychopharmacology, 64, *163–170.*

Anisman, H., Ritch, M., & Sklar, L. S. *(1981). Noradrenergic and dopaminergic interactions in escape behavior: Analysis of uncontrollable stress effects.* Psychopharmacology, 74, *263–268.*

Anisman, H., & Sklar, L. S. *(1979). Catecholamine depletion in mice upon re-exposure to stress: Mediation of the escape deficits produced by inescapable shock.* J Comp Physiol Psychol, 93, *610–625.*

Anisman, H., & Sklar, L. S. *(1981). Social housing conditions influence escape deficits produced by uncontrollable stress: Assessment of the contribution of norepinephrine.* Behav Neural Biol, 32, *406–427.*

Anisman, H., Suissa, A., & Sklar, L. S. *(1980). Escape deficits induced by uncontrollable stress: Antagonis by dopamine and norepinephrine agonists.* Behav Neural Biol, 28, *37–47.*

Birkhimer, L. J., DeVane, C. L., & Muniz, C. E. *(1985). Posttraumatic stress disorder: Characteristics and pharmacological response in the veteran population.* Comp Psychiatry, 26, *304–310.*

Blanchard, E. B., Kolb, L. C., Pallmeyer, T. P. & Gerardi, R. J. *(1982). A psycho physiologic study of post-traumatic stress disorder in Vietnam veterans,* Psychiatr Q. 54, *220–228.*

Blanchard, E. B., Kolb, L. C., Gerardi, R. J., Ryan, P., & Pallmeyer, T. P. *(1986). Cardiac response to relevant stimuli as an adjunctive tool for diagnosing posttraumatic stress disorder in Vietnam veterans.* Behavior Therapy, 17, *592–606.*

Bleich, A., Siegel, B., Garb, R., & Lerer, B. *(1986). Post-traumatic stress disorder following combat exposure: Clinical features and psychopharmacological treatment.* Brit J Psychiatry, 149, *365–369.*

Boehnlein, J. K., Kinzie, J. D., Ben, R., & Fleck, J. *(1985). One year follow-up study of posttraumatic stress disorder among survivors of Cambodian concentration camps.* Am J Psychiatry, 142, *956–959.*

Bourne, P. B., Ruse, R. M., & Mason, J. W. *(1968). 17-OHCS levels in combat: Special Forces "A" Team under threat of attack.* Arch Gen Psychiatry, 19, *135–140.*

Brende, J. O. *(1982). Electrodermal responses in post-traumatic syndromes.* J Nerv Ment Dis, 170, *352–361.*

Brown, M. B., & Fisher, L. A. (1986). Glucocorticoid suppression of the sympathetic nervous system and adrenal medulla. Life Sci, 39, 1003–1012.

Buchsbaum, M. S., Coutsey, R. D. & Murphy, D. L. (1976). The biochemical high risk paradigm: Behavioral and family correlates of low platelet monoamine oxidase activity. Science, 194, 339–341.

Bury, J. S. (1918). Pathology of war neuroses. Lancet, 1, 97–99.

Campbell, C. M. (1918). The role of instinct, emotion and personality in disorders of the heart. JAMA, 71, 1621–1626.

Carroll, B. J., Ieinberg, M., Greden, J. F., Tarika, J., Albala, A. A., Hackett, R. F., Norman, J., Lohr, N., Sterner, M., deVigne, J. P., & Young, E. (1981). A specific laboratory test for the diagnosis of melancholia: standardization, validation, and clinical utility. Arch Gen Psychiatry, 38, 15–22.

Cassella, J. V., & Davis, M. (1985). Fear enhanced acoustic startle is not attenuated by acute or chronic imipramine treatment in rats. Psychopharmacology, 87, 278–282.

Cassens, G., Roffman, M. Kuruc, A., Orsulak, P. J., & Schildkraut, J. J. (1980). Alterations in brain norepinephrine metabolism by environmental stimuli previously paired with inescapable shock. Science, 209, 1138–1140.

Castelluci, V. F., Naurn, A., Greengard, P., Schwartz, J. H., & Kandel, E. R. (1982) Inhibition of adenosine 3'5' monophosphate dependent protein kinase blocks presynaptic facilitation in Aplysia. J Neurosol, 2, 1673–1681

Charney, D. S., Menkes, D. B., & Heninger, O. R. (1981). Receptor sensitivity and the mechanism of action of antidepressant treatment: Implications for the etiology and therapy of depression. Arch Gen Psychiatry, 38, 1160–1180.

Charney, D. S., Breier, A., Jatlow, P. I., & Heninger G. R. (1986). Behavioral, biochemical, and blood pressure responses to alprazolam in healthy subjects: Interactions with yohimbine. Psychopharmacology, 88, 133–140.

Comb, M., Hyman, S. E., & Goodman, H. M. (1987). Mechanisms of trans-synaptic regulation of gene expression. Trends Neurosci, 10, 473–478.

Crile, G. (1940). Results of 152 denervations of the adrenal glands in treatment of neurocirculatory asthenia. The Military Surgeon, 87, 509–513.

Davidson, J., Lipper, S., Kilts, C. D., Mahorney, S., & Hummett, E. (1985a). Platelet MAO activity in posttraumatic stress disorder. Am J Psychiatry, 142, 1341–1343.

Davidson, J. R. T., McLeod, M. N., Turnbull, C. D., White, H. L., & Feuer, E. D. (1980). Platelet monoamine oxidase activity and the classification of depression. Arch Gen Psychiatry, 37, 771–776.

Davidson, J., Swartz, M., Storck, M., Krishnan, R. R., & Hammett, E. (1985b). A diagnostic and family study of posttraumatic stress disorder. Am J Psychiatry, 142, 90–93.

Davis, H. P., & Squire L. R. (1984). Protein synthesis and memory: A review. Psychol Bull, 96, 518–559.

Davis, M. (1980). Neurochemical modulation of sensory-motor reactivity: Acoustic and tactile startle reflexes. Neurosci Biobehav Rev. 4, 241–263.

Davis, M. (1986). Pharmacological and anatomical analysis of fear conditioning using the fear-potentiated startle paradigm. Behav Neurosci, 6, 814–824.

DeLean, A., Hancock, A. A., & Lefkowitz, R. J. (1981). Validation and statistical *analysis of a computer modeling method of quantitative analysis of radioligand binding data for mixtures of pharmacological receptor subtypes.* Mol Pharmacol, 21, 5–9.

Desiderato, O., & Newman, A. *(1971). Conditioned suppression produced in rats by tones paired with escapable or inescapable shock.* J Comp Physiol Psychol, 77, 427–431.

Deutch, A. Y., Tam, S. Y., & Roth, R. H. *(1985). Footshock and conditioned stress increase 3, 4-dihydroxphenylacetic acid (DOPAC) in the ventral tegmental area but not the substantia nigra.* Brain Res, 333, 143–146.

Dobbs, D., & Wilson, W. P. *(1960). Observations on persistence of war neurosis.* Dis Nerv Sys. 21, 40–46.

Dorow, R. R., Horowski, R., Paschelke, G., Amin, M., & Braestrup, C. *(1983). Severe anxiety induced by FG 7142, a beta-carboline ligand for benzodiazepine receptors.* Lancet, 1, 98–99.

Drury, A. N. *(1918). The percentage of carbon dioxide in the alveolar air, and the tolerance to accumulating carbon dioxide in cases of so-called "irritable heart of soldiers."* Heart, 7, 165–173.

Dunner, F. J., Edwards, W. P., & Copeland, P. C. *(1985). Clinical efficacy of alprazolam in PTSD patients.* Program and Papers on New Research, *American Psychiatric Assoc. 138th Annual Meeting, Los Angeles: APA, 50.*

Fifkova, E. *(1985). A possible mechanism of morphometric-changes in dendritic spines induced by stimulation.* Cell Mol Neurobiol, 5, 47–63.

Foote, S. L., Aston-Jones, G., & Bloom, F. E. *(1980). Impulse activity of locus coeruleus neurons in awake rats and monkeys is a function of sensory stimulation and arousal.* Proc Natl Acad Sci USA, 77, 3033–3037.

Frank, J. B., Kosten, T. R., Giller, E. L., & Dan, E. *(1988). A randomized clinical trial of phenelzine and imipramine for Posttraumatic Stress Disorder.* Am J Psychiatry, 145, 1289–1291.

Fraser, F., & Wilson, R. M. *(1918). The sympathetic nervous system and the "irritable heart of soldiers,"* Br Med J, 2, 27–29.

Gibbins, R. J., Kalant, H., LeBlanc, A. E., & Clark, J. W. *(1971). The effects of chronic administration of ethanol on startle threshholds in rats.* Psychopharmacologia (Berl), 19, 95–104.

Goelet, P., & Kandel, E. R. *(1986). Tracking the flow of learned information from membrane receptors to genome.* Trend Neursci, 9, 492–499.

Goodman, P. A., Weiss, J. M., Ambrose, M. J., Cardle, K. A., Bailey, W. H., & Charry, J. M. *(1983). Infusion of a monoamine oxidase inhibitor into the locus coeruleus can protect against stress-induced depression.* Soc Neurosci Abstr, 9, 553.

Goodwin, F., & Bunney, W. E. Jr. *(1971). Depression following reserpine: A reevaluation.* Semin Psychiatry, 3, 435–448.

Grant, S. J., & Redmond, D. E. Jr. *(1983). Locus coeruleus neuronal activity in awake behaving monkeys.* Prog Neuro-Psychopharmacol, 152, #186.

Gudeman, J. E., Schatzberg, A. F., Samsom, J. A., Orsulak, P. J. Cole, J. O., & Schildkraut, J. J. *(1982). Toward a biochemical classification of depressive disorders VI: Platelet MAO activity and clinical symptoms in depressed patients.* Am J Psychiatry, 139, 630–633.*

Harfstrand, A., Fuxe, K., Cintra, A., Agnati, L. F., Zini, I., Wikstrom, A.-C., Okret, S., Yu, Z.-Y., Goldstein M., Steinbusch H., Verhofstad A., & Gustafsson J.-A. (1986). Glucocorticoid receptor immunoreactivity in monoaminergic neurons of rat brain. Proc Natl Acad Sci USA, 83, 9779–9783.

Henke, P. G. (1985). The amygdala and forced immobilization of rats. Behav Brain Res, 16, 19–24.

Hogben, G. I., & Cornfield, R. B. (1981). Treatment of traumatic war neurosis with phenelzine. Arch Gen Psychiatry, 38, 440–445.

Horowitz, M. J. (1973). Phase oriented treatment of stress response syndromes. Am J Psychother, 27, 506–515.

Irwin, J., Ahluwalia, P., & Anisman, H. (1986). Sensitization of norepinephrine activity following acute and chronic footshock. Brain Res, 379, 98–103.

Iverson, S. D. (1984). Cortical monoamines and behavior. In: Monoamine Innervation of Cerebral Cortex. *I. Descarries, T. R. Reader, H. H. Jasper (Eds.). pp. 321–349, New York: Alan R. Liss.*

Jacobs, W. J., & Nadel L. (1985). Stress-induced recovery of fears and phobias. Psychol Rev, 92, 512–531.

Jimenez-Rivera, C., Voltura, A., & Weiss, G. K. (1987). Effect of locus coeruleus stimulation on the development of kindled seizures. Exptl Neurol, 95, 13–20.

Kandel, E. R. (1983). From metapsychology to molecular biology: Explorations into the nature of anxiety. Am J Psychiatry, 140, 1277–1293.

Kolb, L. C., Burris, B. C., & Griffiths, S. (1984). Propranolol and clonidine in the treatment of the chronic post traumatic stress disorders of war. In: Post Traumatic Stress Disorder: Psychological and Biological Sequelae. B. A. van der Kolk (Ed.), 98, 105, Washington, DC.: American Psychiatric Press.

Korf, J. (1976). Locus Coeruleus, noradrenaline metabolism, and stress. In: Catecholamines and Stress. *E. Usdin, R. Kvetnansky, I. J. Kopin (Eds.), pp. 105–111, New York: Pergamon.*

Kosten, T. R., & Krystal, J. H. (1988). Biological mechanisms in post-traumatic stress disorder: Relevance for substance abuse. In: Recent Advances in Alcoholism. Vol VI. *M. Galanter (Ed.), pp. 49–68, New York: Guilford.*

Kosten, T. R., Mason, J. W. Giller, E. L., Ostroff, R., & Harkness, L. (1987). Sustained urinary norepinephrine and epinephrine elevation in post-traumatic stress disorder: Psychoneuroendocrinology, 12, 13–20.

Krystal, H. (1978). Trauma and affects. Psychoanal Stud Child, 33, 81–116.

Kudler, H., Davidson, J., Meador, K., Lipper, S., & Ely, T. (1987). The DST and posttraumatic stress disorder. Am J Psychiatry, 144, 1068–1071.

Larson, J., & Lynch, G. (1986). Induction of synaptic potentiation in hippocampus by patterned stimulation involves two events. Science, 232, 985–988.

Leahy, D. J., Stogin, J. M., Moore, M. R., Losco, R., Lewis, L., Redmond, D. E., (1980). Natural social and nonsocial behaviors associated with fear in cercopishicus aethiops sabeus. Antopolgia Contemporanea, 3, 227.

Leaton, R. N., & Borszcz, G. S. (1985). Potentiated startle: Its relation to freezing and shock intensity in rats. J Exptl Psychol: Animal Behav Processes, 11, 421–428.

Lerer, B., Bleich, A., Kotler, M., Garb, R., Hertzberg, M., & Levin, B. (1987a).

Posttraumatic stress disorder in Israeli combat veterans. Arch Gen Psychiatry, 44, 976–981.

Lerer, B., Ebstein, R. P., Shestatsky, M., Shemesh, Z., & Greenberg, D. (1987b). *Cyclic AMP signal transduction in posttraumatic stress disorder.* Am J Psychiatry, 144, 1324–1327.

Lightman, S. L., & Young, W. S., III. (1987). *Changes in hypothalamic preproenkephalin A mRNA following stress and opiate withdrawal.* Nature, 328, 643–645.

Linnoila, M., Mefford, I., Nutt, D., & Adinoff, B. (1987). *Alcohol withdrawal and noradrenergic function.* Ann Int Med, 107, 875–889.

Lipper, S. Davidson, J. R. T., Grady, T. A., Edinger, J. D., Hammett, E. B., Mahorney, S. L., & Cavenar, J. O., Jr. (1986). *Preliminary study of carbamazepine in posttraumatic stress disorder.* Psychosomatics, 27, 849–853.

Lovinger, D. M., Colley, P. A., Akera, R. F., Nelson, R. B., & Routtenberg, A. (1986). *Direct relation of long-term potentiation to phosphorylation of membrane protein F-1, a substrate for membrane protein kinase C.* Brain Res, 399, 205–212.

McEwen, B. S. (1987). *Glucocorticoid-biogenic amine interactions in relation to mood and behavior.* Biochem Pharmacol 36, 1755–1763.

McEwen, B. S., De Kloet, E. R., & Rostene, W. (1986). *Adrenal steroids receptors and actions in the nervous system.* Physiol Rev 66, 1121–1188.

McIntyre, D. C., & Edson, N. (1981). *Facilitation of amygdala kindling after norepinephrine depletion with 6-hydroxydopamine in rats.* Exptl Neurol, 74, 748–757.

McIntyre, D. C., & Edson, N. (1982). *Effect of norepinephrine depletion on dorsal hippocampus kindling in rats.* Exptl Neurol, 77, 700–704.

Malloy, P. F., Fairbank, J. A., & Keane, T. M. (1983). *Validation of a multimethod assessment of posttraumatic stress disorders in Vietnam veterans.* J Consult Clin Psychol, 51, 488–494.

Mason, J. W. (1968). *A review of psychoendocrine research on the sympathetic-adrenal medullary system.* Psychosom Med, 30, 631–653.

Mason, J. W., Giller, E. L., Kosten, T., Ostroff, R., & Podd, L. (1986). *Urinary free-cortisol levels in posttraumatic stress disorder patients.* J Nerv Ment Dis, 174, 145–149.

Meakins, J. C., & Wilson, R. M. (1918). *The effect of certain sensory stimulation on respiratory and heart rate in cases of so-called "irritable heart."* Heart, 7, 17–22.

Mellman, T. A., & Davis, G. C. (1985). *Combat-related flashbacks in post-traumatic stress disorder: Phenomenology and similarity to panic attacks.* J Clin Psychiatry, 46, 379–382.

Milanes, F. J., Mack, C. N., Dennison, J., & Slater, V. L. (1984). *Phenelzine treatment of post-Vietnam stress syndrome.* VA Practitioner, 15, 40–49.

Minor, T. R., Pelleymounter, M. A., & Maier, S. F. (1988). *Uncontrollable shock, forebrain norepinephrine, and stimulus selection during choice-escape learning.* Psychobiology, 16, 135–145.

Nathanson, J. A., & Redmond, D. E., Jr. (1981). *Morphine withdrawal causes subsensitivity of adrenergic receptor response.* Life Sci, 28, 1353–1360.

Nestler, E. J., & Greengard, P. (1984). Protein Phosphorylation in the Nervous System. *New York: Neurosciences Research Foundation.*

Nies, A., Robinson, D. S., Lamborn, K. R., Lampert, R. P. (1973). *Genetic control of *platelet and plasma monoamine oxidase activity.* Arch Gen Psychiatry, 28, *834–838.*

Peabody, F. W., Clough, H. D., Sturgis, C. C., Wearn, J. T., & Tompkins, E. H. (1918). *Effects of the injection of epinephrine in soldiers with "irritable heart."* JAMA, 71, *1912–1915.*

Perry, B. D., Giller, E. L., Jr., & Southwick, S. M. (1987a). *Altered platelet alpha-2 adrenergic binding sites in post-traumatic stress disorder.* Am J Psychiatry, 144, *1511–1512.*

Perry, B. D., Southwick, S. M., Giller, E. L., Jr. (1987b). *Application of a new paradigm for examining membrane receptors in psychiatric populations.* (abstract) Soc Biol Psychiatry.

Petty, R., & Sherman, A. D. (1979). Reversal of learned helplessness by imipramine. Comm Psychopharmacol, 3, *371–373.*

Petty, F. & Sherman, A. D. (1980). *Regional aspects of the prevention of learned helplessness by desipramine.* Life Sci, 26, *1447–1452.*

Pitman, R. K., Orr, S. P., Forgue, D. F., deJong, J., & Claiborn, J. M. (1987). *Psychophysiologic assessment of posttraumatic stress disorder imagery in Vietnam combat veterans.* Arch Gen Psychiatry, 44, *970–975.*

Post, R. M. Rubinow, D. R., & Ballenger, J. C. (1986). *Conditioning and sensitization in the longitudinal course of affective illness.* Brit J Psychiatry, 149, *191–201.*

Rado, S., (1942). *Pathodynamics and treatment of traumatic war neurosis (traumatophobia).* Psychosom Med, 42, *362–368.*

Rainey, J. M., Aleen, A., Ortiz, A., Yeragami, V., Pohl, R., & Bereliou, R. (1987). *A laboratory procedure for the induction of flashbacks.* Am J Psychiatry, 144, *1317–1319.*

Rasmussen, K., & Jacobs, B. I. (1986). *Single unit activity of locus coeruleus neurons in the freely moving cat. II. Conditioning and pharmacologic studies.* Brain Res, 371, *335–344.*

Redmond, D. E., Jr. (1979). *New and old evidence for the involvement of a brain noradrenergic system in anxiety. In:* Phenomenology and Treatment of Anxiety, W. E. Fann, I. Karacan, A. D. Pakorney, R. L. Williams (Eds.), pp. 153–203, New York: Spectrum.

Redmond, D. E., Jr., & Krystal, J. H. (1984). *Multiple mechanisms of withdrawal from opioid drugs.* Ann Rev Neursci, 7, *443–478.*

Redmond, D. E., Jr., Mass, J. W., Dekirmenjian, H., & Schlemmer, R. F., Jr. (1973). *Changes in social behavior in monkeys after inescapable shock.* Psychosom Med, 35, *448–449.*

Redmond, D. E., Jr., Mass, J. W., Kling, A., Graham, C. W., & Dekirmenjian, H. (1971). *Social behavior of monkeys selectively depleted of monoamines.* Science, 174, *428–431.*

Reinhard, J. F., Jr., Bannon, M. J., & Roth, R. H. (1982). *Acceleration by stress of dopamine synthesis and metabolism in prefrontal cortex: Antagonism by diazepam.* Neuronym-Schmeideberg's Arch Pharmacol, 318, *374–377.*

Reveley, M. A., Reveley, A. M., Clifford, C. A., & Murray, R. M. (1983). *Genetics of platelet MAO activity in discordant schizophrenic and normal twins.* Brit J Psychiat, 142, *560–565.*

Robinson, G. B., & Racine, R. J. (1986). Interactions between septal and entorhinal inputs to the rat dentate gyrus: Facilitation effects. Brain Res, 379, 63–67.

Rubin, R. T., Miller, R. G., Clark, B. R., Poland, R. E., & Arthur, R. J. (1970). The stress of aircraft carrier landings: II. 3-methoxy-4-hydroxypherylglycol excretion in naval aviators. Psychosom Med, 32, 589–597.

Ryan, S. M., Drugan, R. C., Hyson, R. L., & Maier, S. F. (1983). Coping and immunosuppression: Inescapable but not escapable shock suppresses lymphocyte proliferation. Science, 221, 568–570.

Sara, S. J. (1985). The locus coeruleus and cognitive function: Attempts to relate noradrenergic enhancement of signal/noise in the brain to behavior. Physiol Psychol, 13, 151–162.

Seligman, M. E. P., & Maier, S. F., (1967). Failure to escape traumatic shock. J Exp Psychol, 74, 1–9.

Seligman, M. E., Maier, S. F., & Geer, J. H. (1968). Alleviation of learned helplessness in the dog. J Abnormal Psychol, 73, 256–262.

Selye, H. (1936). A syndrome produced by diverse nocuous agents. Nature, 196, 32.

Shavit, Y., Lewis, J. W., Terman, G. W., Gale, R. P., & Lieberskind, J. C. (1982). Opioid peptides mediate the suppressive effect of stress on natural killer cell cytotoxity. Science, 223, 188–190.

Shen, W. W., & Park S. (1983). The use of monoamine oxidase inhibitors in the treatment of traumatic war neurosis: Case report. Milit Med, 148, 430–431.

Sherman, A. D., Sacquitine, J. L., & Pretty, F. (1982). Specificity of the learned helplessness model of depression. Pharmacol Biochem Behav, 16, 449–454.

Sibley, D. R., Streasser R. H., Benovic J. L., Kiefer D., & Lefkowitz, R. J. (1986). Phosphorylation/dephosphorylation of the beta-adrenergic receptor regulates its functional coupling to adenylate cyclase and subcellular distributions. Proc Natl Acad Sci USA, 83, 9408–9412.

Skelton, R. W., Scarth, A. S., Wilkie, D. M., Miller, J. J., & Phelps, A. G., (1987). Long-term increases in dentate granule cell reponsivity responsivitity accompanying operant conditioning. J. Neurosci, 7, 3081–3087.

Skolnick, P., Drugan, R. C., Paul, S. M., & Crawley, J. N. (1984). Learned helplessness induced by an active antagonist of the brain benzodiazepine receptor. Soc Neurosci Abstr, 10, 1069.

Smith, M. A., Davidson, J., Ritchie, H., Kudler, H., Lipper, S., Chappell, P., & Nerneroff, C. B. (1989). Corticotropin-releasing hormone tests in patients with PTSD. Biol Psychiatry.

Stolk, J. M., Vantini, G., Guchhait, R. B., Elston, R. C., Perry, B., & U'Prichard, D. C. (1985). Genetic mechanisms regulating phenylethanolamine N-methyltransferase and their implications for the physiological response to stress. In: Catecholamines and Other Neurotransmitters and Stress. R. Kvetnansky, E. Usdin (Eds.). pp. 435–446, Amsterdam: Elsevier Press.

Stone, E. A., (1975). Stress and catecholamines. In: Catecholamines and Behavior-2: Neuropsychopharmacology. A. J. Friedhoff (Ed.), pp. 31–72, New York: Plenum.

Stone, E. A., Slucky, A. V., Platt, J. E., & Trullas, R. (1985). Reduction of the cyclic adenosine 3',5'-monophosphate response to catecholamines in rat brain slices after repeated restraint stress. J Pharmacol Exp Ther. 237, 702–707.

Svensson, T. H. (1987). Peripheral, autonomic regulation of locus coeruleus noradre-nergic neurons in brain: Putative implications for psychiatry and psychopharma-cology. Psychopharmacology, 92, 1–7.

Tsuda, A., Tanaka, M., Ida, Y., Thujimaru, S., Ushijima, I., & Nagasaki, N. (1986). Effects of preshock experience on enhancement of rat brain noradrenaline turnover induced by psychological stress. Pharmacol Biochem Behav, 24, 115–119.

U'Prichard, D. C., & Kvetnansky, R. (1980). Central and peripheral adrenergic recep-tors in acute and repeated immobilization stress. In: Catecholamines and Stress: Recent Advances. E. Usdin, R., Kvetnansky, I. J. Kopin (Eds.), pp. 299–308, New York: Elsevier North Holland.

Valentino, R. J., Foote, S. L., & Aston-Jones, G. (1983). Corticotropin-releasing factor activates noradrenergic neurons of the locus coeruleus. Brain Res, 270, 363–367.

van der Kolk, B. (1987). Psychological Trauma. Washington DC: American Psychiat-ric Press.

van der Kolk, B., Greenberg, M., Boyd, H., Krystal, J. (1985). Inescapable shock, neurotransmitters, and addiction to trauma: Toward a psychobiolgoy of post trau-matic stress. Biol Psychiatry, 20, 314–325.

Velley, J., Kempf, E., Cardo, B., & Velley, L. (1985). Long-term modulation of learning following locus coeruleus stimulation: Behavioral and neurochemical data. Phy-siol Psychol, 13, 163–171.

Visintainer, M. A., Volpicelli, J. R., & Seligman, M. E. P. (1982). Tumor rejections in rats after inescapable or escapable shock. Science, 216, 437–439.

Walters, E. T. (1987). Site-specific sensitization of defensive reflexes in Aplysia: A simple model of long-term hyperalgesia. J Neursci. 7, 400–407.

Walters, E. T. & Byrne, J. H. (1985). Long-term enhancement produced by activity-dependent modulation of Aplysia sensory neurons. J. Neursci, 5, 662–672.

Weiss, J. M., Stone, E. A., & Harrell, N. (1970). Coping behavior and brain norepi-nephrine levels in rats. J Comp Physiol Psychol, 72, 153–160.

Weiss, J. M., Simson, P. E., Knight, J. A., & Kilts, C. D. (1987). Hyperresponsivity of locus coeruleus is associated with stress-induced behavioral depression. Soc Neu-rosci Abstr, 13, 32.

Woodward, D. J., Moises, H. C., Waterhouse, B. D., Hoffer, B. J., & Freedman, R. (1979). Modulatory actions of norepinephrine in the central nervous system. Fed Proc, 38, 2109–2116.

18. The Body Keeps the Score
Memory and the Evolving Psychobiology of Posttraumatic Stress

Bessel A. van der Kolk

FOR MORE THAN a century ever since people's responses to over-whelming experiences were first systematically explored, researchers have noted that the psychological effects of trauma are stored in somatic memory and expressed as changes in the biological stress response. In 1889 Pierre Janet[1] postulated that intense emotional reactions make events traumatic by interfering with the integration of the experience into existing memory schemes. Intense emotions cause memories of particular events to be disso-ciated from consciousness and to be stored, instead, as visceral sensations (anxiety and panic) or visual images (nightmares and flashbacks). Janet also observed that traumatized patients seemed to react to reminders of the trauma with emergency responses that had been relevant to the original threat but had no bearing on current experience. He noted that, unable to put the trauma behind them, victims had trouble learning from experience: their energy was funneled toward keeping their emotions under control, at the expense of paying attention to current exigencies. They became fixated on the past, in some cases by being obsessed with the trauma, but more often by behaving and feeling as if they were traumatized over and over again without being able to locate the origins of these feelings.[2,3]

Freud[4] also considered the tendency to remain fixated on the trauma to be biologically based: "After severe shock . . . the dream life continually takes the patient back to the situation of his disaster from which he awakens with renewed terror. . . . The patient has undergone a physical fixation to the trauma." Pavlov's investigations[5] continued the tradition of explaining the effects of trauma as the result of lasting physiological alterations. He, and others using his paradigm, coined the term *defensive reaction* for a cluster of

Reprinted by permission from *Harvard Review of Psychiatry*, 1, 263–265. Copyright © by Mosby-Year Book, 1994.

innate reflexive responses to environmental threat. Many studies have shown how the response to potent environmental stimuli (unconditional stimuli) becomes a conditioned reaction. After repeated aversive stimulation, intrinsically nonthreatening cues associated with the trauma (conditional stimuli) can elicit the defensive reaction by themselves (conditional response). A rape victim may respond to conditioned stimuli, such as the approach of an unknown man, as if she were about to be raped again—and experience panic. Pavlov also pointed out that individual differences in temperament accounted for the diversity of long-term adaptations to trauma.

Abraham Kardiner,[6] who first systematically defined posttraumatic stress for American audiences, noted that sufferers of "traumatic neuroses" develop an enduring vigilance for and sensitivity to environmental threat. He stated:

The nucleus of the neurosis is a physioneurosis. This is present on the battlefield and during the entire process of organization: it outlives every intermediary accommodative device, and persists in the chronic forms. The traumatic syndrome is ever present and unchanged.

In *Men Under Stress*, Grinker and Spiegel[7] cataloged the physical symptoms of soldiers in acute posttraumatic states: flexor changes in posture, hyperkinesis, "violently propulsive gait," tremor at rest, masklike facies, cogwheel rigidity, gastric distress, urinary incontinence, mutism, and a violent startle reflex. They noted the similarity between many of these symptoms and those of diseases of the extrapyramidal motor system. Today we understand them to result from stimulation of biological systems, particularly of ascending amine projections. Contemporary research on the biology of posttraumatic stress disorder PTSD, generally uninformed by this earlier research confirms that there are persistent and profound alterations in stress hormone secretion and memory processing in subjects with PTSD.

SYMPTOMATOLOGY

Starting with Kardiner[6] and closely followed by Lindemann.[8] a vast literature on combat trauma, crimes, rape, kidnapping, natural disasters, accidents, and imprisonment[9–12] has shown that the trauma response is bimodal: hypermnesia, hyperreactivity to stimuli, and traumatic re-experiencing coexist with psychic numbing, avoidance, amnesia, and anhedonia. These responses to extreme experiences are so consistent across the different forms of traumatic stimuli that this bimodal reaction appears to be the normative response to any overwhelming and uncontrollable experience. In many persons who have undergone severe stress, the posttraumatic response fades over time, whereas in others it persists. Much work remains to be done to spell out issues of resilience and vulnerability, but magnitude of exposure, previous trauma, and social support appear to be the three most significant predictors for development of chronic PTSD.[13,14]

In an apparent attempt to compensate for chronic hyperarousal, traumatized people seem to shut down: on a behavioral level by avoiding stimuli reminiscent of the trauma, and on a psychobiological level by emotional numbing, which extends to both trauma-related and everyday experience.[15] Thus subjects with chronic PTSD tend to suffer from a numbed responsiveness to the environment, punctuated by intermittent hyperarousal in reaction to conditional traumatic stimuli. However, as Pitman and colleagues[16,17] have pointed out, in PTSD the stimuli that precipitate emergency responses may not be conditional enough: many triggers not directly related to the traumatic experience may precipitate extreme reactions. Subjects with PTSD suffer both from generalized hyperarousal and from physiological emergency reactions to specific reminders.[9,10]

The loss of affective modulation that is so central in PTSD may help to explain the observation that traumatized persons lose the capacity to use affect states as signals.[18] In subjects with PTSD, feelings are not used as cues to attend to incoming information and arousal is likely to precipitate flight-or-fight reactions.[19] Thus they often go immediately from stimulus to response without psychologically assessing the meaning of an event. This makes them prone to freeze or, alternatively, to overreact and intimidate others in response to minor provocations.[12,20]

PSYCHOPHYSIOLOGY

Abnormal psychophysiological responses in PTSD have been observed at two different levels: (1) in response to specific reminders of the trauma and (2) in response to intense but neutral stimuli, such as unexpected noises. The first paradigm implies heightened physiological arousal to sounds, images, and thoughts related to specific traumatic incidents. Many studies[20-25] have confirmed that traumatized individuals respond to such stimuli with significant conditioned autonomic reactions—for example, increases in heart rate, skin conductance, and blood pressure. The highly elevated physiological responses accompanying the recall of traumatic experiences that happened years, and sometimes decades, before illustrate the intensity and timelessness with which traumatic memories continue to affect current experience.[3,16] This phenomenon has been understood in the light of Lang's work,[26] which shows that emotionally laden imagery correlates with measurable autonomic responses. Lang has proposed that emotional memories are stored as "associative networks" that are activated when a person is confronted with situations that stimulate a sufficient number of elements within such networks. One significant measure of treatment outcome that has become widely accepted in recent years is a decrease in physiological arousal in response to imagery related to the trauma.[27] However, Shalev and coworkers[28] have shown that desensitization to specific trauma-related mental images does not necessarily generalize to recollections of other traumatic events as well.

Kolb[29] was the first to propose that excessive stimulation of the central nervous system CNS at the time of the trauma may result in permanent neuronal changes that have a negative effect on learning habituation, and stimulus discrimination. These neuronal changes would not depend on actual exposure to reminders of the trauma for expression. The abnormal startle response characteristic of PTSD[10] exemplifies such neuronal changes.

Although abnormal acoustic startle response (ASR) has been seen as a cardinal feature of the trauma response for more than half a century, systematic explorations of the ASR in PTSD have just begun. The ASR is a characteristic sequence of muscular and autonomic responses elicited by sudden and intense stimuli.[30,31] The neuronal pathways involved consist of only a small number of mediating synapses between the receptor and effector and a large projection to brain areas responsible for CNS activation and stimulus evaluation.[31] The ASR is mediated by excitatory amino acids such as glutamate and aspartate and is modulated by a variety of neurotransmitters and second messengers at both the spinal and the supraspinal levels.[32] Habituation to the ASR in normal human subjects occurs after three to five presentations.[30]

Several studies[33–36] have shown abnormalities in habituation to the ASR in PTSD. Shalev and coworkers[33] found a failure to habituate to both CNS and autonomic nervous system-mediated responses to ASR in 93% of subjects in the PTSD group, compared with 22% of the control subjects. Interestingly, persons who previously met criteria for PTSD but no longer do so continue to show failure of habituation to the ASR (van der Kolk BA. et al., unpublished data, 1991–1992; Pitman RK. et al., unpublished data, 1991–1992), which raises the question of whether abnormal habituation to acoustic startle may be a marker or a vulnerability factor for development of PTSD.

The failure to habituate to acoustic startle suggests that traumatized people have difficulty evaluating sensory stimuli and mobilizing appropriate levels of physiological arousal.[30] Thus the inability of people with PTSD properly to integrate memories of the trauma and the tendency they have to get mired in a continuous reliving of the past are mirrored physiologically by the misinterpretation of innocuous stimuli, such as unexpected noises, as potential threats.

HORMONAL STRESS RESPONSE AND PSYCHOBIOLOGY

PTSD develops after exposure to events that are intensely distressing. Extreme stress is accompanied by the release of endogenous neurohormones, such as cortisol, epinephrine and norepinephrine, vasopressin, oxytocin, and endogenous opioids. These hormones help the organism to mobilize the energy required to deal with the stress; they induce reactions ranging from increased glucose release to enhanced immune function. In a well-functioning organism, stress produces rapid and pronounced hormonal responses. However, chronic and persistent stress inhibits the effectiveness of the stress response and induces desensitization.[37]

Much still remains to be learned about the specific roles of the different neurohormones in the stress response. Norepinephrine is secreted by the locus ceruleus and distributed through much of the CNS, particularly the neocortex and the limbic system, where it plays a role in memory consolidation and helps to initiate fight-or-flight behaviors. Corticotropin is released from the anterior pituitary and activates a cascade of reactions, eventuating in release of glucocorticoids from the adrenal glands. The precise interrelation between hypothalamic-pituitary-adrenal (HPA) axis hormones and the catecholamines in the stress response is not entirely clear, but it is known that stressors that activate norepinephrine neurons also increase the concentration of corticotropin-releasing factor in the locus ceruleus,[38] and intracerebral ventricular infusion of corticotropin-releasing factor increases norepinephrine in the forebrain.[39] Glucocorticoids and catecholamines may modulate each other's effects: in acute stress, cortisol helps to regulate the release of stress hormones via a negative feedback loop to the hippocampus, hypothalamus, and pituitary,[40] and there is evidence that corticosteroids normalize catecholamine-induced arousal in limbic midbrain structures in response to stress.[41] Thus the simultaneous activation of corticosteroids and catecholamines could stimulate active coping behaviors, whereas increased arousal in the presence of low glucocorticoid levels may promote undifferentiated fight-or-flight reactions.[42]

Although acute stress mobilizes the HPA axis and increases glucocorticoid levels, organisms adapt to chronic stress by activating a negative feedback loop that results in (1) decreased resting glucocorticoid levels,[43] (2) decreased glucocorticoid secretion in response to subsequent stress.[42] and '3' increased concentration of glucocorticoid receptors in the hippocampus.[44] Yehuda et al.[45] suggested that increased concentration of glucocorticoid receptors could facilitate a stronger negative glucocorticoid feedback, resulting in a more sensitive HPA axis and a faster recovery from acute stress.

Chronic exposure to stress affects both acute and chronic adaptation: it permanently alters how an organism deals with its environment on a day-to-day basis and interferes with how it copes with subsequent acute stress.[45]

NEUROENDOCRINE ABNORMALITIES

Because there is an extensive literature on the effects of inescapable stress on the biological stress response of animal species such as monkeys and rats, much of the biological research on people with PTSD has focused on testing the applicability of those research findings to human subjects with PTSD.[46,47] Subjects with PTSD, like chronically and inescapably shocked animals, seem to have a persistent activation of the biological stress response after exposure to stimuli reminiscent of the trauma (table 18.1).

Catecholamines

Neuroendocrine studies of Vietnam veterans with PTSD have found good evidence for chronically increased sympathetic nervous system activity in PTSD. One investigation[48] discovered elevated 24-hour urinary excretion of norepinephrine and epinephrine in PTSD combat veterans compared with patients who had other psychiatric diagnoses. Although Pitman and Orr[49] did not replicate these findings in 20 veterans and 15 combat control subjects, the mean urinary excretion of norepinephrine in their combat control subjects (58.0 µg/day) was substantially higher than values previously reported in normal populations. The expected compensatory down-regulation of adrenergic receptors in response to increased levels of norepinephrine was confirmed by a study[50] that found decreased platelet α_2-adrenergic receptors in combat veterans with PTSD compared with normal control subjects. Another study[51] also found an abnormally low α_2-adrenergic receptor-mediated adenylate cyclase signal transduction. Recently Southwick and colleagues[52] used yohimbine injections (0.4 mg kg, which activate noradrenergic neurons by blocking the α_2-autoreceptor, to study noradrenergic neuronal dysregulation in Vietnam

Table 18.1. Biological Abnormalities in PTSD

A. Psychophysiological
   1. Extreme autonomic responses to stimuli reminiscent of the trauma
   2. Nonhabituation to startle stimuli
B. Neurotransmitter
   1. Noradrenergic
      a. Elevated urinary catecholamines
      b. Increased MHPG to yohimbine challenge
      c. Reduced platelet MAO activity
      d. Down-regulation of adrenergic receptors
   2. Serotonergic
      a. Decreased serotonin activity in traumatized animals
      b. Best pharmacological responses to serotonin uptake inhibitors
   3. Endogenous opioids: increased opioid response to stimuli reminiscent of trauma
C. HPA axis
   1. Decreased resting glucocorticoid levels
   2. Decreased glucocorticoid response to stress
   3. Down-regulation of glucocorticoid receptors
   4. Hyperresponsiveness to low-dose dexamethasone
D. Memory
   1. Amnesias and hyperamnesias
   2. Traumatic memories precipitated by noradrenergic stimulation, physiological arousal
   3. Memories generally sensorimotor rather than semantic
E. Miscellaneous
   1. Traumatic nightmares often not oneiric but exact replicas of visual elements of trauma: may occur in stage II or III sleep
   2. Decreased hippocampal volume?
   3. Impaired psychoimmunologic functioning?

---

veterans with PTSD. Yohimbine precipitated panic attacks in 70% of subjects and flashbacks in 40%. Subjects responded with larger increases in plasma 3-methoxy-4-hydroxyphenylglycol (MHPG) than control subjects. Yohimbine precipitated significant increases in all PTSD symptoms.

Corticosteroids

Two studies[42,53] have shown that veterans with PTSD have low urinary excretion of cortisol, even when they have comorbid major depressive disorder. Other research[49] failed to replicate this finding. In a series of studies. Yehuda and coworkers[42,54] found increased numbers of lymphocyte glucocorticoid receptors in Vietnam veterans with PTSD. Interestingly, the number of glucocorticoid receptors was proportional to the severity of PTSD symptoms.

308 BESSEL A. VAN DER KOLK

Yehuda and coworkers[54] also reported the findings of an unpublished study by Heidi Resnick, in which acute cortisol response to trauma was studied in blood samples from 20 rape victims in the emergency room. Three months later, trauma histories were taken and the subjects were evaluated for the presence of PTSD. Development of PTSD after the rape was significantly more likely in victims with histories of sexual abuse than in victims with no such histories. Cortisol levels shortly after the rape were correlated with histories of previous assaults: the mean initial cortisol levels of individuals with assault histories were 15 μg/dl, compared with 30 μg/dl in the control subjects. These findings can be interpreted to mean that previous exposure to traumatic events results either in a blunted cortisol response to subsequent trauma or in a quicker return of cortisol to baseline after stress. That Yehuda and colleagues[45] also found subjects with PTSD to be hyperresponsive to low doses of dexamethasone argues for an enhanced sensitivity of the HPA feedback in traumatized patients.

Serotonin

Although the role of serotonin in PTSD has not been systematically investigated, the facts that decreased CNS serotonin levels develop in inescapably shocked animals[55] and that serotonin reuptake blockers are effective pharmacological agents in the treatment of PTSD justify a brief consideration of the potential role of this neurotransmitter in PTSD. Decreased serotonin in humans has been correlated repeatedly with impulsivity and aggression.[56–58] The authors of these investigations tend to assume that these relationships are based on genetic traits. However, studies of impulsive, aggressive, and suicidal patients, e.g., Green,[59] van der Kolk et al.,[60] and Lewis[61] seem to find at least as robust an association between those behaviors and histories of childhood trauma. Probably both temperament and experience affect relative serotonin levels in the CNS.[62]

Low serotonin levels in animals are also related to an inability to modulate arousal, as exemplified by an exaggerated startle response[62,63] and by increased arousal in reaction to novel stimuli, handling, or pain.[63] The behavioral effects of serotonin depletion in animals include hyperirritability, hyperexcitability, hypersensitivity, and an "exaggerated emotional arousal and or aggressive display to relatively mild stimuli."[63] These behaviors bear a striking resemblance to the phenomenology of PTSD in humans. Furthermore, serotonin reuptake inhibitors have been found to be the most effective pharmacological treatment for obsessive thinking in subjects with obsessive-compulsive disorder[64] and for involuntary preoccupation with traumatic memories in subjects with PTSD.[65,66] Serotonin probably plays a role in the capacity to monitor the environment flexibly and to respond with behaviors that are situation-appropriate, rather than reacting to internal stimuli that are irrelevant to current demands.

Endogenous Opioids

Stress-induced analgesia has been described in experimental animals after a variety of inescapable stressors such as electric shock, fighting, starvation, and cold water swim.[67] In severely stressed animals opiate withdrawal symptoms can be produced either by termination of the stress or by naloxone injections. Motivated by the findings that fear activates the secretion of endogenous opioid peptides and that stress-induced analgesia can become conditioned to subsequent stressors and to previously neutral events associated with the noxious stimulus, we tested the hypothesis that in subjects with PTSD, reexposure to a stimulus resembling the original trauma will cause an endogenous opioid response that can be indirectly measured as naloxone-reversible analgesia.[68,69] We found that 2 decades after the original trauma, opioid-mediated analgesia developed in subjects with PTSD in response to a stimulus resembling the traumatic stressor, which we correlated with a secretion of endogenous opioids equivalent to 8 mg of morphine. Self-reports of emotional responses suggested that endogenous opioids were responsible for a relative blunting of emotional response to the traumatic stimulus.

Endogenous Opioids and Stress-Induced Analgesia: Implications for Affective Function

When young animals are isolated or older ones are attacked, they respond initially with aggression (hyperarousal-fight-protest) and then, if that does not produce the required results, with withdrawal (numbing-flight-despair). Fear-induced attack or protest patterns serve in the young to attract protection and in mature animals to prevent or counteract the predator's activity. During external attacks, pain inhibition is a useful defensive capacity because attention to pain would interfere with effective defense: grooming or licking wounds may attract opponents and stimulate further attack.[70] Thus defensive and pain-motivated behaviors are mutually inhibitory. Stress-induced analgesia protects organisms against feeling pain while engaged in defensive activities. As early as 1946, Beecher,[71] after observing that 75% of severely wounded soldiers on the Italian front did not request morphine, speculated that "strong emotions can block pain." Today, we can reasonably assume that this is caused by the release of endogenous opioids.[68,69]

Endogenous opioids, which inhibit pain and reduce panic, are secreted after prolonged exposure to severe stress. Siegfried and colleagues[70] have observed that memory is impaired in animals when they can no longer actively influence the outcome of a threatening situation. They showed that both the freeze response and panic interfere with effective memory processing: excessive endogenous opioids and norepinephrine both interfere with the storage of experience in explicit memory. Freeze-numbing responses may serve the function of allowing organisms to not "consciously experience" or to not remember situations of overwhelming stress (thus also preventing their learning from experience). We have proposed that the dissociative reactions of subjects in response to trauma may be analogous to this complex of behaviors that occurs in animals after prolonged exposure to severe uncontrollable stress.[68]

DEVELOPMENTAL LEVEL AND THE PSYCHOBIOLOGICAL EFFECTS OF TRAUMA

Although most studies on PTSD have been done on adults, particularly war veterans in recent years a few prospective investigations have documented the differential effects of trauma at various age levels. Anxiety disorders, chronic hyperarousal, and behavioral disturbances have been regularly described in traumatized children (e.g., Bowlby,[72] Cicchetti,[73] and Terr[74]. In addition to the reactions to discrete, one-time, traumatic incidents documented in these studies, intrafamilial abuse is increasingly recognized to produce complex post-traumatic syndromes[75] that involve chronic affect dysregulation, destructive behavior against self and others, learning disabilities, dissociative problems, somatization, and distortions in concepts about self and other.[76,77] The Field Trials for DSM-IV showed that this conglomeration of symptoms tended to occur together and that the severity of the syndrome was proportional to the duration of the trauma and the age of the child when it began.[78]

Although current research on traumatized children is outside the scope of this review, it is important to recognize that a range of neurobiological abnormalities are beginning to be identified in this population. Frank Putnam's as-yet-unpublished prospective studies (personal communications, 1991, 1992, and 1993) are showing major neuroendocrine disturbances in sexually abused girls compared with nonabused girls. Research on the psychobiology of childhood trauma can be profitably informed by the vast literature on the psychobiological effects of trauma and deprivation in non-human primates.[12,79]

TRAUMA AND MEMORY

The Flexibility of Memory and the Engraving of Trauma

A century ago, Janet[1] suggested that the most fundamental of mental activities are the storage and categorization of incoming sensations into memory and the retrieval of those memories under appropriate circumstances. He, like contemporary memory researchers, understood that what is now called semantic, or declarative, memory is an active and constructive process and that remembering depends on existing mental schemata:[3,80] once an event or a particular bit of information is integrated into existing mental schemes, it will no longer be accessible as a separate, immutable entity but will be distorted both by previous experience and by the emotional state at the time of recall.[3] PTSD, by definition, is accompanied by memory disturbances that consist of both hypermnesias and amnesias.[9,10] Research into the nature of traumatic memories[3] indicates that trauma interferes with declarative memory (i.e., conscious recall of experience) but does not inhibit implicit, or nondeclarative, memory, the memory system that controls conditioned emotional responses, skills and habits, and sensorimotor sensations related to experience (figure 18.1). There is now enough information available about the biology of memory storage and retrieval to start building coherent hypotheses regarding the underlying psychobiological processes involved in these memory disturbances.[3,16,17,25]

Early in this century Janet[81] noted that "certain happenings . . . leave indelible and distressing memories—memories to which the sufferer continually

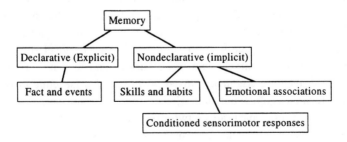

Figure 18.1. Schematic representation of different forms of memory.

returns, and by which he is tormented by day and by night." Clinicians and researchers dealing with traumatized patients have repeatedly observed that the sensory experiences and visual images related to the trauma seem not to fade over time and appear to be less subject to distortion than ordinary experiences.[1,49,82] When people are traumatized, they are said to experience "speechless terror": the emotional impact of the event may interfere with the capacity to capture the experience in words or symbols. Piaget[83] thought that under such circumstances, failure of semantic memory leads to the organization of memory on a somatosensory or iconic level (such as somatic sensations, behavioral enactments, nightmares, and flashbacks). He pointed out:

It is precisely because there is no immediate accommodation that there is complete dissociation of the inner activity from the external world. As the external world is solely represented by images, it is assimilated without resistance [i.e., unattached to other memories] to the unconscious ego.

The State Dependency of Traumatic Memories

Research has shown that under ordinary conditions many traumatized people, including rape victims,[84] battered women,[85] and abused children,[86] have a fairly good psychosocial adjustment. However, they do not respond to stress in the way that other people do. Under pressure they may feel or act as if they were being traumatized all over again. Thus high states of arousal seem selectively to promote retrieval of traumatic memories, sensory information, or behaviors associated with previous traumatic experiences.[9,10] The tendency of traumatized organisms to revert to irrelevant emergency behaviors in response to minor stress has been well documented in animals, as well. Studies at the Wisconsin Primate Laboratory have shown that rhesus monkeys with histories of severe early maternal deprivation display marked withdrawal or aggression in response to emotional or physical stimuli (such as exposure to loud noises or the administration of amphetamines), even after a long period of good social adjustment.[87] In experiments with mice, Mitchell and coworkers[88] found that the relative degree of arousal interacts with previous exposure to high stress to determine how an animal will react to novel stimuli. In a state of low arousal, animals tend to be curious and seek novelty. During high arousal, they are frightened, avoid novelty, and perseverate in familiar behavior, regardless of the outcome. Under ordinary circumstances, an animal will choose the more pleasant of two alternatives. When hyper-aroused, it will seek whatever is familiar, regardless of the intrinsic rewards. Thus animals that have been locked in a box in which they were exposed to electric shocks and then released return to those boxes when they are subsequently stressed. Mitchell and colleagues[88] concluded that this perseveration is non-associative (i.e, uncoupled from the usual reward systems).

Analogous phenomena have been documented in humans: memories (somatic or symbolic) related to the trauma are elicited by heightened arousal.[89] Information acquired in an aroused or otherwise altered state of mind is retrieved more readily when subjects are brought back to that particular state of mind.[90,91] State-dependent memory retrieval may also be involved in dissociative phenomena in which traumatized persons may be wholly or partially amnestic for memories or behaviors enacted while in altered states of mind.[2,3,92]

Contemporary biological researchers have shown that medications that stimulate autonomic arousal may precipitate visual images and affect states associated with previous traumatic experiences in people with PTSD but not in control subjects. In patients with PTSD, the injection of drugs such as lactate[93] and yohimbine[52] tends to precipitate panic attacks, flashbacks (exact reliving experiences) of earlier trauma, or both. In our own laboratory approximately 20% of PTSD subjects responded with a flashback of a traumatic experience when they were presented with acoustic startle stimuli.

Trauma, Neurohormones, and Memory Consolidation

When humans are under severe stress, they secrete endogenous stress hormones that affect the strength of memory consolidation. Based on animal models, researchers have widely assumed that massive secretion of neurohormones at the time of the trauma plays a role in the long-term potentiation (and thus, the overconsolidation) of traumatic memories.[3,46,94] Mammals seem to be equipped with memory-storage mechanisms that ordinarily modulate the strength of memory consolidation according to the strength of the accompanying hormonal stimulation.[95,96] This capacity helps the organism to evaluate the importance of subsequent sensory input according to the relative strength of associated memory traces. The phenomenon appears to be largely mediated by input of norepinephrine to the amygdala[97,98] (figure 18.2). In traumatized organisms the capacity to access relevant memories appears to have gone awry: they become overconditioned to access memory traces of the trauma and to "remember" the trauma whenever aroused. Although norepinephrine seems to be the principal hormone involved in producing long-term potentiation, other neuro-hormones secreted under particular stressful

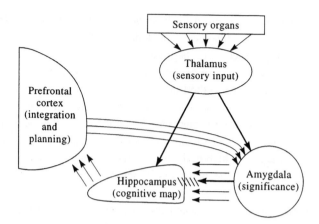

Figure 18.2. Schematic representation of the effects of emotional arousal on declarative memory. The thalamus, amygdala, and hippocampus are all involved in the integration and interpretation of incoming sensory information. Moderate to high activation of the amygdala enhances the long-term potentiation of declarative memory that is mediated by the hippocampus, accounting for hypermnesias for stressful experiences. Excessive stimulation of the amygdala interferes with hippocampal functioning, inhibiting cognitive evaluation of experience and semantic representation. Memories are then stored in sensorimotor modalities: somatic sensations and visual images. These emotional memories are thought to be relatively indelible, but their expression can be modified by feedback from the prefrontal cortex.[3,16,95,98,118]

circumstances (endorphins and oxytocin, for example actually inhibit memory consolidation.[99]

The role of norepinephrine in consolidating memory has been shown to have an inverted U-shaped function:[95,96] both very low and very high levels of norepinephrine activity in the CNS interfere with memory storage. The release of excessive norepinephrine, as well as of other neurohormones such as endogenous opioids, oxytocin, and vasopressin, at the time of the trauma probably plays a role in creating the hypermnesias and amnesias that are a quintessential part of PTSD.[9,10] Interestingly, childbirth, which can be extraordinarily stressful, almost never seems to result in posttraumatic problems.[100] Oxytocin may protect against the overconsolidation of memories surrounding childbirth.

Physiological arousal in general can trigger trauma-related memories: conversely, trauma-related memories precipitate generalized physiological arousal. The frequent reliving of a traumatic event in flashbacks or nightmares probably causes a rerelease of stress hormones that further kindles the strength of the memory trace.[40] Such a positive feedback loop could cause subclinical PTSD to escalate into clinical PTSD,[16] in which the strength of the memories appears to be so deeply engraved that Pitman and Orr[17] have called it "the black hole" in the mental life of the PTSD patient: it attracts all associations to it and saps current life of its significance.

MEMORY, TRAUMA, AND THE LIMBIC SYSTEM

The limbic system is thought to be the part of the CNS that maintains and guides the emotions and behavior necessary for self-preservation and for survival of the species[101] and is critically involved in the storage and retrieval of memory. During both waking and sleeping states, signals from the sensory organs continuously travel to the thalamus, from which they are distributed to the cortex (setting up a "stream of thought"), the basal ganglia (setting up a "stream of movement"), and the limbic system (setting up a "stream of emotions"[102] that determines the emotional significance of the sensory input). Most processing of sensory input occurs outside of conscious awareness, with only novel, significant, or threatening information being selectively passed on to the neocortex for further attention. Because subjects with PTSD appear to overinterpret sensory input as a recurrence of past trauma and because recent studies have suggested limbic-system abnormalities in brain-imaging studies of traumatized patients,[103,104] a review of the psychobiology of trauma would be incomplete without considering the role of the limbic system in PTSD (see also Teicher et al.)[105] Two particular areas of the limbic system have been implicated in the processing of emotionally charged memories: the amygdala and the hippocampus (table 18.2).

Table 18.2. Functions of Limbic Structures and Effects of Lesions

Hippocampus	Amygdala
Functions of limbic structures	
Categorization of experience	Conditioning of fear responses
Creation of a spatial map	Attachment of affect to neutral stimuli
Storage of simple memory	Establishment of associations between sensory modalities
Creation of summary sketch index	
Effects of lesions	
Declarative memory lost	Loss of fear responses
Skill-based memory spared	Meaningful social interaction lost
Immediate memory spared	Declarative memory intact

The Amygdala

Of all areas in the CNS, the amygdala is most clearly implicated in the evaluation of the emotional meaning of incoming stimuli.[106] Several investigators have proposed that the amygdala assigns free-floating feelings of significance to sensory input, which the neocortex then further elaborates and imbues with personal meaning.[101,106–108] Moreover, it is thought to integrate internal representations of the external world in the form of memory images with emotional experiences associated with those memories.[80] After assigning meaning to sensory information, the amygdala guides emotional behavior by projections to the hypothalamus, hippocampus, and basal forebrain.[106,107,109]

The Septohippocampal System

The septohippocampal system, which is adjacent to the amygdala, is thought to record in memory the spatial and temporal dimensions of experience and to play an important role in the categorization and storage of incoming stimuli in memory. Proper functioning of the hippocampus is necessary for explicit or declarative memory.[109] The hippocampus is believed to be involved in the evaluation of spatially and temporally unrelated events, comparing them with previously stored information and determining whether and how they are associated with each other and with reward, punishment, novelty, or nonreward.[107,110] The hippocampus also plays a role in the inhibition of exploratory behavior and in obsessional thinking. Damage to the hippocampus is associated with hyperresponsiveness to environmental stimuli.[111,112]

The slow maturation of the hippocampus, which is not fully myelinated until after the third or fourth year of life, is believed to be the cause of infantile amnesia.[113,114] In contrast, the memory system that encodes the affective quality of experience (roughly speaking, procedural, or "taxon," memory) matures earlier and is less subject to disruption by stress.[112] As the CNS matures, memory storage shifts from primarily sensorimotor (motoric action and perceptual representations (iconic) to symbolic and linguistic organization of mental experience.[83] With maturation, there is an increasing ability to categorize experience and link it with existing mental schemes. However, even as the organism matures, this capacity, and with it the hippocampal localization system, remains vulnerable to disruption.[45,107,110,115,116] Various external and internal stimuli, including stress-induced corticosterone production.[117] decrease hippocampal activity. However, even when stress interferes with hippocampally mediated memory storage and categorization, some mental representation of the experience is probably laid down by means of a system that records affective experience but has no capacity for symbolic processing or placement in space and time (figure 18.2).

Decreased hippocampal functioning causes behavioral disinhibition, possibly by causing incoming stimuli to be interpreted in the direction of "emergency" fight-or-flight) responses. The neurotransmitter serotonin plays a crucial role in the capacity of the septohippocampal system to activate inhibitory pathways that prevent the initiation of emergency responses until it is clear that they will be of use.[110] This observation made us very interested in a possible role for serotonergic agents in the treatment of PTSD.

"Emotional Memories Are Forever"

In animals high-level stimulation of the amygdala interferes with hippocampal functioning.[107,109] This implies that intense affect may inhibit proper evaluation and categorization of experience. One-time intense stimulation of the amygdala in mature animals will produce lasting changes in neuronal excitability and enduring behavioral changes in the direction of either fight or flight.[118] In kindling experiments with animals. Adamec and colleagues[119] showed that, after growth in amplitude of amygdaloid and hippocampal seizure activity, permanent alterations in limbic physiology cause lasting changes in defensiveness and predatory aggression. Preexisting "personality" played a significant role in the behavioral effects of stimulation of the amygdala in cats: animals that are temperamentally insensitive to threat and prone to attack tend to become more aggressive, whereas defensive animals show increased behavioral inhibition.[119]

In a series of experiments, LeDoux and coworkers[118] used repeated electrical stimulation of the amygdala to produce conditioned fear responses. They found that cortical lesions prevent their extinction. This led them to conclude that, once formed, the subcortical traces of the conditioned fear response are indelible, and that "emotional memory may be forever." In 1987 Kolb[29] postulated that patients with PTSD suffer from impaired cortical control over the subcortical areas responsible for learning, habituation, and stimulus discrimination. The concept of indelible subcortical emotional responses, held in check to varying degrees by cortical and septohippocampal activity, has led to the speculation that delayed-onset PTSD may be the expression of subcortically mediated emotional responses that escape cortical, and possibly hippocampal, inhibitory control.[3,16,94,120,121]

Decreased inhibitory control may occur under a variety of circumstances:

under the influence of drugs and alcohol, during sleep (as in nightmares), with aging, and after exposure to strong reminders of the traumatic past. Conceivably, traumatic memories then could emerge, not in the distorted fashion of ordinary recall but as affect states, somatic sensations, or visual images (for example, nightmares[81] or flashbacks)[52] that are timeless and unmodified by further experience.

PSYCHOPHARMACOLOGICAL TREATMENT

The goal of treating PTSD is to help people live in the present, without feeling or behaving according to irrelevant demands belonging to the past. Psychologically, this means that traumatic experiences need to be located in time and place and differentiated from current reality. However, hyperarousal, intrusive reliving, numbing, and dissociation get in the way of separating current reality from past trauma. Hence, medications that affect these PTSD symptoms are often essential for patients to begin to achieve a sense of safety and perspective from which to approach their tasks.

Although numerous articles have been written about the drug treatment of PTSD, to date only 134 people with PTSD have been enrolled in published double-blind studies. Most of these have been Vietnam combat veterans. Unfortunately, until recently only medications that seem to be of limited therapeutic usefulness have been subjected to adequate scientific scrutiny. Because the only published double-blind studies of medications for treating PTSD have involved tricyclic antidepressants and monoamine oxidase (MAO) inhibitors,[122–124] it is sometimes assumed that these agents are the most effective. Three double-blind trials of tricyclic antidepressants have been published;[122,124–126] two showed modest improvement in PTSD symptoms. Although positive results have been claimed for numerous other medications in case reports and open studies, at the present time there are no data about which patient and which PTSD symptom will predictably respond to any of them. Success has been claimed for just about every class of psychoactive medication, including benzodiazepines.[127] tricyclic antidepressants,[122,125,128] MAO inhibitors,[122,129] lithium carbonate.[127] β-adrenergic blockers,[130] clonidine,[130] carbamazapine,[131] and antipsychotic agents. The accumulated clinical experience seems to indicate that understanding the basic neurobiology of arousal and appraisal is the most useful guide in selecting medications for people with PTSD.[124,125] Autonomic arousal can be reduced at different levels in the CNS: through inhibiting noradrenergic activity in the locus ceruleus with clonidine and the β-adrenergic blockers,[130,132] or by increasing the inhibitory effect of the γ-aminobutyric acid (GABA)-ergic system with GABA-ergic agonists (the benzodiazepines). During the past 2 years several case reports and open clinical trials of fluoxetine have been published, followed by our double-blind study of 64 PTSD subjects treated with fluoxetine.[82] Unlike the tricyclic antidepressants, which were effective on either the intrusive (imipramine) or numbing (amitriptyline) symptoms of PTSD, fluoxetine proved to be effective for the entire spectrum of PTSD symptoms. It also acted more rapidly than the tricyclics. The fact that fluoxetine has proved to be such an effective treatment for PTSD supports a larger role for the serotonergic system in PTSD.[66] Rorschach tests administered by "blinded" scorers revealed that subjects taking fluoxetine became able to achieve distance from the emotional impact of incoming stimuli and to use cognition in harnessing emotional responses to unstructured visual stimuli (van der Kolk et al., unpublished data. 1991–1992).

Although the subjects improved clinically, their startle habituation worsened (van der Kolk et al., unpublished data, 1991–1992). The 5-HT_{1A} agonist buspirone shows some promise in facilitating habituation[133] and thus may play a useful adjunctive role in the pharmacotherapy of PTSD. Even newer research has suggested abnormalities of the N-methyl-D-aspartate receptor and of glutamate in PTSD.[134] opening up potential new avenues for the psychopharmacological treatment of this disorder.

The author wishes to thank Rita Fisler, EdM, for her editorial assistance.

REFERENCES

1. Janet P. L'automatisme psychologique. Paris: Alcan. 1889.
2. van der Kolk B A, van der Hart O. Pierre Janet and the breakdown of adaptation in psychological trauma. Am J Psychiatry 1989;146:1530–40.
3. van der Kolk B A, van der Hart O. The intrusive past: the flexibility of memory and the engraving of trauma. Am Imago 1991; 48:425–54.
4. Freud S. Introduction to psychoanalysis and the war neuroses. Standard ed 17: 207–10. Strachey J. trans/ed. London: Hogarth Press, 1919/1954.
5. Pavlov I P. Conditioned reflexes: an investigation of the physiological activity of the cerebral cortex. Anrep G V. trans ed. New York: Dover Publications, 1926.
6. Kardiner A. The traumatic neuroses of war. New York: Hoeber, 1941.
7. Grinker R R, Spiegel J J. Men under stress. New York: McGraw-Hill, 1945.
8. Lindemann E. Symptomatology and management of acute grief. Am J Psychiatry 1944;101:141–8.
9. American Psychiatric Association. Diagnostic and statistical manual of mental disorders. 3rd ed. revised. Washington, DC: American Psychiatric Association, 1987.

320   BESSEL A. VAN DER KOLK

10. American Psychiatric Association. Diagnostic and statistical manual of mental disorders. 4th ed. revised. Washington, DC: American Psychiatric Association, 1994.
11. Horowitz M. Stress response syndromes. 2nd ed. New York: Jason Aronson, 1978.
12. van der Kolk B A. Psychological trauma. Washington, DC: American Psychiatric Press, 1987.
13. Kulka R A, Schlenger W E, Fairbank J A, Hough R L, Jordan B K, Marmar C R. Trauma and the Vietnam War generation: report of findings from the National Vietnam Veterans' Readjustment Study. New York: Brunner Mazel, 1990.
14. McFarlane A C. The longitudinal course of posttraumatic morbidity: the range of outcomes and their predictors. J Nerv Ment Dis 1988;176:30–9.
15. Litz B T, Keane T M. Information processing in anxiety disorders: application to the understanding of post-traumatic stress disorder. Clin Psychol Rev 1989;9: 243–57.
16. Pitman R, Orr S, Shalev A. Once bitten twice shy: beyond the conditioning model of PTSD. Biol Psychiatry 1993;33:145–6.
17. Pitman R, Orr S. The black hole of trauma. Biol Psychiatry 1990;26:221–3.
18. Krystal H. Trauma and affects. Psychoanal Study Child 1978; 33:81–116.
19. Strian F, Klicpera C. Die Bedeutung psychoautonomische Reaktionen im Entstehung und Persistenz von Angstzustanden. Nervenarzt 1978;49:576–83.
20. van der Kolk B A, Ducey C P. The psychological processing of traumatic experience: Rorschach patterns in PTSD. J Traum Stress 1989;2:259–74.
21. Dobbs D, Wilson W P. Observations on the persistence of traumatic war neurosis. J Ment Nerv Dis 1960;21:40–6.
22. Malloy P F, Fairbank J A, Keane T M. Validation of a multi-method assessment of post traumatic stress disorders in Vietnam veterans. J Consult Clin Psychol 1983; 51:4–21.
23. Kolb L C, Multipassi L R. The conditioned emotional response: a subclass of chronic and delayed post traumatic stress disorder. Psychiatr Ann 1982;12:979–87.
24. Blanchard E B, Kolb L C, Gerardi R J. Cardiac response to relevant stimuli as an adjunctive tool for diagnosing post traumatic stress disorder in Vietnam veterans. Behav Ther 1986;17:592–606.
25. Pitman R K, Orr S P, Forgue D F, de Jong J, Claiborn J M. Psychophysiologic assessment of posttraumatic stress disorder imagery in Vietnam combat veterans. Arch Gen Psychiatry 1987;44:970–5.
26. Lang P J. A bio-informational theory of emotional imagery. Psychophysiology 1979;16:495–512.
27. Keane T M, Kaloupek D G. Imaginal flooding in the treatment of post-traumatic stress disorder. J Consult Clin Psychol 1982;50:138–40.
28. Shalev A Y, Orr S P, Peri T, Schreiber S, Pitman R K. Physiologic responses to loud tones in Israeli patients with posttraumatic stress disorder. Arch Gen Psychiatry 1992;49:870–5.
29. Kolb L C. Neurophysiological hypothesis explaining posttraumatic stress disorder. Am J Psychiatry 1987;144:989–95.

30. Shalev A Y, Rogel-Fuchs Y. Psychophysiology of PTSD: from sulfur fumes to behavioral genetics. J Ment Nerv Dis 1995.

31. Davis M. The mammalian startle response. In: Eaton R C, ed. Neural mechanisms of startle behavior. New York: Plenum Press. 1984.

32. Davis M. Pharmacological and anatomical analysis of fear conditioning using the fear-potentiated startle paradigm. Behav Neurosci 1986;100:814–24.

33. Shalev A Y, Orr S P, Peri T, Schreiber S, Pitman R K. Physiologic responses to loud tones in Israeli patients with post traumatic stress disorder. Arch Gen Psychiatry 1993;49:870–5.

34. Ornitz E M, Pynoos R S. Startle modulation in children with post traumatic stress disorder. Am J Psychiatry 1989;146:866–70.

35. Butler R W, Braff D L, Rausch J L, Jenkins M A, Sprock J, Geyer M A. Physiological evidence of exaggerated startle response in a subgroup of Vietnam veterans with combat-related PTSD. Am J Psychiatry 1990;147:1308–12.

36. Ross R J, Ball W A, Cohen M E. Habituation of the startle response in post traumatic stress disorder. J Neuropsychiatry 1989;1:305–7.

37. Axelrod J, Reisine T D. Stress hormones, their interaction and regulation. Science 1984;224:452–9.

38. Dunn A J, Berridge C W. Corticoptropin-releasing factor administration elicits stresslike activation of cerebral catecholamine systems. Pharmacol Biochem Behav 1987;27:685–91.

39. Valentino R J, Foote S L. Corticotropin releasing hormone increases tonic, but not sensory-evoked activity of noradrenergic locus coeruleus in unanesthetized rats. J Neurosci 1988;8:1016–25.

40. Munck A, Guyre P M, Holbrook N J. Physiological functions of glucocorticoids in stress and their relation to pharmacological actions. Endocr Rev 1984:93:9779–83.

41. Bohus B, DeWied D. Pituitary-adrenal system hormones and adaptive behavior. In: Chester-Jones I., Henderson I W, eds. General, comparative, and clinical endocrinology of the adrenal cortex, vol 3. New York: Academic Press, 1978.

42. Yehuda R, Southwick S M, Mason J W, Giller E L. Interactions of the hypothalamic-pituitary adrenal axis and the catechola-minergic system in posttraumatic stress disorder. In: Giller E L, ed. Biological assessment and treatment of PTSD. Washington, DC: American Psychiatric Press, 1990.

43. Meaney M J, Aitken D H, Viau V, Sharma S, Sarieau A. Neonatal handling alters adrenocortical negative feedback sensitivity and hippocampal type II glucocorticoid binding in the rat. Neuroendocrinology 1989;50:597–604.

44. Sapolsky R, Krey L, McEwen B S. Stress down-regulates corticosterone receptors in a site specific manner in the brain. Endocrinology 1984;114:287–92.

45. Yehuda R, Giller E L, Southwick S M, Lowy M T, Mason J W. Hypothalmic-pituitary-adrenal dysfunction in posttraumatic stress disorder. Biol Psychiatry 1991;30:1031–48.

46. van der Kolk B A, Greenberg M S, Boyd H. Krystal J H. Inescapable shock, neurotransmitters and addiction to trauma: towards a psychobiology of post traumatic stress. Biol Psychiatry 1985;20:314–25.

47. Krystal J H, Kosten T R, Southwick S, Mason J W, Perry B D, Giller E L. Neuro-

biological aspects of PTSD: review of clinical and preclinical studies. Behav Ther 1989;20:177–98.

48. Kosten T R, Mason J W, Giller E L, Ostroff R B, Harkness L. Sustained urinary norepinephrine and epinephrine elevation in PTSD. Psychoneuroendocrinology 1987;12:13–20.

49. Pitman R K, Orr S P. Twenty-four hour urinary cortisol and cathecholamine excretion in combat-related post-traumatic stress disorder. Biol Psychiatry 1990; 27:245–7.

50. Perry B D, Giller E L, Southwick S M. Altered plasma alpha-2 adrenergic receptor affinity states in PTSD. Am J Psychiatry 1987;144:1511–2.

51. Lerer B, Bleich A, Kotler M. Post traumatic stress disorder in Israeli combat veterans: effect of phenylzine treatment. Arch Gen Psychiatry 1987;44:976–81.

52. Southwick S M, Krystal J H, Morgan A, Johnson D, Nagy L, Nicolaou A, et al. Abnormal noradrenergic function in post traumatic stress disorder. Arch Gen Psychiatry 1993;50:266–74.

53. Mason J, Giller E L, Kosten T R. Elevated norepinephrine/cortisol ratio in PTSD. J Ment Nerv Dis 1988;176:498–502.

54. Yehuda R, Lowy M T, Southwick S M. Lymphocyte glucortoid receptor number in posttraumatic stress disorder. Am J Psychiatry 1991;148:499–504.

55. Valzelli L. Serotonergic inhibitory control of experimental aggression. Psycho-pharmacol Res Commun 1982;12:1–13.

56. Brown G L, Ballenger J C, Minichiello M D, Goodwin F K. Human aggression and its relationship to cerebrospinal fluid 5-hydroxy-indolacetic acid, 3-methoxy-4-hydroxy-phenyl-glycol, and homovannilic acid. In: Sandler M, ed. Psychopharmacology of aggression. New York: Raven Press. 1979.

57. Mann J D. Psychobiologic predictors of suicide. J Clin Psychiatry 1987;48:39–43.

58. Coccaro E F, Siever L J, Klar H M, Maurer G. Serotonergic studies in patients with affective and personality disorders. Arch Gen Psychiatry 1989;46:587–98.

59. Green A H. Self-destructive behavior in battered children. Am J Psychiatry 1978; 135:579–82.

60. van der Kolk B A, Perry J C, Herman J L. Childhood origins of self-destructive behavior. Am J Psychiatry 1991;148:1665–71.

61. Lewis D O. From abuse to violence: psychophysiological consequences of maltreatment. J Am Acad Child Adolesc Psychiatry 1992; 31:383–91.

62. Gerson S C, Baldessarini R J. Motor effects of serotonin in the central nervous system. Life Sci 1980; 27:1435–51.

63. Dupue R A, Spoont M R. Conceptualizing a serotonin trait: a behavioral model of constraint. Ann NY Acad Sci 1989; 12:47–62.

64. Jenike M A, Baer L, Summergrad P, Minichiello W E, Holland A, Seymour K. Sertroline in obsessive-compulsive disorder: a double blind study. Am J Psychiatry 1990; 147:923–8.

65. van der Kolk B A, Dreyfuss D, Michaels M, Saxe G, Berkowitz R. Fluoxetine in post traumatic stress disorder. J. Clin Psychiatry [1995].

66. van der Kolk B A, Saporta J. The biological response to psychic trauma: mechanisms and treatment of intrusion and numbing! Anxiety Res 1991; 4:199–212.

67. Akil H, Watson S J, Young E. Endogenous opioids: biology and function. Annu Rev Neurosci 1983; 7:223–55.

68. van der Kolk B A, Greenberg M S, Orr S P, Pitman R K. Endogenous opioids and stress induced analgesia in post traumatic stress disorder. Psychopharmacol Bull 1989; 25:108–12.

69. Pitman R K, van der Kolk B A, Orr S P, Greenberg M S. Naloxone reversible stress induced analgesia in post traumatic stress disorder. Arch Gen Psychiatry 1990; 47:541–7.

70. Siegfried B, Frischknecht H R, Nunez de Souza R. An ethological model for the study of activation and interaction of pain, memory and defensive systems in the attacked mouse: role of endogenous opoids Neurosci Biobehav Rev 1990; 14: 481–90.

71. Beecher H K. Pain in men wounded in battle. Ann Surg 1946; 123:96–105.

72. Bowlby J. Attachment and loss. vol 1. New York: Basic Books. 1969.

73. Cicchetti D. The emergence of developmental psychopathology. Child Dev. 1985; 55:1–7.

74. Terr L C. Childhood traumas an outline and overview. Am J Psychiatry 1991; 148:10–20.

75. Cole P M, Putnam F W. Effect of incest on self and social functioning: a developmental psychopathology perspective. J. Consult Clin Psychol 1991; 60:174–84.

76. van der Kolk B A. The trauma spectrum: the interaction of biological and social events in the genesis of the trauma response. J Traum Stress 1988; 1:273–90.

77. Herman J L. Complex PTSD: a syndrome in survivors of prolonged and repeated trauma. J Traum Stress 1992; 5:377–91.

78. van der Kolk B A, Roth S. Pelcovitz D. Field trials for DSM IV. post traumatic stress disorder II: disorders of extreme stress. Washington. DC: American Psychiatric Association, 1992.

79. Reite M, Field T, eds. The psychobiology of attachment and separation. Orlando. Florida: Academic Press. 1985.

80. Calvin W H. The cerebral symphony. New York: Bantam Books. 1990.

81. Janet P. Les medications psychologiques. Paris: Felix Alcan. 1919/1925.

82. van der Kolk B A, Blitz R, Burr W, Hartmann E. Nightmares and trauma. Am J Psychiatry 1984; 141:187–90.

83. Piaget J. Play, dreams, and imitation in childhood. New York: W W Norton. 1962.

84. Kilpatrick D G, Veronen L J, Best C L. Factors predicting psychological distress in rape victims. In: Figley C, ed. Trauma and its wake. New York: Brunner/Mazel, 1985.

85. Hilberman E, Munson M. Sixty battered women. Victimology 1978; 2:460–1.

86. Green A. Child maltreatment. New York: Aronson, 1980.

87. Kraemer G W. Effects of differences in early social experiences on primate neurobiological-behavioral development. In: Reite M, Field T, eds. The psychobiology of attachment and separation. Orlando, Florida: Academic Press, 1985.

88. Mitchell D, Osborne E W, O'Boyle M W. Habituation under stress: shocked mice show non-associative learning in a T-maze. Behav Neurol Biol 1985; 43:212–7.

89. Solomon Z, Garb R. Bleich A, Grupper D. Reactivation of combat-related post-traumatic stress disorder. Am J Psychiatry 1985; 144:51–5.

90. Phillips A G, LePiane F G. Disruption of conditioned taste aversion in the rat by stimulation of amygdala: a conditioning effect, not amnesia. J Comp Physiol Psychol 1980; 94:664–74.

91. Rawlins J N P. Associative and non-associative mechanisms in the development of tolerance for stress: the problem of state dependent learning. In: Levine S, Ursin H. eds. Coping and health. New York: Plenum Press. 1980.

92. Putnam F W. Diagnosis and treatment of multiple personality disorder. New York: Guilford Press. 1989.

93. Rainey J M, Aleem A, Ortiz A, Yaragani V, Pohl R, Berchow R. Laboratory procedure for the inducement of flashbacks. Am J Psychiatry 1987; 144:1317–9.

94. Charney D S, Deutch A Y, Krystal J H, Southwick S M, Davis M. Psychobiologic mechanisms of post traumatic stress disorder. Arch Gen Psychiatry 1993; 50: 294–305.

95. McGaugh J L, Weinberger N M, Lynch G, Granger R H. Neural mechanisms of learning and memory: cells, systems and computations. Naval Res Rev 1985; 37:15–29.

96. McGaugh J L. Involvement of hormonal and neuromodulatory systems in the regulation of memory storage. Ann Rev Neurosci 1989; 2:255–87.

97. LeDoux J E. Information flow from sensation to emotion: plasticity of the neural computation of stimulus value. In: Gabriel M, Morre J, eds. Learning computational neuro-science: foundations of adaptive networks. Cambridge. Massachusetts: MJT Press. 1990.

98. Adamec R E. Normal and abnormal limbic system mechanisms of emotive biasing. In: Livingston K E, Hornykiewicz O, eds. Limbic mechanisms. New York, Plenum Press. 1978.

99. Zager E L, Black P M. Neuropeptides in human memory and learning processes. Neurosurgery 1985; 17:355–69.

100. Moleman N, van der Hart O, van der Kolk B A. The partus stress reaction: a neglected etiological factor in post-partum psychiatric disorders. J Nerv Ment Dis 1992; 180:271–2.

101. MacLean P D. Brain evolution relating to family, play, and the separation call. Arch Gen Psychiatry 1985; 42:405–17.

102. Papez J W. A proposed mechanism of emotion. Arch Neurol Psychiatry 1937; 38:725–43.

103. Saxe G N, Vasile R G, Hill T C, Bloomingdale K, van der Kolk B A SPECT imaging and multiple personality disorder. J Nerv Ment Dis 1992; 180:662–3.

104. Bremner J D, Seibyl J P, Scott T M. Depressed hippocampal volume in posttraumatic stress disorder [New Research Abstract 155]. Proceedings of the 145th Annual Meeting of the American Psychiatric Association, Washington, DC, May 1992.

105. Teicher M H, Glod C A, Surrey J, Swett C. Early childhood abuse and limbic system ratings in adult psychiatric outpatients. J Neuropsychiatry Clin Neurosci [1995].

106. *LeDoux J. Mind and brain: dialogues in cognitive neuro-science. New York: Cambridge University Press, 1986.*

107. *Adamec R E. Partial kindling of the ventral hippocampus: identification of changes in limbic physiology which accompany changes in feline aggression and defense. Physiol Behav 1991; 49:443–54.*

108. *O'Keefe J, Bouma H. Complex sensory properties of certain amygdala units in the freely moving cat. Exp Neurol 1969; 23:384–98.*

109. *Squire L R, Zola-Morgan S. The medial temporal lobe memory system. Science 1991; 253:2380–6.*

110. *Gray J. The neuropsychology of anxiety. An inquiry into the functions of the septo-hippocampal system. London: Oxford University Press. 1982.*

111. *Altman J, Brunner R L, Bayer S A, The hippocampus and behavioral maturation. Behav Biol 1973; 8:557–96.*

112. *O'Keefe J. Nadel L. The hippocampus as a cognitive map. Oxford: Clarendon Press. 1978.*

113. *Jacobs W J, Nadel L. Stress-induced recovery of fears and phobias. Psychol Rev 1985; 92:512–31.*

114. *Schacter D L. Moscovitch M. Infants, amnesics, and dissociable memory systems. In: Moscovitch M. ed. Infant memory. New York: Plenum Press. 1984.*

115. *Nadel L, Zola-Morgan S. Infantile amnesia: a neurobiological perspective. In: Moscovitch M. ed. Infant memory. New York: Plenum Press. 1984.*

116. *Sapolsky R M, Hideo U, Rebert C S, Finch C E. Hippocampal damage associated with prolonged glucocorticoid exposure in primates. J Neurosci 1990; 10: 2897–902.*

117. *Pfaff D W, Silva M T, Weiss J M. Telemetered recording of hormone effects on hippocampal neurons. Science 1971; 172:394–5.*

118. *LeDoux J E, Romanski L, Xagoraris A. Indelibility of subcortical emotional memories. J Cogn Neurosci 1991; 1:238–43.*

119. *Adamec R E, Stark-Adamec C. Livingston K E. The development of predatory aggression and defense in the domestic cat. Neural Biol 1980; 30:389–447.*

120. *Nijenhuis F. Multiple personality disorder, hormones, and memory. Paper presented at the International Conference on Multiple Personality Disorder, Chicago, Illinois, November 5, 1991.*

121. *Shalev A, Rogel-Fuchs Y, Pitman R. Conditioned fear and psychological trauma. Biol Psychiatry 1992; 31:863–5.*

122. *Frank J B, Kosten T R, Giller E L, Dan E. A randomized clinical trial of phenelzine and imipramine in PTSD. Am J Psychiatry 1988; 145:1289–91.*

123. *Bleich A, Siegel B, Garb B, Kottler A, Lerer B. PTSD following combat exposure: clinical features and pharmacological management. Br J Psychiatry 1987; 149:365–9.*

124. *Davidson J R T, Nemeroff C B. Pharmacotherapy in PTSD: historical and clinical considerations and future directions. Psychopharmacol Bull 1989; 25:422–5.*

125. *Reist C, Kauffman C D, Haier R J. A controlled trial of desipramine in 18 men with post-traumatic stress disorder. Am J Psychiatry 1989; 146:513–6.*

126. Davidson J, Kudler H, Smith R. *Treatment of post-traumatic stress disorder with amitriptyline and placebo.* Arch Gen Psychiatry 1990; 47:259–66.

127. van der Kolk B A. *Drug treatment of post traumatic stress disorder.* J Affective Disord 1987; 13:203–13.

128. Falcon S, Ryan C, Chamberlain K. *Tricyclics: possible treatment for posttraumatic stress disorder.* J Clin Psychiatry 1985; 46:385–9.

129. Hogben G L, Cornfield R B. *Treatment of traumatic war neurosis with phenelzine.* Arch Gen Psychiatry 1981; 38:440–5.

130. Kolb L C, Burris B C, Griffiths S. *Propranolol and clonidine in the treatment of post traumatic stress disorders of war.* In: van der Kolk B A ed. *Post traumatic stress disorder: psychological and biological sequelae.* Washington, DC: American Psychiatric Press, 1984.

131. Lipper S, Davidson J R T, Grady T A, Edinger J D, Hammett E B. Mahorney S L, et al. *Preliminary study of carbamazepine in post-traumatic stress disorder.* Psychosomatics 1986; 27:849–54.

132. Famularo R, Kinscherff R. Fenton T. *Propanolol treatment for childhood post-traumatic stress disorder, acute type: a pilot study.* Am J Dis Child 1988; 142: 1244–7.

133. Giral P, Martin P, Soubrie P. *Reversal of helpless behavior in rats by putative 5-HT_{1A} agonists.* Biol Psychiatry 1988; 23:237–42.

134. Krystal J. Neurobiological mechanisms of dissociation. Paper presented at the American Psychiatric Association Meeting, San Francisco, California, May 1993.

PART III

Introduction

Different authorities disagree on the relative values for psychodynamic, cognitive, behavioral, and pharmacological modalities of treatment. I advise the reader to take a both/and, rather than an either/or, stance. That means, in the future, that we can expect an integration of many techniques to emerge out of a central theory. For now we need case formulation and a tailor-made program depending on indices in each individual patient (Horowitz, 1997). Let me also note that I do not endorse the theories or treatments in every paper that I have included. I selected them to enlighten new readers to controversies.

REFERENCE

Horowitz, M. Formulation as a basis for planning psychotherapy treatment. Washington D.C.: Amer. Psychiatric Press, 1997.

19. Stress Response Syndromes
Character Style and Dynamic Psychotherapy

Mardi J. Horowitz

STRESS RESPONSE SYNDROMES are the topic, but the larger aim of this report is to test a model for organizing clinical knowledge. The model integrates variables that characterize current state, personal style, and treatment technique. To reduce information to a coherent level, particular categories along each dimension are designated. The interactions are then examined. Here, a particular domain is circumscribed by state in terms of stress response syndromes, disposition in terms of obsessional and hysterical personality, and by treatment in terms of focal psychodynamic psychotherapy. If this model works for circumscribing a domain and assembling assertions within it, then it can be used with other states, styles, and treatments. The resulting organization of clinical knowledge would allow a clear focus for resolution of disputes about observation and therapy.

RATIONALE FOR CHOICES

State: Stress Response Syndromes

Stress response syndromes have been chosen because the general symptomatic tendencies are well documented, observed across various populations, and usually change rapidly during psychotherapy. External stress events are usually clear and provide the therapist with a point of reference for consideration of other material.

Disposition: Hysterical and Obsessional Neurotic Styles

"Obsessional" and "hysterical" styles are classical typologies in dynamic psychology. Theorization about these styles is at the same level of abstraction

---

Reprinted by permission from *Archives of General Psychiatry*, 31, 768–781. Copyright © by the American Medical Association, 1974.

as theories of stress, in that both stress response syndromes and obsessional and hysterical styles have been described in terms of potentially conscious cognitive and emotional processes. Information processing theory will thus provide a useful language. [1-3]

Technique: Crisis-Oriented Psychodynamic Therapy

The goals of psychotherapy are infinite. Here they will be limited to conceptual and emotional working through of the stress response syndrome to a point of relative mastery, a state in which both denial and compulsive repetition are reduced or absent.

Nuances of techniques such as repetition, clarification, and interpretation will be focused on, since these maneuvers are on an information processing level of abstraction. The nature of the relationship between patient and therapist will also be examined, but the complexities of transference and resistance will not be discussed in detail.

The basic knowledge relevant to each choice will now be summarized and followed by development of their interactions.

The Natural Course of Stress Response Syndromes

Multiple meanings confound the use of the word "stress." In psychiatry, the central application is concerned with the stress event that triggers internal responses and evokes potentially disruptive quantities or qualities of information and energy. A prototype of a stress event is a highway accident and an elaboration of this prototype will be used to provide a concrete reference for what follows.

Before developing this example, some reminders set the stage. Freud and Bruer[4] found that traumatic events were repressed and yet involuntarily repeated in the form of hysterical symptoms. While some "reminiscences" of their hysterical patients stemmed more from fantasy than from reality, the central observation of compulsive repetition of trauma was validated in many later clinical, field, and experimental studies.[5-8] A second common set of stress responses includes ideational denial and emotional numbing. These signs seem antithetical to intrusive repetitions and are regarded as a defensive response.[9-11] Tendencies to both intrusive repetition and denial-numbing occur in populations that vary in predisposition, after stressful events that vary in intensity and quality, and may occur simultaneously in a given person or in patterns of phasic alteration.

There is a common pattern to the progression of phases of stress response. With the onset of the stress event, especially if it is sudden and unanticipated, there may be emotional reactions such as crying out or a stunned uncomprehending daze. After these first emotional reactions and physical responses, there may be a period of comparative denial and numbing. Then an oscillatory period commonly emerges in which there are episodes of intrusive ideas or images, attacks of emotion, or compulsive behaviors alternating with continued denial, numbing, and other indications of efforts to ward off the implications of the new information. Finally, a phase of "working through" may occur in which there are less intrusive thoughts and less uncontrolled attacks of emotion with greater recognition, conceptualization, stability of mood, and acceptance of the meanings of the event.[11-13]

THEORY OF PSYCHIC TRAUMA

Freud's theories about trauma have two important aspects: the neurotic and energic definitions of traumatization. In early theory, a traumatic event was defined as such because it was followed by neurotic symptoms. To avoid circularity, a theoretical explanation of traumatization was necessary. The energic explanation defined as traumatic those events that led to excessive incursions of stimuli. In a series of energy metaphors, stimuli from the outer world were postulated to exceed a "stimulus barrier" or "protective shield." The ego tried to restore homeostasis by "discharging," "binding," or "abreacting" the energy. Energy, instinctual drives, and emotions were often conceptually blended together in this model.[14-15]

While Freud repeated energy metaphors throughout his writings, he also conceptualized trauma in cognitive terms more compatible with contemporary psychodynamic models. As early as 1893 in his lecture "On the Psychical Mechanism of Hysterical Phenomena," he spoke of how one could deal with the affect of a psychic trauma by working it over associatively and producing contrasting ideas.[16] Also, implicit in his formulations of signal anxiety is the concept of ideational appraisal of events and their implications.[17]

The concept of information overload can be substituted for excitation or energy overload.[3,18] Information applies to ideas of inner and outer origin as well as to affects. The persons remain in a state of stress or are vulnerable to recurrent states of stress until this information is processed. It is the information that is both repressed and compulsively repeated until processing is relatively complete. Emotions, which play such an important part in stress response syndromes, are not seen as drive or excitation derivatives, but as responses to ideational incongruities and as motives for defense, control, and coping behavior. This view of the centrality of ideational processing is consistent with French's conceptualization of integrative fields [19] and the concept of emotion with ideational incongruities is concordant with cognitive formulations of emotion,[20] and cognitive-neurophysiological formulations.[21]

Prototypic Example

These generalizations will be given concrete reference in the form of a story. The story is intended as a prototype and will be elaborated in various ways as an exercise. That is, the story will allow a hypothetical constancy of events and problems but a variation in personality style. We shall imagine this story as if it happened to two persons, one with a hysterical neurotic style, the other with an obsessional style. Thus, similar response tendencies to the same stress event can be contrasted in terms of stylistic variations and the nuances of treatment applicable to these variations.

Harry is a 40-year-old truck dispatcher. He had worked his way up in a small trucking firm. One night he himself took a run because he was short-handed. The load was steel pipes carried in an old truck. This improper vehicle had armor between the load bed and the driver's side of the forward compartment but did not fully protect the passenger's side.

Late at night Harry passed an attractive and solitary girl hitch-hiking on a lonely stretch of highway. Making an impulsive decision to violate the company rule against passengers of any sort, he picked her up on the grounds that she was a hippy who did not know any better and might be raped.

A short time later, a car veered across the divider line and entered his lane, threatening a head-on collision. He pulled over the shoulder of the road into an initially clear area, but crashed abruptly into a pile of gravel. The pipes shifted, penetrated the cab of the truck on the passenger's side, and impaled the girl. Harry crashed into the steering wheel and windshield and was briefly unconscious. He regained consciousness and was met with the grisly sight of his dead companion.

The highway patrol found no identification on the girl, the other car had driven on, and Harry was taken by ambulance to a hospital emergency room. No fractures were found, his lacerations were sutured, and he remained overnight for observation. His wife, who sat with him, found him anxious and dazed that night, talking episodically of the events in a fragmentary and incoherent way so that the story was not clear.

The next day he was released. Against his doctor's recommendations for rest and his wife's wishes, he returned to work. From then on, for several days, he continued his regular work as if nothing had happened. There was an immediate session with his superiors and with legal advisors. The result was that he was reprimanded for breaking the rule about passengers but also reassured that, otherwise, the accident was not his fault and he would not be held responsible. As it happened, the no passenger rule was frequently breached by other drivers, and this was well known throughout the group.

During this phase of relative denial and numbing, Harry thought about the accident from time to time but was surprised to find how little emotional effect it seemed to have. He was responsible and well-ordered in his work, but his wife reported that he thrashed around in his sleep, ground his teeth, and seemed more tense and irritable than usual.

Four weeks after the accident he had a nightmare in which mangled bodies appeared. He awoke in an anxiety attack. Throughout the following days, he had recurrent, intense, and intrusive images of the girl's body. These images together with ruminations about the girl were accompanied by anxiety attacks of growing severity. He developed a phobia about driving to and from work. His regular habits of weekend drinking increased to nightly use of growing quantities of alcohol. He had temper outbursts over minor frustrations, experienced difficulty concentrating at work and even while watching television.

Harry tried unsuccessfully to dispel his ruminations about feeling guilty for the accident. Worried over Harry's complaints of insomnia, irritability, and increased alcohol consumption, his doctor referred him for psychiatric treatment. This phase illustrates the period of compulsive repetition in waking and dreaming, thought and emotion.

Harry was initially resistant, in psychiatric evaluation, to reporting the details of the accident. This resistance subsided relatively quickly and he reported recurrent intrusive images of the girl's body. During the subsequent course of psychotherapy, Harry worked through several complexes of ideas and feelings linked associatively to the accident and his intrusive images. The emergent conflictual themes included guilt over causing the girl's death, guilt over the sexual ideas he fantasied about her before the accident, guilt that he felt glad to be alive when she had died, and fear and anger that he had been involved in an accident and her death. To a mild extent, there was also a magical or primary process belief that the girl "caused" the accident by her hitchhiking, and associated anger with her, which then fed back into his various guilt feelings.

COMMENTS

Before continuing with those conflicts triggered by the accident, it is helpful to consider, at a theoretical level, the ideal route of conceptualization that Harry should follow. To reach a point of adaptation to this disaster, Harry should perceive the event correctly; translate these perceptions into clear meanings; relate these meanings to his enduring attitudes; decide on appropriate actions; and revise his memory, attitude, and belief systems to fit this new development in his life. During this information processing, Harry should not ward off implications of the event or relevant associations to the event. To do so would impair his capacity to understand and adapt to new realities.

Human thought does not follow this ideal course. The accident has many meanings sharply incongruent with Harry's previous world picture. The threat to himself, the possibility that he has done harm, the horrors of death and injury, and the fear of accusation by others seriously differ from his wishes for personal integrity, his current self-images, and his view of his life role. This dichotomy between new and old concepts arouses strong painful emotions that threaten to flood his awareness. To avoid such unbearable feelings, Harry limited the processes of elaborating both "real" and "fantasy" meanings of the stressful event.

Because of complex meanings and defensive motives that impede conceptualization, the traumatic perceptions are not rapidly processed and integrated. They are stored because they are too important to forget. The storage is in an active form of memory that, hypothetically, has a tendency toward repeated representation. This tendency triggers involuntary recollections until processing is completed. On completion, the stored images are erased from active memory. [2,8] (This memory is called "active" rather than "short-term" because of the extended duration of intrusive repetitions of stress-related perceptions.) The repetitions, however intrusive, can be adaptive when they provoke resumption of processing. They can be maladaptive when they distract from other tasks, elicit painful emotions, evoke fear of loss of mental control, and motivate pathological defenses.

Defensive operations that oppose repetition can also be adaptive because they allow gradual assimilation rather than overwhelming recognition. Defense maneuvers can be maladaptive if they prevent assimilation, lead to unrealistic appraisals, perpetuate the stress response symptoms, or lead to other problems, such as Harry's alcoholism.

The six problematic themes of Harry's psychotherapy can now be reconsidered as ideational-emotional structures in schematic form. These themes will provide a concrete referent during the ensuing discussion of character style variations. In table 19.1, each theme is represented as a match between a current concept and enduring concepts. Since there is an incongruity between the new and the old, the elicited emotion is also listed.

Three themes cluster under the general idea that Harry sees himself as an aggressor and the girl as a victim. For example, he felt relief that he was alive when someone "had to die." The recollection of this idea elicited guilt because it is discrepant with social morality. He also felt as if he were the aggressor who caused a victim to die because of his wish to live, a primitive concept that someone has to die, and a belief in the magical power of his thought. Similarly, his sexual ideas about the girl before the crash were

Table 19.1. Themes Activated by the Accident

Current Concept Incongruent With "Enduring" Concept→Emotion		
A. Self as "aggressor"		
1. Relief that she and not he was the victim	Social morality	Guilt
2. Aggressive ideas about girl	Social morality	Guilt
3. Sexual ideas about girl	Social morality	Guilt
B. Self as "victim"		
1. Damage to her body could have happened to him	Invulnerable self	Fear
2. He broke rules	Responsibility to company	Fear (of accusations)
3. She instigated the situation by hitchhiking	He is innocent of any badness; the fault is outside	Anger

recalled and were incongruent with his sense of sexual morality and marital fidelity. All three themes are associated with guilty feelings.

Three other themes center around an opposite conceptualization of himself, this time as a victim. Harry is appalled by the damage to the girl's body. It means his body could also be damaged. This forceful idea interferes with his usual denial of personal vulnerability, and is inconsistent with wishes for invulnerability. The result is fear. Harry also conceives of himself as a victim when he recalls that he broke company rules by picking up a passenger. Since the breach resulted in a disaster, and is discrepant with his sense of what the company wants, he believes accusations would be justified and is frightened. "Harrys" with varying character styles would experience this same theme in different ways. A Harry with a paranoid style might project the accusation theme and suspect that others are now accusing him. He might use such externalizations to make himself feel enraged rather than guilty. If Harry had a hysterical style, he might have uncontrolled experiences of dread or anxiety without clear representation of the instigating ideas. Were he obsessional, Harry might ruminate about the rules; about whether they were right or wrong, whether he had or had not done his duty, about what he ought to do next, and on and on.

The last theme cited in table 19.1 places Harry as a victim of the girl's aggression. His current ideas are that she made the disaster happen by appearing on the highway. This matches with his enduring concept of personal innocence in a way that evokes anger. These angry feelings are then represented as a current concept and responses occur to these concepts that again transform Harry's state. His felt experience of anger and his concept of the girl as aggressor do not mesh with his sense of reality. The accident was not her fault and so, as the state of ideas change, his emotional experience (or potential emotional experience) changes. He feels guilty for having irrational and hostile thoughts about her. With this switch from the feelings of victim to the feelings of aggressor, there has been a change in emotions from anger to guilt and, as diagrammed in table 19.1, in state from B3 to A2.

All six themes might be activated by the accident. In "Harrys" of different neurotic character styles, some themes might be more important or conflictual than others. In a hysterical Harry, sexual guilt themes (A3) might predominate. In an obsessional Harry, aggression-guilt (A2), concern for duty (B2), and "self as an innocent victim" themes (B3) might predominate. Other themes, such as fear of bodily vulnerability (B1) and guilt over being a survivor (A1) seem to occur universally.[7,10]

Harry had a period in which there was relative denial and numbness for all the themes. Later, at various times after the accident, some themes were repressed and others emerged; eventually some were worked through so that they no longer aroused intense emotion or motivated defensive efforts. The first emergent themes were triggered by the nightmare of mangled bodies and the daytime recurrent unbidden images of the girl's body. The themes of bodily injury and survivor guilt (A1 and B1) were no longer completely warded off but rather occurred in an oscillatory fashion with periods of both intrusion and relatively successful inhibition. In psychotherapy, these intrusive themes required first attention. The other themes such as sexual guilt emerged later.

General Stratagems of Treatment for Stress Response Syndromes

At least two vectors effect stress response syndomes: the tendencies to repeated representation and the tendencies to inhibited representation to prevent disruptive emotions. The general rationale of treatment is to prevent either extreme denial, which might impede conceptual and emotional processing, or extreme intrusive-repetitiousness, which might cause panic states or secondary avoidance maneuvers. Various "schools" of therapy have evolved techniques for counteracting extremes of denials or repetitious states, and these are tabulated in table 19.2.

Once extreme symptoms are reduced, the task is to bring stress-related information to a point of completion. This "completion" can be defined, at the theoretical level, as a reduction of the discrepancy between current concepts and enduring schemata. The crucial feature is not discharge of pent-up

Table 19.2. Classification of Treatments for Stress Response Syndromes

	States	
Systems	Denial-numbing phase	Intrusive-repetitive phase
Change Controlling processes	Reduce controls Interpretation of defenses Hypnosis & narco-hypnosis Suggestion Social pressure & evocative situations; eg, psychodrama Change attitudes that make controls necessary Uncovering interpretations	Supply controls externally Structure time & events for patient Take over ego functions, eg, organize information Reduce external demands & stimulus levels Rest Provide identification models, group membership, good leadership, orienting values Behavior modification with reward & punishment
Change Information processing	Encourage abreaction Encourage: Association Speech Use of images rather than just words in recollection & fantasy Enactments, eg, role playing, psychodramas, art therapy Reconstructions (to prime memory & associations) Maintenance of environmental reminders	Work through & reorganize by clarifying & educative type interpretive work Reinforce contrasting ideas, eg, simple occupational therapy, moral persuasion Remove environmental reminders & triggers Suppress or dissociate thinking, eg, sedation, tranquilizers, meditation
Change Emotional processing	Encourage catharsis Supply objects & encourage emotional relationships (to counteract numbness)	Support Evoke other emotions, eg., benevolent environment Suppress emotion, eg, sedation or tranquilizers Desensitization procedures Relaxation & biofeedback

excitation, as suggested by the terms "abreaction" and "catharsis," but processing of ideas. To complete the response cycle, either new information must be reappraised or previous concepts must be modified to fit an altered life. Emotional responses will occur during this process when conflicts of meanings are fully considered.

Investigation, in focal psychodynamic treatment, includes examination of conflicts present before and heightened by the immediate situation, as well as the loaded meanings given to stressful events because of prior development experiences and fantasies. Conscious representation is encouraged because it promotes the solving of problems not resolved by automatic, out-of-awareness thought or dreaming. The communicative situation encourages representation and reexamination, and techniques of repetition, clarification, and interpretation enhance the on-going process.[22]

The state of stress imposed by a particular life event may impose a general regression in which developmentally primitive adaptive patterns will be noted, latent conflicts will be activated and more apparent, and increased demand for parental objects will affect all interpersonal relationships. These general regressive signs will subside without specific therapeutic attention, if the state of stress is reduced by working through the personal meanings of the particular life event.

The problem in therapy is to provide tolerable doses of awareness because knowledge of the discrepancies between desire and reality leads to painful emotional responses. On his own, the patient has warded off such knowledge to avoid pain and uncertainty. In therapy, while the affective responses are painful, they are held within bearable limits because the therapeutic relationship increases the patient's sense of safety.[23] In addition, the therapist actively and selectively counters defensive operations by various kinds of intervention. These interventions are, most commonly, clarification and interpretation of specific memories, fantasies, and impulse-defense configurations.

The aim of these techniques is completion of ideational and emotional processing and hence, resolution of stress state rather than extensive modification of character. However, persons of different character structure will manifest different types of resistance and transference during this process. The general techniques will be used with various nuances depending on these dispositional qualities of the patient. As illustration, hysterical and obsessional variations on these general themes will now be considered.

HYSTERICAL STYLE IN RESPONSE TO STRESS

Background

The concept of hysterical character was developed in the context of psycho-analytic studies of hysterical neuroses, even though these neuroses may occur in persons without hysterical character and persons with hysterical styles do not necessarily develop hysterical neurotic symptoms, even under stress. The discussion will briefly develop the "ideal" typology of hysterical style with the assumption that most persons will have only some of the traits and no person will fit the stereotype perfectly.

The main symptoms of hysterical neuroses are either conversion reactions or dissociative episodes.[24] Both symptom sets have been related to dynamically powerful but repressed ideas and emotions that would be intolerable if they gained conscious expression.[4,6] In classical analytic theory, the intolerable ideas are a wish for a symbolically incestuous love object. The desire is discrepant with moral standards and so elicits guilt and fear. To avoid these emotions, the ideational and emotional cluster is warded off from awareness by repression and denial. Because the forbidden ideas and feelings press for expression, there are continuous threats, occasional symbolic or direct break-throughs, and a propensity for traumatization by relevant external situations. While later theorists have added the importance of strivings for dependency and attention ("oral" needs), rage over the frustration of these desires, and the fusion of these strivings with erotic meanings, the correlation of hysterical symptoms with efforts at repression has been unquestioned.[23-27]

Psychoanalysts view hysterical character as a configuration that either *predisposes* toward the development of conversion reactions, anxiety-attacks, and dissociative episodes, or exists as a *separate entity* with similar impulse-defense configurations but different behavioral manifestations. The hysterical character is viewed as typically histrionic, exhibitionistic, labile in mood, and prone to act out.

Because of a proclivity for acting out oedipal fantasies, clinical studies suggest that hysterical persons are more than usually susceptible to stress response syndromes after seductions, especially those that are sadomasochistic; after a loss of persons or of positions that provided direct or symbolic attention or love; after a loss or disfigurement of body parts or attributes used to attract others; and after events associated with guilt about personal activity. In addition, any event that activates strong emotions, such as erotic excitement, anger, anxiety, guilt, or shame, would be more than usually stressful, even though a hysteric might precipitate such experiences by his behavior patterns.

Clinical studies also indicate what kinds of responses may be more frequent in the hysteric during and after the external stress event. Under stress, the prototypical hysteric becomes emotional, impulsive, unstable, histrionic, and possibly disturbed in motor, perceptual, and interpretive functions.

Styles of thought, felt emotion, and subjective experience are of central relevance to the present theses and have been described by Shapiro.[28] He emphasized the importance of impressionism and repression as part of the hysterical style of cognition. That is, the prototypical hysteric lacks a sharp focus of attention and arrives quickly at a global but superficial assumption of the meaning of perceptions, memories, fantasies, and felt emotions. There is a corresponding lack of factual detail and definition in perception plus distractability and incapacity for persistent or intense concentration. The historical continuity of such perceptual and ideational styles leads to a relatively nonfactual world in which guiding schemata of self, objects, and environment have a flat, depthless quality.

Dwelling conceptually in this nonfactual world promotes the behavioral traits of hysterical romance, emphasis on fantasy meanings, and *la belle indifference*. For example, the prototypic hysteric may react swiftly with an emotional outburst and yet remain unable to conceptualize what is happening and why such feelings occur. After the episode he may remember his own emotional experiences unclearly and will regard them as if visited on him rather than self-instigated.

This general style of representation of perception, thought, and emotion lleads to patterns observable in interpersonal relations, traits, and communicative styles. A tabular summary of what is meant by these components of hysterical style is presented below.

Information Processing Style

Short-order patterns—observe in flow of thought and emotion on a topic

> Global deployment of attention
> Unclear or incomplete representations of ideas and feelings, possibly with lack of details or clear labels in communication; nonverbal communications not translated into words or conscious meanings
> Only partial or unidirectional associational lines
> Short circuit to apparent completion or problematic thoughts

Traits

Medium-order patterns—observe in interviews

> Attention-seeking behaviors, possibly including demands for attention, and/or the use of charm, vivacity, sex appeal, childlikeness

Fluid change in mood and emotion, possibly including break-
throughs of feeling
Inconsistency of apparent attitudes

Interpersonal Relations
Long-order patterns—observe in a patient's history
Repetitive, impulsive, stereotyped interpersonal relationships often
characterized by victim-aggressor, child-parent, and rescue or rape
themes
"Cardboard" fantasies and self-object attitudes
Drifting but possibly dramatic lives with an existential sense that
reality is not really real

Shapiro's formulations differ from clinical psychoanalytic opinion in terms
of the stability of such patterns. Shapiro regards the patterns as relatively
fixed, perhaps the result of constitutional predisposition and childhood experiences. Other analysts regard these patterns as more likely to occur during
conflict. The following discussion will not contradict either position, since
both allow us to assume a fixed base line of cognitive-emotional style and an
intensification of such patterns during stress.

Controlling Thought and Emotion: Harry as "Hysteric"

Harry will now be considered as if he responded to stress and treatment in a
typically hysterical manner. One of his six conflictual themes, as described
earlier, will be used to clarify the hysterical mode of controlling thought and
emotion. This theme concerns Harry's relief that he is alive when someone
had to die (See A1, table 19.1).

Considered in microgenetic form, Harry's perceptions of the dead girl's
body and his own bodily sensations of being alive are matched with his fear
of finding himself dead. The discrepancy between his perceptions and his
fears leads to feelings of relief. The sense of relief is then represented as a
conscious experience.

In the context of the girl's death, relief is incongruent with moral strictures.
Harry believes that he should share the fate of others rather than have others
absorb bad fate. This discrepancy between current and enduring concepts
leads to guilt. Harry has low toleration for strong emotions and the danger of
experiencing guilt motivates efforts to repress the representations that generate the emotions.

While repression helps Harry escape unpleasant ideas and emotions, it impedes information processing. Were it not for controlling efforts, Harry might think again of the girl's death, his relief, and his attitudes toward survival at her expense. He might realize that he was following unrealistic principles of thought, forgive himself for feeling relief, undertake some act of penance and remorse if he could not change his attitude, or reach some other resolution of the incongruity between the current concept with his enduring schemata.

If repression is *what* Harry accomplishes, one can go further in microanalysis to indicate *how* it is accomplished in terms of cognitive operations. These operations can be abstracted as if they were in a hierarchy. The maneuver to try first in the hierarchy is inhibition of conscious representation. The initial perceptual images of the girl's body are too powerful to ward off and, immediately after the accident, Harry might have behaved in an "uncontrolled" hysterical style. Later, when defensive capacity was relatively stronger, the active memory images can be inhibited, counteracting the tendency toward repeated representation. Similarly, the initial ideas and feelings of relief might be too powerful to avoid, but later, as components of active memory, their reproductive tendency can be inhibited.

Suppose this inhibition fails or is only partly successful. Warded off ideas are expressed in some modality of representation. In a secondary maneuver, the extended meanings of the ideas can still be avoided by inhibition of translation from initial modes to other forms of representation. Harry could have only his visual images and avoid verbal concepts concerning death, relief, and causation.

A third maneuver is to prevent association to meanings that have been represented. This is again, hypothetically, an interruption of an automatic response tendency. Harry might conceptualize events in image and word forms but not continue in development of obvious associational connections. The purpose would be avoidance of full conscious awareness of threatening meanings.

These controlling efforts are three typically hysterical forms of inhibition: avoidance of representation, avoidance of translation of threatening information from one mode of representation to another, and avoidance of automatic associational connections. If these efforts fail to ward off threatening concepts, there are additional methods. A fourth maneuver is the reversal of role from active to passive. Harry could avoid thinking about his own active thoughts by deploying attention to how other factors (fate, the girl, or the listener to his story) are involved. He could then change the attitude that he was alive because he *actively* wished to be alive, even if another person died, by thinking of one's *passivity* with regard to fate, of the girl's activity in hitch-hiking, and of how she got herself into the accident.

The fifth and last "hysterical" maneuver is alteration of state of consciousness. Metaphorically, if the hysteric cannot prevent an idea from gaining consciousness, he removes consciousness from the idea by changing the organization of thought and the sense of self. Harry used alcohol for this purpose, but no outside agents are necessary to enter a hypnoid state, with loss of reflective self-awareness. These five cognitive maneuvers can be listed as if they were a hierarchy of "rules" for the avoidance of unwanted ideas:

1. Avoid representation
2. Avoid intermodal translation
3. Avoid automatic associational connections (and avoid conscious problem-solving thought)
4. Change self-attitude from active to passive (and vice versa)
5. Alter state of consciousness in order to: (1) alter hierarchies of wishes and fears; (2) blur realities and fantasies; (3) dissociate conflicting attitudes; and (4) alter the sense of self as instigator of thought and action.

The hysteric has further maneuvers, but these extend longer in time. Harry could manipulate situations so that some external person could be held responsible for his survival. This reduces the danger of a sense of guilty personal activity. In terms of very long-range maneuvers, Harry could characterologically avoid experiencing himself as ever fully real, aware, and responsible. He could identify himself with others, real or fantasied, which would make any act, or thought crime, their responsibility and not his.

Clarity in Therapeutic Interventions: An Important Nuance with Persons Who Have Hysterical Style

If the person of hysterical style enters psychotherapy because of stress response symptoms, the therapist will try to terminate the state of stress by helping him to complete the processing of the stress-related ideas and feelings. The activity will include thinking through ideas, including latent conflicts activated by the event, experiencing emotions, and revising concepts to reduce discrepancies. The interpretation of defense may be useful to remove impediments to processing, but the main goal in the present model is to end or reduce a state of stress rather than to alter the character style. Even with such limited goals, character style must be understood and the usual therapy techniques (as in table 19.2) used with appropriate nuances.

These nuances are versions, variations, or accentuations of major techniques such as clarification. One example is simple repetition of what the patient has said. The therapist may, by repeating a phrase, exert a noticeable effect on the hysteric who may respond with a startle reaction, surprise, laughter, or other emotional expressions. The same words uttered by the therapist mean something different from when they are thought or spoken by the hysteric himself; they are to be taken more seriously.

Additional meanings accrue and some meanings are also stripped away. For example, a guilty statement by Harry, repeated by the therapist in a neutral or kind voice, may seem less heinous. More explicitly, to call this "repetition" is to be correct only in a phonemic sense. Actually, the patient hears meanings more clearly, hears new meanings as well, and the previously warded off contents and meanings may seem less dangerous when repeated by the therapist.

Simple repetition is, of course, not so "simple." The therapist selects particular phrases and may recombine phrases to clarify by connection of causal sequences. At first, when Harry was vague about survivorship, but said "I guess I am lucky to still be around," the therapist might just say "yes" to accentuate the thought. A fuller repetition, in other words such as "you feel fortunate to have survived," may also have progressive effects; it "forces" Harry closer to the potential next thought . . . "and she did not, so I feel badly about feeling relief."

Left to his own processes, Harry might have verbalized the various "ingredients" in the theme, might even have painfully experienced pangs of guilt and anxiety, and yet might still not have really "listened" to his ideas. In response to this vague style, the therapist may pull together scattered phrases: "You had the thought, 'Gee I'm glad to still be around, but isn't it awful to be glad when she's dead'?" Harry might listen to his own ideas through the vehicle of the therapist and work out his own reassurance or acceptance. This seems preferable to giving him permission by saying "You feel guilty over a thought that anyone would have in such a situation"; although this is, of course, sometimes necessary. As will be seen, *these simple everyday maneuvers are not as effective with persons of obsessional style.*

Other therapeutic maneuvers oriented toward helping the hysteric complete the processing of stressful events are equally commonplace. To avoid dwelling further on well-known aspects of psychotherapy, some maneuvers are listed in tabular form as applicable to specific facets of hysterical style (table

Table 19.3. Some "Defects" of the Hysterical Style and Their Counteractants in Therapy

Function	Style as "defect"	Therapeutic counter
Perception	Global of selective inattention	Ask for details
Representation	Impressionistic rather than accurate	"Abreaction" & reconstruction
Translation of images & enactions to words	Limited	Encourage talk Provide verbal labels
Associations	Limited by inhibitions Misinterpretations based on schematic stereotypes, deflected from reality to wishes & fears	Encourage production Repetition Clarification
Problem solving	Short circuit to rapid but often erroneous conclusions	Keep subject open Interpretations
	Avoidance of topic when emotions are unbearable	Support

19.3). Each maneuver listed has additional nuances. For example, with some hysterics, interpretations or clarifications should be very short and simple, delivered in a matter-of-fact tone that would serve to counter their vagueness, emotionality, and tendency to elaborate any therapist activity into a fantasy relationship.

Nuances of Relationship with the Hysterical Patient in a State of Stress

Hysterical persons have a low toleration for emotion, although they are touted for emotionality. Because motivations are experienced as inexorable and potentially intolerable, the ideas that evoke emotion are inhibited. If toleration for the unpleasant emotions associated with a stressful event can be increased, then cognitive processing of that event can be resumed. The therapeutic relationship protects the patient from the dangers of internal conflict and potential loss of controls, and so operates to increase tolerance for warded off ideas and feelings. The therapist effects the patient's sense of this relationship by his or her activities or restraint. How this is typically done is also a nuance of technique.

After a stress event, the hysterical patient often manifests swings from rigid overcontrol to uncontrolled intrusions and emotional repetition. *During these swings, especially at the beginning and with a desperate patient, the therapist may oscillate between closeness and distance within the boundaries that characterize a therapeutic relationship.*

The hysteric may consider it imperative to have care and attention. This imperative need has been called, at times, the "oral," "sick," or "bad" component of some hysterical styles.[25,26,29] During the period of imperative need, especially after a devastating stress event, the hysteric may need to experience warmth and human support from the therapist. Without it, the therapeutic relationship will fall apart, the patient may regress or develop further psychopathology. During this phase the therapist moves, in effect, closer to the patient: just close enough to provide necessary support and not so "close" as the patient *appears* to wish.

As the patient becomes more comfortable, he may begin to feel anxiety at the degree of intimacy in the therapeutic relationship because there may be a fear of being seduced or enthralled by the therapist. The therapist then moves back to a "cooler" or more "distant" stance.

The therapist thus oscillates to keep the patient within a zone of safety by sensitive modification of his manner of relating to the patient. Safety allows the patient to move in the direction of greater conceptual clarity.[30,31] Naturally, the therapist's manner includes his nonverbal and verbal cues. This is what the therapist *allows* himself to do in the context of his own real responses and qualities of being. This is *not* role playing. The therapist allows or inhibits his own response tendencies as elicited by the patient.

If the therapist does not oscillate in from a relatively *distant* position, and if the patient has urgent needs for stabilizing his self-concept through relational support, then the discrepancy between need and supply will be so painful that the patient will find it unendurable to expose problematic lines of thought. Inhibition would continue. If the therapist does not oscillate from a relatively *close* position, then conceptual processing will begin but transference issues will cloud working through the stress response syndrome. Neither clarity nor oscillation by the therapist may be a suitable nuance of technique with the obsessional.

OBSESSIVE STYLE IN RESPONSE TO STRESS

Background

Contemporary theory of obsessional style evolved from analysis of neurotic obsessions, compulsions, doubts, and irrational fears. Abraham[32] and Freud[33] believed the obsessional neuroses to be secondary to regressions to or fixations at the anal-sadistic phase of psychosexual development. The manifestations of the neuroses were seen as compromises between aggressive and sexual impulsive aims and defenses such as isolation, intellectualization, reaction formation, and undoing. Underneath a rational consciousness, ambivalent and magical thinking were noted to be prominent. Common conflicts were formed in the interaction of aggressive impulses and predispositions to rage, fears of assault, and harsh attitudes of morality and duty. These conflicts lead to coexistence and fluctuation of dominance and submission themes in interpersonal situations and fantasies.

Salzman[34] emphasized the obsessional's sense of being driven, his strivings for omniscience and control, and his concerns for the magical effects of unfriendly thoughts of both the self and others. Homosexual thoughts may also intrude, although often without homosexual behavior.

Vagueness seems less possible for the obsessional than the hysteric. Since they tend more toward acute awareness of ideas, staying with one position threatens to lead to unpleasant emotions. Seeing the self as dominant is associated with sadism to others and leads to guilt. Seeing the self as submissive is associated with weakness and fears of assaults; hence, this position evokes anxiety. Alternation between opposing poles, as in alternation between sadistic-dominance themes and homosexual-submissive themes, serves to undo the danger of remaining at either pole.[35,36]

To avoid stabilization at a single position and to accomplish the defense of undoing, obsessionals often use the cognitive operation of shifting from one aspect of a theme to an oppositional aspect and back again. The result is continuous change. At the expense of decision and decisiveness, the obsessional maintains a sense of control and avoids emotional threats.[37-39]

While the obsessional moves so rapidly that emotions do not gain full awareness, he or she cannot totally eliminate feelings. Some obsessionals have intrusions of feelings either in minor quasi-ideational form, as expressed in attacks of rage. Even when this occurs, however, the event can be undone by what Salzman calls "verbal juggling." This process includes alterations of meaning, the use of formulas to arrive at attitudes or plans, shifts in valuation from over-to under-estimation, and, sometimes, the attribution of magical properties to word labels.

Shapiro[28] has described the narrowed focus of the mode of attention of the obsessional person, how it misses certain aspects of the world while it engages others in detail. Ideal flexibility of attention involves smooth shifts between sharply directed attention and more impressionistic forms of cognition. The obsessional lacks such fluidity.

He also describes how the obsessional is driven in the course of his thought, emotion, and behavior by "shoulds" and "oughts" dictated by a sense of duty, by his fears of loss of control, and by his need to inhibit recognition of his "wants." In spite of his usual capacity for hard work, productivity, and "will power," the obsessional person may experience difficulty and discomfort when a decision is to be made. Instead of deciding on the basis of wishes and fears, the obsessional must maintain a sense of omnipotence and, therefore, must avoid the dangerous mistakes inherent in a trial-and-error world. The decision among possible choices is likely to rest on a rule evoked to guarantee a "right" decision or else is made on impulse, to end the anxiety. The result of these cognitive styles is an experiential distance from felt emotion. The exception is a feeling of anxious self-doubt, a mood instigated by the absence of cognitive closure.

This discussion has focused on aspects of cognitive style. These are summarized below with common traits and patterns of behavior.

Information Processing Style

Short-order patterns—observe in flow of thought and emotion on a topic

Detailed, sharp focus of attention on details

  Clear representation of ideas, meager representation of emotions

  May shift organization and implications of ideas rather than follow an associational line to conclusion, as directed by original intent or intrinsic meanings

  Avoid completion or decision of a given problem, instead switch back and forth between attitudes

Traits

Medium-order patterns—observe in interviews

Doubt, worry, productivity and/or procrastination

  Single-minded, imperturbable, intellectualizer

  Tense, deliberate, unenthusiastic

  Rigid, ritualistic

Interpersonal Relations

Long-order patterns—observe in a patient's history

Develop regimented, routine and continuous interpersonal relationships low in "life," vividness, or pleasure: often frustrating to "be" with

  Prone to dominance-submission themes

  Duty-filler, hard worker, seeks or makes strain and pressure, does what he "should" do rather than what he decides to do

  Experiences himself as remote from emotional connection with others, although feels committed to operating with others because of role or principles

Controlling Thought and Emotion: Harry as an "Obsessive"

Stressful events may so compel interest that there may be little difference in the initial registration and experience of persons with hysterical or obsessional style. But, short of extreme disasters, the obsessional person may remain behaviorally calm and emotionless in contrast to the emotional explosions of the hysteric. (This report demands such generalizations, but it should be noted that during some events, obsessionals may become quite emotional and hysterics may remain calm. The difference remains in the quality of the person's conscious experience. The hysterical person can have a "hysterical calm" because it is based on an inhibition of some aspects of potential knowledge, no emotion occurs because implications are not known. If and when the obsessional behaves emotionally, it may be experienced by him as a loss of control, one to be "undone" by retrospective shifts of meaning, rituals, apologies, or self-recriminations.)

After a stressful event, the obsessional and the hysteric may both exhibit similar general stress response tendencies, including phases of denial and intrusion. But they may differ in their stability in any given phase. The obsessional may be able to maintain the period of emotional numbing with greater stability, the hysteric may be able to tolerate phases of episodic intrusions with more apparent stability and less narcissistic injury.

During the oscillatory phase, when the uncompleted images and ideas of the current stressful concepts tend to repeated and intrusive representation, the hysteric is likely to inhibit representation to ward off these unwelcome mental contents. The obsessional may be precise and clear in describing the intrusive images, but may focus on details related to "duty," for example, and away from the simple emotion-evoking meanings of the gestalt of the image.

It is during the oscillatory phase of both intrusions and warding off maneuvers that styles stand out in starkest form. Instead of, or in addition to, repressive maneuvers as listed earlier, the obsessional responds to threatened repetitions with cognitive maneuvers such as shifting. By a shift to "something else," the obsessional is able to jam cognitive channels and prevent emergence of endurance of warded-off contents, or to so shift meanings as to stifle emotional arousal. That is, by shifting from topic to topic, or from one meaning to another meaning of the same topic, the emotion-arousing properties of one set of implications are averted.

Treating Harry: Modeled Here as an Obsessional Personality

In discussion of a hysterical Harry, the theme of survival guilt was used as an example. An obsessional Harry might share a tendency toward emergence of the same theme but react to this threat with a style characterized by shifting rather than vagueness and inhibition.

In psychotherapy, Harry begins to talk of the unbidden images of the girl's body. He associates now to his memory of feeling relieved to be alive. The next conceptualization, following the idealized line of working through, outlined earlier, *would be* association of his relieved feelings with ideas of survival at her expense. This cluster *would be* matched against moral strictures counter to such personal gain through damage to others, and Harry *would* go on to conceptualize his emotional experience of guilt or shame (theme A1 in table 19.1). Once clear, he could revise his schematic belief that someone had to die, accept his relief, feel remorse, even plan a penance, and reduce incongruity through one or more of these changes.

Harry does not follow this idealized route because the potential of these emotional experiences is appraised as intolerable at a not fully conscious level of information processing. A switch is made to another ideational cycle in order to avoid the first one. The second cycle is also associatively related to the images of the girl's body. A common element in both ideational cycles allows a pivotal change and reduces awareness that the subtopic has changed.[40]

The pivot for the switch is the idea of bodily damage. In the second ideational cluster, the concept is that bodily damage could happen to him, perhaps at any future time, since it has now happened to her. Through the comparison with his wishes for invulnerability and his dread of vulnerability, fear is aroused (B1 in table 19.1).

While fear is unpleasant and threatening as a potential experience, the switch allows movement away from the potential feelings of guilt (theme A1). When the second theme (B1) becomes too clear, fear might be consciously experienced. The procedure can be reversed with return to A1. Harry can oscillate in terms of conscious and communicative meanings between A1 and B1 without either set of dangerous ideas and emotions being fully experienced.

Harry need not limit switching operations to the two contexts for ideas about bodily damage. He can switch between any permutations of any themes. He can transform, reverse, or undo guilt with fear or anger.[41] He can see himself as victim, then aggressor, then victim, and so forth. These shifts dampen emotional responsivity but reduce cognitive processing of themes.

This does not imply that inhibition of representation will not be found in obsessional Harry or shifts of theme will be absent in hysterical Harry. Obsessional Harry will attempt inhibitions and use his shifts when inhibitory efforts fail. Hysterical Harry might shift from active to passive, as noted earlier, but timing and quality of the shifts would differ. Obsessional Harry would tend to shift more rapidly, with less vagueness at either pole. The shift could occur in midphrase, between an utterance of his and a response from the therapist, or even as virtually simultaneous trains of thought.

It is because of rapid shifts that therapists who attempt clarity with obsessionals may be thwarted in their task. Suppose the therapist makes a clarifying intervention about A1, the survivor guilt theme. Obsessional Harry may have already shifted to B1, his fear of bodily injury, and thus hear the remarks in a noncongruent state. The clarification procedure may not work well because Harry was not unclear or vague in the first place, is not listening from the earlier position, and will undo the therapist's intervention by further shifts. An interpretation to the effect that Harry fears bodily damage as a retribution for his survivor relief and guilt would be premature since, at this point, he has not fully experienced either the fear or the guilt.

Holding to Context: Important Nuances with Persons Who Have Obsessive Character Style

Holding the obsessional to a topic or to a given context within a topic is equivalent to clarifying for the hysteric. Metaphorically, the *obsessional avoids conceptual time where the hysteric avoids conceptual space*. The goal of holding is reduction of shifting, so that the patient can progress further along a given conceptual process. The patient must also be helped to tolerate the emotions that will be experienced when he cannot quickly divert ideas into and out of conscious awareness.

Holding to context is more complicated than clarification. One begins with at least two current problems, such as the dual themes of A1 and B1 in Harry. When the patient is not shifting with extreme rapidity, the therapist may simply hold the patient to either one or the other theme.

The patient will not comply with this maneuver and the therapist must not confuse "holding" with "forcing." Ferenczi,[42] in an effort to speed up analysis, experimented with various ways to make the obsessional stay on topic until intensely felt emotions occurred. For example, he insisted that his patient develop and maintain visual fantasies relevant to a specific theme. During this technical maneuver his obsessional patients did experience emotions, they even had affective explosions, but the transference complications impeded rather than enhanced the therapy.

The therapist has to shift, even though he attempts to hold the patient to a topic. That is, the therapist shifts at a slower rate than the patient, like a dragging anchor that slows the process. This operation increases the progress of the patient in both directions. That is, with each shift, he is able to go a bit further along the conceptual route of either theme, even though he soon becomes frightened and crowds the theme out of mind with an alternative.

The therapist may use repetitions, as with the hysteric, in order to hold or slow the shift of an obsessional patient. But this use of the same maneuver is done with a different nuance. With the hysteric, the repetition heightens the meaning of what the patient is *now* saying. With the obsessional, the repetition goes back to what the patient was saying *before* the shift away from the context occurred. With the hysteric, the repetition may be short phrases. With the obsessional, greater length may be necessary, in order to state the specific context that is being warded off. For example, if Harry is talking about bodily damage and shifts from a survivor guilt context to his fears of injury, then a repetition by the therapist has to link bodily damage specifically to the survivor guilt theme. With the hysteric, such wordy interventions might only diminish clarity.

At times, this more extensive repetition in the obsessional may include the technique of going back to the very beginning of an exchange, retracing the flow carefully, and indicating where extraneous or only vaguely relevant details were introduced by the patient. Reconstructions may add warded off details. This technique has been suggested for long-term character analysis,[31,34] during which defensive operations are interpreted so that the patient increases conscious control and diminishes unconscious restrictions on ideas and feelings. In shorter therapy, aimed at working through a stress, this extensive repetition is still useful, because, during the review by the therapist, the patient attends to the uncomfortable aspects of the topic.

Increased time on the topic allows more opportunity for processing and hence moves the patient toward completion. Emotions aroused by the flow of ideas are more tolerable within the therapeutic relationship than for the patient alone. Also, time on the topic and with the therapist allows continued processing in a communicative state, emphasizing reality and problem solving rather than fantasy and magical belief systems. Identification with and externalization onto the relatively neutral therapist also allows temporary reduction in rigid and harsh introjects that might otherwise deflect thought.

Focusing on details is sometimes a partial deterrent to shifting in the obsessional, just as it may aid clarity with the hysteric. The nuances of focusing on details differ because the purposes differ. In general, the aim with the hysteric is to move from concrete, experiential information, such as images, toward more abstract or more extended meanings, such as word labels for activities and things. The aim with the obsessional is to move from abstract levels, where shifts are facile, to a concrete context. Details act as pegs of meaning in concrete contexts, and make shifts of attitude more difficult. This maneuver utilizes the obsessional's predisposition to details but allows the therapist to specifically select them. Again, the nuance of asking for concrete details is part of the general aim of increasing conceptualization time.

In states where shifts are so rapid as to preclude simple repetition or questioning, the therapist may use a more complex form of repetition. The therapist repeats the event, for example, Harry's intrusive image of the girl's body, and then repeats in a single package the disparate attitudes that the patient oscillates between. For example, the therapist might tell Harry that the image of the girl's body led to two themes. One was the idea of relief at being spared from death that made him feel frightened and guilty. The other was the idea of bodily harm to himself. Were the rate of oscillation less rapid, this form of "packaged" intervention would not be as necessary, since simpler holding operations may be sufficient and the therapist can focus on a single theme.

These efforts by the therapist encroach on the habitual style of the patient. The patient may respond by minimizing or exaggerating the meaning of the intervention. The obsessional is especially vulnerable to threats to his sense of omniscience, especially after traumatic events. If the therapist holds him on a topic, the obsessional senses warded off ideas and feelings and develops uncertainties that cause his self-esteem to fall.

To protect the patient's self-esteem, the therapist uses another technical nuance. He uses questioning to accomplish clarification and topic deepening, even when he has an interpretation in mind. The questions aim the patient toward answers that contain the important, warded off, but now emerging ideas. The obsessional patient can then credit himself with expressing these ideas and experiencing these feelings. The therapist with the hysterical person might, in contrast, interpret at such a moment, using a firm, short delivery, since a question might be followed by vagueness.

To the obsessional, incisive interpretations often mean that the therapist knows something he does not know. A transference bind over dominance and submission arises as the patient either rebels against the interpretation with stubborn denial, accepts it meekly without thinking about it, or both.

Table 19.4. Some "Defects" of Obsessional Style and Their
Counteractants in Therapy

Function	Style as "defect"	Therapeutic counter
Perception	Detailed & factual	Ask for overall impressions and statements about emotional experiences
Representation	Isolation of ideas from emotions	Link emotional meanings to ideational meanings
Translation of images to words	Misses emotional meaning in a rapid transition to partial word meanings	Focus attention on images & felt reactions to them
Associations	Shifts sets of meanings back & forth	Holding operations Interpretation of defense & of warded off meanings
Problem solving	Endless rumination without reaching decisions	Interpretation of reasons for warding off clear decisions

Timing is also important with obsessionals working through stress-activated themes. After experience with a given patient, the therapist intuitively knows when a shift is about to take place. At just that moment, or a trifle before, the therapist asks his question. This interrupts the shift and increases conceptual "time and space" on the topic about to be warded off. These technical nuances are put in a crude, broad context in table 19.4.

Nuances of Relationship with Obsessional Patients in a State of Stress

The oscillation described as sometimes necessary with the hysterical style is not as advisable with the obsessional style. Instead, the therapist creates a safe situation for the patient by remaining stable within his own clear boundaries (eg, objectivity, compassion, understanding, concern for the truth, or whatever his own personal and professional traits are).

The patient learns the limits of the therapist within this frame. It gives him faith that the therapist will react neither harshly nor seductively. This trust increases *the patient's* breadth of oscillation. He can express more aggressive ideas, if he knows the therapist will neither submit, be injured, compete for dominance, or accuse him of evil. Harry could express more of his bodily worries when he knew the therapist would not himself feel guilty or over-responsible.

If the therapist changes with the obsessional's tests or needs, then the obsessional worries that he may be too powerful, too weak, or too "sick" for the therapist to handle. Also, the obsessional may use the situation to externalize warded off ideas or even defensive maneuvers. The therapist shifts, not he. This is not to say the obsessional does not, at times, need kindly support after disastrous external events. But his propensity for shifting makes changes in the degree of support more hazardous than a consistent attitude, whether kindly-supportive, neutral-tough, or otherwise.

Suppose the therapist becomes more kindly as Harry goes through a turbulent period of emotional expression of guilt over survival. Harry may experience this as an increase in the therapist's concern or worry for him. He might shift from the "little" suffering position that elicited the therapist's reaction, to a "big" position from which he looks down with contempt at the "worried" therapist.

Similarly, if the therapist is not consistently tough-minded, in the ordinary sense of insisting on information and truth-telling, but shifts to this stance only in response to the patient's stubborn evasiveness, then the patient can shift from strong stubbornness to weak, vulnerable self-concepts. Within the context of this shift, the therapist comes to be experienced as hostile, demeaning, and demanding.

Unlike the hysteric, then, *the obsessional's shifts in role and attitude within the therapeutic situation are likely to be out of phase with changes in demeanor of the therapist.* The obsessional can chance further and more lucid swings in state when he senses the stability of the therapist.

Transference resistances will occur in spite of the therapist's effort to maintain a therapeutic relationship. The stability of the therapist will be exaggerated by the patient into an omniscience that he will continually test. When negative transference reactions occur, the therapist will act to resolve those that interfere with the goals of therapy. But some transference reactions will not be negative even though they act as resistances. The hysteric may demand attention and halt progress to get it. The obsessional may take an oppositional stance not so much out of hostility or stubbornness, although such factors will be present, as out of a need to avoid the dangerous intimacy of agreement and cooperation. Since the therapist is not aiming at analysis of transference to effect character change, he need not interpret this process.

Instead, with an obsessional patient in an oppositional stance, he may word his interventions to take advantage of the situation.

That is, interventions can be worded, when necessary, in an oppositional manner. Suppose Harry was talking about picking up the girl and the therapist knew he was predisposed to feeling guilty but was warding it off. With a hysterical Harry the therapist might say, "You feel badly about picking up the girl." With an obsessional and cooperative Harry he might say, "Could you be blaming yourself for picking up the girl?" With an oppositional obsessional stance, the therapist might say, "So you don't feel at all badly about picking up the girl." This kind of Harry may disagree and talk of his guilt feelings.

Provided the context is a basically stable therapeutic relationship, one in which the patient has an image of the therapist as objective, kindly, and firmly competent, the inflection need not be the sincere, neutral, firm tone helpful with hysterics. *Slight* sarcasm or *mild* humor may help the obsessional Harry assume a tough position while trying out his own tender ideas.[34]

By sternness, as implied in the above comments, the therapist may have the effect of "ordering" the obsessional to contemplate warded off ideas. This seeming unkindness is kind in that it removes responsibility from the patient and permits him to think the unthinkable. But this sternness, mild sarcasm, or slight humor has to remain a relatively consistent characteristic of the therapist.

This is not as difficult as it may sound, for *these nuances involve what the therapist allows himself to do or not do in natural response to the situation. They are not assumed or artificial roles or traits.* For some therapists, kindliness, openness, gentleness, and a nonjudgmental air are preferable nuances to any toughness, sternness, sarcasm, or honor and may accomplish the same purpose. These latter remarks are meant more as illustrations than assertions because it is here that we encounter that blurred border between the "science" and "art" of psychotherapy.

CONCLUSIONS

This report has taken a state of stress, considered the variations between two dispositional types within that state, and discussed the nuances of psychodynamic psychotherapy aimed at symptom relief. These dimensions, state, typology, and mode of treatment, define a frame of reference. Assertions have been made that are clearly positioned within this frame of reference. For example, stress response syndromes have been characterized by phases of denial and intrusion, hysterical persons have been described as using inhibition of representation to ward off intrusive and repetitive ideas and feelings, and clarity has been posited as an important nuance of their therapy. Obsessional persons were characterized by switching operations for the same purpose and holding operations were asserted to be important nuances of technique in their therapy.

Such assertions involve standard psychiatric knowledge. What is gained through this model is an organization for the systematic assemblage of such knowledge. With clear conceptual positionings of assertions, many of the arguments and divergencies that characterize psychiatry and psychology would fall away in favor of renewed empirical observation and formulation. The key is comparable rather than incongruous levels of abstraction.

To the extent that the model is worthwhile, the assertions here can be specifically challenged. General stress response tendencies may not follow the pathways defined, there may be better ways to typologize what was called "hysterical" and "obsessional," the nuances of focused psychodynamic psychotherapy described may be incomplete or inappropriate. A specific site of disagreement can be localized by following the same dimensions. For example, *an argument about a nuance of treatment would have to be connected with a specific kind of person, in an intrusive-repetitive phase after a stressful external event, involved in psychodynamic treatment aimed at relief of intrusions and resolution of the state of stress.*

While this type of model localizes conceptualization, it may be argued that it defines restrictively small areas. Within the general field of psychopathology and psychotherapy there would be multitudes of such areas. I believe that the field is so large that many specific subdivisions are indicated, and that knowledge will be accumulated and clarified by this method. The complexity is not overwhelming. The present model can be extended by keeping any two dimensions constant while extending the boundaries of the third. For example, extensions may involve other variations of personality, other versions of pathological states, and other views of therapy.

Variations in typology would include narcissistic, schizoid, impulsive, and paranoid personalities. Each would be contrasted with hysterical and obsessional styles of response to stressful life events. Each would be considered in the context of brief dynamic therapy aimed at working through the life event and so central conceptual anchoring would be maintained.

Variations in state would include other formulations of the meaning of a crisis episode. For example, a contrasting view within the framework of brief psychodynamic therapy regards the life events as secondary in importance to enduring conflicts. The predominant state is seen as character patterns rather than phases of stress response. Separation from a lover would be seen as an occasion to work further on dependency-independency conflicts present for a long time.[43,44] Would the same nuances of treatment for varying styles apply in therapy oriented toward character conflicts?

Variations in treatment would maintain the set of stress response syndromes in certain common character types. Other technical approaches would provide contrasting points of view. For example, a behavior therapist would discuss treatment of such intrusive images as noted in Harry. He might advocate such approaches as systematic desensitization and implosion.[45] Learning theory hypotheses would be advanced equivalent to the repetition-until-completion tendency described in this paper. A rationale of treatment would be based on these hypotheses. Assertions would be advanced about how systematic desensitization and implosion work. The behavior therapist might assert that desensitization would be more suitable for hysterical styles because there is a progressive clarification of anxiety-provoking representations and a supportive patient-therapist relationship. He might prefer implosive techniques for obsessional styles, as this method can hold attention to a specific aspect of an ideational complex, provoke emotional response, and engage the patient in a "tough" appearing role-relationship.

These nuances of techniques within a behavior therapy point of view could then be contrasted with the assertions of the dynamic point of view, as well as with other technical possibilities. Nuances across schools might be developed. Hysterical vagueness might be seen as altered by any clarification technique such as role playing, psychodrama, transactional analysis, or gestalt therapy. Obsessional shifting of topics might be seen as altered by any holding technique such as systematic desensitization, implosion, or guided imagery techniques. Contrary assertions would, at least, be assembled at similar levels of abstraction. Disagreements could be resolved by further observation of given types of persons in a given state. In this way we might hope to pass beyond brand names as our professional disagreements become productive rather than schismatic.

REFERENCES

1. *Miller G A, Galanter E, Pribram K:* Plans and the Structure of Behavior. *New York, Henry Holt & Co Inc, 1960.*
2. *Horowitz M J:* Image Formation and Cognition. *New York, Appleton-Century-Crofts Inc, 1970.*

3. *Peterfreund E: Information systems and psychoanalysis: An evolutionary, biological approach to psychoanalytic theory.* Psychol Issues *7:1–397, 1971.*
4. *Freud S, Breuer J: Studies on hysteria, in Strachey J (ed):* Standard Edition. *London, Hogarth Press, 1957, vol 2, pp 185–305.*
5. *Grinker K, Spiegal S:* Men Under Stress. *Philadelphia, Blakiston, 1945.*
6. *Freud S: Beyond the pleasure principle (1920), in Strachey J (ed):* Standard Edition. *London, Hogarth Press, 1953, vol 18, pp 7–64.*
7. *Furst S S: Psychic Trauma: A survey, in Furst S S (ed):* Psychic Trauma. *New York, Basic Books Inc, 1967.*
8. *Horowitz M J, Becker S S: Cognitive response to stress: Experimental studies of a compulsion to repeat trauma, in Holt R, Peterfreund E (eds):* Psychoanalysis and Contemporary Science. *New York, Macmillan Co, vol 1, 1972, pp 258–305.*
9. *Hamburg D A, Adams J E: A perspective on coping behavior: Seeking and utilizing information in major transitions.* Arch Gen Psychiatry *17:277–284, 1967.*
10. *Lifton R J:* History and Human Survival. *New York, Vantage Books, 1967.*
11. *Horowitz M J: Phase oriented treatment of stress response syndromes.* Am J Psychother *27:506–515, 1973.*
12. *Davis D R:* An Introduction to Psychopathology. *London, Oxford University Press, 1966.*
13. *Lazarus R S:* Psychological Stress and the Coping Process. *New York, McGraw-Hill Book Co Inc, 1966.*
14. *Janis I L:* Stress and Frustration. *New York, Harcourt-Brace-Javanovich, 1969.*
15. *Bowlby J, Parkes C M: Separation and loss within the family, in Anthony E J, Kopernik C (eds):* The International Yearbook for Child Psychiatry and Allied Disciplines. *New York, John Wiley & Sons Inc, 1970, pp 197–215.*
16. *Freud S: On the psychical mechanism of hysterical phenomena, in Strachey J (ed):* Standard Edition. *London, Hogarth Press, 1962, vol 3, pp 25–39.*
17. *Freud S: Inhibitions, symptoms and anxiety, in Strachey J (ed):* Standard Edition. *London, Hogarth Press, 1959, vol 20, pp 87–172.*
18. *Appelgarth A: Comments on aspects of the theory of psychic energy.* J Am Psychoanal Assoc *19:379–416, 1971.*
19. *French T:* The Integration of Behavior, Volume 1: Basic Postulates. *Chicago, University of Chicago Press, 1952.*
20. *Lazarus R S, Averill J R, Opton E M: Towards a cognitive theory of emotion, in* Feelings and Emotions. *New York, Academic Press Inc, 1970.*
21. *Pribram K H: Emotion: Steps toward a neuropsychological theory, in Glass D (ed):* Neurophysiology and Emotion. *New York, Rockefeller University Press and Russell Sage Foundation, 1967.*
22. *Bibring E: Psychoanalysis and the dynamic psychotherapies.* J Am Psychoanal Assoc *2:745–770, 1954.*
23. *Greenson R: The working alliance and the transference neurosis.* Psychoanal Q *34:155–181, 1965.*
24. *Janet P:* The Major Symptoms of Hysteria. *New York, Hafner Publishing Co, 1965.*
25. *Easser B R, Lesser S R: Hysterical personality: A re-evaluation.* Psychoanal Q *34:390–405, 1965.*

26. *Marmor J: Orality in the hysterical personality.* J Am Psychoanal Assoc *1:656–675, 1953.*
27. *Ludwig A M: Hysteria: A neurobiological theory.* Arch Gen Psychiatry *27:771–777, 1972.*
28. *Shapiro D:* Neurotic Styles. *New York, Basic Books Inc, 1965.*
29. *Lazare A: The hysterical character in psychoanalytic theory: Evolution and confusion.* Arch Gen Psychiatry *25:131–137, 1971.*
30. *Sandler J: The background of safety.* Int J Psychoanal *41:352–356, 1960.*
31. *Weiss J: The emergence of new themes: A contribution to the psychoanalytic theory of therapy.* Int J Psychoanal *52:459–467, 1971.*
32. *Abraham K: A short study of the development of the libido, viewed in the light of mental disorders, in* Selected Papers. *London, Hogarth Press, 1942.*
33. *Freud S: Notes upon a case of obsessional neurosis, in* Collected Papers. *London, Hogarth Press, 1949, vol 3.*
34. *Salzman L:* The Obsessive Personality. *New York, Science House, 1968.*
35. *Sampson H, Weiss J, Mlodnosky L, et al.: Defense analysis and the emergence of warded-off mental contents: An empirical study.* Arch Gen Psychiatry *26:524–532, 1972.*
36. *Weiss J: The integration of defenses.* Int J Psychoanal *48:520–524, 1967.*
37. *Barnett J: Therapeutic intervention in the dysfunctional thought processes of the obsessional.* Am J Psychotherapy *26:338–351, 1972.*
38. *Schwartz E K: The treatment of the obsessive patient in the group therapy setting.* Am J Psychotherapy *26:352–361, 1972.*
39. *Silverman J S: Obsessional disorders in childhood and adolescence.* Am J Psychotherapy *26:362–377, 1972.*
40. *Klein G S: Peremptory ideation: Structure and force in motivated ideas.* Psychol Issues *5:80–128, 1967.*
41. *Jones E: Fear, guilt and hate.* Int J Psychoanal *10:383–397, 1929.*
42. *Ferenczi S:* Further Contributions to the Theory and Technique of Psychoanalysis. *London, Hogarth Press and the Institute of Psychoanalysis, 1950.*
43. *Sifneos P E:* Short-Term Psychotherapy and Emotional Crisis. *Cambridge, Mass, Harvard University Press, 1973.*
44. *Mann J:* Time Limited Psychotherapy. *Cambridge, Mass, Harvard University Press, 1973.*
45. *Yates A O:* Behavior Therapy. *New York, John Wiley & Sons Inc, 1970.*

20. Witness to Violence

The Child Interview

Robert S. Pynoos and Spencer Eth

ALTHOUGH THERE HAS been a growing awareness of the importance of work with traumatized children such as victims of physical or sexual abuse and kidnapping, there is a larger population of children who have been witness to violence, and suffer from the aftereffects of that psychic trauma (Pynoos and Eth, 1985). For example, the Sheriff's Homicide Division of Los Angeles County estimates that dependent children witness between 10 and 20% of the approximately 2,000 annual homicides in their jurisdiction.

It is difficult to imagine a more harrowing experience than for a child to witness a parent's murder, suicide or rape. Anyone who has attempted to assist children who have recently been so traumatized will understand the difficulty in knowing how to proceed. The child may exhibit many of the characteristics of an acute posttraumatic stress response. As a result, he or she can present as numb or mute. Direct inquiry about the traumatic event may be unproductive, leaving the interviewer feeling stymied and the child further entrenched in detachment. In addition, the child will frequently be in a state of mourning for the lost parent, further complicating the clinical interview.

In this paper, we describe an initial interview technique that has proven successful in helping a psychiatric consultant to engage young children in conversation shortly after witnessing a traumatic or violent event. It is intended for use with children from 3 to 16 years of age. This technique enables the interviewer to gain insight into the child's understanding of the event and to characterize the behavioral and emotional responses in order to provide specific professional support to the child soon after the trauma. The interview technique has undergone a series of revisions as our experience has grown, and particularly as we have learned from the children's own comments about

Reprinted by permission from *Journal of the American Academy of Child and Adolescent Psychiatry*, 25 (3), 306–319. Copyright © by Williams & Wilkins, 1986.

the interview. The interview has proven to be a generic technique applicable for use with children who have witnessed murder, suicide, rape, accidental death, aggravated assault, kidnapping, and school or community violence. To date, we have employed it with over 200 children. In addition, the interview format has been readily taught to other mental health professionals who have themselves successfully used it in a variety of clinical settings.

INTERVIEW FORMAT

This specialized interview technique is designed for use in the initial meeting with a recently traumatized child. It is presented here as a coherent three-stage process: opening, trauma, and closure. The format begins by permitting the child first to express the impact of the trauma in play and fantasy, and through metaphor, by use of a projective free drawing and story telling task. This opening enables the consultant to appreciate the child's preliminary means of coping and defensive maneuvers. Second, the interviewer shifts attention to the actual traumatic episode. In order to foster mastery of the traumatic anxiety, he overcomes the efforts of the child to avoid and deny, and supports a thorough exploration of the child's experience. Finally, the consultant can then assist the child in addressing his or her current life concerns with an increased sense of security, competence and mastery. As with any clinical interview, the suggested order may be modified somewhat as a function of the child's particular responses, but it is important to adhere to the general format. Each major step in the interview process may be depicted through a series of drawings. In our experience, the entire interview requires approximately 90 minutes.

Prior to the interview, it is important to have obtained from the family, police or other sources some description of the family circumstances, the violent event, and the child's subsequent behavior or responses. The interviewer can then be alert to important references or omissions in the child's account.

FIRST STAGE: OPENING

Establishing the Focus. After greeting the child in our usual way, we share that we have had experience in talking to other children who have "gone through what you have gone through." Others can say that they are interested in understanding with the child what it was like to go through what he or she has been through. By making that statement, we establish a focus for the interview, inform the child that he or she is not alone in the predicament, and offer some ego support to the child by our willingness to look together at what has occurred. After these preliminary comments, we do not find it necessary or helpful to have other persons, e.g., family, relatives, or guardians present. We see each child alone in a quiet room.

Free Drawing and Story Telling. Upon being seated, the child is given pencil and paper, and asked to "draw whatever you'd like but something you can tell a story about." The child is reassured that the quality of the drawing is of no concern, and allowed to approach the task without distraction or interference. By stepping aside, the interviewer may encourage the child to attend fully to the creative work. All the children have applied themselves to this task, although there may be an initial period of hesitance. The youngest children, those under 4 years of age, are engaged in play along with their scribbling and are asked similarly "to make up a story." Our emphasis is for the children to begin in whatever manner is most acceptable to them. This approach allows for the child's imagination to be temporarily relieved from reality and superego constraints (Waelder, 1933). The children we have seen have energetically taken to this activity even hours after witnessing a violent event. The drawings and stories vary considerably in their projective style and content, from examples of nearly direct accounts, to richly endowed works of fiction.

Children appear to be more comfortable with this manner of therapeutic engagement than the alternative style of direct inquiry. This opening is seen ultimately to facilitate a later open discussion of the traumatic occurrence. The interviewer hopes by his expression of interest, level of enthusiasm, and occasional playfulness, to encourage the child to regain more spontaneity. This step begins the process of countering the passive, detached stance of the traumatized witness. The interviewer encourages the child to elaborate further on both the drawing and story. This can be done by general questions, i.e., "What happens next?" or by inquiring about some section or detail. Elaboration usually allows the interviewer to gain an initial appreciation of the child's life circumstances.

Traumatic Reference. The key concept in this opening stage is that the violent event remains intrusive on the child's mind and will be represented somewhere in the drawing or story. The interviewer's task is to identify the traumatic references. These may be obvious or obscure, but are invariably present and recognizable.

While telling the story, the child is seen to struggle with unacceptable, painful or frightening feelings which may disguise the traumatic reference. The drawing and story provide clues to the sources of the child's anxiety and means of coping.

We have found four common psychological methods in the preadolescent group to limit or regulate their anxiety within the first weeks after the event. "Denial-in-fantasy" allows the child to mitigate painful reality by imaginatively reversing the violent outcome. The child may provide a more acceptable ending. For example, one 5-year-old whose father, a stunt man, was fatally shot in a family feud, suddenly introduced a safety net after a clown in her story has been maliciously pushed off a high wire. Another group of children avoid reminding themselves of the event by inhibiting spontaneous thought. For instance, an 8-year-old failed to mention the prominent television set he placed in the picture. When asked, he animatedly told of a program in which Bugs Bunny is shot at but safely outruns the attacker's blasts. These children display momentary interruptions of their fantasy elaboration in order to avoid associations to the trauma. A third group cannot at first engage in fantasy. They remain fixed to the trauma and only draw the actual scene. They will without request begin to give an unemotional journalistic but incomplete account of the event. For instance, one 8-year-old introduced himself by saying, "I'm Tommy, my father killed my mother." A fourth group remains in a constant state of anxious arousal, as if to prepare for future danger. In his story, one child emphasized his lack of personal security after his father's murder. This 7-year-old boy told in his story of a kidnapping from a front yard that was once safe to play in. These children will keep themselves preoccupied with thoughts of further harm in lieu of discussing the real event.

SECOND STAGE: TRAUMA

Relieving the Experience

Emotional Release. The transition in the interview from the child's drawing and story telling to the explicit discussion of the violent event is a critical moment for the clinician and child alike. We have found it timely and practical to link some aspect of the drawing or story directly to the trauma. For example, we might say: "I'll bet you wish that:" 1) "Your father could have been saved at the end like the clown," or, 2) "Your babysitter could have gotten away from the man who was about to stab her," or, 3) "By saying what happened over and over again, you would get used to it," or, 4)

"Your father were still here to protect you." What often follows is a profound emotional outcry from the child. Now the child needs to feel the interviewer's willingness to be a supportive presence and to protect the child from being overwhelmed by the intensity or prolongation of the emotional release. The interviewer must be prepared to share in the grief and horror and to offer the child physical comfort.

Reconstruction

Catharsis does not adequately describe the goal of emotional release. Before the child proceeds to "relive the experience," he first must attain a state in which he does not feel too threatened by his emotional responses, a state in which he has the hope, at least, of being able to begin to cope with them. If this is adequately achieved, the child will appear ready to provide a verbal description of the event. The interviewer can then direct the child by suggesting that "Now is a good time to tell what happened and what you saw." The child will recreate the traumatic milieu through various devices. He may first choose to reenact in action or draw the violent scene, but the interviewer must encourage the child to translate the actions or pictorial depiction into words. Props—dolls, puppets, toys, weapons, etc.—are made available. The child may become engrossed in the reenactment play, so that the interviewer must be willing to participate—for instance, acting as the assailant, victim, police or paramedic.

The child should then be supported in his focus on the central action the child witnessed when physical harm was inflicted: the push to the floor, the blow with the fist, the plunge with the knife, the blast of a shotgun, the moment of forced sexual penetration. It may require firm support by the interviewer for the child to draw the particular moment of violence. Although a marked increase in anxiety may precede the child's doing so, afterward the child appears strengthened in his or her mastery of the trauma.

Occasionally, it is not until this step that the pain of the reality is experienced. Again, the interviewer may tactfully facilitate the emotional release by stating, for instance, "I bet you wish the gun had been pointed as you drew it, away from your father, so it would have gone off harmlessly."

Perceptual Experience. We follow this description of the action by addressing the child's sensory experience of the episode: the sight and sound of the gunfire, the screams or sudden silence of the victim, the first sight of blood, the splash of blood on the child's own clothes, the death agony of the victim, and the sirens of the police arrival. This recall can be elicited by a comment such as "Boy, you must have gotten blood on you." In several cases we have been surprised to have the child add that he or she was wearing the very pants which had been stained with blood during the violent episode. In addition, whenever a child describes an intense feeling state, we ask him about the concomitant physical sensation. For example, after a child said "It felt awful," we asked where he felt it. He replied, "My heart hurt, it was beating so fast."

Throughout this account of the traumatic event, the child's selection will be influenced by cognitive development and style, previous history of trauma, violence or loss, and the actual circumstances. The child is also continually attempting to cope with the accompanying affects: helplessness, passivity, fear, rage, confusion, guilt, and even excitement.

The role of the interviewer is to function as a holding environment in order to provide a safe and protected setting so that the child can further work at mastery despite the rising anxiety level. The interviewer does not allow the child to digress from this all-important task. He may need to question the child to ensure that the circumstances and aftermath are fully reviewed. Following completion of the child's account, the interviewer must be sensitive to how physically exhausted and emotionally spent the child may be in contrast to the usual psychiatric session. Relaxation time and snacks should be offered. The child needs to feel that he or she is being adequately cared for during this emotionally challenging time.

Special Detailing

The child may imbue a particular detail with special traumatic meaning (Freud, 1965). These details are of psychodynamic importance and often provide clues to the child's initial identification, for example, with the aggressor, the victim or, we may add, the protector, including the police. One adolescent girl became preoccupied because her mother had been shot while wearing a dress the daughter had lent the mother that morning. A 5-year-old dwelled on whether his deceased mother's legs were broken, in part because he had worn leg casts as a toddler and wished to have her fixed up in that way, too. Another boy painfully recalled having been immediately made to wear the belt used by his father to beat his mother to death in order to hide the evidence. While recognizing the unconscious significance of these details, the immediate goal of the interviewer is to help the child distinguish himself from either the victim or the assailant.

Worst Moment

The interviewer can then proceed to ask about the worst moment for the child. It may not be what an adult would assume, nor even something as yet mentioned. Even young children have sufficient observing ego to reflect on the event and then movingly describe a uniquely painful moment. This may include a memory from earlier in the day or from the violent occurrence or from afterward. One 8-year-old broke down in tears as he told of the moment when he found a razor blade under his suicidal mother's bleeding arm. He had been sent out that day to buy the razor blades, he thought, to make paper mache objects. He cried in total disillusionment. One 7-year-old girl painfully related that her father had called out her nickname as he died from a gunshot wound. A 14-year-old girl described a moment of intolerable anger when in passing the police station her father said, "I'm sorry," having just shotgunned her mother to death. A 5-year-old expressed his intense disappointment that on Christmas Eve Santa Claus had not arrived but a bad man, a killer, instead. This exchange is a particularly empathic moment for the child as he feels especially understood and close to the interviewer.

Violence/Physical Mutilation. The interviewer must now be willing to guide the child to approach the impact of the violence and physical mutilation. Children may be haunted by an unforgettable visual image and may struggle to unburden themselves of the sight. Certain children may insist on drawing a picture of the mutilated or wounded parent. Other children may be more reluctant, but with proper support will draw the horrifying and painful sight.

We have been impressed with the child's need to restore an image of the parent as physically intact or undamaged. In cases of parental death, the funeral offers an opportunity to view the parent as once again restored. Inquiries about this ceremony are especially fruitful. We will also ask if the children have a photograph of their parent and, if one is available, we will look at it with the child during the interview. In addition to aiding the grief process, this step helps the child to invoke earlier, happier images of the parent to counteract the more recent, gruesome sight. However, the validation of external reality and physical death or injury needs to be confirmed and, especially, for the younger child to be concretely represented in play or drawing. Only when children are secure in the belief of their parent's physical death have we seen children speak openly of their grief (Furman, 1974).

Coping with the Experience

Issues of Human Accountability. These are acts of human violence, not of natural disasters. Struggles over human accountability add considerably to the child's difficulty in achieving mastery. As recognized with adults, posttraumatic stress disorder is made more severe and longer lasting when the stressor is of human design, especially human-induced violence (DMS-III; Frederick, 1980; West and Coburn, 1984). As one 12-year-old said, "I'm mad at the way she did go. Because that hurt. I just wanted her to die naturally, not die because someone shot her." The child must confront his awareness and conflicts over who is responsible. He may wish at first to avoid the issue by calling the event an accident, but this provides only superficial relief.

The interviewer explores the issue of whom the child holds accountable for the act, his own understanding of the motive, and the child's conjecture about ways it could have been prevented. For example, we ask "How come it happened?" And then, "What would make someone do something like that?" If the assailant is a stranger, it may be easy for the child to assign blame. However, family violence can throw the child into an intense conflict of loyalty and he may suppress certain thoughts as unacceptable to other family members. The child might have already expressed his view in the story telling. A 7-year-old saw her mother shoot her father as he scuffled with her two brothers, who were trying to protect the mother from further physical assault. Everyone else held the abusive, alcoholic father at fault. However, in her story, this child assigned blame to two young, evil boys who unexpectedly appear and are intent on murderous troublemaking. She clearly missed her father and would not add blame to her memory of him, but neither could she accuse her mother. So she silently held her brothers responsible for the death.

The assignment of responsibility is not always fixed and may be seen to vary during the course of the interview. The child may be most disturbed by thoughts about the victim's actions, for instance, in wondering why the mother would be so provocative as to have yelled at her estranged husband the following: "Go ahead, shoot me. Show the kids what a big man you are."

Inner Plans of Action. We have been particularly impressed by the children's immediate efforts to reverse their helplessness by formulating a plan of action that would have remedied the situation. Lifton (1979) has referred to these cognitive reappraisals after catastrophic loss of life as "inner plans of action" and suggests they are repeatedly used to contend with the "death imprint."

As we have observed, the inner plans of action may seek to alter the precipitating events, to undo the violent act, to reverse the lethal consequences, or to gain safe retaliation. Their content and time frame are developmentally influenced (Eth and Pynoos, 1984).

Because of their limited cognitive skills, the preschool children do not appear to imagine alternate actions they might have taken on their own to prevent or alter the episode. It is they, therefore, who feel the most helpless. They may choose to flee or stay, look or turn away, be attentive, or try to sleep, but all of these are the choices of a passive witness, not a participant. The preschool child may fantasize about outside help having provided needed third party intervention, and, in his play, look to the interviewer to fill this role.

In contrast, school age children do not act as mere witnesses. They can participate, if only in fantasy. They can imagine having called the police, locking doors, grabbing a weapon away from the assailant, even capturing the assailant, before finally offering aid to the victim. Not surprisingly, these inner plans of action are nearly always confined to the day of the event. For example, with the interviewer playing the role of the assailant, one 10-year-old boy acted out how he imagined surprising the murderer, kicking the gun out of his hand, and tossing it to his unarmed father.

Adolescents can imagine alternative actions over a much longer period of time. They do not merely fantasize participation, but can implicate their own action or inaction in a more realistic fashion. One 14-year-old bitterly regretted her failure to unload her father's gun when she had had the chance 2 weeks before. A 17-year-old, boy, in trying to stop the rape of his mother, was overpowered by the assailant in a hand-to-hand knife fight, and, afterward, continued to imagine ways he could kill the man if he ever faced him again.

Especially important are ways the child imagines the parent could have been "fixed up" or aided after the injuries were sustained. For example, the young boy who was concerned with the thought that his mother's legs were broken also had the opportunity to ask a doctor for help during his story play. With the interviewer's aid, he then fixed up the broken legs of his fictional injured race car driver. Furthermore, expression of these particular fantasies may provide enough emotional relief that certain children, who had been reluctant to describe the mutilation, will now do so. One 8-year-old boy enacted a sequence in which he imagined his father is taken by ambulance to the hospital, operated on, the bullet removed, and the wound stitched closed.

With encouragement, he then readily drew the view of the bleeding chest wound that continued to intrude on his mind.

We carefully explore all these cognitive reappraisals (Folkman and Lazarus, 1984) for they are the best indication of the ways the child is troubled by feelings of self-blame for not doing more. Enactment of these "inner plans of action" can offset lingering feelings of personal responsibility.

Punishment or Retaliation. This discussion of blame can raise the question of punishment or retaliation. It may prove difficult for the child because it can reveal unbearable feelings of guilt in some children and frightening fantasies or dreams of revenge in others. In part, these feelings serve to counter the true helplessness at the moment of the violent act. We will allow the children to give full expression to these feelings before reminding them of the realistic limitations to what they could have done at the time. The children often look relieved by permission to imagine the tortures, mutilations, or execution they have reserved for the assailant, and readily draw a picture of "What you'd like to see happen to him." Afterward we will respond, "I see it feels good to imagine getting back at the bad man who stabbed your father," adding "I mean, to be able to do something to him now, when you really couldn't have stopped him at the time."

Counterretaliation. Themes of revenge may be associated with fears of counterretaliation by the assailant. The child may be afraid of the assailant's return and confused over what has actually happened to the suspect. If the assailant is already arrested, the child may be fearful over the future release of the suspect. We are concerned about how rarely the child is reassured about these matters by the police or the local district attorney.

Child's Impulse Control. If the child attributes the assailant's action to anger, hate, rejection, or craziness, etc., it is pertinent to ask, for example, "What do you do when you get angry?" and to explore the challenge to the child's own impulse control. Viewing an open display of violence may not only cause the child to lose trust in adult restraint, but he or she may acutely fear his or her own capability, especially in light of conscious revenge fantasies, and be concerned about the lack of proper external support.

Previous Trauma. After this discussion, it is common for a child spontaneously to mention past traumatic experiences. We have learned from children of further instances of child abuse, violent family deaths, unreported suicidal behavior, physical injuries, or accidents.

Traumatic Dreams. At this point, we inquire about recent dreams that may be remembered. Often a child reports anxiety dreams directly related to the traumatic event. The child may be fearful that the dream represents a portent of the future, not only of being victim of a violent assault, but sometimes becoming an avenging killer, too.

Future Orientation. It is now appropriate to ask the child about his or her concerns for the future, specifically as they relate to the potential dangers in interpersonal relationships. The child may have immediately after the trauma crystallized a vivid and restricted view of his or her own future. One child described how when he grows up he intends to live in an unaccessible fortress surrounded by many guard dogs. Many children stated that they never intend to carry or have children for fear of a similar violent outcome. Even school age children sometimes described changes in career plans for when they got older. For example, one 7-year-old, within days of her father's killing, reported she suddenly decided on a new life ambition, to become a stand-up comic who dressed in rags and made others laugh.

Similarly, the child feels burdened with an awareness of his or her unfortunate legacy. Children will complain about the novelty and stigma of being the child of a parent who died by murder or suicide. For instance, one 11-year-old girl bitterly lamented her status as a daughter of a "man who burned himself to death."

Current Stresses. When sufficient mastery of the traumatic anxiety has been achieved, the child can more actively address the life stresses engendered as a consequence of the traumatic event. He or she may spontaneously and pointedly inquire about placement, or schooling, or be easily encouraged to do so.

We survey a number of the common, easily overlooked issues that may add to the child's distress. These include contacts with the police and legal system changes in living situation or schooling, awareness of media coverage, and concerns about social schemata. We offer to help redress any oversights in the child's care. For example, in going to stay with her grandparents after her mother's murder, a 14-year-old had to abruptly change schools and lost the companionship of her established circle of friends. We were able to arrange to have her old friends visit her at her new home. Exploration of these posttraumatic consequences enables the child to consider the impact of the event on his current life circumstances.

THIRD STAGE: CLOSURE

Recapitulation. The sensitive process of terminating the interview is now begun. The first step is to elicit the child's cooperation in reviewing and summarizing the session. We attempt to make the child's responses seem more acceptable by emphasizing how understandable, realistic, and universal they are. By doing so, we also hope to have the child feel less alone and alienated, and more ready to receive further support from others. The interviewer returns to the initial drawing and story. The link to the trauma may be more clearly indicated perhaps by pointing out a similarity to the child's later reenactment or recounting.

Realistic Fears. It is important to repeat that it is all right to have felt helpless or afraid at the time and then sad or angry. We also make reference to what other children have told us after being in similar circumstances. The threat to the parent is so overwhelming at the time of the violence that many children do not entertain a realistic appraisal of their own personal jeopardy. Afterward, they may ignore, leave unacknowledged, or suppress any fear they might have experienced for their own safety. In one case, we could point out how far away from the shooting the child placed himself in his drawing when in fact he was so close as to have easily been shot himself. This intervention alleviated rather than aggravated the child's anxiety, perhaps by unburdening the child of the need to suppress his fears.

Expectable Course. We share with the children the expectable course for them as they pass through the course of their traumatic reactions. For example, we might say, "There will be times at school when you think about your mom, and feel sad." Or, "You may feel frightened to see a knife at home." Or, "You may jump at the sound of a loud noise," or "You may have some bad dreams but they'll happen less and less with time." We suggest they share these reactions with trusted adults to gain further assistance at these difficult moments.

Child's Courage. The child's beleaguered self-esteem needs support. We may be able to acknowledge the child's bravery. For instance, in one case a 5-year-old scampered out a window and down a fire escape to seek help for her wounded mother. One convenient method is to reflect on the child's performance during the interview, not only telling him what a good job he did but, more important, complimenting him on his courage to engage in such difficult talk. We will actually say, "You are very brave." Children invariably swell with pride upon hearing these words.

Child's Critique. The child is then asked to describe what has been helpful or disturbing about the interview. The children are usually quite candid. They will describe what issue had been "toughest" to talk about, what had been unhelpful, and what made them feel better. In fact, they have been our best teachers. Before we understood the role of suppressed fear, one child turned to one of us and exclaimed, "Boy, was it good to say how afraid I was."

Leave-Taking. As we end the interview, we give expression of our respect for the child and the privilege of having shared the interview experience with him. We then emphasize our availability to be called on in the future. We generally give the child, however young, our professional card with our telephone number. It is important to leave open the opportunity for contact, as often the trauma will be reactivated—on its anniversary date, for instance. At such times many children have sought us out despite the brevity of this initial contact. In those cases where the child has been referred for further treatment we have observed that this consultation with proper closure has facilitated the child's adaptation to the treatment situation.

CASE ILLUSTRATION

Lisa, who is 11 years old, was interviewed 5 days after her mother had been fatally shot by the mother's estranged boyfriend, Jim. On the day of the murder Lisa and her mother were at home babysitting for a neighbor's infant, while Lisa's younger sister was at school. When interviewed, Lisa and her sister were temporarily residing with a cousin and her young children.

The consultant began the interview by inviting Lisa to draw a picture and make up a story about it.

> *Lisa:* We woke up in the morning and we were packing. Then we get into our car and the moving truck. We're loading everything onto the truck and we're moving so that if Jim came back he wouldn't find us, so he can't shoot my mother. That's my mother who is moving the plant. My sister is watering the grass and I'm helping to take the plants off the porch. And everyone is feeling happy.
>
> My mother loves plants. She had house plants and all kinds of plants. I don't really know the name of them but she had lots of plants around the house. She took good care of them. She didn't

really like us helping with the plants because we might do something wrong and they might die. She wanted to take care of them herself.

Right afterward the plants were all given to neighbors except two. These were ones Mother especially grew for me and my sister and cut into the shape of a lion and a hippo. I'm going to make sure to keep watering them.

Consultant (C): This is the kind of story you would have liked to have happen instead of what did.

Lisa: Yes (she begins to cry and is comforted by the interviewer). She had just been offered a job a couple of days before the accident happened. She never had a chance to take it. We could then have afforded to move. Now she's moved to heaven and we're going to have to move somewhere else (she continues to cry and accepts physical consolation).

C: I know it's going to make you sad to talk about some of this.

Lisa: I don't care.

C: Maybe this is a good time to tell what happened (she then begins to describe the actual murder scene and is encouraged to draw a picture of it).

Lisa: This is my mother bundled up on the couch. She's just waking up. The man is right here, talking in front of her face. At first I was just taking a nap and the baby was just in the bedroom. When I came out and saw him with the gun I was so scared, I just stood there looking. He was flicking the gun in her face. He then shot her. He kept shooting her until he got to the door, and then he ran out somewhere.

I waited until I heard our screen door shut, 'cause I didn't want to get shot. Then I ran up to my mother, who was rolling off the couch and she fell on her side. I rolled her over and was talking to her. I was crying and I was mad because I didn't know what to do. I grabbed the phone to call the police but I think they'd already been called by the neighbors. Before the police came I was on the floor with her. Her eyes were down, her eyelids were like half-closed, and her hair was kind of messed up, sticking out. Blood was everywhere. I was trying to open her eyes. I was trying to wake her up—you know, by shaking her face. I thought maybe if I did something wrong she would do something. I tried to listen to her heart and to take her pulse. I couldn't find anything. I'd seen that on a soap opera. I watched with my mother when somebody got shot. Also, you know how when you can't breathe how you press their stomach or something, I was trying to do that so she could breathe, but she wasn't breathing right, and when she took a breath then blood started to come onto the floor. I kept talking to her but she wouldn't talk. I thought if only she could talk then everything could be all right. I just took her hand in mine, and kept shaking it while telling her to hang on. I was crying and I asked God to save my Mommy and I'd be a good girl, but he took her. Afterwards I went and locked all the doors.

C: You tried your best to help her if you could. I'm sure you couldn't stop the bleeding. You worry you should have done more.

Lisa: There was too much blood.

C: Did you get blood on you, too?

Lisa: It was on these pants. These were the pants I was wearing. But they've been washed. I guess I had some right here 'cause I was listening to her heart. Her shirt was full of blood, and when she tried to breathe she made a sound like this (she inhales in a gasping manner) and she did it for a long time. Sometimes I remember how the gun sounded, how loud it was.

C: It's really something to go through.

Lisa: I am not really mad at the fact that she's dead because you know everybody has to go, but I am mad at the way she did go. Because that hurt. I just wanted her to die naturally, not to die of a shooting or stabbing or strangling or something like that.

It just doesn't feel right. Oh, how she died. Like that, horrible. She should have died natural, and maybe I could have been grown because that way I wouldn't have lost a mother truly. I was scared when the police came because first they knocked on the door real loud. But I saw the fire truck and it had a siren on. So I knew it was the police. They didn't barge in as I thought they might have. When the police came I wanted to stay with my mother but they moved me to the next room for awhile.

That's bad that he's not been found yet. I was thinking that my mother would be looking for him and tell me, so then I could tell the police and they'd find him (she draws her mother in heaven).

She is in heaven with God. He has long hair. Jesus had long hair. She's looking down on us. When she sees us cry she cries too. She'll make sure we've all left so if Jim comes back he'll have a big surprise because nobody will be there.

C: Do you get scared?

Lisa: I got scared this morning. I didn't want to go outside because Jim could be somewhere outside. I asked my uncle to get his gun and scare away the man I saw across the street. Maybe we could catch Jim, get him to drop his gun and bring him to the police station.

C: You called it an accident, not murder.

Lisa: Just a name I picked for it. But a man really did it. Murder sounds like when somebody chokes or strangles somebody. I guess I'd say he killed her because that doesn't mean so much physical contact. Maybe if I hadn't woke up she wouldn't be dead. He probably got scared when I saw him with the gun.

C: And he did something terrible to your mother. What makes a person do something like that?

Lisa: I guess hate and anger. He wasn't our friend and she told him she didn't want to see him. I guess he got angry at that.

C: What would you like to see happen to him?

Lisa: I was dreaming that all my cousins and our relatives were dressed, you know, how they put you up against the wall and blindfold you and shoot you. I had the same knife he used to stab my mother and the same gun that he shot her with. Then I went up to him and said, "Do you remember this, now you can feel it." And I stabbed him right where he stabbed my mother. Then I said, "I guess you remember this, too," and then I shot him. Then I moved, and everybody started shooting him (she comments on how good a picture that is to draw). It felt good like I was getting back at him. The hands are behind his back. He's tied up and the scarf is around his neck because we took it off so he could see what happens.

C: Do you know what will happen if he's arrested?

Lisa: He'll go to jail. But I want him to stay in jail for the rest of his life, since he took a life from somebody he ought to get his life down to nothing.

C: There must be times when you get angry at somebody.

Lisa: When I get angry I don't like to show my feelings. I just keep them in. I hold my breath and just don't think about it. But since my mother's death I can't really control it all because the way people treat us it seems like it's all our fault she was dead. The way they're telling us to change so quickly. They want us to do things their way. It's kind of hard for us because we just lost a mother. He must have had a hot temper. When I get mad at my sister now I get afraid I might hit or hurt her. I don't like that.

C: Do you ever think about her relationship with men and what it will be like for you when you get older?

Lisa: I said I'd never get married and have kids, 'cause if me and him fight, something might happen to me where I have to die. Then I will leave my kids just like my mother had to leave. And I don't want to do that to my kids. I had that thought the same day she died. I was thinking about when I have grown kids she'll never be able to see her grandkids in person.

(Toward the end of the interview Lisa began to address some of her current concerns.) We might have to go to an orphanage. I don't want to. Nobody is there like relatives or anything. One reason I don't want to go to a foster home is because they might separate me and my sister. It's bad enough we lost our mother.

C: Remember you told me how well your mother looked after her plants. I think you want somebody to look after you with that much care. You must feel that God is being very unkind in letting this kind of thing happen in your life.

Lisa: Yeah. That sure isn't fair because I understand He wanted her to leave us in this way but why did it have to happen? Or, the least He could have done was wait until a certain age when we could have been on our own.

C: How has it been to talk with me?

Lisa: It made me feel hurt and stuff, but it also made me feel good.

DISCUSSION

Overview

We have described a complete interview format designed to assist children who have witnessed a violent act. The helpless, passive experience of watching the moment or moments of a violent act and its injurious consequences constitutes an immediate psychic trauma for the child (Pynoos and Eth, 1985). The viewing is painful, frightening, and distressing. Our work has been with the most traumatic cases: a parent's suicide, murder, or rape (Eth and Pynoos, 1983; Pynoos and Eth, 1985; Pynoos et al., 1981). We think the "hammer effect" of examining catastrophic violence has brought to light more visibly the processes needed to work with children in many other clinical settings.

Although the technique we have described may appear rigidly structured, in fact, the sessions generally follow the child's lead and are rarely experienced as arbitrary or stifling. It would seem that there is an underlying logic to the interview proceeding in this way. We have been impressed that some child psychiatrists intuitively conduct their initial interviews with traumatized children in exactly this way without consciously recognizing the unique format. Most other clinicians will miss the child's cues and lose the opportunity for ready exploration of the traumatic material. There have been occasions where we have tactfully colluded with the child's avoidance and omitted some component of the interview, only to learn afterward that incomplete mastery of the trauma-related anxiety had been achieved. We caution child therapists who feel inclined to avoid the traumatic material to be aware of countertransference identification with the affected child.

Particular attention must be paid to the final phase of the interview as incomplete closure threatens the effectiveness of the session. Without proper closure the child will be left struggling with traumatic material without adequate enhancement of ego function with which to bind his anxiety. In that situation, the interview can be experienced as unsettling.

This technique has been readily learned by a number of child therapists and applied to their work with a variety of traumatized children. We have noted that some of our colleagues have voiced concern that the interview's focus on the traumatic event could unduly upset an already victimized child. Our extensive experience, supported by the work of several other investigators (Ayalon, 1983; Frederick, 1985) confirms that open discussion of the trauma offers immediate relief and *not* further distress to the child. Recent stress investigators have suggested that there may be an optimum time to provide intervention beyond which it is more difficult to achieve ego restoration and improved affective tolerance (Horowitz and Kaltreider, 1979; van der Kolk and Ducey, 1984).

Childhood Trauma

Recent reviews have discussed the significant psychological impact for children of a wide variety of traumatic experiences (Eth and Pynoos, 1985; Terr, 1984). There is better recognition of the intrapsychic, behavioral, and physiologic changes that can occur. There may be prominent intrusive and avoidant phenomenon, increased states of arousal and incident specific new behaviors. Reports of long-term effects have included pessimistic life attitudes, alterations in personality, diminished self-esteem and disturbances in interpersonal relationships. Because these traumatic sequelae do not necessarily pass with time, there is an obvious need to develop effective methods of therapy intervention.

The landmark paper on the treatment of trauma in childhood was written by Levy (1938). "Release therapy" was specifically devised as a psychotherapeutic technique to resolve symptoms arising from a "definitely known traumatic episode." The child's traumatic anxieties, especially those related to aggressive behaviors inhibited by fear were discharged through directed play. Levy's technique has not received further exploration, in part because of its limited scope.

Analogous Model

In searching for an analogous model of therapeutic trauma consultation, we have been impressed with the resemblance between our technique and that adopted by military psychiatrists for the treatment of soldiers who have viewed a buddy killed or maimed in combat (Fox, 1974; Glass, 1947, 1954; Grinker and Spiegel, 1943; Hendin et al., 1981; Kardiner, 1941; Kolb and Mutalipassi, 1982; Lifton, 1982; Smith, 1982; Teicher, 1953; U.S. Public Health Service, 1943). The principles we share include: 1) the witnessing of extreme violence constitutes a unique, severe, psychic trauma; 2) the importance of "front-line intervention" before maladaptive ego resolution is organized; 3) since "ego contraction" is a primary consequence of the trauma, major efforts are directed at ego restitution and coping enhancement; 4) mastery required an affectively experienced "reliving," including a comprehensive review of the traumatic event; 5) aggressive themes, especially of retaliation, threaten ego restoration and must be fully explored; 6) an "outraged superego" responds to the passivity of the trauma experience by insisting that more should have been done to save the victim, and its demands must be relived by the interview; 7) absent or pathologic grief results from efforts to avoid revoking traumatic anxiety; and 8) sustained mastery can only be achieved through reintegration into the group, family, or community.

Similar interview methods follow from these principles. We remain flexible: at times insisting the child continue, at other times participating theatrically in the reliving of the episode, and occasionally assuming the role of an interested bystander. Whenever stifled grief emerges, we offer open consolation and physical comfort. We underscore the realistic fears associated with a danger, and normalize the anxiety in reexperiencing the event in session. However, the two techniques differ in handling the opening phase of the interview. Since soldiers display traumatic amnesia or disavowal, narcosynthesis or hypnosis were often necessary adjuncts to penetrating these defenses. On the other hand, we have found that children remain consciously aware of the traumatic event, though diminishing its pain through the use of denial-in-fantasy or avoidance.

The Interview

Our interview format is conceptualized as an acute consultation service available to assist the child, the child's family, and the larger social network in functioning more effectively in the aftermath of the child's psychological trauma. The explicit goal is to identify the immediate effects of the trauma, with the child's attention and energy reserved exclusively for this task. The role of the consultant is to serve as an auxiliary ego to provide the encouragement needed to complete the assignment. In this regard, the technique is not unlike Winnicott's (1971) use of the squiggle in his single session consultations.

The choice of a free drawing maneuver is advantageous for several different reasons (Gardner, 1979). Coincidentally, in 1918 on the battlefront at La Fauche, France, drawings were successfully employed to provide access to repressed memories of traumatic scenes (U.S. Public Health Service, 1943). As described, this opening offers a comfortable play activity for the child. His or her own creation then serves as a stimulus for verbalization at a time otherwise known for stony silence. The drawing is referred to often during the remainder of the interview, and as a product of the child's own mind represents an acceptable link to the traumatic situation. As a projective device, the drawing invariably signifies the child's unconscious preoccupation with the traumatic memory. Lifton (1982) has termed this "the indelible image." Since the mode of witnessing the violence was visual, it is appropriate and desirable that the drawing employ that sensory apparatus as well (Horowitz, 1970). According to Piaget and Inhelder (1969): "Drawing . . . should be considered as being halfway between symbolic play and the mental image" (p. 54). By confronting the violent scene on paper, the child begins to distance him-or herself from the traumatic memory. Importantly, the child also initiates motor and verbal activities which counteract the passivity of the traumatic experience. This action helps reverse the sense of helplessness and establish an interpersonal connection, fostering trauma mastery.

Denial in fantasy is one way the child can psychologically avert "objective pain" and danger without disrupting reality testing (Freud, 1937). In tactfully addressing the child's idiosyncratic use of this means of coping, we have been impressed by the immediate restoration of affect heralded by what Horowitz and Kalterider (1979) termed an emotional "outcry." With the ego more tolerant of the painful reality, the child is able, at his or her own pace and manner, to describe the traumatic events.

Sharing the traumatic memories with the consultant begins the process of mastering the traumatic experience. By speaking and playing, the child can partially correct the passive helplessness of the witness role. The session also bolsters the child's observing ego and reality testing functions, which tend to dispel cognitive confusion and encourage active coping (Caplan, 1981). In so doing, the child is assisted to identify traumatic reminders that elicit psychophysiologic reactions, intrusive imagery, and intense affective responses. The goal is to increase the child's sense of being able to anticipate or, at least, manage their recurrence.

Whatever his outward behavior or mood may suggest, the mind of even the young child is preoccupied with inner plans of action in the acute aftermath of a violent trauma. They provide important clues to the child's earliest efforts to master the trauma. Attention to these conscious fantasies enhances the child's understanding of the ways he or she is trying to overcome the helplessness he experienced and is essential to working through of the trauma. It is important to assist the child in distinguishing his or her own aggressive impulses from those of the assailant.

Our child interview is not designed simply to elicit a journalistic recounting of the episode but rather to recapture the child's affective experience of the traumatic events. Exploration of the "worst moment," special detailing, and affectively charged interpersonal exchanges, all assist in this task. Consistent with modern views of autobiographical memory, this form of recall is understood to be subjective reconstruction (Bartlett, 1932; Kris, 1956; Paul, 1967). Rather than dampen all feelings, the child must retain confidence that he or she is not helpless in the face of his or her emotions—that is, neither to fear a loss of impulse control nor a flood of unbearable emotion (Krystal, 1978).

Exploration of the child's revenge fantasies is a key step in this process. It is often followed by a perceivable increase in spontaneity and affective range. In the critique of the interview, children frequently chose the depiction of their revenge fantasy when asked to "point to the drawing that helped the most." We have observed continued affective constriction in children where this step in the interview has not been successful.

Probably the best gauge of the effectiveness of the trauma exploration is the enhanced desire of the child to discuss the subsequent life stresses brought on by the event, and to be actively involved in decisions about his care. Early intervention may therefore be all-important to prevent the traumatized child from passively accepting a series of imposed changes in his life. The child may have constructive ideas about ways in which some things can be done to minimize the continued upset in his or her life. We would especially caution the child expert in regard to custody issues. We have observed that child therapists too often become involved in evaluating a child to render an opinion regarding custody while the child remains untreated for prominent signs of severe posttraumatic stress.

Modifying Factors

There are factors besides the violent event itself which contribute to the child's individual response to the psychic trauma. Age and level of ego development influence his or her experience of the event, initial efforts to cope, and later understanding of responsibility. The preschooler is particularly helpless and passive in the face of danger. He or she will make repeated use of denial in fantasy to restore the parent unharmed after the trauma without imagining ways to prevent or intervene during the episode. Reparative and retaliatory actions must be carried out by adults in their name. Latency age children have expanded their role as witness to include participation, if only in fantasy. They can imagine taking the gun, chasing the assailant, and healing the injured parent. As a consequence, they begin to feel some degree of responsibility and frequently fantasize about personal revenge. The adolescent shows not only preoccupation with the violent act but is also concerned with the interplay of assailant, victim, themselves, and others. They are likely in the interview to emphasize their own behavior during the traumatic episode. Motive, circumstance, and justice emerge as complex issues.

Another consideration is the child's previous experience with psychological trauma. Sadly, many of the children we have interviewed are suffering from the cumulative effect of multiple traumas. Although we begin by focusing on the most recent event, we soon come to discover the preceding series of incidents which never have been previously explored. These children may have come to speak in a manner to lessen the impact of the terror. However, we have not observed them to be immunized or inured by their recent exposure to abuse or violence. The recurrence of intrusive memories of these prior experiences may hamper their recovery from the current trauma, and needs to be addressed. However, the recent event which the child has witnessed is startlingly novel. No observation of previous violence can prepare a child for the sight of a mother's murder. Even the youngest child can identify it as "the beating where Mommy didn't get up and talk again." The interview begins a painful process of opening the child to his or her memories and offering relief through therapeutic contact.

The presence of preexisting psychological conflicts or frank psychopathology handicaps the child in his or her efforts to cope with the impact of the traumatic event and is readily apparent in the session. For example, the presence of an untreated attention deficit disorder interfered by distracting one child from being able to maintain the needed sustained attention even within the therapeutic consultation. Disturbed children are priority candidates for this technique, although further psychiatric intervention is generally indicated.

We would recommend deferring this interview procedure for those children who have themselves been the direct victim of physical injury. Although these children may have also experienced considerable psychological trauma as a consequence of witnessing violence, attention to their own injuries must take precedence. We suggest postponing consideration of the observational insult while the child's ego resources are rightfully centered on his or her bodily damage. As recovery proceeds, the child will then become available to participate actively in this specialized interview technique. This further step is necessary before the child can fully overcome both of these traumas, the physical and psychological.

Benefits

The interview can be helpful for the child in several different ways. After addressing the actual trauma, the child is in a position to more freely concentrate on the grief work and on other critical issues confronting the child in the wake of a family tragedy. We have met with children whose grieving was interrupted by an intrusive memory of the traumatic event, such as the sight of a physically mutilated parent. The interview session relieves the burden of those recollections and the mourning process can be resumed (Eth and Pynoos, 1985).

Following the consultation, many children appear noticeably less alienated and detached. In part, this clinical improvement derives directly from the detailed exploration of the traumatic situation and its consequences. The single session provides immediate relief for the child, at a time when the child is otherwise feeling very badly. As the child begins to feel better in the presence of the trusted consultant, the child reestablishes the capacity to engage in interpersonal relationships. The child's receptivity to human contact, which was nurtured during the session, can then be transferred to others in the child's support network. In effect, the interview functions as a bridge to those caretaking adults available to the child. By so doing, the technique opens the child to therapeutic influences in his or her environment.

Short-term benefits for the child arise from the consultant assuming the role of child advocate. With permission and in the child's presence, we share with the parent or guardian dominant themes of the session and identified traumatic reminders. We also discuss the natural course of traumatic reactions to prepare them to assist the child at home. We might also confer with school and social service personnel. It is especially useful to develop a close affiliation with the judicial authorities, as the child witness to criminal violence can be forced to play a prominent role in criminal proceedings. We have commented on this subject at length elsewhere (Pynoos and Eth, 1984).

Unfortunately, the traumatized child is in a particularly precarious position. Whatever gains may have accrued during the interview process are jeopardized by external factors in the child's social nexus. For instance, placement in the home of a psychotic relative sabotaged the tenuous progress of one orphaned preschool girl. But if the social system is supportive and understanding, then the ego restitution initiated during the session can be consolidated, expanded, and offered as a model for other family members (Polak et al., 1975).

We hesitate to predict that our interview technique will prove to be preventive. Although therapeutic consultations may have long-term benefits, both desired and unanticipated, enough controlled long-term observations of results have not yet been conducted. However, there are initial reports of long-term deleterious consequences arising from childhood trauma (Gislason and Call, 1982) suggesting this to be an important area for in-depth study. In the meanwhile, we can draw upon the psychiatric experience with war neuroses to recommend prompt intervention and full exploration of the trauma. Investigators of adult posttraumatic stress disorders have also argued that there may be an optimum time for intervention, when the intrusive phenomena are most apparent and the associated affect most readily available (Horowitz, 1970; van der Kolk and Ducey, 1984). With promising results reported for adults (Horowitz and Kaltreider, 1979), there is need to investigate the tech-

384   ROBERT S. PYNOOS AND SPENCER ETH

nique and efficacy of brief therapy with children exposed to violence. However, these methods will need modification to take into account important
developmental considerations.

The interview technique, though not explicitly diagnostic, does allow the
consultant to assess the child's adaptation to crisis. Gross indicators of psychopathology are readily apparent, whether they be products of chronic disability or acute decompensation. Hence, the interview serves the purpose of
screening the child for the need for a formal referral for psychiatric evaluation
or treatment. In addition, the technique specifically examines for the presence
or severity of a posttraumatic stress disorder, a common finding in this
population of traumatized children. Those children who require further psychiatric assistance will be able to draw on the positive experience of the
interview to prepare for and accept future therapeutic contacts.

CONCLUSION

We have presented a method of interviewing children who have recently
suffered a personal disaster. It is our contention that the witnessing of extreme
violence constitutes a psychological trauma for the child. The immediate
consequences often include ego contraction, affective intolerance, and estrangement, as well as grief. Despite prominent posttraumatic stress reactions,
children have the capacity and in fact the desire to collaborate with an adult
in directly confronting the traumatic incident soon after its occurrence. Unfortunately, the child's family is often struggling with its own avoidance of
traumatic anxiety. It is therefore essential that the child have the opportunity
to explore the traumatic episode in the reassuring presence of an unaffected
adult (Pynoos and Eth, 1986). Through the use of free drawings and story
telling, the consultant is able to engage the child in an exploration of the
events associated with the experience of overwhelming anxiety. The response
is a sense of immediate relief and a reestablishment of human relatedness.
We hope that this easily learned technique becomes widely available to assist
the many traumatized children at a time of great need.

REFERENCES

Ayalon, O. (1983), Children as hostage. Practitioner, 226:1773–1781.
Bartlett, F. C. (1932), Remembering. Cambridge, Mass.: Cambridge University Press.
Caplan, G. (1981), Mastery of stress: psychological aspects. J. Amer. Psychiat., 138:
    413–420.

Eth, S. & Pynoos, R. (1983), Children who witness the homicide of a parent. Presented at the 1983 annual meeting of the American Academy of Child Psychiatry.

—— *(1984), Developmental perspectives on psychic trauma in childhood. In:* Trauma and Its Wake, *ed. C. R. Figley. New York: Brunner/Mazel.*

—— *(1985), Interaction of trauma and grief in childhood. In:* Posttraumatic Stress Disorder in Children, *Chap. 8, ed. S. Eth and R. Pynoos. Washington, D.C.: American Psychiatric Press.*

Folkman, S. & Lazarus, R. (1984), Personal control and stress and coping processes. J. Pers. Soc. Psychol., *46:839–852.*

Fox, R. P. (1974), Narcissistic rage and the problem of combat aggression. Arch. Gen. Psychiat., *31:807–811.*

Frederick, C. (1980), Effects of natural v. human induced violence upon victims. Evaluation and Change, *Special Issue, 71–75.*

—— *(1985), Children traumatized by catastrophic situations. In:* Posttraumatic Stress Disorder in Children, *Chap. 4, ed. S. Eth & R. Pynoos. Washington, D.C.: American Psychiatric Press.*

Freud, A. (1937), The Ego and Mechanisms of Defence. *London: Hogarth Press.*

—— *(1965),* Normality and Pathology in Childhood. *New York: International Universities Press.*

Furman, E. (1974), A Child's Parent Dies. *New Haven, Conn.: Yale University Press.*

Gardner, R. (1979), Helping children cooperate in therapy. In: Basic Handbook of Child Psychiatry, *Vol. 4, ed. J. D. Noshpitz et al. New York: Basic Books.*

Gislason, I. L. & Call, J. (1982), Dog bite in infancy: trauma and personality development. This Journal, *21:203–207.*

Glass, A. J. (1947), Effectiveness of forward treatment. Bull. U.S. Army Med. Dept., *7:1034–1041.*

—— *(1954), Psychotherapy in the combat zone.* Amer. J. Psychiat., *110:725–731.*

Grinker, R. R. & Spiegel, J. P. (1943), War Neuroses in North Africa: the Tunisian campaign. The Air Surgeon, Army Air Forces, *September. New York: Josiah Macy, Jr. Foundation.*

Hendin, H., Pollinger, A., Singer, P. & Ulman, R. B. (1981), Meanings of combat and the development of post-traumatic stress disorder. Amer. J. Psychiat., *138:1490–1493.*

Horowitz, J. (1970), Image Formation and Cognition. *New York: Appleton-Century-Crofts.*

Horowitz, M. & Kaltreider, N. (1979), Brief therapy of the stress response syndrome. Psychiat. Clin. N. Amer. 2, No. 2, August.

Kardiner, A. (1941), The traumatic neuroses of war. In: Psychosomatic Medical Monograph. *New York: Paul Hoeber, pp. 11–111.*

Kolb, L. & Mutalipassi, L. (1982). The conditioned emotional response: a subclass of the chronic and delayed post-traumatic stress disorder. Psychiat. Ann., *12:979–987.*

Kris, E. (1956), The recovery of childhood memories in psychoanalysis. The Psychoanalytic Study of the Child, *11:54–88.*

Krystal, J. (1978), Trauma and affects. The Psychoanalytic Study of the Child, *33:81–116.*

Levy, D. M. (1938), Release therapy in young children. Psychiatry, 1:387–390.

Lifton, R. J. (1979), The Broken Connection. New York: Simon & Schuster.

—— (1982), The psychology of the survivor and the death imprint. Psychiat. Ann., 12:1011–1020.

Paul, I. H. (1967), The concept of schema in memory theory. Psychol. Issues, 18/19: 218–258.

Piaget, T. & Inhelder, B. (1969), The Psychology of the Child. New York: Basic Books.

Polak, P. R., Egan, D., Vanderberg, R., et al. (1975), Prevention in mental health: a controlled study. Amer. J. Psychiat., 132:146–149.

Pynoos, R. & Eth, S. (1984), The child as witness to homicide. J. Soc. Issues, 40:87–108.

—— (1985), Children traumatized by witnessing of personal violence. In: Posttraumatic Stress Disorder in Children, Chap. 2, ed. S. Eth & R. Pynoos. Washington, D.C.: American Psychiatric Press.

—— (1986), Witnessing violence: special interventions with children. In: The Violent Home, ed. M. Lystad. New York: Brunner/Mazel.

—— Gilman, K. & Shapiro, T. (1981) Children's response to parental suicidal behavior. Presented at the 1981 annual meeting of the American Academy of Child Psychiatry.

Smith, J. R. (1982), Personal responsibility in traumatic stress reactions. Psychiat. Ann., 12:1021–1030.

Teicher, J. D. (1953), "Combat fatigue" or "death anxiety neurosis." J. Nerv. Ment. Dis., 117:232–242.

Terr, L. (1984), Children at risk. In: Psychiatry Update, Vol. III, ed. L. Grinspoon. Washington, D.C.: American Psychiatric Press.

U.S. Public Health Service. (1943), Proceedings of Conference on Traumatic War Neuroses in Merchant Seamen, New York Academy of Medicine (January 28).

van der Kolk, B. & Ducey, C. (1984). Clinical implication of the Rorschach in posttraumatic stress disorder. In: Traumatic Stress Disorder: Psychological and Biological Sequelae, ed. B. Van Der Kolk. Washington, D.C.: American Psychiatric Press.

Waelder, R. (1933), The psychoanalytic theory of play. Psychoanal. Quart., 11:208–224.

West, L. J. & Coburn, K. (1984), Posttraumatic anxiety. In: Diagnosis and Treatment of Anxiety Disorders, ed. R. O. Pasnau. Washington, D.C.: American Psychiatric Press.

Winnicott, D. W. (1971), Therapeutic Consultations in Child Psychiatry. New York: Basic Books.

21. Imagery in Therapy

An Information Processing Analysis of Fear

Peter J. Lang

THE ROLE OF IMAGERY in therapy poses a perplexing question for a natural science of behavior. Philosophers tell us that images are private events available only to human introspection. As their observation cannot be shared or their dimensions measured by any instrument, they cannot be data in a scientific analysis. The founder of systematic desensitization therapy, Joseph Wolpe, recognized this limitation of the subjective construct. Thus, he proposed an alternative view, that images were "specific neural events" which formed part of the pattern or neural sequence previously evoked by specific external stimuli. As they shared a common neurophysiology, the image could "stand in" for an objective stimulus, and the consequences of its manipulation were held to be similar to those that might be occasioned by the object itself. Speaking of desensitization, he states that "a basic assumption underlying this procedure is that the response to the imagined situation resembles that to the real situation" (Wolpe, 1958, p. 139). However, the initiating stimulus in therapy is not the "neural events": it is a set of instructions, which include the admonition to adopt an imaginal set and a description of the things to be imagined. Furthermore, we are unable to manipulate directly the complex neurophysiology implied by Wolpe's analysis. Thus, while the neural image may be an ultimate reality, the practical utility of the concept is limited. Nevertheless, we should not be wholly dismayed. As it is not a knowledge of chemistry which guides the chef to a good bouillabaisse, but knowing which fish to use and how to cook them, so in trying to understand the practical effect of desensitization, the primary task may not be facilitated by reductionism, but by a direct analysis of the information content of the image and the manner of its functional processing.

A starting place for this enterprise is found in a study of systematic

---

desensitization conducted by Lang, Melamed, and Hart (1970). They noted several consistent relationships between physiological reactivity to fear imagery and successful therapeutic outcomes. Subjects who profited from desensitization had faster heart rates during scenes said to evoke fear than during scenes they did not find frightening. Furthermore, successful subjects reported scenes to be unusually fearful during sessions when their tonic heart rates were relatively high. Finally, subjects who improved with treatment showed a systematic reduction in heart rate with repeated scene presentation, which was in turn associated with fewer fear signals. This convariation between verbal report and cardiac activity was not found for those who failed to show improvement with treatment. These data suggest a relationship between the physiology of instructionally evoked imagery and emotional behavior change. More specifically, they imply that the psychophysiological structure of imagined scenes may be a key to the emotional processing which the therapy is designed to accomplish.

In the following pages an information processing analysis of emotional imagery will be described. An effort will be made to show that the image can be a meaningful psychophysiological construct, that it can be defined in terms of measurable response events, and that these responses are controlled by identifiable external stimuli. In the first part of this paper, consideration is given to the recent thought of cognitive psychologists, as they have reexamined issues of imagery processing and storage. It will be argued that affective images are best conceptualized as propositional structures, rather than as reperceived raw, sensory representations. We will show that the former view logically permits experimental manipulation of the image through instructions and development of an imagery taxonomy of stimulus and response components. An experiment will be described which illustrates the utility of this approach. In the second half of the paper the implications of image analysis for an understanding of behavior therapy process and outcome are elucidated. The importance of psychophysiological measurement in therapy is emphasized. Differences are examined between flooding and desensitization, the therapeutic processes initiated by exposure to objective fear stimuli and those prompted by imagery procedures are compared, and therapeutic modeling is analyzed in terms of the propositional image. Finally, a tentative model for fear processing is proposed with suggestions for future research.

IMAGERY PROCESSING AND STORAGE

There are two basic ways in which the imaginal act has been conceptualized. From the first viewpoint, sensory images are presumed to be the primary products of external observation. They are stored in the brain as primitive, nonreducible units, having a fundamental geometric (if visual) or iconic representation in storage. The act of imagining involves the scanning, inward perceiving, or interpreting of this raw harvest of sensory observation. Advocates of the second viewpoint do not assume that the brain is such a silo of unprocessed *appearances*; the brain stores *knowledge* (to use the philosophic terms). We have information about objects or events, not pictures or representations of them. We are culturally conditioned to speak of "seeing" images in the "mind's eye," but this is no more than a compelling metaphor. The phenomenal image masks a more fundamental code. This alternative view begins with the assumption that the image in the brain is more like an elaborated description, an integration of specific affirmations about the world. The image is a functionally organized, finite set of propositions. Such propositions are assertions about relationships, descriptions, interpretations, labels, and tags, which prompt percept-like verbal reports, but which are more basically the units of a preparatory set to respond.

It will be argued in this paper that behavior therapists and researchers in psychopathology should not adopt the picture metaphor, but should embrace the propositional conception of information storage, retrieval, and processing. We are guided in the following argument by an excellent theoretical paper by Pylyshyn (1973), whose explication of this problem is commended to serious students of cognitive imagery.

Pictures in the Head

For many psychologists, the verbal report of an image is viewed as a product of perceptual processing in the absence of an external stimulus. The mental image is a kind of picture in the head, which may be faint and fleeting, or in the case of idetics it may be so vivid as to ape an external observation. As Pylyshyn points out. "The whole vocabulary of imagery uses a language appropriate to describing pictures and the process of perceiving pictures. We speak of clarity and vividness of images, of scanning images, of seeing new patterns in images, and of naming objects or properties depicted in images" (p. 8).

The implications of this language are that object representations are stored in the brain in analog form, that they may be removed from files and "subsequently scanned perceptually in order to obtain meaningful information regarding the presence of objects, attributes, relations, etc." While subjective experience clearly commends this view, there are practical and logical reasons for its rejection. To begin with, the assumption of analog representation places "an incredible burden on the storage capacity of the brain." If the "pictures" held in storage are really in raw form, containing in fine grain the same detail that could have been read off the retina or basilar membrane at the time of external observation, then no serious, current neural theory of memory could explain how the finite sum of cells in the human brain could accommodate this wealth of information. We would be inundated with neuronal snapshots well before the first month of life. Furthermore, the notion that perceptual scanning and interpretation are secondary to a retrieval process introduces a time delay, which is often inconsistent with the rapid efficiency of the brain in reviewing experience and generating behavior. Phenomenological research also prompts a questioning of this view. Remembered scenes, only partially apprehended, are not recalled like jigsaw puzzles with pieces missing. Furthermore, images often seem to have attributional properties that are inextricably wedded to their objective content. Pylyshyn (1973) notes that a chess player may have an image of two pieces that could be described as "being attacked by": a nonchess player would not have this element in his image, although he might report imagining the same spatial relations between pieces on a chessboard. Or similarly, one can have a vivid image of two lovers embracing without any specific sense of who was on the left or who was on the right.

A partial solution to the storage problem might be to assume some kind of limited resolution representation. We could hypothesize a finite number of scan lines, as in a television picture, to be enhanced later by the brain for verbal report, as the computer enhances telemetered pictures of the near planets. A digital code might be even more efficient; however, we now stray even farther from the concept of a primary image. If a teleological statement may be risked, it seems unreasonable to suppose that the purpose of the brain is to provide primary images for human beings to comment on. As Sperry noted many years ago (1952), the purpose of the brain is not to generate perceptual experience but to organize and facilitate responding. If this is true we might expect the image code not to be independent of behavioral function, as are scan lines or digital notation, but to be relational and to incorporate the responding organism. Descriptions of images, particularly emotional images, inevitably contain many of the editorial comments (e.g., "attacking," "embracing") alluded to above. They also include the observer, his point of view, and often his active participation.

The Image as a Propositional Construct

What subjects report about images does not sound like limited-resolution photographs. The reports include both more and less detail than such a system would suggest, as well as the interpretive elements that are not part of raw observations. Any representation having such properties "is much closer to being a description of the scene than a picture of it. A description is propositional, it contains a finite amount of information, it may contain abstract as well as concrete aspects and, especially relevant to the present discussion, it contains terms (symbols for objects, attributes, and relations) which are the results of—not inputs to—perceptual processes" (Pylyshyn, 1973, p. 11).

It is proposed that emotional images, of the sort evoked in the therapeutic context, are best understood as propositional constructions. A proposition is essentially what a string of words assert, e.g., "The book is on the desk." However, this does not mean that the propositions of an image are basically linguistic in form. Bower (1970) makes the distinction between an imagistic memory system and a contrasting verbal-propositional mode of thought and retention. The former is more active in processing concrete information whereas the latter is the common medium for abstract thought. These modes are identified with different hemispheres of the brain, and neurological evidence and studies of recognition memory offer support for the distinction (Sperry, 1968; Nebes, 1974). However, it is reasonable to assume that both of these storage modes have a common underlying code in the functional organization of the brain. We suggest that this deep structure of mentation must be propositional.

This is not meant to deny that so-called short-term memory could involve iconic forms in storage or that there may not be something like spatial schema which underly such phenomena as face recognition. However, when emotion-laden images are evoked in patients, it is long-term storage which is being tapped. "The hypothesis favored here is that the experience of an image itself arises out of 'constructive' processes (Neisser, 1967). The notion is that the units abstracted and interpreted during perception are stored in long-term memory in an abstract format and must be acted on by processes that serve to generate or to produce an experience of an image" (Kosslyn, 1975). Although some might question this view as an explanation of simple visual images, it seems highly consonant with the nature of affective imagery in therapy. These latter images have the property of serial narratives, that obviously include much more than sensory impressions. It is for this reason that they canot be held to simply "stand in" for objective stimuli. They are always processed with response elements as fundamental parts of the structure. In fact, the aim of therapy could be described as the reorganization of the image unit in a way that modifies the affective character of its response elements.

It is proposed that the image we seek to manipulate in using desensitization, catharsis, or flooding techniques is best comprehended as a finite network of specific propositional units which have designating and action functions. The logic of this structure and its underlying neurophysiology is presently unknown. In practice, propositions are often added serially to a diachronic structure. That is to say, the emotional image is not always processed as a complete unit, nor does it necessarily impact on behavior in the abrupt fashion of an external stimulus. Rather, the emotional image is recreated as it is evoked, and propositions may be added to or subtracted from this protean cognitive structure while it unfolds over time. We have noted that the emotional image involves behavior, and it is to be anticipated that this behavior will be measurable. In many practical contexts the emotional image is less usefully conceived of as an internal percept and more valuable when construed as a preparatory set to respond.

EMOTIONAL IMAGERY AND INSTRUCTIONAL CONTROL

We have already been at some pains to emphasize the fundamental, nonlinguistic nature of the hypothesized propositional units. Furthermore, it is clear that emotional images may be evoked and elaborated by nonlinguistic external stimuli, such as models, pictures, or films. However, it is also true that propositional elements can be rendered as statements in a natural language. There is a long history of this enterprise in the written fiction, prose, and poetry of all civilized cultures, and an even more ancient oral tradition which the imagery therapist imitates.

It is therefore proposed as a methodological expedient that the emotional image be considered as a cognitive schema containing a finite set of propositional units, each of which can be represented as a verbal statement or instruction. It is not at all clear at the outset what the basic units of such a structure might be. However, for the purposes of experimental investigation, it is suggested that the emotional image contains at least two fundamental classes of statements: stimulus propositions and response propositions. To the extent that we think of the image as a percept, it is logical to assume that its structure will include descriptors, or assertions about stimuli, e.g., a black snake writhing on the path, and auditorium of staring faces. However, emotional images also invariably contain assertions about behavior, or response propositions: e.g., "My palms are sweating, my heart is racing, I scream. I run away." The response components of the image are often more elaborate than the stimulus elements. They divide themselves naturally into the three response classes that we have come to associate with the empirical analysis of emotion [verbal responses, overt motor acts, and responses of the physiological organs, see Lang (1968, 1971, 1978], as well as propositions which define characteristics of the subject's thinking processes and sense organ adjustments or postural responses that determine point of view. Response propositions representing each of these classes can be observed in the script presented below, created by Watson and Marks (1971, p. 277). It is an example of imagery instructions used in the flooding research on the phobia-reducing effects of exposure to relevant and irrelevant fear stimuli.

Try and imagine yourself at home. You have to go out. You can't avoid it. You're uneasy at the thought. You have to go alone. Your boy is at school, you are on your own. You are already scared. You stumble as you leave your front door. You pull the door to with a bang. By the time you reach the pavement your heart is racing, your mouth is dry, you sweat. Just ten yards further on, past familiar landmarks, the panic starts. You dread losing control, and you shake like a leaf. You feel sick. You feel faint. You feel people are looking at you. You lose control of yourself. You lose control of your body. You vomit. You wet your underwear. You lose control of your mind. You cannot see things clearly. The world is unreal, unclear, seems unfriendly, a terrifying place. You cannot stop yourself from screaming. The noise attracts attention. You scream and scream and scream. Soon a crowd surrounds you. People are afraid to approach you having hysterics as you are, and surrounded by your own vomit. You scream and shout and wave your arms and legs about like a child having a tantrum when it can't get its own way. Your thoughts are muddled, you are confused. You are lost, unable to control yourself, just a few yards away from your home. You continue screaming, crying, yelling, howling. The crowd grows. You go on making an exhibition of yourself. You feel ashamed. You no longer feel grown up and feel you are a baby. No one in the crowd dares to approach you. You make a grotesque spectacle. In a way, some of the crowd enjoy your being out of control. No one comes to help. No one is on your side. All the hysterics fail to make you feel better. In fact, the panic gets worse. The crowd laughs at you, shouts, jeers and points. You feel exposed. You realize they are seeing you as you really are. The panic just goes on. Finally everything goes black.

Image Taxonomy

A tentative propositional catalog is presented in table 21.1, which can be used in classifying imagery instructions for analysis or as a guide to creating balanced scripts for use in treatment and imagery experiments. It is interest-

Table 21.1. Propositional Units of the Emotional Image

Stimulus propositions (auditory, visual, tactile, cutaneous, olfactory, vestibular, anesthetic)
A. Physical details of the object or situation
B. Changes in object configuration
C. Object movement (approach or withdrawal)
D. Physical place or general location
E. Presence or absence of others as observers or participants
F. Comments made by others
G. Pain, location on the body; sharp, dull, etc.
Response propositions
A. Verbal responses
    1. Overt vocalization, out loud comments or expressive cries
    2. Covert verbalizations
        a. Emotional labeling
        b. Self-evaluative statements, e.g., feelings of inferiority
        c. Attribution of attitudes to others
B. Somatomotor events
    1. Muscle tension
    2. Uncontrolled gross motor behavior
    3. Organized motor acts, freezing, approach, avoidance
C. Visceral events
    1. Heart rate and pulse
    2. Body or palmar sweat
    3. Vascular changes, blanching or flushing
    4. Pilomotor response
    5. Salivary response, mouth dry
    6. Respiratory change
    7. Intestinal upset
        a. Vomiting
        b. Incontinence
    8. Urinary dysfunction
D. Processor characteristics
    1. Perception unclear or unusually vivid or distorted
    2. Loss of control over thoughts, cannot think clearly
    3. Disoriented in time or space
E. Sense organ adjustments
    1. General postural changes
    2. Eye and head movements

---

ing to note how few of the statements contained in the Watson and Marks (1971) script actually define stimulus propositions. Most of the flooding instructions assert the responses of the subject. It is clear that some of these statements are hard to classify. Feeling sick, for example, sounds like a stimulus proposition. However, the experience of sickness involves as much behavior as sensation. Thus, our pulse may race, muscles tense, and stomach contract, we have difficulty maintaining a steady hand, and we feel sick. What are usually called feelings may fall into one or several different propositional classes, e.g., stimulus elements, self-referent statements, visceral events, and processor characteristics. Very few details of the internal stimulus configuration actually contribute to the propositional net. Consonant with the view of the emotional image as a response set, its potency is often instructionally augmented more by the elaboration of response propositions than by the refinement of stimulus elements.

It is suggested that the emotional image in the brain of a cooperative patient is more or less consonant with the propositional structure of the administered instructional set. Furthermore, if the image is indeed a preparatory set, we should observe partial responses in imagining subjects which are consistent with the response elements of the script. In point of fact, in many experimental situations, no methodological distinction need be made between the imagery instructions and the hypothesized image in the brain. While this may not be expedient for individuals who idiosyncratically add or subtract from the suggested propositional structure, the instructions will be very close to the image for groups of subjects, whose numbers improve the signal-to-noise ratio. Thus, if elaborate response propositions are part of the instructional set given to one group of subjects and not to another, then the premotor, verbal, and visceral responses during imaging will be relatively augmented for the group so instructed. To modify McLuhan's statement, "the media is the message," the proposed research strategy affirms that the message is the image.

The Somatovisceral Image

In a recent experiment (Kozak & Lang, 1976), we tested the hypothesis that the propositional organization of instructions can be shown to control somatovisceral responses during imagery. All subjects practiced visualizing fearful and neutral materials and were interviewed following each scene. In this context, subgroups were trained in vivid imagination, according to one of two procedures. Group one was instructed to focus on the perceptual content of the scene, to capture it vividly in the "mind's eye." Furthermore, they were verbally reinforced by the experimenter during the interview for describing stimulus detail and elaborating the perceptual content of the reported image. Thus, if a subject imagined that he was outside flying a kite, he was complimented if his postscene description included a mention of such specific elements as "the blue sky," "the sun glistening on the clouds," "the tail of rags, dancing below a bright orange kite."

A second group received instructions which emphasized their somatomotor and visceral responses to the scene. They were told to experience the scene "as if" it were happening, and "to do in the image what you would do in the real situation." Subjects in this group were reinforced during training for reporting response elements, e.g., eyes moving with the spiraling kite, breathing deeply and rapidly as you run through the field, your forehead tense and eyes squinting into the sun. At a final test session, the groups were each given instructions to imagine the same scenes, but with training-related differences in propositional structure. Some of the test scenes involved activities or situations which were not fearful, and others represented emotional confrontations with fear objects. Heart rate, skin conductance, two electromyographic channels, and respiration activity were recorded continuously during the session.

The primary hypothesis of the experiment was strongly supported. For nearly all measures, the groups trained in (and test-instructed with) response propositions generated the largest and most consistent physiological response. Furthermore, individual scenes generated patterns of physiological response which were specific to the propositional structure of the scene. For example, among response-trained subjects, scene scripts which included specific respiratory, heart rate, or muscle tension propositions elicited more activity in these specific response systems than scenes which did not contain these elements. Data on verbal report of scene vividness and feelings of fear were complex, with sex of subject proving to be a highly significant variable. However, response-trained subjects tended to rate their anxiety during fear scenes to be greater than stimulus-trained subjects, relative to each group's verbal response to nonfear material.

In brief, with proper training and instructions, subjects can learn to increase their psychophysiological response in the image context, and this can influence other response systems. In future research, we plan to determine if this training-augmented somatovisceral activity mediates a broad fear behavior change, as was observed for spontaneous scene arousal by Lang et al. (1970). We also plan to manipulate specific verbal and motor act propositions instructionally to determine their specific and general impact on the three systems of affective behavior (Lang, 1971, 1978).

EMOTIONAL IMAGERY AND BEHAVIOR CHANGE

The propositional conception of emotional imagery provides a strategy for the analysis of emotional change which could clarify a variety of unresolved issues in behavior modification research. Specifically, it is suggested that uncontrolled variation in the content of fear imagery accounts for many differences observed by researchers between desensitization and flooding, among *in vivo*, slide or film exposure, and imaginal techniques of fear reduction, as well as between desensitization and modeling.

Despite the many studies of desensitization, little attention has been directed to the effectiveness of image processing during therapy. This is particularly surprising, as the success of therapy (assuming the stimulus substitution theory) must depend at least on the vividness, and perhaps on the affective intensity, of the generated images. Nevertheless, it is a rare experimenter who provides even verbal report data relevant to either quality.

From the perspective presented here, vividness is determined by the completeness of the evoked propositional structure. Thus, subjects reporting vivid images can generally describe them in exquisite detail, providing a large catalog of discriminable stimulus elements. Vividness is also determined by the pattern of response propositions, many of which are measurable during the image experience. For example, a vivid image of a tennis match might include regular, lateral movements of the eyes that are observable in the electro-oculogram.

Affective intensity is defined by the *amplitude* of visceral, verbal, and somatic muscle responses which are associated with the overt emotional state. Thus, an increase in autonomic arousal (e.g., increased heart rate and skin conductance) is expected when subjects visualize more fearful scenes. However, vividness and affective intensity may interact. A change in stimulus propositions (e.g., an increase in proximity to the feared object) presumably involves an augmented visceral response, if vividness is to be maintained. Nevertheless, large autonomic responses can be aversive and may be harder for subjects to generate. Discontinuities in the organization of stimulus and response propositions can then occur.

Verbal reports of vividness and affective intensity are, of course, only loosely coupled to the physiological structure of the image. Individuals who produce vivid images will probably also be able to generate more intense affect. Thus, among sophisticated subjects, moderately high group correlations between reported vividness and affect are to be anticipated (Lang *et al.*, 1970). However, within-subject patterns are predicted less readily. It is easy to confound meanings of affective intensity and vividness, and more arousing images can "seem" more vivid, even when the discriminated details are fewer. On the other hand, the subjects of Lang *et al.* (1970) reported neutral material to be more vivid than images taken from the top of their anxiety hierarchies. It may be that the reported image properties of arousal and clarity parallel the perception of external stimuli, i.e., while moderate arousal improves attention, higher levels of activation prompt response disorganization and a reduction in sensory discrimination.

It is argued here that the therapeutic effect of an image is determined by its propositional structure, the balance between stimulus and response elements, and the interrelated characteristics of vividness and affective intensity. With this general hypothesis in mind, we will now consider the visualization instructions (to the extent they are available) that have been employed in imagery therapy research.

Desensitization and Flooding

The basic structures of the evoked images used in desensitization and in flooding or "implosive" therapy appear to diverge significantly. In desensitization, the therapist's imagery instructions are brief and include primarily what we have called stimulus propositions. A typical scene administered to a socially anxious patient would be: "Imagine that you are standing before a group of twenty spectators just prior to the presentation of an extemporaneous speech." There is no mention of emotional response. The subject would have been previously trained in relaxation and would have been told to relax prior to the scene presentation. However, neither a description of the relaxed posture nor fear arousal is a normal part of the imagery instruction.

From the present perspective, the imagery instructions most often used in desensitization are incomplete. It is the conjunction of stimulus and response propositions which produces a vivid emotional image and, in desensitization, the patient may have to rely wholly on his own resources to generate the important response elements. He may even construe the context as a perplexing and inconsistent response set, i.e., he is told to imagine an emotional context vividly *and* to relax. It is not surprising that subjects resolve this paradox in idiosyncratic ways, some of which can attenuate image vividness and therapeutic effectiveness.

As may be readily observed in the scripts provided by Marks and his coworkers (e.g., Watson & Marks, 1971), imagery instructions in flooding are primarily made up of response propositions, but with enough descriptor statements to tag the context. If we are correct in our assumption that emotional imagery depends on the joint evocation of both propositional classes, then images evoked in flooding could be not only more affectively intense than those prompted in desensitization, but in some cases might be more complete cognitive units and, thus, potentially more vivid. To state the issue more pragmatically, some research has suggested that flooding is more effective than desensitization (e.g., Boulougouris, Marks, & Marset, 1971). It is possible that the response elements of the emotional event were simply more available for processing in flooding than they were during laboratory desensitization, and this accounts for the findings.

It should not be inferred that the induction of intense affective states ensures or facilitates fear change; research suggests that significant emotional change in flooding can occur under drug-induced low arousal (Johnston & Gath, 1973; Marks, Viswanathan, & Lipsedge, 1972). In this context, flooding is tactically very close to desensitization. We hold that the critical requirement for both therapies is that at least partial response components of the affective state must be present if an emotional image is to be modified. Such response components are present in desensitization, if the procedure is not overly asceptic. In the experiment referred to at the outset (Lang *et al.*, 1970), the heart rate responses during fearful images of successful subjects were several beats per minute faster than those of subjects who failed to profit from treatment. Although small, the differences were reliable, indicating that visceral response propositions were indeed being processed in the positive cases.

The most important difference between desensitization and flooding may be the differential emphasis given in these two treatments to stimulus and response components of the image. In desensitization, the stimulus propositions of the images are emphasized. Furthermore, this treatment is undertaken with the patient in a more moderate state of arousal, when discrimination may be best. Using a sensory decision theory analysis, Chapman and Feather (1971) examined the discriminability of reported fear between images evoked at various levels of the anxiety hierarchy. They found greater differential sensitivity in subjects trained in relaxation than in those who were not, and concluded that "the role of relaxation in the therapeutic process is . . . the enhancement of discrimination learning." This view suggests that desensitization is ideally suited to the treatment of focused fears, i.e., the therapist wishes to alter responses to a specific stimulus, but not necessarily to modify more general aspects of the patient's stress response. Consistent with this position, few researchers have questioned the effectiveness of desensitization in the treatment of focal phobia. Furthermore, our own early research (Lang,

1969) supported this idea of specificity. While we found considerable gener-alization of fear reduction after desensitization, as did Paul (1966), we also observed that the degree of effect closely followed the degree of stimulus association.[1]

We have already noted that the scripts used in flooding and implosive therapies emphasize response propositions. Furthermore, these treatments of-ten generate strong affective images, where discrimination may be poor but visceral responses are numerous and intense. For example, in the Stampfl and Levis (1967) procedure an emphasis is placed on maintaining a persistent affective state, and stimulus elements quite remote from the primary fear are often employed. It is interesting to note here that Marks' group has also found that, in flooding, a considerable reduction in specific phobic behavior is prompted by the use of phobia-irrelevant fear image (Watson & Marks, 1971). Furthermore, some investigators (Boulougouris *et al.*, 1971) argue that flood-ing is more successful than desensitization with the diffuse fear of agoraACpho-bics. It could be that treatment of the latter complaint with its characteristic of ubiquitous anxiety, is not very dependent on the patient learning discrimi-nations and that the important element in therapy is the processing of general response components. These facts support the thesis that flooding is less specific in effect than desensitization, and that results are achieved primarily through processing of response elements in the image, which mediate broad changes in the emotional response set.

The above generalizations about desensitization and flooding are made with great hesitation. Recent studies have produced complex results which are difficult to interpret (e.g., Gelder, Bancroft, Gath, Johnston, Matthews, & Shaw, 1973). From the perspective presented here, the critical issue is not whether the therapy is called "flooding" or "desensitization." The important fact is that any evaluation of imagery variables, e.g., duration of the image, frequency and rate of exposure, relevancy of content, or the pertinence of relaxation training, depends on the propositional structure, affective intensity, and vividness of the processed images. This information is available in crude form in the verbal judgments of clients and in the verbal report of stimulus and response propositions which may be systematically gathered at debrief-ing. More important, we must determine that the measurable physiological events occur during imagination, consonant with the image structure and its arousing properties.

To summarize, our view could be construed as an elaboration of the position taken by Wolpe in 1958: The therapeutic use of imagery depends on the modification of an associated psychophysiological state of fear. This state can be defined in terms of three response systems, verbal report, behavioral acts, and somatovisceral events (Lang, 1971, 1978). If extratherapeutic change is to be effected, then irrespective of the treatment's formal structure, components of these responses must be represented in the images processed in therapy. Furthermore, it is incumbent on the researcher, and wise for the journeyman therapist, to confirm their presence during treatment.

Fear Object and Fear Image

The present analysis also raises questions about research comparing imaginal, media, and *in vivo* methods of flooding or desensitization. Such experiments are predicated on the assumption that these methods are different modes of presenting stimuli. However, as we have taken pains to elucidate, the emotional image is not simply a stimulus or a representative of a stimulus. It is both stimulus and response, organized into a processing unit which is as much a behavioral set as an internal percept. Media presentations are to be similarly understood. Indeed, the function of a slide or film is not to present images but to evoke them.

Frightened subjects do not equally avoid all stimulus members of the class of feared objects. The subject's most potent feared object exists as a functional model in the long-term storage of the brain. The external stimulus offered by the experimenter will conform more or less well to this model and, with no other instruction, a bad match may evoke few response propositions of the fear state and little relevant overt behavior. In other words, the objective stimulus defines the descriptors of the image which mediates behavior. However, if a specific test stimulus is poorly chosen, and the subject cannot match it to his fear model, then treatment may be ineffective.

The effect of a media presentation, like a scripted image, depends on the response propositions which are processed with it. Furthermore while a good external stimulus match may facilitate their occurrence, the probability that a complete image unit will be processed is also determined by context, physiological state, and instructions. Thus, Lazarus and his colleagues (Lazarus, Speisman, Mordkoff, & Davison, 1962) studied reactivity to fear films and found that certain instructions, which encouraged an "intellectualization" set or "denial," reduced both autonomic responding and verbal report of fear. Melamed (1969) confirmed this effect of instructions, but showed that it could also be used to increase arousal. In her experiment, the impact of the fear films on visceral reactivity was *augmented* by instructing subjects to become personally involved in the material and to experience the context "as if" it were real.

It is also possible for high tonic levels of sympathetic arousal to render subjects emotionally responsive to a film presentation that might otherwise be less provocative. Schachter (1964) demonstrated this effect for a humorous film, in which subjects who had received injections of epinephrine tended to laugh more while viewing the comedy than undrugged subjects. Furthermore, subjects who had been administered chloropromazine were observed to be significantly less amused than controls. In the same way that instructions can instigate appropriate language response propositions and thus facilitate autonomic responding to media stimuli, the verbal and behavioral components of the emotional image appear to be more readily evoked when subjects are making consonant visceral responses, even though this physiology is generated by emotion-irrelevant factors.

The presentation of fear stimuli in the context of independently generated low arousal is, of course, the treatment method proposed by Wolpe (1958), and the clinical and experimental data indicate that relaxed subjects do report less strong emotional reactions. However, the effects of tonic physiologic state on a subject's response to a film may be complex and difficult to interpret. A moderate increase in arousal facilitates attentiveness (Mackworth, 1969): a very low activation level may be inadequate for image processing. We have already suggested that high levels of sympathetic activity can be distracting and disrupt the integrity of an image. Furthermore, Schachter (1964) has shown that an instructional set that is not consonant with an emotional response can undermine arousal manipulations. Such deflating instructions are sometimes inadvertently communicated by the experimental or clinical context.

It is important to see that pictures and films are not "objective stimuli," but each is a kind of image or thesis. Whether they will actually facilitate imagination and aid the therapeutic task depends on the specifics of their application in the individual case. Furthermore, it is clear that simple instructions can by themselves evoke powerful images, in some cases just because exact details are left to the subject (as in Marks' method of guided fantasy), and the descriptors and response components thus conform most closely to the primary fear model.

Individual Differences

The vividness of the image and, thus, the potential for behavior change depend on the subject's ability to supply the visceral, verbal, and postural responses of emotions. In brief, the effectiveness of imaginal techniques is dependent first on the skill of the therapist in composing and delivering instructions and second on the ability of the patient to self-generate an emotional response. The problem is at least metaphorically parallel to the burden of artistic communication, which is shouldered equally by the creativity of the artist and the aesthetic sensitivity of the viewer.

In part, then, the prognosis of imaginal treatments relative to *in vivo* manipulations will depend on the patients' language control over the visceral and motoric components of emotional responding. Our research on cardiovascular control (Lang, 1975) suggests that the ability to initiate visceral change on instruction is a normally distributed human skill. Thus, some subjects can with a simple command increase heart rate 20 or 30 beats/min or as much as 70 beats/min if provided with proper information and incentives. However, other subjects lack this capacity and do not achieve such instructional control despite extended training.

Imagery instructions can be viewed as another example of verbal control over the somatovisceral system. It is also clear that an imagery control deficit characterizes many patients. Nevertheless, these same patients may show visceral arousal in the context of objective stress. They are autonomically responsive to the presence of fear objects but lack the intentional control over the visceral responses of emotion that we feel is essential to emotional imagery generation. We hypothesize that this group is less capable than the good controllers of processing emotional experience "off-line." It is this group that specifically needs to work with fear stimuli *in vivo*. On the other hand, the subject with language control over arousal can learn prototypic fear-reducing behavior in therapy which he can readily apply in the objective context outside the treatment hour. For this group *in vivo* presentation may well be superfluous.

Image Control and Response Specificity

For nearly all subjects, presentation or the threat of presenting primary fear objects is the surest way to evoke the broadest fear response. However, it is clear from the perspective presented here that the external stimulus is not necessary to all subjects for fear generation. This conforms to clinical experience with patients, many of whom are distressingly capable of frightening themselves with little objective prompting.

The ability to become absorbed in a representation of reality "as if" it were an objective experience was described by the poet Coleridge (1884) as the "willing suspension of disbelief." There are presently very limited data based on the formal assessment of this process in patients. Most experiments have been retrospective, dependent on the vagaries of verbal report, and only a few studies involve the systematic assessment of the evoked image as it is occurring. A potentially useful paradigm was developed by Geer (1974), who examined attentional factors in the processing of sexual images. He found that erotic scripts, which reliably evoked arousal when presented alone, yielded attenuated erectile response when distracting tasks were introduced. These data suggest that competing stimuli of varying strength could be used to measure the saliency of emotional images. Resistance to distraction could become a method for objectively assessing the demand or intensity of emotional response (Geer, 1977). Another method might involve testing the patient's ability to instructionally suppress the visceral propositions of the emotional image in the context of prompting stimuli. Again, the sex researchers provide interesting preliminary data. Barlow (1977) reports that subjects have difficulty suppressing erections instigated by erotic audiotapes relative to erotic visual material, even though the latter yield greater responses. These same questions are relevant to our understanding of fear images, where optimal media impact and set factors must be determined if effective therapeutic processing is to be achieved.

Researchers studying human sexuality have also explored individual differences in image content, and this strategy could be adapted to the study of specific anxieties or phobia. A method has evolved for adjusting the propositional content of the erotic image so as to maximize the concurrent autonomic response. Tapes are presented to subjects repeatedly, progressively eliminating material which does not prompt erection and augmenting those statements which are reliably followed by an increase in penile blood volume. In this manner, specific language controlling the response components of the image are uncovered, and powerful fantasies are tailored to individual subjects. Barlow (1977) reports using this method to explore image contents related to sexual pathology or dysfunction. He notes that patients' verbal reports at interview often poorly label or misidentify the stimuli which prompt their own sexual response. The refining of the emotional image over trials uncovers the truly relevant stimulus contexts which can then become the focus of therapy. A similar procedure could be used to explore patterns of physiological response other than sexual arousal. Weerts and Roberts (1975) recently studied physiological changes occasioned by instructions to image fearful and anger-invoking scenes. Using selected subjects, they found differing autonomic patterns for the two emotions, similar to those originally reported by Ax (1953). The method of successive audiotapes might have further refined this distinction for individual subjects.

Over a decade ago, Graham and his colleagues proposed that specific psychological sets or "attitudes" controlled patterns of physiological responding, and that their repeated instigation underlay much physical disease (Graham, Kabler, & Graham, 1962; Graham, Stern, & Winokur, 1960). For example, they suggested that hypertension involved a feeling of threatened harm and a need to be "ready for anything." Furthermore, they demonstrated that the hypnotic evocation of this "attitude" prompted a predicted blood pressure response. Other attitudes were held to control different physiological response patterns. There has been little effort to replicate this work, although it inevitably finds a place in treatises on psychosomatic medicine. The failure to exploit these insights may stem in part from a methodological failure to focus on the specific elements of the image, i.e., the covariation between a specific instructional set and the physiological response. A propositional analysis of specific fear and anger material, refined over successively presented audiotapes, could very well generate just the kind of psychophysiological patterns Graham hypothesized. They may indeed prove to be reliable and stable for individuals and, once such relationships are established idiosyncratically, communality of content elements could be explored. Thus, it is possible that specific disease entities could sort out in terms of the psychophysiology of specific images. However, the evaluation of this hypothesis depends on the establishment of a more explicit relationship between imagery instructions and physiological response than has previously been sought. In brief, it is not sufficient to say that urticaria is related to "helplessness," ulcer to "deprivation," or tachycardia to "fear." The specific instructional material controlling skin temperature, stomach motility, and heart rate must be isolated before any useful catalog can be generated. In this enterprise, the clinical interview is only a first step. The specific image content must become the independent variable which is tested and refined against the relevant physiological responses.

Modeling and Imagery

The present conception also provides a perspective for the analysis of modeling techniques in fear reduction and suggests what differences would be found between simple exposure to frightening stimuli and observations of others interacting with a feared object. It is clear that the way to alter the fear state is to change the response propositions of the fear image, which we view as a kind of behavioral prototype stored in the brain. The primary response classes of this fear unit are visceral, verbal, and overt acts.

In observing an external model, the subject is provided with a vivid instruction which defines an alternative overt act. If the alternative response is not in the subject's repertoire, e.g., it was a complex social skill that he needs to observe, rehearse, or practice, then the main function of the modeled act would be to demonstrate the skill. The model is a more explicit alternative to verbal instruction for communicating essentially academic information. However, if the desired overt behavior is in the repertoire, but the patient has not been willing to use it in this context (e.g., approaching an object rather than avoiding it), then the effectiveness of the treatment is more likely to depend on changing other components of the emotional response in addition to overt actions. Assuming the topography of the patient's fear includes visceral arousal and somatic muscle tension, we suggest that a filmed model would have to evoke elements of these responses, at least on initial trials, in order to be broadly therapeutic. Furthermore, differences in fear change produced by modeling vs imagery instructions would then depend on the extent to which these physiological elements were instigated and processed in the two procedures. Such competitions between therapy methods can turn out either way, depending on the image potency of the alternative media. Everything depends on the artist-therapist. Is the modeling film successfully realized? Are the imagery instructions well composed and delivered? To some extent psychophysiological analysis will be able to predict the outcome. However, such experiments are really analogous to comparing a novel to a play or film. I believe researchers have many times deceived themselves about the outcome of such contests, simply because they were more creative and/or skilled at developing one set of materials than another.

Despite the above considerations, there may be good practical reasons for choosing modeling instead of instructed imagery for specific treatment situations. For example, modeling may be more effective if the patient's instructional control over the visceral components of emotion is poor. A well made film may have more capacity to evoke the relevant response propositions in such subjects. For this reason, we might expect children to profit less from instructed imagery, on the assumption that their capacity to self-generate emotion is less than that of adults. However, we do not yet have the necessary research to tell us about the development of this capacity. Children are very good at the game of "let's pretend," and at certain ages they may prove superior to adults in generating visceral arousal, whether mediated by verbal or pictorial stimuli.

Covert Modeling

The view taken here is that the fundamental strategy of treatment should be to process the emotional image; the media are a tactical consideration. This fact is highlighted by Kazdin's research (1973, 1974). In his experiments, subjects are asked to imagine models, themselves or others, interacting positively with fear objects. This procedure was dubbed "covert modeling" by Cautela (1971); however, the word modeling seems wholly gratuitous. Kazdin's instructions and those used in flooding or desensitization are the same in that subjects are asked to generate an image unit containing stimulus propositions tagging the fear object. Kazdin's instructions are different because phobic stimuli are combined with verbal and overt response propositions inconsistent with the emotional response. The scene actually involves the covert practice or rehearsal of new, nonphobic behavior.

It is instructive to compare Kazdin's covert coping model and covert mastery model. For coping, "within each scene, the model eventually coped with his anxiety and performed the task calmly. Across all 14 scenes the model became less anxious and more confident so that by the last two scenes there were only confident approach responses" (Kazdin, 1973). In other words, an effort was made to generate emotional imagery in early scenes, and then nonfear responses were gradually substituted. In the mastery condition, the imagined model showed no initial anxiety, he simply interacted with the fear object in a straightforward, fearless manner. "Descriptive phrases in the scenes included performing the tasks without hesitation, while smiling, remaining calm, looking confident, and appearing relaxed" (Kazdin, 1973). There are not enough details provided to permit a detailed propositional analysis of the image scripts and a psychophysiological analysis of the scenes was not undertaken. However, from the material available we might infer some important differences in the response propositions of the images generated, with specific implications for behavioral change. First, there was no specific evocation of visceral arousal. However, to the extent it was present at all, autonomic activation was probably prompted more by the coping than by the mastery scripts. If we are correct in the assumption that evocation of an emotional image depends on the generation of response as well as stimulus propositions, and if this image is indeed critical to behavioral change, then we must presume that greater change would be found after coping instructions. The data did indeed show somewhat more behavior test change for the coping condition. Second, it was the mastery condition that involved extended rehearsal of new, positive self-referent statements, e.g., calm, confident, and relaxed. It is perhaps not surprising to note that the mastery condition yielded slightly more improvement than coping on verbal report measures of reduced anxiety and positive attitudes towards the feared object. In brief, the investigator got out of the experiment more or less what he put into the instructions.

CONCLUSIONS: AN IMAGE FOR THE FUTURE

The purpose of this paper is not to offer a conclusion about the relative effectiveness of different behavior therapies. We do not propose to decide here whether the training of a competing physiological state, the development of new overt coping responses, the encouragement of positive self-referent statements or mere exposure to fear materials is the best vehicle of change. What we have tried to do is define a conceptual context in which we believe such questions would be meaningfully answered.

We have suggested that the narrow definition of the image, as an internal stimulus, is theoretically inadequate and of limited practical utility. We proposed alternatively that the emotional image in the brain is a propositional construct, a finite structure made up of stimulus and response elements which are under limited instructional control. We have tried to show that many components of the image are measurable through concurrent physiological recording and that this provides both a window through which the image can be observed and another vehicle through which it can be modified. Furthermore, we have offered reasoned speculation on the relationship of fear imagery to fear behavior and explored the conditions which increase or decrease the probability of an emotional response.

It is held that fundamental to the emotional response of fear is the prototype fear image contained in long-term storage. This template can be evoked for processing in a variety of ways, through instructions, through pictorial representations, or by objective stimuli. The stored descriptor propositions constitute a model against which external events are tested. If the stimulus does not closely match the prototype, fear is not evoked. However, instructions which provide more information (e.g., "imagine that it is real") can override a mismatch and prompt emotional processing. The processed image is a response set. Thus, an external stimulus which elicits descriptor elements and interpretive propositions will activate the total information unit, including the designated overt behaviors.

It is possible to define the specific conditions which will encourage such processing. Clearly, large parts of the unit can be generated by telling subjects to imagine they are interacting with real stimuli. It should come as no surprise that this is so, as the objective stimulus configuration of most fear stimuli has no fundamental nociceptive property. More intense fear stimuli will not burn the skin or destroy the retina or basilar membrane. Whether a stimulus is present or absent becomes wholly academic, for example, under conditions of attenuated ambient light, when the crucial issue is whether the subject "believes" the stimulus is present. On the one hand, a useful avoidance response is not to "believe" in the fear object and thus not to evoke the image unit with its disruptive response components. However, the conditions prompt equivocation. Whether belief and the fear will be absent or, alternatively, fear will be augmented by the uncertainty, is here a function of idiosyncratic learning. The important consideration is that the objective stimulus is clearly not fundamental to the evocation of either the stimulus or response propositions of the image.

We have already noted that despite the apparent importance of a reality set to the effectiveness of imagery therapy, there is limited objective data on the specific effect of such instructions. Furthermore, we do not routinely determine how well patients will respond to an "as if" set before we proceed to treatment.[2] The large individual differences in the imagery ability of patients needs to be investigated, and methods developed to increase patient responsivity to instructional control.

Clearly, there is much to be learned about fear images and their antecedent relationship to the overt verbal, motoric, and visceral responding in emotion. The methodological assumption of media identity with the image permits us to explore the effects of adding or subtracting information from the image unit. Thus, we can examine the effects on the viscera of the presence or absence of visceral response propositions in the imagery instructions. Similar investigations can be made of self-referent statements and imaginal overt acts. Furthermore, we can explore more explicitly the effects on the image of incongruous or competing propositional units. For example, what are the consequences of instructing subjects to imagine a coping response in the fear context, for the contingent visceral responses of the image, as well as for subsequent overt behavior? Does imagery processing lay down a new response prototype which then becomes the basis for overt behavior change? Can other emotional states (e.g., anger, sexual arousal) be analyzed from a similar conceptual framework, and will this provide a method for examining the interaction of emotional states? We believe the proposed approach opens the way to a serious, systematic exploration of these issues, which will in the next decade greatly increase our understanding of fear processing and perhaps other emotions as well.

NOTES

1. It is possible, of course, to structure desensitization so that relaxation is perceived as a generalized coping response and to treat the desensitization of a specific fear as a prototype for self-treatment (Goldfried, 1971).

2. Goldsmith and McFall (1975) utilized a coaching or rehearsal technique which did consider an aspect of this issue. Subjects were checked repeatedly to see that requested behaviors "fit" their concept of their own behavioral repertoire, i.e., that they could "see themselves" engaging in the response. Modifications were made in the instructed behavior when it was not readily consonant with the prototype image.

REFERENCES

Ax, A. R. The physiological differentiation between fear and anger in humans. Psychosomatic Medicine, 1953, 15, 433–442.

Barlow, D. H. An overview of behavioral assessment in clinical settings. In J. D. Come & R. P. Hawkins (Eds.), Behavioral assessment: New directions in clinical psychology. New York: Brunner/Mazel, 1977.

Boulougouris, J. C., Marks, I. M., & Marset. P. Superiority of flooding (implosion) to desensitization for reducing pathological fear. Behaviour Research and Therapy, 1971, 9, 7–16.

Bower, G. H. Analysis of mnemonic device. American Scientist, 1970, 58, 496–510.

Cautela, J. R. Covert modeling. Paper presented at the Fifth Annual Meeting of the Association for Advancement of Behavior Therapy. Washington, DC, September 1971.

Chapman, C. R., & Feather, B. W. Sensitivity to phobic imagery: A sensory decision theory analysis. Behaviour Research and Therapy, 1971, 9, 161–168.

Coleridge, S. T. [Biographia literaria] (W. G. R. Shedd, Ed.) New York: Harper, 1884 (Originally published, 1817.) Vol. III, p. 365.

Duffy, E. Activation and behavior. New York: Wiley, 1962.

Geer, J. H. Cognitive factors in sexual arousal: Toward an amalgam of research strategies. Paper presented at the meetings of the American Psychological Association. New Orleans, 1974.

Geer, J. H. Sexual functioning—Some data and speculations of psychophysiological assessment. In J. D. Cone & R. P. Hawkins (Eds.), Behavioral assessment: New directions in clinical psychology. New York: Brunner/Mazel, 1977.

Gelder, M. G., Bancroft, J. H. J., Gath, D. H., Johnston, D. W., Mathews, A. M., & Shaw, P. M. Specific and non-specific factors in behaviour therapy. British Journal of Psychiatry, 1973, 123, 445–462.

Goldfried, M. R. Systematic desensitization as training in self-control. Journal of Consulting and Clinical Psychology, 1971, 37, 228–234.

Goldsmith, J. B., & McFall, R. M. Development and evaluation of an interpersonal skill-training program for psychiatric inpatients. Journal of Abnormal Psychology, 1975, 84, 51–58.

Graham, D. T., Kabler, J. D., & Graham, F. K. *Physiological response to the sugges-tion of attitudes specific for hives and hypertension.* Psychosomatic Medicine, *1962, 24, 159–169.*

Graham, D. T., Stern, J. A., & Winokur, G. *The concept of a different specific set of physiological changes in each emotion.* Psychiatric Research Reports, *1960, 12, 8–15.*

Johnston, D. W., & Gath, D. H. *Arousal levels and attribution effects in diazepam-assisted flooding.* British Journal of Psychiatry, *1973, 123, 463–466.*

Kazdin, A. E. *Covert modeling and the reduction of avoidance behavior.* Journal of Abnormal Psychology, *1973, 81, 87–95.*

Kazdin, A. E. *Covert modeling, model similarity and reduction of avoidance behavior.* Behavior Therapy, *1974, 5, 624–635.*

Kosslyn, S. M. *Information representation in visual images.* Cognitive Psychology, *1975, 7, 341–370.*

Kozak, M. J., & Lang, P. J. The psychophysiology of emotional imagery: A structural analysis of image processing. *Material presented as part of an address by the second author to the Netherlands Conference on Biofeedback. Amersfoort, Netherlands, November 25, 1976.*

Lang, P. J. *Fear reduction and fear behavior: Problems in treating a construct. In J. M. Shlien (Ed.),* Research in psychotherapy. *Washington, DC: American Psychological Association, 1968, Vol. III, pp. 90–103.*

Lang, P. J. *The mechanics of desensitization and the laboratory study of human fear. In C. M. Franks (Ed.),* Assessment and status of the behavior therapies. *New York: McGraw-Hill, 1969.*

Lang, P. J. *The application of psychophysiological methods to the study of psychotherapy and behavior modification. In A. E. Bergin & S. L. Garfield (Eds.),* Handbook of psychotherapy and behavior change. *New York: Wiley, 1971.*

Lang, P. J. *Acquisition of heart-rate control: Method, theory and clinical applications. In D. C. Fowles (Ed.),* Clinical applications of psychophysiology. *New York: Columbia University Press, 1975.*

Lang, P. J. *The psychophysiology of anxiety. In H. Akiskal (Ed.),* Psychiatric diagnosis: Exploration of biological criteria. *New York: Spectrum, 1978.*

Lang, P. J., Melamed, B. G., & Hart, J. H. *A psychophysiological analysis of fear modification using an automated desensitization procedure.* Journal of Abnormal Psychology, *1970, 76, 220–234.*

Lazarus, R., Speisman, J., Mordkoff, A., & Davison, L. *A laboratory study of psychological stress produced by a motion picture film.* Psychological Monographs, *1962, 76 (Whole No. 553).*

Mackworth, J. F., Vigilance and habituation. *Harmondsworth, England: Penguin Books, 1969.*

Marks, I. M., Viswanathan, R., & Lipsedge, M. *Enhanced extinction of fear by flooding during waning diazepam effect.* British Journal of Psychiatry, *1972, 121, 493–505.*

Melamed, B. G. The habituation of psychophysiological responses to tones, and to filmed fear stimuli under varying conditions of instructional set. *Unpublished doctoral dissertation. University of Wisconsin, Madison, 1969.*

Nebes, R. D. *Hemispheric specialization in commissurolomized man.* Psychological Bulletin. *1974, 81, 1–14.*

Neisser, U. Cognitive psychology. *New York: Appleton-Century-Crofts, 1967.*

Paul, G. L. Insight vs. desensitization in psychotherapy: An experiment in anxiety reduction. *Stanford, CA: Stanford University Press, 1966.*

Pylyshyn, Z. W. *What the mind's eye tells the mind's brain: A critique of mental imagery.* Psychological Bulletin, *1973, 80, 1–22.*

Schachter, S. *The interaction of cognitive and physiological determinants of emotional state. In L. Berkowitz (Ed.),* Advances in experimental social psychology. *New York: Academic Press, 1964, Vol. 1.*

Sperry, R. W. *Neurology and the mind-brain problem.* American Scientist, *1952, 40, 291–312.*

Sperry, R. W. *Hemisphere deconnection and unity in conscious awareness.* American Psychologist, *1968, 23, 723–733.*

Stampfl, T. G., & Levis, D. *Essentials of implosive therapy: A learning-theory-bared psychodynamic behavorial therapy.* Journal of Abnormal Psychology, *1967, 72, 496–503.*

Watson, J. P., & Marks, I. M. *Relevant and irrelevant fear in flooding.* Behavior Therapy, *1971, 2, 275–293.*

Weerts, T. C., & Roberts, R. The physiological effects of imagining anger-provoking and fear-provoking scenes. *Paper presented at the Society for Psychophysiological Research meetings, Toronto, Ontario, October 1975.*

Wolpe, J. Psychotherapy by reciprocal inhibition. *Stanford, CA: Stanford University Press, 1958.*

22. Treatment of Posttraumatic Stress Disorder in Rape Victims

A Comparison between Cognitive-Behavioral Procedures and Counseling

Edna B. Foa, Barbara Olasov Rothbaum, David S. Riggs, and Tamera B. Murdock

THE PSYCHOLOGICAL sequelae of rape have been conceptualized as posttraumatic stress disorder (PTSD). In a study, Rothbaum, Foa, Murdock, Riggs, and Walsh (1990) found that shortly after the assault, 94% of rape victims met symptomatic criteria for PTSD; 3 months after the assault, 47% of victims still suffered from the disorder. An average of 17 years after the assault, 16.5% of rape victims had PTSD (Kilpatrick et al., 1987). Recent studies have estimated that approximately 25% of American women experienced rape at some point in their lifetime (Koss, 1983). It is therefore imperative that effective therapeutic procedures for PTSD following rape be developed.

PTSD was introduced into the *Diagnostic and Statistical Manual of Mental Disorders* (3rd ed., *DSM-III*; American Psychiatric Association, 1980) as an anxiety disorder. Therefore, the literature on the treatment of PTSD is sparse. However, two types of cognitive-behavioral procedures developed for the treatment of other anxiety disorders have been applied to PTSD sufferers: exposure treatments, in which patients are confronted with the feared memory or situation, and anxiety management training, in which patients are taught a variety of skills to manage anxiety in daily life.

Only one controlled study has been published on the behavioral treatment of PTSD (Keane et al., 1989). In that study, Vietnam veterans either received treatment that included relaxation and imaginal exposure or were assigned to a wait-list control condition. Treated subjects showed a decrease in reexperiencing symptoms, as well as decreased startle reactions, memory and concen-

Reprinted by permission from *Journal of Consulting and Clinical Psychology*, 59, 715–723. Copywright © by the American Psychological Association, 1991.

tration problems, impulsivity, and irritability. The remaining symptoms of PTSD did not improve.

Before the sequelae of rape were conceptualized as PTSD, Veronen, Kilpatrick, and Resick (1978) adapted a cognitive-behavioral treatment program, called *stress inoculation training* (SIT, Meichenbaum, 1974), for rape victims who exhibited persistent fear. Uncontrolled investigations have demonstrated the efficacy of this program in diminishing victims' rape-related fear, anxiety, and depression (Veronen & Kilpatrick, 1982).

In a well-controlled study of three types of group therapy for rape victims, SIT was compared with assertion training, supportive psychotherapy, and a wait-list control group (Resick et al., 1988). All three treatments were equally effective in reducing rape-related symptoms. Improvement was noted on measures of general psychopathology, general fear, and specific fear, as well as intrusion and avoidance symptoms, but not on measures of depression, self-esteem, and social fears. The wait-list control group did not evidence change.

Exposure (systematic desensitization) and anxiety management techniques (cognitive-behavioral therapy) were compared in an uncontrolled study with rape victims (Frank et al., 1988). Both treatments were effective in reducing anxiety and depression with no differences evident between treatments.

Several problems limit the conclusions that can be drawn from the above studies. The Keane et al. (1989) study did not incorporate a control group for nonspecific therapeutic factors. Thus, it is not clear whether improvement was due to the specific procedures employed in the treatment or to nonspecific factors such as therapist contact. The Veronen and Kilpatrick (1982) investigation was uncontrolled and did not include measures of PTSD symptoms. Although Resick et al.'s (1988) study included the necessary experimental conditions, it did not include measures of PTSD symptoms, nor did it control the overlap of potentially important procedures among the various treatment conditions (e.g., elements of exposure were included in two treatments). Frank et al. (1988) did not assign patients randomly to treatments, had no control group, and failed to exclude patients who had been raped shortly before treatment.

The present study sought to address these limitations. We compared the effectiveness of three treatments for reducing posttraumatic stress disorder in rape victims to a wait-list control group (WL). The treatments examined included prolonged exposure (PE), stress inoculation training (SIT), and supportive counseling (SC). SC was included to control for nonspecific therapy effects. There was no overlap of procedures among the treatment conditions.

We predicted that both PE and SIT would significantly reduce PTSD symptoms, more than would SC and WL.

METHOD

Subjects

Subjects were 45 female victims of rape or attempted rape who met *Diagnostic and Statistical Manual of Mental Disorders* (3rd ed., rev., *DSM-III-R*; American Psychiatric Association, 1987) diagnostic criteria for PTSD and who had been raped at least 3 months before participation in the study. The range of time since assault was 3 months to 12 years with a mean of 6.2 years (*SD* 6.7 years). Patients were recruited from three sources: referrals from local professionals and victim assistance agencies, recruitment by local newspaper advertisements, and patients from an assessment study of the response to rape (Rothbaum et al., 1990) who met PTSD criteria 3 months postassault. Diagnoses of PTSD were made by Barbara Olasov Rothbaum on the basis of *DSM-III-R* criteria. Demographic and assault characteristics for the treatment groups are presented in tables 22.1 and 22.2, respectively. Chi-square analyses and analyses of variance (ANOVAs) revealed no differences among the four treatment groups on any demographic measures. ANOVAs on time since assault and on age did not reveal group differences in mean values or variances. With respect to assault characteristics, only one significant difference was detected: Fewer patients who received SIT reported that they had been injured during the assault, $\chi^2(3, N = 45) = 15.33$, $p < .01$.

Exclusion criteria were current or previous diagnosis of organic mental disorder, schizophrenia, or paranoid disorders as defined in the *DSM-III-R*; depression severe enough to require immediate psychiatric treatment, bipolar depression, or depression accompanied by delusions, hallucinations, or bizarre behavior; current alcohol or drug abuse; assault by spouse or other family member; or illiteracy in English. Eligibility for the study was determined through an interview with a master's-or PhD-level psychologist.

Measures

Assessments at pretreatment, posttreatment, and follow-up consisted of clinical interviews conducted by an independent assessor, who was blind to treatment conditions, and self-report questionnaires.

Table 22.1. Demographic Characteristics by Treatment Group

Variable	Total (N = 45)	SIT (n = 14)	PE (n = 10)	SC (n = 11)	WL (n = 10)
Race (%)					
Black	25.0	15.4	30.0	27.3	30.0
White	72.7	84.6	70.0	63.6	70.0
Hispanic	2.3	0.0	0.0	9.1	0.0
Martial status (%)					
Single	52.3	53.8	50.0	45.5	60.0
Married	22.7	23.1	30.0	18.2	20.0
Cohabitating	2.3	7.7	0.0	0.0	0.0
Divorced/separated	22.7	15.4	20.0	36.4	20.0
Income (%)					
Greater than $30,000	25.0	7.7	40.0	36.4	20.0
$20,000–30,000	11.4	15.4	10.0	9.1	10.0
$10,000–20,000	34.1	38.5	10.0	36.4	50.0
Less than $10,000	29.5	38.5	40.0	18.2	20.0
Occupation (%)					
White-collar	29.3	33.3	33.3	20.0	30.0
Secretarial	24.4	33.3	11.1	40.0	10.0
Blue-collar	12.2	8.3	11.1	20.0	10.0
Homemaker	9.8	0.0	11.1	10.0	20.0
Student	24.4	25.0	33.3	10.0	30.0
Time since assault (days)					
M	2,262	1,446	1,981	3,394	2,464
SD	2,484	1,573	2,981	3,156	1,798
Age (years)					
M	31.8	29.3	32.7	34.2	32.0
SD	8.2	6.3	7.3	9.8	9.6

NOTE. SIT = stress inoculation training; PE = prolonged exposure; SC = supportive counseling: WL = wait-list control.

Interviews

Initial interview. The initial interview, lasting approximately 90 min, was conducted at the first assessment only. It contained 305 questions used in previous studies of rape victims (e.g., Resick, 1987). Questions assessed demographics, current daily functioning, PTSD symptoms, alcohol and drug use, assault characteristics, and immediate reaction to the rape. The reliability of the initial interview was established on a pilot sample of 12 victims not included in the current study. Interrater reliability (kappa) was .81.

Assault reaction interview. The assault reaction interview, lasting 30 min, was conducted at each of the remaining assessments. It contained 117 questions selected from the initial interview. These questions assessed PTSD symptoms,

Table 22.2. Assault Characteristics by Treatment Group (in Percentages)

Variable	Total (N = 45)	SIT (n = 14)	PE (n = 10)	SC (n = 11)	WL (n = 10)
Injury					
No	13.3	42.9	0.0	9.0	0.0
Yes	86.7	57.1	100.0	100.0	100.0
Relationship of assailant					
Stranger	55.6	50.0	50.0	63.6	60.0
Acquaintance	44.4	50.0	50.0	36.4	40.0
Duration of assault					
1 min or less	6.7	0.0	0.0	9.1	20.0
2–10 min	15.6	35.7	10.0	0.0	10.0
11–29 min	22.2	14.3	20.0	27.3	30.0
30–59 min	20.0	21.4	20.0	27.3	10.0
60–90 min	8.9	0.0	0.0	18.2	20.0
More than 90 min	26.7	28.6	50.0	18.2	10.0
Weapon used					
No	44.4	42.9	30.0	45.5	60.0
Yes	55.6	57.1	70.0	54.5	40.0
Perception of life threat					
Unlikely	17.8	14.3	20.0	27.3	10.0
Somewhat likely	8.9	14.3	10.0	0.0	10.0
Quite likely	24.4	21.4	20.0	27.3	30.0
Convinced of it	48.9	50.0	50.0	45.5	50.0

NOTE. SIT = stress inoculation training; PE = prolonged exposure; SC = supportive counseling: WL = wait-list control.

changes in lifestyle, sexual behavior, physical and psychiatric problems, and legal issues. Interrater reliability (kappa) was .76.

PTSD severity. Severity of PTSD was calculated by adding the interviewer's severity rating of the following PTSD symptoms: reliving experiences, nightmares, flashbacks, avoidance of reminders and thoughts of the assault, impaired leisure activities (e.g., reduced socializing), sense of detachment, blunted affect, disturbed sleep, memory and concentration difficulties, hyperalertness, increased startle response, feelings of guilt, and increased fearfulness.

A standardized interview of PTSD symptom severity was derived from interview items included in the present study. The reliability of this interview was established on a sample of 28 assault victims not included in the present study. Interrater reliability (kappa) of PTSD diagnosis was .90.

Self-Report Measures

Rape Aftermath Symptom Test (RAST; Kilpatrick, 1988). The RAST is a 70-item self-report inventory that differentiates rape victims from nonvictims.

Internal consistency was .95 and test-retest reliability was .85 over a 2 ½-week interval.

State-Trait Anxiety Inventory (STAI; Spielberger, Gorsuch, & Lushene, 1970). The STAI contains 20 items for state anxiety and 20 items for trait anxiety. Test-retest reliability for state anxiety was .40. Internal consistency ranged from .83 to .92. The trait-anxiety scale was not included in the study because it is designed to measure a stable characteristic that was not hypothesized to respond to a short-term intervention.

Beck Depression Inventory (BDI; Beck et al., 1961). The BDI is a 21-item inventory measuring depression. Split-half reliability was .93 Correlations with clinician ratings of depression ranged from .62 to .66.

Expectancy of therapeutic outcome. The perceived credibility of each active treatment was assessed by questions that were rated on a 1-9 Likert type scale. The total score ranged between 3 and 27.

Motivation for Behavior Change Scale (MBCS; Cautela, 1977). The MBCS is an 8-item scale completed by the therapist to assess the degree of motivation and compliance exhibited by the patient during treatment.

Procedure

Assessment

Evaluations. Eligible patients were randomly assigned to one of the four conditions. After 10 patients were entered into the wait-list condition, subsequent admissions were randomly assigned to one of the three treatment groups. The assigned treatment was described to the patients, and the pretreatment assessment was conducted. Additional assessments were conducted at posttreatment and approximately 3 months ($M = 106.33$ days, $SD = 34.65$) after treatment.

Treatment

Treatment was conducted by six female therapists with master's or doctoral degrees in psychology or clinical social work who were hired specifically for this project. Therapists were trained in the various treatments by Edna B. Foa and Barbara O. Rothbaum. Specifically, exposure treatment was taught by Foa, a recognized expert in this type of treatment. Foa and Rothbaum were trained by Kilpatrick and his colleagues, who developed the SIT program for rape victims. Foa and Rothbaum were also trained by a therapist affiliated with the Philadelphia Chapter of Women Organized Against Rape to learn supportive counseling for rape victims. The remaining therapists were trained by Foa and Rothbaum through direct observation of ongoing treatment. Therapists differed with respect to their theoretical orientation and treatment preferences but were assigned randomly to treatment conditions in the current study.

Treatment sessions were conducted individually and consisted of nine biweekly 90-min sessions, lasting 4 ½ weeks. Control subjects were placed in a wait-list condition for the same length of time. To ensure the integrity of the treatment procedures, therapists were supervised biweekly by Foa. Each therapy session was monitored during supervision to examine possible deviations from protocol. No gross deviations were detected; subtle deviations were noted, and suggestions for correction were provided by the supervisor. Nonparametric (Kruskil-Wallace) tests were conducted to examine possible therapist effects. The therapists did not differ in the percentage of improvement demonstrated by their patients on any of the seven outcome measures used in the current study.

Prolonged exposure (PE). The first two sessions were devoted to information gathering through the initial interview described above, explanation of treatment rationale, and treatment planning. The next seven sessions were devoted to reliving the rape scene in imagination (imaginal exposure). Patients were instructed to relive the assault by imagining it as vividly as possible and describing it aloud using the present tense. The patient repeated the rape scenario several times for a total of 60 min per session. The patient's narratives were tape-recorded, and patients were instructed to listen to the tape at least once daily as homework. Additional homework involved in vivo exposure to feared and avoided situations judged by the patient and the therapist to be safe.

Stress inoculation training (SIT). The procedures included in this treatment program were adapted from Veronen and Kilpatrick (1983). The first session was devoted to information gathering through the initial interview described above. The session terminated with breathing exercises to diminish anxiety that may have been elicited by the interview. During the second session, the treatment method was described to the patient, a rationale for treatment was given, and an explanation for the origin of fear and anxiety was presented.

The next seven sessions were devoted to instruction in coping skills. During the third and fourth sessions, the patients were taught deep muscle relaxation and controlled breathing. In the fifth session, they were taught thought stopping to counter ruminative or obsessive thinking (Wolpe, 1958). The sixth session was devoted to cognitive restructuring (Beck et al., 1979; Ellis, 1977), the seventh to guided self-dialogue (Meichenbaum, 1977), the eighth to covert modeling, and the ninth to role playing. No instructions for exposure were included.

Supportive counseling (SC). Supportive counseling followed the nine-session format, gathering information through the initial interview in the first session and presenting the rationale for treatment in the second session. During the remaining sessions, patients were taught a general problem-solving technique. Therapists played an indirect and unconditionally supportive role. Homework consisted of the patient's keeping a diary of daily problems and her attempts at problem solving. Patients were immediately redirected to focus on current daily problems if discussions of the assault occurred. No instructions for exposure or anxiety management were included.

Wait-List Control (WL). WL subjects were informed that they would receive treatment in 5 weeks. During this period, they were contacted by a therapist between assessments to determine whether emergency services were required. Following an assessment at the end of the wait-list period, patients were randomly assigned to either PE or SIT.

RESULTS

Preliminary Analyses

Sixty-six victims met inclusion criteria and were offered treatment; 11 victims refused treatment and did not return for pretreatment assessment. Of the 55 victims who began treatment, 17 were assigned to SIT, 14 to PE, 14 to SC, and 10 to WL. Dropout rates were not significantly different across the treatment groups, $\chi^2(3, N = 55) = 3.34$, p; mt.30, and were as follows: PE 28.6%, SIT 17.6%, SC 21.4%, and WL 0%. The 10 dropouts differed from completers on three variables: A greater percentage of them had an income less than \$10,000, $\chi^2(3, N-55)-10.95$, $p < .05$, and were blue-collar workers, $\chi^2(5, N = 55) = 10.34$, $p < .05$. Dropouts also scored higher on the RAST than did completers, $F(1, 53) = 10.72$, $p < .01$. Subsequent analyses were conducted on data from the 45 completers. Analyses of variance (ANOVAs) revealed no significant differences among groups on initial severity of PTSD symptoms, other measures of psychopathology, or expectancy of treatment outcome for the active treatments.

Treatment Effects

Analyses were conducted in two stages. The immediate effects of treatment on the measures of psychopathology were examined with a 2×4 multivariate analysis of variance (MANOVA; Occasion [pretreatment, posttreatment] $\times$ Treatment [SIT, PE, SC, WL]), with occasion as a repeated measure. This was followed by a series of 2×4 ANOVAs. Effects of treatment at follow-up were examined with a 3×3 MANOVA (Occasion [pretreatment, post-treatment, followed-up] $\times$ Treatment [SIT, PE, SC]). This was followed by a series of 3×3 ANOVAs. Patients who were initially on WL were excluded from the latter analyses.

Immediate effects of treatment. Means and standard deviations for each of the dependent measures at pre-and posttreatment are presented in table 22.3. The MANOVA on the outcome measures revealed a significant main effect of occasion, $F(1, 36) = 60.76$ $p < .001$, and a significant Measure $\times$ Occasion interaction, $F(6, 216) = 28.52$, $p < .001$.

The ANOVA on PTSD severity revealed a significant main effect of occasion, $F(1, 41) = 101.69$, $p < .001$, modified by a significant Treatment $\times$ Occasion interaction, $F(3, 41) = 5.38$, $p < .005$. Simple effects analyses revealed a significant difference among treatment groups at posttreatment, $F(3, 41) = 5.38$, $p < .005$. Simple effects analyses revealed a significant difference among treatment groups at posttreatment, $F(3, 40) = 3.04, p < .05$, but not at pretreatment. Post hoc pairwise comparison using Tukey's HSD test indicated that the SIT group showed greater symptom reduction than did the SC and WL groups. Simple effects analyses also revealed significant pre-post changes for all four groups, $F(1, 41) = 75.67$, $p < .001$; $F(1,41) = 32.38, p < .001$; $F(1, 41) = 13.10, p < .002$; and $F(1, 41) = 7.30, p < .02$, for SIT, PE, SC, and WL, respectively.

The effects of treatment on each of the three PTSD symptom clusters (avoidance, intrusion, arousal) were also examined. An ANOVA on avoidance symptoms revealed a main effect of occasion, $F(1, 41) = 22.27, p < .001$, modified by a Treatment $\times$ Occasion interaction, $F(3, 41) = 9.56, p < .001$. Simple effects analyses revealed significant group differences at posttreat-ment, $F(3, 41) = 3.43, p < .05$, but not at pretreatment. Post hoc tests on posttreatment data indicated that patients in the SIT group were less avoidant

Table 22.3. Pretreatment and Posttreatment Means and Standard Deviations

Measure	SIT (*n* = 14)	PE (*n* = 10)	SC (*n* = 11)	WL (*n* = 10)
PTSD severity				
Pretreatment				
M	24.48	25.78	24.39	24.43
SD	6.62	5.01	6.62	4.64
Posttreatment				
M	11.07	15.40	18.09	19.50
SD	3.97	11.09	7.13	7.18
Avoidance symptoms				
Pretreatment				
M	6.48	6.50	5.42	5.70
SD	2.02	3.13	2.76	2.01
Posttreatment				
M	2.43	4.10	5.18	6.00
SD	1.95	4.33	2.56	2.62
Intrusion symptoms				
Pretreatment				
M	5.64	5.28	5.17	5.30
SD	1.92	1.02	2.67	2.26
Posttreatment				
M	1.64	3.40	3.82	3.90
SD	1.28	3.17	2.44	1.45
Arousal symptoms				
Pretreatment				
M	11.24	12.27	12.09	11.47
SD	2.22	1.58	2.40	2.43
Posttreatment				
M	6.36	7.20	8.27	8.50
SD	2.84	3.55	2.94	3.87
RAST				
Pretreatment				
M	141.00	141.69	124.00	131.60
SD	22.46	48.66	39.21	31.32
Posttreatment				
M	91.20	88.70	98.91	102.22
SD	36.72	60.92	54.40	58.80
STAI-state				
Pretreatment				
M	54.39	58.10	55.40	57.10
SD	6.90	11.72	11.30	13.20
Posttreatment				
M	37.15	41.50	43.73	49.90
SD	7.58	13.77	16.80	13.80
BDI				
Pretreatment				
M	19.43	19.60	18.01	19.90
SD	10.99	9.41	10.62	8.67
Posttreatment				
M	9.86	13.40	15.36	15.40
SD	6.76	14.22	13.96	9.71

NOTE. SIT = stress inoculation training; PE = prolonged exposure; SC = supportive counseling: WL = wait-list control. PTSD = posttraumatic stress disorder; RAST = Rape Aftermath Symptom Text; STAI = State-Trait Anxiety Inventory; BDI = Beck Depression Inventory.

than were those in the SC and WL groups. Simple effects analyses also revealed pre-post differences for the SIT and PE groups, $F(1, 41) = 45.34$, $p < .001$, and $F(1, 41) = 11.39$, $p < .005$, respectively, but not for the SC or WL groups.

Analysis of intrusion symptoms also showed a significant effect of occasion, $F(1, 41) = 28.82$, $p < .001$, modified by a Treatment $\times$ Occasion interaction, $F(3, 41) = 2.81$, $p = .05$. Simple effects analyses revealed significant group differences at posttreatment only, $F(3,41) = 3.07$, $p < .05$. However, post hoc comparisons failed to detect differences among groups. Simple effects analyses revealed significant occasion differences for the SIT and PE groups only, $F(1,41)$ 31.39, $p < .001$, and $F(1,41) = 4.97$, $p < .05$, respectively. A significant main effect of occasion was revealed for the arousal symptoms, $F(1, 41) = 107.82$, $p < .001$. No significant treatment main effect or Treatment $\times$ Occasion interaction was detected.

Self-report measures of psychopathology were also examined using 2 $\times$ 4 ANOVAs: Occasion (pretreatment, posttreatment) $\times$ Treatment (SIT, PE, SC, WL), with occasion as a repeated measure. ANOVAs revealed main effects of occasion on the RAST, $F(1,37) = 39.06$, $p < .001$; BDI, $F(1,41) = 25.94$, $p < .001$; and STAI, $F(1, 40) = 49.23$, $p < .001$. No main effects of treatment or Occasion $\times$ Treatment interactions were detected, suggesting that all groups improved equally on these measures.

Effects of treatment at follow-up. Only patients with follow-up data were included in these analyses, and patients previously on the waiting-list were excluded. Means and standard deviations for the dependent measures at pretreatment, posttreatment, and follow-up are presented in table 22.4. A 3 $\times$ 3 MANOVA: Occasion (pretreatment, posttreatment, follow-up) $\times$ Treatment (SIT, PE, SC), with occasion as a repeated measure, revealed a significant main effect of occasion, $F(2,38) = 19.69$, $p < .001$, modified by both a significant Scale $\times$ Occasion interaction, $F(12, 228) = 8.91$, $p < .001$, and a significant Treatment $\times$ Measure $\times$ Occasion interaction, $F(12, 228) = 2.27$, $p < .005$.

A 3 $\times$ 3 ANOVA conducted on PTSD symptom severity revealed a significant effect of occasion, $F(2, 48) = 51.25$, $p < .001$, modified by a significant Treatment $\times$ Occasion interaction, $F(4, 48) = 2.67$, $p < .05$. Simple effects analyses revealed that all three groups improved significantly, $F(2, 48) = 24.14$, $p < .001$; $F(2, 48) = 23.87$, $p < .001$; $F(2, 48) = 8.59$, $p < .002$, for SIT, PE, and SC, respectively, over the course of the study. The three groups differed significantly in the severity of PTSD symptoms only at the posttreat-

Table 22.4. *Posttreatment and Follow-up Means and Standard Deviations*

Measure	SIT ($n = 9$)	PE ($n = 9$)	SC ($n = 9$)
PTSD severity			
Pretreatment			
M	24.30	25.01	25.25
SD	6.10	4.64	6.33
Posttreatment			
M	9.89	13.56	19.78
SD	4.20	10.00	5.65
Follow-up			
M	12.33	10.44	16.11
SD	9.59	8.22	9.37
Avoidance symptoms			
Pretreatment			
M	6.41	6.09	5.44
SD	2.35	3.01	2.53
Posttreatment			
M	2.11	3.44	5.78
SD	2.26	4.04	2.33
Follow-up			
M	2.44	3.00	3.67
SD	2.74	3.12	2.74
Intrusion symptoms			
Pretreatment			
M	5.82	5.48	5.32
SD	1.98	.85	2.92
Posttreatment			
M	1.67	2.89	4.11
SD	1.41	2.89	2.32
Follow-up			
M	2.89	2.00	4.11
SD	3.02	2.40	3.66
Arousal symptoms			
Pretreatment			
M	11.11	12.00	12.48
SD	2.27	1.42	1.86
Posttreatment			
M	5.56	6.78	8.90
SD	2.24	3.49	1.86
Follow-up			
M	6.44	5.00	7.56
SD	4.67	3.00	3.97
RAST			
Pretreatment			
M	139.83	146.24	129.88
SD	20.86	42.95	37.40
Posttreatment			
M	96.50	89.00	109.38
SD	48.14	65.94	57.82
Follow-up			
M	86.50	61.00	123.38
SD	50.37	62.09	72.50

Measure	SIT ($n = 9$)	PE ($n = 9$)	SC ($n = 9$)
STAI-state			
Pretreatment			
M	54.44	58.62	58.42
SD	6.39	10.53	9.68
Posttreatment			
M	36.67	41.62	47.38
SD	7.62	14.23	18.17
Follow-up			
M	37.56	32.38	50.00
SD	15.36	6.99	19.35
BDI			
Pretreatment			
M	15.11	19.88	21.38
SD	9.17	10.62	8.28
Posttreatment			
M	6.78	12.75	19.00
SD	6.48	15.97	14.40
Follow-up			
M	10.33	6.38	15.88
SD	11.68	7.56	10.20

NOTE. SIT = stress inoculation training; PE = prolonged exposure; SC = supportive counseling: WL = wait-list control. PTSD = posttraumatic stress disorder; RAST = Rape Aftermath Symptom Text; STAI = State-Trait Anxiety Inventory; BDI = Beck Depression Inventory.

ment assessment, $F(2, 24) = 4.51$, $p<.03$. Post hoc tests revealed that all three groups improved between pretreatment and posttreatment assessments. None of the groups improved significantly between posttreatment and follow-up; however, the PE group showed a trend ($p<.07$) toward improvement.

The ANOVA on avoidance symptoms revealed a significant main effect of occasion, $F(2, 48) = 18.43$, $p<.001$, modified by a significant Treatment $\times$ Occasion interaction, $F(4, 48) = 3.62$; $p<.02$. Simple effects analysis indicated that all three groups improved significantly from pretreatment to follow-up, $F(2, 48) = 14.98$, p; lt.001; $F(2, 48) = 7.30$; $p<.005$; $F(2, 48) = 3,38$, $p<.05$, for SIT, PE, and SC, respectively. Post hoc analyses revealed that SIT and PE groups improved significantly between pretreatment and posttreatment. None of the groups changed significantly between posttreatment and follow-up. Again, the groups differed significantly only at the posttreatment assessment, $F(2, 24) = 3.47$, $p<.05$.

Results of the analyses of the intrusive and arousal symptoms clusters revealed main effects of occasion, $F(2, 48) = 17.61$, $p<.001$; $F(2, 48) = 51.06$, $p<.001$, respectively. Post hoc tests revealed that the groups improved significantly between pretreatment and posttreatment assessments but not between posttreatment and follow-up. No significant changes were detected on the RAST, STAI, or BDI between posttreatment and follow-up.

Clinical significance of treatment effects. Treatment response was also examined through a series of chi-square tests comparing the percentage of patients in each of the treatment groups who showed clinically significant improvement on PTSD symptoms. Following the suggestion of Jacobson and Traux (1991), a patient was designated as significantly improved if her posttreatment (follow-up) scores were more than two standard deviations below the mean of the pretreatment sample. At posttreatment, all four groups were included in the analyses. At follow-up, waiting-list patients were excluded from the analyses, and the three treatments (SIT, PE, SC) were compared.

At posttreatment, the four groups differed in the percentage of patients who improved on PTSD symptoms, $\chi^2(3\ N = 45) = 9.61$, $p<.05$: 71% ($n = 10$) of the SIT patients and 40% ($n = 4$) of the PE patients were significantly improved at posttreatment. In contrast, only 18% ($n = 2$) of the SC and 20% ($n = 2$) of the WL group showed significant improvement in PTSD symptoms. At the follow-up assessment, the three treatment groups (SIT, PE, SC) did not differ with respect to the number of improved patients. Sixty-seven percent ($n = 6$) of the SIT group, 56 % ($n = 5$) of the PE group, and 33% ($n = 3$) of the SC group were significantly improved at follow-up. These results converge with those obtained through ANOVAs.

Similar chi-square analyses were conducted to examine differences comparing the percentage of patients in each group who did not meet diagnostic criteria for PTSD at the posttreatment and at follow-up assessments. Again, wait-list patients were excluded from the follow-up analyses.

At posttreatment, the four groups differed significantly in the percentage of patients who met diagnostic criteria for PTSD $\chi^2(3\ N = 45) = 10.18$, $p<.05$. Fifty percent ($n = 7$) of the SIT patients and 40% ($n = 4$) of PE patients no longer met criteria for PTSD. In contrast, 90% ($n = 10$) of the SC group and all of the WL patients retained the diagnosis at posttreatment. The three treatment groups (SIT, PE, SC) did not differ in the percentage of PTSD patients at follow-up. In both the SIT and PE groups, 55% ($n = 5$) of the patients did not meet PTSD criteria; 45% ($n = 4$) of the SC group did not meet diagnostic criteria for the disorder.

Using Spearman-Brown and Pearson correlations, the demographic and assault characteristics presented in tables 22.1 and 22.2 were correlated with all outcome variables at posttreatment and follow-up in a search for potential outcome predictors. Similarly, therapist ratings of treatment compliance were correlated with outcome measures. None of these variables were significantly correlated with treatment outcome.

DISCUSSION

We examined the relative efficacy of three treatments in ameliorating chronic posttraumatic stress disorder in rape victims and compared them with a wait-list control condition. We hypothesized that stress inoculation training (SIT) and prolonged exposure (PE) would relieve trauma-related symptoms more effectively than would supportive counseling (SC) or no treatment (WL). The results partially supported our hypothesis. SIT was the most effective treatment in reducing PTSD symptomatology immediately after treatment. PE was also found to be an effective treatment. Unexpectedly, SC and WL conditions improved arousal symptoms of PTSD, but not intrusion and avoidance symptoms. Three and one-half months after treatment termination, PE appeared to be the superior treatment. Thus, although SIT appeared to be the most effective treatment in the short term, PE appeared to be the most effective treatment in the long term.

The superiority of SIT and PE over the other two conditions was evidenced only on PTSD symptoms. On other measures of psychopathology, no significant group differences emerged. Nevertheless, means of the four psychopathology measures in the present study (PTSD, RAST, STAI, BDI) revealed a consistent picture: Immediately after treatment, patients who received SIT showed the least pathology, followed by PE, SC, and WL, respectively. However, at follow-up, patients who received PE evidenced the most improvement, followed by those who received SIT, with patients receiving SC showing the least improvement.

How can this reversal between PE and SIT be explained? We suggest that the procedures included in SIT produce immediate relief, as they are aimed at anxiety management. It is conceivable that after treatment terminated, some patients did not continue to employ SIT techniques, as is necessary for lasting improvement. The procedures utilized in PE, on the other hand, are expected to produce temporarily high levels of arousal, as patients are asked to repeatedly confront the rape memory. These procedures, however, are thought to lead to permanent change in the rape memory and hence to durable gains. The mechanisms by which exposure treatments have been hypothesized to produce change in the trauma memory, referred to as emotional processing, have been discussed at length elsewhere (Foa, Steketee, & Rothbaum, 1989;

Rachman, 1980). They include habituation to feared stimuli, reevaluation of the probability of threat in feared situations, and changes in the negative valence associated with fear responses.

Depression and anxiety decreased significantly following all treatments as well as during the wait-list period. These results seem to indicate that mere contact with a therapist is sufficient to ameliorate nonspecific distress. Whereas such contact may help to reduce general distress, the results of our study indicate that it is not sufficient for alleviating PTSD symptoms.

Our finding that SIT was effective in reducing rape-related psychopathology is consistent with those of Veronen and Kilpatrick (1982) and of Resick et al. (1988). Also consistent with our findings are Resick et al.'s results indicating no difference between counseling and SIT on measures of general psychopathology. However, Resick et al.'s results differ from ours in two ways. First, they did not detect the posttreatment trend for SIT's superiority over other treatments, possibly due to the overlap of procedures mentioned earlier. And second, they did not find improvement during the wait-list period, perhaps because their WL patients were not contacted as frequently as were ours.

The finding that PE was effective in ameliorating PTSD is consistent with Keane et al.'s (1989) results. However, in our study, PE reduced all three symptom clusters of PTSD, whereas Keane et al.'s Vietnam veterans evidenced improvement on intrusion and arousal symptoms but not on avoidance. This may be due to procedural differences in administering the exposure treatment. In the present study, PE consisted of recounting the trauma imaginally without relaxation and of confronting feared situations in vivo; Keane et al.'s treatment included imaginal recounting of the traumatic experience combined with relaxation and no in vivo exposure. Perhaps the relaxation hindered patients from experiencing high anxiety during exposure and thereby diminished the efficacy of treatment. Indeed, anxiety reaction and its decrease during exposure treatments have been found to be positively related to treatment outcome (Kozak, Foa, & Steketee, 1988; Lang, Melamed, & Hart, 1970). Additionally, the absence of improvement in avoidance symptoms in the Keane et al. study may have been due to the absence of in vivo exposure, which is thought to be the most active ingredient in the reduction of avoidance in anxiety-disordered individuals (Marks, 1987).

Two issues inherent in the study of rape victims should be noted. Approximately half of the women scheduled for initial evaluations did not attend their scheduled appointments, and 19% of those offered treatment declined. This reluctance may be due to a tendency of rape victims to avoid confrontation with the rape memory, which is one of the symptoms of PTSD (for a more extensive discussion see Rothbaum & Foa, 1992). Additionally, unlike other anxiety-disordered individuals (e.g., obsessive-compulsives, agoraphobics), rape victims do not seem to define themselves as "patients." Consequently, they seem less likely to comply with therapeutic demands including timely appearance in the therapist's office. It should also be noted that rape is underreported, and many rape victims are reluctant to seek treatment for their symptoms. This seems to be particularly true for lower socioeconomic status individuals. Therefore, the extent to which the present results can be extended to other samples of rape victims is unknown.

In interpreting the current results, two possible limitations should be considered: First, the use of only female therapists in the study limits its generalizability. However, this issue may not pose a serious limitation because most rape victims' treatment centers employ primarily women as therapists. More important, the fact that the principal authors provided training and supervision in all of the treatments may have introduced experimental bias effects. Also, it is difficult to assess the impact of the fact that therapists conducted therapies that may have been contrary to their preferences.

Two issues have arisen from the present study that need to be addressed in future research. First, the findings that SIT produced superior immediate symptom reduction and PE seemed to produce superior improvement at follow-up suggest that an optimal program should combine both treatments. Such a program is presently being investigated. Second, SIT, as practiced by rape researchers, includes several procedures, but no data about their relative efficacy is presently available. The administration of SIT might become more efficient if inert procedures were eliminated.

REFERENCES

American Psychiatric Association. (1980). Diagnostic and statistical manual of mental disorders (3rd ed.). Washington, DC: Author.

American Psychiatric Association. (1987). Diagnostic and statistical manual of mental disorders (3rd ed., rev.). Washington, DC: Author.

Beck, A. T., Rush, A. J., Shaw, B. F., & Emery, G. (1979). Cognitive therapy of depression. New York: Guilford Press.

Beck, A. T., Ward, C. H., Mendelsohn, M., Mock, J., & Erbaugh, J. (1961). An inventory for measuring depression. Archives of General Psychiatry, 4, 561–571.

Cautela, J. R. (1977). Behavior analysis forms for clinical interventions. Champaign, IL: Research Press.

Ellis, A. (1977). The basic clinical theory and rational-emotive therapy. In A. Ellis &

R. Grieger (Eds.), Handbook of rational-emotive therapy. (pp. 3–34). New York: Springer.

Foa, E. B., Steketee, G., & Rothbaum, B. O. (1989). Behavioral/cognitive conceptualization of posttraumatic stress disorder. Behavior Therapy, 20, 155–176.

Frank, E., Anderson, B., Stewart, B. D., Dancu, C., Hughes, C., & West, D. (1988). Efficacy of cognitive behavior therapy and systematic desensitization in the treatment of rape trauma. Behavior Therapy, 19, 403–420.

Jacobson, N. S., & Traux, P. (1991). Clinical significance: A statistical approach to defining meaningful change in psychotherapy research. Journal of Consulting and Clinical Psychology, 59, 12–19.

Keane, T. M., Fairbank, J. A., Caddell, J. M., & Zimering, R. T. (1989). Implosive (flooding) therapy reduces symptoms of PTSD in Vietnam combat veterans. Behavior Therapy, 20, 245–260.

Kilpatrick, D. G. (1988). Rape aftermath symptom test. In M. Hersen & A. S. Bellack (Eds.). Dictionary of behavioral assessment techniques (pp. 366–367). Oxford, UK: Pergamon Press.

Kilpatrick, D. G., Saunders, B. E., Veronen, L. J., Best, C. L., & Von, J. M. (1987). Criminal victimization: Lifetime prevalence, reporting to police, and psychological impact. Crime and Delinquency, 33, 479–489.

Koss, M. P. (1983). The scope of rape: Implications for the clinical treatment of victims. The Clinical Psychologist, 38, 88–91.

Kozak, M. J., Foa, E. B., & Steketee, G. (1988). Process and outcome of exposure treatment with obsessive-compulsives: Psychophysiological indicators of emotional processing. Behavior Therapy, 19, 157–169.

Lang, P., Melamed, B., & Hart, J. D. (1970). A psychophysiological analysis of fear modification using automated desensitization. Journal of Abnormal Psychology, 31, 220–234.

Marks, I. M. (1987). Fears, phobias, and rituals: Panic, anxiety, and their disorders. Oxford, UK: Oxford University Press.

Meichenbaum, D. (1974). Cognitive behavior modification. Morristown, NJ: General Learning Press.

Meichenbaum, D. (1977). Cognitive-behavior modification: An integrative approach. New York: Plenum Press.

Rachman, S. (1980). Emotional processing. Behaviour Research and Therapy, 18, 51–60.

Resick, P. A. (1987). Reactions of female and male victims of rape and robbery (Final Report, NIJ Grant No. MH37296). Washington, DC: National Institute of Justice.

Resick, P. A., Jordan, C. G., Girelli, S. A., Hutter, C. K., & Marhoefer-Dvorak. S. (1988). A comparative outcome study of behavioral group therapy for sexual assault victims. Behavior Therapy, 19, 385–401.

Rothbaum, B. O. & Foa, E. B. (1992). Exposure therapy for rape victims with post-traumatic stress disorder. The Behavior Therapist (1992).

Rothbaum, B. O., Foa, E. B., Murdock, T., Riggs, D., & Walsh, W. (1990). Post traumatic stress disorder in rape victims. (Unpublished manuscript.)

Spielberger, C. D., Gorsuch, R. L., & Lushene, R. E. (1970). Manual for the State-

Trait Anxiety Inventory (self-evaluation questionnaire). *Palo Alto, CA: Consulting Psychologists Press.*

Veronen, L. J., & Kilpatrick, D. G. *(1982, November).* Stress inoculation training for victims of rape: Efficacy and differential findings. *Presented in a symposium entitled "Sexual Violence and Harassment" at the 16th Annual Convention of the Association for Advancement of Behavior Therapy, Los Angeles, CA.*

Veronen, L. J., & Kilpatrick, D. G., *(1983). Stress management for rape victims. In D. Meichenbaum & M. E. Jaremko (Eds.),* Stress reduction and prevention *pp. 341–374. New York: Plenum Press.*

Veronen, L. J., Kilpatrick, D. G., & Resick, P. A. *(1978, November).* Stress inoculation training for victims of rape. *Paper presented at the Association for the Advancement of Behavior Therapy, Chicago.*

Wolpe, J. *(1958).* Psychotherapy by reciprocal inhibition. *Stanford, CA: Stanford University Press.*

23. Efficacy of the Eye Movement Desensitization Procedure in the Treatment of Traumatic Memories

Francine Shapiro

STRONG INTEREST in post traumatic stress disorder (PTSD) was brought to the forefront by the treatment of Vietnam veterans (Figley, 1978). At the same time, the feminist movement forced a reevaluation of the treatment of rape victims (Largen, 1976), so that rape is listed second only to combat in the DSM III categorization of PTSD.

It is well accepted that the response to memories of specific traumatic events is the primary factor in the manifestation of PTSD-related symptoms (Keane *et al.*, 1985). In treating the specific memories, behavior modification exposure techniques such as Systematic Desensitization (Wolpe, 1958) and flooding (Stampfl and Levis, 1967) have been used (Fairbank and Keane, 1982). However, both of these procedures are hampered by serious drawbacks in their clinical use.

Systematic Desensitization (SD) which has proven quite efficacious in reducing or eliminating phobias, entails a process by which the anxiety-producing cues are ranked according to levels of subjective disturbance. The lowest ranking cues are then introduced for approximately 6 sec, followed by a period of intense relaxation. While counter conditioning and extinction have been posited as the controlling mechanisms in this procedure (cf. Kazdin and Wilcoxon, 1976), Wolpe (1954) argues that the state of relaxation is incompatible with the state of anxiety and the phobic cue is thereby desensitized by means of reciprocal inhibition.

According to Wolpe (1954, 1982), in order for desensitization to be effective, prolonged training in deep relaxation (approximately nine sessions) is

Reprinted by permission from *Journal of Traumatic Stress* 2 (2), 199–223. Copyright © Plenum Publishing, 1989. The present chapter does not include the entire methodology of EMDR as currently used. A full description of procedures to be employed in clinical or research practices is found in: *Eye Movement Desensitization and Reprocessing: Basic Principles, Protocols, and Procedures* by Francine Shapiro. New York: Guilford Press, 1995.

required and only low levels of disturbance are amenable to the treatment in each session. Thus, many sessions are necessary to proceed through the hierarchy before the goal of desensitizing the total anxiety response is achieved. Perhaps because of the number of relaxation and desensitization sessions necessary, or because the traumatic cues associated with a rape or many Vietnam incidents are not amenable to hierarchical arrangement, SD has not found more widespread use in the treatment of PTSD.

With flooding it is possible to address traumatic events at a high level of disturbance. However, as with SD there are certain problems with this procedure. During the implementation of flooding, the client is asked to relive the event in exaggerated detail which produces intense anxiety throughout the sessions. Between five and nine sessions are usually required to eliminate the anxiety. Therefore, while this procedure can be effective, there continues to be an expressed concern in the therapeutic community regarding the forced elicitation of such high anxiety in clients for prolonged periods (Fairbank and Brown, 1987). In addition, flooding (as well as SD) has been criticized for failing to address irrational cognitions or to offer generalizable coping skills (Becker and Abel, 1981; Kilpatrick et al., 1982; Kilpatrick and Best, 1984). Consequently, cognitive therapy techniques have been used to supplement the behavioral techniques in order to reorient clients toward self-acceptance.

The consensus in the behavioral community is that both cognitive and exposure techniques are necessary for the treatment of traumatic memories. However, the difficulties already discussed regarding SD and flooding indicate a treatment need for a desensitization procedure that can address highly traumatic incidents in a short period of time without exacerbated anxiety on the part of the victim while at the same time incorporating a cognitive reconstruction.

The investigator has developed a technique, the Eye Movement Desensitization (EMD) procedure, which on the basis of clinical observation appeared to be extremely promising in the treatment of traumatic memories and stress-related symptoms. The primary component of the EMD procedure is the generation of rhythmic, multi-saccadic eye movements while the client concentrates on the memory to be desensitized. The effect of saccadic eye movements was discovered accidentally by the author when she noticed that recurring, disturbing thoughts were suddenly disappearing and not returning. Careful self-examination ascertained that the apparent reason for this effect was that the eyes were automatically moving in a multi-saccadic manner while the disturbing thought was being held in consciousness. The effect was that the thought disappeared completely and if deliberately retrieved was without its previously disturbing emotional correlate. The author then began to make systematic use of these movements to study the effect and later proceeded to generate the saccades in a large number of volunteers and clients in order to investigate further the therapeutic possibilities. The EMD procedure examined in the present study thus evolved from the clinical observations garnered during hundreds of treatment sessions.

In the EMD procedure clients are requested to follow with their eyes the therapist's finger, which is moved very rapidly from side to side 10-20 times as a means of eliciting from them rhythmic, bilateral saccadic eye movements, while they simultaneously visualize the traumatic event and internally repeat the associated irrational cognition or negative self-statement (i.e., self-assessment). Preliminary testing suggested that the procedure had the capacity to (1) desensitize a highly traumatic memory within a short period of time (one session) without intense and prolonged anxiety; (2) produce a cognitive restructuring of the verbalized self-statement or assessment, along with a redefined visual representation; and (3) cause congruent and substantial behavioral shifts.

Since the preceding observations were anecdotal, the present study was carried out to examine the efficacy of the EMD procedure in a systematic and controlled manner.

METHOD

Design

Twenty-two volunteer subjects suffering from traumatic memories were randomly divided into a Treatment Group, which received the EMD treatment, and a Control Group, which received a placebo treatment. Each group was measured before, during, and after their respective treatments on anxiety level and belief in the validity of the desired cognition concerning their traumatic memory. Also measured were the subject's presenting complaints. Identical statements, questions, and number of measurements were used for both groups in order to control for subjects' expectations and other placebo effects, and for the possibility that mere exposure to the traumatic incident would cause desensitization.

For ethical reasons, the EMD procedure was administered to the Control Group after they had participated in the placebo condition. While affording treatment to the Control Group prevented a between-groups analysis of follow-up results, it did provide the opportunity for a within-groups analysis in which the Control Group after the placebo was compared to the same group after the EMD procedure (delayed treatment condition).

Follow-up tests of the effectiveness of the treatment were obtained at 1 and 2 months after the initial session.

Subjects

Five males and 17 females served as subjects. All were volunteers referred from (1) the Mendocino, CA Community Assistance in Assault and Rape Emergency (CAARE) Project which treats rape/assault/molestation victims; (2) the Parents United Group, which treats adult survivors of childhood molestations; (3) the Fort Bragg, CA, Vietnam Veterans Outreach Program; or (4) independent therapists.

All referrals were previously diagnosed by their counselors as PTSD victims. An additional five subjects were mental health professionals who desired relief from traumatic memories that continued to cause them distress (e.g., intrusive thoughts, nightmares, intimacy problems). Subjects' ages ranged from 11 to 53 years, with a mean of 37 years. They came from all walks of life, including unemployed blue collar workers, professional mental health workers, and a psychiatrist. Education level was congruent with employment (i.e., ranged from elementary school education to postgraduate studies).

All referrals were accepted as subjects based upon the criteria of a long-standing (i.e., 1 or more years) traumatic memory and related symptomatology (e.g., flashbacks, intrusive thoughts, sleep disturbances, intimacy problems). One subject had undergone severe mental and physical abuse, while all others had experienced either rape/molestation or Vietnam War combat incidents. The number of years that these traumatic memories had persisted ranged from 1 to 47 years, with a mean of 23 years. The length of therapy ranged from 2 months to 25 years, with a mean of 6 years. Other symptoms and their frequencies were: flashbacks (range = 1/month-6/week; mean = 3/week); intrusive thoughts (range = 5/week-6/day; mean = 12/week), and sleep disturbances (range = 2/week-5/week; mean = 4/week).

Measurements

The dependent variables were anxiety level, belief in the validity of the desired cognitions, and presenting complaints.

The level of anxiety related to the traumatic memories was assessed by means of an 11-point (0 = no anxiety; 10 = highest anxiety possible) Subjective Units of Disturbance scale (SUDs; Wolpe, 1982). This instrument has been found to correlate with objective physiological indicators of stress (Thyer et al., 1984) and is customarily used to assess anxiety level during the SD procedure. Pulse rates were also recorded in order to monitor any undue disturbance on the part of the subject.

Irrational cognitions are a part of PTSD and cognitive therapy serves to restructure these beliefs (DeFazio et al., 1975; Keane et al., 1985). Therefore, the second quantitative measurement entailed first eliciting from subjects the words that best described their irrational belief about the traumatic memory, then asking them to verbalize the belief that they desired as a replacement, and finally, while concentrating on the traumatic memory, to indicate on a 7-point (1 = completely untrue; 7 = completely true) Semantic Differential scale the current strength of this alternate belief. With regard to the latter, subjects were instructed to respond in terms of their "gut feelings" rather than their intellect. This measure, which was created by the author, is referred to as the Validity of Cognition scale and was assumed, on the basis of its face validity, to provide a rapid assessment of cognitive structure.

The subjects' presenting complaints were also used as an index of potential therapeutic effectiveness. At the initial session subjects were interviewed regarding presenting symptoms including flashbacks, intrusive thoughts, and sleep disturbances, and their frequency during the preceding month. These were used as baseline data and were corroborated by therapists, spouses, and parents. The primary presenting complaints for each of the subjects are listed in tables 23.1 and 23.2 of "Results."

Procedure

At the outset of the 50-min initial session (Session 1), subjects in both Treatment and Control Groups were requested to read and sign a release form, indicating that, although "not guaranteed," their participation in the experiment might have "possible benefits" for their specific complaints. They were asked to enumerate and quantify their presenting complaints (e.g., number of intrusive thoughts during the preceding week). They were then instructed to describe the memory from which they wished relief in terms of who was involved and what had happened. They were asked to isolate a single picture that represented the entire memory (preferably the most traumatic point of the incident) and to indicate who and what was in the picture.

Table 23.1. *Primary Presenting Problems for Individual Subjects in Treatment Group for Session 1 and 1- and 3-Month Follow-Up*

Subject	Session 1 Primary problem	Follow-up	
		1-Month	3-Month
1	Flashbacks	Eliminated[a]	E[b]
2	Intrusive thoughts	Decreased	I[c]
3	Nightmares	Eliminated[a]	E
4	Lack of trust in men	Decreased	I
5	Flashbacks	Eliminated	E
6	Nightmares	Eliminated[a]	E
7	Daily headaches/panic	Eliminated	E
8	Flashbacks	Eliminated	E
9	Insomnia	Eliminated	E
10	Flashbacks	Eliminated	E
11	Intrusive thoughts	Decreased	E

[a] Only one dream the night of Session 1 which resolved without fear. No nightmares for the remainder of period.
[b] E, Eliminated.
[c] I, Improved.

Table 23.2. *Primary Presenting Problems for Individual Subjects in Control (Delayed Treatment) Group for Session 1 and 1- and 3-Month Follow-Up*

Subject	Session 1 Primary problem	Follow-up	
		1-Month	3-Month
1	Insecurity in groups	Decreased	I[a]
2	Lack of trust in men	Decreased	S[b]
3	Intrusive thoughts	Decreased	S
4	Flashbacks	Eliminated	E[c]
5	Insomnia	Eliminated	E
6	Insomnia	Eliminated	E
7	Nightmares	Unavailable	
8	Lack of trust in men	Decreased	I
9	Flashbacks/panic	Eliminated	E
10	Flashbacks	Eliminated	E
11	Intrusive thoughts	Eliminated	E

[a] I, Improved.
[b] S, Same as 1-month follow-up.
[c] E, Eliminated.

In order to assess their belief statement about the incident, they were then asked "What words about yourself or the incident best go with the picture?" Most subjects expressed such belief statements as "I am helpless," "I should have done something," or "I have no control." If the subject experienced difficulty in generating an assessment statement, the investigator provided assistance by explaining the concept of negative self-assessments and gave examples. Alternatively, the researcher might ask them to describe their feelings about the past incident and then suggest some alternatives. Only those belief statements that were recognized by the subjects as applicable to them and the incident were used, and where possible the subjects' own words were quoted.

Subjects were then directed to imagine both the traumatic scene and the words of the belief statement and to assign a SUDs level to them. They were then asked how they would like to feel instead and to supply a new belief statement that reflected the desired feeling (e.g., "I have control," "I am worthy," "I did the best I could"). The subjects were then requested to judge by means of the 7-point Validity of Cognition scale how true the new statement felt to them and this response was recorded.

Next, subjects were told that: "What we will be doing is often a physiology check. I need to know from you exactly what is going on with as clear feedback as possible. Sometimes things will change and sometimes they won't. I may ask you if the picture changes—sometimes it will and sometimes it won't. I'll ask you how you feel from '0' to '10'—sometimes it will change and sometimes it won't. I may ask if something else comes up—sometimes it will and sometimes it won't. There are no 'supposed to's' in this process. So just give as accurate feedback as you can as to what is happening, without judging whether it should be happening or not. Just let whatever happens, happen."

Treatment Group

Subjects in the Treatment Group were instructed to visualize the traumatic scene, rehearse the negative statement (e.g., "I am helpless"), and follow the investigator's index finger with their eyes. The investigator then caused subjects to generate a series of 10–20 voluntary, bilateral, rhythmic saccadic eye movements by moving her index finger rapidly back and forth across their line of vision. The finger was located 12–14 in. from the face and was moved from the extreme right to the extreme left of the visual field at the rate of two back-and-forth sweeps per second. The distance of one sweep was approximately 12 in. The investigator's finger moved either (1) in a diagonal across the midline of the face from the subjects' extreme lower right to extreme upper left (i.e., chin-level to contralateral brow-level) or (2) horizontally at mid-eye level from the extreme right to extreme left of the subjects' visual field.

Two of the subjects were unable to follow the moving finger and thus for these subjects the investigator used a two-handed approach in which she placed the index finger of each hand on opposite sides of the subject's face at eye level and alternately lifted each finger. The subject was instructed to move the eyes to the raised finger which was at the extreme left or right limit of the visual field.

Each grouping of 10 to 20 two-directional saccadic eye movements is considered to be one set. After each set of saccades, the subjects were asked to: "Blank it (the picture) out, and take a deep breath." They were then asked to bring up the picture and words again, to concentrate on the anxiety level generated, and to provide a SUDs level rating from "0" to "10." At the times that the SUDs levels were taken, subjects were occasionally asked such questions as "Did the picture change?" or "What do you get now/Does anything else come up?" Their answers were used as barometers of change since they often revealed new insights, perceptions, or alterations of the picture (e.g., "The picture seems further away"; "I didn't do anything wrong"). If an answer revealed that a new associated limiting belief had arisen, this belief was often included with the original statement during the next set.

When the SUDs level reached "0" or "1" (after 3–12 sets of saccades), the subject's belief in the validity of the desired cognition was tested by asking: "How do you feel about the statement (desired cognition) from '1'— completely untrue to '7'—completely true." The EMD procedure was terminated only when no other trauma or competing cognition was revealed and self-reported anxiety level was at "0" or "1." In five cases, anxiety was found to be reduced but validity of cognition had not reached "6" or "7." In these cases, two or three additional sets of eye movements, while pairing the previously traumatic memory with the positive self-statement, were sufficient to raise validity of cognition to the desired level.

If another memory and /or cognition was determined to be interfering, the entire procedure was repeated on the new material. The latter situation is exemplified in the case of the Vietnam veteran who was working to accept as valid the cognition: "I can be comfortably in control." When asked to respond to the validity of the statement after the original image had been desensitized, he responded: "I am not worthy to be comfortably in control." This cognition of "lack of worth" was related to a different trauma which needed to be desensitized, and then still another trauma was revealed having to do with "failure." When these two additional traumas were desensitized, he was able to give a "7" rating to the words: "I can be comfortably in control."

Control Group (Placebo Condition)

In order to match the two groups on exposure to the traumatic memory, subjects in the control group were asked to describe the memory (with an emphasis on the specific traumatic scene) in full detail, indicating who was involved, what the environment looked like, and exactly what happened. This provided a modified flooding procedure. During the description, the investigator interrupted the subjects seven times at approximately 1–1 ½-min intervals to ask for a new SUDs level (i.e., How does it feel now from "0" to "10"?) This paralleled the procedure for the Treatment Group subjects who had been interrupted 3–12 times to obtain these measurements. As with the Treatment Group, subjects in the Control Group were then asked if the picture had changed or if anything new was coming to mind. After they answered the questions they resumed the detailed description of their memory.

Following the seventh measure of the SUDs level, the statement was checked on the Validity of Cognition scale which completed the control procedure.

Finally, in order that the Control Group receive the presumed benefit of the therapy, the EMD procedure was administered in exactly the same fashion as for the Treatment Group and is referred to as the delayed treatment condition.

Thus, before treatment was administered, the Treatment Group and the Control Group were comparable on (1) initial expectancy of the treatment's effectiveness, (2) exposure to the traumatic memory, (3) occurrence of repeated interruptions and identical questioning, and (4) number of SUDs and Validity of Cognition measurements obtained. They differed in that only the Treatment Group (1) held the desired cognition along with the traumatic memory in mind, (2) engaged in repeated eye movements, and (3) blanked out the memory and took a deep breath at the end of a given set of eye movements. This complex of events thus represents the EMD procedure.

Follow-Up

One and three months after Session 1, subjects were rescheduled for ½-hr interviews (1-and 3-Month Follow-Up Sessions) in order to measure the long-term effects of the treatment. They were asked to visualize the original traumatic memory and to give a SUDs rating regarding the anxiety generated by it. The positive belief statement that had been used at Session 1 was then repeated to them and they were asked to provide a rating on the Validity of Cognition scale. The subjects' previous complaints regarding intrusive thoughts, sleep disturbances, psychological numbing, etc. were reviewed and a new assessment given by them regarding intensity/severity of these complaints (e.g., numbers of intrusive thoughts, nightmares, etc.) over the preceding month. In most cases (i.e., 18 out of 22) subjects' reports were verified by therapist, spouse, or parent.

RESULTS

The efficacy of the treatment procedure was measured in terms of (1) SUDs level, (2) validity of cognition, (3) pulse rate, and (4) presenting complaints.

Subjective Units of Disturbance (SUDs)

Group means for the SUDs measures obtained in Session 1 are presented in fig. 23.1. As indicated under "Procedure," the Control Group was first tested

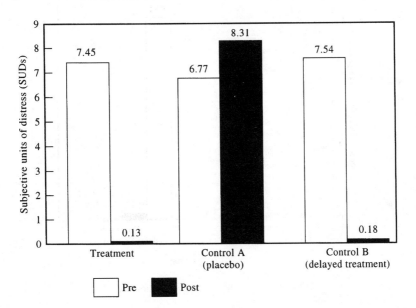

Figure 23.1. Mean subjective units of disturbance for Treatment, Control A (placebo) and Control B (delayed treatment) groups in Session 1.

in the placebo condition and subsequently in the delayed treatment condition (also referred to in fig. 23.1 as Control A and Control B). The first analysis entailed a comparison of SUDs scores for Treatment and Control A. The data for Session 1 were subjected to a Treatment/Control × Pre/Post analysis of variance with repeated measures on the second factor. Both main effects were statistically significant, although it is clear from an examination of fig. 23.1 that the most important result was the interaction, $F(1, 20) = 44.46$, $p < 0.001$. A simple effects analysis revealed that the interaction was due to a highly significant ($p < 0.001$) pre-post drop in the SUDs level for the Treatment Group and no pre-post change ($p > 0.05$) for the Control Group.

In order to examine the effect of treatment on the Control Group, a Placebo/Delayed Treatment × Pre/Post analysis of variance was carried out. A statistically significant interaction, $F(1, 10) = 39.52$, $p < 0.001$ was obtained which, according to simple effects analyses, was due to a highly significant ($p < 0.001$) pre-post decline in SUDs level for the delayed treatment condition. As indicated in the previous analysis, the pre-post difference for the Control Group was nonsignificant ($p > 0.05$).

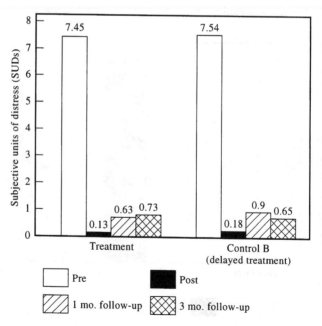

Figure 23.2. Mean subjective units of disturbance for Treatment and Control B (delayed treatment) groups in Session 1, and 1-month and 3-month follow-up.

Figure 23.2 presents the mean SUDs levels for the Treatment Group and Control (delayed treatment) Group for Session 1 and 1-and 3-month Follow-Up Sessions. These data were subjected to a 2 × 4 analysis of variance in which the first factor was Treatment/Delayed Treatment and the second was Session 1 Pre/Session 1 Post/1-Month Follow-Up/3-Month Follow-Up. A statistically significant effect was obtained for the second factor, $F(3, 57) = 132.55$, $p < 0.001$. Simple effects analyses indicated that for neither the Treatment nor the Control Group (delayed treatment) were the differences among the post-, 1-Month Follow-Up, or 3-Month Follow-Up measures statistically significant ($p > 0.05$). Thus, as seen in fig. 23.2, the significant main effect resulted from a very sharp pre-post decline in SUDs level in Session 1 for both Treatment and Control Groups, with levels remaining essentially the same through the 3-month Follow-Up.

Validity of Cognitions

The mean validity of cognition scores for Treatment, Control A (placebo condition), and Control B (delayed treatment condition) Groups are presented in fig. 23.3. The data for Treatment and Control A Groups were subjected to

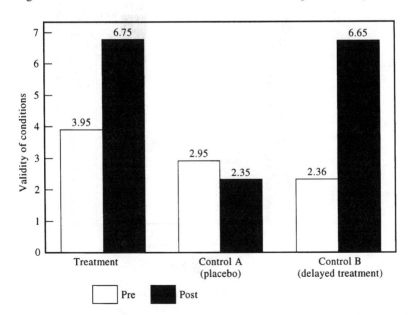

Figure 23.3. Mean validity of cognitions for Treatment, Control A (placebo) and Control B (delayed treatment) groups in Session 1.

a Treatment/Control A × Pre/Post analysis of variance. The interaction was statistically significant, $F(1, 19) = 43.193, p < 0.001$. Simple effects analyses indicated that the pre-post increase in validity of cognitions for the Treatment Group was highly statistically significant ($p < 0.001$), while the difference for the Control A Group was non-significant ($p < 0.05$). Also revealed by these analyses was a statistically significant difference between the Treatment and Control A Groups ($p < 0.05$) on *pretreatment* validity of cognition. This was unexpected, in that the two groups were treated identically through the pretreatment condition and is apparently due to chance. Reexamination of the data indicated that the difference was apparently due to one subject in the Treatment Group who began with the maximum validity of cognition score.

In order to examine the effect of treatment on the Control Group (right two-thirds of fig. 23.3), a Placebo/Delayed Treatment × Pre/Post analysis of variance was carried out. The statistically significant interaction, $F(1, 10) = 40.09, p < 0.001$ was demonstrated by means of simple effects analysis to be the result of a sharp pre-post increase in validity of cognition level as a result of delayed treatment ($p < 0.001$), but no pre-post difference for the placebo

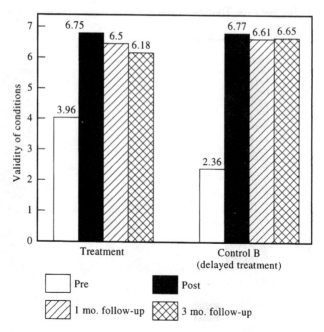

Figure 23.4. Mean validity of cognition for Treatment and Control B (delayed treatment) groups in Session 1, and 1-month and 3-month follow-up.

condition. Figure 23.4 presents the mean validity of cognition values for the Treatment and Control (delayed treatment) Groups for Session 1 and 1-and 3-month Follow-Up Sessions. These data were subjected to a 2 × 4 analysis of variance. Both the effect factor of Session 1 Pre/Session 1 Post/1-Month Follow-Up/3-Month Follow-Up, $F(3, 51) = 79.88$, $p < 0.001$, and the interaction, $F(3, 51) = 6.22$, $p = 0.001$, were statistically significant. Simple effects analyses revealed that the difference between pretreatment and the remaining three conditions was statistically significant ($p < 0.001$) for both Treatment and Control (delayed treatment) Groups. Thus, the increases for both groups were substantial and the high degree of validity of cognition produced by the therapeutic procedure was maintained for both groups through the 3-Month Follow-Up Session. As previous analyses have indicated, there was also an unexpected and unexplained difference between the two groups in the pretreatment condition, which led to the interaction.

Pulse Rate

As noted earlier, pulse rate was obtained as a means of monitoring any severe emotional distress that might be experienced by the subjects, perhaps requiring termination of the session. Fortunately, such an extreme reaction never occurred. It was realized subsequent to the experiment that this measure might represent an index of the effectiveness of the therapeutic treatment. The highest pulse rate occurring during the subjects' first elicitation of the memory was noted for each of the three sessions. A mean decrease of 13 pulses/min was obtained for both Treatment and Control (delayed treatment) Groups between Session 1 and the 1-Month Follow-Up Session, a drop that was maintained at the 3-Month Follow-Up Session.

Unfortunately, no pulse rate data were obtained for placebo and delayed treatment conditions of the Control Group at the end of Session 1. Therefore the results are only suggestive because the lack of comparison data at the end of Session 1 makes it impossible to rule out habituation to the experimenter and the environment as the cause for the decline in pulse rate. Nevertheless, it is important to note that the lowered pulse rates during the initial probe measures at the three sessions are congruent with the reduced self-reported SUDs levels and subsequent behavioral changes.

Primary Presenting Problems

The treatment effect in regards to the alleviation of primary presenting symptoms, as reported by the subjects, is presented in tables 23.1 and 23.2. All

subjects reported either a decrease or total elimination of the primary presenting problem during the 1-Month Follow-Up Session. At the 3-Month
Follow-Up Session subjects reported either a maintenance or improvement of
the 1-month condition. All of the related nightmares and flashbacks had been
eliminated. Thoughts of the incident had totally disappeared or, in the case of
three subjects, were extremely rare and without emotional impact. All subjects
reported a higher level of self-esteem and over-all functioning and, when
previously problematic, an increased intimacy in relationships. Subjects who
were in therapy at the time of the EMD treatment maintained contact with
their primary therapists, who in all cases, verified that presenting complaints
had been eliminated or substantially reduced immediately following the EMD
treatment session. In all but four of the remaining cases, subject reports were
verified by parent or spouse.

Examples of typical subjects' reports are as follows:

A subject who had reported a life-long history of one or two violent,
fearful dreams per week reported that only one violent dream had occurred
the night following the treatment. On this occasion, however, he had felt no
fear and in the dream had "ritually bowed to his Samurai enemies." They
had then "joined forces" and, since that night, he had had no other violent or
fearful dreams. He stated that this was the first period of his life that he could
remember having no nightmares and feeling consistently "good and confident, without breaks." His wife reported that he no longer slept fitfully, and
that he seemed much calmer and relaxed at home since the session.

One Vietnam veteran who had had flashbacks, intrusive thoughts, and
nightmares for 21 years regarding a particular incident also reported only one
subsequent nightmare. He reported that there was "no power to it" and had
arrived at the realization that "the person cutting my throat was me." No
other frightful dreams had occurred and only infrequent intrusive thoughts
but "none have power anymore." He also reported himself to be calmer on
all related issues and memories.

One other Vietnam veteran was treated for three different memories (see
"Procedure" section). Panic attacks that had afflicted him daily were reduced
to only one during the 1-month period, flashbacks related to planes overhead
had been eliminated, and he had been able to gain and maintain an erection
for the first time in 3 years. Changes seemed directly attributable to the
content of the three memories treated: (1) feeling out of control, (2) a bomb
exploding in Vietnam, and (3) a failed sexual encounter.

Other subjects reported changes in a variety of long-standing problems.
One subject who had been orally raped as a child, 40 years ago, had flashback

feelings of panic and a gagging sensation in her throat several times a week. Since the treatment session, thoughts of the incident caused no upset, and the panic/gagging sensation had been totally eliminated. Another subject reported that daily headaches had ceased following treatment.

One 11-year-old subject who had been molested over a prolonged period had been so traumatized that she was unable to bring up the molestor's face. However, she was nonfunctional in school because her teacher's face would "turn into someone who would hurt" her. The same thing would happen to the faces of people on the street and she would freeze, seeing "some weird guy who wants to kidnap a kid." She was desensitized by having her picture the molester's shirt and pants and "imagine/pretend seeing his face." There have been no flashbacks since and she has been functioning again at school over the 3-month period. Her mother also reported that for many months the child had been regularly experiencing violent nightmares which caused her either to wake up screaming or to throw herself out of bed. Her mother stated that the nightmares had been totally eliminated after the treatment session.

Patterns

While the following patterns were unexpected by the investigator, they should be carefully reviewed for the purposes of study replication or clinical intervention.

Mismatch

An important pattern that emerged in this experiment was a consistent anxiety desensitization on each trial, except when a mismatch of picture, cognition, or feeling had occurred. Seventy percent of the Treatment Group subjects revealed a consistent decrease from start to finish in SUDs levels from one set to the next as compared to the Control Group which remained the same or increased (except for one placebo effect). At any time that a decrease failed to occur after two sets the subjects were asked if the picture, words, or feelings had changed. Without exception, one of these factors had shifted, causing a mismatch to occur. For instance, the cognitive component "It was shameful," which went with the feeling of guilt and shame, no longer applied to the feeling of sadness which had replaced it. In this instance the cognition was replaced with the words, "How sad" and the procedure continued to desensitize the trauma.

Likewise, the picture of the traumatic incident may have switched to an earlier incident which required a different set of cognitions. In this case a different, appropriate cognition was applied to the new incident and that traumatic memory was desensitized before returning to the original picture. These observations seem to indicate that associated traumas are also revealed by the process in a "peel back" fashion. Each of the previous traumas must be desensitized in turn before continuing with the original picture. In these cases, the original picture will often generate less anxiety when reactivated after the older trauma has been treated.

Other cases involving a pictorial mismatch occurred when the traumatic picture changed into a less upsetting form. For instance, one subject reported that the "leering face" she was imagining had changed to a "smiling face." In other instances, the image of the rapist disappeared totally, leaving a neutral environment. In these cases, it seemed appropriate to return to the original picture when possible which continued the desensitization procedure.

Parenthetically, it should be noted that the traumatic picture may change to a more neutral one and that the subject will be unable to retrieve the original image. In this case, it is possible to continue the desensitization, if it has ceased, by changing the cognition to a more appropriate one (i.e., replacing it with the desired cognition). When the original picture or a facsimile can be retrieved, it is preferable to continue desensitization with it in mind rather than the altered version.

Occasionally, a subject may have taken upon him-or herself to switch the auditory component to the desired positively worded statement. If this was done, it appeared that the desensitization automatically stopped, as indicated by the reported SUDs levels. Upon discovering the nature of the mismatch, the investigator had to direct the subject to return to the original statement before proceeding and a decrease in SUDs level immediately followed. As indicated, the lack of desensitization after two sets meant that some form of mismatch had occurred and once the problem was identified and the components realigned, the SUDs level decreased immediately with the next set of eye movements.

Progressions

Subjects also reported watching the traumatic incident unfold into a subsequent scene or memory. Other subjects reported a progressive difficulty in retrieving the image, fuzziness, lack of clarity, etc. While the subjects remained aware of the actual event and what occurred, the reaction to the event along with pictorial representations was altered.

Another consistent pattern to appear between each set of saccades was that subjects spontaneously generated new insights and perspectives that were part of a logical train of thought involved in a successful and ecological therapeutic assessment of the situation (e.g., changing "I was to blame" to "I was very young" to "I did the best I could" to "It wasn't my fault"). Regardless of the amount of previous psychological exposure, age, or experience, the subjects consistently generated new insights and perspectives that were congruent with the progressive desensitization process.

In addition, the natural progression of emotions from the stage of denial through fear or guilt, through anger to sadness to relief and acceptance was evident in many subjects. Just as the picture often changed after each set of saccades, so too did emotions. In fact, a subject would first evince extreme anger at the memory, and after the next set of saccades would break into tears. The sorrow would be intense for a period of approximately 1–2 min and then would subside. The next set of saccades would then bring out a sense of relief, etc. One subject whose memory of her molestation had only recently surfaced vividly, forcefully "exploded" into tears and cried for about 1½ min. When asked how she felt, she replied "I feel as though I have just been exorcised."

These observations pointed to a progression, on the kinesthetic level, of the therapeutic process. Each stage of emotions, although lasting only 1–2 min, seems to clear the emotion out of the system while setting the stage for the next emotional state. The stages listed above from denial to acceptance are standard steps of healing for the trauma victim that normally occur over a period of days, months, or years. However, the EMD procedure seems to trigger an abreactive response and "contract" the therapeutic process to a matter of minutes.

DISCUSSION

Efficacy

The evidence clearly indicates that a single session of the EMD procedure is effective in desensitizing memories of traumatic incidents and changing the subjects' cognitive assessments of their individual situations. Furthermore, these effects were maintained for a 3-month period and were accompanied by behavioral shifts which included the alleviation of the subjects' primary presenting complaints.

Additional support for the efficacy of the treatment is found in the within-subject comparison of the Control Group subjects in their placebo and de-layed treatment conditions. It should be noted, however, that since all subjects in this group were exposed to the placebo condition before the delayed treatment procedure (i.e., order was not counterbalanced), these results are only suggestive.

Alleviation of presenting complaints occurred for all subjects. Subjects reported that flashbacks and nightmares were eliminated and that intrusive thoughts were either completely absent or much fewer in number. When intrusive thoughts did occur, they were of the memory without anxiety and the pretreatment negative cognition no longer applied.

Not only did all subjects report the elimination or substantial reduction of intrusive thoughts and sleep disturbances, but those with relationship and self-esteem problems experienced a substantial alleviation of symptoms and indi-cated a more positive quality of life since the initial treatment.

Experimenter Bias and Subject Expectancy

In the present study the experimenter and author were one in the same. Thus it is legitimate to be concerned with the possibility of demand characteristics, unintentional experimenter bias, and subject expectancies as alternate expla-nations of the results. Several factors mitigate against this possibility. First, many of the subjects entered the present study expressing grave doubts about the likelihood of success, and thus were biased against supporting the exper-imental hypothesis. During the EMD process, these subjects would frequently express surprise and disbelief, spontaneously making statements such as: "This is too easy"; "This can't be happening"; "I don't believe this." This reaction was also repeated by many subjects with respect to the longevity of treatment effect. No attempt was made by the investigator to assuage their concerns before, during, or after the treatment session.

The use of standardized disclaimers, instructions, and questioning through-out the study should have helped to maintain the same level of expectancy for the two groups. In addition, subjects had been previously in therapy for a mean of 6 years. The lack of treatment effect during that time and the marked changes produced when the EMD procedure was implemented argues against the possibility that expectancy alone was responsible for the present desensi-tization and behavioral shifts.

An argument against experimenter bias as the cause of the present results was the sheer magnitude of the effects. It is very unlikely that subtle, uninten-tional cues from the experimenter could account for the substantial pre-post shifts in SUDs and the validity of cognition levels observed in Session 1 or that these effects as well as the concomitant behavioral shifts (e.g., total cessation of flashbacks and nightmares) would be maintained for 3 months. Independent evaluations by primary therapists, spouses, and parents verified the subjects' reports and indicated that behavioral changes were substantial and stable.

Still, another indication that a specific treatment effect, independent of demand characteristics, occurred was the consistent pattern of desensitization processing for the subjects. No prior description or rationale for the success of either the treatment or the control procedure was given. However, except for three subjects (one Treatment and two Control) who took two trials to begin desensitization, all subjects began to show effects after one trial of the EMD procedure. For the Control Group, delayed treatment began to desensitize the memory as soon as the procedure began, regardless of the amount of anxiety generated during the placebo condition. Further, since all subjects were told that much of what was being done was a physiology check and change was not consistently expected (i.e., consistency was counter-demanded) this pattern indicates that the procedure rather than expectancy or placebo was the salient factor.

In addition, the mismatch phases (see "Results") were the only instances that deterred the treatment effect, and immediate desensitization resumed when the mismatch was addressed. As previously noted, this pattern, and the finding that subjects tended to switch to an earlier related trauma in way of a "peel-back" pattern, were not anticipated by the investigator. This fact, and the patterned consistency of subjects' desensitization responses, indicates that the EMD procedure is not confounded by extraneous variables and represents a standardized procedure with a predictable effect. In addition, both findings seem congruent with Lang's (1977, 1979) bioinformational theory of emotional imagery by indicating a propositional network of memory/imagery cues and a concurrence of stimulus, response, and interpretive (e.g., cognitive assessment) information which need to be aligned for optimal desensitization.

Ecological Validity of Subject Response

Only two subjects showed a sharp (i.e., more than "2") rise in SUDs level at the Follow-Up Sessions. One subject had experienced a placebo effect in the placebo condition and thus in this instance the EMD procedure was inaugurated with an artificially low SUDs level. The only other subject who revealed a sharp increase in SUDs level (i.e., "0" at the end of Session 1 and "4" at the 1-Month Follow-Up Session) seemed to do so because of pertinent environmental factors. This subject's results were confounded by the fact that she was informed that the man who had raped her was still residing in the area, and was concerned that he would rape her again as he had threatened. At the follow-up, she described her feelings as "two-thirds" better than before. She reported that when she heard about him through mutual acquaintances, she felt more detached and more in control and considered her present emotions (i.e., SUDs rating of "4" rather than the pretreatment rating of "8") to be "very realistic" under the circumstances. The treatment effect was also evidenced by the fact that her main presenting problem of intrusive thoughts had been totally eliminated.

The results of the preceding case indicate that certain fears voiced by the therapeutic community (Fairbank and Brown, 1987; Kilpatrick and Best, 1984; Kilpatrick et al., 1982) regarding the possible problems with flooding and/or SD with respect to the desensitization of *ecologically valid* fears does not apply to the EMD process. In other subjects who showed a SUDs level higher than "0" at Follow-Up Sessions, the emotion was often indignation or anger at the person who had violated them, rather than feelings of anxiety or guilt. Therefore, the small rise in SUDs level indicated by the data appeared to be primarily based on a new assessment of the situation that was congruent with the validity of the positive cognition they had adapted, and which was maintained during the 3-month period.

Generalization

Subjects reported that memories that were related to the traumatic incident treated in the first session were also generally desensitized. Thus, other incidents of molestations by the same individual, or incidents with a sufficient number of similar cues and associations, no longer caused anxiety. This finding is congruent with the reports of Fairbank and Keane (1982) regarding the effects of flooding in the treatment of PTSD-related memories and with the generalization of extinction effects (Levis and Boyd, 1979). Specifically, it was discovered at the 3-Month Follow-Up Session that all related memories evoked exactly the same response as the treated memory with respect to the kinds of emotions and levels of intensity as the treated memory. This makes the EMD treatment extremely efficacious as a single-session treatment for multiple rapes, molestations, and similar combat experiences.

Underlying Mechanisms

While the present investigation was not designed to explain how EMD works, some conjectures may be made. Other behavioral treatments of traumatic memories (e.g., SD and flooding) have included exposure to memory, relaxation, and manipulation or interruption of vivid imagery. Since EMD has been successful in directly addressing highly traumatic memories in one session, without relaxation (i.e., in many clinical instances without even the deep breath), and without, in some cases, a vivid picture of the event, some other factor must be essential. Furthermore, since in both SD and EMD the client is asked to picture the disturbing event for 6–10 sec and then to discontinue the image, some factor other than this interruptive procedure causes the immediate desensitization of high SUDs level trauma since SD is not effective for trauma desensitization without a hierarchical approach (Wolpe, 1954, 1982).

Exposure to the memory alone does not appear to be the crucial factor in the effectiveness of the EMD procedure since, in the case of flooding, imaginal, and *in vivo* exposure procedures, the traumatic fear stimuli initially cause a rise in anxiety which does not begin to decrease in less than approximately 25 min of continuous exposure (Chaplin and Levine, 1981; Foa and Kozak, 1986). This is congruent with the experience of the placebo condition in which SUDs level increased during the approximately 8 min of exposure to the memory. However, unlike any other reports of the direct desensitization of high level traumas, the EMD treatment and delayed-treatment condition produced a decrease of 1–5 SUDs units within the first 3 min of treatment and a complete desensitization in 10–40 min. The only subject to exceed a 50-min session was the veteran (described in "Results") who was treated for three traumatic memories in 90 min.

It would therefore appear, congruent with the author's personal experience, that the crucial component of the EMD procedure is the repeated eye movements while the memory is maintained in awareness. If so, it is of interest to speculate how eye movements might produce these results.

The author believes that one of the most potentially fruitful areas of study involves Pavlov's (1927) theory of psychotherapeutic effect and the basis of neurosis which involves a balance between excitatory and inhibitory processes. As cited by Wolpe (1954), "If at a given locus of the cortex excitation and inhibition come into conflict with each other at high intensity, the neural elements concerned may be unable to bear the strain and so undergo a pathological change by which the balance is overthrown; and then the animal presents neurotic symptoms. In accordance with this hypothesis, the essence of therapy would be to restore the balance . . ." (p. 220).

Within the present paradigm, the concept of information processing of the trauma "frozen state" should be examined. It may be suggested that pathological neural changes caused by a traumatic overload (as claimed by Pavlov, 1927) "freeze"/maintain the incident in its original anxiety-producing form (complete with representational picture and cognitions of negative assessment). This pathological change of neural elements blocks the usual progression of continued information processing to a resolution. Thus the incident is maintained in active memory and triggered as intrusive thoughts, flashbacks, and nightmares (Horowitz and Becker, 1972). Rhythmic, bilateral saccadic movement along with an alignment of cognition and pictorial image which connects to the physiologically stored traumatic memory may (1) restore the balance, (2) reverse the neural pathology, and (3) allow the information processing to proceed to resolution with a consequent cessation of intrusive symptomatology.

Specifically, this theory assumes that the effect of the traumatic incident is excitatory in nature and causes the imbalance of neural elements. The rhythmic multi-saccadic movement may be the body's automatic inhibitory (or excitation releasing) mechanism, just as unconscious material surfaces and may be partially desensitized during the dream (REM) state of sleep. The EMD process, therefore, reciprocally inhibits the excitatory phase (which is correlated with symptoms of anxiety) and may be strong enough to return balance to the neural elements. This return of functional information processing would manifest itself as a desensitization of the traumatic memory and a concomitant decline in the symptomatically high SUDs level. As the balance is gradually restored, the pictorial, cognitive, and kinesthetic information is processed and their representations, as reported by the subjects, are progressively altered and resolved causing a cessation of symptomatology.

This hypothesis is also supported by additional information in neurobiology regarding the effects on memory of the alteration of synaptic potential due to repetitive low-voltage current (Barrionuevo et al., 1980). It is possible that the repetitive multi-saccadic movement of the EMD procedure duplicates these results through the neuronal bursts which typify saccadic movement, as suggested by numerous studies of saccades (e.g., Monty and Sender, 1976; Leigh and Zee, 1983; Gale and Johnson, 1984). Both experimental and clinical observations, therefore, indicate that this hypothesis deserves further investigation.

FINAL REMARKS

Since the present study represents the seminal work on the EMD technique, as much information as possible has been included regarding the procedure for purposes of study replication and further investigation. However, it should be emphasized that more detailed explanations may be necessary in order for other experimenters/therapists to achieve the 100% success-rate revealed in this study. Every attempt has been made to standardize the procedure, but there are points in the process where the experimenter must make a decision to take a new tack (e.g., backtrack to the original picture, attend to an alternative cognition, pursue a newly revealed memory). However, the specific components of EMD (i.e., eye movements, picture/cognition, "blanking out," and deep breath are a constant in all instances. Therefore, the author is convinced that enough information has been given here to achieve complete desensitization of 75–80% of any individually treated trauma-related memory in a single 50-min session.

In addition, it must be emphasized that the EMD procedure, as presented here, serves to desensitize the anxiety related to traumatic memories, not to eliminate all PTSD-related symptomatology and complications, nor to provide coping strategies for the victims. It has been necessary for the author to work with some clients (Vietnam veterans, rape/molestation victims, and ritual abuse victims from age 5 to 74) for a number of sessions before the wide range of problems for a given individual were resolved. The results have been profoundly successful, with an average treatment time of five sessions, as well as modified EMD instructions to the client for personal use. However, it seems to the author that supplemental training for clinicians in the EMD procedure will be necessary for full therapeutic success.

So far four therapists have been trained by the author in the EMD procedure, and all are achieving excellent results with trauma victims during one-session desensitizations and multisession clinical interventions. The fact that other therapists have successfully used EMD strengthens the contention that it is a standardized treatment procedure, not requiring special and perhaps unspecifiable personal characteristics of the present investigator.

In conclusion, these findings open many research possibilities regarding the neurobiological basis of saccades and their connection to memory, information processing, and desensitization effect in the treatment of stress-related symptomatology. Further, the information processing patterns revealed by the subjects open some interesting avenues in regard to the memory network itself. Studies are presently underway to investigate the various components of EMD and a variety of possible treatment effects.

REFERENCE

American Psychiatric Association (1980). Diagnostic and Statistical Manual of Mental Disorders *(third edition), APA, Washington.*

Barrionuevo, G., Schottler, F., and Lynch, G. (1980). The effects of repetitive low frequency stimulation on control and "potentiated" synaptic responses in the hippocampus. Life Sci. *27:2385–2391.*

Becker, J. V., and Abel, G. G. (1981). Behavioral treatment of victims of sexual assault. In Turner, S. M., Calhoun, K. S., and Adams, H. E. (eds.), Handbook of Clinical Behavioral Therapy, *Wiley, New York.*

Chaplin, E. W., and Levine, B. A. (1981). The effects of total exposure duration and interrupted versus continuous exposure in flooding therapy. Behav. Ther. *12:360–368.*

DeFazio, V., Rustin, S., and Diamond, A. (1975). Symptom development in Vietnam veterans. Am. J. Orthopsychiat. *43:640–653.*

Fairbank, J. A., and Brown, T. (1987). Current behavioral approaches to the treatment of post-traumatic stress disorder. Behav. Ther. *3:57–64.*

Fairbank, J. A., and Brown, T. (1987). Heterogeneity of post-traumatic stress reactions. Behav. Ther. *10:242.*

Fairbank, J. A., and Keane, T. M. (1982). Flooding for combat-related stress disorders: Assessment of anxiety reduction across traumatic memories. Behav. Ther. *13:499–510.*

Figley, C. R. (1978). Psychosocial adjustment among Vietnam veterans. In Figley, C. R. (ed.), Stress Disorders among Vietnam Veterans: Theory, Research, and Treatment, *Brunner/Mazel, New York.*

Foa, E. B., and Kozak, M. J. (1986). Emotional processing of fear: Exposure to corrective information. Psychological Bull. *99:20–35.*

Gale, A., and Johnson, F. (eds.) (1984). Theoretical and Applied Aspects of Eye Movement Research, *Elsevier, New York.*

Horowitz, M. J., and Becker, S. S. (1972). Cognitive response to stress: Experimental studies of a 'compulsion to repeat trauma.' In Holt, H. G., and Peterfreund, E. (ed.), Psychoanalysis and Contemporary Science *(Vol. 1), Macmillan, New York.*

Kazdin, A. E., and Wilcoxon, L. A. (1976). Systematic desensitization and nonspecific treatment effects: A methodological evaluation. Psychological Bull. *83:729–758.*

Keane, T. M., Zimering, R., and Caddell, J. M. (1985). A behavioral formulation of Posttraumatic Stress Disorder in Vietnam veterans. Behav. Ther. *8:9–12.*

Kilpatrick, D. G., and Best, C. L. (1984). Some cautionary remarks on treating sexual assault victims with implosion. Behav. Ther. *15:421–523.*

Kilpatrick, D. G., Veronen, L. J., and Resick, P. A. (1982). Psychological sequelae to rape:Assessment and treatment strategies. In Doleys, D. M., and Meredith, R. L. (eds.), Behavioral Medicine: Assessment and Treatment Strategies, *Plenum, New York.*

Lang, P. J. (1977). Imagery in therapy: An information processing analysis of fear. Behav. Ther. 8:862–886.

Lang, P. J. (1979). A bio-informational theory of emotional imagery. Psychophysiology 16:495–512.

Largen, M. A. (1976). History of women's movement in changing attitudes, laws and treatment toward rape victims. In Walker, M. J., and Brodsky, S. L. (eds.), Sexual Assault, Heath, Lexington, Mass.

Leigh, R. J., and Zee, D. (1983). The Neurology of Eye Movements, F. A. Davis, Philadelphia.

Levis, D. J., and Boyd, T. L. (1979). Symptom maintenance: An infrahuman analysis and extension of the conservation of anxiety principle. J. Abnorm. Psychol. 88: 107–120.

Monty, R. A., and Senders, J. W. (eds.) (1976). Eye Movements and Psychological Processes, Lawrence Erlbaum Assoc., Hillsdale, N.J.

Pavlov, I. P. (1927). Conditioned Reflexes. G. V. Anrep (Trans.), Liveright, New York.

Stampfl, T. G., and Levis, D. J. (1967). Essentials of implosive therapy: A learning-theory-based psychodynamic behavioral therapy. J. Abnorm. Psychol. 72:496–503.

Thyer, B. A., Papsdorf, J. D., Davis, R., and Vallecorsa, S. (1984). Autonomic correlates of the subjective anxiety scale. J. Behav. Ther. Exp. Psychiatr. 15:3–7.

Wolpe, J. (1954). Reciprocal inhibition as the main basis of psychotherapeutic effects. Arch. Neurol. Psychiatr. 72:205–226.

Wolpe, J. (1958). Psychotherapy by Reciprocal Inhibition, Stanford University Press, Stanford, Calif.

Wolpe, J. (1982). The Practice of Behavior Therapy, Pergamon Press, New York.

24. Levels of Functional Impairment Following a Civilian Disaster

The Beverly Hills Supper Club Fire

Bonnie L. Green, Mary C. Grace, Jacob D. Lindy, James L. Titchener, and Joanne G. Lindy

CIVILIAN DISASTERS potentially constitute a noteworthy mental health problem in the United States and elsewhere. Hewitt and Sheehan (Note 1) and Dworkin (Note 2) reported 836 natural disasters from 1947 to 1973 in which 100 or more people were killed or injured or in which at least $1 million worth of damage was incurred. Recently, man-made disasters seem on the increase; for example, airplane crashes, building collapses, and nuclear accidents. Such incidents are receiving the increased attention of mental health professionals as evidence indicates that disastrous events may have severe and lasting effects (e.g., Gleser, Green, & Winget, 1981; Leopold & Dillon, 1963; Titchener & Kapp, 1976).

In order to determine the extent to which such events require psychological attention (i.e., how many people are affected and how severely), one must examine a range of disastrous events that provide information about impairment. Although some authors have reviewed published studies and tried to draw conclusions about "effects of disaster" from the standpoint of type and severity of response (e.g., Chamberlin, 1980; Kinston & Rosser, 1974; Tierney & Baisden, 1979), with few exceptions, the data are compiled as if disasters were interchangeable, rather than distinct and possibly different types of events.

As shown by Green (1982), however, it is possible to classify disasters objectively along several dimensions that differentiate them from each other. Although conceptual schema offered to date are far from exhaustive, certain aspects have been noted that are helpful in placing events along a continuum with regard to severity. Some factors are suddenness and duration (Barton,

Reprinted by permission from *Journal of Consulting and Clinical Psychology*, 51 (4), 573–580. Copyright © by the American Psychological Association, 1983.

1969; Berren, Beigel, & Ghertner, 1980), threat to life, bereavement and prolongation of suffering (Berren et al., 1980; Gleser, Green, & Winget, 1981), and scope of the impact (Barton, 1969; Gleser et al., 1981; Tierney & Baisden, 1979). Green (1982) suggested an additional dimension identifying the centrality of the disaster to a geographic community. All of these dimensions have implications for the psychological impact of an event, and any event can be so classified.

In addition to the features of the disaster itself, there are methodological factors that affect *estimates* of impairment rates, such as sampling of subjects, level of data, how "cases" are identified, and time of follow-up (Green, 1982). Variability in these factors from one study to the next make it nearly impossible to draw conclusions about differential effects by type of disaster.

A partial solution to this problem would be for investigators to collect comparable types of data from one study to the next. This would eliminate one of the methodological sources of error, and direct comparisons would be possible. Additionally, findings need to be understood in the context of other aspects of methodology, particularly sampling. Investigators should also consider their findings in light of the "actual" disaster dimensions (Green, 1982) previously mentioned. If these steps are consistently taken, we will indeed develop better estimates of mental health needs following specific types of disaster.

The present study reports on a particular civilian, man-made disaster, the Beverly Hills Supper Club fire. The supper club burned to the ground in May of 1977 (Memorial Day weekend). Of the over 2,000 people there that night, 165 people died of burns or smoke inhalation and many others were injured. An extensive research project was conducted by the Fire Aftermath Center, set up in the Department of Psychiatry, University of Cincinnati Medical Center, and funded by the State of Ohio. The center had outreach, treatment, and research components. Data regarding the extent of impairment found in the 147 subjects who were interviewed 1 year after the fire will be set forth in this report, as well as 2-year data on 88 of these subjects. The discussion places the fire-survivor sample in the context of other samples, disaster and non-disaster, and explains how the fire might be best characterized with regard to the dimensions of disasters previously mentioned. In addition, two subsamples that differed with regard to the type and extent of stress suffered are examined.

METHOD

Subjects

Subjects were 89 women and 58 men recruited through an extensive outreach effort. These efforts included newspaper articles, television and radio interviews describing the clinical work of the Fire Aftermath Center, possible psychological consequences of disaster, and the research that was being conducted on long-term effects. The telephone number of the Center was given. Outreach began when the Center was funded (November, 1977) and continued through the first anniversary of the fire (May, 1978). Extensive coverage was given by the local media immediately preceding the first anniversary. Contacts were also made with leaders of groups that had attended the nightclub together the night of the fire, and with community agencies. Finally, an extensive telephone outreach was instituted to next-of-kin and other survivors whose names were taken from a Kentucky State Police list. The telephone contact team was made up of experienced clinicians who called to enlist people's help in studying long-term effects of disaster by coming to the Center for a research interview. Letters preceded the calls explaining their purpose, and a tear sheet was attached that people could return if they wished *not* to be called. In all, about 500 individuals were contacted. Numbers and characteristics of people coming via the various modes are detailed elsewhere (Lindy, Grace, & Green, 1981). The majority of initial assessments (80%) took place within 2 months of the first anniversary of the fire.

For outreach purposes, an attempt was made to define individuals who were likely to be at psychological risk following the event (Lindy et al., 1981). The broad groupings used, and, thus, subjects included in the study, were as follows: (a) endangered—nightclub patrons and employees, (b) families of victims or survivors, and (c) rescue workers. The two latter groups were not present at the club when the fire broke out.

Procedure

All subjects, however recruited, were asked to call the Fire Aftermath Center. This was seen as demonstrating some motivation for follow through with regard to the research interview and/or treatment. At that time, the intake secretary collected basic demographic data, referral source, status of the subject vis-à-vis the fire (e.g., patron), and whether the person was interested in treatment as well as the research interview. All subjects had the general research procedure explained to them at this time. Interviewers were then given these names and scheduled their own appointments. For treatment subjects, appointments were scheduled in collaboration with the therapist so that the research interview could be done first. Thirty subjects initiated treatment. Ten treatments met full criteria for completed psychotherapy for grief or trauma (Lindy, Green, Grace, & Titchener, Note 3). All subjects were recontacted for follow-up approximately 12 months after their initial interview.

Interviewers

The interviewers were two graduate psychiatric nursing students and two medical students, all women. These women received extensive training prior to the start of the project, particularly on administering and rating the Psychiatric Evaluation Form (described below).

Instruments

The present report focuses on levels of psychopathology found at 1 and 2 years after the fire. The measures that will be described are those dealing with level of functioning and degree of stress, to set the sample in the appropriate context. Other instruments were also administered and will be described in a later report (Green, Grace, & Gleser, Note 4) on factors that predict degree of long-term impairment (also see Green, 1981).

Intensity of stress. The quantification of the objective stressfulness of the fire experience was based on scales similar to those developed during an investigation of the Buffalo Creek flood (Gleser et al., 1981). The scales were devised a priori, and direct questions were asked to ensure that the information needed was obtained. A number of specific stresses were measured. The stress scales relevant to the present report were as follows: (a) Bereavement scores were based on the closeness of the relationship to people lost. If multiple people were lost, the closest relationship was scored. (b) Life threat scale measured amount of warning and whether a person was actually in contact with smoke or encountered obstacles in escaping. A scale of extent of physical injury was also used. These scales can be found in table 24.1.

Table 24.1. Stress Scales

Bereavement
0 = no one
1 = acquaintance
2 = co-worker
3 = friend
4 = very close friend
5 = member of household
Life Threat
1 = no pushing, shoving
2 = smoke present, but no pushing or shoving
3 = smoke, pushing/shoving
4 = pulled out by another
Injury
1 = no injury
2 = slight injury
3 = broken bones, smoke inhalation, etc.

Subjective stress. A 1 to 10 scale was used in which individuals were asked to rate their own perception of total stressfulness of their fire experience, considering any aspects they thought relevant.

Psychopathology. The Psychiatric Evaluation Form (PEF; Endicott & Spitzer, 1972; Spitzer, Endicott, Mesnikoff, & Cohen, 1968) was chosen as the primary outcome measure. The PEF consists of 19 six-point rating scales for such symptoms as anxiety, belligerence, depression, alcohol abuse, social isolation, disorganization, and so forth; several role impairment scales; and an Overall Severity scale. A rating "1" indicates no evidence of the symptom and "6" indicates "extreme" impairment. Scale descriptions are fairly explicit as to the criteria to be considered in making a rating. A structured interview insures that all areas will be covered so that the rater can make the appropriate judgments. Scale ratings can be summed up to yield scores that are more comprehensive.

The Symptom Checklist, Revised Version (SCL-90R, Derogatis, 1977) was used to measure symptoms reported by the subject. It consists of a series of 90 symptoms or behaviors (e.g., getting into frequent arguments, trouble falling asleep, feeling hopeless about the future, crying easily, etc.), which the subject rates as characteristic of himself or herself during the past week on a 5-point (0–4) scale. The present study specified the past month. Items are then combined into nine clusters. The first five clusters have been empirically validated (somatic complaints, obsessive-compulsive, interpersonal-sensitivity, depression, and anxiety) whereas the last four are more experimental (hostility, phobic anxiety, paranoid ideation, and psychoticism). Clusters on the SCL are highly intercorrelated but show some convergent validity with similarly named scales from the PEF (Gleser, Green, & Winget, 1978; Green, Gleser, Stone, & Seifert, 1975).

These measures were administered in the context of a 1½-hour initial interview covering the subject's description of his or her fire experience (from which the stress ratings were made), a life events inventory, questions about coping with fire stress, and social support networks. The follow-up interview was similar but somewhat shorter due to the deletion of the fire description.

Preliminary analyses of objective stress and outcome measures were conducted. These included cluster analyses on the individual PEF and SCL-90 scales and generalizability studies on the PEF and stress scales. These analyses are described in more detail elsewhere (Green, 1981). The generalizability coefficient takes into account not only the relative ordering of subjects, but mean differences among raters as well. Figures for the PEF cluster scores ranged from .52 to .90; the coefficient for the global Overall Severity rating was .77. The stress measures had the following coefficients: Bereavement, .94; Life Threat, .92; and Injury, .82. For purposes of the present report, the PEF scales were used separately with emphasis on the Overall Severity rating. For the SCL-90, the Global Severity Index (GSI) was used, as well as the Hostility subscale score.

RESULTS

Because of the small numbers of subjects in the family ($n = 23$) and rescue worker ($n = 7$) groups, they were combined for purposes of data analysis into a "Not at fire" group, even though the nature of their experiences was different and the latter group was actually on the scene. They were not, however, passive victims and came to the fire voluntarily to help others. Initially, data were also examined by sex.

Table 24.2 shows the demographic characteristics of the four subsamples. The average age of the group was close to 40 years, and 8.8% of the sample was black. On the average, subjects had completed some college. The overall educational level was 14.0. Only 8% of subjects had less than a high school diploma, while a third had completed at least a bachelor's degree. The majority of subjects in all groups (70% overall) were married at the time of the initial interview.

The majority of the sample at the fire had been seated in the Cabaret

Table 24.2. Demographic Information by Sex and Fire Status

Variable	At fire Males ($n = 48$)	Females ($n = 69$)	Not at fire Males ($n = 11$)	Females ($n = 19$)
Age				
M	39.22	36.32	39.18	41.26
SD	13.6	12.17	17.17	17.88
Race				
White	92	91	91	89
Black	8	9	9	11
Marital status				
Single	21	19	9	16
Married	69	71	82	58
Divorced	6	4	9	11
Widowed	4	6		16
Education				
M	14.94	13.59	13.27	13.63
SD	2.40	2.08	2.28	2.22
Fire status				
Patron	88	88		
Employee	12	12		
Family			73	79
Rescue worker			27	21
Referral source				
Self	8	6	18	32
Indirect	19	16	64	58
Telephone				
Outreach	73	78	18	10

NOTE. Except for Ms and SDs, values given are percentages, which may not add to 100 due to rounding.

Room, the largest room in the club. It had the most congestion, the most dangerous fire, and the highest level of toxic gases and smoke to inhale.

Eighty-eight percent of subjects at the fire were patrons of the club. The other 12% were employees working there that night. For the not at fire group, 77% were family members and 23% were rescue workers.

A discrepancy between the two status groups is evident when the method by which they reached the Fire Aftermath Center is examined. Only 7% of the at fire group was self-referred, whereas 27% of the not at fire group came by this means. The majority of family and rescue workers (60%) came to the Center by way of indirect referral (e.g., family, physician, community agencies). The majority of the at fire group (76%) was recruited by the telephone outreach team.

Levels of Stress and Psychopathology at 1 Year

Table 24.3 shows means and standard deviations for the various measures of stress and psychopathology at 1 year, by fire status. No mean differences by sex emerged on any of the global scales. Consequently, men and women were combined for statistical comparisons and analyses.

Examination of the stress measures shows that, by definition, the not at fire subjects received no scores on the Life Threat or Injury scales, but they had significantly higher bereavement scores than the at fire group. They also reported significantly higher levels of subjective stressfulness of the overall event approximately a year later.

The psychopathology of the not at fire group was higher as well. These differences reached significance on both of the global ratings, and on the Hostility subscale of the SCL-90.

As a slightly different way of viewing the data, percentages of subjects showing different levels of impairment on selected scales of the PEF have been included (see table 24.4). The figures show that Anxiety was the predominant symptom and that only 16% of the sample could be rated "none" on this variable. About one third of the subjects were rated none on Overall Severity and Depression. Twenty percent of the total sample was rated moderately to severely impaired on Overall Severity.

Table 24.3. Levels of Stress and Psychopathology at 1 Year by Fire Status

Variable	At fire (n = 117)		Not at fire (n = 30)	
	M	SD	M	SD
Stress				
Bereavement	1.39	1.69	2.97	1.61*
Life threat	2.20	.84		
Injury	1.36	.66		
Subjective	6.30	5.20	8.40	2.50*
Psychopathology				
PEF overall severity	2.09	1.17	3.07	1.31*
SCL-90—GSI	.70	.65	.98	.73*
SCL-90—hostility	3.43	4.40	6.06	5.60*

NOTE. PEF = Psychiatric Evaluation Form; SCL-90 = Symptom Checklist-90; GSI = Global Severity Index.
    * t tests indicate differences significant at $p < .05$.

Table 24.4. Percentage of Subjects Receiving Different Ratings on the Psychiatric Evaluation Form Individual Scales of Overall Severity, Anxiety, and Depression at 1-Year Postfire

	At fire	Not at fire	Total
Overall severity			
1. None	41	15	36
2. Minimal	28	24	27
3. Mild	18	22	18
4. Moderate	9	27	14
5. Severe	3	12	5
6. Extreme	1	—	1
Anxiety			
1. None	20	9	16
2. Minimal	29	19	27
3. Mild	19	37	23
4. Moderate	21	22	22
5. Severe	11	13	12
6. Extreme	0	—	—
Depression			
1. None	32	13	28
2. Minimal	31	21	28
3. Mild	15	15	16
4. Moderate	16	22	18
5. Severe	4	29	9
6. Extreme	2	—	1

NOTE. Percentages may not add to 100 due to rounding.

Dropouts from the Research Study

Of the original 147 subjects who were interviewed approximately 1 year after the fire, 88 returned for follow-up (2 years postfire). The dropouts included 30% of the not at fire subjects and 43% of subjects at the fire. Although a few of these individuals could not be located and had probably moved out of town, the vast majority of dropouts were those who did not want to be reinterviewed. Demographically, the dropouts and remainers were similar. The dropout group tended to be slightly more impaired at 1 year on the psychopathology measures; however, the differences reached significance only for the global SCL-90 score for subjects at the fire. Dropouts had a mean GSI of .81, whereas the remainder GSI was .54.

Changes in Psychopathology from First to Second Year

Table 24.5 shows means and standards deviations on the various psychopathology measures at the initial and the follow-up (2 year) interview for the 67 at fire subjects and the 21 not at fire subjects who had both interviews. Correlated t tests were done for each measure for each group.

For Overall Severity on the PEF, the not at fire group decreased significantly between 1 and 2 years. Their decrease on the Hostility Subscale of the SCL-90 reached significance as well, while the global SCL-90 score nearly did ($p<.06$). For the at fire group, the only change was a significant *increase* in the Hostility subscale.

Percentages of subjects receiving the various scale point ratings on Overall Severity, Anxiety, and Depression on the PEF showed that, 2 years postfire, about one half of the subjects received a rating of "none" on Overall Severity, as compared to 35% at 1 year. The proportion of subjects receiving ratings of "none" on the other two scales increased as well. The proportion of moderate to extreme ratings decreased to 10% for Overall Severity, and to 22% and 11% for Anxiety and Depression, respectively.

Table 24.5. Means and Standard Deviations at Initial and Final Follow-Up for Reinterviewed Subjects by Status Group

Outcome	At fire (n = 67)		Not at fire (n = 21)	
	Initial	Follow-up	Initial	Follow-up
PEF Overall severity				
M	1.91	1.72	3.00	2.19**
SD	1.08	.97	1.34	1.29
Symptom Checklist-90 GSI				
M	.54	.56	.80	.64*
SD	.47	.50	.66	.07
Hostility				
M	3.40	4.20**	6.10	4.10**
SD	.46	.52	1.30	1.10

NOTE. PEF = Psychiatric Evaluation Form; GSI = Global Severity Index.
*$p < .06$ **$p < .05$.

DISCUSSION

The goal of the present report was to present psychological findings based on an in-depth assessment of a sample of disaster survivors and to place those findings in three contexts: the level of impairment found as it compared to other samples of disaster and nondisaster survivors, the nature of this particular disaster, and the methodological framework within which the study was done.

The first point to note is how the sample compared with others. In the present study the measures used to assess psychological functioning were specifically chosen to allow a comparison of findings with other studies in clinical and nonclinical settings. This was possible with both the PEF and the SCL-90. Using the Overall Severity rating on the PEF, the subjects at the fire had similar scores to a nonpatient sample. The nonpatient sample used for comparison consisted of 87 friends and relatives of psychotherapists in the New York area and was part of the validation studies done on the PEF (Endicott & Spitzer, 1972). Subjects not at the fire resembled a noncrisis outpatient sample. This outpatient sample of 325 was drawn from private and clinic outpatients in the New York City area (Endicott & Spitzer, 1972).

Data were also available on the PEF from a study done locally in a crisis clinic that conducts brief focal psychotherapy (Green et al., 1975). Ratings for the at fire group were significantly lower ($M = 2.09$) than those of the crisis group ($M = 3.76$) at the beginning of treatment $t(165) = 9.6$, $p<.001$. The not at fire group ($M = 3.02$) was also significantly lower, $t(78) = 3.2$, $p<.01$, but the difference was not as great.

The only disaster study with which to compare the PEF results was one examining the Buffalo Creek flood (Gleser et al., 1981). For purposes of comparison, the 2-year scores from the present study were used, since the results reported on the Buffalo Creek survivors were obtained at 2 years. Combined Overall Severity scores for the at fire and not at fire samples ($M = 1.8$) indicated much less impairment for the present subjects than for the flood sample ($M = 3.4$).

The SCL-90 also located the total fire sample somewhere between outpatients and normals. The two Beverly Hills samples were significantly less impaired than a validation sample of psychiatric outpatients; however both samples were significantly more impaired than a validation sample of 974 normals on the Global Severity Index of the measure (Derogatis, 1977).

Scores on the SCL-90 were also compared to two samples of subjects seen at Three Mile Island (TMI) after the nuclear accident there (Bromet, Note 5).

That study examined mothers of preschool children and workers at the TMI plant as well as psychiatric patients at 9 months and 1 year after the accident. Subjects in the present sample showed somewhat higher scores than the mother and worker groups at one year.

With regard to changes between the first and second year, a decrease in levels of pathology occurred only for subjects not at the fire. These decreases brought them to a level more similar to that for the at fire subjects. Thus, at 2 years they resembled normals on the PEF and were between normals and outpatients on the SCL-90. No decreases were noted for the at fire group. With the PEF, this was at least in part due to the fact that the scores were so low to begin with. On the SCL-90, however, there was potentially some room for change. On the Hostility subscale, a significant *increase* in distress was noted. There is no obvious explanation for this finding. It certainly raises the possibility that certain psychological effects of a traumatic experience may persist or increase over time. Decreases in the not at fire group may also have been partially due to the higher proportion of treatment subjects in this group (57% as opposed to 11%).

Methodologically, several issues are relevant to the present study. It has been suggested that in-depth clinical interviews are more likely to turn up psychopathology than are checklists of symptoms (Dohrenwend, 1975). That does not seem to be the case in the present study. Whether measured by the PEF (the clinical interview) or the SCL-90 (a checklist of symptoms), the sample could be similarly characterized—as falling somewhere between normals and outpatients. These measures were moderately correlated ($r = .66$). If this similarity in classification holds up in other studies, it will be encouraging since studies using different types of instruments may be somewhat comparable.

The timing of the study definitely puts it in the category of long-term effects. Whether the anniversary of the fire caused some exacerbation of symptoms is impossible to tell. Measuring functioning at two points in time allowed some examination of the "natural course" of the symptoms. The findings of decreased psychopathology at 2 years for the not at fire group did parallel those from another study that measured effects over time (Gleser et al., 1981).

Sampling issues were also highlighted in the present study. As pointed out by Green (1982) there are two major aspects of sampling that determine how impaired a sample of disaster victims will look; how the sample is obtained and the definition of the affected population. If the sample is from a particular subpopulation it may not be representative of the population as a whole. For example, some studies have focused on a hospitalized sample or on people who have lost their homes. Yet these variables have been shown to affect degree of impairment found (e.g., Bennett, 1970; Gleser et al., 1981; Melick, 1978). The differences in psychopathology between the at fire and not at fire groups highlights this point. The subsample not at the fire was exclusively bereaved family members or rescue workers, that is, a highly stressed group. The at fire group was less bereaved. They had an average loss of a relationship between an acquaintance and a coworker. Those not at the fire showed an average loss at the level of a friend. Of that group, 68% lost a close friend, relative, or loved one. The total sample consisted of volunteers for a research project and people interested in treatment. It is not clear whether volunteers are likely to be more or less impaired.

Conceptually, differences might also be expected depending on how the population is defined. In the present study, the population was not obvious since the disaster did not happen to a particular community. The patrons and employees of the nightclub were clearly part of the population. Additionally some relatives were highly traumatized by their visits to the temporary morgue to identify bodies, as were rescue workers who handled the dead. For both clinical and research purposes, the population of interest was defined as including all of these groups.

The nature of the disaster itself is of particular interest if we are to define our understanding of psychological effects of such events. Although the Beverly Hills fire had a large number of deaths, relative to most disasters, there were several other aspects that might limit psychological casualties. Although the onset was sudden, with little or no warning, the duration of the impact was short, the potential for recurrence was low, and physical suffering was usually not prolonged. In addition, the disaster did not devastate the geographic community of the survivors (it was a peripheral disaster). Thus, survivors were able to return to intact communities and relatively intact support systems and they were not displaced. As noted previously, survivors of the Buffalo Creek flood had much higher impairment rates. Congruent with these rates, their entire community was devastated, many people were displaced, and suffering was prolonged.

In summary, the factors that contribute to how impaired a sample of disaster survivors is found to be are complex, and obtained impairment rates are determined by methodological factors as well as actual differences in the nature of a particular disaster. However, it is possible to specify many of these factors to help place the findings in a context. The impact of some of the factors is best understood by comparing one disaster to another (e.g., differences between central and peripheral disasters), using similar instruments and sampling procedures. Other factors, representing individual differences in experience, like degree of bereavement suffered, degree of life threat, and role of the survivor, vary within a disaster and probably are most easily examined within that context. The present report was an attempt to present findings from a particular study in a way that highlighted the various factors involved in making comparisons from different disasters. It is hoped that the report will both provide information about a particular type of disaster and encourage other investigators to attend more closely to the issues involved in making generalizations.

NOTES

1. Hewitt, K., & Sheehan, L. *A pilot survey of global natural disasters of the past twenty years* (Natural Hazards Research, Working Paper 11). University of Toronto, 1969.

2. Dworkin, J. *Global trends in natural disasters* 1947–1973 (Natural Hazards Research, Working Paper 26). University of Toronto, 1973.

3. Lindy, J. D., Green, B. L., Grace, M. C., & Titchener, J. L. *Psychotherapy with survivors of the Beverly Hills Supper Club fire*. Manuscript submitted for publication, 1983.

4. Green, B. L., Grace, M. C., & Gleser, G. C. *Prediction of psychological risk following a disaster: A model using the Beverly Hills Supper Club fire*. Manuscript submitted for publication, 1983.

5. Bromet, E. *Three Mile Island: Mental Health Findings*. University of Pittsburgh, Western Psychiatric Institute, Pittsburgh, 1980.

REFERENCES

Barton, A. H. Communities in disaster: A Sociological Analysis of Collective Stress Situations. *New York: Doubleday, 1969.*

Bennett, G. *Bristol Floods 1968. Controlled survey of effects on health of local community disaster.* British Medical Journal, *1970, 3, 454–458.*

Berren, M. R., Beigel, A., & Ghertner, S. *A topology for the classification of disasters. Community Mental Health Journal, 1980, 16, 103–111.*

Chamberlin, B. C. *Mayo seminars in psychiatry: The psychological aftermath of disaster.* Journal of Clinical Psychiatry, *1980, 41, 238–244.*

Derogatis, L. R. SCL-90 R Version manual—I. *Baltimore, Md.: Johns Hopkins University, 1977.*

Dohrenwend, B. P. *Sociocultural and social-psychological factors in the genesis of mental disorders.* Journal of Health and Social Behavior, *1975, 16, 365–392.*

Endicott, J., & Spitzer, R. L. What! Another rating scale? The Psychiatric Evaluation Form. Journal of Nervous and Mental Disease, 1972, 154, 88–104.

Gleser, G. C., Green, B. L., & Winget, C. N. Quantifying interview data on psychic impairment of disaster survivors. Journal of Nervous and Mental Disease, 1978, 166, 209–216.

Gleser, G. C., Green, B. L., & Winget, C. N. Buffalo Creek revisited: Prolonged psychosocial effects of disaster. New York: Academic Press, 1981.

Green, B. L. Prediction of long-term psychosocial functioning following the Beverly Hills fire. (Doctoral dissertation, University of Cincinnati, 1980). Dissertation Abstracts International, 1981, 41, 3919B. (University Microfilms No. 8107489).

Green, B. L. Assessing levels of psychological impairment following disaster: Consideration of actual and methodological dimensions. Journal of Nervous and Mental Disease, 1982.

Green, B. L., Gleser, G. C., Stone, W. N., & Seifert, R. F. Relationships among diverse measures of psychotherapy outcome. Journal of Consulting and Clinical Psychology, 1975, 43, 689–699.

Kinston, W., & Rosser, R. Disaster: Effects on mental and physical state. Journal of Psychosomatic Research, 1974, 18, 437–456.

Leopold, R. D., & Dillon, H. Psycho-anatomy of a disaster: A long-term study of post-traumatic neuroses in survivors of a marine explosion. American Journal of Psychiatry, 1963, 119, 913–921.

Lindy, J. D., Grace, M. C., & Green, B. L. Survivors: Outreach to a reluctant population. American Journal of Orthopsychiatry, 1981, 51, 468–478.

Melick, M. E. Life change and illness: Illness behavior of males in the recovery period of a natural disaster. Journal of Health and Social Behavior, 1978, 19, 335–342.

Spitzer, R. L., Endicott, J., Mesnikoff, A. M., & Cohen, M. S. The Psychiatric Evaluation Form. New York: Biometrics Research, 1968.

Tierney, K. J., & Baisden, B. Crisis intervention programs: A source book and manual for smaller communities (U.S.D.H.E.W., Publication No. ADM 79–675). Washington, D.C.: U.S. Government Printing Office, 1979.

Titchener, J. L., & Kapp, F. T. Family and character change at Buffalo Creek. American Journal of Psychiatry, 1976, 133, 295–299.

25. Pharmacotherapy for Posttraumatic Stress Disorder

Matthew J. Friedman

O F APPROXIMATELY 1,000 articles cited in the 1986 edition of Arnold's bibliography on combat-related posttraumatic stress disorder (PTSD) (1), less than 20 address pharmacotherapy for PTSD. Instead, most of the current literature has focused on the history, epidemiology, symptomatology, diagnosis, and nonpharmacological psychotherapeutic treatment of PTSD. There may be three reasons for this apparent lack of interest in pharmacotherapy for PTSD. First of all, PTSD appears to be the quintessential psychological disorder in which exposure to a stimulus (catastrophic stress) is followed by a conditioned emotional response and negatively reinforced avoidance behavior. Probably no other disorder in *DSM-III* can be conceptualized by classic learning theory (i.e., two-factor theory [2]) as well as PTSD can. Second, there has been strong resistance in some psychiatric circles to acknowledging the validity of PTSD as a diagnostic entity. In fact, pockets of such resistance even exist at some facilities within the Veterans Administration, despite the large number of psychiatric patients with combat-related PTSD. Third, there has been little time since the publication of *DSM-III* for systematic evaluation of either the biological correlates or the clinical psychopharmacology of PTSD.

Among clinicians who do accept the validity of this diagnosis, PTSD has rekindled old therapeutic controversies. Questions about the efficacy of amobarbital-induced narcosynthesis have received new interest after decades of neglect in the published literature (3). There are proponents of long-term hospitalization who argue that effective treatment for severe PTSD requires at least 3 months of intensive inpatient psychotherapy and that standard 2–3-week hospitalizations can achieve little more than symptom reduction or crisis intervention (4). Another controversy concerns the proper role of pharmacotherapy in the treatment of PTSD.

Reprinted by permission from *American Journal of Psychiatry*, 144, 281–285. Copyright © by the American Psychiatric Association, 1988.

Many proponents of intensive psychotherapy for PTSD complain that medication is counterproductive. While conceding that relief of some PTSD symptoms can be achieved through pharmacotherapy, they argue that not only does such superficial improvement fail to affect the core disease but also such symptomatic improvement may so distract patients from the major therapeutic agenda that they terminate treatment prematurely. This is an old controversy—as old as the introduction of the first psychotropic agents into psychiatric practice—and it fails to acknowledge research showing that psychotherapy and pharmacotherapy are usually complementary treatments (5). On the other hand, there is sufficient evidence to support the idea that drugs may be an inadequate treatment for this disorder (6).

This review should be considered an interim report on rational pharmacotherapy for PTSD. Rational pharmacotherapy is possible either when the pharmacological action of an effective drug will reverse the biological alterations associated with a specific disorder or when double-blind trials have demonstrated the efficacy of a given drug for a given disorder. With regard to biological correlates of PTSD, a few studies have appeared which suggest that people who meet the *DSM-III* criteria for PTSD may also have a unique pathophysiological profile which is distinct from that of panic disorder or affective illness. With regard to the clinical psychopharmacology of PTSD, to my knowledge no double-blind trials have been published to date (although a number are currently in progress), but there is a small body of open trials and case reports that can be reviewed at this time.

BIOLOGICAL CORRELATES OF PTSD

It is reasonable to suggest that any disorder which can persist for decades (7) is associated with measurable biological alterations, but there is little research on this question. The few biological investigations of PTSD that have been conducted can be categorized as studies of alterations in sympathetic arousal, the neuroendocrine system, and the sleep/dream cycle.

Psychophysiological research has indicated that patients with PTSD exhibit higher levels of sympathetic nervous system activity and reactivity. Earlier findings in uncontrolled studies by Dobbs and Wilson (8) on EEG alpha rhythm, heart rate, and respiration rate and by Gillespie (9) on muscle tension were confirmed and extended by Blanchard et al. (10), who compared male Vietnam veterans with PTSD to age and sex-matched nonveteran control subjects. The PTSD patients showed higher baseline heart rates, systolic blood pressure, and forehead electromyogram (EMG) responses. More importantly, these PTSD patients exhibited significantly greater physiological responses to an audiotape of combat sounds played at gradually increasing volume levels. The heart rate, systolic blood pressure, and EMG responses of PTSD patients were so much greater than those of control subjects that blind raters correctly classified them 95.5% of the time. Similar results have been obtained in other laboratories (11, 12).

Mason et al. (13, 14) showed that PTSD patients had a significantly higher urinary norepinephrine/cortisol ratio than patients with bipolar disorder, major depressive disorder, paranoid schizophrenia, and undifferentiated schizophrenia. The authors suggested that higher urinary norepinephrine levels are consistent with psychophysiological findings which show increased sympathetic nervous system activity and reactivity (10–12). Lower urinary cortisol levels are consistent with earlier findings which suggested that denial and psychological defenses can exert a strong suppressive effect on urinary corticosteroid levels (15–21).

Research on sleep and dreaming also suggests that there may be a unique biological pattern associated with PTSD. Veterans with combat-related PTSD exhibit sleep abnormalities such as increased REM latency, less REM sleep, diminished stage 4 sleep, and reduced sleep efficiency (22–25). Kramer believes that PTSD is essentially an arousal disorder. He and Kinney showed that patients with PTSD are much more physiologically reactive than control subjects to nonspecific auditory stimuli during sleep (26). In addition to an abnormal sleep pattern, disturbed dreaming is a prominent abnormality in chronic PTSD (27, 28). Friedman (29) noted that traumatic nightmares associated with PTSD do not fit into either of Kramer's nightmare categories (27): they do not meet criteria for REM-related dream anxiety attacks nor are they typical of a stage 4 night terror/nightmare syndrome. Furthermore, van der Kolk and associates (28) showed that traumatic nightmares may arise out of various stages of sleep and are not confined to REM sleep alone.

To summarize, all biological research to date is consistent with the hypothesis that chronic PTSD is a hyperarousal state associated with excessive sympathetic nervous activity. Van der Kolk et al. (30), extrapolating from the animal model of inescapable shock, hypothesized that the hyperarousal, traumatic nightmares, and flashbacks that characterize PTSD are related to long-term potentiation of locus ceruleus pathways to the hippocampus and amygdala. They also suggested that such hyperreactivity is further enhanced by fluctuations in endogenous opioid levels in response to reexposure to traumatic situations.

Kindling is another neurobiological model with potential applicability to

PTSD. Post and Kopanda (31) suggested that endogenous catecholamines might kindle limbic nuclei in the same way as cocaine, thereby producing endogenous schizophrenic or manic-depressive psychosis. Similarly, the chronic sympathetic hyperarousal observed in PTSD patients might also kindle limbic nuclei, thereby producing a relatively stable neurobiological alteration. Such a hypothesis would explain why untreated PTSD can persist for decades (7). It suggests that carbamazepine might be an effective treatment for PTSD. It also suggests that benzodiazepines and other γ-aminobutyric acid agonists or synergists should be particularly efficacious for treatment of PTSD, since benzodiazepine receptor binding is increased substantially during the development of limbic kindling (32–34).

CLINICAL PSYCHOPHARMACOLOGY

The current literature on the pharmacotherapy of PTSD consists entirely of reports of open trials and case reports. A number of double-blind trials are in progress, but none have been reported. It seems that any pharmacological agent which can dampen the hyperarousal associated with PTSD should have a palliative if not curative role in treatment. Therefore, it is not surprising that the drugs which have been reported to be effective are clonidine, tricyclic antidepressants, monoamine oxidase inhibitors (MAOIs), propranolol, lithium, and benzodiazepines (29, 35–37). Kolb et al. (38) conducted successful trials of clonidine and propranolol in patients with chronic combat-related PTSD. Lithium (37, 39) has also been found effective in treating chronic PTSD.

There are several reports on the efficacy of the MAOI phenelzine (40–43). MOAIs are attractive agents to consider because they are antipanic agents, antidepressants, and powerful inhibitors of REM sleep. Phenelzine may not be the best alternative for combat veterans with PTSD because of the high rate of alcoholism and chemical abuse/dependency observed in this population (44). Therefore, it may have wider applicability for survivors of sexual trauma or natural disasters, for whom rates of alcoholism are probably much lower.

Tricyclic antidepressants have been used the most in treating PTSD. Although no reports of controlled trials have been published, several reports attest to the effectiveness of these agents (29, 45–47). Tricyclics (especially imipramine) dampen hyperarousal through their antipanic action, reduce intrusive recollections, suppress flashbacks, and reduce traumatic nightmares. In addition, the antidepressant action of tricyclics is of great value, since so many patients with chronic PTSD also meet the *DSM-III* criteria for major depression. The tricyclics are less risky than MAOIs to prescribe for patients with alcohol or substance abuse/dependency problems. Finally, since tricyclics enhance endogenous opioids through potentiation of synergistic serotoninergic mechanisms (48), their effectiveness in PTSD may also be attributed to their modulation of the sharp fluctuations in endogenous opioids postulated by van der Kolk and associates (30) in their inescapable-shock model of PTSD.

Benzodiazepines are effective (37) and may have unique applicability if kindling has a role in the pathophysiology of PTSD. Obviously, they should be prescribed with caution for patients with alcoholism, chemical dependency, or a previous history of drug addiction (29). Currently, there is considerable interest in the unique triazolobenzodiazepine alprazolam because of its demonstrated antipanic and antidepressant properties (49, 50). However, there is growing concern about addiction and withdrawal problems with this drug (51, 52).

Antipsychotic agents have no place in the routine treatment of PTSD. Even paranoid-type symptoms and the unique hallucinatory experiences known as flashbacks are usually treated effectively by reducing the level of arousal with tricyclic antidepressants or other agents that I have mentioned. Neuroleptics are, of course, the drugs of choice for frank psychosis, but it is quite unusual in chronic PTSD. Indications for prescribing neuroleptics for patients with PTSD include aggressive psychotic symptoms (frequently paranoid), overwhelming anger, self-destructive behavior, and frequent flashback episodes characterized by visual and auditory hallucinations of traumatic events (29, 36).

It is important to note that pharmacotherapy alone is rarely sufficient to provide complete remission of PTSD. Symptom relief provided by medication enables the patient to participate more thoroughly in individual, behavioral, or group psychotherapy.

DIAGNOSTIC CONSIDERATIONS

Most drugs that are effective for PTSD are also useful both in major depression and in panic disorder. This is true not only for tricyclics and MAOIs but also for alprazolam. In addition, major depression and panic disorder share many of the same symptoms as PTSD. Therefore, it is useful to review current knowledge about the biology and clinical psychopharmacology of each of these disorders in order to clarify their distinguishing features as well as their similarities.

In addition to their responsivity to tricyclics, MAOIs, and lithium, patients with PTSD and those with major depression have many symptoms in common, such as dysphoria, guilt, grief, anhedonia, irritability, social withdrawal, and insomnia. Such similarities, however, should not obscure some of the fundamental differences between these two disorders. Major depression and PTSD differ on a number of sleep characteristics. 1) There is diminished REM sleep in PTSD and excessive REM sleep in major depression. 2) REM

latency is increased in PTSD and diminished in major depression. 3) Dreams and nightmares appear in REM and non-REM sleep of patients with PTSD but only in REM sleep of those with major depression. There also appear to be endocrinological differences with regard to the corticosteroid system. Major depression is often associated with an abnormal dexamethasone suppression test (DST) result, indicating hyperactivity of the hypothalamic-pituitary-adrenocortical axis (53). Although no studies of the DST in PTSD have been published to my knowledge, PTSD appears to be a hypoadreno-cortical state, as indicated by lower urinary free cortisol levels (13,14). Sympathetic arousal and anxiety appear to be hallmarks of PTSD (10–12), whereas they are both less prominent and more variable in major depression. Finally, propranolol is an effective treatment for PTSD (38) but may exacerbate depressive symptoms in individuals with a diathesis for major depression (54).

There are also similarities between PTSD and panic disorder. Both disorders are associated with sympathetic hyperarousal and sudden surges of anxiety. Both respond to tricyclic antidepressants, MAIOs, and propranolol (38, 55). Both disorders are often associated with depressive symptoms. It has been postulated that locus ceruleus dysregulation plays a major role in panic disorder (56) as well as in PTSD (30). And, finally, it has been suggested that PTSD flashbacks meet the *DSM-III* criteria for panic attacks (57). There are important differences between the disorders, however. In panic disorder, attacks are spontaneous and primarily physiological in nature, whereas PTSD attacks are triggered by a meaningful stimulus and are primarily meaningful psychological events. Stage 4 sleep is reduced in PTSD but significantly increased in panic disorder (58). A familial tendency toward the spontaneous development of panic disorder has been demonstrated (59), whereas PTSD is never spontaneous and occurs only after exposure to catastrophic stress. Marijuana can precipitate panic attacks in patients with panic disorder (60, 61, and manuscript by S. M. Fishman et al.) but appears to have a calming effect on combat veterans with PTSD. Finally, we await a systematic evaluation of sodium lactate infusion in PTSD patients to see whether it can precipitate attacks, as it can in panic disorder (62).

To summarize, PTSD, major depression, and panic disorder all appear to have unique biological profiles despite a considerable overlap in symptoms and responsivity to tricyclics and MAOIs.

MESHING TREATMENT WITH SYMPTOMS

In *DSM-III-R* the diagnostic criteria for PTSD (pp. 247–248) have been modified in a way that is more consistent with the embryonic biological characterization of this disorder. The four criteria are 1) exposure to catastrophic stress, 2) reexperiencing the trauma spontaneously or after exposure to emotionally charged stimuli through intrusive recollections, nightmares, or flashbacks, 3) persistent avoidance of emotionally charged stimuli through numbing of responsiveness, avoidance of charged stimuli, or psychogenic amnesia, and 4) persistent hyperarousal as indicated by insomnia, irritability and rage, difficulty concentrating, hypervigilance, and increased startle response. It appears that target symptoms under the second and fourth criteria (intrusive recollections and sympathetic arousal, respectively) are most responsive to pharmacotherapy. Avoidant symptoms such as alienation, detachment, and psychic numbing rarely respond to medication unless depression is also present. This is reminiscent of the observation that neuroleptics attenuate the positive but not the negative symptoms of schizophrenia.

CONCLUSIONS

It is clear that there is no definitive pharmacological treatment for PTSD. Drug treatment alone is never sufficient to alleviate the suffering in PTSD. Pharmacotherapy is primarily useful as an adjunct to psychological (intrapsychic and/or behavioral) treatment of PTSD. Drug-mediated attenuation of intrusive or hyperarousal symptoms facilitates therapeutic work on guilt, grief, intimacy, rage, moral pain, and other issues.

It also appears that catastrophic exposure to trauma is followed by stable biological alterations in the sympathetic nervous system, neuroendocrine system, and sleep/dream cycle. Such alterations appear to be unique to PTSD and distinguish it both from major depression and from panic disorder despite similarities in symptomatology. It is hoped that better understanding of the biological correlates of PTSD will lead to a rational pharmacotherapy for this disorder.

REFERENCES

1. Arnold A: Selected Bibliography, II: Post-Traumatic Stress Disorder With Special Attention to Vietnam Veterans, XXV Revision. Phoenix, Ariz, VA Medical Center, 1986
2. Keane T M, Zimering R T, Caddell J M: A behavioral formulation of posttraumatic stress disorder in Vietnam veterans. Behavior Therapist 1985; 8:9–12
3. Kolb L C: The place of narcosynthesis in the treatment of chronic and delayed stress reactions of war, in The Trauma of War Stress and Recovery in Vietnam Veterans. Edited by Sonnenberg S M, Blank A S, Talbott J A. Washington, DC, American Psychiatric Press, 1985
4. Arnold A L: Inpatient treatment of Vietnam veterans with post-traumatic stress disorder. Ibid
5. Conte H R, Plutchik R, Wild K V, et al.: Combined psychotherapy and pharmacotherapy for depression. Arch Gen Psychiatry 1986; 43:471–479
6. Birkhimer L J, DeVane C L, Muniz C E: Posttraumatic stress disorder: characteristics and pharmacological response in the veteran population. Compr Psychiatry 1985; 26:304–310
7. Archibald H C, Tuddenham R D: Persistent stress reaction after combat: a 20-year follow-up. Arch Gen Psychiatry 1965; 12:475–481
8. Dobbs D, Wilson W P: Observations on persistence of war neurosis. Dis Nerv Syst 1961; 21:40–46
9. Gillespie R D: Psychological Effects of War on Citizen and Soldier. New York, W W Norton, 1942
10. Blanchard E B, Kolb L C, Pallmeyer T P, et al.: A psychophysiological study of post traumatic stress disorder in Vietnam veterans. Psychiatr Q 1982; 54:220–229
11. Malloy P F, Fairbank J A, Keane T M: Validation of a multimethod assessment of posttraumatic stress disorders in Vietnam veterans. J Consult Clin Psychol 1983; 51:488–494
12. Brende J O: Electrodermal responses in post-traumatic syndromes. J Nerv Ment Dis 1982; 170:352–361
13. Mason J W, Giller E L, Kosten T R, et al.: Urinary free-cortisol in posttraumatic stress disorder. J Nerv Ment Dis 1986; 174:145–149
14. Mason J, Giller E L, Kosten T R, et al.: Elevated urinary norepinephrine/cortisol ratio in posttraumatic stress disorder, in New Research Program and Abstracts, 138th Annual Meeting of the American Psychiatric Association. Washington, DC, APA, 1985
15. Friedman S B, Mason J W, Hamburg D A: Urinary 17-hydroxycorticosteroid levels in parents of children with neoplastic disease. Psychosom Med 1963, 25:364–376

16. Wolff C T, Friedman S B, Hofer M A, et al.: Relationship between psychological defenses and mean urinary 17-OHCS excretion rates, I: a predictive study of parents of fatally ill children. Psychosom Med 1964; 26:576–592

17. Wolff C T, Hofer M A, Mason J W: Relationship between psychological defenses and mean urinary 17-OHCS excretion rates, II: methodological and theoretical considerations. Psychosom Med 1964; 26:592–609

18. Mason J W: Clinical psychophysiology: psychoendocrine mechanisms, in American Handbook of Psychiatry, vol 4. Edited by Reiser M. New York, Basic Books, 1975

19. Katz J, Weiner H, Gallagher T E, et al.: Stress, distress and ego defenses: psychoendocrine responses to impending breast tumor biopsy. Arch Gen Psychiatry 1970; 23:131–142

20. Knight R B, Atkins A, Eagle C J, et al.: Psychological stress, ego defenses and cortisol production in children hospitalized for elective surgery. Psychosom Med 1979; 41:40–49

21. Poe R O, Rose R M, Mason J W: Multiple determinants of 17-hydroxy-corticosteroid excretion in recruits during basic training. Psychosom Med 1970; 32:369–378

22. Lavie P, Hefez A, Halperin G, et al.: Long-term effects of traumatic war-related events on sleep. Am J Psychiatry 1979; 136:175–178

23. Schlossberg A, Benjamin M: Sleep patterns in three acute combat fatigue cases. J Clin Psychiatry 1978; 39:546–549

24. Kramer M, Kinney L, Scharf M: Sleep in delayed stress victims. Sleep Research 1982; 11:113

25. Kramer M, Kinney L: Is sleep a marker of vulnerability to delayed posttraumatic stress disorder? Sleep Research 1985; 14:181

26. Kinney L, Kramer M: Sleep and sleep responsivity in disturbed dreamers. Sleep Research 1985; 14:140

27. Kramer M: Dream disturbance. Psychiatr Annals 1979; 9:50–60

28. van der Kolk B, Blitz R, Burr W, et al.: Nightmares and trauma: a comparison of nightmares after combat with lifelong nightmares in veterans. Am J Psychiatry 1984; 141:187–190

29. Friedman M J: Post-Vietnam syndrome:recognition and management. Psychosomatics 1981; 22:931–943

30. van der Kolk B, Greenberg M, Boyd H, et al.: Inescapable shock, neurotransmitters, and addiction to trauma: toward a psychobiology of posttraumatic stress. Biol Psychiatry 1985; 20:314–325

31. Post R M, Kopanda R T: Cocaine, kindling, and psychosis. Am J Psychiatry 1976; 133:627–634

32. McNamara J O, Bonhaus D W, Shin C, et al.: The kindling model of epilepsy: a critical review. CRC Critical Reviews in Clinical Neurobiology 1985; 1:341–391

33. Morita K, Okamoto M, Seki K, et al.: Suppression of amygdalakindled seizures in cats by enhanced GABAergic transmission in the substantia innominata. Exp Neurol 1985; 89:225–236

34. Tietz E I, Gomez F, Berman R F: Amygdala kindled seizure stage is related to altered benzodiazepine binding site density. Life Sci 1985; 36:183–190

35. Yost J: The psychopharmacologic treatment of the delayed stress syndrome in Vietnam veterans, in Post-Traumatic Stress Disorders of the Vietnam Veteran. Edited by Cincinnati William T. Disabled American Veterans, 1980
36. Walker J I: Chemotherapy of traumatic war stress. Milit Med 1982; 147:1029–1033
37. van der Kolk B A: Psychopharmacological issues in posttraumatic stress disorder. Hosp Community Psychiatry 1983; 34:683–691
38. Kolb L C, Burris B C, Griffiths S: Propranolol and clonidine in treatment of the chronic post-traumatic stress disorders of war, in Post-Traumatic Stress Disorder: Psychological and Biological Sequelae. Edited by van der Kolk B A. Washington, DC, American Psychiatric Press, 1984
39. Kitchner I, Greenstein R: Low dose lithium carbonate in the treatment of post traumatic stress disorder: brief communication. Milit Med 1985; 150:378–381
40. Hogben G L, Cornfield R B: Treatment of traumatic war neurosis with phenelzine. Arch Gen Psychiatry 1981; 38:440–445
41. Levenson H, Lanman R, Rankin M: Traumatic war neurosis and phenelzine (letter). Arch Gen Psychiatry 1982; 39:1345
42. Shen W W, Park S: The use of monoamine oxidase inhibitors in the treatment of traumatic war neurosis: case report. Milit Med 1983; 148:430–431
43. Milanes F J, Mack C N, Dennison J, et al.: Phenelzine treatment of post-Vietnam stress syndrome. VA Practitioner, June 1984, pp. 40–47
44. Branchey L, Davis W, Lieber C S: Alcoholism in Vietnam and Korea veterans: a long term follow-up. Alcoholism: Clinical and Experimental Research 1984; 8: 572–575
45. Burstein A: Treatment of post-traumatic stress disorder with imipramine. Psychosomatics 1982; 25:681–687
46. Falcon S, Ryan C, Chamberlain K, et al.: Tricyclics: possible treatment for posttraumatic stress disorder. J Clin Psychiatry 1985; 46:385–389
47. Blake D J: Treatment of acute posttraumatic stress disorder with tricyclic antidepressants. South Med J 1986; 79:201–204
48. Malseed R T, Goldstein F J: Enhancement of morphine analgesia by tricyclic antidepressants. Neuropharmacology 1979; 18:827–829
49. Sheehan D V: Current perspectives in the treatment of panic and phobic disorders. Drug Therapy 1982; 7:179–193
50. Feighner J P, Aden G C, Fabre L F, et al.: Comparison of alprazolam, imipramine and placebo in the treatment of depression. JAMA 1983; 249:3057–3064
51. Higgitt A C, Lader M H, Fonagy P: Clinical management of benzodiazepine dependence. Br Med J 1985; 291:688–690
52. Noyes R Jr, Clancy J, Coryell W H, et al.: A withdrawal syndrome after abrupt discontinuation of alprazolam. Am J Psychiatry 1985; 142:114–116
53. Carroll B J, Feinberg M, Greden J F, et al.: A specific laboratory test for the diagnosis of melancholia: standardization, validation, and clinical utility. Arch Gen Psychiatry 1981; 38:15–22
54. Griffin S G, Friedman M J: Depressive symptoms in propranolol users. J Clin Psychiatry 1986; 47:453–457
55. Ravaris C L, Friedman M J, Hauri P: Xanax and Inderal in panic and agorapho-

bic outpatients, in New Research Program and Abstracts, 139th Annual Meeting of the American Psychiatric Association. Washington, DC, APA, 1986

56. *Redmond D E Jr, Huang Y H: New evidence for a locus coeruleus-norepinephrine connection with anxiety. Life Sci 1979; 25:2149–2162*

57. *Mellman T A, Davis G C: Combat-related flashbacks in posttraumatic stress disorder: phenomenology and similarity to panic attacks. J Clin Psychiatry 1985; 46:379–382*

58. *Hauri P, Friedman M J, Ravaris C L: Sleep in agoraphobia with panic attacks. Sleep Research 1985; 14:128*

59. *Sheehan D V: Current concepts in psychiatry: panic attacks and phobias. N Engl J Med 1982; 307:156–158*

60. *Keeler MH: Adverse reaction to marijuana. Am J Psychiatry 1967; 124:674–677*

61. *Moran C: Depersonalization and agoraphobia associated with marijuana use. Br J Med Psychol 1986; 59:187–196*

62. *Pitts F N Jr, McClure J N Jr: Lactate metabolism in anxiety neurosis. N Engl J Med 1967; 277:1329–1336*

26. An Epidemiological Study of Psychic Trauma and Treatment Effectiveness for Children after a Natural Disaster

Rosemarie Galante and Dario Foa

O N NOVEMBER 23, 1980, a devastating earthquake struck the rugged rural mountain region of central Italy. The death toll in this sparsely populated area was surprisingly high. Over 4000 people lost their lives and tens of thousands lost their homes in the 116 villages damaged by the earthquake. Particularly affected by the tragedy were the children of these communities. They were affected not only by the earthquake but also by the unfortunate circumstances that surrounded the tragedy and augmented the number of fatalities and psychic trauma. The children's memories of those events were to dominate their lives long after the seismic shocks that had destroyed their world subsided.

Those charming mountain-top medieval villages with their narrow, steep, and winding streets became instant and horrendous death traps as the mortar and stone structures collapsed. The streets were immediately inundated with tons of rubble which blocked all escape routes. This nightmare "no-escape" situation was one of the themes that plagued the children. Another disturbing aspect was related to the rescue efforts.

Due to their isolation, the destruction of communication lines, and Italy's small emergency relief resources, there were at times delays of 2 and 3 days before help arrived. In the long wait the survivors made vain efforts to dig out the victims, who pleaded for rescue for days before dying. The children, who were witnesses to these pathetic scenes, later recalled with precision the time when each victim was last heard from. They later made constant references to those moments.

This additional loss of life, attributed by the earthquake victims to the failure of emergency assistance, provoked a bitterness and hostility that made

Reprinted by permission from the *Journal of the American Academy of Child Psychiatry*, 25 (3), 357–363. Copyright © by Williams & Wilkins, 1986.

the disaster relief even more difficult. The children were affected by their own reactions to these scenes as well as by the angry responses of their families and communities.

In an attempt to make up for this initial delay in response and to supplement the relief forces, there was a great deal of volunteering from public and private sectors. Each regional government took responsibility for a part of the disaster area. The region of Lombardy (which includes Milan) assisted the six villages at the epicenter. Disaster relief teams were formed consisting of health, sanitation, education, and mental health professionals. The University of Milan participated in this effort. We at the medical psychology department were given the task of working with the children.

It was deceptively easy sitting in an office at the University to project our part of the relief services. One of our team (D.F.) was to handle the problems with the local personnel in reopening the schools and the other (M.G.) was to work with the traumatized children of the six villages. Although eventually implemented, this plan almost did not survive the first impact with the chaotic reality of the situation. After a somber reassessment of the problems involved we realized that our prior experience was not an adequate preparation to enable us to respond to the needs of these children.

In the first days after the earthquake the children displayed a wide range of disturbed behaviors. They were apathetic, aggressive, and even at times assaultive. Behaviors were extreme and exaggerated. Their reactions were certainly understandable since they had been subjected to scenes of sudden and prolonged death, had lost their homes and all their belongings, and lived in the unrecognizable remnants of their community. Helping the children seemed an immense and impossible task. In spite of the urgency of the situation we decided it was imperative to research what others had done in working with disaster-related traumas in order to have an idea about what we might expect to accomplish.

In the event of a disaster, children have been identified as being among the more susceptible elements of the population to suffer from posttraumatic stress syndrome (PTSS) (Frederick, 1982). In a summary of the findings of different disasters, it was found that, in three-quarters of the children, symptoms were still evident 2 years after the traumatizing event. A review of the psychiatric literature that relates to the general phenomena of psychic trauma in children provides some understanding of why children are particularly vulnerable.

Bowlby (1973), in his well-known work on loss in children, states that any unwilling separation from the caretakers of a child gives rise to emotional distress, and personality disturbances. He also pointed out that children's problems are often overlooked while others in the family respond to a loss. The children's rebuffed feelings often fuel problems that emerge long after. Since the family's response is such an important (though obvious) factor, it is often cited in the literature.

Caplan (1964) also considered the family reaction to be a deciding factor in how well the members cope with and recover from their trauma. He predicted the onset of disorganized behaviors when normal defense mechanisms (individual or collective) fail to cope with a hazardous situation. Without normal support systems (as when all family members are subject to danger), recovery becomes more difficult.

The Buffalo Creek children, who suffered traumas after a devastating flood, showed no improvement with the passage of time (Newman, 1976). All children were found to be affected (including children born after the event). Newman found a correlation between the family's reaction, developmental level of the child, the amount of exposure to the trauma, and the degree of psychic trauma. Treatment was recommended to counteract the negative effects.

There are few studies that describe follow-up or treatment after a traumatic event. Most studies describe the crisis interventions that are made at the time. One of the few to deal with treatment after the events is that of Terr.

Terr (1981), in her work with psychic trauma of kidnap victims, speaks of the long-lasting effects of the trauma. She found that symptoms may not be observed by the parents for up to a year after the trauma. Among the symptoms were: fears of recurrence, fears of other trauma, repetitive relating of the trauma, and "playing" the trauma. She reported a reduction in symptoms in many cases after brief counseling.

Another study describes counseling in a traumatic situation with children involved in an earthquake. Howard and Gordon (1972) after the San Fernando earthquake found that counseling coupled with community outreach was important in making contact with the large numbers of children manifesting symptoms. Although brief counseling was effective in most cases, 1-year follow-ups showed that some children still had symptoms.

In summary, there seems to be agreement on a few basic points. Children can be expected to develop symptoms of stress and trauma after a disaster. These symptoms are more likely to occur when the family is also involved. These symptoms tend to be long-lasting and do not necessarily disappear with the passage of time. Children suffering loss may be particularly susceptible even though their problems may not emerge for years. Given that some children do not show outward signs of disturbance they tend to be overlooked by the adults around them after a loss. Brief counseling, though useful, is not completely effective in relieving long-lasting symptoms.

It seemed that our Italian children met every criteria for being susceptible to developing long-lasting psychic trauma. We therefore decided that we should broaden the length and the scope of our planned intervention in the area.

Our revised project for our six villages consisted of three phases:

Phase 1. Pretesting. Six months after the earthquake all the children were tested to discover the numbers and location of children at "risk." We were fortunate in finding a screening instrument that had been validated on an Italian population sample, the Rutter Children's Behavior Questionnaire for Completion by Teachers. A score of nine or more on the Rutter scale indicates that the child is at "risk" of developing neurotic or antisocial disturbances (Zimmerman-Tansella et al., 1978).

Phase 2. Treatment. The treatment program was implemented in the village with the highest number of children at "risk."

Phase 3. Posttesting. Eighteen months after the earthquake all children were retested (a year after pretesting).

Realizing that in such chaotic field conditions we could not hope to conduct a rigorous investigation we nevertheless attempted to answer a few basic questions that could enable us to fulfill our commitments in a meaningful manner.

We were interested in knowing if: (1) there would be a higher percentage of children at risk in the villages that had suffered the most destruction; (2) children who had suffered deaths in the family would have a higher number of at risk scores than those who did not; and (3) children who had been part of the treatment program would have a greater reduction in the number of at risk scores than those who had not.

PHASE 1

Method

Subjects

The questionnaire has been completed for all the first through fourth graders in the six villages studied (total 300).

Procedure

Six months after the earthquake the questionnaire was distributed to the elementary school teachers by research assistants (psychology interns). At the same time the children were asked to draw a house, a tree, and a person (by the research assistants).

A chi square (χ^2) analysis was performed on the at-risk scores in relationship to deaths in the family. A χ^2 analysis was also used to determine the appropriateness of the Rutter scale used on the earthquake children by comparing them with the Verona sample of the first through fourth graders (data from an unpublished manuscript, Zimmerman [1977]). The overall death, damage, and destruction in the individual communities and at risk scores were compared.

Results

A significant correlation between deaths in the family and at-risk scores occurred only in Calabritto and in the total scores (table 26.1).

Although there were great differences in the proportion of at-risk scores between the villages, these differences were not always related to the amount of damage, destruction, and death in that community (table 26.2).

An analysis of the totaled scores of Verona and the earthquake area revealed no significant differences in the two populations (χ^2, $p<0.10$). (All three phases of the project will be discussed together at the conclusion of this report.)

Table 26.1. Death and Risk Scores[a]

Village	6 Months after	18 Months after
Calabritto	0.001	NS
Caposele	NS	NS
Conza	NS	NS
Laviano	NS	NS
Pesco Pagano	NS	NS
Teora	NS	NS
Total	0.000	NS

*NS = not significant.

Table 26.2. Damage and At-Risk Scores

| | Total damages | | | Rutter scores 1–4 grades | |
| | | | | Assessed after 6 months | |
Village	Damaged homes (%)	Destroyed homes (%)	Deaths (%)	Total no.	Percent risk
Calabritto	95	80	8	62	47
Caposele	85	60	1	40	8
Conza	100	100	25	41	20
Laviano	100	100	37	35	43
Pesco Pagano	80	60	8	77	9
Teora	95	65	3	45	9

PHASE 2

Method

Subjects

Subjects included all of the first through fourth grade elementary school children of Calabritto (this village was selected for treatment because there were the largest number of children at risk).

Procedure

For 1 academic year at approximately monthly intervals one of the investigators (M.G.) conducted a week-long series of group sessions. Each group of four met for 1 hour, once, during each series of sessions. The first introductory session was held in the classroom; all others were held in a separate room. The treatment program was the same for all grades first to fourth) with adjustments made in language to keep the treatment age-appropriate. Notes were taken on each child, for each session, and a frequency count of all earthquake-related behaviors was taken and compared with other behaviors on a checklist.

Treatment Program

Session 1. Objective: To give permission to communicate openly, particularly about the earthquake. Activity: Drawing while listening to stories about San Francisco's recovery from earthquakes and its seismic proof constructions.

Session 2. Objective: To openly discuss fears and to demonstrate that being afraid was a common shared reaction. Activity: Children drawing while listening to a story about a child who is afraid but too timid to ask for help. This was followed by a discussion of their drawings and their feelings. (They told what they did when they were afraid.)

Session 3. Objective: To discuss myths and erroneous beliefs about earthquakes. Activity: Children drawing while listening to a story about a child being afraid of earthquakes recurring because he did not understand how they occurred. This was followed by the children's talking about their beliefs and a "lesson" on earthquakes.

Session 4. Objective: To involve the children in an active discharge of feelings about the earthquake and place the earthquake in the past. The activity consisted of making a large joint drawing of Calabritto and furnishing it with small toys (cars, dolls, and furniture). This inevitably simulated a spontaneous "acting out" of the earthquake. The focus was on what they did *after* the earthquake to resume a normal life.

Session 5. Objective: To release the power of the images of the deaths and focus on building the future. Activity: Role-playing (with a drawing of Calabritto that included the cemetery) and funeral rituals. The future of the "New Calabritto" was then planned.

Session 6. Objective: To develop the idea that one is not a "victim of the fates" but could take an active part in one's own survival. Activity: Role-playing being parents, teaching children to survive in various emergency situations, i.e., floods, earthquakes, and accidents.

Session 7. Objective: To give the children an opportunity to bring up whatever they chose to in "closing." The activity was a free drawing and discussion.

Analysis of Data

Clinical observations were made of each child for each session. From the notes taken a frequency count was made of all fears mentioned and of all earthquake-related issues (fig. 26.1).

Results

During the first session the children interacted with each other rather than with the investigator. They were either extremely aggressive (active fighting)

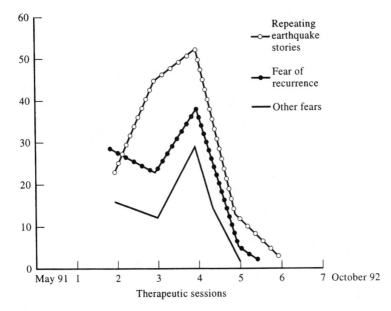

Figure 26.1. Comparison of frequency count of behaviors with participation in treatment.

or silent and apprehensive. In spite of their disruptive or distracted behavior they were attentive to the story.

The drawings were full of menacing features and the environment tended to be threatening. The children did not draw the earthquake or their destroyed village. Some of the children began to speak about the earthquake. A third-grade boy said, "My uncle called for help during the night. He talked until 3 in the morning, then he died. When he was dug out he was cut in half." This and other accounts were repeated in a hurried matter-of-fact tone of voice.

In Session 2 many of the children spoke about the earthquake. There was a repetitious, monotonous, well-rehearsed air to all these earthquake stories. Some spoke of omens. A second-grade boy said, "Ten days before the earthquake my uncle said that we would all die together. He died with my aunt and cousins." Others had anniversary fears. Many stated calmly, "On Nov. 23, there will be another one." There were also fears of all kinds of impending doom. A second-grader said, "Every night when I go to bed I think that the world will split in half at Calabritto and I will fall to the center. Will I get burned?" The children seemed to be trying to prepare and protect themselves against their fears of recurrence of a disaster.

Session 3 was characterized by a sharp increase in expression of fears and retelling of the earthquake stories. Comments ranged from open expressions of fears to complete denial: a 7-year-old girl said, "Sometimes I just suddenly start screaming." Another stated, "Sometimes I just start yelling 'Earthquake!' 'Earthquake!' " A third, reflecting denial, said, "It's no use to be afraid or cry. I never cry." There were strange comments that were interjected as their defenses began to break down: "Even the dogs cried after the earthquake. The end of the world is coming in 19 years." This statement was spoken in a hushed tone by a second-grade boy (whose dog had died in the earthquake). A third-grade girl seemed to reassure herself when she said, "The old should die. The young should live." Session four was the high point of repetition of earthquake stories and the relaying of all types of fears.

By Session 4 the children had moved into the prefabricated schools and homes. Instead of taking a step forward with the attainment of these eagerly awaited developments, they regressed to the earlier exaggerated ways of behaving. Consistent with those exaggerated emotions their attachment to the investigator became intense. Their drawings (which were done in addition to the group project) began to have symbolic references to their actual losses. A seemingly cheerful 8-year-old girl drew two figures and omitted the lower half of their bodies. Her mother had remained paralyzed from the waist down as the result of earthquake injuries. A typical comment on the playing of "earthquake" by an 8-year-old demonstrated how his attempts to limit the disaster were quickly overcome by his fears: "I don't want any wars. No one dies or gets hurt. Maybe I get hurt, but not in a war, in an accident. Killers arrive and kill everyone. We send for the police. Then there is a big earthquake and we take everyone to the cemetery. Then we have a big party and forget about it."

By Session 5, the children had developed a passionate and possessive attachment to the investigator. They were also strongly involved in the session. They seemed to want to put order in the untidy and capricious disaster by killing off everyone in the "earthquake" game. A fourth-grade girl comments, "First there is a volcanic eruption and that family all dies. The people are left sorry. Then there is an earthquake and everyone dies. Well, maybe three people lived. They went to another valley but they wished they died because they had no one left. So they killed themselves." This was accompanied by shaking of the table, a simulation of the rumble of the earthquake, and gleeful laughter. The children were delighted to fit the disaster into a more comprehensible scheme; everyone has the same fate. At this point the first open reference to their losses was made in their drawings. For instance, one 7-year-old drew a picture of his friends in a mausoleum.

Session 6 was much less intense than the preceding sessions. The children continued to participate in the role-playing but in a much more relaxed mood. There was almost no talk of fears in spite of the stimulating disaster scenes. The children planned the future with some skepticism but the doubts were related to realistic issues rather than apocalyptic fears.

Session 7 was the closure session. The children drew and chatted about everyday issues. There was no mention of earthquake-related themes.

The frequency count on the behavioral checklist showed a dramatic drop in all earthquake-related fears and other fears after the role-playing of the earthquake.

PHASE 3

Method

Subjects

The first-through fourth-grade elementary school children who were present at the pretest.

Procedure

Eighteen months after the earthquake (1 year after the pretesting) the questionnaire was redistributed to the same teachers by different research assistants (psychology interns).

Analysis of Data

A χ^2 analysis was performed on the correlations between pre-and posttest scores in the different villages and of the correlation between the posttest score and the deaths in the family.

Results

There was a significant difference in the pre-and posttest test scores in three villages. In Calabritto and Teora there was a decrease in at-risk scores. In

Table 26.3. Correlation Between At-Risk Scores Before and After Interventions (1–4th Grades)[a]

Village	6 Months after		18 months after		*p*	Risk
	Total no.	Percent at risk	Total no.	Percent at risk		
Calabrito	62	47	62	34	0.01	−
Caposele	40	8	40	20	0.05	+
Conza	41	20	41	20	0.01	
Laviano	35	43	35	43	NS	
Pesco Pagano	77	9	77	24	NS	
Teora	45	9	45	7	0.01	−

*NS = not significant.

Caposele there was an increase (table 26.3). In the posttest scores there was no significant correlation between deaths and at-risk scores.

DISCUSSION

Our hypothesis that there would be a greater reduction of at-risk scores in the children who had been in the treatment program was confirmed. Not only the at-risk scores but also the "frequency of expressed fears" dropped significantly.

The children themselves made it clear that they had a strong need of the sessions. They fought to be the first to enter and had to be evicted at the end. On more than one occasion irate children bombarded the prefab treatment room with stones, attempting to storm their way back in after their turn was over. This could not be explained as a need for art and drama. These activities were already offered by the school and were poorly attended. The children seemed to want to work through the feelings that were not expressed in routine retelling of the earthquake stories.

Many of the same reactions reported by Terr (1981) were present in these children. The children spoke of an infinite variety of real and fantastic fears. They spoke of omens and had fears of a recurrence around the anniversary of the earthquake. There were also instances of reenactment behaviors as when the children would absentmindedly break into the sound of the earthquake rumble. All of this came to an abrupt halt after the dramatizations of the earthquake.

The children seemed to need an opportunity to master the earthquake experience as well as discharge feelings. The acting out of the disaster appeared to give them a chance to regain a feeling of control over their environment. After the dramatizations they were able to respond to an implicit suggestion to put the earthquake in the past by actively planning their future. The children needed a structured experience in order to begin to master and overcome their traumatic fears.

Our hypothesis that there would be more children at risk among those who had suffered a death in the family was not confirmed. Although there were differences in the pretesting at the time the posttesting was done (18 months after the earthquake) these differences had disappeared.

Either the children are more resilient than previously expected or community loss may be less traumatizing than individual loss. Another possibility is that this screening instrument is not sensitive to the kinds of problems that may have been generated. Other measures of the Calabritto children have been taken and are awaiting analysis. This further exploration could provide more definitive answers to this question.

Another hypothesis that was not confirmed was the hypothesis that related to the amount of destruction being correlated with at-risk scores. It is interesting to explore why this hypothesis was not confirmed.

In considering why there were inconsistent results in the communities, we can eliminate predisaster differences. The communities share a common historical and cultural background that goes back approximately a thousand years. Therefore, an examination of the differences in the response to the event itself and the aftermath of the disaster is in order.

In all of the villages the experiences were essentially the same, with the exception of Laviano and Calabritto. The differences in these two communities were that they lacked coordination since the community leaders were either absent or missing. The effect was to delay many essential services including the resumption of regular school service.

The schools were particularly needed to keep the children occupied. The parents spent most of their time besieging the relief headquarters demanding better services. This not only absorbed their time and energy but also provoked a state of anger that was constant. Their bitterness was augmented by their awareness that the "others" (other villages) were "doing better." The families were strained and infuriated. Since the importance of the effect of the families has already been discussed, this in great part could explain the poor performance of these children.

A community that did surprisingly well was Conza. Just as the lack of coordinated leadership in the emergency situation was deleterious at Calabritto and Laviano, so the presence of effective support systems was positive in the case of Conza. In spite of the fact that the village had been rebuilt in a new location (as in Laviano) the children were doing very well. The school principal informed us with pride that in the first days after the earthquake the children were gathered (first under a tree and then under a tent) to enable them to express their feelings. It appears that as in the treatment program in Calabritto the opportunity to openly work through the fear and grief is critical.

The only other village where there was a significant decrease in at-risk scores is Teora. Once again we have evidence that instead of neglecting or attempting to avoid earthquake issues in Teora they were frequently brought out. They even self-published a book entitled *Teora Before and After*.

Open treatment of earthquake issues is important. It is still open for discussion if it is important that this be handled by specially trained personnel.

CONCLUSIONS

Children seem to be more resilient than they might be expected to be in the event of a disaster if a few basic needs are met: (1) most important is the availability of their family support systems. If the family is in a position to respond to the child instead of being absorbed by other issues the child seems to do better; (2) it appears to be helpful if the daily routine is quickly reestablished. Rapid resumption of school services is important; and (3) children are able to profit by a structured opportunity to discuss and work through their fears and disaster experiences.

The working through of their fears could be handled by local trained personnel and would not necessarily require a specially trained professional. This would permit a larger number of children to benefit by the treatment program.

The example of Conza and Teora confirms our conclusions. With or without a treatment program, given the minimum of these conditions, children can begin the long process of overcoming the negative effects of their tragic experience.

REFERENCES

Bowlby, J. (1973), Attachment and Loss, *Vol. 2. New York: Basic Books.*
Caplan, G. (1964), Principles of Preventive Psychiatry. *New York: Basic Books.*
Fredrick, C. J. (1982), Children of disaster. *Paper read at the International Association of Child and Adolescent Psychiatry and Allied Professions, Dublin, Ireland.*

Howard, S. J & Gordon, N. S. (1972), Mental health intervention in a major disaster. NIMH research grant MH 21649–09. Child Guidance Clinic, San Fernando, Calif.

Newman, C. J. (1976), Children of disaster: clinical observations at Buffalo Creek. Amer. J. Psychiat., *133:306–312.*

Terr, L. C. (1981), Psychic trauma in children: observations following the Chowchilla school-bus kidnapping. Amer. J. Psychiat., *138:14–19.*

Zimmerman, C. (1977), Unpublished manuscript.

Zimmerman-Tansella, CH., Minghetti, S., Tacconi, A. & Tansella, M. (1978), The children's behavioral questionnaire for completion by teachers in an Italian sample. Preliminary results. J. Child Psychol. Psychiat., *19:167–173.*

27. Vicarious Traumatization

A Framework for Understanding the Psychological Effects of Working with Victims

I. Lisa McCann and Laurie Anne Pearlman

Tom, a married man in his late 20s and father of two young children, was frequently disturbed by intrusive images involving danger befalling his loved ones. He became obsessed with safety precautions and was hypervigilant about strange noises in his house. As a result, he often woke up suddenly in the middle of the night, fearing that a prowler was in the house. Despite the absence of evidence of immediate danger, he would lie vigilant in his bed for several hours before finally dropping off to sleep. These recurrent feelings of impending danger disrupted his sleep pattern and left him with a pervasive sense of anxiety and vulnerability.

Joan, a single parent and mother of two school-aged daughters, often attended school functions with other parents in the community. During one event, she observed a father stroking the hair of his young daughter, an exceptionally beautiful little girl. Suddenly, she experienced a vivid image of the father forcibly sodomizing the child, an image associated with feelings of disgust and anxiety. She quickly found a friend to talk to and consciously pushed the ugly image out of her mind. She reflected later that she often found herself distrustful of other people's motives, particularly where the potential abuse of children was involved.

Ann, a single woman in her 30s, would awaken in a cold sweat after experiencing a vivid, recurrent nightmare of being raped brutally at knife point. She would turn on all the lights and lie awake until the dawn broke. After these nightmares, she reported feeling vulnerable and exposed. Over the subsequent weeks she experienced intrusive thoughts about knives and became fearful of being around knives.

What do these three people have in common? Are they experiencing the

Reprinted by permission from the *Journal of Traumatic Stress*, 3 (1), 131–149. Copyright © by Plenum Publishing, 1989.

psychological aftereffects of incest, rape, or some other traumatic violation? Indeed, these people are evidencing some of the cardinal signs and symptoms of the aftermath of a serious victimization. The nightmares, fearful thoughts, intrusive images, and suspicion of other people's motives are common among persons who have been victimized. However, neither Tom, Joan, nor Ann has directly experienced a victimization or catastrophe. What they do have in common is that they are all mental health professionals who spend a significant proportion of their professional time doing therapy with or studying persons who have been victimized. Although all of them have advanced degrees and training, including supervision in the treatment of victims, they are not immune to the painful images, thoughts, and feelings associated with exposure to their clients' traumatic memories. These reactions can occur as a short-term reaction to working with particular clients, as described in the literature on countertransference in work with victims (e.g., Blank, 1987; Danieli, 1981; Lindy, 1988) or as a long-term alteration in the therapist's own cognitive schemas, or beliefs, expectations, and assumptions about self and others.

Therapists who work with victims may find their cognitive schemas and imagery system of memory (Paivio, 1986) altered or disrupted by long-term exposure to the traumatic experiences of their victim clients. In this paper, we describe this transformation and provide a new theoretical context for understanding this complex phenomenon. Through the explication of the trauma-related alterations in the therapist's cognitive schemas, we build upon the existing literature to provide a systematic basis for assessing and understanding therapists' unique responses to clients' traumatic material. Our work at the Traumatic Stress Institute, a private mental health organization devoted to the treatment of trauma survivors, has shaped our thinking about this issue as well as providing the case material presented in this paper.

In the past two decades, mental health professionals have shown an unprecedented interest in the psychological aftermath of victimization (e.g., Figley, 1985, 1988; Horowitz, 1976; Lifton, 1973; van der Kolk, 1987). This interest has extended to a wide variety of victimizing events. While an extensive knowledge base exists on the psychological consequences of traumatic experiences for victims, less attention has focused on the enduring psychological consequences for therapists of exposure to the traumatic experiences of victim clients. Persons who work with victims may experience profound psychological effects, effects that can be disruptive and painful for the helper and can persist for months or years after work with traumatized persons. We term this process "vicarious traumatization."

First, we review previous conceptualizations of the client's impact on the psychotherapist and the psychotherapeutic process. Next, we apply our constructivist self-development theory to understanding the psychological impact of working with victims. Finally, we discuss the implications of this theory for clinicians who work with trauma victims.

PREVIOUS CONCEPTUALIZATIONS

Burnout

Working with victims clearly has much in common with working with any difficult population, such as seriously ill persons, victims of poverty, or persons with very severe psychiatric or social problems. Burnout refers to the psychological strain of working with difficult populations. From a social learning theory (Rotter, 1954) point of view, burnout might be conceptualized as the state in which one's minimal goals are too high and are not changed in response to feedback.

The symptoms of burnout have been described as depression, cynicism, boredom, loss of compassion, and discouragement (Freudenberger and Robbins, 1979). The research on burnout among therapists suggests the following as contributing factors: professional isolation, the emotional drain of always being empathetic, ambiguous successes (Bermak, 1977); lack of therapeutic success, nonreciprocated giving and attentiveness (Farber and Heifetz, 1982); and failure to live up to one's own (perhaps unrealistic) expectations, leading to feelings of inadequacy or incompetence (Deutsch, 1984). Although the burnout literature has not specifically addressed the effects of working with victims, these concepts are clearly relevant.

Working with victims may produce symptoms of burnout in mental health professionals for a number of reasons. Victims of undisclosed traumas may present with chronic, entrenched symptoms that are difficult to treat and require long-term therapy. Furthermore, trauma victims may be reluctant to focus on traumatic memories, a source of potential frustration for the therapist. Finally, helpers who understand victimization as a reflection of social and political problems may feel hopeless about the potential impact of individual psychotherapy upon the root causes of crime and violence.

We believe that burnout among therapists who work with victims has special meanings. That is, symptoms of burnout may be the final common pathway of continual exposure to traumatic material that cannot be assimilated or worked through. The symptoms of burnout may be analogous to the trauma survivor's numbing and avoidance patterns in that each reflects an inability to process the traumatic material.

Although the burnout literature is relevant to working with trauma victims, we concur with others (e.g., Danieli, 1981; Haley, 1974) that the potential effects of working with trauma survivors are distinct from those of working with other difficult populations because the therapist is exposed to the emotionally shocking images of horror and suffering that are characteristic of serious traumas.

Countertransference

The countertransference literature provides additional useful background for understanding this complex phenomenon. Countertransference traditionally has referred to the activation of the therapist's unresolved or unconscious conflicts or concerns. Freudenberger and Robbins (1979) write: "(in therapy), the therapist's old scars and injuries are constantly rubbed anew" (p. 287). Similarly, Farber (1985) suggests that the work of psychotherapy may reactivate therapists' early experiences and memories.

Within the victimization literature, countertransference has more broadly incorporated the painful feelings, images, and thoughts that can accompany work with trauma survivors. Haley (1974) originally described the intense and sometimes overwhelming emotions that can be evoked by exposure to images of atrocities or abusive violence reported by Vietnam veterans. In reporting her own reactions to hearing about atrocities experienced by her clients, Haley describes feeling "numbed and frightened" and cautions therapists to confront their own sadistic and retaliatory wishes. Blank (1984) states that persons who work with Vietnam veterans must face the darkest side of humanity and forever be transformed by it. Scurfield (1985) suggests that work with these clients may stir up ambivalent, negative, or moral/judgmental feelings in the therapist and suggests the importance of confronting one's own feelings of aggression, rage, grief, horror, loss of control, and vulnerability. Margolin (1984) describes therapists' reactions to Vietnam veterans as centering around existential anxiety about death and non-being. Furthermore, Blank (1987) describes cases in which therapists experience an intrusion of their own unresolved traumatic experiences, including unresolved Vietnam experiences. With regard to work with incest survivors, Herman (1981) suggests the danger for female therapists of overidentification with the victim and rage at the perpetrator. In contrast, male therapists may experience overidentification with the aggressor.

The most comprehensive models of countertransference reactions among therapists who work with victims cite the following issues and themes. In her work with therapists who work with Holocaust survivors, Danieli (1981) found empirical validation for some of the following themes: guilt, rage, dread and horror, grief and mourning, shame, inability to contain intense emotions, and utilization of defenses such as numbing, denial, or avoidance. In a similar model, Lindy (1988) identified a number of symptom patterns that emerged in therapists in their work with Vietnam veterans. These included nightmares, intrusive images, reenactments, amnesia, estrangement, alienation, irritability, psychophysiologic reactions, and survivor guilt.

Finally, within the area of victimization, there is evidence that persons close to the victim, such as family members, may suffer signs and symptoms of traumatization similar to those of the victim. This concept has been described by Figley (1983) as secondary victimization. For example, there is evidence that children of Nazi concentration camp survivors (Danieli, 1985; Freyberg, 1980) and Vietnam combat veterans (Kehle and Parsons, 1988 may experience social and psychological difficulties. Critical incident stress, an acute type of posttraumatic stress disorder (PTSD), has also been observed in emergency workers who are at the scene of environmental disasters or accidents involving loss of life (Mitchell, 1985).

Overall, the above writings suggest that exposure to the traumatic experiences of victims may be hazardous to the mental health of people close to the victim, including therapists involved in the victim's healing process. These different literatures parallel the two lines of thinking in the field of traumatic stress which place different emphases on whether characteristics of the stressor or individuals' personal characteristics determine their responses to trauma. That is, the literature on burnout parallels the focus on characteristics of the stressor in that it suggests that the therapist is distressed because of the nature of the external event (isolation, difficult client population, and so forth). On the other hand, the countertransference literature parallels the focus on preexisting personal characteristics to the extent that it attempts to explain the individual's responses as a function of his or her previous unresolved psychological conflicts. Constructivist self-development theory is interactive in that it views the therapist's unique responses to client material as shaped by both characteristics of the situation and the therapist's unique psychological needs and cognitive schemas.

In addition, we understand the effects on therapists as pervasive, that is, potentially affecting all realms of the therapist's life; cumulative, in that each client's story can reinforce the therapist's gradually changing schemas; and likely permanent, even if worked through completely. This notion has been written about somewhat more broadly in the past. Jung (1966) originally conceived that an "unconscious infection" may result from working with the mentally ill. English (1976) describes this process as follows: "As the emotional needs and distresses of people in difficulty were presented to me, I not only felt them through a process of empathy, but I also found I tended to absorb them within myself as well" (p. 193. Chessick (1978) also hypothesizes that conditions of depression and despair in one's clients (which he calls "soul sadness") can be contagious. Farber (1985) cites evidence that the client can transfer his or her pathology to the therapist. Finally, in a recent book on the personal impact of doing psychotherapy, Guy (1987) cites research which supports the notion that doing psychotherapy can be dangerous to the psyche of the therapist.

Within the area of victimization, others (Blank, 1987; Danieli, 1981; Lindy, 1988) have described a similar phenomenon, generally using the rubric of countertransference, while also raising questions about the adequacy of that construct to explain the phenomenon. Our notion of vicarious traumatization is somewhat broader than countertransference, as it implies that much of the therapist's cognitive world will be altered by hearing traumatic client material. It is our belief that all therapists working with trauma survivors will experience lasting alterations in their cognitive schemas, having a significant impact on the therapist's feelings, relationships, and life. Whether these changes are ultimately destructive to the helper and to the therapeutic process depends, in large part, on the extent to which the therapist is able to engage in a parallel process to that of the victim client, the process of integrating and transforming these experiences of horror or violation.

CONSTRUCTIVIST SELF-DEVELOPMENT THEORY

The material we present here expands upon our previous work and provides a new theoretical perspective for understanding and working with therapists' reactions. In previous papers (McCann et al., 1988a,b), we described a new theoretical model for understanding psychological responses to victimization. That work focused on the complex relation among traumatic life events, cognitive schemas about self and world, and psychological adaptation. We have elaborated that model into a theory of personality we call constructivist self-development theory, described more fully elsewhere (McCann and Pearlman, 1991b). In this paper, we focus primarily on the portion of the theory that describes psychological needs and cognitive schemas.

The cognitive portion of the theory is built upon a constructivist foundation. The underlying premise is that human beings construct their own personal realities through the development of complex cognitive structures which are used to interpret events (e.g., Epstein, 1989; Mahoney, 1981; Mahoney and Lyddon, 1988). These cognitive structures evolve and become increasingly complex over the life span as individuals interact with their meaningful environment. Piaget (1971) described these cognitive structures as schemas. These schemas or mental frameworks include beliefs, assumptions, and expectations about self and world that enable individuals to make sense of their experience. Some of these basic schemas for experience involve beliefs and assumptions about causality, the trustworthiness of sense data, identity, and self-world relations (Mahoney, 1981).

An extensive review of the literature on adaptation to trauma (McCann et al., 1988b) revealed five fundamental psychological needs: safety, dependency/trust, power, esteem, and intimacy. In later elaborations of our work (McCann and Pearlman, 1991b), we have expanded the needs of interest to include independence and frame of reference.

The cognitive manifestations of psychological needs are schemas. Our major hypothesis is that trauma can disrupt these schemas and that the unique way that trauma is experienced depends in part upon which schemas are central or salient for the individual. In this paper, we assert that working with trauma survivors can also disrupt the therapist's schemas in these areas. The therapist's unique reactions will be determined by the centrality or salience of these schemas to himself or herself. In addition to the focus on schemas, our current work (McCann and Pearlman, 1991a,b) includes more emphasis on the imagery system of memory, as well as ego resources and self-capacities. In this paper, we will focus primarily on changes in cognitive schemas and in the imagery system, both areas particularly relevant to understanding vicarious traumatization.

Cognitive Schemas

Beliefs, expectations, and assumptions about the world are central to many current notions about the effects of victimization. Janoff-Bulman (1985) asserts that victimizing life events challenge three basic assumptions or beliefs about the self and the world: the belief in personal invulnerability; the view of oneself in a positive light; and the belief in a meaningful, orderly world. Similarly, Taylor and Brown (1988) have reviewed the evidence that illusions about self and world are adaptive and enhance self-esteem and mental health.

Epstein (1989) presents four basic assumptions which he asserts are disrupted by trauma. These include the beliefs that the world is benign, the world is meaningful, the self is worthy, and people are trustworthy. The work of Roth and her colleagues (Roth, 1989) draws upon and provides empirical support for Epstein's conceptualization. Our work is consistent with this thinking.

Therapists may experience disruptions in their schemas about self and world when they work with trauma victims. These changes may be subtle or shocking, depending upon the degree of discrepancy between the client's traumatic memories and the therapist's existing schemas. Below, we describe how disruptions in these schemas may be associated with certain emotions or thoughts in the helper.

Dependency/Trust

Through their clients, therapists who work with victims are exposed to the many cruel ways that people deceive, betray, or violate the trust of other human beings, as well as the ways people can undermine those who depend upon them, as is often the case with child victims. This may well disrupt the therapist's schemas about trust. As a result, therapists may become suspicious of other people's motives, more cynical, or distrustful. In the case example of Joan, presented above, we find a helper who works with many incest survivors questioning the motives of parents at her child's school function. In our case conferences about victims, we sometimes observe ourselves expecting the worst from people in our clients' interpersonal worlds. For example, a therapist reporting on a new intake said, "I bet I know how this case is going to come out. The father is probably molesting the daughter, the mother has abandoned her emotionally, and everyone else is looking the other way." Startled by what she had just said, this therapist reflected, "I can't believe I'm saying this. I used to believe that most people are trustworthy and that some people are not. Now I believe just the opposite."

Safety

Images involving a loss of safety, including threats or harm to innocent people, may challenge the therapist's schemas within the area of safety. This will be particularly disruptive if the helper has strong needs for security. The case example of Tom, the therapist who awoke one night with fearful images of being violated by a prowler, involves a therapist who works with many victims of acute traumas, such as crime or rape. In this instance, the therapist strongly identified with his middle class suburban clients who were victims of a burglary. His own fearful images closely corresponded to the images they reported in therapy. In other instances, the connection between the client's images and the therapist's response is not as readily apparent. For example, the helper might experience increased thoughts and images associated with personal vulnerability, such as loved ones being killed in a car accident. Therapists who work with victims of rape or other crime may experience a greater need to take precautions against such a violation. Overall, clinicians who work with victims of random violence or accidents may experience a heightened sense of vulnerability and an enhanced awareness of the fragility of life.

Power

Persons who have been victimized often find themselves in situations of extreme helplessness, vulnerability, or even paralysis. Exposure to these traumatic situations through the client's memories may evoke concerns about the therapist's own sense of power or efficacy in the world. In our experience, helpers with high needs for power are likely to be greatly impacted by the powerlessness reported by their clients. This can at times lead therapists to urge clients inappropriately to take action rather than to help clients understand the meanings of their responses. It is not uncommon to hear rape counselors report that they are taking self-defense classes, no doubt to increase their own sense of power as well as safety. In addition, therapists whose power needs are threatened may find themselves becoming more dominant in social or work situations. One therapist who works with crime victims states that he often fantasizes about how he would protect his family in the event of a criminal victimization. Sometimes these fantasies are brutal or retaliatory, expressing his need to reaffirm his beliefs in his own personal power. Another therapist spoke of wondering how she would respond if she were raped. Sometimes these thoughts became obsessional, as she would replay various rape scenarios over and over in her mind. To the extent that this leads to constructive self-protective action, whether by client or therapist, it is positive. Yet it can become dysfunctional if it leads to inappropriate attempts to control others or anger about one's inability to do so.

Alternatively, a therapist may express a heightened awareness of the illusory nature of control over capricious or unexpected life events. One therapist expressed this by stating, "I realize now how little control I really have over life or death. All that I have worked for can be destroyed in an instant and nothing I do now can prevent that from happening." In extreme cases, a therapist may find himself or herself experiencing feelings of helplessness, depression, or despair about the uncontrollable forces of nature or human violence.

Independence

Trauma survivors, such as victims of rape or other crime, often experience a disruption in their need for independence, such as restriction in their freedom of movement and a diminishment in personal autonomy. One of the therapists in our setting works with many rape and other crime victims. Several of her clients are women with high needs for independence who have experienced a profound diminishment in personal freedom since the victimization. One survivor continues to be terrorized by her assailant, resulting in her decision to move back into her family's home, an event that profoundly disrupted her independence. Her therapist found herself identifying with her client's loss of independence and described experiencing dreams in which she was similarly trapped and confined. While discussing these clients in a case conference, she reflected on how painful it would be "to lose my sense of personal control and freedom in my life" while another therapist, for whom safety was a more salient issue, focused on the sense of personal vulnerability this case elicited in her. For the therapist with strong needs for independence, the identification with clients who have lost a sense of personal control and freedom can be especially painful.

Esteem

We use esteem to refer to the need to perceive others as benevolent and worthy of respect. Persons who are violated or harmed through the uncaring, cruel, or malicious intentions and acts of other human beings may experience diminished esteem for other people or the human race in general.

The helper may also find his or her own view of human nature becoming more cynical or pessimistic. A therapist who had previously held an idealistic view of human nature, reflecting her training in humanistic psychology, experienced a painful shattering of her belief systems after working at the Institute for a year. In case conferences, she would often comment "I can't believe that people treat each other like this" and describe how distressing it was to encounter so much human cruelty. The discrepancy between her own positive schemas about human beings and the reality of the terrible abuses people perpetrate made this a particularly salient and painful issue for her. This diminished view of humanity may be associated with feelings of bitterness, cynicism, or pessimism. Therapists may experience a sense of anger at other people and the world in general as they reflect on the potential malevolence of others. This is a very painful experience as it involves a loss of youthful idealism. On an existential level, therapists may find themselves reflecting on the problem of human perversity and pondering the fate of the human race.

Intimacy

Trauma victims often experience a profound sense of alienation from other people and from the world in general. This experience is most often described in Vietnam veterans who found themselves at odds with a world to which they no longer connected (Lifton, 1973). Therapists who work with victims may experience a sense of alienation that results from exposure to horrific imagery and cruel realities. This alienation may be reinforced by other professionals who view the work they are doing with disdain or repulsion. Too often, therapists are asked "How can you listen to such terrible things day after day?" We met a rape crisis counselor at a professional meeting; when asked what kind of work she did, she paused briefly, told us, then pulled in her breath and pulled back slightly, as if waiting for a shocked response. Indeed, she eventually explained with some relief, that was the type of response she ordinarily received. Just as the victim often feels stigmatized (Bard and Sangrey, 1985), so too may the therapist exposed to these horrors experience an uncomfortable sense of separateness from family, friends, or coworkers. This sense of separateness is compounded by the requirement for confidentiality in psychotherapy, which precludes one's ability to reveal the disturbing traumatic material. This of course stands in the way of a sense of connection with others, and, unchecked, may grow into a deep sense of alienation. Finally, other professionals may assume that the therapist chose this particular field of study because of his or her own unresolved conflicts. This too can contribute to a sense that one is stigmatized because of one's association with the field of traumatic stress.

Frame of Reference

The need to develop a meaningful frame of reference for experience is a fundamental human need (Epstein, 1989; Fromm, 1955; Lecky, 1945; Rogers,

1951; Snygg and Combs, 1949). This need is represented cognitively in part in schemas related to causality, or individuals' attributions about why events occur. Traumatized individuals often reflect repeatedly upon the question, "Why did this happen to me?" Similarly, therapists may try to understand why an individual experienced a traumatic event. This can become destructive if it takes the form of victim-blaming. For example, a client reported that her previous therapist of several years minimized the importance of her incest experience, focusing instead on why she had allowed the incest to continue into young adulthood. Therapists can commit another serious therapeutic error by focusing on the possible motives of the assailant or perpetrator. A woman whose former boyfriend tried to murder her reported that her therapist asked her many more questions about the boyfriend, his family, and his history, than about herself. This seems to reflect the therapist's rather than the client's need to assign causality. The client interpreted the therapist's behavior as the latter's unwillingness to hear her pain, and terminated therapy prematurely.

Another, perhaps more subtle, alteration in frame of reference schemas can also be quite distressing. If therapists' schemas are continuously challenged by clients' reports of traumatic experiences, they can experience an overall sense of disorientation. Without the opportunity to process their experiences, therapists, like clients, can respond to this with a pervasive and unsettling sense of uneasiness.

The Memory System

Therapists who listen to accounts of victimization may internalize the memories of their clients and may have their own memory systems altered temporarily or permanently. The following sections describe how the therapist's memory system may be affected by exposure to the traumatic memories of clients. These alterations in memory may become intrusive or disruptive to the helper's psychological and interpersonal functioning.

Disruptions in Imagery

The imagery system of memory (Paivio, 1986) is most likely to be altered in vicarious traumatization. Like the trauma victim, therapists may experience their clients' traumatic imagery returning as fragments, without context or meaning. These fragments may take the form of flashbacks, dreams, or intrusive thoughts (Horowitz, 1976) and constitute what some believe to be the hallmark of PTSD (Brett and Ostroff, 1985). These images may be triggered by previously neutral stimuli that have become associated with the clients' traumatic memories. In the case of Ann, presented earlier, the therapist experienced a nightmare that replicated the rape of one of her clients. Another clinician reported the uncanny experience of having a "flashback" that replicated that of one of her clients. This therapist, who works with many Vietnam veterans, found herself staring at a young Vietnamese waitress while ordering food in a restaurant. She described the following experience: "I found myself experiencing a vivid image of hiding in a rice paddy, watching for the enemy. Suddenly, a young Vietnamese girl spotted me and I knew, with horror, that I would have to kill her." The therapist recalls experiencing this as her own memory because the image was so vivid and powerful. These examples suggest that the client's memories may become incorporated into the memory system of the therapist. The images can then be triggered by what previously was a neutral stimulus.

We also believe that the imagery that is most painful to therapists often centers around the schemas related to the therapist's salient need areas. That is, a therapist for whom safety is salient will likely recall those images that are associated with threat and personal vulnerability, while another, for whom esteem is more central, may focus in on images involving extreme degradation or cruelty at the hands of others. Likewise, the imagery that is recollected can produce a temporary state of disequilibrium as the schemas accommodate or change. Thus, what is recollected in the imagery system of memory is colored by schemas, which are encoded in the verbal representation system of memory (Paivio, 1986). Likewise, the memories (both imagery and verbal components) produce changes in the schemas as the latter accommodate to new realities.

Disruption in the imagery system of memory is often associated with powerful affective states (Bower, 1981; Paivio, 1986). Therapists may report a variety of uncomfortable emotions resulting from their work with victims, including sadness, anxiety, or anger. These feeling states may be activated and within conscious awareness or they may be repressed and out of conscious awareness. Some therapists, particularly those who are unable to process their emotional reactions, may experience denial or emotional numbing. These latter reactions may occur when therapists are exposed to traumatic imagery that is too overwhelming, emotionally or cognitively, to integrate. These feelings may be too overwhelming because the therapist's own capacities for affect regulation or self-soothing are overtaxed or because the traumatic experiences are too discrepant with the therapist's own meaning systems or schemas.

In brief, therapists may experience alterations in their own imagery system of memory through their work with traumatized clients in which they reexperience or avoid various components of their client's traumatic memories. For the most part, alterations in one's memory system are probably transient in nature. However, we believe that these traumatic memories can become permanently incorporated into the therapist's memory system. This is likely to occur when the material is particularly salient to the therapist, relating closely to his or her psychological needs and life experience, and when the therapist does not have the opportunity to talk about his or her experiences of the traumatic material.

SUMMARY

In the previous sections, we provided a theoretical conceptualization of the profound psychological impact of working with trauma victims, which we refer to as vicarious traumatization. Elsewhere we apply constructivist self-development theory to the conceptualization of unique human beings who experience trauma (McCann and Pearlman, 1991b). Just as trauma alters its victims, therapists who work with victims may find themselves permanently altered by the experience. The unique effects on therapists can be more fully understood within this theoretical framework.

The Transformation of Vicarious Traumatization

In *Civilization and Its Discontents*, Freud (1930/1961) expresses a dim view of human nature that reflects the painful awareness of the cruelty of the world and human beings:

... (people) are not gentle creatures who want to be loved, and who at most can defend themselves if they are attacked; they are, on the contrary, creatures among whose instinctual endowments is to be reckoned a powerful share of aggressiveness. As a result, their neighbor is for them not only a potential helper or sexual object, but also someone who tempts them to satisfy their aggressiveness on him, to exploit his capacity to work without compensation, to use him sexually without his consent, to seize his possessions, to humiliate him, to cause him pain, to torture and to kill him. *Homo homini lupus*. (Man is a wolf to man) (p. 58).

Is it inevitable that helpers who work with victims adopt this grim view of Freud's, a view that is both realistic and despairing? Is it possible to have a more optimistic view of humanity than Freud, without denying the harsh reality of violence and aggression? How can the helper be aware of and ameliorate these potential harmful effects, transforming images of horror and violence through his or her own healing process?

Therapists may experience painful images and emotions associated with their clients' traumatic memories and may, over time, incorporate these memories into their own memory systems. As a result, therapists may find themselves experiencing PTSD symptoms, including intrusive thoughts or images and painful emotional reactions. The helper must be able to acknowledge, express, and work through these painful experiences in a supportive environment. This process is essential if therapists are to prevent or ameliorate some of the potentially damaging effects of their work. If these feelings are not openly acknowledged and resolved, there is the risk that the helper may begin to feel numb or emotionally distant, thus unable to maintain a warm, empathetic, and responsive stance with clients.

Helpers must understand how their own schemas are disrupted or altered through the course of this work and also shape the way they respond to clients. Our theory can be helpful in identifying the areas within the therapist where disturbances might exist. For example, therapists for whom safety schemas are salient or disturbed may find it very anxiety-provoking to work with crime, rape, or accident victims. This work can challenge their own beliefs in personal safety, resulting in a tuning out or avoidance of the client's memories. It is thus important for the helper to assess which of the seven need areas are particularly salient for him or her. This is important because the therapist's reactions to trauma survivors will be shaped by his or her own schemas.

It is important to tap into potential sources of support in one's professional network. The helper should first avoid professional isolation by having contact with other professionals who work with victims. These contacts can provide opportunities for emotional support for one's work in addition to the professional and intellectual support they offer. Professionals within a geographical area might organize support groups for helpers who work with victims. These support groups can be facilitated by experienced professionals who are sensitive to the personal effects of working with victims. Such groups can be focused around three major issues: normalizing the reactions helpers experience in the course of this work; applying constructivist self-development theory to understanding one's specific reactions; and providing a safe environment where helpers feel free to share and work through reactions that are painful or disruptive.

In our two-hour weekly case conference, we spend the first hour discussing and conceptualizing difficult victim cases (with client consent). In the second hour, we move into more personal discussions about what this means to us and how each of us responds to the painful experiences of victims. We refer to this as "feelings" time. As we have grown to trust each other and to allow ourselves to be vulnerable with one another, we have found this time together powerful and meaningful. At times, we have had to process not only our own individual reactions, but also the way in which particularly traumatic cases can affect the entire organization. At times, we struggle with two competing needs: the need to verbalize the traumatic imagery we are attempting to work through and the need to protect our colleagues from the stress of assimilating new traumatic material. The way we have attempted to resolve this is to talk openly about this dilemma and attempt to find a balance between the two needs. At times, we have had to tell each other that we cannot handle hearing details of a particular case because our own personal resources are at a low ebb or because we have particular difficulty assimilating certain types of traumatic material, such as serious violence against children. Fortunately, because the group is large enough, there is usually at least one other clinician who can listen and talk about any particular case. Providing a safe, supportive context for processing these issues is clearly essential to making this format positive and productive.

To this end, it is important that the group members avoid pathologizing the responses of helpers. Just as PTSD is viewed as a normal reaction to an abnormal event, we view vicarious traumatization as a normal reaction to the stressful and sometimes traumatizing work with victims.

While there is no doubt that countertransference reactions that arise from the therapist's own psychic conflicts are also important, we do not presume that the therapist's own unresolved issues always underlie these reactions. On the other hand, therapists' own unresolved victimizations of early childhood experiences can contribute to the process of vicarious traumatization. These reactions should not be viewed necessarily as a sign of psychopathology, but rather as an area of potential growth for the helper. Over the course of this personal exploration, the helper may conclude that he or she needs to work through these more personal issues in his or her own therapy.

Finally, the theory states that individuals will experience and construe events according to their own needs and schemas. As therapists learn more about their own psychological needs, they will be able to process traumatic material more effectively and limit its impact upon their schemas.

In essence, the process of working through vicarious traumatization is parallel to the therapeutic process with victims. We do not offer a quick fix approach to psychological issues that will require continual awareness, monitoring, and processing for those who work with many victims. As the authors were finishing the final touches on this manuscript in an office at home, workers were in the house installing a burglar alarm system. We reflected on the irony of writing an article on this topic while this was happening, as the need for the alarm system was a direct result of disruptions in safety schemas in our work with many crime victims. That our lives have changed in permanent ways must be acknowledged, along with the inherent losses and pain associated with this process.

We have found it useful to share with each other coping strategies that help us ameliorate some of the potential hazards of this work. The coping strategies that have emerged from our weekly discussions include: striving for balance between our personal and professional lives; balancing a clinical caseload with other professional involvements such as research and teaching that can replenish us; balancing victim with nonvictim cases; being aware of and respecting our own personal boundaries, such as limiting evening or weekend work; developing realistic expectations of ourselves in doing this type of work; giving ourselves permission to experience fully any emotional reactions of which we are aware; finding ways to nurture and support ourselves; engaging in political work for social change; and seeking out nonvictim-related activities that provide hope and optimism. Furthermore, it has been important for us to be aware of our conflict areas or unresolved traumas that are reactivated by the therapeutic process.

In a recent article on how mental health professionals cope with working with difficult cases, Medeiros and Prochaska (1988) found evidence that the coping strategy "optimistic perseverance" is adaptive. We concur that maintaining optimism and hopefulness in the face of tragedy is an essential component to making our work with victims possible. To this end, we also try to acknowledge and confirm the many positive experiences in our work as well as the positive impacts this has had on ourselves and our lives. It is important to remind ourselves and others that this work has enriched our lives in countless ways. In our case conferences, we also share the many personal rewards that are inherent in this work. There is a tremendous sense of personal meaning that evolves from knowing that we are involved in an important social problem by making a contribution toward ameliorating some of the destructive impact of violence on human lives. For some of us, an outcome of our enhanced awareness of social and political conditions that lead to violence has been greater social activism. Other positive effects include a heightened sensitivity and enhanced empathy for the suffering of victims, resulting in a deeper sense of connection with others; increased feelings of self-esteem from helping trauma victims regain a sense of wholeness and meaning in their lives; a deep sense of hopefulness about the capacity of human beings to endure, overcome, and even transform their traumatic experiences; and a more realistic view of the world, through the integration of the dark sides of humanity with healing images. Although we may be sadder but wiser, it is important to acknowledge the many ways this important work has enriched our own lives as well as countless others.

REFERENCES

Bard, M., and Sangrey, D. (1985). The Crime Victim's Book (second edition), Basic Books, New York.

Bermak, G. E. (1977). Do psychiatrists have special emotional problems? Am. J. Psychoanal. 37:141–146.

Blank, A. S. (1984). Psychological Treatment of War Veterans: A Challenge for Mental Health Professionals, Paper presented at the ninety-second annual convention of the American Psychological Association, Toronto, August, 1984.

Blank, A. S. (1987). Irrational reactions to post-traumatic stress disorder and Vietnam veterans. In Sonnenberg, S. M. (ed.), The Trauma of War: Stress and Recovery in Vietnam Veterans, American Psychiatric Association Press, Washington, D.C.

Bower, G. (1981). Mood and memory. Am. Psychologist 36:129–148.

Brett, E. A., and Ostroff, R. (1985). Imagery and post-traumatic stress disorder: An overview. Am. J. Psychiatry 142:417–424.

Chessick, R. D. (1978). The sad soul of the psychiatrist. Bull. Menn. Clin. 42:1–9.

Danieli, Y. (1981). Therapists' difficulties in treating survivors of the Nazi Holocaust and their children. Diss. Abstr. Int. 42:2947-B.

Danieli, Y. (1985). The treatment and prevention of long-term effects and intergenerational transmission of victimization. A lesson for Holocaust survivors and their families. In Figley, C. R. (ed.), Trauma and Its Wake: The Study and Treatment of Post-Traumatic Stress Disorder, New York, Brunner/Mazel, pp. 295–313.

Deutsch, C. J. (1984). Self-reported sources of stress among psychotherapists. Prof. Psychol. Res. Pract. 15:833–845.

English, O. S. (1976). The emotional stress of psychotherapeutic practice. J. Acad. Psychoanal. 4(2): 191–201.

Epstein, S. (1989). The self-concept, the traumatic neurosis, and the structure of personality. In Ozer, D., Healy, J. M., Jr., and Stewart, A. J. (eds.), Perspectives on Personality (Vol. 3), JAI Press, Greenwich, Conn.

Farber, B. A. (1985). The genesis, development, and implications of psychological-mindedness among psychotherapists. Psychotherapy 22:170–177.

Farber, B. A., and Heifetz, L. J. (1982). The process and dimensions of burnout in psychotherapists. Profess. Psychol. 13:293–301.

Figley, C. R. (1983). Catastrophes: An overview of family reaction. In Figley, C. R., and McCubbin, H. I. (eds.), Stress and the Family: Coping with Catastrophe (Vol. 2), Brunner/Mazel, New York, pp. 3–20.

Figley, C. R. (ed.), (1985). Trauma and Its Wake: The Study and Treatment of Post-Traumatic Stress Disorder, Brunner/Mazel, New York.

Figley, C. R. (1988). Toward a field of traumatic stress. J. Traum. Stress 1:3–16.

Freud, S. (1930/1961). In Strachey, J. (ed.), Civilization and Its Discontents, Norton, New York.

Freudenberger, H., and Robbins, A. (1979). The hazards of being a psychoanalyst. Psychoanal. Rev. 66(2): 275–296.

Freyberg, J. T. (1980). Difficulties in separation-individuation as experienced by off-spring of Nazi Holocaust survivors. Am. J. Orthopsychiatry 50:87–95.

Fromm, E. (1955). The Sane Society, Rinehart, New York.

Guy, J. D. (1987). The Personal Life of the Psychotherapist, Wiley, New York.

Haley, S. A. (1974). When the patient reports atrocities: Specific treatment considerations in the Vietnam veteran. Arch. Gen. Psychiat. 30:191–196.

Herman, J. L. (1981). Father-Daughter Incest, Harvard University Press, Cambridge, Mass.

Horowitz, M. J. (1976). Stress Response Syndromes, Jason Aronson, New York.

Janoff-Bulman, R. (1985). The aftermath of victimization: Rebuilding shattered assumptions. In Figley, C. R. (ed.), Trauma and Its Wake: The Study and Treatment of Post-Traumatic Stress Disorder, Brunner/Mazel, New York, pp. 15–35.

Jung, C. J. (1966). Psychology of the transference. The Practice of Psychotherapy (Vol. 16, Bollingen Series), Princeton University Press, Princeton, NJ.

Kehle, T. J., and Parsons, J. P. (1988). Psychological and Social Characteristics of Children of Vietnam Combat Veterans, Paper presented at the Annual Meeting of the National Association of School Psychologists, Chicago, April, 1988.

Lecky, P. (1945). Self-Consistency, A Theory of Personality, Island Press, New York.

Lifton, R. J. (1973). Home from the War, Simon and Schuster, New York.

Lindy, J. D. (1988). Vietnam: A Casebook, Brunner/Mazel, New York.

Mahoney, M. J. (1981). Psychotherapy and human change processes. In Harvey, J. H., and Parks, M. M. (eds.), Psychotherapy Research and Behavior Change, Master lecture seies, American Psychological Association, Washington, D.C., pp. 73–122.

Mahoney, M. J., and Lyddon, W. J. (1988). Recent developments in cognitive approaches to counseling and psychotherapy. Counsel. Psychologist 16(2): 190–234.

Margolin, Y. (1984). What I Don't Know Can't Hurt Me: Therapist Reactions to Vietnam Veterans, Paper presented at the ninety-second annual convention of the American Psychological Association, Toronto, August, 1984.

McCann, L., and Pearlman, L. A. (1991a). Constructivist self-development theory as a framework for assessing and treating victims of family violence. In Stith, S., Williams, M. B., and Rosen, K. (eds.), Violence Hits Home, Springer, New York.

McCann, L., and Pearlman, L. A. (1991b). Through a Glass darkly: Understanding and Treating the Adult Trauma Survivor through Constructivist Self-Development theory, *Brunner/Mazel, New York.*

McCann, L., Pearlman, L. A., Sakheim, D. K., and Abrahamson, D. J. (1988a). *Assessment and treatment of the adult survivor of childhood sexual abuse within a schema framework. In Sgroi, S. M. (ed.),* Vulnerable Populations: Evaluation and Treatment of Sexually Abused Children and Adult Survivors, Vol. 1, *Lexington Books, Lexington, Mass., pp. 77–101.*

McCann, L., Sakheim, D. K., and Abrahamson, D. J., (1988b). *Trauma and victimization: A model of psychological adaptation.* Counsel. Psychologist *16:531–594.*

Medeiros, M. E., and Prochaska, J. O. (1988). *Coping strategies that psychotherapists use in working with stressful clients.* Prof. Psychol. Res. Pract. *1:112–114.*

Mitchell, J. T. (1985). *Healing the helper. In National Institute of Mental Health (ed.),* Role Stressors and Supports for Emergency Workers, *NIMH, Washington, D.C., pp. 105–118.*

Paivio, A. (1986). Mental Representations: A Dual Coding Approach, *Oxford University Press, New York.*

Piaget, J. (1971). Psychology and Epistemology: Toward a Theory of Knowledge, *Viking, New York.*

Rogers, C. R. (1951). Client-Centered Therapy, *Houghton Mifflin Co., New York.*

Roth, S. (1989). Coping with sexual trauma. *Unpublished manuscript.*

Rotter, J. B. (1954). Social Learning and Clinical Psychology, *Prentice-Hall, Englewood Cliffs, N.J.*

Scurfield, R. M. (1985). *Post-trauma stress assessment and treatment: Overview and formulations. In Figley, C. R. (ed.),* Trauma and Its Wake: The Study and Treatment of Post-Traumatic Stress Disorder, *Brunner/Mazel, New York, pp. 219–256.*

Snygg, D., and Combs, A. W., (1949). Individual Behavior, *Harper and Row, New York.*

Taylor, S., and Brown, J. D. (1988). *Illusions and well-being: A social-psychological perspective on mental health.* Psychological Bull. *103:193–210.*

van der Kolk, B. A. (1987). Psychological Trauma, *American Psychiatric Press, Inc., Washington, D.C.*

28. Empathic Strain and Countertransference

John P. Wilson and Jacob D. Lindy

In RECENT YEARS the study and treatment of posttraumatic stress disorder (PTSD) has grown at an exponential rate, reflecting not only the accumulation of scientific data and clinical knowledge but the worldwide pervasiveness of the events that cause PTSD and associated psychological conditions (Wilson & Raphael, 1993). Simultaneously, mental health professionals have attempted to assist victims of trauma and disaster through the use of modern techniques of psychotherapy, counseling, psychopharmacology, and behaviorally oriented approaches to treatment (Figley, 1985; Lindy, 1989; McCann & Pearlman, 1990; Ochberg, 1988). At present, however, there are only a few empirical studies that have been designed to evaluate psychotherapy outcome and to determine which modalities of treatment are most effective with different types of clients (Foa, Rathbaum, Riggs, & Mardock, 1991). The availability of such studies in the future will enable more systematic clinical programs to be developed in regard to training psychotherapists. Recently, a growing awareness has emerged of the importance of therapists' reactions and countertransference processes in the treatment of PTSD (Danieli, 1988; Lindy, 1985, 1989; McCann & Pearlman, 1990; Wilson, 1989). It is the purpose of this chapter to focus on issues that affect empathy and the treatment outcome of PTSD.

THERAPIST'S CONFRONTATION WITH TRAUMATIZED CLIENTS

Clinical work with trauma victims brings the clinician close to the "soul" of the pain and injury. Although the nature and severity of the specific issues that a trauma survivor with PTSD faces in the task of healing and psychologically integrating a traumatic experience varies from person to person (Och-

Reprinted by permission from "Empathic Strains and Countertransference." In J. P. Wilson and J. D. Lindy, eds., Countertransference in the Treatment of PTSD, 5–30, New York: Guilford Press, 1994.

berg, 1988; Wilson, 1989), survivors and victims who seek help often suffer from painful memories of the events and distressing affective states that may alter the structure of the self. As observed by Lifton (1988), traumatic events may cause a disequilibrium in psychoformative processes and lead to defensive attempts (e.g., withdrawal, aggressive compensation, psychic numbing) to protect the injured self-structure and personal sense of vitality and wholeness. Moreover, although there are alternative pathways of posttraumatic adaptation in the course of life cycle development, *the traumatized individual seeks a safe environment, a therapeutic sanctuary, in which to engage in an interpersonal relationship that facilitates recovery and movement toward integrating the stressful experience within the ego-structure in ways that are no longer distressing or disruptive of adaptive functioning* (see Herman, 1992, for a discussion).

Empathy and Empathic Strain in PTSD[1]

Although the client suffering from PTSD initially presents in a variety of ways, ranging from extreme psychic numbing and avoidance of self-disclosure to being psychically overloaded and feeling emotionally distraught and unable to modulate distressing affects (McCann & Pearlman, 1990), the treatment of this disorder usually follows a predictable path. In the early phase of treatment, the "trauma story" is explored and the therapist attempts to establish trust, rapport, and openness (Lindy, 1993; Wilson, 1989). Therapists listen in an empathic and nonjudgmental way to clients' descriptions and interpretations of what happened to them in the trauma (Ochberg, 1993). The creation of a "safe-holding" environment (Winnicott, 1960) is crucial to the establishment of mutual trust in the therapeutic process. We believe that the capacity for sustained empathy is pivotal for the recovery process—as the trauma unfolds, as new affect and imagery develops, and as trauma is placed in a newer meaning system. In our opinion, the clinician's capacity for genuine empathy is the *sine qua non* for laying the groundwork that enables the patient to perceive that the therapeutic context is a situation of security and protection, and a proper place to express anxiety and feelings of vulnerability. A similar position has been espoused by Maroda (1991), who states:

Essentially, the first year [of treatment] is devoted to developing the relationship and setting the stage for the expression of the transference. Basic trust and empathy are the primary concerns—the patient wants to know that his therapist understands, is reliable and trustworthy, and is genuine in his desire to help him. In this initial stage, the self psychological approach to treatment is very effective. Sustained empathic inquiry is ideal because the patient is telling his story and is seeking some symptom relief for the pain or crisis that brought him to treatment in the first place. (p. 67)

Achieving empathy requires the ability to project oneself into the phenomenological world being experienced by another person. While empathy is an integral part of any therapy, in the treatment of PTSD and allied conditions *sustained empathic inquiry* is both more necessary and more difficult to maintain. This empathic stance enables the therapist to help the client through traumatization to the point where its aftereffects can be successfully integrated into the individual's self-structure. Sustained empathic inquiry is also vital to the creation of a safe-holding environment, a milieu in which the client's reactions to victimization can be normalized and one that offers reassurance that what the client is experiencing is a human reaction to abnormally stressful life events. Yet it is no simple matter to maintain empathy when the treatment setting itself becomes a crucible into which aspects of the trauma become transferred. Rather, empathy is a complex enterprise in which the therapist must also be aware of his or her own partial identification with the client's phenomenological framework—in other words, therapists working with these patients *must* take into account the processes of countertransference.

Slatker's (1987) review of the literature on countertransference (which is consistent with our view) indicates that a rupture of empathy results in the loss of an effective therapeutic role, that is, one that permits sustained empathic inquiry into the patient's processing of traumatic memories and the undermodulated affect associated with cognitive processes, which operate on all levels of consciousness in the trauma patient. The factors that cause *empathic strain* in the therapeutic relationship are potential determinants of *affective reactions* (ARs) in the therapist. Although ARs are common in treatment, intense ARs can lead to negative countertransferential reactions (CTRs) by diminishing the capacity for sustained empathic inquiry and thereby producing a temporary rupture in the therapeutic role stance. Therapy-rupturing CTRs diminish the ability of the therapist to maintain the safe-holding environment necessary for recovery from PTSD. Yet, given the enormity of the therapist's task in containing intense trauma affect, which by definition is the human response to conditions outside the range of usual life experiences, countertransference tendencies should be anticipated. It is for this reason that we seek to understand the place of CTRs in the psychotherapy of trauma survivors.

Clearly, empathy, identification, and countertransference are interrelated processes. Slatker (1987), for example, has argued that the relation between empathy and countertransference depends on what he terms *counteridentification*, as well as on identification with the client's inner world of affect and psychological being. Here Slatker suggests that through the process of counteridentification "the analyst both identifies with the patient and at the same time pulls back from that identification so as to view the patient's conflict with objectivity" (p. 203). From this viewpoint, "empathy is based on counter-identification; indeed it is counter-identification that permits our empathy to be therapeutically useful. But counter-identification is also a component of countertransference, and if it operates imperfectly, whereby objectivity is not achieved, then the analyst's negative countertransferential reactions can cause empathy to diminish or to vanish altogether" (p. 203).

Affective Reactions, Sources of Empathic Strain, and Countertransference

The concept of countertransference as a clinical construct originates in Freud's essays on the technique of psychoanalysis (1910). The most thorough early monograph (Racker, 1968) distinguishes countertransference along several lines and introduces projective identification as a central mechanism. Many subsequent clarifications, refinements, and revisions have been proposed by analysts and other psychodynamically oriented therapists (see Slatker, 1987, for a review). Unfortunately, definitions vary, as do the prominent intrapsychic model (Isaacharoff & Hunt, 1978). The focus of this book does not permit us to discuss these variations, other than to note that (1) authors now employ an object relations intrapsychic model more often than a classical structural model; (2) authors define CTR more inclusively, as opposed to the earlier view of CTR as subjective and idiosyncratic; and (3) authors tend to advise therapists to work with countertransference insights through supervision and to disclose them rather than to seek their elimination as the treatment goal. Depending upon author and definition, the concept of countertransference has been regarded variously as controversial, important, irrelevant, or central to the outcome of psychotherapy.

Transference and Countertransference in the Treatment of PTSD: Trauma-Specific Transference

The terms *transference* and *countertransference* traditionally refer to the reciprocal impact that the patient and the therapist have on each other during the course of psychotherapy. In the treatment of PTSD and comorbid states, transference processes may be *trauma specific* (Brandell, 1992; Danieli, 1988; Lindy, 1985, 1988; McCann & Pearlman, 1990; Wilson, 1988, 1989) and/or generic in nature, originating from pretraumatic, life course development as well as from traumatic events.

Trauma-specific transference (TST) reactions are those in which the patient unconsciously relates to the therapist in ways that concern unresolved, unassimilated, and ego-alien aspects of the traumatic event. These reactions include affective states, behavioral tendencies, and symbolic role relationships. In the context of a safe-holding environment, the TST reaction includes the tendency of the client to focus on the particular dynamics of the traumatic life event. The client casts the therapist into one or more trauma-specific roles through the transference process.

The therapist, in a complementary manner, may feel as though he or she has entered one of these particular roles as part of the countertransference process. Countertransference positions (role enactments) range from positive (the therapist becomes a fellow survivor or a helpful supporter, rescuer, or comforter near the trauma) to negative (the therapist becomes a "turncoat" collaborator or hostile judge). In the worst case (most often following empathic error), the therapist may be seen as the perpetrator during a reenactment in the therapy.

The shape of the therapy is likely to arise from the ambivalence and paradoxes of these various positions and the capacity of the therapist to recognize their nuances and complexities. For example, some Holocaust survivors may be clear in their hatred for Nazi perpetrators but more mixed in their disdain for collaborators (e.g., Nazi *Kapos*). Some Vietnam veterans may think of themselves as perpetrators as well as survivors; they may even respect the enemy and identify faulty American political policy as the perpetrator. Rape victims have no fellow survivors, and they discover that judges may recapitulate the perpetrator's role. Hostages may see their perpetrators as rescuers (e.g., Stockholm syndrome). Incest survivors may have had to turn for comfort to their perpetrators, while having no fellow victim or true comforter at all. In fact, small children who are repeatedly exposed to terrifying trauma and molestation may have no choice but to invent out of their imagination new personalities to fulfill the roles, such as protector and avenger, left vacant by adults during their trauma (e.g., multiple personality disorder and dissociative tendencies).

Trauma situations combine the emotional terror of each of these roles differently. Later, as dynamic relations play out in treatment, failures in therapist empathy are likely to evoke both negative transference reactions, in which the therapist is seen as a negative trauma figure, and negative CTRs, in which the therapist begins to feel as if he or she were in one of these roles vis-à-vis the client. These are critically important moments in the treatment and must be understood in order for the treatment to survive.

Sophie's Choice: A Historical-Fictional Example of Trauma-Specific Unconscious Reenactment from World War II Nazi Germany

One of the classic literary illustrations of unconscious reenactment processes and TST is found in William Styron's (1979) novel *Sophie's Choice*, in which the Nazi Holocaust survivor, Sophie, developed a sadomasochistic relationship after the war with her lover, Nathan. Delusional and obsessed with the glory and power of Nazi Germany, the psychotic Nathan brutally acts out against Sophie his grandiose and paranoid vision of Nazi omnipotence. His actions further victimize Sophie, whose psychic condition is fragile and depressed. Intertwined in their self-destructive relationship, as portrayed in the novel and motion picture, they reenact the traumatic choice forced on Sophie by the Nazi SS officer at the death camp's receiving platform: She had to determine which of her two young children would live. As portrayed by Styron (1979), Sophie's helplessness, confusion, terror, and indecision over having to choose which of her children would live or die form the nucleus of her posttraumatic symptomatology. In the pathology of their relationship, Nathan symbolically becomes many objects for Sophie, such as the revived child who had been sacrificed to the Nazis. An affair with him captures a carefree, spontaneous life of which both of them had been deprived. In another reenactment, Nathan becomes the Nazi who had rejected Sophie's brief attempt at seduction to save her children on the exit ramp. Through Nathan, she finally seduces him, then murders them both for their "crimes." Tragically, she symbolically reunites with her lost child by her dual suicide with Nathan. Viewed from the perspective of PTSD, Sophie's relationship with Nathan is a symbolic form of reenactment, driven by powerful, undermodulated affect, grief, and self-recrimination, all of which are highly trauma specific. The readers and audience of *Sophie's Choice* are cast in the role of overwhelmed witnesses to the Nazi atrocity. As the story unfolds we may be drawn in feeling the guilt of the surviving child, despair for the dead child, rage at the Nazi, or turmoil at Sophie's frantic yet empty life, finally explained by her impossible choice. Each of these positions ultimately confronts us with existential shame. Were we to be her therapists, each of these positions would be a potential point for empathic strain and powerful CTRs.

THE ELEMENTS OF COUNTERTRANSFERENCE AND THEIR RELATION TO PTSD

As the complement to transference, countertransference has been defined as a process that "denotes all those reactions of the analyst to the patient that may help or hinder treatment" (Slatker, 1987, p. 3). This brief definition calls attention to several elements of central significance to our understanding of the process of countertransference.

First, there are reactions of the therapist to the patient, which are *indigenous* to the context in which therapy occurs. Second, these reactions may enhance or disrupt therapeutic engagement. Third, they may be *complementary* or *concordant*. Racker (1968) distinguished concordant countertransference from complementary countertransference. In the first instance, therapists respond to the dilemma of their patients by identifying with some aspect of their plight, such as a wish (to survive), a defense (denial), or an ideal (courage). In a complementary countertransference, the therapist identifies with a role or intrapsychic vantage point that captures that plight from another perspective than the survivor's intrapsychic search for understanding. For example, in a trauma case the therapist may temporarily feel like the perpetrator victimizing the patient rather than empathizing, or like the patient's own harsh superego that is criticizing the patient rather than empathizing with his plight.

Fourth, the transference-countertransference sequence is an *interactive* process and may stimulate reactions (e.g., emotional states, memories, fantasies, creative insights) in *both* the patient and the therapist. As noted initially by Winnicott (1949), the interactive processes of treatment make countertransference inevitable, including *objective* and *subjective* forms of reaction. Gorkin (1987) has reviewed this distinction between objective and subjective reactions. "What is of primary interest to me," he writes, "is that type of response which is the counterpart, or expectable, response to the patient's personality and behavior—objective countertransference. I distinguish this type of countertransference from the kind of response that is due to the analyst's personal conflict or idiosyncrasies—subjective countertransference" (pp. 34–35). Maroda (1991) has revived Racker's (1968) seminal concept of *dual unfolding*: "transference unfolds in conjunction with the countertransference. . . . From an interpersonal perspective, the countertransference can be as important as the transference, and the person of the therapist can be almost as important as the person of the patient" (Maroda, 1991, pp. 69–70).

Slatker's (1987) careful study of the psychoanalytic literature on countertransference reveals a wealth of insight about this complex phenomenon that is applicable to the treatment of PTSD. The concept of dual unfolding further informs us that countertransference is a *multidimensional phenomenon* that includes (1) ARs, (e.g., guilt, shame, anxiety, tension), which are part of a psychobiological capacity for empathy; (2) cognitive reactions (e.g., fantasies, mental associations); and (3) dispositions to act in idiosyncratic or need-based ways toward the client as part of an ongoing interpersonal process (e.g., prosocial advocacy, rescuer reactions).

In the treatment of PTSD and allied conditions, the potential for developing both objective and subjective CTRs is quite significant because of the intensity of the transference process presented by a trauma survivor (McCann & Pearlman, 1990; Mollica, 1988; Wilson, 1989). Survivors of extremely stressful life events disclose trauma stories that are laden with affective intensity and descriptions of human experiences that so often and so far exceed the boundaries of a "just, equitable, and fair world" that they cause the therapist to be taken aback and temporarily dislodged from an empathic, objective, and nurturing professional role. Consider the following case example:

Teresa, a woman in her 20s, disclosed to her counselor the following trauma story regarding her internment in a South American prison for political dissenters. Her captors demeaned and abused her sexually, using rape in all its human forms. Next, they unleashed specially conditioned Alsatian dogs that intimidated, threatened, and bit her, drawing blood from her breasts. The dogs then had sexual intercourse with her. During these events the captors watched, laughed, and made humiliating and disparaging remarks. Next, her captors beheaded her two young children while forcing her to watch. They kicked her children's decapitated heads as "soccer balls." Finally they placed her in an isolation cell and carried out a mock execution.

The counselor who was helping this client was badly shaken during the session when the trauma story was told and sought relief from the tension she experienced throughout the hour of treatment. Her AR was such that she was overwhelmed by the content of the trauma story, which raised personal issues for her, as she was herself a woman in prime childbearing years.

As the consultant, I (JPW), too, was powerfully affected by the counselor's intense, emotionally charged need to sort our her personal reactions to the torture victim who was her client. As I listened intently, I visualized the scenes the counselor described, a technique that not only assisted me in recognizing the counselor's feelings of helplessness, terror, anger, fear, and uncertainty, but also generated in me feelings of anger and the need to "set things right."

The powerful emotions evoked in this case are not uncommon in work with victims of trauma and disaster who suffer from PTSD, depression, anxiety, and injuries that "bruise the soul" (Simpson, 1993). The traumatized individual seeks help to let go of pain, confusion, and feelings of vulnerability. Yet, in order to do so, the survivor must find a safe-holding milieu in which the therapist can maintain an empathic stance with firm interpersonal boundaries, a milieu in which the dual unfolding process will enable the client to successfully work through the phases of recovery (Horowitz, 1986). Because the power of affect is so intense, the therapist must attend to countertransference processes in the treatment of PTSD. In these cases, countertransference can lead to empathic strain which, if unmanaged, will cause a rupture of empathy and a loss of therapeutic role.

The Groundwork of the Forbidden

It is now presumed that the psychotherapy of trauma survivors presents the therapist with uniquely intense encounters with trauma clients because of the types of events that cause PTSD. As Lifton (1967) observed many years ago in his pioneering work with Hiroshima survivors of the atomic bomb, the encounter with death and massive destruction, the perceived threat to the bases of human existence, and the need to generate meaning result in the difficult task of reformulating the significance of the event for the survivor. For most victims who suffer the personally painful damage to their well-being, it is their ongoing attempt to put the experience to rest with new meaning and insight that brings them into treatment.

The patient's trauma story may reveal an overwhelming tragedy, a situation of coercive vulnerability, involvement as a victim in sinister activities of depravity, or a description of torment, pain, suffering, and loss. In listening to such stories, the therapist reels with the enormity of the trauma as it affects the patient. At the same time, the traumatized patient's attitudes, demeanor, and affect can also activate forbidden impulses and fantasies in the therapist, responses occurring in addition to the common range of Type I (avoidance) and Type II (overidentification) CTRs.

One of us (JPW) has presented the vignette of Teresa to hundreds of trauma counselors as a point of departure for discussion. Common responses among professionals are disgust, anger, sadness, denial, revulsion, and fear. Universally, counselors find the trauma story horrendous, and they are powerfully struck, if not immediately overwhelmed, by the image of a mother watching torturers kicking her children's decapitated heads. They sense a profound discomfort and disequilibrium as they consider what Danieli (1988) refers to as "existential shame." Moreover, these reactions occur within the safe and sterile environment of ongoing education and training. What if they had encountered Teresa themselves?

It should be noted that the therapist in this horrible case was able to hear the whole story, a story that began with sexual degradation and ended with mock execution. The torturers deliberately set out to degrade their prisoner sexually, to equate her political position with a feeling of disgust about herself, to punish her as though she were a criminal, and finally to leave her with the memory of anticipating a randomly timed, imminent execution as though she deserved it.

Countertransference to the first phase of the torture, while also evoking disgust and horror, might additionally elicit hints of forbidden feelings — such as arousal, voyeurism, erotic sadistic or masochistic impulses, identification with the aggressor — that might frighten the counselor by casting him or her in the perpetrator's role. Although the therapists' reactions might be quickly hidden from view, such countertransference phenomena could have interrupted the trauma story. From a more traditional point of view, one could also suggest that such fleeting fantasies or ARs should have been condemned as idiosyncratic, or at least disregarded as shameful and pathological. However, it could alternatively be argued that the therapist who was aware of such forbidden fantasies might discover a hidden organizing feature of the trauma experience, namely that, subjectively speaking, the torture survivor may still be confused or disoriented by the (invalid) fear that her action or inaction provoked the abusers' excesses and set the whole tragedy in motion. By seeing herself in an interactional context with her torturers, she might reveal the horrible "reality" that she continues to feel ashamed that these despicable actions were carried out even though she was helpless to stop them, or worse, that she believes that somehow she deserved the abuse.

In the psychotherapy of PTSD, *the groundwork of the forbidden* must be acknowledged as part of the domain of CTRs that occur as the dual unfolding process evolves during the course of treatment. The activation of *forbidden impulses*, like less extreme CTRs, contains information that can assist in the successful treatment of a patient by illuminating trauma-specific themes of transference. In fact, because these reactions are expectable, we must work to create the proper psychological and physical space for them to be acknowledged and shared with colleagues.

MODES OF EMPATHIC STRAIN: THERAPISTS' REACTIVE STYLES

Empathic strain results from those interpersonal events in psychotherapy that weaken, injure, or force beyond reasonable limits a salutary therapeutic response to the client. Countertransference processes are only one source of empathic strain, yet we believe that in the treatment of PTSD, CTRs are perhaps the primary cause of treatment failure.

Building on the seminal works of Slatker (1987), Danieli (1988), Lindy (1988), Parson (1988), Wilson (1989), Maroda (1991), and Scurfield (1993), it is possible to construct a schema for understanding modalities of empathic strain in the treatment of PTSD. Figure 28.1 illustrates these forms of empathic strain in a two-dimensional representation, based on Type I and Type II modes of CTRs divided by objective and subjective countertransference processes. As noted earlier, objective CTRs are expectable affective and cognitive reactions experienced by the therapist in response to the personality, behavior, and trauma story of the client, whereas subjective CTRs are personal reactions that originate from the therapist's personal conflicts, idiosyncracies, or unresolved issues from life course development.

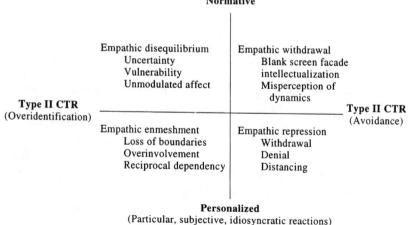

Figure 28.1. Modes of empathic strain in countertransference reactions (CTRs)

Type I and Type II modes of countertransference refer respectively to the primary tendencies of counterphobic avoidance, distancing, and detachment reactions as opposed to tendencies to overidentify and become enmeshed with the client. Type I CTRs typically include forms of denial, minimization, distortion, counterphobic reactions, avoidance, detachment, and withdrawal from an empathic stance toward the client. Type II CTRs, in contrast, involve forms of overidentification, overidealization, enmeshment, and excessive advocacy for the client, as well as behaviors that elicit guilt reactions.

As figure 28.1 illustrates, the combination of the two axes of countertransference processes produces four distinct modes or styles of empathic strain, which we have identified as (1) empathic withdrawal, (2) empathic repression, (3) empathic enmeshment, and (4) empathic disequilibrium. Although a therapist may experience one style or reaction pattern more than another, it is possible to experience any or all of the modes of empathic strain during the course of treatment with a traumatized client.

Empathic withdrawal is a mode of countertransference strain that occurs when the therapist experiences expected affective and cognitive reactions during treatment, and he or she is predisposed by defensive style and personality characteristics toward Type I avoidance and detachment responses. In this mode, a rupture occurs in the empathic stance toward the client. The result is often the loss of capacity for sustained empathic inquiry due to overreliance on the "blank-screen" conventional, or recently taught (for new therapist) therapeutic techniques. These reactions block the painful task of integrating the trauma experience and may lead the therapist to misperceive or misinterpret the behavior and psychodynamics of the client on the basis of the therapist's previous assumptions.

A similar process occurs in *empathic repression*, in which the transference issues of the patient reactivate conflicts and unresolved personal concerns in the therapist's life. Thus, a subjective reaction, combined with a disposition toward a Type I CTR, may be associated with repressive countermeasures by the therapist. His or her inward focus on areas of personal conflict is likely to be associated with an unwitting withdrawal from the therapeutic role and denial of the full significance of the clinical issues being presented by the client.

The third mode of strain, *empathic enmeshment*, is the result of the therapist's tendency toward Type II CTRs coupled with subjective reactions during treatment. In this mode of empathic strain, the clinician leaves the therapeutic role by becoming overinvolved and overidentified with the client. The most common consequence is pathological enmeshment and a loss of role boundaries in the context of treatment. In the treatment of PTSD, therapists with a personal history of trauma and victimization are especially vulnerable to this mode of empathic strain and may unconsciously attempt to rescue traumatized clients as an indirect way of dealing with their own unintegrated personal conflicts. Perhaps the greatest danger that occurs within this mode of empathic strain is the potential for the therapist to unconsciously reenact personal problems through pathological enmeshment. When this occurs it not only causes an abandonment of the empathic stance toward the person seeking help but may lead to secondary victimization or intensification of the transference themes that the patient brought to treatment in the first place.

Empathic disequilibrium, as figure 28.1 indicates, is characterized by a disposition to Type II CTRs and the experience of objective reactions during treatment, especially in work with patients suffering from PTSD and comorbid conditions. This mode of strain is characterized by somatic discomfort, feelings of insecurity and uncertainty as to how to deal with the client, and more. It occurs commonly in therapists who experience either Type I or Type II CTRs. In the case example described earlier in this chapter, the therapist indicated that she felt overwhelmed, tense, vulnerable, and uncertain of her own capacity to bind anxiety, and she experienced increased physiological arousal. She stated that she felt somewhat insecure in regard to her ability to adequately treat the torture victim, despite having worked quite successfully with other torture victims in the past. In particular, her objective CTR included vivid images of seeing the heads of the murdered children on the ground being sadistically abused by the victim's captors. These visual images and her natural identification with the woman as a mother and brutalized person were associated with an extreme state of autonomic nervous system arousal. Her concern following the session was that if she could not more effectively modulate her affect she would not be successful in her clinical efforts. An associated concern centered around her fear that the torture victim might become further isolated from sources of help or even worse, commit suicide.

This case illustration also indicates that empathic overarousal is associated with powerful ARs (e.g., anxiety, motor tension) and cognitive processes (e.g., images of sadistic torture) that extend beyond the therapy hour in distressing ways and are associated with self-doubt, feelings of vulnerability, and a need to discharge the therapist's hyperaroused state.[2]

To some degree the type of countertransference a given clinical encounter will evoke is a function of the role of helper. Clinicians and practitioners occupy many roles, such as rescue workers on the scene of a disaster, consultants to primary caregivers immediately after industrial and school trauma, or advisors to survivors during litigation proceedings (as with rape victims and children who witness murder). They are also experts in financial restitution proceedings regarding disability and compensation, and in legal proceedings regarding criminal charges.

Within psychotherapy, clinicians are called on to take trauma histories and to elicit the trauma story. Clients call on clinicians to protect and rescue, to judge and to accept, to constrain and to advocate, to comfort, and to endow with meaning. Each of these roles may reflect some unresolved aspects of the trauma experience and become the fulcrum around which the countertransference of withdrawal and enmeshment occurs.

Later in work of this nature, the client may begin to reexperience trauma-related feelings that he or she feels are activated in the here and now of the therapy. The former torture survivor, for example, may feel that the therapist is failing to protect her from harsh, current political forces that are blocking immigration and thereby persecuting her anew. She may feel that the therapist is judging her for sacrificing her children to her political cause, irreverently dismissing her attachment to her dead children, or failing to hear her sadness and pain at now feeling inhibited sexually (thereby disrespecting her sexuality). As each of these elements in the trauma situation is partially reenacted and transferred onto the treatment, new trauma-based countertransferences may appear, impairing empathy by rupture, repression, enmeshment, or over-arousal, until these processes are understood as part of the dual unfolding of the treatment.

Individual Variations in Modes of Empathic Strain

We realize that elaborating a two-dimensional model for a topology of countertransference has its limitations as well as its value, and we do not mean to say that *all* relevant CTRs to PTSD fit neatly into one of the four quadrants. For example, CTRs may also need to be categorized in terms of affect range and intensity, trauma role reenacted, defense cluster mobilized, symptom experienced by therapist, or segment of the treatment frame distorted. Neither do we wish to imply a static mode, one that confines CTR in a given treatment to one quadrant. Indeed, there is more likely a dynamic interplay among quadrants over time in a single case. Nevertheless, this model provides an important starting point, one that includes rather than excludes other descriptive dimensions and, for purposes of clinical use, establishes an important point of orientation.

THE IMPACT OF EMPATHIC STRAIN AND COUNTERTRANSFERENCE ON THE PSYCHOTHERAPY OF TRAUMA SURVIVORS

Next we turn to an analysis of the factors that determine CTRs and how CTRs, in turn, affect the phases of stress recovery and potentially cause pathological results to the client.

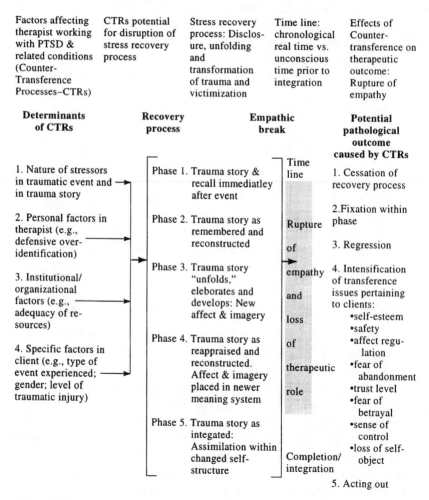

Factors affecting therapist working with PTSD & related conditions (Counter-Transference Processes–CTRs)	CTRs potential for disruption of stress recovery process	Stress recovery process: Disclosure, unfolding and transformation of trauma and victimization	Time line: chronological real time vs. unconscious time prior to integration	Effects of Countertransference on therapeutic outcome: Rupture of empathy
Determinants of CTRs	**Recovery process**	**Empathic break**		**Potential pathological outcome caused by CTRs**
1. Nature of stressors in traumatic event and in trauma story	Phase 1. Trauma story & recall immediatley after event		Time line	1. Cessation of recovery process
2. Personal factors in therapist (e.g., defensive over-identification)	Phase 2. Trauma story as remembered and reconstructed		Rupture of	2.Fixation within phase
3. Institutional/ organizational factors (e.g., adequacy of re-sources)	Phase 3. Trauma story "unfolds," eleborates and develops: New affect & imagery		empathy and loss of	3. Regression 4. Intensification of transference issues pertaining to clients: •self-esteem •safety
4. Specific factors in client (e.g., type of event experienced; gender; level of traumatic injury)	Phase 4. Trauma story as reappraised and reconstructed. Affect & imagery placed in newer meaning system		therapeutic role	•affect regu-lation •fear of abandonment •trust level •fear of betrayal •sense of control •loss of self-object
	Phase 5. Trauma story as integated: Assimilation within changed self-structure		Completion/ integration	5. Acting out

Figure 28.2. Countertransference effects on recovery from trauma and victimization.

Figure 28.2 presents a conceptual schema of countertransference effects in the treatment of trauma survivors. This schema is a general model that attempts to illustrate how CTRs cause a rupture of empathy and lead to a loss of the therapeutic role stance essential for sustained empathic inquiry. Of particular importance are the potential pathological consequences caused by an empathic break between the therapist and the client suffering from PTSD.

Factors Associated with CTRs

We believe that there are at least four major categories that contain determinants of CTRs: (1) the nature of stressor dimensions present in the trauma and the trauma story, (2) personal factors in the therapist/helper, (3) institutional organizational factors affecting the therapist and the therapeutic process, and (4) specific characteristics in the client.

As figure 28.2 indicates, each of these four categories of CTRs has the potential to affect the specific phases of the stress recovery process and cause a rupture of empathy. Further, when an empathic break does occur, it may cause a pathological outcome such as (1) cessation of the recovery process, (2) fixation within a phase, (3) regression, (4) intensification of transference, and (5) forms of acting-out behavior.

The Nature of Stressor Dimensions Present in the Trauma and in the Trauma Story

Table 28.1 summarizes the key elements that comprise the four categories of determinants of CTRs. The first set of factors common to work with trauma survivors concerns the therapist's reactions to the trauma story as presented by the client. With refugee torture victims, for example, the trauma story typically contains accounts of extremely stressful life experience that involves injury, threat, mutilation, bereavement, humiliation, degradation, defilement, the confrontation of moral dilemmas, and exposure to death, dying, destruction, and chaos. During treatment, the therapist typically experiences strong ARs to the client's account and reliving of the traumatic event. Beyond that, of course, therapists react to their own images and understanding of the traumatic event through the mechanism of partial identification and counteridentification (Slatker, 1987). Thus, the complexity of countertransference can be seen in the multileveled way in which the therapist reacts to a particular client in the transference-countertransference, dual unfolding process.

Table 28.1. Factors That Interact in Determining the Nature, Quality, and Dynamics in CRTs in Work with Survivors of Trauma/Victimization

I. The Nature of Stressor Dimensions Present in the Trauma and the Trauma Story
   Complexity and type of stressor (natural vs. human origin)
   Grotesqueness, death, injury, mutilation, abuse
   Stage in life cycle at exposure
   Role(s) in event
   Moral dilemmas during event
   Degree of psychological ensnarement by perpetrator of events
   Duration, severity, frequency of exposure or victimization
   Personal role relations in event
   Degree of community involvement
II. Personal Factors in Therapist/Helper
   Personal beliefs, religious values, ideological systems, and preconceptions
   Defensive styles and dispositions
   Personal "historical" data from own life experiences
   Degree of training and experience with trauma and victimization
   Motivation to work in trauma field
   Theoretical assumptions about personality and life cycle development
III. Factors in the Client Relevant to Understanding CTRs
   Age, race, gender, ethnicity, and cultural dimensions
   Role in traumatic event (e.g., perpetrator, victim, witness)
   Personality characteristics
   Defensive and coping styles
   Level of traumatization and injuries
   Cultural differences affecting the cognitive process of trauma
   Pretrauma ego strength or premorbidity
   Type of traumatic event experienced
   Family dynamics and background factors
IV. Institutional/Organizational Factors Relevant to the Therapeutic Process
   Political context: Supportive versus oppositional
   Attitudes toward client population
   Adequacy of resources that help or hinder treatment
   Availability of "network" affiliations and resources to aid in treatment
   Internal or external mechanisms to provide necessary support for helpers
   Flexibility versus rigidity to change in existing organizational health care structures

Countertransference includes reactions to the traumatic event (e.g., torture), the reliving of the trauma story by the distressed client (e.g., anguish, pain, bereavement), the social status characteristics (e.g., age, gender), and the role relations of the survivor (e.g., mother of murdered children).

Historical Events and Personality Characteristics in the Therapist

It is a truism to say that the therapist brings his or her own personality characteristics and idiosyncracies to the treatment situation. These include personal beliefs and ideological systems, defensive styles and personality traits, education, and personal "historical" data from life experiences relevant to the trauma circumstance.

In work with persons suffering from PTSD, the degree of training and education for work in the field of traumatic stress can significantly influence the disposition to Type I and Type II CTRs. Therapists with little training or preparation to work with trauma survivors often report being overwhelmed by the self-disclosure of a profoundly disturbing life experience by a client with a history of trauma or abuse. If unmanaged by supervision or peer consultation, a Type I or Type II CTR may cause a rupture of empathy and disrupt progress in treatment. It is also important to critically examine the therapist's motivation to work with trauma survivors. A personal history of trauma or abuse in childhood, for example, can affect the type of CTR experienced. Moreover, it can create additional difficulty in the dual unfolding process because the client's personal struggle to integrate his or her own trauma experience can stimulate conscious or unconscious reenactment and reliving processes in the therapist as well.

Personality Characteristics of the Client

A broad range of factors in clients with PTSD can influence countertransference processes. Included in this list are demographic characteristics (e.g., race, gender, age, cultural attributes), personality characteristics and defensive styles, the type and degree of traumatization and immediate trauma-related support, pretrauma ego-strength, and the psychosocial history of the client. These factors may facilitate or hinder the process of dual unfolding and the therapist's partial identification or counteridentification with a particular trauma survivor.

In our case example of the refugee victim of torture, the counselor, herself a young woman, identified with the gender, age, and role status of the client (i.e., a mother of two children). She identified with the victim as a woman raped by male captors and dogs. She also had a special appreciation of the victim's struggle to start life over again after fleeing her native culture.

The client was a survivor with PTSD, but she was also an indigent, single woman living alone in one of the most populated cities in the world. She was poor, lonely, and suicidal. The counselor, dedicated and compassionate, was strongly affected by the sheer emotional intensity of the trauma story as it unfolded in their work together and by the current life circumstances of the torture survivor as they added secondary stressors to her life. In her effort to maintain an empathic stance, the counselor shared the woman's sadness and desolation.

By imagining various different therapists working on Teresa's case, we see that there could be many combinations of forces affecting her interaction with them and the nature of their empathic strains and countertransferences. For example, would a male therapist's countertransference be the same as a female's? Would an older woman's resemble a younger woman's? Or, in another variation, would a male torture survivor evoke similar or different emotions? In discussing this case in training workshops, we have found that many male therapists who hear the story of the torture victim and her children experience degrees of anger and rage, and they often have fantasies of killing the captors. Yet, other male therapists describe their reactions as avoidance, distancing, or revulsion. Race, ethnicity, culture, and political orientation affect Type I and Type II reactions as well. All of this points to the need for systematic, controlled, empirical studies of the complex interactive processes affecting countertransference mechanisms in the psychotherapy of trauma survivors.

Institutional/Organizational Factors Relevant to CTRs

Although many mental health professionals work in organizations that have policies, procedures, methods, and rules that affect the care of clients, the impact of these institutional variables is neither well understood nor often studied empirically. One notable voice in this wilderness has been Arthur Blank (1985, 1993) in his studies of the irrational reactions to work with Vietnam veterans. Blank noted that until the U.S. Department of Veterans Affairs agreed to provide quality care to Vietnam-era veterans, that organization had institutionalized many obstacles to the development of needed health care programs, especially for the treatment of PTSD. These obstacles ranged from negative, stereotypic attitudes toward Vietnam veterans to the lack of recognition of PTSD as a clinical entity and the absence of adequate facilities to carry out readjustment counseling.

The example of the U.S. Department of Veterans Affairs and the difficulties faced by many of its professional health workers undoubtedly applies to other mental health agencies and the parent bureaucratic bodies that fund them. From our perspective, the concern is that institutions may be *supportive* of or *oppositional* to the efforts made by mental health care providers; *flexible* or *rigid* in responding to innovation, change, and improvement of services; *self-contained* or *collaborative* in efforts at net-working with allied agencies for the benefit of the client with PTSD; and *nurturing* or *indifferent* in providing adequate mechanisms of support for the service providers themselves. What is clear, however, is that when institutions fail to create an environment in which the service provider feels that he or she is part of a cooperative team with shared values and a commitment to aid victims of trauma, the impact on that service provider is likely to be a negative one, which creates a dual form of countertransference: one toward the institution and one toward the client who accesses that agency for help.

In summary, it is possible to discern that the four categories of counter-transference we have listed in table 28.1 all interact with each other, at least in a logical way, if not empirically. Survivors of trauma with symptoms, reactions, or a diagnosis of PTSD tell their trauma stories through the filter of their unique personality styles, cultures, and life experiences. Similarly, the therapist helping the trauma survivor is a person with distinct personality attributes, a professional role, and a psychosocial history as well. Together they meet in a common psychological space for purposes of working to facilitate healing, recovery, and psychological integration from a traumatic past life event. The context of this task occurs in a private practice or within an organization that employs the helping professional. What then ensues is a joint relationship, a psychological and spiritual encounter, where together they try to understand events and profoundly disturbing experiences that alter the course of people's lives, so that they can attempt to understand the meaning of why the trauma occurred.

If this process goes well, the helper will be able, in a metaphorical sense, to "dance" delicately and gracefully with the survivor in a safe space that enables the survivor to feel his or her human vulnerability and to grow from it, and thus to overcome victimization, with a new sense of meaning and personal well-being. This metaphorical dance will not be easy for either participant, and they will encounter crises, impasses, and moments during which the whole enterprise will be at risk of fracture and a premature ending.

MANAGEMENT OF THERAPIST DISEQUILIBRIUM IN THE TREATMENT OF PTSD

Given the ubiquity of empathic strain in working with trauma survivors and the consequent tendency toward CTRs, the question of management of the resultant disequilibrium in the therapist is a matter of utmost importance for treatment outcome. Among the memories likely to be activated are those of the therapist's own traumatic past. Among the affects likely to be stirred are the therapist's own reactions had he or she been in the trauma situation. Managing and working through these dysphoric affects and memories is an awesome, at times overwhelming, task, and the pressure to disclose unresolved affect prematurely to the client as a means of discharge can be intense. As a corollary, a need to avail oneself of peer support and supervision/consultation may even be an absolute, as in the case example. However, the private working through is both necessary to the therapist's self-understanding and an essential ingredient in communicating understanding to the survivor.

On the other hand, in treating PTSD the therapist cannot maintain a "blank screen" and fail to validate legitimate feelings. Before some trauma survivors are able to tell their stories or unconsciously permit partial reenactment in treatment, they may need to know the trauma credentials of the therapist. They may also need to test the therapist to ascertain that the hearer of the trauma story will be humane, sensitive, and compassionate. These are the nutrients in the "soil" that permit recovery work to grow. In fact, one essential difference between treating trauma survivors and other clients is the therapist's stance: What in another context is termed "disclosure," and considered counterproductive, may in this context define essential elements in the working alliance.

SIGNS OF DEFENSIVENESS AND COUNTERTRANSFERENCE IN THE PSYCHOTHERAPY OF TRAUMA SURVIVORS

Defensive behavior by the therapist is typically counterproductive to the successful treatment of PTSD. Maroda (1991) suggests that defensiveness is in itself a sign of a countertransference problem, regardless of the factors that led to the use of defenses. She suggests that signs of defensiveness include attitudes of derision, condescension, criticalness, judgmental postures, passive repetition of past interpretations that were rejected, and problems around scheduling appointments. The latter includes forgetting appointments, double-scheduling, rescheduling, or canceling appointments. Other clues to defensiveness include a fear of being out of control with a patient or a narcissistic belief in one's special talents in working with trauma survivors.

Table 28.2 summarizes four sets of indicators of CTRs in the psychotherapy of trauma survivors: (1) physiological and physical reactions, (2) affective reactions, (3) psychological reactions, and (4) behavioral symptoms. These four categories were derived by talking extensively with our colleagues in the field who work with trauma survivors (i.e., members of the International Society for Traumatic Stress Studies). For example, nearly all stated that

Table 28.2. Factors Indicative of CTRs in Therapist/Helper

I. Physiological and Physical Reactions
      Symptoms of increased ANS arousal
      Somatic reactions to trauma story or therapy as a contextual process
      Sleep disturbances
      Agitation
      Inattention, drowsiness, or avoidance reactions
      Uncontrolled and unintended displays of emotion

II. Emotional Reactions
      Irritability, annoyance, or disdain toward client
      Anxiety and fear reactions
      Depression and sadness reactions
      Anger, rage, hostility reactions
      Detachment, denial, avoidance, or numbing reactions
      Sadistic/masochistic reactions
      Voyeuristic and sexualized reactions
      Horror, disgust, dread, or loathing reactions
      Confusion, psychic overload, overwhelmed reactions
      Guilt, shame, embarrassment reactions

III. Psychological Reactions
      Detachment reactions based on defenses of intellectualization, rationalization, isolation, denial, minimization, fantasy
      Overidentification based on defenses of projection, introjection, denial

IV. Signs and Behavioral Symptoms of CTRs That May Be Conscious or Unconscious
      Forgetting, lapse of attention, parapraxes
      Leave therapeutic role stance of empathy
      Hostility, anger toward client
      Relief when client misses appointment or wish that client not show for session
      Denial of feelings and/or denial of need for supervision/consultation
      Narcissistic belief in role of being gifted specialist in PTSDExcessive concern/identification with client
      Psychic numbing or emotional constriction
      Self-medication as numbing
      Loss of boundaries during therapy
      Totalistic, concordant, complementary reactions

---

physical reactions were common (e.g., headaches, increased motor tension, flushing, sleeplessness, increased autonomic nervous system [ANS] arousal), and were a salient clue that countertransference was at work.

The range of emotional reactions that are part of CTRs spans the continuum of human emotions and varies from one therapist to another, depending on the attributes of the client and the nature of his or her traumatic experi-

Table 28.3. Glossary of Terms Relevant to Countertransference Processes

Affective reaction (AR)	The experience of affect by the therapist in response to transference reaction by the client
Counteridentification	The process by which the therapist attempts to maintain objectivity in treatment by examining his or her identification with the client in an empathic role stance
Countertransference reactions (CTRs)	The affective, somatic, cognitive, and interpersonal reactions (including defensive) of the therapist toward the client's story and behaviors
Dual countertransference	CTRs toward two or more objects at the same time (e.g., a client and an institution where therapist is employed)
Dual unfolding process	The evolving nature of the transference-countertransference process in the course of treatment
Empathy	The psychobiological capacity to experience another person's state of being and phenomenological perspective at a given moment in time
Empathic strain	Interpersonal events in psychotherapy that weaken, injure, or force beyond due limits a salutary response to a client
Objective CTRs	Expectable and indigenous ARs by the therapist during the course of treatment
Safe-holding environment	D. W. Winnicott's term for a therapeutic context that is perceived by the client as a safe, protective environment that can successfully contain or hold the emotional difficulties of the client that led to treatment
Subjective CTRs	ARs manifested by the therapist to the transference that are idiosyncratic and particular and may involve personal conflicts that are unresolved
Sustained empathic inquiry	The capacity of the therapist to remain in an empathic role stance toward the client throughout the course of treatment
Transference	The process and behaviors by which a client relates to the therapist in a manner similar to that in past relationships with significant others
Trauma specific transference (TST)	Transference reactions that are specifically associated with unmetabolized elements of the traumatic event and which usually involve symbolic and other forms of reenactment with the therapist
Trauma story	The account of the trauma survivor of his or her experience in a traumatic event
Type I CTRs	CTRs that involve forms of denial, detachment, distancing, or withdrawal from the client
Type II CTRs	CTRs that involve forms of overidentification, enmeshment, or overidealization of the client

ence. Many therapists stated that increased tension, somatic reactions, irritability, and numbing were common reactions, especially if there was not adequate supervision, peer consultation, or other opportunities to defuse their personal reactions after prolonged contact with trauma survivors. Table 28.2 also indicates that therapists may develop behavioral symptoms indicative of CTRs, such as lapses of attention, relief when a client misses an appointment, or hostility toward the client who is vulnerable and dependent for help. Parapraxes, excessive identification with the client's experiences, or increased drug or alcohol use as self-medication are also employed to reduce states of arousal, tension, or fatigue.

The importance of recognizing and properly managing CTRs in the treatment of PTSD is critical to the maintenance of sustained empathic inquiry. Maroda (1991) states that "failure to express or analyze the countertransference, particularly at critical moments in the treatment process, can result in long impasses, untimely terminations, and treatments that run their course dominated not by the transference, but by the countertransference" (p. 156). Given the therapeutic objective—to help survivors heal—the importance of countertransference in this population is pivotal to the successful transformation of trauma and the restoration of human integrity.

NOTES

1. Table 28.3 at the end of this chapter contains a glossary of terms and their definitions for this chapter and throughout the book.

2. It is interesting to note that one consequence of empathy is that the therapist may experience degrees of hyperarousal that are proportional to the level of hyper arousal the patient manifests as part of their PTSD. Clearly, this is a type of dual unfolding in the dynamics of transference and countertransference.

REFERENCES

Blank, A. S. (1985). Irrational reactions to PTSD and Vietnam Veterans. In I. Sonnenberg, A. S. Blank, & J. A. Talbott (Eds.), The trauma of war (pp. 69–99). Washington, DC. American Psychiatric Press.

Blank, A. S. (1993). Vet centers: A new paradigm in delivery services for victims and survivors of traumatic stress. In J. P. Wilson & B. Raphael (Eds.), The international handbook of traumatic stress syndromes (pp. 915–925). New York: Plenum Press.

Brandell, J. (1992). Countertransference in psychotherapy with children and adolescents. Northvale, NJ: Jason Aronson.

Danieli, Y. (1988). Confronting the unimaginable: Psychotherapists' reactions to victims of the Nazi Holocaust. In J. P. Wilson, Z. Harel, & B. Kahana (Eds.), Human adaptation to extreme stress (pp. 219–237). New York: Plenum Press.

Figley, C. R. (Ed.). (1985). Trauma and its wake (Vol. I). New York: Brunner/Mazel.

Foa, F. B., Rathbaum, B. O., Riggs, D. S., & Mardock, T. B. (1991). Treatment of post-traumatic stress disorder in rape victims: A comparison between cognitive-behavioral procedures and counseling. Journal of Consulting and Clinical Psychology, 59(5), 715–723.

Freud, S. (1910). Future prospects for psycho-analytic therapy. Standard Edition, 11, 141–142. London: Hogarth Press, 1962.

Gorkin, M. (1987). The uses of countertransference. Northvale, NJ: Jason Aronson.

Herman, J. (1992). Trauma and recovery. New York: Basic Books.

Horowitz, M. (1986). Stress response syndromes. Northvale, NJ: Jason Aronson.

Isaacharoff, A., & Hunt, W. (1978). Beyond countertransference. Contemporary Psychoanalysis, 14, 291–310.

Lifton, R. J. (1967). Death in life: The survivors of Hiroshima. New York: Touchstone.

Lifton, R. J. (1988). Understanding the traumatized self: Imagery, symbolization, and transformation. In J. P. Wilson, Z. Harel, & B. Kahana (Eds.), Human adaptation to extreme stress (pp. 7–32). New York: Plenum Press.

Lindy, J. D. (1985). The trauma membrane and other clinical concepts derived from psychotherapeutic work with survivors of natural disaster. Psychiatric Annals, 15(3), 153–160.

Lindy, J. D. (1988). Vietnam: A casebook. New York: Brunner/Mazel.

Lindy, J. D. (1989). Transference and post-traumatic stress disorder. Journal of American Academy of Psychoanalysis, 17, 397–403.

Lindy, J. (1993). Focal psychoanalytic psychotherapy of posttraumatic stress disorder. In J. P. Wilson & B. Raphael (Eds.), The international handbook of traumatic stress syndromes (pp. 803–811). New York: Plenum Press.

Maroda, K. J. (1991). The power of countertransference. New York: Wiley.

McCann, I. I., & Pearlman, I., (1990). Psychological trauma and the adult survivor. New York: Brunner/Mazel.

Mollica, R. (1988). The trauma story: The psychiatric care of refugee survivors of violence and torture. In F. Ochberg (Ed.), Post-traumatic therapy and victims of violence (pp. 295–315). New York: Brunner/Mazel.

Ochberg, F. (Ed.). (1988). Post-traumatic therapy and victims of violence. New York: Brunner/Mazel.

Ochberg, F. (1993). Post-traumatic therapy. In J. P. Wilson & B. Raphael (Eds.), The international handbook of traumatic stress syndrome (pp. 773–785). New York: Plenum Press.

Parson, E. (1998). Post-traumatic stress disorder: Theoretical and practical considerations for psychotherapy of Vietnam War veterans. In J. P. Wilson, Z. Harel, & B. Kahana (Eds.), Human adaptation to extreme stress (pp. 245–279). New York: Plenum Press.

Racker, II. (1968). Transference and countertransference. New York: International Universities Press.

Scurfield, R. M. (1993). Treatment of post-traumatic syndrome disorder among Viet-

nam veterans. In J. P. Wilson & B. Raphael (Eds.), The international handbook of traumatic stress syndromes *(pp. 879–889). New York: Plenum Press.*

Simpson, M. (1993). Traumatic stress and the bruising of the soul: The effects of torture and coercive interrogation. In J. P. Wilson & B. Raphael (Eds.), The international handbook of traumatic stress syndromes *(pp. 667–685). New York: Plenum Press.*

Slatker, E. (1987). Countertransference. *Northvale, NJ: Jason Aronson.*

Styron, W. (1979). Sophie's choice. *New York: Random House.*

Wilson, J. P. (1988). Understanding the Vietnam veteran. In F. Ochberg (Ed.), Post-traumatic therapy and victims of violence *(pp. 227–254). New York: Brunner/Mazel.*

Wilson, J. P. (1989). Trauma, transformation, and healing: An integrative approach to theory, research, and post-traumatic therapy. *New York: Brunner/Mazel.*

Wilson, J. P., & Raphael, B. (Eds.). (1993). The international handbook of traumatic stress syndromes. *New York: Plenum Press.*

Winnicott, D. W. (1949). Hate in the countertransference. International Journal of Psycho-Analysis, 30, *69–74.*

Winnicott, D. W. (1960). Countertransference. In Maturational processes and the facilitating environment *(pp. 158–165). New York: International Universities Press, 1965.*

Index

About the Editor

MARDI HOROWITZ began his studies on stress with investigation of unbidden and recurrent visual images. This led to his first book, *Image Formation and Cognition,* now in its third edition as *Image Formation and Psychotherapy.* The clinical studies led him to development of empirical methods for the laboratory study of intrusive phenomena, using reliable and valid measures of reports of such conscious experiences. Emerging from such research studies, he developed the *Impact of Events Scale,* which has become an international standard in investigations of stressor life experiences.

A combination of clinical, field, and laboratory-experimental studies led to his now-classical book, *Stress Response Syndromes,* which is also now in its third edition. For this book and the related papers Dr. Horowitz received several awards, including the highest honors received by psychiatric investigators in America: the Foundation's Fund Prize of the American Psychiatric Association and the Strecker Award of the Institute of the Pennsylvania Hospital. This line of work helped objectify several syndromes, including most importantly the development of the official diagnosis of *Post Traumatic Stress Disorders.*

Subsequent work on the etiology of stress-induced disorders led Dr. Horowitz to focus on the dimensions from normal to pathological grief reactions. He clarified important mental processes involving personality based issues, as in his book *Person Schemas and Maladaptive Interpersonal Patterns.* He illuminated the configurations of shock mastery and reschematization as interacting causes of experiences and behaviors, leading to treatment-oriented works such as his *Personality Styles and Brief Psychotherapy* and *Formulation as a Basis for Planning Psychotherapy Treatment.* Most recently, he published his central theory in the book *Cognitive Psychodynamics: From Conflict to Character.*